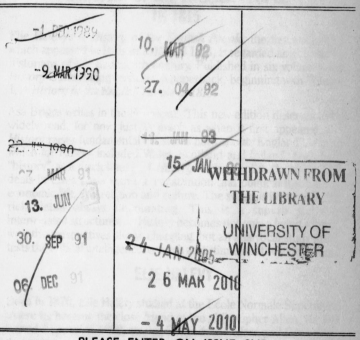

Halevy ... *losophic Radicalism* and
Em... ...died in 1937.

ARK

ELIE HALEVY
A HISTORY OF THE ENGLISH PEOPLE IN 1815
INTRODUCTION BY ASA BRIGGS

ARK PAPERBACKS
London and New York

First published in Great Britain in 1924
ARK edition 1987
ARK PAPERBACKS is an imprint of
Routledge & Kegan Paul Ltd.
11 New Fetter Lane, London EC4P 4EE

Published in the USA by
Routledge & Kegan Paul Inc.
in association with Methuen Inc.
29 West 35th Street, New York, NY 10001

Printed in Great Britain
by Cox & Wyman Ltd
Reading

Library of Congress Cataloging in Publication Data
Halévy, Elie, 1870–1937.
A history of the English people in 1815.
Translation of: Angleterre en 1815, v. 1. of the
author's Histoire du peuple anglais au XIXe siècle.
Bibliography: p.
Includes index.
1. Great Britain—History—1789–1820. 2. England—
Civilization—19th century. I. Title.
DA521.H3513 1987 941.07′3   87–969

British Library CIP Data also available
ISBN 0-7448-0067-6 (pbk)

CONTENTS

FOREWORD

I

Élie Halévy's *A History of the English People*, the first volume of which appeared in Paris in 1912 and 1913, is regarded as a classic by most historians of the nineteenth century. Like many classics, it is less well-known that it used to be. In 1937, the year when Halévy died, it was one of the first Pelican paperbacks, but that edition has long been out-of-print. Nor has the French edition been kept continuously in print either, although Hachette reissued it between 1973 and 1975. This new edition deserves to be widely read, for now, just as much as when it first appeared, the *History* raises fundamental questions both about "England", a term which for Halévy included Wales, Scotland and Ireland, and about "history" as a discipline. Even more important, Halévy, a philosopher before he was a historian, attempted with imagination and system to answer them.

A History of the English People falls into different volumes, published in French and translated into English at quite different times. The chronology is important. It is the very first volume, published in 1912 and 1913, which is most magisterial—*England in 1815*, which deals in three parts with the constitution and political institutions, economic life and religion and culture. The sweep is impressive, the rich detail always illuminating. This is a superb study of a structure or rather of inter-related structures. Moreover, it poses a proposition which preoccupied Halévy. Despite profound contradictions in its policy and in its economy, Britain in 1815 was spared a revolution, Halévy maintained, through the stabilizing moral influence of evangelical religion, particularly Methodism. As a result, it was able to establish itself as a country of freedom, "of voluntary obedience, of an organisation freely initiated and freely accepted." Halévy had turned to Methodism, which he described as "a well chosen subject", in 1904 and hoped to write a book on it, but because he learned that another Frenchman was already engaged in such an enterprise he was content with two important but little-known articles which appeared in the *Revue de Paris* in 1906. They were not translated into English until 1971. The work on Methodism subsequently directly influenced the *History*.

There was far more, however, in the first volume of the *History* than what has come to be known as the "Halévy thesis", a supreme example of the kind of thesis about which historians like to argue. There is, for example, a very striking account of economic structure which begins not with English industry but with Irish agriculture, and there is an unusually thorough analysis of British public finances. Despite all the research which has been carried out since—and in total it has been somewhat patchy—Halévy's first volume does not look out-of-date.

Volume II of his *History*, which turned from structures to narrative and dealt with Britain from Waterloo to the beginnings of the Reform Bill crisis in 1830, was not published until 1922—four years after the end of the First World War, which for Halévy marked the beginning of what he called "the era of tyrannies". The volume appeared in parallel with a further chronological volume covering the period from 1830 to 1841, from the Reform Bill crisis to the coming to power of Sir Robert Peel in 1841.

These two chronological volumes are necessarily somewhat different in approach from the first analytical volume, although as the story unfolds Halévy continues to focus attention on the "self-governing" characteristics of the English. He starts with events, but since he is particularly interested in the making of policies and the forces which account for them, he is concerned at every point with "causes". The two volumes, well received at the time, remain the fullest and best documented narrative history of Britain during these years. Halévy brought the provinces into the picture as well as the metropolis, although his version of events is much as it would have been seen by men in power or by men anxious to drive them out of power. Yet, not surprisingly, ideas figure in the pattern as much as personalities or interests.

It was not until 1924 that the first English translation of Halévy appeared, Halévy's Volume I, to be followed two years later by his Volume II, now called "The Liberal Awakening" and a year after that (1927) by his Volume III, now called "The Triumph of Reform". By then Halévy had published the first part of a Volume V in French in 1926, having taken a strategic and in retrospect controversial decision not to continue his narrative at that stage beyond 1841. Interrupting his chronology, he took up the narrative again in 1895, a point in time three years after his own first momentous visit to England as a young man of twenty-two. He was writing about the England that he remembered in what he called an "Epilogue".

Between then and 1914, when the narrative covered in his "Epilogue" was to end, Halévy had frequently crossed the Channel and had got to know personally many of Britain's most interesting personalities. There was inevitably a difference of experience, therefore, which affected the way in which he dealt with the two periods from 1815 to 1841 and from 1895 to 1914. Yet there were other differences. He himself wrote at the beginning of the "Epilogue" that "the period between 1895 and 1914 does not belong to the British nineteenth century as I understand it." Indeed, it was a prologue to the twentieth century as much as an epilogue; and while once again religion figured in Halévy's analysis, in this case "the decline of that individualist form of Christianity in which Protestantism generally consists, and a revival of Catholicism or more generally of the Catholic forms of faith", a thesis more open to challenge even than his first thesis, Halévy dwelt too on "the simultaneous decline of economic individualism" and "the growth of socialism". The "Epilogue" ended with Britain declaring war on Germany.

The first part of the "Epilogue" was not translated into English until 1929, and the fact that it was now given the title *Imperialism and the Rise of Labour* was apposite in that this was the year when Britain's second Labour government came into office, if not into power. Halévy himself, born into a comfortable family, had always been interested in "socialism" in its British as well as in what seemed to him to be its contrasting "continental" forms, and before and after the First World War he had followed the fortunes of the Labour Party as methodically as he had followed the fortunes of Sir Robert Peel in his first two volumes. He knew the Webbs, and Graham and May Wallas were friends whose opinions he trusted.

The second part of his "Epilogue", now called *The Rule of Democracy, 1905–1914*, did not appear in London until 1934, when democracy almost everywhere was under threat. It was in that year that Halévy, increasingly pessimistic about Europe's future, gave an interesting lecture to the Royal Institute of International Affairs in Chatham House, subsequently published in its journal *International Affairs*, "Socialism and the Problem of Democratic Parliamentarianism", and this was later reprinted in France in his *Era of Tyrannies*, a collection of essays, articles and papers published posthumously one year after his death in 1937 and translated into English in 1965. The volume demonstrates that liberty was Halévy's ultimate value. He believed that not only the First World War but the aftermath of that war had placed it increasingly in danger. Moreover, England no longer seemed immune from the threat to it. He described his subject in 1934 as "universal", not "national", and set out "from a view point which is not English to see what shape this problem takes for England".

Nine years before that, in 1928, only one year before the publication in London of his *Imperialism and the Rise of Labour*, his remarkable doctoral thesis, *The Growth of Philosophic Radicalism*, which had first appeared in French as long ago as 1901, appeared in London. It did as much as his *History* to establish Halévy's reputation in Britain. A definitive work, it is concerned, like the *History*, with basic questions which always preoccupied Halévy—the relationship between interests and opinions, between ideas and policies, and between intellectual history and social history.

In retrospect, it is plain that what he wrote in it about Jeremy Bentham and the development of "philosophic radicalism", a different philosophy from "popular radicalism", drew Halévy further away from philosophy and deeper and deeper into history, and English history at that. Yet he maintained a deeply philosophical cast of mind and developed a comparative approach to history. He never sought easy explanations nor was he ever satisfied with rhetoric: he probed deep and pondered long. And as the sequence of events in the 1930s moved towards a new war, he became more and more interested in socialism within and between countries without ever becoming a socialist. In relation to contemporary events he was never willing to attribute what was happening to the policies of "statesmen". "The wisdom or folly of our statesmen is merely the reflection of our own wisdom or folly", he maintained. Bentham would have concurred.

Before Bentham there had been Socrates and Plato. The first review Halévy wrote was of a new study of Plato published in 1893, and his first book, which appeared in 1896, was called *La théorie platonicienne des sciences*, "The Platonic theory of the Sciences": it examined the Platonic dialogues. The influence of Plato on Halévy's move from philosophy to history was clearly recognized by his childhood friend, Léon Brunschvicg, who wrote after Halévy's death that:

> if Plato had had at heart, above all else, the aspiration to overcome for the safety of
> his city state the opposition between purely speculative criticism and purely
> empirical politics, Halévy's labours are to be explained by his fidelity to Plato's
> inspiration. . . . In the eyes of Élie Halévy, the linking of theory and practice is the
> end and justification of the philosophical enterprise.

To that enterprise Halévy continued to contribute. He had founded the *Revue de métaphysique et de morale* in collaboration with Xavier Léon, a review committed not to faith but to reason, and he was very active as a member of the small and select Société française de philosophie, founded in the same spirit as the *Revue*. For many years he edited the *Supplement* to the *Revue*, and he joined in most of the discussions of the society—they often took the form of dialogues—with philosophers who in the early twentieth century included Bergson, Durkheim and Georges Sorel. In 1902 Halévy offered a powerful critique of a paper by Georges Sorel on historical materialism, and between 1902 and 1923 he made substantial contributions to a "vocabulaire technique et critique de la philosophie", a study of philosophical terms, organised by the Society: they included entries on "political economy", "liberalism", "individualism", "collectivism", "ideal" and "utopia". Throughout his life Halévy rejected materialist interpretations of history, the subject of another of his entries: "the basis of history," he wrote plainly in 1929, "is idealistic, not materialistic, and idealism makes revolutions and wars." He approached Marx, about whom he knew a great deal, via Thomas Hodgskin, the British socialist (about whom he wrote a monograph in 1903) and Sismondi, who figured prominently in his later works and whose importance he clearly appreciated.

Halévy's characteristic plainness of statement did not mean that he neglected economic history, as his contributions to the "vocabulaire" and the contents of the second part of the first volume of his *History of the English People* demonstrate. In one sense, however, the Halévy thesis was a *riposte* to interpretations of English history which rested on theories of historical materialism. "If the materialist interpretation of history is to be trusted," he wrote in the first volume of his *History*, "if economic facts explain the course taken by the human race in its progress, the England of the nineteenth century was surely, above all other countries, destined to revolution, both political and religious. But it was not to be so. . . . To find an explanation we must pass on to another category of social phenomena—to beliefs, emotions, and opinions, as well as to the institutions and sects in which these beliefs, emotions and opinions take a form suitable for scientific enquiry."

As Halévy turned from philosophy to history he retained, even strengthened, his sense that he was concerned with "scientific enquiry". When he had finished his essays on Methodism and began to work out plans for his *History* in 1905, he told his friend, Célestin Bouglé, that history—and he added the adverb "unfortunately"—was "the only way for me to do science. Better physics or astronomy. But I can't do them, and I look where I can for explanatory connections." There were plenty of these in his thesis on philosophic radicalism which he presented one year before he argued with Sorel, for in it he examined the dichotomy in utilitarian thinking between the assumption that different interests had to be identified artificially to promote "the greatest happiness of the greatest number" and the view of political economists that there was a natural identity of interests. According to the first assumption there was a role for the legislator: according to the second view there was an invisible hand. Acceptance of the first assumption pointed to the need for political reform: acceptance of the second pointed to the need for commercial freedom. It was only by turning to the detailed history of England between 1776 and 1832, which he broke down into three shorter periods, that Halévy could disentangle "contradictions" and find "explanatory connections". Yet his account of how Jeremy Bentham became a radical left a place for accident as well as for necessity.

While Halévy's doctoral thesis is rightly taken as being directly "connected" with the later *History*, there were other forces leading him towards it, and before he began it he had already produced a subsequently little noticed book specifically on England, *L'Angleterre et son empire*, "England and her Empire", in 1905. Research on his thesis took him to England once or more every year during the late 1890s, when there was more talk, much of it strident, of the expansion of the British Empire than ever before, and *L'Angleterre et son empire* was a topical book, suggested by his brother Daniel. His occasional letters to Bouglé, in particular, describe important extensions of his knowledge and experience of Britain, but two of the most interesting of his letters were to his mother and father in December 1900 when he was correcting his Latin thesis—a required item for his doctorate—in a London which for once in December was bright, not cold, and free from fog. Britain was caught up in the Boer War, and there were many signs of ill-feeling between Britain and France.

"If a war were to break out with England," Halévy wrote, "we would be massacred as *dreyfusards*, without even having the time to take refuge on a battle-field." Halévy had taken a keen interest in the Dreyfus case, which would figure prominently in any full biography of him: "I was an anti-clerical, a democrat, and, a republican," he wrote later. "I was a Dreyfusard. But I was not a socialist" and at the time he complained of *les exaltés* who called themselves socialists because they believed that Dreyfus was innocent. He was already comparing France with England and drawing parallels and contrasts. When the novelist Émile Zola was being attacked in France for his support of Dreyfus, Halévy was reading how Joseph Priestley's house was destroyed by a Birmingham mob in 1793. At once he saw connections. England seemed quiet then while France was bitterly torn, and in 1898, when he visited Cambridge, Halévy wrote of "one football match succeeding another".

The Boer War, of course, changed the mood. Halévy followed its fortunes with fascination, once noting briefly in 1900 that what was happening in Africa was "not glorious" for the English, but adding that he did not believe that "the clock had yet struck for them". Perhaps one day it would. He had become keenly interested in Britain's changing role in the world, and had written in 1898 that, the day when a universal Anglo-Saxon federation was created, England will have become "a sort of historical museum", visited by young men from America, Australia and Rhodesia who wanted to study "the origins of Americanism".

From 1898 onwards, for almost forty years Halévy gave a course of lectures on British political ideas at the *École libre des sciences politiques*, founded soon after the defeat of France in 1871, and from 1901 onwards he alternated this course with a course on the history of European socialism, in which Marx was "the pivot". Both courses were frequently revised in the light of travel as well as of research, and he hoped to turn the latter into a published history. There was a landmark in his personal life when in October 1901 he married Florence Noufflard, a woman of character and charm, with whom he continued his travels—they spent their honeymoon at Portofino. They worked in close collaboration at his home. His friends were her friends and they carried out historical research together. She was to survive him and live until 1957. During the Second World War she and a group of colleagues and students, "Les amis d'Élie Halévy", prepared for the press three posthumous works, among them an *Histoire du socialisme européen*, with a preface by Raymond Aron, and a volume of his unfinished British History from 1841 to 1852, *Le Milieu du Siècle, 1841–1852*, edited by Paul Vaucher. This still left a forty-three year gap in his British narrative, filled in only sketchily, in far less depth and in a very different style, by R. B. McCallum in his *Victorian Years* published in 1951, the year of the centenary of the Great Exhibition.

II

What kind of man was Halévy and how did he come to know Britain so well and to write about it so superbly whether he was discussing the English "miracle" of the nineteenth century or the "decline" of the twentieth century? He was clearly an outstanding expositor. "While lecturing," a distinguished pupil recalled, "he stood there erect, with hands on the back of the chair, or else sat up very straight, tall and strong, with his head high. . . . The whole amphitheatre was held with passionate intensity by his voice, which was even and full, on occasion ironic or testy. His sentences . . . reached eloquence by the mere purity of his stripped style."

Behind the lecture room there was always the study. Julian Benda wrote in 1938:

> I see him again as he was in his study—a tall, slim, elegant man, the perfect model of the aristocratic republican. I see him as he was, so simple, so little pontifical. . . . When, on reading his books I discover once again how much learning, disinterested labour, lofty vision and original thought this simplicity concealed, I realise that it has been granted to me, at least once in my life, to draw near to a great master of the human heart and mind.

Those were pictures of Halévy as he had appeared in his prime. He would have been the first to recognise, however, that to understand him you had to go back to the beginning. When he was thirteen, he began to keep a diary, although he made only intermittent entries in it, the last of them when he was twenty. They include factual details about his background and clear-cut statements of his outlook and intention. This is the first of the key sources which have to be tapped for an understanding of him. Extracts from it, which need to be carefully checked with the original, were published in France in Alain's *Correspondence avec Élie et Florence Halévy* (1958).

In his first entry Halévy notes that he was born in Étretat in September 1870, two days after the Battle of Sedan, the German breakthrough in the Franco-Prussian War. His father, Ludovic Halévy, was an opera librettist and producer, who worked closely with Offenbach and Bizet and wrote the libretto of *Carmen*: his great-grandfather had been a cantor of the synagogue. His grandfather, Léon, was secretary to St Simon in succession to Auguste Comte, before marrying a Catholic. Élie's mother was a Protestant, however, and Élie himself was brought up in that minority faith. His great-uncle, Jacques, was a composer, and his maternal grandfather was a well-known clockmaker. His paternal grandmother's father was an architect. Another ancestor was the chemist, Marcellin Berthelot, a champion of university reform.

There were several contrasting strands, therefore, in Halévy's inheritance. There were also many different kinds of visitors to his family home first in Paris and then, not very far away in the woods at Sucy-en-Brie, where his father bought *la Haute Maison* in July 1893. One of the friends, Hippolyte Taine, had already established his reputation *inter alia* as a writer on England: his *Notes sur l'Angleterre* (1872), later translated into English, continues to be read and quoted. Another friend was the artist, Dégas.

Halévy attended the Lycée Condorcet, where he won prizes—in philosophy—and was far ahead of his contemporaries, among them some of his closest friends then and later—Brunschrieg and Léon. Another contemporary was Marcel Proust who confessed that he was somewhat intimidated by him. His English teacher was Mallarmé. From 1889 to 1892 Halévy studied at the École Normale Supérieure, a nursery of French talent: there he met the philosopher, Alain Émile Chartier, who also became an intimate friend, as did Bouglé.

As a student Halévy proved himself very much of an individualist, lively but critical and well aware of the pressures of collective interests in the world of ideas and even on his own life. He was determined to sustain independence of mind and freedom of action. He had been born well off, but he did not want to take advantage of this: "I more and more dislike having a future that I have neither earned nor deserved", he wrote while still at the Lycée. Conventional attitudes to "honour" disgusted him: so, too, did love of glory or riches. Sincerity, he proclaimed, was his declared object. He wanted to free himself of partisan prejudices. "I hope in setting down my thoughts," he wrote in 1890, "to give them the appearance of an order, a necessity external to myself that I can impose on myself." In his last diary entry in February 1891 he argued that "the moral point of view is also the logical point of view."

Having successfully completed his first agrégé examinations—and having already made journeys abroad, the first of them to Italy—Halévy arrived in London for the first time in October 1892. First impressions are interesting, and this was a very special visit for a young man, as his letters reveal. One of the first people he met was Henry James, who told him that he wished that more of his novels were translated into French. Two of the first things Halévy did were to go to the opera at Covent Garden (several times) and to buy a book of Kipling's verses. Politics came second, although within a week of his arrival he had lunch with the Fisher Unwins, lively publishers, who introduced him to people of interest whom they felt he should meet. The "so pretty" Mrs Fisher Unwin was the daughter of the politician Richard Cobden, who was to figure in the English title of one volume of his *History*, but it was of more interest to Halévy at his first lunch with them that he met the Sickerts than that he talked about Cobden. Art, literature and music were major preoccupations. "Dégas reigns over English art", he wrote home. "The verses of William Morris", he went on, "were unequalled for boredom." "Everyone in our class", he also observed, "speaks Italian".

From London Halévy moved to Oxford, a place which he was to visit frequently in the future, and he attended a number of lectures there, complaining of the difficulty of finding philosophers of stature in England: Englishmen found it more congenial to read poetry or, while they were undergraduates, to row on the river. Halévy also had an uninspiring hour with the Master of Balliol, Benjamin Jowett, in his "sumptuous apartment", conscious that he was not impressing the great man. Cambridge he found more lively than Oxford, Ireland at this stage less interesting than Scotland (though he was to write illuminating letters from Ireland on a visit with his wife in 1903, to be referred to in his "Epilogue"). Halévy was obviously enjoying his first visit which lasted until the spring of 1893. "Dear mother," he began one letter in English, immediately passing over to French, "I am enjoying myself so much that the prospect of returning to France disgusts me." In another letter he felt it necessary to explain that he was still thinking in French and dreaming in French. "The secret of happiness," he told his mother in November 1892, "was to distrust the English and to live in England."

I am deeply grateful to Halévy's niece and literary executor, Dr Henriette Noufflard Guy-Loé, for her kindness in letting me read and quote from these early unpublished Halévy letters, vivid and spontaneous, which I studied at her home, in the room where Halévy worked, in Sucy-en-Brie. She has translated many of them and fully recognized their historical significance. The longer Halévy stayed in Britain, the more the impressions and the contacts multiplied. The focusing came later. It was fortunate that as a young man he met Oscar Browning, talker of talkers, heard General Booth, the leader of the Salvation Army, speaking more of soup than of God, attended a gathering of the Society for Psychical Research, went to the House of Commons and after speeches by Gladstone (*l'air très vieux*), and Balfour, listened to Joseph Chamberlain and John Morley (Chamberlain, he thought, spoke the better of the two). He also read Ruskin and pondered on advertisements for Pears soap: civilisation by soap was not skin-deep.

There were later visits to England during the 1890s—and they soon became annual—but Halévy continued to travel far more widely than this, visiting Tunisia and Algeria, for example, in 1896 and Spain in 1900. In the process, as Tocqueville had done, he sought clues to the interpretation of the development and prospects of the countries which he visited. It was completely in character when in 1894 he asked himself in Berlin whether or not socialism was the form taken by industrialism in a country where there was a cult of military and administrative discipline.

It was England, however, which soon stood out, particularly after he started working on Bentham in 1896. "*Une paix admirable règne ici,*" he wrote from Jesus Lane, Cambridge in 1898. Yet the Boer War, the subject of many gripping letters, fascinated him, and after it ended he fortunately continued to find much to grip him. "England begins to be interesting for the sociologist," he wrote to Bouglé in July 1903, though he feared that Durkheim and his colleagues were incapable of turning away from totem and taboo.

From Bentham Halévy himself turned to John Stuart Mill. "Have you ever heard of Harriet Taylor?" he asked his father in September 1900. Two years earlier he had told Bouglé that he was studying the history of ideas in England around 1800, noting that there had been no revolution. In further interesting letters to Bouglé, posted in London in 1900, he expressed his doubts about what Bouglé called "philosophie réelle" and explained his growing interest not in the workings of the mind but in "social tissue".

If through such letters—as in retrospect—Halévy's study of philosophic radicalism seems to lead directly to the later *History*, his first open venture into history, *L'Angleterre et son empire*, owed more to his immediate reactions to changing British politics and the role of Chamberlain in particular. In July 1896 he had told a friend that he would not write a history of England but would write a philosophy of history instead. The first book he wrote, however, was not philosophical in character. Nor was it a book standing on its own. It was published in a series, with parallel volumes on American imperialism by Henri Hauser and on German economic development by

François Delaisi, who was to specialize later in what he called "political mythology". Halévy's treatment of British foreign policy in 1905 was strictly chronological and for the most part factual, and what remains most interesting about it in the light of Halévy's whole career is that in many places it offers intimations of Halévy's "Epilogue". During the first part of the century, he maintained, "England" followed a liberal foreign policy: English governments "intervened" in Europe always "to defend liberal institutions against absolute powers", and they did not "intervene" outside Europe where their interest, the paramount concern in policy-making, was to ensure free trade. During the second half of the century, however, this policy underwent a "revolution". England then had no "reason" to "intervene" in Europe—or at least abstained from intervening—but followed an imperialist policy outside Europe. It was a policy which Halévy did not like.

In his *History* Halévy was to be more critical of Palmerston (and Canning), when he dealt with foreign policy earlier in the century, than he was in 1905, and he explained his shift in terms of the First World War which had changed his views of them. (He wrote an article on Palmerston in the *Revue des Sciences Politiques* in 1921 with the pointed title "How Palmerston passed for a great man"). It was never true that Halévy was more interested in domestic politics than in foreign politics. In an age when diplomatic history enjoyed great prestige he argued the need to examine "the interior structures of a society", but he never minimised the importance of "foreign affairs" as some later historians of Britain have done. It was a strength in this connection that he never took official documents for granted, although after 1918 he accepted an invitation to serve on the Commission that published the official French documents on the origins of the First World War.

It must have been very soon after the publication of *L'Angleterre et son empire* that Halévy wrote his now famous articles on Methodism which provide yet another lead into his later *History*. "I am going to England to cultivate my garden and to study Methodism," he told Bouglé in July 1905. He had always been interested in religion—and liked to attend diverse religious services as a young man—although as he told Alain in September 1887 he was "neither Protestant nor Catholic nor Jew". Indeed, if he had a preference, he claimed jokingly, it was for Buddhism. Four years earlier he had expressed himself opposed to all new religions: better to be a Stoic than a Christian, a Christian than a Babist. A letter from London in 1898 described how, after attending a mass in an Anglican Church, St Alban's, Holborn, he would tell anyone seeking "a sumptuous version of Christianity" to become a Protestant. (Note the pejorative use of the world "sumptuous" as in the case of his descriptions of Jowett's room.)

Halévy's sense of late nineteenth century religion in England being drawn back into ancient ritual was founded in experience, but he wanted to generalize. "The core of his work", he told Xavier Léon, when he was working on Methodism in Oxford in 1905, was "to define those two forms of Christian religious exaltation which are called Catholicism and Protestantism."

He was studying them, however, he insisted, as he would have studied Buddhism or Babism. As a necessary part of the study he went to Methodist services, including a London open air meeting conducted by "the Methodist pope of the neighbourhood" in July 1905: it was followed by an indoor meeting, "extraordinary, mystic, benign, exalted, such as I had never before seen." Again, there is a word which stands out—the word "exalted".

Halévy learnt in the course of careful research among the papers—and absorbing as that could be, it could scarcely be described as "exalting"—that another *normalien*, Augustin Léger, was also carrying out research on Methodism, and this may have speeded his intention to publish his own researches in article form. More important, it may have led him more quickly into the project of writing a *History*. "I am getting to know England extremely well by studying the Methodists," he told his mother in July 1905. He had always contemplated a *History*, he informed Bouglé two weeks after he had learned of Léger's activities, explaining that he already had five or six green boxes in his study concerned with the project.

There is evidence, indeed, that as early as 1896, when he was turning to Bentham, Halévy was meditating on whether to produce "a theory of society, a theory of modern democracy or a history of England". The danger, he added, was that if one were to study England exclusively as a historical theme one might become an Anglophile, a danger which he had readily admitted in an earlier letter to Bouglé. Yet what, he asked, could he do about it? He was already a great admirer of England. "For two centuries England had given Europe lessons in politics." He continued to hold the same view throughout his life, claiming in the 1930s that the only European countries which set an example were Britain, Holland and the Scandinavian states.

While he was preparing his *History* in visits not only to London but to Birmingham, Manchester and Leeds. Halévy also continued to ask big questions, some of them concerning the future as well as the past, some philosophical in character. What would India be like if the British left it? he asked in 1907. Why were French politics so "frivolous" and what would be the consequences? was a question he asked a year later. In the same year Alain was expressing scepticism about all historical concepts. "Between one concept and another the facts have never been able to decide, not even in a laboratory.. . . One always finds what one is looking for." In 1909 Alain touched obscurely on what *his* History of England would be like, which suggests (unfortunately Halévy's letters to Alain do not survive) that he had been discussing Halévy's *History* with him. He pointed out, if it needed pointing out, that David Hume, himself a sceptic, had been both a philosopher and an historian.

There was to be disappointment before the first volume of Halévy's *History* appeared in 1912, for the first publisher to whom it was sent, Colin, turned it down in December 1910, possibly because Halévy stated unambiguously that it would be the first of four or five volumes. It was on the eve of a visit to England that its unhappy author told his friend, Lucien Herr, in a letter of 26 December 1910 that he was going to London to correct a manuscript perhaps "destined never to find a publisher". He asked Herr to glance at it for him and to give his opinion about how the public—or Halévy added significantly, "different publics"—would respond to it. Did it not have a more general interest than Max Leclerc, the publisher who had read it, had believed? Could not a different publisher be found? Halévy told Herr not to breathe a word of this even to his most intimate friends, Léon, Bouglé and Chartier (Alain), and in a further letter written four days later he added that he had been uneasy about telling even Herr about his problems and hoped that he would not bother to read the manuscript line by line.

The letter of 30 December is important first because it sets out some of Halévy's own feelings as a historian at this crucial moment in his life and, second, because it elicited the warmest and most encouraging responses from Herr. Judge the book, Halévy told Herr, as if you were its only public. After carefully outlining his approach, his table of contents and the reasoning behind the order of his chapters, he set out part at least of what later came to be called the Halévy thesis, his basic proposition that it was the "evangelical revival" of the eighteenth century (he did not mention Methodism specifically) which explains the "tempered" nature of liberalism and of English individualism in the nineteenth century, which "little by little rendered impossible the formation of reactionary and revolutionary parties of the continental kind."

That this was only part of what at this stage sounded rather a vague thesis is evident. So, too, is Halévy's emphasis on other elements in his manuscript – his work on judges and on naval and military officers; his economic description and his analysis; his determination to describe the fortunes and attitudes of "each class in the nation". Halévy was not the first or the last historian to affirm that there were many things in his book which had never previously appeared in either a French or an English account of English history and that his general interpretation was more systematic and complete than that of any earlier historian. He had one particular anxiety, however, which was special to himself. Did he think, he asked Herr—and now he did mention Methodism—that there was too much about religion in his text to appeal to Colin? If so, there was no way around it, for it was, in the details of theology and religious practice that he discovered the *base explicative de mon ouvrage*, the explanatory core of his work. If he risked boring those who were interested in religion it was a risk that had to be taken.

"I do not have the vice or the talent," he concluded, "to write a history book like Ferrero or Victor Bérard", now forgotten men. Nor could he cut bits and pieces out. If Colin had rejected the text, there would be even more objections from Hachette. Nor did he wish to bury himself, like Ostrogorski, in the cellars of "la maison Lévy". Nevertheless, it was Hachette which was to publish the first volume of the *History* in 1912 and to continue the venture.

Fortunately, Herr's reply to Halévy, dated 4 January 1911, survives. He had spent a day and a half on the text and found the *History "de premier ordre"*, first-class. He wished Halévy had consulted him first before approaching

Colin, for his friend Charles Seignobos, who knew something about England, was "all powerful" in that business. One difficulty was that the external aspect of the text looked "prodigiously massive, compact and *terrible.*" Another was that there were some awkwardnesses of style. Yet the general impression would surely be favourable—the impression of force, penetration and comprehensiveness coupled with an obvious skill in construction. Leclerc might have wanted a less austere work: so might other publishers. In his view Hachette would be the best and he was sure that Hachette would accept it.

There are few other such letters, but obviously the confidence of Hachette enabled Halévy to proceed. He was, as always, methodical and committed, and happily his friends were as pleased with the results as Herr had been. Alain, a good critic, who observed percipiently that there was one thing missing from the great Volume I—a chapter on "private life"—love, marriage, adultery, scandals, education of children . . . births, deaths, etc., told Halévy, however, after opening the volume that he recognised him in every page. "The soil is good for your feet." And in a later letter he changed the metaphor with the words "I have the impression that your great machine is in action and that it will make its noise in the world."

Halévy's Volume II had already been started in the year that Volume I appeared, although because of the First World War it was not until 1922 that it was actually published. The War, in which Halévy served as a volunteer in the French Medical Service, not only stopped him from visiting England but forced him to stop publishing. He had written only one article in 1916—a review of Pasquet's *London and the Workers of London*, and the only other work he wrote between 1916 and 1918 was an anonymous little book *La part de la France*, addressed to American soldiers upon the entering of the United States into the War in 1917.

Significantly, Halévy always had an audience of devoted American historians: indeed, the most detailed studies of his career as an historian have been written by Americans, looking at England from outside just as Halévy had done. In 1948 Professor J. Bartlett Brebner of Columbia University, a dedicated teacher who was as keenly interested as Halévy in the ambivalent utilitarian heritage, published a sympathetic study of him; in 1950 Professor Charles Gillispie of Princeton University, wrote an appreciation in the *Journal of Modern Scholarly History*; in 1971 Professor Bernard Semmel wrote a valuable introduction to Halévy's studies of *The Birth of Methodism in England*; in 1965 Professor R. K. Webb translated *The Era of Tyrannies* (with a preface); and in 1975 Professor Melvin Richter, who had already written about Halévy in the *International Encyclopedia of the Social Sciences*, with the indispensable assistance of Dr Guy Loé, prepared a full bibliography of Halévy's signed works; and in 1980 Myrna Chase published "an intellectual biography" of him.

III

For British readers, old and new, Halévy's *History*, the first volume of which now re-appears, will have a special point. With the great French historian as a guide, history becomes not only a living subject, with the perspectives always changing, but an analytical study which tests the critical intelligence as much as it stimulates the imagination. Halévy lived long enough to observe and to assess by 1923, when his second volume appeared, how much the perspectives of 1912 had already changed. For him the Great War of 1914 to 1918 had been a terrifying crucible into which much had been poured and out of which much that was newly terrifying came. He was not surprised by its advent, but he was deeply disturbed by its consequences. For modern British readers the Second World War has to be taken into account also. It had even greater consequences for Britain than the First.

There is a gap almost as long as the nineteenth-century Halévy gap between the end of the Second World War and the uncertain present. Yet Halévy's way of writing history encourages the reader to ask his own questions, including questions relating to what has happened since 1945, and they are bound to be many. Does "England" still offer "lessons" to Europe and the world and, if so, what are they? Did it buy perpetual immunity from revolution? Was it, *pace* Halévy, "a good thing" that it did not have a revolution in the late eighteenth or early nineteenth century? What have been the implications for "England" and Europe of joining the European Economic Community?

In one of his essays on Saint-Simonian doctrine reprinted in *The Era of Tyrannies* he had quoted a passage from St Simon, eloquent but misleading, which had obviously influenced his own interpretation of English history:

> Separated from the continent by the sea, England ceased to have anything in common with the people who live there, while creating a natural religion and a government different from all the governments of Europe. Her constitution was founded, not on prejudices and customs, but on what must be the basis of every constitution at all times and places, the freedom and happiness of the people.

St Simon had added, however, that Europe would reach its ultimate organisation only "if all its nations, each one governed by a parliament, would recognize the supremacy of a general parliament superior to all national governments and invested with the power to settle their disputes."

Halévy's own answers to such questions would have been bound to be pertinent, for his personal relationship with "England" between 1918 and 1937 became even closer than it had been before the deluge. He made many new friends, among them Sir Ernest Barker, and built up his own English public to which he attached special importance. Before he gave his Chatham House lecture in 1934 he had written several papers about industrial relations in Britain—the first of them in 1919—had been presented with an honorary doctorate at Oxford University in 1926 and had delivered the Rhodes Lecture there in 1929, to be published in 1930 with what was to become an all-too familiar title, *The World Crisis of 1914–1918*. There were links too, some of them curious, between the different elements of Halévy's increasing involvement. Thus, when he received his honorary degree in 1926 it was at the time of the general strike, when British industrial relations reached an unprecedented point of collision, and when he gave the Rhodes Lecture the world economic depression had already begun. He wrote a vivid and interesting letter describing the rituals of the honorary degree ceremony (he also had an honorary doctorate from the Sorbonne, where long ago he had refused a professorship), and the awkward travelling arrangements necessary to get there because of the strike; when he got back to London, the strike was over.

Arrangements for the English translation and publication of his book were, of course, his biggest preoccupation, and there are interesting letters to and from his translator, E. I. Watkin, and his publisher, Ernest Benn, who had taken over T. Fisher Unwin. In a translator's preface to *The Age of Peel and Cobden* (1947) Watkin noted that it was as long ago as 1913 that he had begun his translation of Halévy's *History* and that he felt himself fortunate "to have been permitted to continue the translation to the end": indeed, he considered this last volume of his translation to be "a tribute to M. Halévy's memory." Watkin, an author in his own right, was a Catholic whose philosophical and religious position was very different from Halévy's, yet he insisted that he belonged to "the liberal tradition of individual freedom of which M. Halévy is the sympathetic historian." Certainly Sir Ernest Benn, the publisher, second baronet, belonged to that tradition, although to a more militant element in it than that represented by Halévy. Born five years after Halévy and outliving him by seventeen years, he left behind one stirring book of his own, *Confessions of a Capitalist* (1925). "From 1925," his biographer noted, "individualism was the very kernel of Ernest Benn's life."

Halévy considered Watkin to be an "able translator" who at times was capable of making what to him were modifications of the text, and he had a rather sharp-edged correspondence with him about religion and liberty in 1927. He also noted modifications on the part of the publisher in 1934 and even thought of writing to *The Times Literary Supplement* drawing attention to some of them. The one modification that really disturbed Halévy was the omission by the publisher of references in the French text of the *Epilogue* to Edward VII's private life—his mistresses—and to his "relations" with armament firms. For Halévy this was an example of almost childish timidity. "If you have skimmed through my work you will admit that it is austere and gives no space to scandal."

H. A. L. Fisher, writing from the Warden's lodgings in New College, Oxford, felt that Halévy was right to complain, but advised silence in public until someone pointed out the discrepancies. Halévy's publishers did not apologize. "We are quite definitely of the opinion," wrote Gordon Robbins on their behalf, "that we should be wrong to allow such (references) to appear in a book carrying our imprint." Yet he added that "the last thing we want you to think is that our action implies any kind of criticism of you or your writing. . . . This is an extremely friendly partnership in which we both do our best for the book."

The partnership continued after Halévy's death. The last article of his that he saw published was in 1937 for *Les Cahiers de Radio Paris*: it was concerned with Anglo-French relations between 1882 and 1914. He had never got back, as he had wished, to the years of the Halévy gap. Time caught up with him. In his preface to *The Age of Peel and Cobden* Paul Vaucher, who was responsible for putting the French collection together in 1946, described Halévy's intentions. He would have written two further volumes of the *History*. For the first volume, which covered the period from 1853 to 1865, he had already collected a large number of notes. It would have consisted of three books—Book I, "The Crimean War and its Sequel, 1853–1859"; Book II, "The Ideas of 1860"; and Book III, 'The End of an Epoch, 1859–1865'. Presumably the death of Palmerston accounted for the choice of the final date. The second volume was not prepared: it would have been devoted to Gladstone and Disraeli and would inevitably have forced Halévy to consider fully the changing role of the political party in the processes of opinion and policy making. The way would thus have been open for the beginning of the *Epilogue* where Halévy found himself in a new world.

He never disguised his view that his own opinions had been formed in the nineteenth century before the *Epilogue* began and that the twentieth century had never greatly appealed to him by comparison. It had got off to a bad start. Yet as he wrote in 1907 in his essay on "St. Simonian Economic Doctrine", "The nineteenth century is gone; we are beginning to understand it." His *History* is above all a necessary key to its understanding. Even without any introduction or commentary it stands firm by itself.

ASA BRIGGS
Worcester College

INTRODUCTION

Every student, either of the past development or of the present working of British institutions, must be grateful for the fact that M. Élie Halévy's well-known History is to appear in an English translation.

Vol. I was first published in French in March 1912. The completion and publication of the later volumes was interrupted by M. Halévy's duties during the Great War, but Vols. II and III (bringing the History to 1841) appeared in 1923, and there is now every prospect that the work will soon be completed and carried on to 1914.

Meanwhile, this first volume, on "England in 1815," is not only a self-contained analysis of English conditions at the date from which the History starts, but an admirable instance of M. Halévy's method and point of view. Anyone who will open this volume and read a few pages will be convinced of M. Halévy's enormous learning and strict impartiality. But it is only when reading the volume as a whole that one comes to understand in what respects it differs from other English histories either of this or earlier periods.

A great English historian declared that history was "past politics," and readers of M. Halévy's later volumes will find that the greater part of his work falls under that definition—especially if it is taken to include the relation between the policy of England and the policy of other Powers. But past politics can be written about in several different ways. A historian may give us an accurate description of such political events as the passing of laws, the rise and fall of parties, and the making of wars and treaties ; and he may combine his narrative of political events with an analysis of the characters and motives of the statesmen who have been directly responsible for those events. Both these elements, set out with meticulous care, and drawn from an independent analysis of contemporary sources, will be found in M. Halévy's volumes. But the outstanding importance of his work lies in the fact that he has accepted a third and more difficult task. He has tried to explain *why* statesmen found it possible in one year to pass laws and carry through executive policies which were impossible in another year, and even why it was that statesmen found themselves in different years desiring to pass different measures.

So far the only interpretation of history in that sense has been based upon an analysis of economic forces—the growth of new forms of industry and finance, the extensions of overseas trade, the commercial rivalry of

nations, the appearance of economic " class-consciousness " and the like—
and on a deduction from that analysis of the resulting legislation.
M. Halévy—and it is this which constitutes the essential originality of
his method—denies that economic changes, or the personal characters of
statesmen, or even the forms of political constitutions, are the only, or,
in the case of English history, even the most important factors in national
evolution.   Other histories of England have sometimes interposed isolated
chapters on " Literature, Science and Religion," as interruptions to a
narrative of political events.   M. Halévy presents the growth of ideas
and of the feelings arising from ideas as essential factors in his analysis
of causes and effects.   On page 335, for instance, after stating that " in
no other country of Europe have social changes been accomplished with
such a marked and gradual continuity" as in England, he goes on to say :
" The source of such continuity and comparative stability is, as we have
seen, not to be found in the economic organization of the country.   We
have seen, also, that it cannot be found in the political institutions of
England. . . .   To find it we must pass on to another category of social
phenomena—to beliefs, emotions and opinions, as well as to the institutions
and sects in which those beliefs, emotions and opinions take a form suitable
for scientific inquiry."

A few English writers like Professor Dicey and Mr. C. R. Fay have
successfully attempted such a synthesis for particular periods and aspects
of our nineteenth-century history.   No one would, I think, claim that
they have approached M. Halévy either in the width of their range or
the depth of their detailed knowledge.

M. Halévy in his Preface appears to deny himself any claim to be
a specialist researcher into original sources.   Those who notice throughout
his book the use which he has made of little-known contemporary material,
and even of the forbidding mass of evidence in old newspapers, will not
be so modest on his behalf.   But on two points—the growth of the
characteristically English utilitarian philosophy, and the history of English
religion from 1750 to 1850—he is not only a researcher but the only
researcher who has examined those subjects both with scientific thorough-
ness and with scientific detachment.   His three volumes on " La Formation
du Radicalisme philosophique " (Librairie Félix Alcan, 1901) show that
he is not only himself an original thinker on the problems concerned, but
that he is the only living man who has ever been through and reduced
to intellectual order the enormous mass of Bentham's manuscripts now
deposited in the library of University College, London.   And it was a
happy instinct which led him, after his Bentham researches, to the studies
which resulted in his articles in the *Revue de Paris*, August and September
1906, on " La Naissance du Méthodisme en Angleterre."

At first sight Evangelical Christianity and non-Christian Radicalism
would seem to be at the opposite poles of human thought.   But when,
forty years ago, I first became a practical politician, I discovered how

strong was the tradition of a working alliance between the two forces. On some of the most interesting pages of this volume (e.g. 509–11) M. Halévy explains the causes of this apparent paradox by showing the high, almost ascetic seriousness which both groups shared, and which, in spite of Wilberforce's social conservatism, and James Mill's grim anti-pietism, brought them together whenever humanitarian work had to be done. Both groups shared in the destruction of the slave trade and of slavery, and M. Halévy quotes (p. 510 n) Bentham's declaration, " If to be an anti-slavist is to be a saint, saintship for me. I am a saint ! " Both groups worked together on the British and Foreign School Society in the early struggles for popular education. Lord Shaftesbury, the saint, was surprised to find that his most effective allies in the fight for factory regulation were to be found among men who rejected both his constitutional and his religious opinions. And when in 1865 Governor Eyre's case revived the problem of slavery, John Stuart Mill appeared as an ally of the evangelical missionaries. It is his sensitive understanding of such facts—due perhaps in part to his belonging to a family in which the traditions of French Protestantism and French Liberalism were united—which has enabled M. Halévy to carry out his purpose of making us " realize the complexity and variety of the strands which, woven together, compose the facts of history" (p. xxvii). M. Halévy not only knows the English tradition and is capable at times of smiling at it ; he has the additional quality which is necessary for full understanding, in that he really likes the Englishness of the English people.

Many readers will seek to find in M. Halévy's work a helpful analogy between the position of England after 1815 and her position a hundred years later, after the Peace of Versailles. The analogy is, of course, in many respects very close. One follows with a keen sense of recognition his account of our blind efforts after Waterloo, in a society disorganized both by war and by industrial invention, to regulate the distribution " of functional activities and economic rewards " (p. 227). M. Halévy himself has told me how, when he returned to his house after the war, and took up again the sheets which recorded (in Vol. II) his conscientious but comparatively uninterested researches into the controversies of 1816 to 1819 as to the resumption of the gold standard and the rate of exchange of paper money, he found that the old facts had suddenly acquired a new and menacing vividness. But to me the re-reading of Vol. I has rather brought home the profound intellectual differences between the two situations. The whole conception of the universe which in different ways was shared by men so unlike as Peel and Wilberforce, Whately and Wordsworth, Shaftesbury and Gladstone, has, apparently, as an effective factor in social and political events, disappeared for ever. A hundred years hence, in estimating the intellectual forces of our own time, a future historian may have to search not so much in the records of the churches as among the obscure proceedings of working-class propagandist organiza-

tions, and to trace the relations of those proceedings to the conclusions of the twentieth-century biologists and psychologists, and of
the historians and poets who in each generation undertake the ever-
fresh duty of reinterpreting the past.

In writing his history M. Halévy has followed the old custom (unfortunately abandoned, under the influence of Lord Acton, by the *Cambridge
Modern History*) of giving full references to his authorities. I can
imagine nothing more delightful for a special student of any period or
section of English nineteenth-century history than to acquire the habit
of looking up M. Halévy's references. · He will realize how stern has been
the effort of compression which has enabled M. Halévy to bring his book
within its present compass. But he will also understand how well founded
is M. Halévy's gentle reproof to English scholars that " it is impossible
to regard as sufficient the monographs already written, which deal
with particular aspects or special points of English History " (p. ix).
We created during the nineteenth century our Civil Service on principles
then new, but since largely imitated elsewhere. No English account of
that process exists. The industry and insight of Mr. and Mrs. Webb have
brought the history of English Local Government up to 1835, but nothing
exists corresponding to their work for the all-important period which
followed 1835. The histories of nineteenth-century English religion
are partisan compilations or chatter about Newman. Is it too much to
hope that M. Halévy may not only instruct some of our younger students
of history, but may stimulate them by his example to efforts like his own ?

GRAHAM WALLAS.

PREFACE

I am well aware of my boldness in undertaking to write the history of the English people during the 19th century. Even in the case of very distant periods, for which the evidence is more scanty, historians are distrustful of works covering a wide field and prefer monographs to a synthesis. Such an attitude seems even more justifiable in the study of modern times, where the investigator feels himself at first quite overwhelmed by the mass of evidence at his disposal. Nevertheless I am, I think, in a position to plead in my favour several extenuating circumstances.

In the first place, it is impossible to regard as sufficient the monographs already written, which deal with particular aspects or special points of English history. To justify the labours of specialists attempts must be made from time to time to utilize their researches for a more general history : such is the aim of this book. It does not fall within my province to relate in detail the events of military, diplomatic or constitutional history, but rather, by considering together all its various aspects, to depict British civilization and society as a whole, and to show how the different orders of social phenomena—political, economic and religious—combined with each other and reacted on each other. Perhaps, by the very fact of employing this synthetic method, I shall avoid a fault common among writers of monographs. Man inevitably generalizes, even when he is at pains to avoid generalization. The historian, who deliberately sets himself to study Society under one aspect alone, unconsciously comes to consider this aspect as possessing a special importance above the others, and even as being the key to their explanation. And he will thus come to teach according to the special class of phenomena which he studies, either a political or a religious or an economic philosophy of history. The method here followed, precisely because its object is less narrowly limited, is better able to guard against excessive simplifications and to make us realize the complexity and variety of the strands which, woven together, compose the facts of history.

Moreover, when we study the history of modern Europe, or, to speak more particularly, that of modern England, we are surprised to find how inadequate are the detailed researches which have been made in this field. To take first religious history. Despite their importance, we possess no really scientific work dealing with the dissenting sects, nor even, which is still more surprising, with the Church of England. Or, again, to take economic history. There is certainly no lack of works dealing with the condition of the workers or technical improvements, but there are very few works indeed which discuss the industrial, commercial or financial organization of the employers. It would be easy to multiply examples of this deficiency, and here perhaps lies the greatest danger attendant upon the exclusive employment of the monograph.

It is obvious that really valuable work is impossible without a division of labour. But it is often forgotten that there can be no rational division of labour without a preliminary coordination, and that it is the province of general history to effect this coordination by guiding the researches of specialists. I hope that my book, by exposing the lacunæ in our knowledge, and bringing to light our uncertainty or ignorance on many points of importance, will contribute towards the filling of these gaps and towards the substitution of knowledge for uncertainty and ignorance. May the theories advanced in this work afford fresh stimulus to special studies, which will complete, correct, if need be confute, these very theories. I have no higher ambition.

From another point of view, I am aware of my boldness. A Frenchman, I am undertaking a history of England. I am attempting the study of a people to whom I am foreign alike by birth and by education. Despite copious reading, visits to London and the provinces, and frequent intercourse with different circles of English society, I have nevertheless been obliged to learn with great difficulty, and in a manner which would seem necessarily artificial, a multitude of things which even an uneducated Englishman knows, so to speak, by instinct. I fully realize all this. Nevertheless I am firmly convinced that the risks I have taken were risks well worth the taking.

In the first place, where the national life of England differs from that of my native land, I may claim to possess a valuable capacity for wonder. To an Englishman, English society is the whole of society, the ideal society. Buckle, in a work celebrated half a century ago, avowedly treated all forms of human civilization as so many deviations from the true norm of civilization, the civilization of Great Britain. Very different is the attitude of the observer from abroad. A great number of characteristics which, being familiar to the natives from birth, have come to form part of their intellectual and moral nature, are for him matter of astonishment—whether of admiration or disapproval is indifferent—and demand from him an explanation. Indeed, of all the nations of Europe, it is perhaps the English whose institutions must, in many respects, be regarded as being beyond the institutions of other people, paradoxical, " unique." In short, because I am French, my knowledge of English life is, indeed, more external than would have been the case were I a native Englishman, but on the other hand, for that very reason it is perhaps more objective.

Moreover, whatever the differences between English and continental life, we must beware of exaggerating their importance. To be sure, the Frenchman feels himself in a foreign land when he crosses from Calais to Dover, but how insignificant the difference would seem to an Asiatic traveller from Calcutta or Pekin. Between Latin Catholicism and Anglo-Saxon Protestantism there seems a wide gulf, but what is it to the distance which divides European Christianity as a whole from Brahminism? The European nations at the present day are, indeed, in a very ambiguous position. Divided one from another by strong passions, they are nevertheless in many respects internationalized by common interests, by a common outlook on life, and by a common literary and scientific culture. The institutions or ideas which one nation has neither borrowed from nor imparted to their neighbours will be found on analysis to be few indeed. The difference between the nations of Europe consists after all not so much in the elements which compose their national character, as in the different proportions in which are combined, in each nation, elements common to most or all. The great political invention of modern England has been representative democracy. The invention, however, has spread and is still spreading, and with increasing rapidity, throughout Europe—indeed the entire world. Indeed, representative government bids fair to become part of the common inheritance of mankind. How, then, have these representative institutions of England been built up? Along what lines have they been developed and modified? What laws governed the process? Parliamentary government alike in the State, the factory and the Church had become an almost sacred tradition to the nineteenth-century Englishman. What were the causes, what the forces, which had produced this effect? These problems are of interest to all Europeans. For their study all Europeans are competent.

June, 1912.   E. H.

I must express my thanks to M. Lucien Herr, Librarian of the Ecole Normale Supérieure, who read my work in manuscript and assisted me with his advice; and also to Miss Eileen Power, Girton College, Cambridge, Shaw research student of the London School of Economics and Political Science, who kindly undertook some researches for me in London.

E. H.

TRANSLATOR'S NOTE

For the translation of the first and third books I am responsible, Mr. Barker for the translation of the second book. I may, perhaps, add that the translation has been twice read by M. Halévy, to whose kind help I am indebted for a large number of most valuable suggestions and criticisms.

E. I. WATKIN.

BOOK I

POLITICAL INSTITUTIONS

POLITICAL INSTITUTIONS

1748. Montesquieu, in his *Esprit des Lois*, proposed the political institutions of England as a model to the Governments of the Continent. At that time the Whigs held office in England. The feature of the British Constitution which excited Montesquieu's admiration was the guarantees it provided for the liberty of the subject. For Montesquieu the best and freest type of constitution was the " mixed " or moderate constitution, which combined the distinctive principles of monarchy, aristocracy and democracy. Such a constitution was to be found in England. And again the best and freest type of constitution was that in which there is a clear-cut separation between the three departments of government—the legislature, the executive and the judicature. This also was to be found in the British Constitution.

1815. We now find the Whigs defeated and demoralized, reduced to the condition of a permanent Opposition. With scarcely an interruption for over thirty years past the Cabinets had been Tory, supporters of the Royal Prerogative. Aboukir and Trafalgar, Salamanca and Vittoria, Waterloo, the two Treaties of Paris had bestowed upon the Tory programme the undeniable consecration of success. What, then, had taken place since Montesquieu wrote? Had England passed through revolutions and *coups d'état*? Most certainly not.

In England itself Montesquieu's theory continued to be the classical interpretation of English constitutional law. Blackstone, the great Tory jurist, in his *Commentaries on the Laws of England*, is generally content to follow in the steps of the *Esprit des Lois*. An examination, therefore, of the political institutions of England, as they existed in the opening years of the 19th century, raises a very delicate problem. That problem is to understand the development by which a theory elaborated to defend a constitution regarded by the Whigs as essentially a free constitution served fifty or sixty years later to defend a constitution denounced by the Whig Opposition as oppressive and reactionary. Was it that the constitutional forms, without being directly violated or abolished, had been worked in a manner foreign to their true intention and thus perverted? Or was it rather that the reactionary movement had affected not the Constitution itself, which remained intact, but the public opinion of the country, freely expressed through the forms

3

of this very Constitution ? Perhaps the Liberalism of 1748 no longer satisfied the demands of the Liberals of 1815. Or was the Constitution after all freer than would be imagined from the Opposition complaints ? The very ease with which these complaints found expression, together with the fact that the Government was compelled to meet the grievances of the Opposition with a host of partial concessions, proves how hard it is to arrive at an adequate definition, a definition that will do justice to all the complex factors at work, of the period known to historians as the Tory Reaction.

CHAPTER I

THE EXECUTIVE.   THE JUDICATURE.
THE ARMY.   THE NAVY

THE KING.   THE CABINET.   THE CENTRAL
GOVERNMENT.

The King.   His Sons.   The Prince Regent.

WHEN George III ascended the throne he was not satisfied, as had been the first two monarchs of his dynasty, to be merely a German prince, well paid by the English aristocracy for acting as a figure-head in London.   He wished to effect in his personal interest a restoration of the royal authority, which had been so weakened of late, and to govern England as the other European sovereigns governed their countries, as he himself governed his electorate of Hanover.   The Tory Reaction dates from his accession.   But what, after all, had been the success of this new policy of King George ?   His personal popularity in 1815 is certainly beyond dispute.   The gentry had always admired in him his tastes for country life and sport, and was not scandalized by his indifference to literature, science and art. The middle classes prized his strict virtue, even his bigoted Protestantism.   The vast majority of Englishmen shared his prejudices against Catholic emancipation, his stubborn determination to carry on the war with France.   We must not, however, forget that the monarch and his Court were marked by a German pedantry and formality which had given frequent offence.   Moreover, he had been for a long period the victim of intrigues among parliamentary cliques, exposed to the insults of London journalists, to hostile demonstrations by the mob, to the attempts of assassins.   It was, in fact, only in 1810, when King George, who had already several times been deprived temporarily of his reason, became permanently insane, that he won the unbounded veneration of the people.[1]   His misfortunes won him sympathy as his virtues had won him respect : monarchy in England became a

---

[1] Campbell, *Lives of the Chancellors*, vol. vi. p. 211 n.   " I have heard a high legal dignitary, now no more, say : ' It is a remarkable circumstance that George III, at the commencement of his reign, when in the full possession of his faculties, was abused, ridiculed, thwarted and

harmless fetish. The King George of 1815, blind, deaf and insane, exactly realized the ideal of a puppet king, so dear to the eighteenth-century Whigs, and the puppet became the popular idol. Thus at the very moment of triumph for the party, which is commonly believed to represent the principle of autocracy, the cause of constitutional government won a brilliant victory. The insanity of the King of England made not the slightest change in the government of the country. The same Cabinet, supported by the same majority, remained in office. In fact, if we were to confine our attention to the proceedings of the Government, we should be unable to distinguish between the time when England possessed a monarch and the time when she possessed only the shadow of a monarch.

But perhaps the Royal Family boasted a member sufficiently intelligent, energetic and influential to assume the government of the country, when the King himself had become incapable of rule? No; among the numerous sons of King George not one was fit to govern. With the exception of the sensible but insignificant Duke of Cambridge, and the Duke of Sussex, a Liberal and a friend of reform, who had, however, lost caste by his marriage with Lady Augusta Murray, all the Princes were objects of universal hatred or scorn. Even when they had inherited their father's virtues, they made those very virtues odious. Their love of discipline was tyrannical, narrow, stupid. The Duke of Clarence, who served in the Navy, drove his subordinates to exasperation. In 1798, despite the flattery he received from Nelson, the King was forced to recognize his unfitness for command. The Duke of Kent, a religious man and a philanthropist, caused a mutiny at Gibraltar by his excessive zeal for the repression of drunkenness in the Army. He also was compelled to resign. The Press was on the watch to expose and exploit the scandals caused first by one then by another of the Princes. When Mrs. Jordan, the celebrated actress, lived with the Duke of Clarence as his avowed mistress, rumour declared that he was supported by her earnings. The Duke of York, the favourite son of King George and the Commander-in-Chief of the Army, was considered a man of virtue and a good administrator. Then it was discovered that he kept a mistress and that his mistress had organized with his connivance a regular trade in commissions. The affair caused widespread scandal, a parliamentary inquiry was instituted, and the Duke had to retire into private life for two years. The Duke of Cumberland, perhaps the most intelligent of the King's sons, made himself particularly unpopular by his unbending Toryism. One morning he was found by his bedside wounded, while in an adjoining apartment his valet was lying wounded to death. Despite the verdict of an impartial jury, report accused him of murder and of infamous

almost driven into exile; but when he was deprived of his reason, the nation, falling prostrate before him, called out: A God! A God!'"

vices.[1] To hide himself from popular view he withdrew to the Continent, to return in 1815 married to the Princess of Salm, a lady of doubtful reputation. To support his new establishment he asked Parliament for a higher grant in the Civil List. The House of Commons, after a most insulting debate, refused his request. And what, finally, can be said for the weak and contemptible Prince of Wales who from 1810 onwards exercised the functions of Prince Regent ?

Before his regency he was only known to the public by his constant squabbles with his father and by his equally constant requests to the nation for money. One of the regular occupations of Parliaments for many years was the payment of the Prince's debts. By a promise to put his finances in order, to pay off his creditors and to increase his income, the nation at last secured his marriage. He had one daughter by his wife Princess Caroline of Brunswick. After the child's birth the couple separated and the wretched story of their quarrel began. The Prince of Wales considered himself an unofficial leader of the Opposition. The Whigs therefore took the part of the husband, the Tories of his wife. But later on, when the Prince became Regent, he became at the same time a Tory. Henceforward he found his supporters in the Tory ranks, while the Whigs espoused the cause of the injured Princess. And the Prince brought discredit on both parties in turn, as he joined first the one, then the other. To be sure, he was no country squire like his father and brothers. He had pretensions to intellectual culture. Sheridan had been his intimate friend. At their first meeting he won the heart of Thomas Moore, the poet. Scott, whom he entertained at luncheon, left his presence intoxicated with delight and loyalty. But that was not the way to become popular in England. The public forgave his drunkenness, his quarrelling, his immorality, for these were manly vices. The public could not forgive his effeminacy, his cowardice, which had become a byword, and his persistent desire at the age of fifty to be not only the most fashionable but the most handsome man of his time, the Adonis of European aristocracy. Four hostile Courts : such was the sight presented by the English Royal Family at the beginning of 1815. In a small and simply furnished house at Windsor the old Queen was watching over the last years of her husband, a mental and physical wreck. The Prince of Wales kept up a royal establishment at Carlton House, where he entertained lavishly. His morganatic wife, Mrs. Fitzherbert, to whom he had been secretly wedded according to the rites of the Catholic Church, a woman universally respected, had been forsaken. The Marchioness of Hertford was now the favourite, and she and her set—the Marquis of Hertford, the Marquis of Yarmouth, and the Marquis of Headfort—led the Prince and distributed his

[1] For the scandal of the Duke of Cumberland, see Lady Anne Hamilton, *Secret History of the Court of England*, vol. i. pp. 156-99.

patronage. Kensington Palace was the headquarters of the Princess of Wales. She was a poor, brainless creature, whose head had been turned by the court paid to her by the men of letters, statesmen and leaders of fashion, who wished to annoy the Prince Regent. Meanwhile at Warwick House Princess Charlotte, the daughter of the Prince and Princess, led a dreary and commonplace existence. Her father loathed her and in his jealousy tried to get rid of her. He decided to give her in marriage to the Prince of Orange, who would remove her to Holland. The Princess resisted the scheme and took shelter with her mother. To fetch her home the Prince had to send a regular embassy of ministers, headed by the Lord Chancellor. The middle class and the populace of London joined in the quarrel, and not on the side of the Regent.

When the allied sovereigns visited London after the victories of 1814, the English were not slow to show them how little they respected their rulers. Whenever the Prince drove out in his carriage, whenever he appeared at the theatre, the mob either kept a complete silence or booed. Whenever Princess Charlotte appeared there was an outburst of applause. When these monarchs attended a sitting of the House of Commons, the Opposition raised a full debate on the Regent's behaviour to the two Princesses, in which his vices were denounced, their sufferings deplored.[1] Such were the facilities afforded by the institutions of Great Britain to the open and legal expression of public contempt for the disorders of the Royal Family. Despite fifty years of the Tory reaction England was not governed by a Court. Whether the head of the State were popular like George III or unpopular like the Regent, was in England a matter of less importance than might be expected. For he could not exercise the control over the Government that was exercised by the head of the State in every other European country.

The Influence of the Crown. The Quarrel between the two Parties.

Of what grievance, then, since the Tory reaction began, did the Whig leaders complain ? They feared lest the King should, to use the phraseology of the time, compensate for his diminished " prerogative " by the increase of his " influence." By prerogative we are to understand the constitutional rights of the King, derived from legislation or custom, by influence the indirect action of the King

---

[1] *Creevey Papers*, vol. i. p. 195 sqq., letters to his wife, June 14 and 21, 1814. " All agree," he writes in the letter of the 14th, " that Prinny (the Prince of Wales) will die or go mad. He is worn with fuss, fatigue and *rage*." See also a letter from Lord Grenville to the Marquis of Buckingham, May 9, 1814 (*Court of England under the Prince Regent*, vol. ii. p. 75). " We are full of nothing but very ridiculous preparations for very foolish exhibitions of ourselves to foreign sovereigns (if they do come here) in that character which least of all becomes us—that of courtly magnificence. Our kings never have, and I hope they will never be able, to come near their neighbours in that respect."

upon Parliament by his employment of the means of corruption at his disposal—distribution of money and especially distribution of places.[1] According to the theory of the division of powers, while Parliament makes the laws, it is the office of the King to carry them into execution, or more accurately, to choose the executive. It would seem, therefore, from the very nature of the Constitution, that the State departments, the Government offices, must be under the immediate control of the head of the executive. Such departments were the Treasury, the Exchequer, the Secretaryships of State, the Board of Trade, the Board of Control, and the Military Departments. All the offices through which the revenues were collected, Customs Duties, Excise and Direct Taxes, were subordinate to the Treasury. The First Lord of the Treasury was usually the Prime Minister. The Exchequer, at the head of which was the Chancellor, was also a dependency of the Treasury. Immediately the Budget had been passed, the audit of the national receipts and expenditure took place in the Exchequer. The three Secretaries of State were the Home Secretary, the Foreign Secretary and the Secretary of State for War.[2] The Board of Control supervised (controlled) the administration of India. The Military Departments were the Admiralty, the War Office and the Artillery Office, also the Military Treasury or the Paymastership of the Forces. The most coveted offices were by no means always those which from their functions were in a position to exert the most direct influence on the national policy. They were the offices which disposed of the greatest number of places, possessed the most extensive "patronage." The Treasury and the Admiralty had richer prizes to bestow than the Foreign or the Home Office.[3] According to the Whigs, all these offices and places constituted the sphere of royal influence. Moreover, a host of abuses which had grown up in the Government departments made the possession of administrative posts even more desirable, and thereby increased the power of the Government in whose hands lay the nomination to these places.

The system by which Government officials were remunerated was nothing less than a scandal. In addition to their fixed salary

[1] Burke, "Thoughts on the Cause of the Present Discontents," 1770 (*Works*, vol. ii. pp. 229 sqq.).

[2] For the history and administration of the three Secretaryships of State, see H. of C., April 3, 1816 (*Parl. Deb.*, vol. xxxiii. p. 892 sqq.). For the respective powers of the Secretary of State for War and the Head of the War Office, see Bulwer, *Life of Lord Palmerston*, vol. i. p. 124.

[3] *Journal of Lady Holland*, September 20, 1806 (vol. ii. p. 184). "Lord Howick is *now* desirous of retaining the Admiralty : he is satisfied of the impolicy of giving up such a mine of patronage, and has, in idea, been long enough in possession of the Foreign Office to be weary of it, but unluckily it is too late. The Foxites have not *one* office which has patronage annexed to it." *Ibid.*, January 20, 1811 (vol. ii. p. 285). In the course of negotiations between Grey and Grenville for the formation of a ministry, Grenville said he was prepared to accept the Home Office on condition that the patronage hitherto belonging to the Treasury were transferred to that Department.

they received additional emoluments and fees, which were in some cases determined by the amount of money which passed through their hands. Hence it was to their interest, in direct opposition to the interest of the taxpayer, that the State should receive and expend the largest possible sums. Equally scandalous was the management of accounts in the public offices at the end of the 18th century. Each department possessed its departmental treasury, and these treasuries were mutually independent. Between the time when a Government official received money from the Treasury and the time when he paid it out to his subordinates, or again between the time when he received the taxes and the time when he paid them into the Treasury, he could make whatever use of this money he pleased ; he could even deposit it in a bank at interest. It was, therefore, to his profit to keep the money in his hands as long as possible, a procedure by no means for the advantage of the national finances.[1] Nor was this all. There were a very large number of posts which were not considered as entailing on their holders any obligation to perform, in return for a reasonable salary, any function of social utility, but as positions of power which carried with them a pension and were purely a reward for services rendered in other spheres, either to the country as a whole or to a party.[2] The administration had thus, as all the world knew, become choked with offices, officially classed as sinecures,[3] posts without any useful service attached, posts whose remuneration was out of all proportion to the service performed, posts whose salary was taken by one man while a deputy did the work at a lower rate. By a judicious distribution of " places " the King was able to create dependents, to buy a body of supporters, and with their help to prevent the free expression in the House of Commons of the national will.

All this formed the burden of Whig complaints. Very different was the language of the Tories, the party which at the end of the 18th century was known as " the King's friends." According to them the working of the representative institutions, as they operated in England, was a source of danger to the prosperity, indeed to the very existence, of the country. It was by no means the case that foreign policy and home government were subject to the control of the people ; they were, on the contrary, the sport of aristocratic cabals, determined by the intrigues and caprices of a handful of noble families. The King had become the head of a new party—a party superior to contending factions—whose sole aim was to defend the permanent interest of the entire nation. " To check as much as may be possible the

---

[1] As long as the system of remuneration by fees continued, each of the four Tellers of the Exchequer drew in war-time about £25,000 a year.

[2] John Morley, *Burke*, p. 165.

[3] For a list of the administrative sinecures in existence about 1815, see *First, Second and Third Report from the Select Committee on Sinecure Offices*, June 20, 1810, June 18, 1811, April 23, 1812, and *First Report from the Select Committee on Finance*, March 27, 1817.

spirit of party appears to be one of the first duties and noblest employments of a King." Thus wrote the Tory, Thomas Gisborne.[1] Who could blame George III for seeking the aid of new men to resist the heads of the great "connections" (the Cavendishes, the Russells), and for bestowing his patronage on these supporters? "The House was not of that aristocratic spirit," said Lord Castlereagh, "that would deprive men of humble birth but of great talents of any participation in the administration of the State."[2] On this interpretation—an interpretation, moreover, by no means indefensible—administrative posts were the stake in a contest between the King and the great Whig families. A severe and an unfair contest, the Tories might well add, so great was the preponderance in the British Constitution of the power of Parliament and of the aristocracy over the power of the Crown.

According to the constitutional divisions of powers, replied the Whigs, it was part of the Royal Prerogative to choose the Officers of State, and this right enabled the King to exercise an illegitimate influence which endangered the balance of powers. This would certainly have been the case had the division between the executive and the legislature been carried out in practice as strictly as the theory demanded. But a mixed or complex Constitution like that of Great Britain is unable from its very nature to define with mathematical accuracy the sphere of each of the powers of government. Each of the powers encroached on the spheres of the others. The question was whether or no these encroachments were favourable to the Royal Prerogative.

Blackstone regards the King as not merely the head of the executive, but also as "a constituent part of the supreme legislative power," and ascribes to him in this capacity the right to reject any measure passed by Parliament which failed to meet with his approval.[3] That is to say, he ascribes to him a right of veto on the joint decision of both

---

[1] Gisborne, *Duties of Man*, ed. 1795, vol. i. pp. 57–58. Gisborne continues: "To countenance it is to encourage interested nobles and aspiring commoners, factious orators, needy and profligate adventurers to combine in bands and confederacies for the purpose of obtruding themselves into all the offices of Government, and under the name and garb of servants of imposing on the Monarch and on the people chains too strong to be broken."—Cf. *ibid.*, pp. 51, 634. Cf. *Diary of Lord Colchester*, vol. i. p. 322, Hardwicke to Addington, October 24, 1801: "The great object to the King's Minister in the exercise of patronage must be the management of the Parliament and the quiet and orderly government of the country."

[2] H. of C., March 29, 1813 (*Parl. Deb.*, vol. xxv. p. 400). Cf. H. of C., May 4, 1812, speech of the Chancellor of the Exchequer: "It was only by such places as these that the Crown had now the power of prevailing on men to accept of offices who were not completely independent in their fortunes, and who were obliged to look to their own exertions for the maintenance and provision of their families" (*Parl. Deb.*, vol. xxii. p. 1171).

[3] *Comm.* 261. It must be added that the Tory lawyers were not in agreement upon this point. When the question of Catholic Emancipation came up in 1795 George III inquired of Lord Kenyon, the Chief Justice of the King's Bench, and through him of the Attorney-General, Sir John Scott (the future Lord Eldon), whether his coronation oath did not oblige him in conscience to veto any measure of Catholic Emancipation. Lord Kenyon and Sir John Scott replied in the negative. (See G. T. Kenyon, *Life of Lord Kenyon*, p. 305 sqq., and in particular pp. 317 and 320.)

Houses. And this veto would be a clear gain for the prerogative. But, as a matter of fact, the Tory monarch never had occasion, after his accession to the throne, to put into practice the doctrine of Blackstone. Whenever there arose a difference of opinion between the King and his Cabinet about a Bill adopted by the latter, one of two things always happened. Either the majority in Parliament shrank in the disturbed condition of Europe from a constitutional crisis, and therefore consented to postpone the matter to avoid a conflict, or the King dissolved Parliament, and on his appeal to the country the electors returned a majority favourable to the royal wishes. George III never encroached on the functions of the legislature, nor did he ever attack directly the established constitutional customs which secured the independence of Parliament against the Crown, nor even those customs which constituted a perpetual encroachment of the legislature upon the functions proper to the head of the executive. It is true that, despite repeated attempts, the eighteenth-century Whigs never succeeded in placing the Government departments under the control of committees of Parliament, and in thus securing the complete subordination of the executive to the legislature.[1] But it is equally true that the heads of these departments, the Cabinet Ministers, were members of Parliament, and responsible to Parliament for the measures they took, the appointments they made, and for the way in which they carried out the presumed wishes of the national representatives. In the Cabinet [2] both powers, the legislative and the executive, were confused, but a separation also was made, unnoticed by Montesquieu—a separation, namely, between the agents of the executive who carried on the actual work of government and the head of the executive—who was, moreover, by a fundamental principle of the Constitution irresponsible for the acts of his agents. Such had been the working of Government under the first two Georges, and despite the personal interference of George III in politics it had changed little, if at all, since. As much as King George, indeed more than the King, William Pitt, the Prime Minister, embodied the new and victorious Toryism. Pitt's parliamentary dictatorship, which covered the last fifteen years of the 18th

[1] See the incidents which led to the formation of the Board of Trade and Plantations in 1696 : *Parl. Hist.*, vol. v. p. 977 ; Burnet, *History of his Own Time*, ed. 1833, vol. iv. p. 294 ; Burke, *Speech on Economical Reform, Works*, vol. iii. pp. 325 sqq. ; East India Bill, 1783, see *Annual Register*, 1784, p. 59 ; Lecky, *England in the 18th Century*, vol. v. pp. 231 sqq.

[2] It must be added, if we would speak with perfect accuracy, that not all the responsible Ministers belonged to the Cabinet, nor were all the members of the Cabinet always consulted on matters of grave importance. See *Journal of Lady Holland*, March 8, 1807 (vol. ii. p. 211) : " There is an expedition to be undertaken, which, on account of Erskine's extraordinary imprudence in talking, is to be kept a secret from the Cabinet and only known to a few." For the constitution of the Cabinet at this period see the interesting details in Lord Holland's *Memoirs of the Whig Party*, vol. ii. pp. 84, 87, 88. This distinction between an " inner " and an " outer Cabinet " was even more strictly maintained in the 18th century. See Anson, *Law and Custom of the Constitution*, 2nd ed., vol. ii. pp. 100 sqq.

century, did not differ materially from the dictatorship of his father, thirty years earlier. And his father had been a leader and tribune of the Whigs.

Further, the Whigs accused the King of underhand and indirect attempts to undermine the Constitution. By these very accusations, however, they bore testimony that the King was too weak to attempt its open violation. In fact, not only had the prerogative not increased during the reign of George III ; it had actually decreased. On his accession King George had renounced, by an act of grace, the revenues derived from the hereditary possessions of the Crown, and had expressed his desire that these revenues should henceforth be collected in the same fashion as the other national revenues and included in the Civil List.[1] Later he had been obliged to acquiesce in a limitation of his right to grant pensions. Henceforward the amount disbursed in pensions might not exceed a definite figure, separately fixed for England, Scotland and Ireland.[2] Impeachment was a quasi-judicial procedure employed by Parliament to secure the responsibility of the executive officials. In 1791 the Crown lost the power to stop proceedings by dissolving Parliament.[3] On two occasions, in 1788 and in 1811, when the King had become incapable of government, Parliament refused to proceed by way of address, and to invite the Prince of Wales to assume the Regency by right of birth. On both occasions Parliament took upon itself to nominate, by a special Act, the head of the executive and to define the limits of his authority, and on both occasions it was the Whigs who supported the hereditary principle, because they favoured the claims of the Prince of Wales and because the Prince was considered their leader. It was the Tories who secured, in opposition to the Whigs, the triumph of the old Whig doctrine of the supremacy of Parliament.

The Whig opposition denounced also the management of the Government departments. Here, certainly, they had good cause for complaint : the abuses were scandalous. But these abuses dated from the period of Whig rule, and the only complaint that could fairly be brought against the Tory Ministries was that they had failed to

---

[1] See 1 Geo. III, cap. 1.

[2] See 22 Geo. II, cap. 82 ; 33 Geo. III, cap. 34 (Ireland) ; 50 Geo. III, cap. 111 ; May, *Constitutional History*, vol. i. pp. 215, 217.

[3] 26 Geo. III, cap. 96 ; 45 Geo. III, cap. 125 ; Pellew, *Life of Lord Sidmouth*, vol. i. p. 81 ; Adolphus, *British Empire*, vol. i. p. 291 ; *Parl. Hist.*, vol. xxix. pp. 523, 543 ; Anson, *Law and Custom of the Constitution*, vol. i. pp. 365–366. Nevertheless, after the impeachment of Lord Melville (1804), impeachment fell into disuse ; " laid aside," writes Townsend (*Memoirs of the House of Commons*, vol. ii. p. 356), " like the battle-axe of Richard Cœur de Lion, too heavy for modern arms to wield with effect ; or, like the sword of the Black Prince or a relic in the Sanctuary, rather an object of reverence than of terror, more honourable in its rust than in its edge. May it long continue in abeyance, like another valued privilege of the Commons— their power of refusing the supplies—undisturbed as the royal veto." The age of contests between the Crown and Parliament had gone by ; new problems of a different character were now demanding solution.

abolish them when they succeeded to power. And these abuses, it might be argued, far from favouring the despotic aspirations of the Crown, were, on the contrary, calculated to perpetuate the supremacy in the executive of the Whig aristocracy.

A body of officials, drawn from the middle or lower classes and poorly paid, would be animated by feelings of jealousy towards the aristocracy. On such officials a monarch, greedy of power, could rely for support in a struggle against the arrogant pretensions of the heads of the great families. But it was to satisfy the claims of this aristocracy that those offices of wealth and influence, those sinecures of which we have spoken, had been instituted.[1] And these high officials, securely entrenched in their bureaus, bid the Crown defiance. The English aristocracy had laboured, and with success, to establish the rule that the permanent civil servants were irremovable.[2] Every office conferred for life was deemed, by the lawyers and by Parliament, the freehold of its occupant; therefore no Government post could be taken from its occupant or suppressed, nor even could its character be changed without violating the right of private property.[3] It was even an established custom to grant certain posts in reversion.[4] The patent which conferred the post provided that on the holder's death it should revert to his son or to some other person specified. Some-

---

[1] Even the reformers recognized this, and admitted that the sinecures, if properly distributed, would at least serve to maintain the position of the old aristocracy. "They now serve," writes Cobbett (*Political Register*, March 1, 1806), "or ought to serve, the purpose of rewarding public services—services well known and universally acknowledged; and, which is not less essential to the maintenance of the monarchy and the welfare of the State, for the purpose of upholding and cherishing those amongst the ancient nobility and gentry, who otherwise might fall into a state that would inevitably bring disgrace upon rank, and would, thereby, leave us no aristocracy but that of wealth, ten thousand times more grinding and insolent than the lords of the worst of feudal times." Edmund Burke, twenty-five years earlier, had used similar language in his speech on Economical Reform (*Works*, vol. ii. pp. 238–239): "When we look over this Exchequer list, we find it filled with the descendants of the Walpoles, of the Pelhams, of the Townshends—names to whom the country owes its liberties, and to whom His Majesty owes his crown. May such fountains never be dried up! May they ever flow with their original purity, and refresh and fructify the commonwealth for ages." Accordingly, while demanding a reduction of the salaries attached to these valuable sinecures, he did not demand their total suppression.

[2] When in 1810 the King was seized with madness, and confusion reigned in the Cabinet, Lord Grenville, one of the leaders of the Opposition, took advantage of his position as Auditor of the Exchequer to embarrass the Government by opposing his veto to every issue of money to the Treasury (*Court of England under the Prince Regent*, vol. i. p. 15).

[3] Burke, *Speech on Economical Reform*, 1780 (*Works*, vol. iii. p. 308). The Tellerships of the Exchequer had been reformed in 1784 and the emoluments reduced to a fixed salary of £4,000. But the actual holders were left in undisturbed enjoyment of the enormous emoluments to which they had been entitled before the reform. The Marquis of Buckingham, one of the Tellers unaffected by the reform, did not die till 1813 and it was only at his own request that Lord Camden's Tellership could be reformed in 1819 (59 Geo. III, cap. 43).

[4] *Or for Joint Lives with Benefit of Survivorship.* In 1782 a patent was issued to confer the post of Clerk of the Parliament after the death of Mr. Ashley Cowper, then eighty years of age, on Samuel Strut and George Rose in reversion. George Rose succeeded to the post in 1795, and it brought him an annual income of £3,278. He secured the reversion of it for his eldest son. (*Diaries . . . of George Rose*, vol. i. pp. 25 sqq. Cobbett, *Paper against Gold*, Letter 27, July 20, 1811; *Political Register*, vol. xx. p. 69.)

times the patent even nominated three successive holders of the same office. Thus was constituted in the Government departments of England a species of mortmain. We must add that by 1813 the higher officials had lost their former right to sell the subordinate posts. The result of all this was that even in the departments where, as head of the executive, we might have expected to find him absolute, King George was no Sovereign, but merely an overlord. In many respects the bureaucracy of London presented the characteristics of an hereditary feudalism.[1]

" It is our purpose," contended the Opposition speakers, " by a reform of the administration, to prevent the establishment in our midst of a powerful bureaucracy under the control of a despotic monarch." " Your contention is absurd," replied the supporters of the Government. " These very abuses, at which you exclaim, effectively limit the Royal Prerogative and protect the aristocracy against the Crown." We cannot be surprised that public opinion watched with an ever-increasing scepticism a dispute in which both parties were obviously fighting for their own interests. When in 1784 the issue had been whether the East India patronage should be entrusted to a parliamentary commission or to a Minister nominated by the Crown, the country had plainly declared in favour of the King and against the great parliamentary families. Quite recently, in 1812, when the Whigs were about to take office, they had attempted to prevent the Prince Regent from choosing the officers of his household without consulting the Cabinet. The attempt failed ; victory rested with the Regent, and the leaders of the Opposition realized, to their disgust, that public opinion did not support them.[2] The nation's one desire was the reform of abuses, whoever might benefit by them, and the middle classes were delighted that, in part owing to the pressure of the new democratic ideas, in part to the exigencies of party warfare, this reform had already begun.

Administrative Reform.

Reform dated from the moment that George III showed his intention to exploit the old abuses for his own ends. The Whigs took alarm, and attempted to become once more the champions of popular rights. Edmund Burke, the great Whig orator, opened, in

[1] Miss Edgeworth, *Patronage*, chap. ix : " Thus the forms of homage and the rights of vassalage are altered, the competition for favour having succeeded to the dependence for protection ; the feudal lord of ancient times could ill compete in power with the influence of the modern political patron."

[2] See Thomas Grenville's letter to the Marquis of Buckingham, June 10, 1812 (*Court of England under the Prince Regent*, vol. i. p. 379). On this matter cf. *ibid.*, vol. i. pp. 355-357 : Minute of a conversation between Lords Grey and Grenville and Lord Moira, June 6, 1812 ; H. of C., January 16, January 27, 1812 ; H. of L., February 7, 1812 (*Parl. Deb.*, vol. xxi. pp. 151 sqq., 331 sqq., 689 sqq.).

1780, the campaign in favour of "economical reform," [1] or, as we should term it, of administrative reform. During five years of successive political crises the question of "economical reform" was the burden of all the important debates. When the Whigs—Fox and his friends—were in opposition they loudly demanded reform from the King's friends. If they succeeded to an interval of office they were at once reproached by their opponents for slackness and hesitation in carrying out their programme. Two important commissions [2] were appointed, and issued a series of reports which reviewed all the Government departments, criticizing abuses and suggesting reforms. The length of time was reduced during which the Government funds would be at the disposal of the heads of departments, who moreover lost, in certain cases, the right to the usufruct of these funds. In some cases a system of fixed salaries was substituted for that of remuneration by "fees." The number of useless posts was reduced, also of posts where the work was done by a deputy. Treasury, Exchequer, Customs, Excise, Admiralty, all were reformed.[3] Pitt, the Tory Premier, wished to contrast his policy of active reform with the inertia of the Whig oligarchy in its days of power.

There followed the French Revolution and the Napoleonic War. Pitt and Burke were reconciled and belonged henceforward to the same party, the party formed to defend all the old traditions, even all the old abuses, against Jacobin propaganda. And the war led to lavish expenditure. Instead of economies in the offices already existing, new offices were brought into existence, a Secretaryship of State for War, a Board of Artillery.[4] But five years had not elapsed before

---

[1] *Speech on Economical Reform*, 1780 (*Works*, vol. iii. pp. 229 sqq.). The reader will find a general view of the reform movement, together with an appreciation of the work accomplished —an appreciation inspired naturally enough by Governmental optimism—in the speech delivered by George Rose in the House of Commons on June 2, 1809, and published by the speaker as a pamphlet entitled *Observations respecting the Public Expenditure and the Influence of the Crown*, 1810. Bentham published a reply, his *Defence of Economy against the Right Hon. Edmund Burke* (*Works*, vol. v. pp. 278 sqq.).

[2] 20 Geo. III, cap. 54 : " For appointing and enabling Commissioners to examine, take and state the public accounts of the Kingdom ; and to report what balances are in the hands of accountants which may be applied to the public service, and what defects there are in the present mode of receiving, collecting, issuing, and accounting for public money ; and in what more expeditious and effectual and less expensive manner the said services can in future be regulated and carried on for the benefit of the public." 25 Geo. III, cap. 19 : " For appointing Commissioners to inquire into the fees, gratuities, perquisites, and emoluments which are or lately have been received in the several public offices to be therein mentioned ; to examine into any abuses which may exist in the same ; and to report such observations as shall occur to them for the better concluding and managing the business transacted in the said offices." See H. of C., February 17, March 8, 1785 (*Parliamentary Register*, vol. xvii. pp. 180 sqq., 344 sqq.).

[3] 22 Geo. III, cap. 75 (offices in the Plantations) ; 22 Geo. III, cap. 81, and 23 Geo. III, cap. 82 (Paymaster of the Forces) ; 22 Geo. III, cap. 82 (Civil list) ; 23 Geo. III, cap. 82 (Exchequer) ; 24 Geo. III, cap. 38 (Tax Office : Exchequer) ; 25 Geo. III, cap. 31 (Treasureship of the Navy) ; 25 Geo. III, cap. 52 (for better auditing public accounts) ; 27 Geo. III, cap. 13 (Customs and Excise) ; 29 Geo. III, cap. 64 (Customs).

[4] The Treasury reform begun in 1782 was completed in 1793. The Reports were issued in 1789, 1792 and 1793. In consequence of two reports issued by the Commissioners of the

the agitation for reform began once more. When Pitt asked Parliament in 1797 for the nomination of a commission of inquiry into the public finances, Parliament exacted an extension of its scope. Like the commission appointed fifteen years earlier, it was to review all the Government departments and to take into consideration the reforms already effected and those which were still necessary.[1] After the Peace of Amiens and the resumption of hostilities, as the Government lost prestige, the reform movement became more active. Lord St. Vincent reformed the administration of the Navy,[2] the Duke of York reformed the War Office.[3] Lord Melville, the First Lord of the Admiralty, was accused of speculating for his personal profit with the funds temporarily entrusted to his charge. This brought up the whole question of the subordinate treasuries, and in 1806 a Coalition Ministry, containing the Whig leaders, settled the matter by an Act which embraced all the public departments.[4] A scandal made public in 1809 led to the passage of a Bill prohibiting the sale of Government offices.[5] In 1812 a Bill for the abolition of sinecures was introduced. This Bill provided for the employment of the money thus saved to establish a pension fund for retiring officials. The Bill was twice rejected by the Lords, but in the course of the debates an important sinecure, the Paymastership of Widows' Pensions, was suddenly abolished. This was a deliberate insult offered to the Prince of Wales, whose intimate friend, Lord MacMahon, was Paymaster.[6] The custom of granting

Customs appointed in 1789, a Bill for the abolition of the fees paid to the "Outdoor Officers" of the Customs was prepared in 1792. But there the matter rested. It is remarkable that the reform was suspended coincidently with the outbreak of hostilities.

[1] H. of C., March 13, 1797 (*Parliamentary Register*, vol. lxiv. pp. 27 sqq.). The Reform Bills passed in consequence of the Commission were 38 Geo. III, cap. 89 (Abolition of Salt Board, its work was transferred to the Excise); 38 Geo. III, cap. 86 (Abolition of sinecures in the Customs); 39 Geo. III, cap. 83 (Abolition of the auditors of the Land Revenue in England and Wales).

[2] 93 Geo. III, cap. 16: "For appointing Commissioners to inquire and examine into any irregularities, frauds or abuses which are or have been practised by persons employed in the several naval departments therein mentioned, and in the business of Prize Agency; to report such observations as shall occur to them, for preventing such irregularities, frauds and abuses—for the better conducting and managing the business of the said departments and of Prize Agency in future." Continued 45 Geo. III, cap. 46, until the end of the next session of Parliament.

[3] 45 Geo. III, cap. 47: "To appoint Commissioners to inquire and examine into the public expenditure in the conduct of public business, in the military departments there mentioned; and to report such observations as shall occur to them for correcting or preventing any abuses and irregularities and for the better conducting and managing the business of the said departments; to continue in force for two years, and from thence until the expiration of six weeks after the commencement of the then next session of Parliament."

[4] 46 Geo. III, cap. 141. See *Annual Register*, 1806, pp. 78 sqq. To this general Act we must add a number of special Acts dealing with the reorganization of the system of accounts in the Government offices. Pitt's Cabinet initiated the movement by the Act, 45 Geo. III, cap. 58, dealing with the Paymastership-General.

[5] 49 Geo. III, cap. 126.

[6] On the question of sinecures see H. of C., February 10, July 7, 1807; February 5, May 31, 1810; January 9, March 24, May 4, June 15, 1812; February 12, 1813; H. of L., May 18, 1813 (*Parl. Deb.*, vol. viii. p. 703, vol. ix. p. 745, vol. xv. p. 311, vol. xvii. p. 227, vol. xxi. p. 112, vol. xxii. pp. 162, 1159, vol. xxiii. p. 468, vol. xxiv. p. 506, vol. xxvi. p. 220). When

administrative posts in reversion fell into disuse. The Cabinet of 1806 boasted that it had made no grants of this kind,[1] and although in 1815 the practice had not yet been definitely abolished, it had been suspended for the previous eight years by a series of temporary Acts.[2]

Historians are too much in the habit of regarding the *ancien régime* in England as a solid block which did not begin to crumble till about 1832. In reality a great reform movement began about 1780, and although this movement undoubtedly died down during the anti-Jacobin reaction, during the last years of the war it was once more in full swing. To this fact is due the radical difficulty which faces us when we seek to define exactly the state of British society during the early years of the 19th century. Not only was that society highly complex, it was also in a state of flux. Take, for instance, the administration and its abuses. The Tories were undoubtedly right in insisting that the system owed its origin and character to the Whigs, and had been constructed to reduce to a minimum the authority of the head of the executive over the agents of the executive. Sometimes indeed, for instance, during the early years of William Pitt's Ministry, the Tories had even played the part of reformers. But by 1815 they were pledged to the defence of all the abuses employed by the eighteenth-century Whigs to secure their power ; for that power was now in Tory hands. It was the leaders of the Whig Opposition who, to storm the citadel occupied by the Regent's advisers, were battering to pieces the old edifice of Whig aristocracy.

THE JUDICATURE. JUDGES AND BARRISTERS.

Lawyers : Solicitors. Barristers. Judges.

Montesquieu distinguished between the legislature and the executive. He made a further distinction between " the executive power in matters pertaining to international law," in short, the executive proper, and the " executive power in matters relative to the civil law." [3]   In other

on May 6, 1812, Fremantle informed the Marquis of Buckingham of the Government defeat on the Sinecure Offices Bill, he added, " There never was a Bill so full of absurdity and impracticability ; but the object of it was one which the House of Commons are now wild upon " (*Court of England under the Prince Regent*, vol. i. p. 288).

[1] H. of C., February 10, 1807, Lord Henry Petty's Speech (*Parl. Deb.*, vol. viii. p. 703).

[2] 48 Geo. III, cap. 50 ; 50 Geo. III, cap. 88 ; 51 Geo. III, cap. 1 (Regency Sec. 9) ; 52 Geo. III, cap. 40.   See the Parliamentary Debates : H. of L., August 4, 1807 ; H. of C., January 25, April 11, 1808, April 24, 1809, January 31, 1810 (a motion by Bankes in favour of an Office in Reversion Bill was adopted by acclamation.   An amendment by the Chancellor of the Exchequer received only two votes, one of these being the vote of the Chancellor himself), April 5, 1811, January 28, February 7, 1812 ; H. of L., February 17, 1812 ; H. of C., April 5, 1812 ; H. of L., March 24, 1812, July 8, 1814 ; H. of C., July 19, 1814 ; H. of L., June 12, 1815.   (*Parl. Deb.*, vol. ix. p. 1044, vol. x. p. 96, vol. xi. p. 18, vol. xiv. p. 191, vol. xv. p. 251, vol. xix. p. 712, vol. xxi. pp. 381, 691, 825, vol. xxii. p. 151, vol. xxviii. pp. 632, 791, vol. xxxi. p. 716.)

[3] *Esprit des Lois*, Book II, chap vi.

words, if the principle of the separation of powers is to be completely applied there must be a separation between the judicature and the two other powers. On this point Blackstone followed Montesquieu, but was careful to modify a doctrine no doubt too republican for his liking. According to Montesquieu, if the independence of the Bench is to be duly secured, the judges must be taken from the mass of the people, they must be partially liable to challenge, and must be the peers of the accused. But these independent judges which Montesquieu regarded as essential to a good constitution and which he did in fact find in England, were not the judges but the juries. We find nothing of all this in Blackstone, who, in the passage where he defines the nature of judicial independence, makes no allusion whatever to the jury system. We will therefore do well to neglect the jury, provisionally at least, and be content to inquire to what extent the English judicial system did in reality carry out the theory of the separation of powers, as we find it laid down by Blackstone. " Indeed," writes Blackstone, " that the absolute power claimed and exercised in a neighbouring nation is more tolerable than that of the Eastern empires, is in great measure owing to their having vested the judicial power in their Parliaments, a body separate and distinct from both the legislative and executive : and if ever that nation recovers its former liberty, it will owe it to the efforts of those assemblies." [1] But this very institution which in France embodied so perfectly the principle of the separation of powers was lacking in England. In England the Bar and the Bench did not constitute a caste. A legal career was open to the ambition and the talents of the poorest, and it led to the very highest positions in society. On the lowest rung of this ladder we find the attorneys, or, to employ the more dignified term now coming into general use, the solicitors. [2] One of the sources of their prosperity was the numerous services which they were in a position to render to the great landed proprietors. Did a landowner find the personal management of his farms irksome and difficult ? He made a solicitor his agent and put all business in his hands. Or did he find a difficulty in performing his duties as a magistrate ? He made a solicitor his salaried clerk, who prompted him and did all the real work. Or again, was he moved by political ambitions to stand for a borough or a county ? A solicitor was indispensable to watch over his interests, take part in local intrigues and distribute money in his client's name. Thus the solicitors grew wealthy while the great families, whose agents they were, spending

[1] 1 *Comm.* 269.

[2] Miss Edgeworth, *Patronage*, chap. xxii : " Solicitor Babington, by the by, pray tell Rosamund in answer to her question whether there is an honest attorney, that there are no such things as attorneys now in England—they are all turned into solicitors and agents, just as every *shop* is b ecome a *warehouse*, and every *service* a *situation*." Number of solicitors in 1800 in London, 1,800 ; 3,500 in the provinces (Gneist, *Verfassungs und Verwaltungsrecht*, vol. i. p. 509).

recklessly, were impoverished, sometimes even ruined.[1] But, drawn from the people the solicitors continued to be of the people. They were a body without prestige, a body separated from the barristers by a social abyss. The latter, to be sure, could not dispense with the services of the former. But for that very reason professional etiquette forbade them ever to do anything that would have the appearance of courting the favour of solicitors or of paying court to them for briefs. And apparently with the 19th century the rules of the Bar became even stricter on this point than they had been in the 18th. Lord Campbell informs us that in the 18th century Pratt remained a long while briefless because he would not invite solicitors to his dinner parties nor dance with their daughters ; and that Wedderburn, on the other hand, built up a large body of clients by canvassing the City solicitors for briefs. But such practices were a thing of the past, and Campbell remarks that professional snobbery had now been pushed to absurdity.[2]

Active, wealthy, intelligent, but without social standing, the solicitors had every inducement to become a discontented class in revolt against a system which condemned them to a position of social inferiority. John Frost, one of the leading " Jacobin " agitators in 1794, was a solicitor. About the same period Burke made it a reproach against the new democracies of France and America that they were governed by solicitors. It would, nevertheless, be a mistake to suppose that the established order of society was ever in any danger from the grievances of the English solicitors ; for they were comforted by the knowledge that it was in their power to win for their children the standing which they could never obtain for themselves. A solicitor's son, called to the Bar, possessed the most favourable opening for a brilliant career. His father recommended him both to his clients and to his fellow solicitors. He had learnt his profession in his father's office, and his fellow students, when in due course they became solicitors, brought their cases to him. The three most eminent Lord Chancellors in the 18th century were the sons of solicitors, and of the three, two had not even been to the University. After 1792 the prestige attaching to the military profession was much raised by the constant wars, and, moreover, the increase in the forces made a great many new openings in the Army for the younger members of the aristocracy. This rendered access to the Bar even easier than before. And the moment

---

[1] See the complaints of the first Marquis of Lansdowne (Fitzmaurice, *Life of Lord Shelburne*, vol. ii, pp. 345–6) : " . . . Of all the follies, the greatest is that which formerly was practised and is still continued in some great families, that of having some considerable lawyer or some eminent man of business at a considerable salary to audit your accounts. There is a family whose fortune was entirely made by the father's auditing the accounts of different estates, which many of the owners were infinitely more capable of auditing."

[2] Campbell, *Lives of the Chancellors*, vol. v. p. 232, vol. vi. p. 56.

a solicitor's son began to practise at the Bar he felt himself a member of the governing class and shared its snobbery.[1]

The four great Inns at the City gates, where swarmed the entire population of lawyers, were in fact four large aristocratic clubs, recruited by free cooptation. In this district between the City of London and the Borough of Westminster, the English kings had founded in the 13th century an institution intended to provide young men of good family with a school of jurisprudence. Soon, however, those for whose benefit the Inns of Court had been established forsook them and went to Oxford or Cambridge to complete their education. Nevertheless, it still remained fashionable, the gentlemanly thing, to read for the Bar. Sons of landed gentlemen, of officers in the Army, of merchants, of solicitors, the London barristers were well aware that the vote which had conferred upon them the privileges of the Bar had also admitted them into good society. They met at definite periods as a disciplinary court, a Bench, whose function it was to secure the observance of the rules of the corporation. In 1807 the Benchers of Lincoln's Inn had decided that no one who had received payment for writing in the newspapers might henceforth be called to the Bar. To procure the abolition of this rule required all the influence of the Press, a campaign of three years and a long debate in Parliament, in which all the lawyers present dissociated themselves from the action of their senate.[2]

Since barristers were men of the world who prided themselves on having nothing of the theorist or the pedant about them, they took care that the Inns of Court should bear no resemblance to Universities provided with an organized teaching staff. The old aristocratic England was not enamoured of learning. In 1799 it required all the energy of the Chancellor, Lord Loughborough, to obtain from the Benchers of Lincoln's Inn permission for Mackintosh to deliver a course of lectures on the law of nature.[3] His course lasted two years. On its conclusion the old order was restored, the experiment was never repeated; the traditional contempt for scientific principles, the established routine, resumed their sway. To be present each term

---

[1] H. of C., March 23, 1810 (Stephen's Speech) : " That profession was in a pre-eminent manner the patrimony of the people at large. . . . In other professions, as the Church or Army, hereditary claims or fortune might facilitate preferment ; but at the Bar, a profession which was a much more frequent road to rank and fortune, no such extrinsic advantages were of any avail. On the contrary, it was proverbial, that a necessity arising from poverty in the early part of life was almost the only source of splendid success at the Bar " (*Parl. Deb.*, vol. xvi. p. 375). See, on the other hand, Miss Austen, *Sense and Sensibility*, chap. 19. " . . . The law was allowed to be genteel enough ; many young men who had chambers in the Temple made a very good appearance in the first circles, and drove about town in very knowing gigs." The number of barristers in 1810 = 598, in 1820 = 880, in 1821 = 820 (Gneist, *Verfassungs und Verwaltungsrecht*, vol. i. p. 503).

[2] See the Debates, H. of C., March 23 and 26, 1810 (*Parl. Deb.*, vol. xvi. pp. 27, 45). Cf. *Diary of Lord Colchester*, March 23, 1810, vol. ii. p. 240.

[3] Campbell, *Lives of the Chancellors*, vol. vi. pp. 288–290.

at a fixed number of dinners in hall formed the only obligation imposed by the rules. The students dined at the Lower Table. At the High Table the Benchers enjoyed a better-cooked dinner, which they had earned by a two years' apprenticeship at the Lower Table. The food was good, the drinking heavy. If a student wanted to work, it was for him to procure the means of instruction. He could become a clerk in a solicitor's office or, perhaps, attach himself to one of the barristers of inferior rank, specialists in matters of procedure and intermediate between barristers and solicitors, who were called special pleaders and who for the last twenty years had been earning a livelihood by coaching pupils for the Bar.

Then came the time to practise. The wealthiest and most fashionable of the young barristers spent the season at Bath, and during the circuits, when they followed the Westminster judges into the provinces on their yearly round of assizes, they made quite a stir by their fashionable style of living. And to maintain his position the poor barrister was obliged, as far as possible, to imitate his wealthier confrères. So grievous is the yoke of snobbery. In London he must keep a clerk and occupy chambers where solicitors and their clients came to consult him. This entailed a rent of £40 to £60 a year. During the two circuits in which he took part every year he was obliged to spend over £80 in the course of ten weeks. The horse on which he rode from town to town was a costly item, and it was considered beneath the dignity of the profession to pass the night at a common inn.[1] The first years were often years of great hardship. Good friends, however, or the lucky chance of a successful case, might make the reputation of our youthful barrister. Henceforth he will leave to others the inferior business of the profession, such as procedure, the drawing up of notaries' documents or the coaching of pupils, and from a junior barrister will become a leader. In future all his work will consist in conducting important cases and in the practice of oratory. He will become Serjeant-at-Law and King's Counsel, and exchange his woollen gown for silk. Quite a large number of barristers made £4,000 a year. Sir Samuel Romilly received from £15,000 to £16,000 a year Nothing was beyond the reach of a successful barrister; there was no office or title to which he might not aspire.[2]

Parliament was open to him. For parliamentary government is essentially government by oratory. But neither the country gentlemen who composed the great mass of the Tory Party nor the heads of " the great Revolution families " who led the Whigs were necessarily orators. They therefore called the barristers to their assistance, found them

---

[1] For the expenses of a London barrister see Cottu, *Administration de la Justice Criminelle en Angleterre*, pp. 145–146.

[2] Charles Abbott refused a judgeship in 1808. As a barrister he was making £8,000 a year and would have lost too much by joining the Bench (Townshend, *Lives of Eminent Judges*, vol. ii. p. 245).

seats, and offered them later a position in their Cabinets as the Crown lawyers, Attorney-General and Solicitor-General. These were extremely lucrative posts, posts moreover which not only allowed their holders to continue to accept private briefs, but also, by the prestige which they conferred, sent them a large influx of business.

The other positions in the Cabinet brought in less money and occupied more time. But there were the sinecures and grants in reversion to secure pecuniary compensation to those who accepted such offices and to their immediate heirs. The " black squadron " [1] of lawyers acquired an ever-increasing influence in the councils of the Tory Party, from the day when the barrister William Pitt reorganized it after the American War till the moment when the barrister Addington found himself at the head of a Cabinet in which barristers abounded. To be sure, they were far from popular. An Opposition orator denounced " this weak and idiotic administration," not one of whose members " had landed or indeed any other kind of property, and which was merely a parcel of second-rate lawyers and needy adventurers." [2] " The present ministers," Horner wrote scornfully, " are almost all lawyers, bred upon the lowest benches of the forum." [3] But after all Horner was himself a lawyer, and it was not only on the Tory side of the House that the brunt of the debate was borne by lawyers. Among the Whig lawyers in Parliament were Horner himself, Romilly the leading light of the London Bar, and Brougham the great man from Edinburgh.[4] The demagogue, Cobbett, who attacked both parties, invited in 1812 the electors of Bristol to vote against the Whig Romilly, simply because he was a barrister. " We have been brought," he wrote, " to our present miserable state by a lawyer-like policy defended in lawyer-like debates." [5]

A barrister could also be made a judge of one of the four higher

---

[1] See Sir John Scott to his brother, 1790 (Campbell, *Lives of the Chancellors*, vol. vii. p. 103). In a list of the Members of the House of Commons in 1815, forty-seven names were those of lawyers. We must not, however, forget that a certain number of those put down as lawyers were young men of good family who had been called to the Bar but did not practise.

[2] H. of C., November 29, 1810 (*Parl. Deb.*, vol. xviii. p. 107)—Speech of General Mathew, and January 2, 1811 (*Parl. Deb.*, vol. xviii, p. 660)—Sheridan's speech. Sheridan compares the Ministry to a new Directory. Only a Carnot, he said, was wanting to make the resemblance perfect. " There is, however, one similitude—that at the head of the French Directory, as well as now of our own, there was a lawyer of the name of Reubel." Cf. Ward, *Letters to Ivy*, October 1809 (pp. 85–6). " Lord Liverpool takes the Department of War and Colonies. Richard Ryder succeeds him as Home Secretary. Quaere. Will the duties of that high office allow him leisure to audit my Lord Stafford's accounts, which he has hitherto done and received for it an annual douceur of £2,000 ? "

[3] F. Horner to J. A. Murray, May 22, 1810 (*Correspondence*, vol. ii. p. 43).

[4] In 1818 Creevey told Wellington that he would like to see Romilly Leader of the Opposition in the Commons. Wellington replied : " The House of Commons never likes lawyers." " So I " (Creevey) " said that was true generally, and justly so, but that poor Horner had been an exception, and so was Romilly ; that they were no ordinary, artificial, skirmishing lawyers, speaking from briefs, but that they conveyed to the House, in addition to their talents, the impression of their being really sincere, honest men (*Creevey Papers*, vol. i. p. 278).

[5] *Political Register*, July 4, 1812 (vol. xxii. p. 9).

courts of Westminster. In all there were twelve judgeships between the three Common Law courts—the King's Bench, Common Pleas and Exchequer. Each of these courts had a president, the Chief Justice or Chief Baron and three " Puisne " judges. The fourth court, known as the Court of Equity, possessed one judge, the Lord Chancellor, who was assisted by a Master of the Rolls and also, since 1813, by a Vice-Chancellor. The number of these posts was obviously very small, but on that very account the greater was the prestige attaching to them. It might happen that the judges were men of no birth, hampered by unsuitable wives, former mistresses or uneducated and unpolished women of the lower middle class. Nevertheless, they were treated with respect by the noblest families of the land, took rank with the bishops, and were received in state in the provinces. The Lord Chancellor held a position apart from the other judges, for he was a Cabinet Minister. The importance of this office had increased since Lord Eldon held it. An intransigent Tory, a great judge, an unwearied intriguer, he had succeeded, after having been the political adviser and friend of George III, in gaining the intimate friendship of the Prince Regent. It seemed as if the office of Lord Chancellor had become irremovable, and the chief judge of the kingdom was also a perpetual vicar of the Government.

The Relation of the Judicature to the Other Powers.

With a judiciary thus constituted what became of the classic theory of the division of powers ? If the judicature and the legislature were to be kept separate, a judge should have been incapable of sitting in the House of Commons; but though this was certainly the custom, it was no absolute rule. There was an entire class of judges, namely the Welsh, to whom it did not apply at all. These judges were all eligible to a seat in the Commons. Consequently they were always, or nearly always, chosen from the Members of the House, and their nomination was always a reward for political services. Three years before our date the nomination to a judgeship, during a general election, of William Kenrick, the proprietor of the Borough of Bletchingley, had caused a public scandal.[1] The same principle also required

[1] H. of C., June 12, 1809 (Romilly's speech) : " . . . that for the last thirty years the Welsh judges, with only three exceptions, had been chosen from among gentlemen of the profession who were Members of that House (*Parl. Deb.*, vol. xiv. p. 989). F. Burton, one of the Welsh judges, had, on March 8, 1809, vigorously defended the Duke of York. The Chancellor of the Exchequer ascribed the violent campaign carried on by the Opposition against the privilege of the Welsh judges to the ill-feeling they cherished against Burton. See June 1, 1809 : " As to the proposition of excluding the Welsh judges from the House of Commons, if such a regulation were at present adopted it would appear to be pointed at an individual who had always been most zealous in the discharge of his public duties " (*Parl. Deb.*, vol. xiv. p. 857). For the nomination of Kenrick see *Morning Chronicle*, October 31, 1812 : " The late advancement of a member of the Household, the Clerk of the Kitchen, but the proprietor of the Borough of Bletchingley, to a Welsh judgeship shows that there is nothing so sacred in the Constitution which Ministers would not sacrifice to augment their numbers."

that no judge could ever be a Member of the Upper House. But the Chancellor, by the very fact of his appointment, entered the House of Lords, and the posts of Chief Justice and Chief Baron also brought with them a peerage. George III established the custom that the judges of the higher courts should always be knighted on promotion to the Bench; and he could advance later to the peerage those among the judges whom he considered sufficiently rich to support the position. In the lifetime of George III, thirteen lawyers entered the House of Lords through a seat on the Bench, three others after previous membership of the Lower House where they had taken an active part in politics. These new peers were of widely different origin. Lord Erskine was a son of the Earl of Buchan, Lord Ellenborough of a Bishop of Carlisle. But Lord Eldon, on the other hand, was the son of an obscure merchant, who had made a fortune out of the Newcastle collieries, and Charles Abbott, who was soon to receive a peerage, was the son of a Canterbury wigmaker. In all sixteen lawyers, practising or retired, had been raised to the peerage, a number equal to that of the ennobled sailors and soldiers.

Extenuating circumstances were pleaded on behalf of this confusion of powers. It was maintained that these Law Lords, though adherents of the rival parties, had learnt to work together in the impartial discharge of their judicial functions. But, if that were the case, the customs of the country, for reasons which remain to be investigated, had effected what its institutions would have failed to effect. Nor was the House of Lords only a legislative assembly; it was also a Court of Justice. It heard appeals from all the higher courts of England, Scotland and Ireland. For the trial of Peers it was a criminal court both of first and last instance. It was certainly the custom that the great body of Peers abstained from taking part in debate whenever the House was discharging its judicial functions, and left the conduct of business to those of their body who were also professional judges. But this was after all no more than a custom—a custom, moreover, which was only observed when the House of Lords sat as a Court of Appeal. When the Peers tried a fellow Peer on a criminal charge all the Peers acted as judges. In short, the British Constitution allowed a judge to exercise, in addition to his judicial functions, the functions of a legislator. It allowed a legislator to exercise, in addition to his legislative functions, the functions of a judge. And to these two instances of a confusion of powers we must add yet a third. A judge was permitted, as we shall see, in the very exercise of his judicial functions, to be in the strictest sense a legislator.

"The scope of judgments," wrote Montesquieu, "should be limited so rigidly that they can never amount to more than an exact statement of the law. If they might be an expression of the judge's private opinion, the members of society would live in ignorance of the exact nature of the obligations binding upon them." In other words, Montesquieu would not permit the independence of the judicature to encroach upon the other powers. According to him, the function of the judge was to apply, secure from external pressure and from underhand influence, but with the most scrupulous precision, the laws enacted by the legislature. Here, then, we find another point on which Montesquieu's theory fails to correspond with his British model. In the 18th century the British Parliament legislated very little. As regards the English civil law, not only was there no code, but it would even be true to say that there were no laws. A respect for the common law—that is for the general principles of jurisprudence, drawn from the accumulated legal decisions of past centuries—formed the sole rule of English law that prevailed in the three courts of Common Pleas, King's Bench, and Exchequer. To be sure the Court of Chancery, unlike these three courts, judged in equity. But what, then, was this equity? Was it the Roman law which was administered by this court in the distant past when it was an ecclesiastical court of Canon law? For such an interpretation of equity, an intention on the Chancellors' part to apply the Roman law would have been insufficient; the Chancellors must also have possessed a sufficient knowledge of that law to be capable of applying it. But this was not the case. Was equity, then, as others maintained, the common sense of the judge, who, neglecting precedents, took into consideration only the character of the case before him? If so, the decisions would be purely arbitrary, since the judge would professedly be emancipated from all control. Or was it, to follow a third interpretation, a system of legal principles, resembling in its main features the jurisprudence of the other courts, and equally empirical? So, on the whole, it was understood by Lord Eldon. After all, then, the four courts framed their decisions on the same general principles, and thus all worked together in the gradual development of English law.

Each trial was in practice a professional conference between the judges and the barristers on either side, all of whom were members of the same body, trained in the same school, and differing only in their rank in the legal hierarchy; and the object of this conference was to discover how the former decisions of the courts should be applied to the new case. Through these applications, the ancient law, the secret of the profession, was inevitably altered by those who claimed only to maintain its integrity. The periods during which certain great judges discharged their functions were epoch-making in the history of English law. Lord Eldon, for example, reformed both commercial law and the law of marriage. English civil law is judge-made law in the formation of which the legislature has had no share.

The confusion of the two powers is obvious. In fact, English statesmen of the 18th century were not concerned to separate the judiciary and the legislature. Their interest was confined to one problem alone—how best to secure the complete protection of both powers, the judicial and the legislative alike, against the encroachment of the executive. To understand how the British institutions effected a separation between the executive and the judicature we must return once more, not to Montesquieu, but to Blackstone, and examine how far Blackstone's teaching was realized in fact. According to Blackstone, the separation between the executive and the judicature consisted in the delegation by the kings of their judicial power " to the judges of their several courts." These judges, he continues, " are the grand depositaries of the fundamental laws of the kingdom, and have gained a known and stated jurisdiction, regulated by certain and established rules, which the Crown itself cannot now alter but by Act of Parliament." [1] Since the reign of William III they had been irremovable, holding their places no longer *durante bene placito* (during the King's pleasure), but *quamdiu se bene gesserit* (during good behaviour), and could only be removed by a joint address of both Houses.[2] Under the first two Georges the Crown still retained the right to deprive the judges on the accession of a new monarch ; but when the Tory monarch, George III, ascended the throne, he yielded this remnant of the prerogative.[3] In this way, according to Blackstone, the independence of the judges was assured. But we must not forget that in their irremovability the position of the judges hardly differed from that of the other high officials, all of whom, in virtue of an unbroken practice, if not of a definite law, were coming to be considered irremovable. In England the judicature formed a branch of the executive, constituted for all intents and purposes like the other branches, and like them protected against any attempt at control by the nominal head of the executive.

The judges were appointed by the King through the Lord Chancellor and at his advice. We might, therefore, expect that the nominations of judges were always party nominations. As a matter of fact, certain traditional usages guaranteed in England the independence of the Bench, still suspect, despite judicial irremovability, and prevented the natural effects of the political institutions. Custom compelled an absolutely impartial choice of judges from among the most well-known barristers.[4] But the rule was not without exception.

---

[1] *Comm.* 1, 267.   [2] 13 Will. III, cap. 2.
[3] 1 Geo. III, cap. 23.   One judge had been removed after the death of George I, two after the death of George II.
[4] *Morning Chronicle*, October 31, 1812 : " The nation has not been much accustomed to see promotion in our Courts of Justice conferred as in the Church and other departments of the State, and will be deeply indignant if they observe a preference of the claims of favouritism or

During the early years of the 19th century the Attorneys-General and the Solicitors-General claimed, as of right, the presidency of the high courts, when those positions fell vacant.[1] And they were professedly party men. Again, custom forbade the promotion of the Puisne Judges of the three high courts to the presidency of their courts. The custom checked intrigues.[2] But this rule also had its exceptions. 1817 was to see the promotion of Charles Abbott, after he had been in succession Puisne Judge of the Common Pleas and of the King's Bench, to be Chief Justice of the King's Bench. There was, moreover, nothing to prevent a Chief Justice, who presided over the Common Pleas, from aspiring to pass through the Common Pleas into the King's Bench, or to become Lord Chancellor. Again, custom forbade the judges ever to appear at Court—in other words, to do anything that would appear like soliciting favours. But what was there to prevent them frequenting the Prime Minister and the other members of the Cabinet ? Here, indeed, we are face to face with the decisive question, and the independence of the judicial Bench as against royal interference will depend on the answer. To what extent were the Ministers, as agents of the royal power, inclined to violate established usages in order to carry out the personal policy of George III or the Regent ? To what extent, on the other hand, as Members of Parliament and responsible to Parliament, was it their interest to defend, in opposition to the head of the executive, customs which safeguarded the independence of his subordinates ?

We must now consider a glaring example of confusion between the judicature and the executive. According to Blackstone, " nothing is more to be avoided in a free constitution than uniting the provinces of a judge and a Minister of State." [3] Now, as far as the three courts of Common Pleas, King's Bench and Exchequer are concerned the British Constitution practically succeeded in avoiding this danger. We say " practically," because Lord Mansfield, the Chief Justice of the King's Bench, had been allowed for a long period during the early years of the reign to attend almost openly all the Cabinet meetings, and Fox seems to have been astonished at the violent opposition aroused when in 1806 he offered a seat in his Cabinet to Lord Ellenborough, who occupied the same position as

corruption to the fair pretensions of personal qualifications." Since the *Morning Chronicle* was an Opposition paper, its testimony is valuable.

[1] See a memorandum by Lord Eldon, who, moreover, protests against this claim, and Twiss, *Life of Lord Eldon*, vol. ii. pp. 510–12. Cf. Lord John Russell, *Essay on the English Government*, 1823, pp. 410–11 : " The . . . offices . . . of Attorney and Solicitor General imply a determination to support the measures of Government when called upon, as thoroughly as the interests of any private client whom a lawyer undertakes to defend. The path to the office of judge very frequently, and to the office of Lord Chancellor almost always, passes through these offices. It follows, that the road of ambition for a lawyer is to attach himself to the governing party in the State."

[2] Cottu, *Administration de la Justice Criminelle en Angleterre*, pp. 141–2.

[3] *Comm.* 1, 269.

Lord Mansfield.[1] But there was a fourth court whose president, the Lord Chancellor, was an ex-officio member of the Cabinet. And, like the other Ministers, he was removable. He was in truth a Minister, without the title, who was regarded as more dependent than his colleagues on the royal pleasure, and less bound by the joint decisions of the Cabinet than his fellow Ministers. It was the Chancellor who appointed in the provinces the justices of the peace and the officers of the militia. It was urged that, since as judge he tried civil not criminal cases, his performance of strictly executive functions did not endanger the liberty of the subject. But it was his office to judge "petitions of right" in which the subject was plaintiff against the Crown. And when a peer was tried by his fellow peers he presided over the trial in his capacity of Lord High Steward. During the sessions of Parliament, his powers were limited, for his function in the House of Lords was merely that of president. When, however, the House was not sitting he had to decide all cases. He possessed authority to summon a fixed number of peers to act as jurors, and he exercised with their assistance precisely the same functions as the Lord Chief Justice exercised in the King's Bench or Common Pleas. In the person of the Lord Chancellor the separation of the judicature and the executive was frankly disregarded. But it remains to inquire to what extent, in reality, this high officer of State could or would become, in the Cabinet, the agent of an arbitrary and despotic policy. Here also the question of the degree of independence of the judicature, as against the executive, has brought us back to that other question, the question of the independence of the executive itself as against the head of the executive.[2] But, as we have already seen, the institution of a responsible Cabinet answered the latter question unfavourably to the royal authority.

[1] See the Debates, H. of L., March 3, 1806 (*Parl. Deb.*, vol. vi. p. 253) ; H. of C., March 3, 1806 (*id. ibid.*, p. 286). See especially a speech by Canning (*id. ibid.*, p. 298). In a letter to Wilberforce of February 4, 1806 (*Private Papers of Wilberforce*, pp. 125 sqq.), Lord Ellenborough pleads extenuating circumstances : " . . . In accepting it I have stipulated that I should not be expected to attend except on particularly important occasions, and on such occasions some of my predecessors and particularly Lord Mansfield has, I understood, been called upon for his advice, and indeed, in virtue of my oath as Privy Councillor, I am bound to give that advice when required." Chester was a County Palatine with its independent courts, composed of a Chamberlain and of a Chief Justice. In 1814 the Government conferred on Sir William Garrow, the Attorney-General, the post of Chief Justice of Chester. Sir William Garrow resigned his seat as Member for Eye, but remained Attorney-General. See Romilly's proposals, H. of C., March 1, 1814 (*Parl. Deb.*, vol. xxvii. p. 338).

[2] As regards the desirability of a separation between the legislature and the judiciary, Lord St. John publicly disputed Montesquieu's doctrine (H. of L., March 3, 1806, *Parl. Deb.* vol. vi. p. 261). " Such a doctrine in that House could never be recognized as a part of the law or Constitution of England, where it had uniformly been the practice to blend, in repeated instances, the judicial and legislative character. This served to prove how little, relative to the Constitution of this country, could be gathered from Montesquieu. He should look to better sources for information upon that subject, namely the Statute Book, and the practice and usage of the country." Cf. the Speech delivered by Fox on the same day in the House of Commons (*Parl. Deb.*, vol. vi. p. 308).

Abuses. The Beginnings of Reform.

All the abuses whose existence we have noticed in the other branches of the administration were rife in the English courts of law. Here also were sinecures and posts whose salary was paid to the nominal holder, while a subordinate did the work. Here also was the system of remuneration by "fees," which gave the Bench a direct interest in prolonging proceedings, so that the delays of the English law, especially in the Court of Chancery, had become proverbial. And to these abuses we must add the sale by the judges of a number of subordinate posts. This practice still subsisted in the courts after its abolition in 1809 in the executive departments. Even in cases where the judge did not possess the right to sell a post, he stipulated with the nominee for a share of the fees, and only a fixed proportion, and that as small as possible, was left for the petty official. All these abuses had aroused the same protest from public opinion as the abuses in the other branches of the administration. Bentham, the apostle of reform in civil and criminal law, in the penal system and in the administration of justice, had begun to gather round him a group of enthusiastic disciples ; and here, as elsewhere, the reform of abuses had already begun. The reform of the Scottish courts in 1807 had demonstrated that it was possible to improve the administration of justice without undermining the fabric of society.[1] Nevertheless, legal reform was evidently being effected more slowly than the reform of the civil service, for it had to face exceptionally powerful obstacles.

Bitter were the complaints of the interminable length of suits pending in the Court of Chancery. Lord Eldon, instead of simplifying the procedure, created a new post, that of Vice-Chancellor.[2] The post was created to provide a pension for a faithful servant of the Tories, Sir Thomas Plumer, the Attorney-General. A cry was raised for the abolition of remuneration by fees and the sale of posts. The judges replied that, if their perquisites were suppressed, their salary would be insufficient to provide them a livelihood. They demanded and demanded successfully, as a condition precedent to any reform, that their salaries should be raised and retiring pensions granted whose amount was fixed by statute.[3] Indeed, the very nature of the English legal

---

[1] 48 Geo. III, cap. 151. On this reform see Cockburn, *Memorials of his Time*, pp. 219 sqq., 244 sqq., and *Life of Jeffrey*, vol. i. pp. 176-7 ; Romilly, *Memoirs*, vol. ii. pp. 165 sqq. Walter Scott criticized the reform in an article in *The Edinburgh Annual Register* (1808, Part II, pp. 342 sqq.). Cf. Lockhart, *Life of Walter Scott*, vol. iii. pp. 266 sqq. See also for a widely different standpoint, Bentham, *Scotch Reform considered with Reference to the Plan proposed in the late Parliament*, 1808 (*Works*, vol. v. pp. 1 sqq.).

[2] 53 Geo. III, cap. 24.

[3] H. of C., March 27, April 20, April 27, May 15, 1809 ; H. of L., June 13, 1809. Debate on the Sale of Offices Prevention Bill (*Parl. Deb.*, vol. xiii. p. 820, vol. xiv. pp. 113, 268, 573). H. of C., June 1, 12, 1809. Judges' Salaries Bill (*Parl. Deb.*, vol. xiv. pp. 833, 988).—An Act of 1799 had raised the salary of the Master of the Rolls and of the Chief Baron of the Exchequer to £4,000, of the Puisne Judges of the three Common Law Courts to £3,000,

institutions must, it would seem, have a tendency to perpetuate abuses. There was no clearly defined separation between the barristers and the judges, and consequently no professional rivalry between them. The reformers, therefore, necessarily failed to find in the barristers wholehearted allies in their campaign against a body of which the barristers themselves formed part. Nor was there any definite separation, and therefore no hereditary feud between the judges and the aristocracy of which Parliament was composed. This made it impossible to expect from Parliament a crusade against the disorders of the judiciary.

The organization of the judiciary was, as we have seen, ill-defined. Once again we are compelled to correct Montesquieu's interpretation of the British Constitution. His two definitions of that constitution— a constitution based on the division of powers, a mixed constitution— are not equivalent, and the latter is the more accurate. The British Government was not a Government in which all the powers were clearly distinguished. It was rather a Government in which all the constituent parts were confused, and in which all the powers mutually encroached. King George III was mistaken in his belief that he could take advantage of this confusion to increase surreptitiously the influence of the executive over the two other powers. In reality a mass of usages, already over a century old, usages which the Tory reaction was powerless to overthrow, protected both the judges and the other officers of State against the despotic tendencies of the chief of the executive. In short, all the powers were indeed confused, but in such fashion that this confusion must always operate to the detriment of the monarchy. This conclusion has been already verified by our examination of the departments of the central government, but it will strike us even more forcibly as we proceed to examine the local government and the manner in which the capital judged and administered the provinces.

LOCAL JUSTICE AND LOCAL GOVERNMENT.

The Central Government and the Provinces. The Justices of the Peace.

We will examine first the administration of justice in the provinces. The only paid judges recognized by the British Constitution were the judges of the capital, who sat in Westminster Hall ; the only barristers

and had conferred on the Crown the right to grant the officials of the Westminster Courts retiring pensions statutorily graded. These pensions ranged from £2,000 to £4,000 (39 Geo. III, cap. 110). The Act of 1809 raised the salary of the Chief Baron of the Exchequer to £5,000, that of the Puisne Judges to £4,000, and added £400 to the salaries of the Chief Justice of Chester and of the Welsh Judges (49 Geo. III, cap. 127). Gneist, *Verfassungs und Verwaltungsrecht* (vol. i. p. 495), gives an inaccurate account of the Act of 1799, and *omits altogether* the Act of 1809.

in England belonged to the London Bar. At first sight this appears an extremely centralized system; but the legal administration of England was not in reality so centralized as would appear at first sight. Had every Englishman been obliged to come up to London to obtain justice, the provinces would have been left without any judicial administration. But a system had been devised by which, without the creation of provincial courts, the English judges were enabled to deal with crimes and offences committed in the provinces. Once a year in the four northern counties, twice a year in the other counties, the judges of the Common Law Courts went on circuit in groups of two to try civil and criminal cases. But these representatives of the capital made but a passing appearance in the provinces. They had barely arrived before they went away. The country was left to make its own provision for the maintenance of law and order. So with the other branches of administration. The London Government required local agents to collect its revenues, and as the population grew larger and wealthier, and the budgets heavier, more agents became necessary. There were the postal officials. To manage 61 mail-coaches, 4,000 horses and 54 packet-boats, the State, it has been estimated, maintained some 1,500 officials; [1] and there were the customs officers, with a whole host of searchers, surveyors, coast-waiters, tide-surveyors, tide-waiters, watermen, coal meters, riding officers and masters of revenue cutters—in all 9,000 officials for the three kingdoms. There were also the agents of the Treasury, comptrollers of stamps, collectors of the direct taxes, and, above all, the 7,500 excisemen who collected the duties on articles of consumption. The total number of these officials approached 25,000. [2] But this number, though it aroused the ire of Opposition orators, was in reality by no means excessive, if we take into account the needs of a large Empire.

In England the central government did nothing to secure the public safety, provided no schools, made no roads, gave no relief to the poor. With the one exception of the postal service, the State performed no function of immediate benefit to the taxpayer. In the eyes of the public the State appeared only as the power that enlisted men and levied taxes. The local representatives of the central government were sorry creatures, ill paid, without prestige, unpopular. And

---

[1] Great Britain 1,129, Ireland 347. See *A Return of the Number of Persons Employed* . . . 1828. Adolphus, *British Empire*, vol. ii. pp. 37–8, makes out, on the other hand, about 4,000 postal employees of all ranks.

[2] 24,598 officials in 1815. In 1797 there were only 16,267 (*A Return* . . . 1828). These official statistics give higher figures than those accepted alike by writers who supported or opposed the Government. See Colquhoun, *Wealth . . . of the British Empire*, p. 124 : 3,500 persons in the superior civil offices, 18,000 in the inferior civil offices. This gives a total of 21,500 officials. Cf. H. of C., June 24, 1822 (Bonnet's speech, *Parl. Deb.*, New Series, vol. vii. pp. 1309–10) : " There were between 18,000 and 20,000 civil officers whom the Crown nominated and paid. . . . There was, in fact, a large army in the Customs and Excise —a body equal in number to the standing army kept up in this country in the good old times."

of all the excisemen were the most unpopular. The inquisitorial powers conferred upon them by law, their authority to tax the subject uncontrolled, like the collectors of the direct taxes, by the local aristocracy, had made them for over a century a living symbol of arbitrary government. Even Blackstone, staunch Conservative as he was, did not attempt to defend this form of taxation. "The rigour and arbitrary proceeding of excise laws seem," he wrote, "hardly compatible with the temper of a free nation." [1]

And, as we should expect, the landed gentry exploited this hostility of public opinion to destroy the influence which the agents of the central government might otherwise have opposed to their own. In 1782 all collectors of taxes, direct and indirect alike, had been deprived as a body of the franchise. [2] This step was a direct blow to the influence which the Crown could exercise at an election, and tightened the grasp of the landed proprietors on the local administration. The landlords were, indeed, the true rulers of the English provinces. From among them, according to a long-established custom, was chosen the body of justices of the peace. A host of subordinate functions, both administrative and judicial, were discharged by these magistrates, whose number was indeterminate and varied with each county. A succession of statutes had assigned to them these diverse duties. In some cases they were to administer justice individually, in others the law demanded the cooperation of at least two magistrates. They must also meet at regular intervals in specified places, and at those meetings they were assisted by a clerk. The meetings were of three kinds—Special Sessions, Petty Sessions, and Quarter Sessions. The Quarter Sessions were held every three months in solemn state, and all the magistrates of the county were supposed to attend. The justices were unpaid. Their functions were regarded as an honour, and were assigned by the executive to men who were sufficiently rich and sufficiently disinterested to devote their leisure to the public service. No expert legal knowledge was required of a magistrate. It was considered that he would judge well enough by the light of common sense. Formerly the magistrates had been assisted by a certain number of professional judges, but this old precaution had fallen gradually into disuse without any protest being raised. [3]

[1] 1 *Comm.* 318. Blackstone, to clear the British Crown of responsibility, adds that the Excise is an institution of republican origin. "Though Lord Clarendon tells us that to his knowledge the Earl of Bedford (who was made Lord Treasurer by King Charles I), to oblige his Parliament, intended to have set up the Excise in England, yet it never made a part of that unfortunate Prince's revenue, being first introduced, on the model of the Dutch prototype, by the Parliament itself after its rupture with the Crown."

[2] 22 Geo. III, cap. 41. Cf. H. of C., May 6, June 14, 1785 (*Parliamentary Register*, vol. xviii. pp. 220 sqq., 501 sqq.), debates on Beaufoy's motion " to bring in a Bill for the purpose of correcting and defining the jurisdiction of the Commissioners of Excise, and for extending the right of trial by jury."

[3] Gneist, *Verfassungs und Verwaltungsrecht*, vol. ii. p. 178. S. and B. Webb, *English Local Government*, vol. i. pp. 302–3. Blackstone, in the passage which he devotes to the justices

The functions performed by the justices of the peace were primarily judicial. For a large number of petty offences they had the right either to pass an immediate sentence sitting alone or in pairs, or to refer the case to Quarter Sessions, a court itself composed of magistrates. But they performed administrative functions also. Suppose, for instance, a bridge fell into ruin. The magistrates summoned before their Bench the inhabitants of the parish in which the bridge was situated and ordered them to pay for its repair. If we call this sum, which the parishioners were compelled to pay, a fine for previous neglect, the decision may be considered a judicial sentence ; if, however, we call it a rate, the decision must be considered an administrative act. But of all the functions performed by the magistrates one of the most important was precisely that of approving the parish rates, the rate for the upkeep of the roads and the poor rate, and of fixing the amount of the county rate. Since such an important part of English law, the " common law," is case-made law, the magistrates, thus at once judges and executive officials, possessed the power to determine from time to time what actions fell within the scope of the old statutes which regulated local government ; and by increasing at their pleasure the number of these actions, they were able to extend their jurisdiction, and to impose an ever-increasing number of obligations on the inhabitants of the county. The Courts of Quarter Sessions were genuine legislatures engaged in building up from quarter to quarter a new code of law under the pretext of interpreting the old. In this capacity they put together during the last years of the 18th century a complete poor law, first in one county, then in another, acting on their own initiative, without any interference by the central government. Yet once again we may ask, what becomes of the classic doctrine of the separation of powers ? The county magistrates unite in their person the judicial, the legislative and the executive power.[1] Montesquieu does not even mention the justices of the peace. Nevertheless, with the responsible Cabinet they are the most original and the most characteristic of all British institutions.

If, indeed, we were to take into consideration only the letter of the various statutes which defined the organization and determined the jurisdiction of the justices of the peace, the entire institution would appear to have been designed for the express purpose of maintaining the control of the central government over the provinces.[2]

of the peace (1 *Comm.* 351,2), cites two statutes, passed during the 18th century, which expressly declare the assistance of professional judges to be henceforward unnecessary (26 Geo. II, cap. 27 ; 7 Geo. III, cap. 21).

[1] On this confusion of powers see especially S and B. Webb, *English Local Government* Book II, The County (vol. i. pp. 419, 445, 533 sqq. *et passim*).

[2] This adherence to the letter of the law seems to us the radical error of Gneist—an error which to some degree detracts from the value of the important works in which for the first time the importance of the institution of justices of the peace in the British Constitution has been

Till the 14th century those entrusted with the preservation of the peace in the provinces either held this charge by prescriptive right, or in virtue of the tenure of their lands, or had been elected by the freeholders. Edward III introduced a system of direct nomination by the Crown, and shortly afterwards he conferred upon these officials, together with the title of justices, authority to try felonies.[1] By this means the justices of the peace served to strengthen the power of the central government and of the monarchy. Nominees of the Crown, the magistrates were in theory removable by the Crown. They were not representatives chosen by the county for the work of local government. They were the representatives in the county of the central government, appointed by that government to control the units of local administration, the parishes and the hundreds. They had, moreover, encroached on the autonomy of these units. They appointed in each parish the constable, charged with the police of the district; [2] the surveyor of the highways,[3] responsible for the upkeep of the roads; and the overseer of the poor, who administered the Poor Law. It is true that the magistrates must be residents of the county and own in their county land bringing in a net annual income of at least £100—this to guarantee the aristocratic character of the institution. But their authority emanated from the State. Thus in many of its features the institution of the justices of the peace would seem at first sight an instrument of monarchic centralization. It would appear to have been devised for the express purpose of securing the necessary control of the central government over the entire social fabric.

But to understand the spirit of a law, we must learn how it is applied in practice and the manner in which that application has in the course of time been altered; and it is indisputable that, as regards the magistrates, the 18th century in England had been a period of decentralization—a period during which the central government had relaxed its control over the justices of the peace. Since the Stuart Restoration, but above all since the Revolution of 1688, the law had increased the number of cases triable by Quarter Sessions as a court of final instance, without power of appeal from " their decisions to the high court judges." [4] Legally, the magistrates continued to be

clearly brought out. It is the mistake of a lawyer, and of a Continental lawyer, who imagines the gentry who ruled the English counties after the model of the German nobility, a body far more hierarchic and bureaucratic.

[1] 1 Edw. III, st. 2, cap. 16; 4 Edw. III, cap. 2; 18 Edw. III, st. 1, cap. 2.

[2] In strict law the constable was appointed by the Court Leet. (For the Court Leet, an administrative and judicial institution of feudal character and origin, see S. and B. Webb, *English Local Government*, vol. ii. pp. 21 sqq.) When the Court Leet fell into abeyance, the Law (13 and 14 Car. II, cap. 12 and 15) provided that in default of the Court Leet the justices of the peace were to have the right to appoint the constables, and in the vast majority of cases they appointed them in practice.

[3] 3 and 4 William and Mary, cap. 12.

[4] 5 William and Mary, cap. 11; 8 and 9 Will. III, cap. 33; 1 Anne, cap. 18 and 55; 5 Geo. II, cap. 19; Gneist, *Verfassungs und Verwaltungsrecht*, vol. ii. pp. 168–9.

removable, but they came more and more to be regarded as irremovable.[1] They were certainly Crown nominees, and in theory the royal choice was uncontrolled. But the custom had been established for over a century that they should always be chosen on the recommendation of the Lord-Lieutenant of the county. By custom the office of Lord-Lieutenant was given to the largest landowner of the county, and it required very exceptional circumstances, a political crisis of extraordinary gravity, for the King and his Prime Minister to make use of their right to deprive a Lord-Lieutenant.[2] In reality, therefore, it was not the King, but the head of the local aristocracy, an official holding his position for life, who, after a more or less explicit understanding with the body of justices, made new promotions from the ranks of the county landowners. Thus the body of magistrates was coincident with the good society of the district. To be admitted into their ranks by the purchase of land, or by performing the wearisome and costly duties of High Sheriff, was the honour coveted by all the *nouveaux riches* of the neighbourhood.

The composition of the Bench varied with the period and the locality. Formerly the Anglican clergy had been ineligible, but as a result of the Protestant revival of the 18th century, a more serious understanding of religion and the increased favour shown by public opinion to Christian beliefs, their presence on the Bench was now tolerated, even desired. During the last forty years great numbers of clergy had become magistrates. If we may credit certain accounts, over half the justices sitting at the sessions were clergymen.[3] Was the Bench also open to financiers and to manufacturers ? That depended on the district. In Lancashire the magistrates were exclusive and the cotton-spinners were debarred from a Bench offended by their too recent wealth, disgusted by their vulgarity.[4] In the south-west, on the other hand, the manufacture of woollen cloth was an old-established industry. The manufacturers belonged to old county families, the aristocracy of the district. In the southern counties the London financiers and bankers possessed sufficient wealth and influence to make their way on to the Bench. Here, too, there is an absence of clearly defined boundaries. England possessed no close castes. But, generally speaking, it is true to say that if the Bench of magistrates

---

[1] S. and B. Webb, *English Local Government*, vol. i. pp. 380–1.

[2] The Earl of Carlisle, Lord-Lieutenant of the East Riding in 1780 ; the Duke of Norfolk, Lord-Lieutenant of the West Riding in 1798.

[3] Cobbett's *Political Register*, May 22, 1811, vol. xix. p. 1256 : "In the country more than two-thirds, I believe, of those who attend at the Sessions are clergymen of the Church of England." Cf. Hume's speech, H. of C., April 18, 1833 (*Parl. Deb.*, Third Series, vol. xvii. p. 282) : ". . . the Sessions of whom one-half was . . . composed of clergymen." According to S. and B. Webb, there were 1,354 clerical J.P.s in 1832—that is to say, a quarter of the entire body (*English Local Government*, vol. i. p. 384 n.). The custom on this point varied with each county. See Wakefield, *Ireland*, vol. ii. p. 339.

[4] See the Debates, H. of C., May 12, 1813 (*Parl. Deb.*, vol. xxvi. p. 100).

was in part drawn from those outside the old landed aristocracy, the extent to which this was the case exactly measured the proportion in which, under the influence of novel conditions, this aristocracy had itself absorbed new elements.

Distinctive Features of the British System of Civil Administration.

We have termed the British Constitution a mixed Constitution. We should be equally right to characterize it as a decentralized Constitution. Not only were all the powers of government confused, the head of the State, and this is of the first importance, was powerless, or almost powerless. At the summit of the political edifice were the Ministers, who controlled the preparation of new legislation, and the national executive. The King was not responsible for their acts. At its base the justices of the peace judged, administered and legislated, and to their hands the central government abandoned the greater part of local government. No doubt the country gentlemen, the old landed families, were deeply attached to the Tory cause ; but they were equally jealous of their independence, and nowhere were the old prejudices against every kind of administrative centralization, against any sort of bureaucracy, more powerful than among the gentry. These prejudices had triumphed in 1688, with the conquest of power by the Whigs, but this triumph would not have been so final or so complete had not the deepest rooted sentiments of the Whigs been shared by their bitterest foes. Thus the Tory reaction, by strengthening the hold of the Tory gentry over local government, confirmed the predominance in the British Constitution of what may be termed the Whig principle. English society was freed from State control and left to govern itself. " In England," wrote one of his correspondents to Lord Eldon, " the machine goes on almost of itself, and therefore a very bad driver may manage it tolerably well." [1]

The system which we have described was anything but democratic. The justice of the peace was an aristocrat who, without the assistance of a jury and without any regular procedure, decided a host of questions, very largely affecting his property. And from the same class were taken both the House of Commons, which made the laws, and the Cabinet, which directed the general policy of the country. Moreover, it is clear that the same institutions might appear at the beginning of a century favourable, at its close unfavourable, to the liberties of the people. In 1688 and in the years following, the King regarded himself, and was regarded by public opinion, as the Sovereign. It was always to be feared that he would attempt to make his sovereignty absolute, and the independence of his authority enjoyed by all the powers

[1] Twiss, *Life of Lord Eldon*, vol. ii. p. 443. Lord Redesdale to Lord Eldon, December 19, 1821. " It is not so in Ireland," adds Lord Redesdale.

of the State constituted a deliberate limitation of the prerogative, a system of constitutional guarantees against royal despotism.   At the opening of the 19th century it was the people who in America, in France, in England even, had asserted, or were about to assert, their claim to sovereignty ; it was therefore against the people that the three Powers now maintained their independence.   It was no longer the Whigs, it was the Tories who supported institutions whose significance had changed, while their form remained the same. And now the King presided over the league formed by the three Powers for the defence of their autonomy against the new claimant to sovereignty.

But while this must be said to explain the attacks made upon the established institutions about 1815 by English democrats, we must not therefore regard the system as a tyranny, and ignore the elements of genuine liberty which it contained.   Doubtless among the enormous number of magistrates was to be found more than one petty tyrant, ready to abuse the powers conferred upon him by law, to terrorize the proletariat.   We have only to think of Caleb Williams' persecutor in Godwin's famous novel.   But are we to regard such a man as typical of his order ?   Others, clergy and laymen alike, won the admiration of their contemporaries by their humanitarian zeal.   Typical of a far more numerous body of magistrates is Fielding's Squire Western, a hard drinker, a big eater, a keen hunter, the despot of his family circle, a lover of good cheer, universally popular.   Even the most determined reformers regarded the magistrates with indulgence. "The system of magistracy," declared Whitbread in 1807, " had its defects ; but in what other country was there a body so excellent ? " [1]   Their administration of justice appears to have been on the whole easy-going and kindly, their administration of the Poor Law lax, even wasteful. But the magistrates cannot altogether claim the credit for this mildness and generosity.   In reality they only wanted not the will to oppress, but the means of oppression.

By their obstinate struggle against the King and his Ministers, and by their final reduction of the control of the central government to almost nothing, the landed gentry had at the same time deprived themselves of the help of the central government to suppress popular disorder.   Without the assistance of a large and well-organized body of police, what force was at the disposal of the magistrates isolated on their several estates, and swamped in the mass of agricultural labourers or factory hands ?   We have but to read Wesley's Diary to realize how impotent were the guardians of law and order in the English country districts.   Whenever the open-air sermons of the great Methodist preacher occasioned a riot among the people, what time was lost in the search for a magistrate, and even when he did at last arrive, how

[1] H. of C., July 13, 1807 (*Parl. Deb.*, vol. ix. p. 803).

great was his difficulty in calming the storm without any armed force at his disposal or other means save persuasion or trickery! As the urban centres multiplied, the inadequacy of this patriarchal and rustic system became increasingly evident. To check the growth of crime, Parliament made the penal code even more severe than before. At the end of the 18th century well-nigh two hundred offences were capital.¹ A few police measures had also been adopted. Barracks containing small bodies of soldiery had been established in the country districts. In London a certain number of stipendiary magistrates had been provided, who were assisted by police officers.² Towards the end of 1811 an outbreak of crime in London excited a panic not only in the capital but throughout the entire country. The papers noticed the formation in the most widely separated localities of police associations, voluntary unions of the leading gentlemen of the district.³ Obviously the aggravation of penalties for crime was but a clumsy expedient to compensate for the extreme uncertainty of its repression. But the national optimism opposed an obstinate resistance to the organization of a State police throughout the country. Under the Tories England remained fundamentally what it had been in the days of Whig rule—a country governed without police. To palliate the evils of such a system men reckoned on the phlegmatic temperament of the people, and on the rarity of murders and acts of revenge. The public was prepared, if necessary, to put up with a certain amount of disorder, if it was the price of freedom. "They have an admirable police at Paris," wrote John William Ward, "but they pay for it dear enough. I had rather half-a-dozen people's throats should be cut in Ratcliffe Highway every three or four years than be subject to domiciliary visits, spies, and all the rest of Fouché's contrivances." ⁴

---

¹ Blackstone, 4 *Comm.* 18–19. Stephen, *History of the Criminal Law in England*, vol. i. pp. 469 sqq. Remark in the same passage his reflections on the non-enforcement of these penalties.

² 32 Geo. III, cap. 53 (a temporary measure renewed regularly). See S. and B. Webb, *English Local Government*, vol. i. pp. 573 sqq.

³ For Chelsea see the *Morning Chronicle*, January 14, 1812 : " The Committee appointed by the inhabitants of Chelsea put their patrol of ten men in motion on Sunday night. These men are relieved at midnight by a second party, who patrol till daylight. It is highly honourable to the Gentlemen of the Parish who have voluntarily tendered their services to superintend the conduct of this patrol. The first patrol on Sunday night was conducted by Thomas Bonnor, Esq." For Morpeth and Bolam see *Newcastle Chronicle*, February 1, 1812 ; for Heaton and Jesmond *ibid.*, March 27, 1813.

⁴ *Letters to Ivy*, December 27, 1811 (p 146). Cf. *Morning Chronicle*, January 6, 1812 : " We have heard much in praise of the admirable effects of the Police in Paris. Certainly the Police of Paris is most dexterously contrived for the purpose of tyranny, but that it is so very efficacious in the prevention of the blackest crimes that deform and afflict human nature we much question."

THE NAVY.

The Army and the Constitution. The Navy.

From our account of the national executive, we purposely omitted the officials entrusted with the armed defence of the country against foreign enemies. For the importance of their office and the power at their disposal entitle them to separate consideration. The British Constitution recognized, as part of the Royal Prerogative, the command of the Army and the Fleet. To the King belonged " the sole supreme government, command and disposition . . . of all forces by sea and land." [1] This maxim, affirmed under Charles II, had not been disputed after the overthrow of the Stuarts. It was defended by appeal to the principle of a mixed constitution. Blackstone observes that monarchy is best suited to supply the Army with the necessary direction and unity of organization. " It follows," he wrote, " from the very end of its institution, that in a monarchy the military power must be trusted in the hands of the Prince." [2] But here danger lies. If, in a mixed constitution, the monarchy admittedly represents the principle of authority and discipline, so indispensable to the existence of a good army, must it not for this very reason endanger the balance of the constitution into which it has been admitted ? It is by the support of a large, obedient and well-equipped army that a dynasty can free itself from the control of a rebellious people or a jealous aristocracy. The Whigs of 1688, taught by the history of seventeenth-century England, adopted the necessary precautions to render the military prerogative of the sovereign harmless to the liberties of the people. George III, therefore, in his desire to strengthen his authority, should surely have made it his first consideration to undo in this sphere, before any other, the results accomplished by the anti-monarchic policy of the Whigs. But to measure the success of this reaction, and to determine what was the actual position of the armed forces of England after sixty-six years of Whig policy and thirty of Tory, it is important at the outset to make a clear distinction between the Navy and the Army.

England maintained a very large navy. In 1792, at the opening of the great war, she possessed, according to the official statistics, a fleet of ships of the line almost double the French Fleet, close on 160 vessels as against a little over 80. But, on the other hand, such a large proportion of ships were unfit for service that the real superiority of the British over the French Fleet scarcely amounted to a sixth.[3] Moreover, by joining forces France, Spain and Holland could oppose to the

---

[1] 13 Carl. II, cap. 6. [2] 1 *Comm.* 262.
[3] James, *Naval History*, vol. i. pp. 52–3. British Line = 158, French Line = 82 (pp. 45, 86). Here, and in what follows, we have not given the figures for the frigates ; they would not alter the balance between the two navies.

158 British ships of the line 295 ships of the line of the same class.[1] Ten years later, after the Peace of Amiens, England possessed, according to the official figures, 104 ships of the line in commission, 98 ships of the line in ordinary or in course of construction, making up a total of 202 ships, to which France could now oppose only 39, and France, Spain and Holland together only 118. Taking into consideration only the vessels capable of immediate service, Addington estimated about this time that the British Fleet was superior to the three hostile fleets by 60 ships of the line.[2] In 1806, after Trafalgar, the superiority of the British Navy was even greater. The figures then were : vessels in commission—128 ships of the line and 15 ships of fifty ; ships in ordinary or in course of construction—88 ships of the line and 19 ships of fifty. Total : 250 ships. France possessed only 19 ships of the same class, Spain 57, Holland 16. Total : 92. England now possessed more ships than all the other European fleets combined, who could only oppose to England's 250 ships of the line, 239 ships of the line, including ships of fifty.[3] In 1812, at the critical moment when Napoleon on the verge of his sudden collapse had formed against England a European coalition, France had once more a fleet of about 100 ships of the line. If we add to these the 42 ships of the line in the Baltic which constituted the combined fleets of Russia, Sweden and Denmark, we have a total of some 140 units. But to these England opposed 250 units of the same class and of these ships 100 or 150 were in commission.[4]

Such was the strength of the British Navy towards the end of the great war. Its overwhelming superiority dates from this period. But this enormous increase of the Fleet did not affect, nor could have affected, the political institutions of the country. If on the conclusion of peace public opinion insisted on a reduction in naval expenditure, it was because the national debt was large and the Navy cost very dear. No

[1] James, *Naval History*, vol. i. pp. 50 sqq. Holland 49 ships of the line, Spain 76, Portugal 6, Russia 40, Denmark 24, Sweden 18. But we must not forget that the six Portuguese ships were commanded by English officers and at the disposition of the British Government, nor that out of the forty-nine Dutch " ships of the line " a good number were not entitled to the appellation.

[2] H. of C., December 2, 1802 (*Parl. Hist.*, vol. xxxvi. p. 1039). For slightly different figures see James, *Naval History*, vol. iii. pp. 164 sqq.

[3] Adolphus, *British Empire*, vol. ii. pp. 199–200. For slightly different figures see William Burney, *The British Neptune* . . ., 1807, and James, *Naval History*, vol. iv. Appendix No. 14.

[4] *Quarterly Review*, September 1812, Art. II, *Pering and Money on Shipbuilding* (vol. viii. p. 55). Brenton, *Naval History*, vol. iv. p. 6. For slightly different figures for the British Fleet see James, *Naval History*, vol. vi. Appendix No. 20, and Chevalier, *Histoire de la Marine française*, vol. v. p. 3. On the conclusion of peace France was compelled to surrender thirty-one ships of the line to the Allies, and she lacked the money to equip those still left to her. This made it possible for England to effect with security a great reduction in her naval budget. See Brenton, *Naval History*, vol. v. pp. 359 sqq. He gives very different figures for the British Fleet, lower by about a half. This difference is due to the fact that Brenton here leaves out of account the ships in course of construction or in ordinary. See also Laignel, *Changements opérés dans la Marine anglaise*, 1819.

ulterior motive of a political character, no anti-militarist feeling, inspired the Opposition speakers. A fleet could neither defend a Government against a rebellion, nor cause a revolution, nor effect a *coup d'état*. We must reserve, therefore, the constitutional question till we treat of the Army ; as regards the Navy, it does not exist. This fact explains the universal popularity enjoyed by the naval officers and their crews. They protected the safety of all, threatened the liberty of none. And in this universal popularity we shall discover the cause to which alone, to the exclusion of any other factor, the naval power of the nation was ultimately due.

The Fleet.

Was it the numerical superiority of the British Fleet that won the victory ? Obviously it was not, for at the outbreak of hostilities this superiority was far from indisputable. Or was it, perhaps, to the better quality of their vessels, to the perfection of their equipment, that the British sailors owed their first successes ? On the contrary, even after twenty years of victory, the existence of such a superiority in equipment was very doubtful. From the time when Peter Pitt in 1646 built the first English frigate, the *Constant Warwick*, after a French model,[1] and Sir Anthony Dean in 1674 built the *Harwich* in imitation of the French *Superbe*,[2] the British man-of-war had been a copy of the French. The English consoled themselves by the reflection that if the French constructed better vessels than they could build, they were masters of the art of capturing their ships and of employing them against the nation that had launched them.[3] Between 1793 and 1815 the British captured from the French and their allies 113 ships of the line and 205 frigates. Of these 83 ships of the line and 162 frigates became British men-of-war.[4] The *Pomone* taken in 1794, the *Hoche* taken in 1799, were for a long time reckoned among the best ships that England possessed.[5]

And how did the dimensions of the English compare with the dimensions of the foreign men-of-war ? The *Cæsar*, built by the English in 1793, did not attain the dimensions of the *Foudroyant*, captured from the French in 1758. The *Queen Charlotte*, built in 1810, was smaller than the Spanish *San Josef*, taken in the Battle of Cape St. Vincent in 1797. The *Howe* and the *St. Vincent*, ships of 130 built in 1815, were even smaller than the *Commerce de Marseille* of 120, taken at

---

[1] James, *Naval History*, vol. i. pp. 22–3. The very word frigate is of French and Mediterranean origin (*ibid.*, p. 20).

[2] *Quarterly Review*, January 1815, Art. 7. Sepping's *Improvements in Shipbuilding*, vol. xii. p. 450.

[3] See H. of C., January 7, 1795, Admiral Gardner's speech (*Annual Register*, 1795, p. 166).

[4] James, *Naval History*, vol. iii. p. 357 ; vol. vi. p. 505.

[5] Brenton, *Naval History*, vol. i. p. 244 ; vol. ii. p. 365.

Toulon in 1794. And at the very moment when the Admiralty put them on the stocks, the Americans put on the stocks five vessels whose keel measured 200 feet in length as against the 170 feet of the two British ships.[1]

But if the designs of the Continental shipwrights were bolder and more skilful, was not perhaps the English workmanship superior, both in the public dockyards and in the yards of private builders? This was certainly the cherished belief of the Englishman. According to him, in England theory was not as in France divorced from practice; English engineers were actual workmen, who built their ships to a large extent with their own hands, and had the advantage of the lessons taught by first-hand experience.[2] But was this belief after all well founded?[3] When the British engineers set themselves, according to the traditional plan, to copy a French type, they prided themselves on introducing into every vessel a number of alterations. But almost always these alterations were not improvements. Often they were positive defects which hindered the navigation of the vessel. Lord Collingwood's correspondence is full of complaints on this head.[4] Or, if not defects, they were too insignificant to be a decided advantage, while at the same time sufficiently important to break the unity of the squadrons. When Nelson was in command off Cadiz, his eighteen ships represented no less than seven distinct types. Each type required a special sort of mast, sail and yard, so that if a vessel were disabled, the others could not supply her with the means to repair the damage. Perhaps the British men-of-war were even worse constructed in 1815 than half a century earlier. A growing fleet had required continual and always hasty repairs. The average life of a man-of-war during the opening years of the 19th century was estimated by optimists at fifteen years, by those less optimistic at eight.[5] Not a few first-class vessels fell to pieces after five or even three years' service. How does

[1] *Quarterly Review*, January 1815, Art. 7, Sepping's *Improvements in Shipbuilding* (vol. xii. pp. 444 sqq.). Brenton, *Life of Lord St. Vincent*, vol. i. pp. 67–8. Brenton, *Naval History*, vol. i. p. 42, and vol. ii. p. 564. (Dimensions of some of the most approved ships in His Majesty's Navy.) *An Enquiry into the . . . state of the . . . Navy, by an Englishman*, pp. 16 sqq.

[2] *Quarterly Review*, November 1810, Art. 2, *The Natural Defence of an Insular Empire* (vol. iv. pp. 313 sqq.).

[3] For all the following see the *Quarterly Review*, September 1812, Art. 2, *Pering and Money on Shipbuilding* (vol. viii. pp. 28 sqq.).

[4] *Life*, vol. ii. p. 77. Letter to Lord Mulgrave, December 11, 1807 : " . . . The *Endymion* is complaining very much, owing to her enormous masts, which are more than can be secured. On this subject I must observe to your Lordship, that the wall-sided ships, and those heavy masted, are a continual burden upon the docks and arsenals ; while the ships of the old establishment, as the *Terrible, Saturn, Zealous, Queen*, and such whose sides fall in, are most to be depended on in winter for service." *Ibid.*, vol. ii. pp 310–11. Letter to Blackett, February 18, 1809 : " I was then on my way to Naples with my ship in a very ricketty and bad condition, from an ill-judged experiment which the Surveyors of the Navy were making, in the mode of securing the vessels. . . . We have now replaced all the copper bolts with iron ones. . . ."

[5] *Quarterly Review*, article above mentioned (vol. viii. p. 32). Cf. Brenton, *Life of St. Vincent*, vol. ii. p. 234.

this compare with the *Royal William*, built at Portsmouth in 1719, which took part in the Gibraltar expedition of 1782, and which in 1812 still carried the Port Admiral's flag at Spithead ; or the *Barfleur*, built in 1768, and the *Montague*, launched in 1779, both of which were still effective ships in 1812 ? [1]

In 1809 an Order in Council established in the naval college at Portsmouth a superior class of shipwrights' apprentices. Twenty-five young men, after a difficult entrance examination, were taught the theory and practice of shipbuilding. On the completion of their course they cruised for one year, "during which," the order directed, "they shall mess with the officers, and be treated in all respects as gentlemen." [2] But this attempt to form in England an expert body of naval engineers, in imitation of the French naval engineers, was still too recent to have produced the results that might be expected. In one point alone during the last thirty years had any real improvement in technique been effected. Lord Howe and Sir Home Popham, by their method of signalling, had enabled the commander of a squadron to exercise a stricter and more continuous control over his subordinates, to make his orders more definite, and to alter them in the course of the battle. Naval tactics were transformed by the innovation. Formerly two hostile fleets never joined battle, unless they could oppose an equal number of ships of the same class. Drawn up in two parallel lines, they would manœuvre about with a view to direct collision ; and the battle was reduced to a series of single combats, ship of the line against ship of the line, frigate against frigate. Now, however, the English Fleet had been rendered capable of concerted movements. Sometimes it would attempt to pass along the front of the hostile fleet, to surround the ships in the van, and to destroy them by force of numbers before the ships in the rear had time to come to their assistance. These were the tactics adopted at Aboukir. Sometimes it would make a flank attack and pierce the enemy's line in one or two places. His van was then left to drift, while the ships in the rear were destroyed one by one, as the wind drove them into the attacking squadron. These were the tactics of Cape St. Vincent and Trafalgar.[3] These combined

[1] Cf. Brenton, *Naval History*, vol. i. pp. 15–16. The *Phœnix* (Spanish), of eighty guns, taken by Sir George Rodney in the year 1780, and called the *Gibraltar*, was supposed to have been fifty years old at the time of her capture. She was built at Havannah of solid mahogany, and in 1810 she was cruising in the bay as an effective ship.

[2] *Quarterly Review*, article above mentioned (vol. viii. p. 31).

[3] The exponent of these new tactics was John Clark of Eldin, in his treatise on naval tactics (1782). He in turn seems to have made use of the theories of Continental tacticians. See Brenton, *Life of St. Vincent*, vol. ii. Lord St. Vincent's letter to Lord Howick, June 2, 1806 : ". . . Not having Mr. Clark's treatise on naval tactics with me, I am unable to give you a detailed opinion upon the influence it has had in the several victories our fleets have obtained over those of France, Spain and Holland since its publication. I would not for the world subtract from the merits of Mr. Clark, which I have always admitted ; yet, on referring to the encyclopædia, wherein are copious extracts from the pamphlet, I perceive evident signs of compilation from Père le Hoste down to Viscount de Grenier. In truth, it would be difficult for

movements were, however, only possible in a small number of important battles, and a careful study of these very battles [1] will reveal the impotence of the admirals to prevent the speedy degeneration of the struggle into a disordered mêlée, in which the victory was decided by luck, by the ardour of the crews, or by the skill and energy of individual captains. After all, naval tactics had changed little in the course of a century. A contemporary of the first Pitt, or even of William of Orange, would not have felt lost had he to serve under Lord St. Vincent or Nelson. The vessels were still at the mercy of favourable or unfavourable winds. They were still the same conglomerations of planks, all of which shifted several inches when the vessel was launched, and which afterwards were only kept together at all by the external pressure of the water in which they were plunged, and fell apart as soon as they were brought on to dry land. The industrial revolution, which during the last forty years had been transforming manufactures, had not as yet affected the methods of war. In the Navy the age of iron and steam had not begun. Events of revolutionary significance had taken place in the naval history of the great Powers, but there had been no corresponding revolution in the construction and equipment of men-of-war. [2]

The Crews.

We have failed to discover in the material equipment of the British Navy the secret of British sea power ; we must therefore seek it in the character of the men who manned the vessels. But although we are now closer to the solution of the problem, many difficulties still face us. It is easy to misunderstand the true nature of the causes to which was due the bravery of the crews and their officers.

It has been often said that since England possessed the largest mercantile marine of the entire world, she never found any difficulty in recruiting from her trading vessels the experienced seamen necessary to

the ablest seaman and tactician to write upon the subject without running into one or all the French authors." Certainly the French were not slow to learn the tactical principles of St. Vincent and Nelson. In 1811, at the Battle of Lissa in the Adriatic, we find these tactics employed, though unsuccessfully, against the British Fleet (Brenton, *Naval History*, vol. iv. p. 547).

[1] Brenton, *Naval History*, vol. iii. p. 474 (extract from Collingwood's report on the Battle of Trafalgar) : ". . . As the mode of our attack had been previously determined on, and communicated to the flag officers and captains, few signals were necessary, and none were made, except to direct close order as the lines bore down."

[2] Whitbread (H. of C., April 24, 1815) complained that the new steam and hydraulic engines were still ignored by the Admiralty ; "that the improvements which to a wonderful extent had been made in all the private concerns of the country, were so slow in finding their way into the public establishments, and especially the dockyards. . . . In the same place, and almost in the same spot, at Portsmouth, where Mr. Brunnell's improvements were carrying on—improvements that, two or three centuries ago, would have had their ingenious author hanged for witchcraft—trucks were to be seen in a public department that would disgrace one of those American tribes whose boundaries were so lately the cause of contentions " (*Parl. Deb.*, vol. xxx. p. 809).

man her squadrons. But we must not forget that at the outbreak of a war the merchant shipping was scattered in every quarter of the globe. The country, therefore, could not obtain from her merchantmen the enormous complement of men required by the sudden emergency.[1] As the war continued, the nature of the problem changed, but its solution became no easier. The pay of sailors in the merchant service, at all times high, was raised still higher as the risks of navigation became greater. In the port of London the average pay of a sailor before the war ranged from £1 5s. to £1 15s. On the declaration of war it was raised immediately to £3 15s. By 1800 it had risen to four, by 1804 to five guineas. The State could not attempt to compete against such high rates.[2] Moreover, the British Government had no wish to transfer to the Royal Navy the crews of the Merchant Service. On the contrary, its aim was to maintain a navy sufficiently powerful to secure to as many merchant vessels as before the war, if not to an even larger number, a safe passage over the seas of both hemispheres ; and the feat was actually accomplished. Between 1792, when war was declared, and 1812, when the naval forces reached their maximum, the number of sailors increased from 36,000 to 114,000.[3] During the same time the numbers engaged in the Merchant Service increased from 118,000[4] to 165,000 men.[5] But to obtain this result the Admiralty was driven to every conceivable expedient.

The traditional method was the press gang. The United Kingdom was divided into twenty-six stations. In each of them a captain, assisted by a number of lieutenants, directed the operations of small press gangs, and in time of war possessed the right to seize the first comer and to dispatch him to serve in the Fleet either while the war lasted or for an indeterminate number of years.[6] The procedure was of dubious legality. All that the jurists could say in support of impressment was that, having been practised from time immemorial, it had become a part of the common law, the unwritten law of the

[1] A. T. Mahan, *Types*, pp. 447–8.

[2] The increase of pay during 1815 was £1 15s. See *Editorial Review*, No. 81, October 1824, Art. 8, *Abolition of Impressment* (vol. xli. pp. 154 sqq.).

[3] Sea Service Supplies, 1793 = 20,000 seamen ; additional = 16,000 (not including 5,000, later 4,000 marines, soldiers employed in naval warfare, but not in the navigation of the vessels). 1812 = 113,600 seamen, exclusive of 31,400 marines (James, *Naval History*, vol. i. p. 378 ; vol. vi. p. 494).

[4] 118,386 (Macpherson, *Ann. of Comm.*, vol. iv. p. 260).

[5] *Account of the number of vessels, with . . . the number of men and boys . . . which belonged to the several parts of the British Empire*, on September 30th, in the years 1812, 1813, 1814. The figures for 1812 = 165,030.

[6] In peace the power of impressment was submitted to certain restrictions. In the City the signature of the civil magistrate was necessary. To impress a fisherman required the formal sanction of two justices of the peace. Those engaged in the whale fishery of the North of Scotland were exempt while on their way to the fishing stations. Ferrymen were also exempted (Adolphus, *British Empire*, vol. ii. pp. 223 sqq. Brenton, *Naval History*, vol. i. pp. 50 sqq.). In time of war, however, an Act suspending these exceptions was usually passed. American War, 19 Geo. III, cap. 75. Napoleonic War, 38 Geo. III, cap. 46.

realm, or that, although it had never been instituted by Statute, many statutes presupposed its existence, and that it was in consequence contained indirectly in the written or statute law.[1] But an attempt to have recourse to more regular methods proved unsuccessful. In imitation of Colbert, William III had sought to introduce a species of naval registration. Thirty thousand sailors enrolled in a Government register were to hold themselves, in return for certain privileges, in constant readiness to serve. These privileges comprised a small annual pension, a larger share of the prizes, a better chance of promotion and the guarantee of support for themselves and their families in case of sickness, incapacitation or old age. The Opposition protested, represented the registered as reduced, by the very fact of their registration, to a sort of legal slavery, and succeeded in obtaining the repeal of the statute.[2] The eighteenth-century Whigs preferred, as more in harmony with the spirit of a free constitution, the irregular method of the press to the bureaucratic order, temporarily introduced by William III. Once admitted, the press could be worked in two ways. The press officers could make it their object to carry off from the coast districts the men whom they considered the most likely to make good sailors. It was then that their tyranny assumed its most odious aspect, since the press gangs made choice of the men who were not only the strongest but also the most intelligent and of the best character, and tore them from their families. There occurred many a heart-rending scene when a sailor, just returned from a long voyage, was seized on the threshold of his father's home and carried off anew, never perhaps to behold his native village again. And bloody frays took place along the coast when the press gang was out. There were even actual battles with gunfire between the whale-fishers of the north and the vessels of the Admiralty, when the latter attempted to capture the whalers on board their fishing-boats. Or the press officers could employ another method, and in the endeavour to make their proceedings less unpopular, might endeavour a friendly understanding either with the captains of the Merchant Service or with the local authorities in the selection of men for the service of the State. In 1795 in every British port an embargo was laid on all English vessels, and the owners were obliged, each in proportion to the number of men in his employ, to furnish between them a total of 19,867 men. This also was impressment. But in this form it left the owners and captains of the Mercantile Marine free to select for the Navy the worst elements of their crews. At the same time in the towns the justices of the peace and other magistrates were called upon to surrender to the Admiralty, for service in the Navy, specified classes of vagabonds and criminals. The Royal Navy thus became, as far as the large towns

---

[1] Blackstone, 1 *Comm.* 918–19.
[2] 7 and 8 Will. III, cap. 21 ; 7 Anne, cap. 21.

of the kingdom were concerned, a cheap convict station or prison. Whenever a strike broke out at a port among the crews of the merchantmen, the owners and the press officers soon arranged the removal and disappearance of the leaders.[1] The sailors obtained by these methods were not always the worst. The smugglers of the Kentish coast were in great request as pilots with the commanders of the British Navy. But, allowing for exceptions, crews thus recruited must as a general rule have been worth very little.

Moreover, even these sources were insufficient for the Admiralty. Still more men were needed, and since they could not be had at home, they were sought abroad. In 1793 Parliament suspended an article of the Navigation Act, which provided that the crews of English vessels should be entirely composed of Englishmen.[2] But it was not only for the Merchant Service, it was for the Royal Navy that sailors were drawn from every country under the sun. It was useless for the Directory to decree that every sailor not of British nationality who was captured on a British man-of-war should be put to death. The threat was childish, since the Directory never made any prisoners at sea. In 1796 Collingwood, while cruising off Toulon, captured on French vessels a number of Austrian deserters and prisoners, whom Massena was taking from Genoa to Toulon. Massena had intended to make French soldiers of them. Collingwood turned them into British sailors. " In my ship's company," he wrote to a friend, " I have some of all the States in Germany—Austrians, Poles, Croats, and Hungarians—a motley tribe." [3]

When a little later the English complained that their sailors deserted to seek higher pay in the American Merchant Service, the Americans replied that an equal number of their citizens served in the British Navy. Collingwood, in 1807, admitted the truth of their statement.[4] Once more we may ask what could be the possible value in war of such a medley as this ? [5]

---

[1] Whitbread denounced the abuse in the House of Commons (June 1, 1814) : " Three men had been impressed as riotous persons, at the desire of some other persons. Thus was this power of impress, illegal and oppressive as it was in itself, perverted from its legitimate object." To this Croker replied : " The Admiralty was innocent. The execution of the impress warrants rested with the officers of the ports only. . . . It was a favour to a master of a merchant ship, when the impress officers were obliged to take some men from his vessels, to allow him to choose those whom he would wish to remain " (Parl. Deb., vol. xxvii. p. 1039). See, on the other hand, the Newcastle Chronicle, February 20, 1812 : " Monday, near thirty riotous seamen were taken on the Tyne at Shields and lodged safe in His Majesty's ship Transit. The peace of this port has frequently been disturbed, under pretence of demanding more wages ; but now positive orders are given by the Admiralty to the commanding officer here to impress such lawless hands and send them to the Nore."

[2] 33 Geo. III, cap. 26. An Act permitting three-fourths of the crews of merchantmen to consist of foreigners.

[3] Letter to J. E. Blackett, September 25, 1796 (Life, vol. i. pp. 43–4).

[4] Letter to Vice-Admiral Thornborough, October 18, 1807 (Life, vol. ii. p. 66). On quite a small number of ships there were, he reckoned, 217 American sailors.

[5] Once more recourse was had to the offer of bounties for those who would join voluntarily (Brenton, Naval History, vol. i. pp. 49, 168). But the scheme obtained a very poor success.

In 1797, when the British Navy was on the eve of its most splendid victories, mutiny broke out on all the fleets. The disorders began on the Channel Fleet, then at anchor in Portsmouth harbour. The sailors had presented to Admiral Howe petitions demanding higher pay. When he refused they went on strike, for their mutiny can be termed by no other name. The strike lasted an entire month, from April 15th to May 14th, and completely paralysed the activity of the British Fleet off Brest and Cherbourg. On May 20th the North Sea Fleet at anchor near the mouth of the Thames mutinied, put the officers in irons, proclaimed a common sailor " President of the Floating Republic," blockaded the port of London, and did not surrender until June 20th. In July the infection spread to the fleet cruising off Cadiz,[1] under the command of Sir John Jervis. Sir John occupied the crews with constant expeditions, and, while satisfying the just demands of the sailors, did not shrink from making examples of offenders. By these means he was able to prevent the mutiny from becoming universal, perhaps even the desertion of the fleet to the enemy. But the disorder continued for the next four years. In 1798 the crews of the *Pompey* and the *Neptune* mutinied, and were on the verge of surrendering the two vessels to the enemy. This actually happened the same year in the case of another vessel, the *Hermione* off Porto Rico, and in the following year a sloop carrying twenty cannon deserted off Brest.[2] In 1801 Lord St. Vincent has still to admit " the *deplorable state* of the discipline of the Navy." [3] When, after the Peace of Amiens, the British Government decided to send a fleet to the Barbadoes, the sailors, who had been expecting to be disbanded almost at once, proclaimed their dissatisfaction with the order and refused to start. Sixteen of the ringleaders were put to death.[4]

But such stern repression appears to have been altogether the exception in the history of the British Navy. Numerous were the concessions made to appease the mutinous spirit of the sailors. All

See Brenton, *Naval History*, vol. i. p. 49 n. : " One of these wretched objects, on coming on board a ship of war with £70 bounty, was seized by a boatswain's mate, who, holding him up by the waistband of his trousers, humorously exclaimed : ' Here is a —— that cost a guinea a pound.' There were few, if any, seamen among them ; and the term ' quota-man ' or ' lord mayor's man ' was supposed to comprise everything that was base and contemptible among sailors."

[1] Collingwood, Letter to J. E. Blackett, June 27, 1797 : " . . . The seamen, I am persuaded, would never have revolted from good order ; but consider, with such a fleet as we have now, how large a portion of the crews of the ships are miscreants of every description, and capable of every crime ; and when these predominate, what evils may we not dread from the demoniac councils, and influence of such a mass of mischief ? " (*Life*, vol. i. p. 63).

[2] Brenton, *Naval History*, vol. ii. pp. 286, 435 sqq. Chevalier, *Marine française*, vol. iv. p. 24.

[3] Brenton, *Life of St. Vincent*, vol. ii. p. 56.

[4] Brenton, *Naval History*, vol. ii. pp. 559 sqq. ; *Life of Lord St. Vincent*, vol. ii. pp. 100–2 ; *Diary of Lord Colchester*, vol. i. pp. 396 sqq. ; Pellew, *Life of Lord Sidmouth*, vol. i. p. 363.

the demands of the Portsmouth mutineers were granted and not a man punished. The mutiny of the North Sea Fleet was certainly repressed more sternly. It was one of those second insurrections by which governments are not taken unawares. And in such cases the government is apt to make the leaders of the second mutiny atone for its feebleness in dealing with the first. Nevertheless, even then, the Cabinet was obviously anxious to punish as few as possible. And those who were condemned to imprisonment were pardoned on the first opportunity.[1] Nor did the mutinous fleet forfeit any of the concessions already obtained for all sailors by the Portsmouth mutineers. Henceforward the crews received a larger share of the prizes. The pay of the petty officers and of the first-class sailors was raised by 5s. 6d. a month, that of the second-class sailors by 4s. 6d. In 1806 the Fox-Grenville Ministry granted a further increase—5s. for petty officers, 4s. for first-class sailors, 2s. for the other sailors.[2] Sir John Jervis, Lord St. Vincent since his great victory in 1797, reformed and mitigated naval discipline ; he took care that the men were properly fed, and provided for the first time a special cabin for the sick.[3] Though corporal punishment was not abolished, the best admirals, such as Nelson and Collingwood, employed it as seldom as possible. Sometimes during a whole year not a single sailor was flogged on board their fleets.[4] The following incident will sufficiently prove the anxiety of the Admiralty to show its care for the common sailors. In 1812 a naval lieutenant in command of a sloop killed, in a fit of rage, an infantry sergeant of the marines who had been guilty of insubordination. He was condemned to death and executed. Nor was he even shot ; he was hanged like a common murderer.[5]

Were these attempts to conciliate the feeling of the crews successful ? Undoubtedly they enjoyed a measure of success. After 1801 the British Navy witnessed no more mutinies on a large scale. All the same the *moral* of the sailors continued to be far from satisfactory. In 1810 Admiral Patten accused the sailors of being " in the habit of deeming both mutiny and desertion as privileges attached to their situation." He complained also that the warrant officers were " men of inferior or doubtful characters, who encourage mutiny, wink at desertion, and sometimes join the seamen in both these alarming transgressions." [6] The community of speech rendered

---

[1] Brenton, *Naval History*, vol. ii. p. 119.

[2] Clowes, *Royal Navy*, vol. iv. p. 171.   H. of C., April 25, 1806 (*Parl. Deb.*, vol. vi p. 908).

[3] Brenton, *Life of St. Vincent*, vol. i. p. 342.

[4] *Life of Collingwood*, vol. i. pp. 68, 78.

[5] The condemned had been recommended by the court martial to the mercy of the Government. It was nevertheless decided to proceed with the execution (Brenton, *Naval History*, vol. iv. p. 15).

[6] *The Natural Defence of an Insular Empire*, quoted in the *Quarterly Review*, in the article above mentioned, vol. iv. pp. 329, 331.   For other criticisms see Miss Edgeworth, *Patronage*,

it peculiarly easy for English deserters to be naturalized as citizens of the United States. This gave rise to a series of diplomatic representations which finally led to a war between England and America. Never had the methods of recruiting for the Navy been the object of sharper criticism than during the years immediately preceding 1815.[1]

The Officers.

If the sources from which the crews were drawn, and, in consequence, their discipline left so much to be desired, did the peculiar excellence of their officers compensate for these defects in the organization of the Navy ? So the English believed, and their belief was in many respects well founded. Though, generally speaking, to become a naval officer a man must belong to the governing classes of the country, the aristocracy or the gentry, the rule was not absolute. To become a midshipman gentle birth was not essential, nor even wealth, provided the consent of a commander were obtained.[2] A little boy, fourteen or fifteen, sometimes only eleven years old, would be entrusted by a parent to a friend who was in command of a frigate or of a ship of the line. On board, under his master's supervision, he would learn at the same time both the theory and the practice of his profession. He would serve for four years as landman or able volunteer, for two years as midshipman or master's mate, and at the end of the six years would be ready to pass his examination for lieutenant. Formerly it had been the practice to postpone the moment of embarkation by a convenient fiction. At the age of eleven or twelve, the child's name was entered in the ship's log-book, but the registration was a mere form, and two or three years would pass before he actually joined the ship.[3] But such practices had been entirely given up, and about 1815 the ablest commanders were beginning to regard with disfavour both the excessively early age at which for so many children life on board began, and the insufficiency of their theoretical attainments for the position of a naval officer.[4] Some of these midshipmen took a dislike to the life and left the Navy for the Army.[5] Those who remained were proud

chap. xxiii.—H. of C., March 18, 1824 ; G. W. Butler's petition, speeches of Hume and Sykes (*Parl. Deb.*, New Series, vol. x. p. 1220).—*Editorial Review*, October 1824, Art. 8, *Abolition of Impressment* (vol. xli. pp. 151 sqq.).

[1] H. of C., April 24, 1815. Whitbread's speech (*Parl. Deb.*, vol. xxx. p. 812).

[2] An Order in Council had even laid down the conditions under which a quartermaster or a pilot could become a lieutenant without passing through the rank of midshipman (Adolphus, *British Empire*, vol. ii. p. 233). And a certain Captain Coghlan, who belonged to the Merchant Service before he joined the Navy, who was at once given the honorary rank of captain (Brenton, *Naval History*, vol. ii. p. 510 ; vol. v. p. 100).

[3] Brenton, *British Navy*, vol. i. pp. 79–80.

[4] Collingwood, *Life*, vol. i. pp. 100, 120 ; vol. ii. p. 240.

[5] Campbell, *Lives of the Chancellors*, vol. vi. p. 377 ; *Journal of Lady Holland*, vol. ii. p. 259. It was only the want of means that kept Thomas Erskine in the Navy (Campbell, *ibid.*, p. 373).

to contrast the difficulties of the earlier stages of their career with the ease with which commissions in the Army could be obtained by influence or wealth.

At the age of nineteen, the midshipman passed his examination for a lieutenancy. He could then be promoted, either by seniority after ten years' service, or as the reward of some brilliant exploit after at least two years' service, to be captain of a sloop. A year later he might perhaps be made a post-captain, in command of a frigate or ship of the line. The next stage was the command of a squadron. After this, if he showed the capacity, he might become commodore, and then in turn rear-admiral, vice-admiral, admiral, finally perhaps admiral of the entire fleet. These positions were the object of keen competition ; but the duties were peculiarly onerous.

It was not enough for the commander of a squadron to be an able strategist, a good tactician. Ruling, as he did, a small floating city, which might perhaps comprise ten or even twenty thousand souls, he had need to prove himself a statesman. He must be able to secure obedience from the sailors and harmony among the officers of all ranks. He must provide for the maintenance of all under his command, and must therefore be able to determine beforehand when and where the crews should disembark to revictual the ships with fresh meat and water. It was his duty, moreover, to treat, as the representative of his fleet and nation, with the governments of the countries off whose shores he was cruising—allied governments, hostile governments, neutral governments, and, most of all, governments that waited on the vicissitudes of war and revolution and became friendly and hostile in turn, between one cruise and the next. Sometimes the home authorities invested an admiral with the powers of a plenipotentiary ; but he was always obliged to play the part of a diplomatist. Lord Collingwood, who commanded in the Mediterranean, had not only to blockade the port of Toulon and to protect the Sicilian coasts ; he had also to conduct negotiations with the Sultan of Morocco, the Bey of Algiers and the Bey of Tunis, and on his own responsibility to treat with them as the representative at once of his squadron, of the Court of St. James and the Court of Palermo.

So long as Spain remained hostile, he must take care, while fighting her, to spare her as much as possible in the hope of detaching her sooner

" . . . My second objection is, that I would be obliged to keep company with a most abandoned set of people that would corrupt my morals ; whereas in the Army, though they be bad enough, yet I should have the advantage of choosing my company where I pleased, without being constrained to any particular set." But in order to enter the Army he would have been obliged to purchase a commission, and for that reason alone, he joined the Navy. For the difficulties which the midshipman found in living on his scanty pay which was, moreover, only due at intervals of six months, see *A Letter . . . on the . . . Condition of Officers in the Royal Navy*, by a Post-Captain, 1811, pp. 8–10. This little work was published by the author as a supplement to the work published in the preceding year by Admiral Patten, which dealt with the condition of the common sailors.

or later from the French alliance. It was for him to decide, without waiting for orders from London, what should be the attitude of his fleet to the Porte. At one time he must enter into friendly negotiations with the Sultan, at another he must send ships to bombard him.[1] Sir James Saumarez, the commander of the Baltic Fleet, earned the thanks of the nation not only by the number of hostile convoys that he intercepted, but also by the skill with which, after Sweden had joined the Napoleonic League and England no longer possessed a single friend in the Baltic, he had succeeded in maintaining good relations with that country, in continuing to revictual in Swedish ports and in paving the way, by his diplomacy, for the defection of Bernadotte.[2]

Such hard work deserved its pay. The admiral of the fleet received up to £1,800 a year, an admiral £1,260, a vice-admiral £880, a rear-admiral £630. An admiral or vice-admiral, when holding the chief command, received in addition 20s. a day for table expenses.[3] But to obtain a correct idea of the sums actually received by the commander of a squadron, we must add to this fixed remuneration the enormous emoluments derived from occasional sources, from prizes captured from the enemy, whether from men-of-war or merchantmen. A quarter of the prize went to the crew of the ships which had effected the capture, a quarter to the midshipmen, the mates and other petty officers, an eighth to the lieutenants and masters. This left three-eighths for the captain, but if the vessel formed part of a squadron, the admiral had a right to one of these three-eighths.[4] This was, of course, a very unreliable source of income, and the prizes by no means always corresponded with the importance of the victories won. During the closing years of the 18th century a naval officer might make his fortune in a day, if he happened to meet a Spanish vessel laden with gold from the mines of America.[5] The Battle of Trafalgar, on the other hand, brought the victors nothing.[6] The sharing of

---

[1] Mahan, *Types*, pp. 424–5.   [2] Mahan, *Types*, pp. 424–5.

[3] Adolphus, *British Empire*, vol. ii. pp. 228–9, gives the rate of pay per diem. The figures given above were obtained by multiplying his figures by 360.

[4] *Ibid.*, vol. ii. p. 241.

[5] In 1793 the *San Iago*, which was carrying £25,000,000 in specie, yielded £50,000 to Lord Hood, and £30,000 to each of the captains of the squadron (Brenton, *Naval History*, vol. i. pp. 193–4). When in 1799 two Spanish frigates were captured off Cape Finisterre, every captain received over £40,000, every lieutenant over £5,000, every warrant officer close on £2,500, and the midshipmen and petty officers were left with £800 to divide amongst them, and the common sailors with £200 (Brenton, *Naval History*, vol. ii. pp. 381–2).

[6] Collingwood, *Letter to Lady Collingwood*, October 25, 1806 : " They have used us shabbily about that whole business ; for the poor seamen who fought a battle that set all England in an uproar, and all the poets and painters at work, have not at this moment received one sixpence of prize money " (*Life*, vol. i. pp. 338–9). Cf. Clarke and MacArthur, *Life of Nelson*, vol. i. p. 132. Letter of Nelson to his wife after the capture of Toulon : " I believe the world is convinced that no conquests of importance can be made without us ; and yet, as soon as we have accomplished the service we are ordered on, we are neglected. If Parliament does not grant something to this fleet, our Jacks will grumble ; for here there is no prize money to soften their hardships ; all we get is honour and salt beef."

prize money was, moreover, a highly contentious business and gave rise to innumerable squabbles. These were in the first instance disputes with the Admiralty ; [1] for the proceeds of the sale of enemy ships, captured before the declaration of war, but on which an embargo had been laid, belonged to the Admiralty. And this raised the question whether or no war had been declared previous to the capture of a particular vessel. Again, men-of-war which had been taken by the enemy and afterwards regained were also prizes of the Admiralty and not of the crew of the ship that had made the capture. Suppose, then, an English ship after her capture by the enemy had been refitted and completely transformed in a French port. If she should subsequently be recaptured, ought she to be regarded as a new vessel to which the Admiralty had no claim ? [2] Then there were disputes among the officers. Suppose an admiral who had captured a convoy had detached two or three ships from his fleet a few hours before the engagement. Were the officers in command of these vessels to blame for the ill-timed order ? Did they not belong to the squadron ? Had they not therefore a right to a share of the prize ? [3] For five years Nelson and Lord St. Vincent were at law with each other over a claim to the sum of £3,000, the commander's portion of prizes made in 1799 by Lord St. Vincent's fleet after his departure for England.[4]

As a further inducement to good service, and also as some compensation to officers still poor after brilliant victories, the Government had in reserve titles of nobility, honours of all kinds, commemorative medals, military decorations. The Order of the Bath, which in 1815 comprised only a very small body of knights, was a much-coveted distinction. The rules which governed the grant of titles had been clearly fixed by custom. A captain who in obedience to orders performed some striking feat received a knighthood. A commander of a squadron who had shown originality in his interpretation of the admiral's orders, and whose initiative had led to a decisive success, or who had taken a subordinate part in winning an important victory, was made a baronet.[5] An admiral, a vice-admiral, even a rear-admiral might aspire to a peerage. If the new peer were poor, a pension would be conferred upon him, to enable him to keep up his position. From the list of the higher naval officers, who received a peerage during the reign of George III, we are able to form a sufficiently accurate idea of the classes from which the commanders of the British Navy were drawn. Three of these new peers were younger sons

---

[1] Brenton, *Naval History*, vol. iv. p. 41.

[2] See the case of the *Castor*, 1793 (Brenton, *Naval History*, vol. i. pp. 362–3).

[3] The case was called in legal terminology one of "constructive assistance" (Brenton, *Naval History*, vol. ii. pp. 400–1).

[4] Pettigrew, *Life of Nelson*, vol. ii. p. 271.

[5] See a curious letter from Lord St. Vincent to Lord Spencer, March 7, 1799 (Brenton, *Life*, vol. ii. pp. 348–9).

of great houses, and three were of good family—two of the latter, Lord Collingwood and Lord Duncan, from the landed gentry. Two were the sons of soldiers who had never risen to the rank of colonel. Two were sons of poor barristers. Nelson and the two Hoods were sons of clergymen. Lord Exmouth was of quite humble origin. His father had been in command of a mail boat in Dover harbour.[1]

The organization, therefore, of the naval command, theoretically at least, would seem to have been as excellent as the methods employed by the British Government to obtain crews were defective. The apprenticeship to the profession was difficult, promotion open to merit, and the career could lead to the highest dignities of the realm. But we must not forget that the conditions under which promotion was given in the Navy were a source of constant complaints, quarrels and insubordination among the officers. Whig ideas had always prevailed in the British Navy. Naval men maintained that, while the land army belonged to the King, the fleet was essentially a constitutional and a parliamentary force. When, some years earlier, the Government had placed a crown above the anchor on the naval ensigns, the change is said to have been resented as an insult.[2] The two leaders of the most advanced democrats, Lord Cochrane, himself a rear-admiral, and his friend, Sir Francis Burdett, bombarded the House of Commons with the grievances of the naval officers.[3] Seamen have an instinctive distrust of ministries and public offices, of the interference of the incompetent land lubber in naval business. And now that the Government seemed settled in Tory hands, the traditional Whiggery of the Fleet became all the stronger. The sailors well knew the influence exerted by electioneering considerations on the choice of pilots at Dover. This was, they alleged, the reason why so many ships were lost at sea or taken by the enemy.[4] They complained that the same

[1] We must not regard as a naval peerage the title of Baron Pierrepont and Viscount Newark, conferred in 1796 on Charles Herbert Pierrepont, M.P. for the county of Nottingham, and formerly a Port Captain. But if, to the fifteen naval peerages of England, we add five peerages of Ireland, we shall find that four out of these new Irish peers belonged to great families; only one, Lord Shuldham, was the son of a clergyman.

[2] Moore relates this in his Diary (November 28, 1818), on Tierney's authority, without, however, guaranteeing its truth. He goes on: "The Prince, at one time, thought of giving red waistcoats and breeches to the Navy; at another time he is reported to have said, upon some consultation for a change of their costume: 'D——n them; dress them now how you will, you cannot make them look like gentlemen.'"

[3] H. of C., July 10, 1807. Lord Cochrane's speech (Parl. Deb., vol. ix. pp. 754 sqq.).

[4] Lord St. Vincent, Letter to John Robinson, Esq., March 30, 1801 (Brenton, Life, vol. ii. p. 61). Lord John Russell, English Government, 1823 ed., p. 416. "The Navy, being under the direction of a Cabinet Minister, is not so purely conducted [as the Army under a Prince of the Royal Family]. Many an officer owes his advance, many a civil servant his place, to an election interest."—Sir Charles Napier, The Navy, pp. 22–4. An Enquiry into the . . . state of . . . the Navy, by an Englishman, pp. 23 sqq., and 44–5: "The whole number of post-captains who compose the present list amounts to about 840: of these I estimate about 450 to have attained their rank from merit and long service, leaving 390 who, I really believe, have risen purely by private patronage and borough interest." But we must not imagine that these nominations through influence were of a nature to render the body of naval officers more

influences affected promotions, and agreed with Lord Collingwood that "a hole or two in the skin will not weigh against a vote in Parliament." [1]   If the rules of seniority were strictly observed, the sailors ascribed it to the desire to encourage among young men of good family the notion that they had a right to rapid promotion without having to work for it. [2]   If, on the other hand, the rules of seniority were broken, they were ready with the cry of favouritism, of arbitrary preference.

When in 1798 Nelson received the command of the Mediterranean Fleet, nothing short of a mutiny among the officers was the result. The malcontents were led by two in high command, Sir William Parker and Sir John Orde, who considered that their rights had been violated.[3]   At the same time, Lord St. Vincent on the Atlantic was bewailing the insubordination which prevailed throughout his fleet : "Mutinous spirits among the lower orders, and factious discontents in a few of the higher." [4]   He was obliged to maintain his authority against simultaneous attack from both quarters, and in another letter written shortly afterwards he ascribed the insubordination of the crews "entirely" to "the licentiousness of the officers." [5]   Later on Nelson himself took offence before Alexandria at the bestowal of an independent command upon Sir Sidney Smith, the personal friend of Pitt. Three years afterwards, he feigned indisposition because he was ordered to serve under the aged Sir Hyde Parker, whose promotion he attributed to political influence. In 1804 similar bickerings took place in the Pacific between Sir Edward Pellew and Sir Thomas Troubridge.[6] In 1811 a letter from Rear-Admiral Fremantle to the Marquis of Buckingham reveals the entire fleet in open revolt against Admiral Cotton, and awaiting impatiently the change of Cabinet which would replace him by another admiral.[7]

These complaints of the officers were not, however, always justified. Surely we cannot blame the Government for sending Nelson in 1798 to win the Battle of Aboukir. On the contrary, the impartiality

aristocratic. Their effect was quite the contrary, when the nominations were inspired by electioneering considerations. " It is no disgrace," continues our writer, " to the post-captains of the English Navy, who have many lords amonst them, that these are also the worthy offspring of tailors, shoemakers, farmers, ale-house keepers, sailors, pilots, haberdashers, drapers, milliners, and in fact every calling under the sun."

[1] Lord Collingwood, *Letter to Captain Clavell*, October 20, 1809 (*Mem. and Corr.*, 1828, p. 483).

[2] Brenton, *Life of St. Vincent*, vol. ii. p. 60 ; *Life of Collingwood*, vol. ii. pp. 313, 333.

[3] See a long letter from Collingwood in Brenton, *Life of St. Vincent*, vol. i. pp. 425-6.

[4] Letter to Lady Spencer, December 27, 1798 (Brenton, *Life*, vol. i., pp. 369-370).

[5] Letter to A. MacDonald, May 16, 1801 (Brenton, *Life*, vol. ii. p. 665). Cf. Letter to the Marquis of Clanricarde, *ibid.*, pp. 66, 67. Cf. also a letter written later to Rear-Admiral Markham, April 9, 1801 (*Life*, vol. ii. pp. 256-7) : " My opinion has long been that the supplies of fresh beef have been too frequent ; but a discontinuance under me would produce a clamour among the officers, from whence all our evils have originated, and you well know how soon seditious expressions are conveyed from the ward-room to the gun-deck."

[6] Osler, *Life of Admiral Viscount Exmouth*, pp. 218 sqq.

[7] *Court of England under the Prince Regent*, vol. ii. pp. 54-5. Letter of March 1, 1811.

displayed by the Admiralty on many occasions is quite remarkable. We find, for instance, in 1794 Sir John Jervis and Sir Charles Grey, both influential Whigs, entrusted by Pitt with the command of the expedition sent against the French Colonies in the West Indies. Again, in 1809 an important command was given to Lord Cochrane, the demagogue. But, whether justified or no, the lack of discipline among the officers was undeniable. Never was it displayed more undisguisedly than after the victory of the Aix Ronds in 1809. Rear-Admiral Eliab Harvey, who was second-in-command, inveighed openly on the bridge of the admiral's ship against the commander-in-chief, Lord Gambier. The latter was obliged to bring him before a court martial and deprive him of his command. Lord Cochrane, to whose fireships the victory was chiefly due, now came forward to accuse Lord Gambier of allowing the remnants of the French Fleet, by the slowness of his movements, time to take refuge in the Charente. On his return to London he declared himself prepared, should a vote of thanks to Lord Gambier be moved in Parliament, to vote and speak, as a Member of the House, in opposition to the motion. To clear himself in the eyes of the public Lord Gambier was forced to demand a trial by court martial. There was no law to prevent an officer on active service taking his seat in Parliament. In 1815 the House of Commons contained ten naval officers, including an admiral, three vice-admirals and three rear-admirals. Naval officers were thus enabled, between cruises, to make the nation witness of their quarrels.[1] Despite the Tory reaction, the British Navy had kept the traditional independence and insubordination, whose manifestations were so astonishing to the Continental observer.

One further touch remains to complete our picture of the spirit prevalent in the British Navy. One of the grievances put forward by the mutineers of the North Sea Fleet was "That they were not allowed to keep the Sabbath day holy, and that the fiddler had been ordered or permitted to play to them on Sunday."[2] Their ringleader, Richard Parker, on his condemnation to death, presented the Fleet with the spectacle of an edifying end. At his execution he drank a glass of wine, saying, as he drank it, "I drink first to the salvation of my soul and next to the forgiveness of my enemies," and then knelt in prayer.[3] When Nelson had given his orders on the morning of

[1] The admirals took umbrage at this, and while by no means disposed to sacrifice their own privileges, demanded that they should not be allowed to ordinary captains. See St. Vincent's letter to Lord Howick, October 18, 1806 (Brenton, *Life*, vol. ii. pp. 316–17) : " If you will, my good lord, bring a Bill into Parliament to disqualify any officer under the rank of rear-admiral to sit in the House of Commons, the Navy may be preserved ; but, while a little drunken, worthless jackanapes is permitted to hold the seditious language he has done, in the presence of flag officers of rank, you will require a man of greater health and vigour than I possess to command your fleets."

[2] Brenton, *Naval History*, vol. i. p. 425, ed. 1823, p. 284, 1836.

[3] *Ibid.*, vol. i. p. 442, ed. 1823, p. 296, 1836.

the Battle of Trafalgar, he retired into his cabin and composed the following prayer : " May the great God, whom I worship, grant my country, and for the benefit of Europe in general, a great and glorious victory. . . . Amen. Amen. Amen." [1] Very different would have been the language and deaths of French mutineers at Brest or Toulon. Napoleon and his generals did not prepare for battle in this way. For the last fifty years a powerful movement of religious enthusiasm had been stirring the public mind to its depths. Perhaps this unanimity of religious sentiment, this feeling of reverence and fear of God, had already begun to modify the insubordinate temper of the sailors. But we witness as yet only the first symptoms of the new spirit. The English fleets about the year 1800 still represented the old England of the 18th century, riotous and insubordinate. The ships that won the day at Camperdown, Cape St. Vincent and Aboukir were commanded by undisciplined officers, and manned by mutinous crews. Nevertheless, the British Fleet, in spite of its disunion, proved overwhelmingly superior to the fleets of the enemy. In the hour of battle, admirals, officers and men were reconciled and swooped down upon the enemy's ships " like a falcon on her prey." Why was this ? What was the secret of their strength ? It was that they had the country behind them, and they knew it. [2]

The Navy and Public Opinion.

In France the national territory had been threatened on the Eastern frontier. Since Valmy, it had been in this quarter that the soldiers knew there were laurels for the winning and dangers worth the daring. All the while the French sailors felt themselves forgotten on board their ships, neglected by the public, left as though to languish in exile. In the minds of their fellow-countrymen they were an altogether secondary force. They displayed in consequence a second-rate *moral*. The British public had, on the contrary, been accustomed for a century past to regard the sea as the source of England's wealth and greatness. As we have seen, it is a mistake to suppose that because the Mercantile Marine of Great Britain was of such importance, it furnished a ready supply of sailors to the Royal Navy. The importance of the Merchant Service did, however, familiarize Englishmen with the sea. For them the sea had no terrors—only attraction. It was, moreover, the sea that separated the United Kingdom from the rest of the world, and constituted the national frontier. England was a besieged country on whose ramparts the sailors mounted guard. All eyes were fixed upon them. Unable to endanger the Constitution of the Realm, they secured the prosperity, the safety, the very existence of the nation. Jack Tar, with his peculiar three-coloured dress, his wide breeches,

[1] Brenton, *Naval History*, vol. iii. p. 448, ed. 1823.
[2] Collingwood, letter to his wife, February 17, 1797 (*Life*, vol. i. p. 47).

his flowing jacket, his hair hanging in pigtails down his neck, was the popular hero ; and his warlike ardour naturally grew with the enthusiasm he inspired.

The truth of the foregoing observations may be confirmed from a different point of view. We have only to consider the events of the last ten years of the war. Napoleon had realized that he could never hope to inspire French sailors with the enthusiasm which possessed his soldiers. He devised accordingly a new naval strategy, better suited to the timidity of his captains and their crews. Henceforward, the French vessels should remain in the ports, always in great number, always apparently on the verge of sailing. They would thus, while carefully avoiding an engagement, compel the British Fleet to keep a constant watch off Antwerp, Brest, Rochefort, and Toulon. The British ships were left to rot on the open sea, while their crews were demoralized by inaction. Nelson, a stern commander, dull and commonplace everywhere save on the poop of his vessel, a born leader and fighter, had been the hero of the first period of the war. The melancholy and conscientious Collingwood, condemned to constant wandering over lonely seas, without the joy or even the hope of victory, and succumbing at last to the weary burden seven years after he had left his native land, was the hero of the second period. And Napoleon's new strategy proved up to a certain point successful. The British Fleet, reduced to inactivity, lost thereby some of its former popularity, and with it some of its old fighting spirit. " It is not the fashion for young men to be seamen now," wrote Collingwood regretfully.[1] The sailors, conscious that the favour of the public was passing from them, became embittered and discontented. They contrasted their scanty pay and small pensions with the enormous incomes with which politicians satisfied their greed.[2] Bitterly they compared their lot with that of the officers in the Army. Why, they asked, had only one peerage been granted to a sailor since 1807 ? After Waterloo a democratic innovation had been made, and a commemorative medal been given to all who took part in the battle—to the common soldiers as well as to the officers. Why, queried the sailors, had not the Government thought of this before, when the conquerors of Trafalgar were to be rewarded ?[3] In 1816 a Member of Parliament, who persisted in bringing before the House the grievances of the naval officers, was scarcely granted a hearing and his voice was drowned by a babel of conversation.[4] The prestige of the Navy had suffered an eclipse.[5] Nelson had belonged to the already distant age of Pitt and

[1] Letter to Lord Radstock, April 13, 1807 (*Mem. and Corr.*, ed. 1823, p. 248).
[2] H. of C., May 11, 1810. Lord Cochrane's speech (*Parl. Deb.*, vol. xvi. pp. 1,006 sqq.).
[3] Brenton, *Naval History*, vol. iv. pp. 496-7.
[4] H. of C., March 29, 1816. Forbes' speech (*Parl. Deb.*, vol. xxxiii. pp. 735 sqq.).
[5] For an expression of this discontent and for the complaints of the commercial ports that merchantmen were insufficiently protected against the American Navy, see *An Enquiry into the . . . state of the . . . Navy, by an Englishman*, pp. 39 sqq.

Fox, Wellington was now the national hero. When in 1812 war
with America broke out, the British crews fought badly, and suffered
a series of defeats which, although of no real importance, were ridiculous and humiliating. Meanwhile the army in Spain was winning
victory after victory.

THE ARMY.

The Anti-Militarist Tradition in England.

"To render the executive sovereign incapable of tyranny," wrote
Montesquieu, "the armies entrusted to him should consist of citizens,
and should be of the same mind as their fellow-citizens, as was the case
at Rome down to the time of Marius. There are but two possible
means to obtain this. Either those who serve in the Army should
possess sufficient wealth to pledge their good conduct towards the
other citizens, and should be enlisted for a year only, as was done at
Rome, or if there be a standing army, and the soldiers be drawn from
the worst order of the people, the legislature must possess the authority
to disband the forces at pleasure, and the soldiers must dwell with the
civilians, having no separate camps, barracks or forts." [1] Blackstone,
in his *Commentaries*, reproduces Montesquieu's language almost verbally.[2]
Indeed, the problem stated by Montesquieu was the very problem
which confronted the English Parliament throughout the 18th century.
How could an anti-militarist party, indeed an anti-militarist nation,
maintain a standing army without ceasing to be anti-militarist? There
is nothing to show that Montesquieu had England in his mind when
he put forward the former of his two expedients, and suggested an
army composed of propertied men with a personal stake in the preservation of public liberty, and enlisted only for a very short period.
Nevertheless, the English "militia," as it had been termed since the
17th century, corresponded in many respects to this description. It
was neither a professional nor a standing army, nor was it separate
from the rest of the nation. In its modern form, its organization
rested on two statutes passed shortly after the Restoration.[3] The
supreme command belonged to the King, but he could not call out
the militia for service overseas. The King appointed the lord-
lieutenants, who commanded the militia of each county, but it was
the lord-lieutenants, not the King, who appointed the subordinate
officers. Every one possessing an annual income of £500 from real
or of £600 from personal estate was obliged to furnish a cavalry-

---

[1] *Esprit des Lois*, Book II, chap. vi.   [2] 1 *Comm.* 413–14.
[3] 13 Car. II, cap. 6. An Act declaring the sole right of the militia to be in the King,
and for the better ordering and disposing the same. 13 and 14 Car. II, cap. 3. An Act for
ordering the forces in the several counties of this kingdom.

man and his horse. Every one with an income of £50 from real or £60 from personal estate was obliged to furnish an infantryman. The manœuvres did not exceed fifteen days a year. There were no special courts or code for the punishment of crimes and breaches of discipline committed in the militia during this period.[1] In course of time new statutes were enacted, which sometimes increased, but at others diminished the Royal Prerogative in respect of the militia.

This prerogative would, indeed, have been practically abolished, had not a Bill which passed the Commons in 1756 been thrown out by the Lords. It was, on the contrary, markedly strengthened by the important Act of 1757.[2] This Act provided that in each county a list should be drawn up of all capable of bearing arms. The number of militiamen to be furnished by each county should be fixed yearly by law. Those who must actually serve should be designated by ballot, but those drawn should be allowed to pay a substitute. Henceforward the Crown should nominate not only the lord-lieutenants but also the adjutants and sergeants, and was to possess a veto on the nomination of any officer whatsoever. All this was so much gain for the Royal Prerogative. And moreover, for the first time the militia when under arms was now subjected to the jurisdiction of courts martial. But we must not overlook the fact that another provision of this very statute counterbalanced all that was unduly favourable to the prerogative in its other articles. A colonel must possess an income derived from real estate of at least £400 a year, a lieutenant-colonel or major must possess £300 a year from the same source, a captain £200, a lieutenant £100, an ensign £50.[3] Thus the hierarchy of rank in the local militia was made to reproduce exactly the social hierarchy of the county landowners. The organization of the militia was essentially the application to the military sphere of the system of the Justices of the Peace. And in fact the body of officers were chosen from the upper classes by cooptation, a cooptation controlled by lord-lieutenants who were in practice irremovable. Certainly the militia was no democratic institution, but still less was it royalist. At the accession of George III it was still what it had been at the time of the downfall of the Stuarts—the army of the nation in opposition to the standing army, the army of the King. "The circumstance," declared Wilberforce, "which rendered our militia so dear to us, as a constitutional force, was its being officered by country gentlemen— men of property, of family, of domestic connections, of personal influence,

---

[1] 30 Geo. II, cap. 25. [2] 30 Geo. II, cap. 25.

[3] The great consolidating Militia Act of 1786 (26 Geo. III, cap. 107, § 5) altered this scale of incomes. For colonels and lieutenant-colonels the qualifying income was raised respectively to £1,000 and £600, for majors and captains it was fixed at £200. In the case of lieutenants and ensigns the income demanded was lowered to £50 and £20 respectively, and those two inferior grades were thrown open to persons with only personal estate if their income amounted to £1,000 a year for a lieutenant, or £500 a year for an ensign.

whose arms were in no conjuncture likely to be turned against their country." [1]

It was, nevertheless, impossible that a State which desired to interfere in European politics, to dispatch expeditions to the Continent, to acquire colonies, could be content with nothing more than a militia. Moreover, the very organization of the militia presupposed an agricultural nation, consisting of landed proprietors great and small, and their tenants. How could such a system survive the industrial revolution, in the course of which vast urban centres grew up all over the land—towns where the traditional grades of rural society were blurred, indeed destroyed ? We must add that the popular anti-militarism of the English rendered the satisfactory execution of the Militia Acts very difficult. The quasi-conscription established by the Act of 1757 aroused keen discontent, widespread complaints, even the beginnings of revolt. Large numbers of those drawn by the ballot availed themselves of the permission granted by the Act to purchase a substitute ; but we can hardly call a militia of paid substitutes in any true sense a militia. A force of this kind, so far as the common soldiers were concerned, was a professional army ; the sole difference being that their services, instead of being bought by the State, had been bought by private individuals chosen at haphazard, and the cost therefore did not appear in the budget.

In their hatred of bureaucracy, eighteenth-century Englishmen refused to fulfil the conditions under which alone they would have been able to form a citizen army. Whig England was therefore compelled to establish a standing army. Parliament resigned itself to the inevitable, and confined its efforts to the diminution of an evil recognized as necessary, by the application of the principles formulated by Montesquieu in the passage quoted above. The Mutiny Act, renewed each year, fixed the number of men whom the executive would have the right to maintain under arms. The figure thus fixed was a maximum, which might not be exceeded, though it need not be reached. The legal maximum had always been kept as low as possible, and the effective force of the British Army before the American War barely exceeded 17,000 men. The Mutiny Act also settled the amount of the grant made to the executive for the support of the standing army for one year. Therefore, by a legal fiction, the professional army was not, strictly speaking, a standing army, but was engaged and paid for one year only. The troops were, in Blackstone's words, " *ipso facto* disbanded at the expiration of every year, unless continued by Parliament." [2]

Moreover, there did not exist, as in the case of the Navy, the constitutional force of the country, a permanent statute, passed once for all by the two Houses, defining military offences and determining

---

[1] H. of C., June 19, 1798 (*Parl. Hist.*, vol. xxxiii. p. 1508).   [2] 1 *Comm.* 413.

a corresponding scale of penalties, together with the composition of the military tribunals and the procedure to be followed. The Mutiny Act conferred on the executive every year, and for one year only, the right to punish by courts martial, and in accordance with their procedure and code, cases of desertion and insubordination ; and an ineradicable prejudice forbade the quartering of the troops in barracks. That the separation between the life of the soldiers and the life of the civil population might be minimized, British soldiers throughout the whole of the 18th century were billeted in private lodgings, as a general rule at the inns. This was one of those peculiar usages which distinguished England from the rest of Europe and satisfied the nation that it was really free. Blackstone, content as a rule to explain and justify existing institutions, was not satisfied even with all these precautions against militarism. He desired that a fixed portion of the Army, on the expiration of the period for which they had been engaged, should be compelled to return to civil life. He questioned whether courts martial, such as they were found in the British Army, were after all indispensable. When their authority was extended to the militia, he declared them a danger to the national liberty.[1]

The Tory Reaction and the Army.

Such were the military institutions of Great Britain when George III ascended the throne with the avowed intention of changing a system expressly devised to weaken the Royal Prerogative. Throughout the earlier years of his reign he sought in vain to extract from his Colonial Empire the resources necessary for the maintenance of a large standing army freed from the control of Parliament. The attempt not only failed ; it cost England her American colonies. But to all appearance he had succeeded better since the outbreak of the war with France in 1792.

His first victory had been gained in 1795, when he secured the appointment of his son, the Duke of York, to the newly created post of Commander-in-Chief. Henceforward, side by side with the Ordnance and War Offices controlled by Members of Parliament, stood the military offices of the Horse Guards, where a Prince of the Blood ruled. The Adjutant-General and the Quartermaster-General became, so to speak, his head clerks, and took advantage of the obscurities in the statutory definition of the functions of the Commander-in-Chief to extend their powers continually at the expense of the other departments. The Duke of York, who had received his military training at Berlin, attempted to introduce Prussian principles and methods into the British Army. His active policy made him popular with the Court party and with professional soldiers ; but it aroused great suspicion among the members of the old Opposition, who waged

[1] 1 *Comm.* 415.

a war without truce against him. When Fox became a Cabinet Minister in 1806, he secured the institution of a military council [1] to assist and control the Duke of York in the administration of the Army. From the debates in Parliament, while this Cabinet was in office, we can see plainly what ill-feeling had been produced at Court by the demand of the Whigs.[2] Three years later, when the Tories were in power, the Whigs renewed their attack.

They chose a time when all the expeditions on the Continent were unsuccessful—the moment also when the grave scandal was made public which the Opposition exploited to compel the resignation of the Duke of York. The head of the War Office at that time, the young Lord Palmerston, attempted to utilize the Duke's resignation to prevent the complete subordination of the departments under his own control to those under the authority of the Commander-in-Chief. He sought to effect an amicable arrangement by which their respective functions should be so apportioned that everything concerning the appointment of officers and military discipline would emanate from the Commander-in-Chief, while on the other hand the entire control of the finances of the Army would be restored to the War Office.[3] But he failed to obtain a definite settlement of the matter, and two years had not passed before the Duke of York was back in office. The Duke thus shared the glory of the victories won by the Army during the concluding years of the war. His chief aim now—to be fulfilled in 1820—was the election to Parliament of his military secretary. By this means—so, at least, he hoped—the Secretary for War would no longer be the sole representative of the Government for military purposes in the House of Commons. Side by side with him, even it might be in opposition to him, would sit the mouthpiece of the Commander-in-Chief.[4]

To the stronger control of the executive over the organization of the Army, corresponded the rapid abandonment of the old antimilitarist tradition. " No barracks " had been the popular cry in the 18th century—the soldier when off duty must remain a citizen and live among his fellow-citizens. In 1792 Pitt created by warrant the military post of Barrackmaster-General ; he employed the extraordinary

[1] He had made this demand first in 1803. See H. of C., December 9, 1803. " He thought it necessary that there should be a responsible military council, to govern the whole affairs of the War Department ; although he felt a great personal respect for the Commander-in-Chief, he should not so far flatter him as to say that he was alone capable of governing that department. It was evident besides, that his high birth put him above responsibility " (*Annual Register*, 1804, p. 21).

[2] H. of C., April 3, 1806, Lord Castlereagh's speech (Military Establishments of the Country) ; April 17, 1806, General Tarleton's speech (Military Opinions relative to the Army) ; April 30, 1806, Canning's speech (Repeal of Additional Force Bill).—(*Parl. Deb.*, vol. vi. pp. 691, 783, 977.)

[3] Bulwer, *Life of Lord Palmerston*, vol. i. pp. 124 sqq. Cf. Lord Palmerston's Memorandum on the Office of Secretary at War, August 16, 1811 (Clode, *Military Forces*, vol. ii. pp. 689 sqq.).

[4] Clode, *Military Forces*, vol. ii. pp. 343-4.

revenue derived from the special war taxes in erecting barracks without having first obtained the sanction of Parliament. The indirect method which he deemed it necessary to adopt proves what violent opposition he must have expected to encounter had he asked the preliminary consent of the Commons.

But although the Opposition protested to good effect against the waste of public money, and succeeded after a series of official inquiries in checking the waste and in obtaining a reform of the organization established in 1792, the fact remains that, so far as the barrack system was concerned, Pitt won the day. At the opening of the war the British Government possessed in its forty-three forts and garrison towns quarters sufficient for no more than 20,847 men—artillery-men and infantry.[1] In 1815, 155 barracks, all recently constructed, afforded quarters for 16,854 cavalry and 138,410 infantry.[2] The old system of billeting the troops among the inhabitants had been definitely abandoned. "No standing army" was still the cry, or at least, if a standing army be indispensable, it must not be a large one. But in the course of the long struggle in which all Europe was involved, both parties had come to agree that it was impossible to do without a large army, and in pursuit of that end had radically changed the relations established by the tradition of a century between the militia and the standing army.

We have already seen that, since the early years of the reign, the militia had been no longer, strictly speaking, a citizen army ; it had tended more and more to consist of professional soldiers attracted by the bounty given to substitutes. What reason, then, could there be to confine these men to home defence, while others taken from the same class of society, and recruited by identical methods, were sent abroad to fight on the Continent or further still, in America or Asia ? It was impossible to justify an organization which drained the sources from which the regular army was recruited, a system which gave to a labourer out of work or a tramp the choice between enlistment for life with the regulars for a bounty of less than £8 sterling, and enlistment for five years only in the county militia for a bounty which might exceed £20. Already during the first war Pitt had attempted to break down the barrier which divided the two forces, and by a series of temporary statutes, passed in 1795,[3] 1798[4] and 1799,[5] had authorized the enlistment of a certain number of militiamen in the regular army. In 1803, after the conclusion of the Peace

---

[1] Clode, *Military Forces*, vol. i. p. 223.
[2] Adolphus, *British Empire*, vol. ii pp. 393 sqq., gives details as to the barracks and the number of men quartered in each. See, for a slightly earlier period, figures somewhat higher in the *Second Report of the Commissioners of Military Inquiry*, Appendix No. 4 (A), 1806.
[3] 33 Geo. III, cap. 83 (Artillery and Marines), Clode, *Military Forces*, vol. i. pp. 2 and 3.
[4] 38 Geo. III, cap. 17.
[5] 39 Geo. III, cap. 106. Clode, *Military Forces*, vol. i. pp. 284–5.

of Amiens, every one knew that a renewal of hostilities was inevitable. Addington seized the opportunity to superimpose upon the militia an "additional force," [1] which was simply a new militia, in its composition practically identical with the old, but with the difference that the soldiers of this reserve were authorized, indeed encouraged, to join the regulars. [2]

The results proved unsatisfactory and the system was abandoned. Nevertheless, in 1804 Pitt reorganized Addington's "additional force." [3] Raised for a period of five years, the "additional force" was to be employed solely for home defence, but was also to constitute the normal source from which the regular army would draw recruits, and was to be closely united with the regulars. With every regular battalion there would correspond a battalion of the "additional force," the depôt battalion ; and the old militia was so managed that, while its independence was respected, its importance was diminished. Henceforward it was not to exceed 51,000 men ; all in excess of this figure were to be induced to take service at once with the regulars. [4] The standing army came to be regarded less and less as an anomaly, an "excrescence," [5] of the British Constitution. It was now the "regular" army, and the other forces were in comparison of subordinate and secondary importance. It was no longer maintained that a professional army was in itself unconstitutional. It was merely argued that the militia and the standing army were two counter-balancing forces, as in the Political Constitution were the Parliament and the Crown. [6]

Even the representatives of the old Whig Party gave way. In 1802 we find Fox still declaring it his opinion that in time of peace a small standing army was a better defence of the country than a larger

---

[1] 43 Geo. III, cap. 82, § 33 ; 83, § 31 ; 85, § 28.

[2] See Fortescue, *County Lieutenancies and the Army*, p. 71 : ". . . Very soon rumours were current that the officers were putting the largest clothes upon the smallest men, giving them misfitting shoes, and applying other such methods of petty tyranny in order to force them to take service at once with the Regulars."

[3] 44 Geo. III, cap. 56, 66, 74.

[4] 45 Geo. III, cap. 31. Fortescue, *County Lieutenancies and the Army*, p. 145.

[5] Blackstone, I *Comm.* 412 : "When the nation was engaged in war, more veteran troops and more regular discipline were esteemed to be necessary, than could be expected from a mere militia . . . which are to be looked upon only as temporary excrescences bred out of the distemper of the State, and not as any part of the permanent and perpetual laws of the kingdom."

[6] See Canning's speech, H. of C., April 30, 1806 : ". . . The right hon. gentleman is endeavouring to lay the foundation of a large regular army, while he is sapping all the other establishments which ought constitutionally to accompany it. The right hon. gentleman may perhaps tell me that the checks and balances to which I allude are mere creatures of the imagination ; for that it is utterly improbable that our militia or volunteers should in any instance be drawn out against the line. God forbid they should ! But look, sir, at the analogy of our civil Constitution ; what is it but a system of mutual checks and balances, which have a sure though silent operation on each other ? Such is likewise the operation of our checks upon our standing army " (*Parl. Deb.*, vol. vi. p. 988). Cf. H. of C., June 18, 1804, Addington's speech : " We, sir, possess a constitutional army. . . . I think, sir, that army should always be commensurate with what is called the regular military force of the empire. . . . This House . . . should never forego this truly constitutional principle " (*Parl. Deb.*, vol. ii. p. 727).

body of troops.[1] Only a few months later, however, he retracted the opinion he had previously held and asked for a regular army "as numerous and as strong as possible." [2] In 1806, when he was one of the heads of the Coalition Cabinet, he allowed Windham, the Secretary for War, to strengthen the Army,[3] to attract recruits by a system of short-term enlistments,[4] and to procure the adoption by Parliament of a Bill providing that 4,000 Irish militiamen should pass annually into the line regiments.[5] Lord Castlereagh, Windham's Tory successor at the War Office, instituted a "local militia" in which no substitutes were allowed, and no bounty given, a force exclusively territorial. In this militia military training could be given every year to as many as 300,000 men.[6] But he returned, at the same time, to Pitt's system, and by a series of temporary Acts allowed the Army to draw the necessary recruits from the old militia. An Act of 1807 authorized two-fifths of each militia regiment to enlist in the line. This Measure rendered 30,000 men available for the regular army.[7] An Act of 1809 conceded 28,500 men,[8] a further Act of 1811 10,000 men every year.[9] And again in 1813 the Crown was authorized to take a further 30,000 men from the militia, the sole condition imposed being that no militia regiment should be allowed to fall below a quarter of its strength. The militiamen sent to the Peninsula, in accordance with the provisions of this Act, were to retain during their foreign service the appellation of militiamen, and were to form distinct battalions or regiments under the command of their own officers.[10] By this Measure, in defiance of traditional principles, the militia was formally employed on foreign service. But we do not need this Act to measure the extent to which the militia had degenerated. It was now nothing more than a school where professional soldiers were trained for service in the line, "a recruiting, or . . . a crimping fund for the supply of the regular army." [11]

In the first year of the war the Government had believed that 46,000 men in Europe with 10,000 men in the East Indies would be a sufficient army. In 1801, immediately before the Peace of Amiens, the Ministry asked Parliament for the necessary credits to maintain a regular army of 193,000 men. Even during the truce

[1] H. of C., December 8, 1802 (*Parl. Hist.*, vol. xxxvi. pp. 1,083 sqq.).

[2] H. of C., July 18, 1803.

[3] 46 Geo. III, cap. 90. See Windham's speech, H. of C., April 3, 1806, and that of Fox himself, May 6, 1806 (*Parl. Deb.*, vol. vi. pp. 652 sqq. ; vol. vii. pp. 22 sqq.).

[4] 46 Geo III, cap 66. Schedule. Clode, *Military Forces*, vol. ii. pp. 28–9.

[5] 46 Geo. III, cap. 124.   [6] 48 Geo. III, cap. 111, 150.

[7] 47 Geo. III, Sess. 2, cap. 55, 57.

[8] 49 Geo. III, cap. iv. Fortescue, *County Lieutenancies and the Army*, p. 223.

[9] 51 Geo. III, cap. 20, 30. *Ibid.*, p. 254.

[10] 54 Geo. III, cap. 1, 17, 20. To enable His Majesty to accept the services of a proportion of the militia out of the United Kingdom, for the vigorous prosecution of the war.

[11] H. of C., May 9, 1809, Lord Fitzwilliam's speech (*Parl. Deb.*, vol. xiv. p. 436).

that followed, the number of effective troops never fell below 78,000.
The figure of 200,000 men had been exceeded since 1807, that of
250,000 men since 1812.[1] After the first entry of the Allies into
Paris and the first restoration of the peace in Europe, the Government
was still able to obtain the sanction of the Commons in November
1814 for an army of 204,000 men.[2] Even after Waterloo the
Ministry was prepared to ask the Commons for an army of 150,000
men. If we subtract 20,000 men serving in the East Indies and
30,000 men employed in the occupation of French territory, we are
left with a garrison of 100,000 in the United Kingdom.[3] The Tories
had succeeded in enabling the Government to establish a larger army
than England had ever before possessed. But was the value of
the British Army in proportion to its size? Moreover, did this
enormous increase of numbers necessarily endanger the balance of the
Constitution? Before we are in a position to answer this double
question, we must describe the organization of the regular army. We
shall find it an aristocratic organization, and therefore in perfect harmony with the organization of all the other executive departments.

Privates and Officers.

The British Army was recruited by voluntary enlistment. The
kingdom was divided into recruiting districts. At the head of each
district was a paymaster, who directed the labours of recruiting sergeants
and civil agents, or crimps.[4] Other methods, indeed, were sometimes
employed to obtain the necessary men. During the 18th century
several statutes had authorized the conscription of able-bodied vagabonds.[5] Up to 1815 the governors of prisons were granted the right
to shorten the imprisonment of a certain number of criminals, on
condition of their enlistment. Three regiments of the army in Portugal
had been recruited by this method.[6] But the former method had not
been employed at all since 1780, and the latter was only employed
under exceptional circumstances. Wellington could therefore assert
with perfect sincerity twenty years later[7] that *never* had any
other method of recruiting been in use save that of voluntary
enlistment. This was, as we saw, by no means the case with

---

[1] For these figures, consult further the Parliamentary Debates on the annual introduction
of the Army Estimates (Fortescue, *County Lieutenancies and the Army*, *passim*). The statistics
are hard to interpret; sometimes the officers, the foreign soldiers in the pay of the British
Government, and the artillery are included—at others excluded.

[2] 204,386 men, 55 Geo. III, cap. 20.

[3] See especially H. of C., 2 February 26, 27 and 28, 1816 (*Parl. Deb.*, vol. xxxii. pp. 841,
843, 909, 955).

[4] Adolphus, *British Empire*, vol. ii. pp. 286–7.

[5] Clode, *Military Forces*, vol. ii. pp. 18–19.

[6] *Ibid.*, vol. ii. pp. 13 sqq.

[7] *Report from . . . Commissioners . . . into Military Punishments, Minutes of Evidence*,
p. 321.

the Navy. What, then, was the reason of this difference between the two services ? Like the sailors, the soldiers were enlisted for an indeterminate period. They had no more, or rather they had even less, chance than the sailors of promotion to the rank of officer. At rare intervals a recruiting sergeant might save enough money to purchase an ensign's commission.[1] In time of war it might happen that a non-commissioned officer was rewarded for a deed of bravery by promotion ; ten years of warfare had produced many such cases.[2] But ensigns who had risen from the ranks could never rise to a higher grade ; " the ensigncy was their marshal's baton." [3] Their manners were bad, and their heads could not stand the hard drinking. They were made to feel that they were out of place, and very soon threw up their commission. We must not forget that the Government, yielding to the pressure of democratic opinion, had shown their eagerness to ameliorate the conditions of military service. The bounties on enlistment had been enormously raised. From the 16th century to the Peace of Utrecht they had been kept, roughly speaking, at the figure of £2. They had risen to three guineas during the American War. By 1803 they had reached the amount of £7 12s. 6d., by 1814 that of sixteen guineas.[4] The rate of pay had increased proportionately, and was now double the pay of a French or Prussian soldier.[5] Since 1799 it had been the custom to collect for the information of their families the names of soldiers who had been killed or wounded. In 1806 Windham not only raised the retiring pensions, but decided at the same time, despite Tory protests, that these pensions should no longer be regarded as favours granted at the pleasure of the Government, but that twenty years' service should entitle a soldier to retire on a pension. In 1811 and 1812, in consequence of an active campaign in the Press, regulations were made to render the punishment of flogging less frequent and less severe.[6] But the true reason why the War Office found less difficulty

[1] Fortescue, *County Lieutenancies and the Army*, p. 105.

[2] The *Quarterly Review* (vol. xiii. p. 420) deplored this mixture of classes, which it ascribed to two causes—" the principles introduced by the French Revolution, and the long war which it entailed upon Europe."

[3] Foy, *Guerre de la Peninsule*, vol. i. p. 237. Cf. *Report from . . . Commissioners . . . into Military Punishments* (*Minutes of Evidence*, p. 329). The Duke of Wellington's evidence : " I believe that in the Peninsula I gave every commission I had to give away either to gentlemen volunteers or to non-commissioned officers." He adds, however, that very few of the latter had remained in the Army. " They are not persons that can be borne in the society of the officers of the Army."

[4] Clode, *Military Forces*, vol. ii. pp. 4–5, 19, and Fortescue, *County Lieutenancies and the Army*, pp. 74, 130.

[5] Clode, *Military Forces*, vol. i. p. 106. It had been fixed at 1s. a day in 1797 Since then it had been increased by reducing the deductions made to cover various expenses. After all such deductions had been made the common soldier actually received 2½d. a day (Foy, *Guerre de la Peninsule*, vol. i. p. 230).

[6] Article 22 of the Mutiny Act of 1811 (51 Geo. III, cap. 8) empowered courts martial to punish with imprisonment, not only, as hitherto, with the lash. . . . See the protests of

than the Admiralty in obtaining the necessary recruits was, after all, economic. Seamen could earn in the Merchant Service the wages of skilled labourers—wages moreover which, on account of the risks of navigation, rose whenever war was declared, that is to say at the very moment when the Navy was most in need of sailors. In the Army, on the other hand, the pay was practically equal to the wages earned by an unskilled labourer in the country or in the great industrial centres.[1] But the development of English manufactures during the last thirty years had made the condition of the workmen extremely uncertain. Sometimes they were attracted in crowds to the towns, where the factories were constantly growing in size and number. At others a crisis of over-production threw them on to the streets without work or food. For these unemployed the Army was a welcome refuge, and the parish authorities were only too glad to be relieved by the State from the burden of their maintenance. At the beginning of the 18th century the English had ascribed the superiority of Marlborough's troops to the fact that they were recruited from the small landowners, the country yeomen. During the Seven Years' War they had taken credit for the utilization in their Highland regiments of the savage virtues of Northern Scotland, so lately reduced to order. The regiments that were now winning the Peninsula victories were composed of discarded factory hands.

All officers' commissions, from the ensign's to the lieutenant-colonel's, were on sale.[2] Crown and Parliament had attempted after 1688 to abolish the abuse ; but the attempt had not proved successful and the Government had contented itself with minimizing the evil, by subjecting it to a series of official regulations. An officer was no longer allowed to sell his commission to the first purchaser. He continued to receive the purchase money, but the State selected the purchaser. Nor was an officer permitted any longer to fix his own price—an official scale of prices was established. Nor could he any longer sell his commission at any time he chose, but only after twenty years' service or on account of ill-health contracted in the Army. Neither was an officer any longer permitted to purchase his com-

the *Courier*, a semi-official organ, February 25, 1811. In 1812 a confidential circular from the Commander-in-Chief forbade courts martial to inflict " on any pretext whatsoever " more than 300 lashes. The circular adds : " Sufficient attention has not been paid to the *prevention of crime*. The timely interference of the officer, his personal intercourse, and above all his personal example, are the only efficacious means of preventing military offences " (*Report from H.M.'s Commissioners for Inquiring into . . . Military Punishments . . .*, 1836, *Minutes of Evidence*, p. 303).

[1] Clode, *Military Forces*, vol. i. p. 489. Table showing the pay and allowance of the soldier and agricultural and town labourer.

[2] The practice is so general as to be almost universal. It extends to at least three-fourths of all the officers appointed to fill commissions. (*Report from Select Committee on Army and Navy Appointments*, 1833, Appendix, p. 273. The Duke of Wellington's memorial.) The Crown reserved the right to dispose of the commission of every officer who had been promoted without having purchased his rank, or had fallen in the field.

mission whenever he chose. No one could become captain until he had served three years, major until he had served seven years, lieutenant-colonel until he had served nine years.[1] Again, the purchase money no longer passed directly from the purchaser to the vendor. The State interposed between them, and in some cases did not pay over the whole price to the retiring officer, but kept back a portion to form a "reserve fund" from which to improve half-pay, and to relieve the widows and orphans of officers and privates. Nevertheless, for all these reforms the purchase system still survived and would survive for many a year to come.

The Treasury looked with favour on a custom which enabled a system of retiring pensions to be organized without apparently costing the nation a single penny.[2] Advocates of the constitutional oligarchy defended the abuse both as making it difficult for soldiers of fortune to become officers and as weakening the control of the central government over the Army. Officers who had purchased their rank naturally came to regard their commissions as title-deeds to a property. Although the validity of this contention was of very dubious legality,[3] and had never been admitted by the courts, it was nevertheless inevitable that the purchase system should to some extent protect the subordinate officers against their superiors and against the Government departments. One thing, at any rate, is certain ; the officers of the British Army were financially independent of the Government. An ensign in the infantry drew £80 a year, but he had paid £400 for the right to draw it. If, therefore, we deduct the interest on the capital expenditure, we find that in reality he only received £60 a year. A lieutenant-colonel drew £405 a year, but had paid £3,500 for his commission. When, therefore, all deductions had been made, he actually received only £230 a year.[4] In legal terminology his pay was *honorarium non merces*.[5] In the higher ranks, which were not for sale, the pay was indeed higher,[6] but here there were restraints of another sort on the action of the authorities. From the rank of colonel to that of field-marshal promotion went by seniority. Favouritism

---

[1] Foy, *Guerre de la Peninsule*, vol. i. p. 248.

[2] Communication from the Duke of Wellington to Lord Hill. *Report from Select Committee on Army and Navy Appointments*, 1833, Appendix, p. 274.

[3] *Rules and Regulations respecting Appointment, Promotion and Retirement in the Army*. Report of Commissioners . . . into Naval and Military Promotion and Retirement, 1804, Appendix, pp. 285–6.

[4] Foy, *Guerre de la Peninsule*, vol. i. pp. 245–6.

[5] Clode, *Military Forces*, vol. i. p. 106 ; vol. ii. pp. 115–16.

[6] Till 1814 an officer above the rank of colonel, whatever that might be, was honorary colonel of a regiment and only received a colonel's pay In 1833 Wellington estimated the total remuneration of a colonel in the cavalry at £1,400 a year (that is his pay with the profit which he made on the supply of uniforms to the regiment), and that of a colonel in the infantry at £1,100 a year. It was only in 1814 that a regulation was made by which generals as such were to be paid at the rate of £1 18s a day, lieutenant-generals at the rate of £1 5s. (*Report . . . on Army and Navy Appointments*, 1833, pp. 273, 276).

or influence of any kind was thus impossible. The Government could not even promote an officer, as a reward for some brilliant exploit, without at the same time promoting all the officers of the same rank who had received their commissions before him. The Opposition speakers were wrong to regard the excessive increase of the general staff as due to royal favour. The increase was the inevitable result of applying a rule which deprived the commander-in-chief of all freedom of choice in the nomination of the higher officers.

Theoretically, the purchase system was no doubt rather plutocratic than aristocratic. Wealth was an indispensable qualification for an officer, birth was not. There was nothing to prevent a wealthy city merchant buying a commission for his son, and thereby purchasing his admission into the aristocracy of the kingdom. When Mrs. Clarke, the Duke of York's mistress, organized her traffic in promotions, there is nothing to show that she ever troubled to inquire into the birth or standing of her clients. Certain great families had entertained for a long time past strong prejudices against a military career.[1] The British aristocracy, as it was seen in the Army, appeared to a foreign observer like General Foy of a mixed character and hard to define— "a blend of noble birth, financial and mercantile interests, talent, the nominees of Government, wealth derived from manufactures or land." [2] Nevertheless, the officers were, as a body, aristocratic, certainly more aristocratic than the officers of the Navy.[3] For the *nouveaux riches* the Army was, after all, far from a good way to enter society, and the poor were practically excluded from it. Fifteen generals were raised to the peerage under George III ; of these only three came of obscure birth. Twelve of these fifteen officers had been raised to the peerage since 1792 and all the twelve except one, Lord Harris, the son of a curate, belonged to noble or very good families.[4] There can be no doubt that it was because the officers were taken from the landed aristocracy, and because that aristocracy was the dominant power in Parliament, that soldiers were so numerous in the Commons. In 1812 thirty-four were elected. The English officer was essentially an

[1] Wellington, *Memorandum on the . . . Discipline of the Army*, April 22, 1829 : " The British Army . . . disliked by the inhabitants, particularly by the higher orders, some of whom never allow one of their family to serve in it " (*Dispatches*, vol. viii. p. 344). We may compare with his language a passage from *Lady Holland's Journal* (October 19, 1799, vol. ii. pp. 32–3) : " Lord G. is raising a regiment, and is appointed Lieutenant-Colonel. I am sorry he throws away very excellent abilities upon a profession where so little is required—at least, as it is practised in this country ; and I believe as a good patriot one ought to hope it may for ever remain as insignificant as it has done hitherto." But these prejudices were weakening (*ibid.*, August 21, 1793, vol. ii. p. 16) : " The young men of fashion and birth are bit with a military mania ; they all aim at attaining a martial air, and a reputation for strictness in their militia discipline."

[2] Foy, *Guerre de la Péninsule*, vol. i. p. 239.

[3] Perhaps this is the reason why there were more soldiers than sailors in the House of Commons. Among the members were two generals, fifteen lieutenant-generals, eight major-generals, three lieutenant-colonels, two majors, a captain, and three colonels of militia.

[4] We may add five military peerages of Ireland—all aristocratic.

aristocrat, for whom camp life was but the continuation of the life on his country estate, to which he had been accustomed from infancy. War was a sport like any other, only rougher and more dangerous. When a young man scarcely sixteen years old bought an ensign's commission and joined a regiment, he found a non-commissioned officer, without prospect of promotion to a higher rank, ready to advise him and to cover his inexperience. And in this old sergeant who inspired or interpreted his orders, the young officer would recognize the old servant who in days gone by on the family estate taught him to ride or to shoot.

We are by no means disposed to make light of the advantages in an army, as elsewhere, of aristocratic institutions. If they are freely accepted, and deliberately willed by all the members of a society, even by those who do not themselves belong to the governing oligarchy, they are calculated to spread among all ranks a collective pride, which is a source of energy and power. "When each class," wrote Alison, the Tory historian, "is respectable and protected in itself, it feels its own importance, and often disdains to seek admission into that next in succession ; the universal passion for individual exaltation is the offspring of a state of society where the rights and immunities of the humbler ranks have been habitually, by all persons in power, trampled under foot." [1] The English officer was proud to be a member of an aristocracy which, if not the most exclusive, was most certainly the most solid in the world. The soldier was proud to occupy his position in the hierarchy of the British Army. Whether a common soldier or a non-commissioned officer, the mere fact of serving, without hope of promotion, in the British Army made him in very deed an aristocrat among the soldiers of the other European armies. It would be true to say that the British Army was an army of snobs, and that the universal snobbery produced here a maximum of good results. But we must not, on the other hand, ignore the numerous defects and disorders, forgotten in the intoxication of the final victory.

Lack of Discipline in the Army.

The discipline of the British Army was very imperfect. "The Bishop of Killala," wrote Lady Holland in 1800, "yields the palm of superiority to the English for their *dexterity* in pillaging and in plunder ; indeed, compared with every European army, save the Papal one, it is the only *excellence* in candour we can admit them to lay claim to." [2] Since Lady Holland penned these words the English had learnt to conquer, but their indiscipline was Wellington's constant complaint.[3] All the reforms introduced by him to render the sentences

---

[1] Alison, *History of Europe*, vol. xii. p. 22.
[2] *Journal of Lady Holland*, March 22, 1800, vol. ii. pp. 61–2.
[3] Letter to A. J. Villiers, May 31, 1809 (*Dispatches*, vol. iii. p. 262): ". . . I have, I say, been of opinion that the British Army could bear neither success nor failure, and I have

of the courts martial in time of war prompter and more certain, failed to effect their object. After the defeat at Burgos the soldiers left the ranks during the retreat on Ciudad Rodrigo, just as they had left the ranks three years earlier after the victory of Talavera during the retreat on Badajoz ; and never did Wellington issue a more severe order of the day than that which he then addressed to the officers and non-commissioned officers of his army. The soldiers left the ranks after Vittoria, on the very eve of invading French territory, just as they had left the ranks four years earlier, when they had compelled Soult and his army to evacuate the province of Oporto. In the hour of battle the British Army had no rival, but it was impossible to keep it in good order during the long marches which preceded and followed the battles. The English generals were never, indeed, faced with an organized mutiny of their troops, like the naval mutiny at the Nore. The English private was no deliberate rebel who mutinied on principle ; [1] but disorder, drunkenness and plunder were chronic diseases of the expeditionary force in Spain and Portugal. The aristocratic organization was one of the causes, if not the essential cause, of this permanent state of indiscipline.

The English officer was a man of fashion, who regarded war as a sport, not a science. The Academy at Woolwich was confined to the engineers, and it was only in 1799 and 1802 that the Duke of York founded at High Wycombe and Great Marlow military schools, modelled on those of France, Austria and Prussia. [2] It was calculated

had manifest proofs of the truth of this opinion in the first of its branches in the recent conduct of the soldiers of this army. They have plundered the country most terribly." To the same, September 18, 1809 (*Dispatches*, vol. iii. p. 488) : " I really believe that more plunder and outrage have been committed by this army than by any other that ever was in the field." To Lord Liverpool, January 24, 1810 (*Dispatches*, vol. v. p. 704) : " The outrages committed by the British soldiers belonging to this army have become . . . enormous." To Lord Bathurst, July 2, 1813 (*Dispatches*, vol. vi. p. 575) : " It is quite impossible for me or any other man to command a British army under the existing system. We have in the service the scum of the earth as common soldiers ; and of late we have been doing everything in our power, both by law and by publications, to relax the discipline by which alone such men can be kept in order, . . . etc., etc." See, however, in the *Report from . . . Commissioners . . . into Military Punishments*, 1836 (*Minutes of Evidence*, pp. 316-27), Wellington's extremely favourable evidence as to the discipline of the Peninsula army. We must not, indeed, forget that this evidence was not given till above twenty years after the events. But on the other hand, even Wellington's contemporary evidence should not be accepted without reserve. (1) He was a man who belonged to good society, not a soldier of fortune, and therefore would be more shocked by the disorders of camp life than one of Napoleon's generals would have been. (2) His complaints of the lack of discipline among his troops cease immediately the army has entered France ; the condition of Spain incited to indiscipline and pillage.

[1] Napier, *History of the Peninsular War*, vol. iii. p. 271. We must except the Indian Army, in which mutinies had been frequent during the previous half-century, but in making this exception we must take into account two facts : (1) The Indian Army served under very exceptional conditions ; (2) the mutinies were not mutinies of soldiers against their officers, but mutinies of the Company's officers, with the support of their troops, against the commander-in-chief and the government of the Company. See, for these mutinies, an able article in the *Quarterly Review*, February 1811, Art. 8, *India : Disturbances at Madras* (vol. v. pp. 140 sqq.) ; also John Malcolm, *Observations on the Disturbances in the Madras Army in* 1809, 1812.

[2] Adolphus, *British Empire*, vol. ii. pp. 364–6 ; Fortescue, *History of the British Army*, vol. iv. pt. 2, pp. 926–7.

in 1815 that of 276 pupils of the higher grade, 114 had served or were serving as staff officers, and 651 pupils of the lower grade had already entered the Army.[1] This was little enough. It is also obvious that the new institution had not had time to bear fruit during the Peninsular War. Moreover, the candidate for a commission was under no obligation to pass through the Government school. When he joined his regiment, the average English officer, possessed no more knowledge than that which he had managed to pick up at a preparatory school between the ages of ten and fifteen. The British staff officers in 1815 were still regarded by the whole of Europe as the most incompetent in the world. " Nobody in the British Army," wrote Wellington, " ever reads a regulation or an order as if it were to be a guide for his conduct, or in any other manner than as an amusing novel ; and the consequence is, that when complicated arrangements are to be carried into execution . . . every *gentleman* proceeds according to his fancy ; and then, when it is found that the arrangement fails (as it must fail if the order is not strictly obeyed), they come upon me to set matters to rights and thus my labour is increased tenfold." [2] The officers thrown all together in a foreign land formed a large aristocratic club, divided into sets, and without any clearly determined order of precedence. There was, indeed, the precedence of official rank. But this came into collision with the precedence of social rank ; and the organization of the British Army was less hierarchic than that of any other army in the world. The Army was composed of isolated regiments, which were not coordinated in regular groups, in army corps, in divisions, in brigades ; neither was the precedence of social rank decisive. Since Pitt had multiplied peerages, they had lost much of their value. The scion of an old country family was little disposed to treat with deference the son of a lord of yesterday's creation. General Foy remarks with disgust that " duels between officers of unequal rank, although severely punished, are by no means uncommon." [3] The mess was a veritable council of war, held daily, where every officer criticized freely the acts of the general. It contained both Whigs and Tories. The Whigs were pessimists, predicted final defeat, were ready to demonstrate the inutility of the victories already won, the impossibility of opposing a permanent resistance to the vast armies of Napoleon. When the Army was in retreat they were triumphant, and the malcontents of every kind would then swell the Opposition party among the staff officers. Letters, written by officers to friends in London, soon found their way into the newspapers. During the British retreat in Portugal before the advance of Massena's army the disorder became intolerable. " The temper,"

[1] H. of C., June 2, 1815, John Hope's speech (*Parl. Deb.*, vol. xxxi. p. 591).
[2] Letter to Colonel Torrens, December 6, 1812 (*Dispatches*, vol. vi. p. 201).
[3] Foy, *Guerre de la Peninsule*, vol. i. p. 244.

exclaimed Wellington, " of some of the officers of the British Army gives me more concern than the folly of the Portuguese Government.
. . Whether owing to the Opposition in England, or whether the magnitude of the concern is too much for their minds and their nerves, or whether I am mistaken and they are right, I cannot tell ; but there is a system of croaking in the Army which is highly injurious to the public service, and which I must devise some means of putting an end to, or it will put an end to us." [1]   The evil continued notwithstanding, and was lamented by Wellington to the end.   The contention of the apologists of the English system that this system was at the same time and for the same reasons an aristocratic and a free system was indeed correct—in this sense at least, that the ruling class, both in the Army and elsewhere, was in reality a vast deliberative assembly which " governed itself," unfettered by the control of any clearly defined authority.   Such a system was sheer anarchy, a government of the Polish type.   Why, then, did not England perish like the kingdom of Poland ?

The indiscipline of the troops is to be explained by the same causes as the indiscipline of the officers.   Wellington cast about him in vain

---

[1] Wellington, letter to Charles Stuart, September 11, 1810 (*Dispatches*, vol. iv. p. 274). Cf. Lord Liverpool to Wellington, September 10, 1810 (Yonge, *Life of Lord Liverpool*, vol. i. p. 335). See further, Wellington's letters to Lord Liverpool, January 2, 1810 (*Dispatches* vol. iii. p. 671) : " I wrote to you the other day about general officers.   I only beg you not to send me any violent party men.   We must keep the spirit of party out of the Army, or we shall be in a bad way indeed."   To Lord Liverpool, May 15, 1811 (*Dispatches*, vol. v. pp. 21–2) : " It is to be hoped that the general and other officers of the Army will at last acquire that experience which will teach them that success can be attained by attention to the most minute details ; and by tracing every part of every operation from its origin to its conclusion, point by point, and ascertaining that the whole is understood by those who are to execute it."   To Lord Liverpool, May 28, 1812 (*Dispatches*, vol. v. p. 682) : " I cannot prevail upon the general officers to feel a little confidence in their situation.   They take alarm at the least movement of the enemy, and then spread the alarm and interrupt everything."   To Colonel Torrens, September 13, 1812 (*Dispatches*, vol. v. pp. 73–4) : " I am sorry to say that the perpetual changes which we are making, owing to the infirmities or the wounds, or the disinclination of the general officers to serve in this country, are by no means favourable to the discipline and success of the Army ; and don't augment the ease of my situation."   To Colonel Torrens, July 18, 1813 (*Dispatches*, vol. vi. p. 604) : " I am sorry that I can't recommend X for promotion. . . . I had had him in arrest since the battle for disobeying an order given to him by me verbally. . . .   If discipline means . . obedience to orders as well as military instruction, we have but little in the Army.   Nobody ever thinks of obeying an order.   All the regulations, etc., are so much waste paper."   To Lieutenant-Colonel Barns, February 9, 1814 (*Dispatches*, vol. vii. p. 310) : " It is extraordinary that resistance to authority should be so frequent as it is by the British officers and soldiers of the Army. . . .   It has lately been so frequent, and the instances attended by such serious consequences, that it is necessary that I should endeavour to prevail upon general courts martial to mark their disapprobation of such conduct more forcibly, etc."   We should notice how Gisborne, an extremely conservative moralist and a Tory, defines an officer's duty of obedience in his *Duties of Man*, vol. i. pp. 287–8 : " Every individual officer who is called into active service is bound to investigate the justice of the war in which he engages, to the utmost extent of his abilities and information. . . .   If he should be thoroughly convinced that his own country is the culpable aggressor in the quarrel, or deems the probability to be very greatly on that side, it is his indispensable duty to resign his employment. . . .   Will it be said that it is his part to obey and leave the State to answer for the guilt ?   This is not the argument of a considerate man or of a Protestant."

for a means to establish discipline in his army. He ascribed the evil to the fact that England was not governed despotically like the Continental nations. A commander might, indeed, try the experiment of keeping the soldiers under arms the whole day long, confining them strictly to camp or barracks between the drills, and only permitting them to go into a town in bands under the supervision of a corporal ; but the soldiers would find such a regular life an intolerable burden. It were better to allow them more liberty, with the knowledge that for grave offences or crimes they would incur very severe penalties.[1] Were conscription employed the discipline of the troops would be greatly improved. But the English would not accept this system of slavery, and it remained, therefore, to make the best possible out of an army recruited from the rabble.[2] Again, the English officer made it his first point of honour to be a gentleman. The rules of his class obliged him to keep his distance from the non-commissioned officers and privates. He had joined the Army to fight, not to perform the wearisome duties of an accountant or a jailor. There was therefore nobody in the British Army, either in the infantry or in the cavalry, whose particular duty it was to do the work which in Continental armies fell to the subalterns. The charge of everything that makes up the daily life of an army—of marching formations, of pitching the camp —was left to the non-commissioned officers. The latter formed with the privates a world apart, a world unknown to the officers, and recruited from the lowest strata of the population. For such the Army was a school of moral discipline only because their previous degradation had been so extreme. They were left to discipline themselves as best they could and would, that is to say, very ill indeed. Even when by chance the officers had the desire to enforce order in the lower ranks, they proved themselves the most ignorant and blundering of rulers.[3] To sum up, the aristocratic constitution of the Army was to blame for the indiscipline of the troops, not only because of itself it involved the dangers as well as the advantages of freedom, but above all because it prevented the officers getting to know their men. The British Army was that of a bygone age, in essentials still the same as in the days of Marlborough. But, in the interval, Frederick II and Napoleon had created a new type of military organization.

The Final Triumph. Wellington.

Nevertheless, the British Army had been victorious. Eight years of uninterrupted success had obliterated the memory of the humiliating

---

[1] Wellington, *Memorandum . . . on the Discipline of the Army*, 1829 (*Dispatches*, vol. viii. p. 347).

[2] *Dispatches*, vol. viii pp. 345, 350.

[3] Wellington, *Memorandum . . .* (*Dispatches*, vol. viii. p. 346). Cf. Foy, *Guerre de la Peninsule*, vol. i. p. 241.

defeats which it had suffered in Flanders and Holland, defeats now fifteen to twenty years old, and had demonstrated, in the opinion of a Tory writer, "the inherent superiority of the British race." To be sure, we must not forget, that when the English victories began, the Russians at Friedland and the Austrians at Essling had already shown that it was possible to offer successful resistance to the French. The English, moreover, conquered in a country where for the first time the French found to their discomfiture that the lower orders did not behold with joy, or even with equanimity, the overthrow of their Government. The changed circumstances acted differently on the spirit of the two armies. While the *moral* of the British Army rose, the *moral* of the French Army declined. Wellington is the typical figure of this period of the war. His name does not mark an epoch in the history of modern strategy or tactics. He must not be expected, like Napoleon, to reduce an entire campaign to a single battle, nor like Napoleon, to conquer a kingdom within a few weeks by a fixed date and according to a prearranged plan. Each time that in imitation of his rival he attempted to conclude a campaign by a march on the capital, as in 1809 and in 1812, his rash victories had been followed by perilous retreats. Had Napoleon been in command of his Spanish army in July 1809, instead of being at Wagram, Wellington's army would perhaps have been annihilated. In 1812, if the Grande Armée had not been on its way to Russia, it is highly doubtful whether Wellington's army would have been left secure and entire in Portugal. He was not even a great tactician. In the hour of battle he trusted entirely to the bravery of his troops, to their coolness, and to the solid resistance they offered to the enemy's charge, to wear out the ardour of the French. Had he wished to do more than this, he would have been obliged first to reorganize his army, which, though steady, was heavy and slow-moving, always encumbered with baggage and unable to undertake anything without having first secured its retreat and communications with the sea. He preferred to take it as he found it. The man of the moment, he relied on circumstances and adapted himself to the situation. This is the secret of his greatness.

When he first arrived in Portugal, he cherished no ambition to march from Lisbon to Madrid, from Madrid to Paris. One day Sir Brent Spencer, his principal lieutenant, asked the Duke what his plans were. "It would," he said, "be a great misfortune to the army if it were to lose you ; but still you might be killed, and I think it necessary that I should ask you what are your plans, in order that I may be able to carry them out in case I should unfortunately succeed to the command of the army." "Plans," replied Wellington, "ah, plans. I haven't got any plans, except that I mean to beat the French. If I can't do it in one way, I will in another."[1] With the situation he

[1] *Memoirs and Correspondence of Lord Combermere*, vol. i. p. 192.

hoped and despaired by turns, but he always remained true to his vocation. When Napoleon undertook the conquest of the entire civilized
world, he was attempting a task which exceeded the power of man.
Wellington looked for victory neither to the genius of his subordinates,
nor to his own, but to the force of events. After Talavera and before
Massena's invasion of Portugal, he all but despaired of success ; but
Massena's attempt failed. The French no longer acted with their
accustomed decision. They lacked the personal command of Napoleon.
They divided their forces, wasted time over sieges, in short made war
in the old style. This was, of course, all to the advantage of an army
of the old style, like the British. Witness the events of 1812, the
year of the Russian campaign and of Wellington's victory at Salamanca ;
or again the events of 1813, the year that witnessed the German
campaign, and the rout of King Joseph at Vittoria. Wellington
then crossed the Bidassoa and entered France. It was the triumph
of common sense over genius.

Wellington had yet to confront Napoleon face to face. At
Waterloo, Napoleon gave him the opportunity, and Wellington's
military career closed with a brilliant victory. He did not, however,
take any particular pride in his triumph. Before the battle he complained incessantly of the soldiers who had been placed under his
command, and were not his old soldiers of the Peninsular War. "To
tell you the truth," he wrote to a Minister, "I am not very well pleased
. . . with the manner in which the Horse Guards have conducted
themselves towards me. It will be admitted that the army is not a
very good one. . . . I am overloaded with people I have never seen
before, and it appears to be purposely intended to keep those out of
my way whom I wished to have." [1] In a letter written a few days
later he employs stronger language : "I have got," he wrote, "an
infamous army, very weak and ill-equipped, and a very inexperienced
staff." [2] Even when the victory had been won, he was annoyed to
see it unduly magnified. In the efforts that he made to discourage
men of letters from writing its history, there is evident, besides considerable irritation at the inaccuracy of accounts composed by civilians,
the fear that the historians, if by chance they should arrive at a knowledge of the real facts, would publish many instances of indiscipline
and weakness best forgotten.[3] "I am," he wrote, "really disgusted

[1] Letter to Earl Bathurst, May 4, 1815 (*Supplementary Dispatches*, vol. x. p. 219).
[2] Letter to General Lord Stewart, May 8, 1815 (*Dispatches*, vol. viii. p. 66). He continues :
" In my opinion they are doing nothing in England. They have not raised a man ; they have
not called out the militia either in England or Ireland'; are unable to send me anything ; and
they have not sent a message to Parliament about the money. The war spirit is therefore
evaporating, as I am informed."
[3] Letter to ———, Esq., August 8, 1815 (*Dispatches*, vol. viii. pp. 231–2) : " The history
of a battle is not unlike the history of a ball. Some individuals may recollect all the little events
of which the great result is the battle won'or lost ; but no individual can recollect the order in
which, nor the exact moment at which, they occurred, which makes all the difference as to their

with, and ashamed of, all that I have seen of the Battle of Waterloo. The number of writings upon it would lead the world to suppose that the British Army had never fought a battle before." [1] He disliked the troops under his command and regretted the army which he had lead to victory at Talavera, at Salamanca and at Vittoria, an army whose faults were now forgotten, and with which he would fain have shared his final triumph. When a few months after Waterloo he gave it as his opinion that " the best troops we have, probably the best in the world, are the British infantry," he is careful to add " particularly the old infantry that has served in Spain." [2] Was it, then, the excellence of Wellington's strategy that secured the victory of an army raised in haste and of very inferior calibre? On the contrary, never had Wellington's strategy been more feeble than in the operations immediately preceding Waterloo. Perhaps the peculiar circumstances of his " situation, neither at war nor at peace, unable on that account to reconnoitre the enemy and ascertain his position by view," [3] made it very difficult for him to receive information as to the movements of the French Army. But, on the other hand, he enjoyed the exceptional advantage that his theatre of action was the frontier of a country divided against itself and swarming with royalist agents, where therefore he could learn from spies all that his position made it impossible to discover by means of patrols. Whatever the reason Wellington scarcely foresaw an attack, and although on his arrival in Belgium at the commencement of April he entertained keen apprehensions on this score, they seem to have faded as the moment of the actual attack drew near. If, indeed, he foresaw an attack at all, he expected that it would be " between the Lys and the Scheldt," [4] or " between the Sambre and the Scheldt," or on both lines simultaneously, or perhaps " from the front." [5] And after all he refused to credit the report that Napoleon would be on the frontier by June 13th. " I judged," he wrote, " from his [Napoleon's] speech to the legislature that his

---

value or importance. Then the faults or the misbehaviour of some gave occasion for the distinction of others, and perhaps were the cause of material losses ; and you cannot write a true history of a battle without including the faults and misbehaviour of part at least of those engaged. Believe me, that every man you see in a military uniform is not a hero ; and that, although in the account given of a general action such as of Waterloo many instances of individual heroism must be passed over unrelated, it is better for the general interests to leave those parts of the story untold, than to tell the whole truth." Cf. letters of June 23 and September 12, 1815 (*Dispatches*, vol. viii. pp. 163, 259).

[1] To Sir John Sinclair, April 28, 1816 (*Dispatches*, vol. viii. p. 331).

[2] To Earl Bathurst, October 23, 1815 (*Dispatches*, vol. viii. p. 285 : ed. 1838, vol. xii. p. 668).

[3] To the Prince of Orange, May 11, 1815 (*Dispatches*, vol. viii. p. 78 : ed. 1838, vol. xii. p. 375).

[4] Secret Memorandum, May 1, 1815 (*Dispatches*, vol. viii. p. 51 : ed. 1838, vol. xii. p. 337). To General —— (*Dispatches*, vol. viii. p. 21 : ed. 1838, vol. xii. p. 294).

[5] To Lieutenant-General Lord Stewart, May 8, 1815 (*Dispatches*, vol. viii. p. 85 : ed. 1838, vol. xii. p. 360).

departure was not likely to be immediate. I think we are now too strong for him here." [1] And on June 15th he was engaged in arranging a combined invasion of France by the three allied armies, when he learnt that Napoleon had outflanked his left and had attacked the Prussian outposts. The battle had now begun and these raw troops, who had never yet seen war, and were regarded with contempt by their own general, atoned, by a resistance worthy of the Peninsula veterans, for the incompetent strategy of their commander. The genius of Napoleon had not failed him. The plan he had formed would undoubtedly have given him the victory, could battles be won by plans. He thrust his army like a wedge between the left flank of the English Army, which he had taken by surprise, and the Prussian right flank. It was his intention to thrust Wellington's army to the left and Blücher's to the right, to crush each in turn, and then to march upon Brussels. But the spirit of his troops was no longer what it had been ten years earlier, at Austerlitz or Jena. It was now the enemy who were the most determined on victory. The Prussians, far from scattering before the onslaught, kept up an obstinate resistance, and finally retreated in good order ; and the French had so lost heart that they would not pursue nor even make sure of the direction of their retreat. The British Army came off even better, repulsed Ney's attacks, and only retreated on Brussels at the news of the Prussian retreat and to avoid isolation. Of the two generals, Wellington and Blücher, who combined the retreat of both armies to concentrate them in the rear ? If it was Wellington, then it must be admitted that his plans contributed to the final success, but, after all, when Blücher joined him on the evening of the 18th the French defeat was already assured, after a day of promiscuous slaughter, the details of which, according to his own subsequent avowal, Wellington had failed to grasp. " The battle," he wrote, " began, *I believe*, at eleven. *It is impossible to say when each important occurrence took place nor in what order.* . . . Repeated attacks were made along the whole front of the centre of the position by cavalry and infantry till seven at night. *How many I cannot tell.* . . . Napoleon did not manœuvre at all. He just moved forward in the old style in columns, and was driven off in the old style." [2] Of the Allies 22,000 men had been slain or wounded, of the French 40,000. The campaign was concluded with a truly Napoleonic celerity. The French Army broke up after Waterloo, just as the Prussian Army had dispersed, nine years before, after Jena. On June 29th the Allies arrived for the second time beneath the walls of Paris.

[1] To General Lord Lynedoch, June 13, 1815 (*Dispatches*, vol. viii. p. 135 ; ed. 1838, vol. xii. p. 462).
[2] *Dispatches*, vol. viii. pp. 244, 186. Letters to ———, Esq., August 17, 1815, and to Lord Beresford, July 2, 1815 (ed. 1838, vol. xii. pp. 610 and 529).

The Survival of Anti-Militarism.

Victory had been won ; peace seemed at length assured ; and the constitutional problem called for solution. What, in time of peace, was to become of this vast standing army, the creation in its entirety of the last twenty years ? Could the Government make up its mind to disband it ? If, however, it were not disbanded, was it possible to keep so large a number of men under arms without endangering those anti-militarist traditions which were an essential part of the British Constitution ? We may grant that on this point the fears of the Liberal Opposition appear at first sight well founded, for nowhere else were the effects of the Tory reaction so evident. Already, in 1814, the dissatisfaction of the Whigs had found expression in Parliament. The Government had decided to keep under arms during peace a certain number of militia regiments arbitrarily selected. The scheme was denounced as unconstitutional, and was the subject of heated debates.[1] And the opening months of 1816 were to witness far more vehement protests. What, asked the Opposition speakers, could be the meaning of these reviews, of these parades ? Why did the Regent open Parliament not, as was the custom, in civil dress, but in field-marshal's uniform and cocked hat ? Why was an entire district of London put into a state of siege whenever he gave an entertainment at Carlton House ? [2] When the Earl of Essex and Lord Milton were stopped in Pall Mall by a Horse Guard who was standing sentry and obliged to turn back, they raised a discussion in both Houses and declared the Constitution in danger.[3] What, again, was the significance of so many new institutions, all infused with a novel spirit : institutions such as the Royal Military Asylum, which received the orphans of soldiers, and trained them from infancy for service in the Army, in complete segregation from the civil population ; the Royal Military College, where young men of good family were educated on the Prussian system ; and the Military Club, composed exclusively of officers who wished, no doubt, to form a caste, to become a nation within the nation ? [4]

But in reality these complaints were as silly as they were noisy. The analysis already made of the military institutions of Great Britain is their sufficient refutation. In England the regular army was not of a nature to become the tool of royal despotism. It was not the

[1] H. of C., November 21 and 28, 1814, Romilly's motion (*Parl. Deb.*, vol. xxix. pp. 378, 563). Cf. May 18, 1815, Lord Folkestone's speech (*Parl. Deb.*, vol. xxxi. p. 266). It is doubtful whether or no the contention of the Opposition was legally valid. Cf. Clode, *Military Forces*, vol. i. p. 49.

[2] H. of C., February 28, 1816, Lord Folkestone's speech (*Parl. Deb.*, vol. xxxii. p. 965) ; April 10, 1816, Lord Folkestone's speech (*Parl. Deb.*, vol. xxxiii. pp. 1158, 1159).

[3] H. of L., April 5, 1816. H. of C., April 4, 1816 (*Parl. Deb.*, vol. xxxiii. pp. 930, 950).

[4] H. of C., February 28, 1816, Lord Folkestone's speech (*Parl. Deb.*, vol. xxxii. p. 965). Cf. June 2, 1815, Bennett's speech (*Parl. Deb.*, vol. xxxi. p. 590).

army of an autocrat, but an aristocratic, anarchic and decentralized army. Indeed, even those who denounced the new militarism did not venture to predict a *coup d'état* in the near future. Their sole complaint was that the increase in the staff put a larger number of places at the King's disposal, and thereby augmented, to use the stock phrase, "the influence of the Crown." [1] But that influence was itself limited. Though abuses were rampant in the British Army, they were not new. Neither King George, nor the Regent, nor the Duke of York was responsible for them. Like the abuses in all the other branches of the administration, they dated from the period of Whig rule. Far from strengthening, they paralysed the action of the Government.

A professional army, commanded by soldiers of fortune, may possibly endanger the stability of political institutions ; but in England the military and political institutions were in perfect harmony. The same men commanded the Army and governed the State. It was by no means unusual for a country gentleman to purchase an ensign's or cornet's commission for his son—not that he might become a professional soldier, but that he might " see life," might " become a man of the world." Once the young man had attained the rank of lieutenant, he would leave the Army, marry and settle down in his native county, there to perform those administrative functions which were his by a right to all intents hereditary. Even those officers who aspired, and with success, to the higher ranks, saw with equanimity the final conclusion of peace. They knew that by right of birth they would find, either as county magistrates or as Members of Parliament, places awaiting their occupation in the ranks of civil society. They were even prepared at need to acquiesce in a reduction of the Forces. A new type of anti-militarism was now growing up, based entirely on economic—not, as formerly, on constitutional grounds.[2] A large army cost dear, England was overburdened with taxation and the officers who sat in Parliament—whether retired or active mattered little— were landowners as well as soldiers. They desired the abolition of the income tax and this involved a reduction of the army estimates. Attached more closely to their class than to their profession, they were thus rendered incapable of forming a distinct military party at Westminster. But without leaders the British Army could never become a Prætorian guard ; and conversely, even had the officers possessed

[1] H. of L., March 15, 1816, Lord Lansdowne's speech (*Parl. Deb.*, vol. xxxiii. pp. 305 sqq.). Cf. Lord John Russell, *English Government and Constitution*, ed. 1823, pp. 410–11 : " After the peace there were not less than 600 generals in the English service. In 1780 we had 2,000 military officers ; at present we have 19,000 on full and half pay. In 1780 we had about 1,800 naval officers ; at present we have about 8,400 on full and half pay ; thus making about 27,000 officers in Army and Navy only." See also Lord Castlereagh's reply to these complaints, February 13, 1816 (*Parl. Deb.*, vol. xxxii. p. 455).

[2] H. of C., November 28, 1814, Baring's speech (*Parl. Deb.*, vol. xxix. p. 591). H. of L., March 15, 1816, Lord Lansdowne's speech (*Parl. Deb.*, vol. xxxiii. pp. 305 sqq.).

the desire to employ the Army for the repression of any movement that threatened the interests of the propertied classes, they would have needed soldiers willing to yield them blind obedience. There was, however, but little community of interest or feeling between the officers and the privates. The Army lacked *esprit de corps*. The common soldier, out of touch with his officers, and an object of distrust to the people, who regarded him either as an idle good-for-nothing living at their expense or as a particularly well armed and dangerous policeman, lost, when confronted with a riot at home, that invincible confidence which he had displayed so often when fighting a foreign foe. When grave disturbances broke out in London in the February of 1815, it even happened that soldiers disobeyed orders and took part with the rioters.[1] In spite of a defective organization the British Army had been victorious. Owing to that defective organization, the victories won by the British Army did not endanger the traditional liberties of the nation.

FOREIGN POLICY OF THE BRITISH GOVERNMENT

Britain Commands the Sea and Arbitrates on the Continent.

There was certainly no reason of national security to prevent the English reducing their expenditure on the Army. England had now no enemies to fear. After a war extending over more than a century the power of France was at length broken. Carthage had conquered Rome. It was the triumph of British diplomacy under both its aspects ; the maritime and the continental policy of England had alike proved successful.

At sea England enforced as a belligerent rights which the other nations considered tyrannical. The diplomatic representatives of Great Britain claimed for the ships of their nation the right to stop, search, seize and bring into their ports the vessels of neutral Powers, merely undertaking to release them later, if it were proved to the satisfaction of an English jury that they were not enemy's ships in disguise, and to allow them to retain their cargo, if it were also proved judicially that the cargo, like the vessel, was really neutral. England also claimed the right to establish fictitious blockades, and to order her privateers to seize any neutral vessel whose destination was supposed to be one of the ports arbitrarily chosen, though their access was not actually being blocked by a single British vessel.

The British Court of Admiralty pronounced that " Great Britain,

---

[1] Twiss, *Life of Lord Eldon*, vol. ii. p. 263 : " I brought into the house by their collars two of the mob, and told them that they would be hanged. One of them bid me look to myself, and told me that the people were much more likely to hang me than I was to procure any of them to be hanged. They were sent before a J.P., but the soldiers said they would do their duty as soldiers, but they would not be witnesses." Cf. *Annual Register*, 1816, pp. 115 sqq., for the unpopularity of the English soldiers at Glasgow.

in virtue of her insular position, *blockaded naturally* all the Spanish and French ports." [1] England claimed in addition the right to stop and search neutral vessels—not only merchantmen but, if necessary, even men-of-war—to discover whether there were any English deserters on board and to carry off presumed deserters, without any form of trial, to serve in the British Navy. The exercise of these rights was essential to the naval supremacy of Great Britain, and the naval supremacy to which Great Britain now aspired was itself essential to her very existence ; for the time had arrived when her manufactures had exceeded her agriculture, and she was therefore compelled to obtain from abroad at least a considerable portion of her food supply. Foreign nations had protested again and again against the British claims, and with French encouragement and support had leagued together to withstand them. In the end, however, they found themselves compelled to submit. Without the British alliance they could not hope to shake off the far heavier yoke of Napoleonic despotism. At sea Great Britain claimed, and claimed successfully, absolute sovereignty. On land, however, the situation was reversed, and since all the nations of Europe, with the exception of Great Britain, were continental rather than maritime powers, the British Government was able, with every appearance of truth, to pose before the other rulers of Europe as the disinterested arbiter of international justice.

The policy of the British Government was not, nor had been since 1792, a policy of annexation. It is true that the late war had extended the British Colonial Empire. In India, a British protectorate had been imposed upon the Sultan of Mysore, upon the Nizam and upon the Mahratta confederation. The British troops had occupied Delhi, and over ninety thousand square miles of territory had been annexed. Along the coast the territories of the three presidencies had been joined up, in the interior the East India Company was extending in all directions its supremacy and its influence. Ceylon, the Cape, Mauritius, Santa Lucia and Tobago were all new conquests in the Indian Ocean or in the West Indies. But we must not regard this growth of the Empire as the result of a preconceived design. It was by mere chance, indeed almost reluctantly, that the British Government had made all these conquests. The disasters of the American War had rendered the policy of colonial expansion so distasteful to the English that they had even abolished the Secretaryship of State " for the Colonies." [2] When Pitt introduced his India Bill to enlarge the control of the Government over the East India Company, he expressly declared all projects of conquest in India " repugnant to the wish, the honour, the policy of this nation." [3] Later, indeed, to safe-

---

[1] Fauchille, *Du Blocus Maritime*, p. 7. [2] 22 Geo. III, cap. 82, § 1.

[3] 24 Geo. III, cap. 25. Preamble to Art. 34 For the Indian policy of the Government subsequent to 1784 see H. of C., April 11, 1791, Lord Porchester's speech (*Parl. Deb.*, vol. xxix. pp. 125 sqq.).

guard the factories on the coast of India from attacks by the French agents, first at Seringapatam, later on the Jumna, it was found necessary to dispatch military expeditions into the interior. When, however, a succession of wars followed, the Board of Control, the Directors of the Company and political and financial circles generally, took alarm. Orders were sent to the Governor-General, Lord Wellesley, to conclude peace as soon as possible. He resigned, and a series of treaties, provisional compromises, were botched up with the Mahratta chiefs. Or, again, consider the negotiations for peace with America. Though Great Britain would not yield an inch where her naval rights were concerned, she was prepared to abandon all claims of territorial aggrandizement. The United States were even permitted to thrust a wedge of their territory between Canada and New Brunswick. The Treaty of Paris left Martinique and Guadeloupe to France, together with her right of fishery on the Newfoundland coast, and even her factories on the shores of India, on condition that no armies were kept there. Holland received back Java, Denmark all her colonies. Even the colonies that were not given up were not retained for the sake of territorial expansion. Like the Ionian Islands, Malta and Gibraltar in Europe, those colonies were regarded by the British statesman simply as strategic centres, or naval stations.[1] St. Helena, Simon's Bay and Mauritius would enable British ships on the voyage to India to take in supplies of fresh water and fresh meat.

England, however, had a large surplus population, more hands than she could employ, more mouths than she could feed. Surely it was high time to organize emigration to the new colonies, or at least to some of them. Apart from the exceptional case of Australia, a penal colony to which English convicts were deported, the British Government does not seem even to have thought as yet of this solution of the problem of over-population.[2] Even when in the near future a movement of emigration would take shape of itself, altogether apart from Government intervention, the Ministry would not behold it without anxiety. For the British colonists would naturally look to the Mother Country for help against the enterprises of other colonizing nations, or the attacks of the native races ; and the Home Government was by no means disposed to pay for the military expeditions

---

[1] See the debates on the Treaty of Paris, H. of C., June 29, 1814. Lord Castlereagh justified the colonial concessions made to France on the principle " that it was expedient fully to open to France the means of peaceful occupation, and that it was not the interest of this country to make her a military and a conquering, instead of a commercial and a pacific nation." He defended the annexation of Mauritius " not on account of any commercial advantages resulting from its possession, but because in time of war it was a great maritime nuisance, highly detrimental to our commerce. In the two past wars, the injury to our commerce by the occupation of the Mauritius on the part of the enemy, as a cruising station, was incalculable " (Parl. Deb., vol. xxviii. p. 462).

[2] A solution already being urged by the Malthusians (Quarterly Review, vol. xii. p. 41, October 1814, art. on Australia).

which the colonists would demand. The time would, moreover, come when the colonies would claim a right to self-government, a Parliament and a responsible Cabinet; and England had not forgotten the troubles occasioned by the constant disputes in the old colonies between the popular assembly and "the Council" which represented the Home Government.[1] Neither had she forgotten how she had lost already the larger part of her North American colonies.

To prevent a repetition of that disaster the British Government struggled to maintain as strict a control as possible over the newly acquired colonies.[2] In the intention of the Ministry, these colonies were never to be more than fortified positions under military control. No doubt the governing aristocracy profited from the extension of the Colonial Empire, where lucrative sinecures were plentiful; but that aristocracy was subject to the constant pressure of middle-class opinion— the opinion not only of manufacturers and merchants, but of the entire body of investors. The colonial sinecures were denounced like all other sinecures, and like them were threatened with abolition.[3] In short, despite so many naval victories, the England of 1815 showed no signs of "imperialism."

Still less did she entertain the desire to make conquests on the Continent of Europe. The King of England was now once more King of Hanover; but the union of the two Crowns was soon to cease; nor did his Ministers allow the English Sovereign to make use of the power of Britain in the interest of his German electorate. The British Government claimed to play on the Continent the part of an impartial mediator. Throughout the war England had interpreted her belligerent rights in the sense most favourable to the inhabitants of the country under invasion and most inconvenient to herself. She had never permitted her armies to live, like Napoleon's, at the expense of the country.[4] They were either obliged to purchase with ready money the necessary provisions, or these were brought by sea at no slight expense. On the conclusion of peace England intervened between the victors and the vanquished. In 1814 she had obtained the signature by the Powers of a separate treaty with France—that the French Govern-

---

[1] *Memoirs and Correspondence of Lord Castlereagh*, vol. viii. p. 198. Letter to the Duke of Manchester, February 11, 1809: "The pretension of the Assembly" (of Jamaica) "to all the rights and privileges of the House of Commons is quite absurd; they have no other privileges than those naturally arising out of or connected with the colonial and limited purposes for which, *by the act of the Crown*, they have been created. The control of the Army does not belong to them. Inquiries on their part into the conduct of military officers, in the sense the Commons inquire at home, are quite foreign to their jurisdiction." For difficulties of the same sort at Barbadoes 1818–1820, see *Memoirs and Correspondence of Lord Combermere*, vol. i. pp. 256 sqq.

[2] Egerton, *A Short History of British Colonial Policy*, p. 260.

[3] For these colonial sinecures see the *Second Report . . . on Sinecure Offices*, June 18, 1811, and especially the *Third Report . . .*, April 23, 1812; also the Debates on the Colonial Offices Bill, H. of C., March 22, 28, 29, April 18, 25, May 6, 1814 (*Parl. Deb.*, vol. xxvii. pp. 339, 365, 375, 434, 522, 731).

[4] Not even in India. See Alison, *History of Europe*, vol. xi. pp 108–9.

ment might be reconstituted in time to be represented at the Congress of Vienna, and to take part in the settlement of Europe. At Paris, both before and after the Hundred Days, Wellington constituted himself the protector of the French whom he had conquered, and opposed on their behalf the brutality of the Prussian troops and the unreasonable demands of the Prussian diplomats.

Not a soul in Europe, however, with the possible exception of a handful of Liberal statesmen and publicists, showed any real gratitude to England for her policy of arbitration. The very impartiality put forward so ostentatiously by the English appeared somehow cold and unsympathetic. Brought face to face with the English, all the other peoples of Europe—Frenchmen and Spaniards, Latins, Teutons and Slavs—were conscious of a common bond, they felt that the wars which had divided them during the past twenty-five years were after all civil wars ; and asked themselves by what right a foreign nation interfered in their quarrels, to lecture them on morals and statesmanship. The British troops were often disconcerted to find themselves the object of general dislike in the very country which they had just liberated, while with the process of time the memory of French rule was losing its bitterness.[1] How to calm the obstinate suspicion of Continental Governments and peoples was a problem which embarrassed the English diplomatists, and it was complicated by another problem. In England, as in no other European country, public opinion was alert and ready to criticize the actions of the Government. England was the sole country in which, according to constitutional forms universally respected, the entire policy of Europe was the daily subject of a public debate.[2] Though the Tories were in power, she remained *par excellence* the free country among the nations of Europe. English diplomatists were at times able to profit by the pressure thus exerted upon them by public opinion. They could on occasion protract negotiations, and declare themselves powerless to come to any definite agreement until the matter had been referred to London and they were assured of the support of Parliament. More usually, however, they found the control of public opinion a burden and a weakness. It made it difficult for them to arrive at the most suitable formulæ to define the new settlement of Europe.

---

[1] Foy, *Guerre de la Peninsule.* Brenton, *Naval History*, vol. iv. pp. 117–18.

[2] Sir James Mackintosh to Horner, Paris, December 12, 1814 : " Nobody can be here without feeling the great hatred entertained against us by all ranks and parties. It has been a little abated during the last three weeks by the debates of the House of Commons, which have been more important, and I hope more beneficial, on the Continent, than at any former period of our parliamentary history. The general Continent wanted an organ, and the only popular assembly in Europe partially supplied it. You gave the sanction of a public body to the principles of common sense ; and you have certainly contributed to all the success which may attend Talleyrand in his new office of assertor of justice and protector of weakness " (*Memoirs and Correspondence of Francis Horner*, vol. ii. pp. 223–4). On his return to London, Mackintosh made use of practically the same expressions in his important speech in Parliament on April 27, 1815 (*Parl. Deb.*, vol. xxx. p. 891).

The European Problem : its Difficulty.

Was it simply a question of " restoring " the state of Europe previous to 1792, of re-establishing on their thrones all the "legitimate" dynasties, and thus obliterating as completely as possible every memorial of the long period of revolutionary upheaval, of maintaining the mutual independence of the nations, and of preserving intact the old political and religious traditions ? Such was, indeed, the desire of the Allies in 1814 and 1815 ; but difficulties were raised in London. The anti-Jacobin party in England had been formed by a coalition of the Tories and the great majority of the Whigs. The political philosophy of the new coalition had been formulated by a Whig. According to Burke and his school equality was synonymous with tyranny, aristocracy with freedom. A century after the death of Louis XIV, the British upper classes could still believe that in defending their privileges they were defending the liberties of the nation and the political freedom of Europe. English "legitimism" was a totally different thing from Continental legitimism.

In the train of the British armies the system of parliamentary government had spread throughout the whole of Western Europe. The national pride even of the Tories was flattered by the adoption in turn by Sicily, Spain, France, and Holland of Constitutions modelled on the Constitution of Great Britain.[1] They had certainly some hesitation in believing that the peoples of the Continent were worthy to receive, or even capable of understanding, institutions of such sovereign excellence. They considered the Sicilian Constitution too oligarchic,[2] the Constitution of Cadiz too Jacobin,[3] and feared that the French Parliament would prove but a clumsy imitation of the Parliament of Westminster.[4] But if the awkwardness of Continental

---

[1] H. of C., June 29, 1814, Canning's speech (*Parl. Deb.*, vol. xxviii. p. 451).

[2] Mr. A. Court to ——, Palermo, January 5, 1815 (*Memoirs and Correspondence of Lord Castlereagh*, vol. x. p. 237). Lord Sheffield to Abbot, November 6, 1812 (*Diary and Correspondence of Lord Colchester*, vol. ii. pp. 408–9). Cf. a curious memorandum by an anonymous writer printed among Lord Castlereagh's letters (vol. viii. pp. 217 sqq.). It dates from the year 1810 and is entitled *Some Account of the Present State of Sicily*. The author advocates the introduction into Sicily and the other Mediterranean islands of popular institutions under a species of British protectorate.

[3] For a discussion of this Constitution, see the *Edinburgh Review*, September 1814, Art. 5, *Cortes of Spain* (vol. xxiii. p. 361). See also Lord Castlereagh's letter to Sir Henry Wellesley, Paris, May 10, 1814 (*Memoirs and Correspondence of Lord Castlereagh*, vol. ix. p. 462); also Wellington to Lord Bathurst, January 27, 1813 (*Dispatches*, vol. vi. pp. 255–6).

[4] E. Cooke to Lord Castlereagh, Foreign Office, April 14, 1814 : " Such a House of Lords ! without family, property, character." For the Upper House, cf. Lord Castlereagh's letter to Lord Liverpool, Paris, April 20, 1814 (*Memoirs and Correspondence of Lord Castlereagh*, vol. ix. p. 481) ; also Wellington to Dumouriez, Paris, November 26, 1814 : " Everything is new here, and as you know, new things, especially when they are of a complicated nature, do not work well. . . . Everybody is poor and, what is worse, their institutions prevent any family becoming wealthy and powerful " (*Dispatches*, vol. xii. p. 192, translated from the French). See also in the *Edinburgh Review*, September 1814, Art. 11, *Paris in 1802–4* (vol. xxiii. pp. 483–4), extracts from the journal of an English traveller in Paris. See further the *Diary of Lord Colchester* (kept during his stay at Paris), October 9, 1815 : " Arbuthnot brought me a string of

attempts at parliamentary government inspired the English Tory with feelings of scornful condescension, the brutal depotism of the newly restored monarchs filled him with disgust and horror. It was in Spain that the British policy was most completely stultified. Ferdinand VII restored the Inquisition, abolished the Constitution, and imprisoned or executed the leading Liberals, the very men who admired most fervently the fundamental principles of English political and social life. To re-establish his depotism the Spanish King employed troops paid with British gold and led by British officers. The Opposition at Westminster raised violent protests, and the Ministry scarcely dared to defend their action.[1] They were well aware—their ambassador at Madrid had informed them of it[2]—that every success of absolutism in the Peninsula was so much loss to British influence. Already in 1815, before the time of Canning and the revolt of the Spanish colonies, an incompatibility of principle was evident between England and her Allies of 1813. Scarcely four months after Waterloo the rulers of the great Continental Powers asked the Prince Regent to sign the agreement, known as the Holy Alliance. Lord Castlereagh, to whom the communication of their request had been entrusted, expressed his regret that he was compelled to lay before a British Sovereign " this piece of sublime mysticism and nonsense." After deliberation the Cabinet declared itself unable to advise the Regent to give his adhesion. It was unconstitutional for the Sovereign to conclude on his own responsibility an alliance with a foreign monarch. His power was confined to the ratification of a treaty concluded in due form, signed already by a plenipotentiary and to which the great seal had been affixed.[3]

The foreign policy of the Tory Government was confronted with fresh difficulties when it came to rearranging the map of Europe. An exact restoration of the territorial arrangements previous to 1792 did not present itself, even to the English Cabinet, as a prudent policy. The galaxy of petty States in Western Germany and Northern Italy had long exposed Central Europe to French influence and invasion. If the balance of power in Europe were to be maintained, it was essential that a barrier of States should be set up sufficiently large to offer a serious resistance to France. In other words, that policy

questions proposed by the French Ministers, about the principles and forms and examples of managing the practical part of the English Government, proving their entire ignorance of the subject." October 11th : " Heard an authentic and curious account of the state of the French Ministry, and their utter ignorance of all the forms and principles of the British Government which they profess to emulate " (vol. ii. p. 557).

[1] The Cabinet even admitted that were any intervention in Spain admissible, it would be against absolutism. H. of C., November 15, 1814, Mr. Baring's motion for papers relating to Spain. Wellesley Pole's reply (*Parl. Deb.*, vol. xxix. p. 200).

[2] *Memoirs and Correspondence of Lord Castlereagh*, vol. x. p. 509 sqq. Cf. vol. x. pp. 25–6, Lord Castlereagh to Sir Henry Wellesley, May 10, 1814.

[3] Yonge, *Life of Lord Liverpool*, vol. ii. pp. 226 sqq.

of "territorial groups" which Napoleon had employed in favour of France must now be employed against her. In agreement with the rest of Europe, Great Britain demanded that the Scheldt should be opened to free navigation, that Antwerp should be declared a free port, and that the Spanish Netherlands should form one kingdom with Holland. But when these points had been secured, neither the British Government nor the British public had any interest in bringing about the universal absorption of petty States by their more important neighbours. The indifference of Great Britain formed a striking contrast to the greed displayed by Russia, Prussia and Austria. Nor did the Opposition speakers fail to exploit this indifference. They refused to recognize in the new States, artificially created by international diplomacy, the free countries, the collective persons which Britain had defended against the aggression of Napoleon. In language of the most pronounced conservatism, Mackintosh pronounced the panegyric of "the ancient and magnificent system" which had been bestowed on Europe by the Peace of Westphalia, and preserved intact until the partition of Poland and the French Revolution. He complained that, despite the overthrow of Napoleon, the Napoleonic system was still maintained—the sole difference being that the dictatorship of Europe, then wielded by a single man, was now in the hands of a triumvirate.[1] The Ministers questioned could find nothing to reply.

Public opinion was first aroused by the Norwegian question. In virtue of an agreement concluded with England, Bernadotte had obtained as the price of his defection the separation of Norway from Denmark and its annexation to Sweden. The Norwegians thus delivered to a new master rose in arms. Had not the Swedes effected a speedy conquest of Norway, it is extremely doubtful whether Parliament would have permitted the British Government to fulfil the terms of the treaty by giving active assistance to the Swedish Army.[2] The annexation of Genoa by Piedmont next kindled popular indignation, an indignation the more intense because Lord William Bentinck, the British plenipotentiary in Italy and a convinced Whig, had lavished on the Genoese the most solemn promises of liberty.[3] As regards

---

[1] H. of C., April 27, 1815, motion relating to the transfer of Genoa (*Parl. Deb.*, vol. xxx. pp. 891 sqq.). Cf. Whitbread's speech, February 9th and 13th, March 6th (*Parl. Deb.*, vol. xxix. pp. 697, 726, and vol. xxx. p. 13). We should notice also Ponsonby's exclamation during the debates of February 13th, when the Chancellor of the Exchequer refused to reply : " Mr. Speaker, I wish you would cast your eyes upon that bench, and say if there is a single person there who dares contradict what has been asserted. And if you do cast your eyes upon them, I should be glad to know what your emotions are—whether you most pity or condemn them ? (Hear, hear and laughter.)"

[2] See Lord Liverpool's letters to Castlereagh and Wellington, September 2, 1814 (Yonge, *Life of Lord Liverpool*, vol. ii. pp. 21-2, 24). For the Norwegian question, see *Edinburgh Review*, April 1814, No. 45, Art. 4, *Transference of Norway* (vol. xxiii. pp. 102-3).

[3] H. of C., February 13, April 27, 1815, and April 7th. Papers relating to Genoa, presented by command of the Prince Regent (*Parl. Deb.*, vol. xxix. pp. 727 sqq. ; vol. xxx. pp. 901 sqq. and 387 sqq.). For the part played by Lord William Bentinck in Sicily, see *Court of*

Germany, the King of Prussia had concluded an agreement with his close ally, the Emperor of Russia, to divide the possessions of the King of Saxony, who to the very end had refused to join the Allies. According to the terms of this arrangement Russia was to secure the Grand Duchy of Warsaw, Prussia, Saxony itself. This compact threw out of gear all the calculations of British diplomacy ; for Great Britain had no desire to see this increase of Russian influence and territory. Was there not reason to fear lest the Tsar, now become so powerful by the downfall of France, would ally himself with the United States to defend the rights of neutrals at sea ? Might he not cherish designs of conquest in Turkey, perhaps even in India ? [1] What the English Cabinet would really have liked, was a close alliance with Prussia and Austria, since these two Powers formed a barrier between Western and Eastern Europe. Since this was impossible, the Ministry was forced to be content with an agreement with France and Austria against Russia and Prussia. In the early months of 1815 a treaty of alliance was signed with the two former Powers. A joint military demonstration, perhaps even an expedition, was expected ; but further difficulties arose. In Italy Murat had succeeded in keeping his throne, with the support of Austria—which not only gave him a formal guarantee of undisturbed possession, but even promised him an increase of territory in the north. England and France, however, feared the possibility of a secret understanding between Murat at Naples and Napoleon in banishment at Elba, and desired the restoration of the Bourbons to the Neapolitan throne, as being at once clients of the British Government and relations of Louis XVIII. Public opinion in London made use of all these questions of foreign policy, which threatened to cause a war at any moment, as pretexts for criticism of the Cabinet. In January Lord Castlereagh, the English plenipotentiary at Vienna, was hurriedly recalled. A session of Parliament was about to open, the political situation was extremely difficult, and the Ministry dared not face the debates unless Lord Castlereagh were present in person to justify his diplomacy to the Commons.

Was an outbreak of war really imminent during the early months of 1815 ? The British Cabinet, at any rate, were most strongly opposed to war, and whenever Wellington at Paris, or Lord Castlereagh at Vienna, displayed any inclination towards a war or even an offensive alliance, Lord Liverpool wrote from London to urge a more peaceful course. "There is no mode," he wrote, " in which the arrangements in Poland, Germany and Italy can be settled con-

<hr />

England under the Prince Regent, vol. i. pp. 199, 200. Compare also the councils of moderation addressed to Lord William by Lord Castlereagh, April 3 and May 7, 1814 (*Memoirs and Correspondence of Lord Castlereagh*, vol. ix. pp. 429 sqq. ; vol. x. p. 18).

[1] *Quarterly Review*, October 1815, *Elphinstone's Account of Caubul* (vol. xiv. pp. 154-5). The writer of the article, however, makes light of such fears.

sistently with the stipulations of the Treaty of Paris which is not to be preferred, under present circumstances, to a renewal of hostilities between the Continental Powers." [1] For any war that might break out in any part of Europe would very soon become general and kindle a revolution. At the close of 1814, Lord Liverpool still hoped that two or three years of peace would suffice to calm the excitement of popular feeling throughout Europe, and that diplomatists would then again be able, without peril to the established order of society, to provoke "a war . . . not different in its character and its effects from any of those wars which occurred in the 17th and 18th centuries, before the commencement of the French Revolution." [2]

The Hundred Days shattered the illusion. All the rulers of Europe agreed with one consent to weaken France, to impose upon her a heavy war indemnity, to narrow her frontiers, to plant garrisons on her territory. All divergencies of interest were obliterated by the common dread of Napoleon. The peace of Europe was thus securely established. The epoch of dynastic wars had gone by. Nor would even the democratic Opposition demand a war for the emancipation of the peoples of Europe from the despotic rule of the league of monarchs. In fact, the desire for a policy of peace and retrenchment was universal. The majority even of the Ministerialists supported the Opposition against the Cabinet in their demand that the heavy burden of taxation should be alleviated. Such an alleviation was not, however, feasible so long as the British Army was maintained on a war footing, and subsidies were paid to Continental Powers. "Very few persons give themselves any anxiety," wrote Lord Liverpool on January 16th to Lord Castlereagh, "about what is passing at Vienna, except in as far as it is connected with expense." Again, on February 20th he insists in an alarmist letter : "Many of our best friends think of nothing but the reduction of taxes and war establishments. The country at this moment is peace mad." [3]

The Weakness of the Executive.

The preceding observations have abundantly proved that the constitution of the British Government about the year 1815 must be regarded, despite the reactionary tendencies of the Tories, as essentially free.

[1] Lord Liverpool to Lord Castlereagh, December 23, 1814 (Yonge, *Life of Lord Liverpool*, vol. ii. p. 85).

[2] Lord Liverpool to Lord Castlereagh, September 25, 1814 (Yonge, *Life of Lord Liverpool*, vol. ii. p. 31). He expresses himself in practically identical terms in a letter to Wellington which is attributed by Yonge to the month of November (vol. ii. pp. 81–2). Cf. letters of Lord Liverpool to Wellington, September 2, 1814 ; to Lord Castlereagh, November 2, 1814, and December 23, 1814 ; to Wellington, December 31, 1814 (Yonge, *Life of Lord Liverpool*, vol. ii. pp. 24, 29, 51, 100).

[3] *Memoirs and Correspondence of Lord Castlereagh*, vol. x. p. 241 ; *Supplementary Dispatches of . . . Wellington*, vol. ix. p. 573.

We are to understand by this, in the first place, that the various branches of the administration constituted together a system of securities against bureaucratic centralization and military despotism ; for their nature rendered it impossible for the head of the executive to employ a handful of bureaucrats to oppress the majority of his subjects. England was a nation richly provided with the means of war, but her principal arm of warfare was her navy, and no navy, however strong, can ever be a source of danger to public liberty. And although the English had reluctantly yielded to the pressure of circumstances and now maintained a large standing army, this army of mercenaries had neither the means nor the desire to seize the reins of government and alter the Constitution. When, however, we say that England was, in the sense above defined, a free country, we are far from terming it a democracy. Such a definition would, indeed, be widely remote from the truth. To be sure, the British aristocracy was very open, for it was constantly receiving new accessions from the Bar, the Army and commerce. Nevertheless, it was essentially an aristocracy of wealthy landed proprietors, who controlled both the central and the local government of the country. Hence the progress of democratic institutions during the 19th century necessarily followed, in England, a course very different from that which it was to follow in the other countries of Europe. On the Continent the bureaucratic State was already in being, and nothing more was required than the transference to other hands of this pre-existent machinery and its employment for novel purposes. In England the machinery itself had to be created.

Nevertheless, in terming it aristocratic we have not given a sufficient definition of the English system of government. Though predominantly aristocratic, it was not undiluted aristocracy. We have already had occasion to remark the presence in the British Constitution of influences which counteracted the influence of the ruling aristocracy, for all its firm grasp of power and greedy appropriation of the prizes of government. The aim of the Whig campaign for the reform of administrative abuses which opened about the year 1780, was to deprive the Crown of one of the sources of its power and thereby to fortify indirectly the political privileges of the aristocracy. Since, however, it was that very aristocracy which profited so largely by these abuses, it lost at least as much as the monarchy lost by the progress of administrative reform. A force from without, the pressure of public opinion, pushed the reformers forward and carried them further than they would ever have been led by considerations of private interest. Our study of the foreign policy of Great Britain has shown that English diplomatists and statesmen, from the very fact that they had been nurtured in the tradition of self-government and were members of a ruling aristocracy, viewed with uneasiness the despotic tendencies of the Continental monarchs. And it happened very frequently in their dealings with the Continental nations that they found themselves compelled, by the pressure of public opinion, to show sympathy with a democratic policy by no means in harmony with the interest of their class. And we have also seen how in the provinces the system of aristocratic self-government left public opinion a partial control over local government. For the landowners had at their disposal neither police nor military force to defend them against insurrection. To assure the permanence of the existing system, therefore, they were obliged to take account of the opinion of those whom they governed. Nor is this all that can be said. The control exerted over the governors by the governed found further expression in a number of positive institutions, which formed part of the Constitution of the Kingdom. To these we have already made passing allusion ; we must now undertake their detailed analysis.

CHAPTER II

THE LEGISLATURE AND THE SUPREMACY OF PUBLIC OPINION

THE REPRESENTATIVE SYSTEM OF THE UNITED KINGDOM.

The Different Possible Forms of Popular Self-Government.

THREE, and only three, possible methods are conceivable by which a people could govern itself. The entire body of citizens might meet as frequently as possible to pass laws and to nominate officials to execute the laws. This is government by public meeting, the direct government of the people by the people. Or a limited number of individuals might be designated by lot, or selected according to any kind of predetermined order—according to seniority, if you like, for that would serve the purpose as well as anything else. Those chosen few would discharge in turn the functions of government. This would be government by rotation. Or again, the entire body of citizens might assemble, at fairly distant intervals, not to legislate or appoint the executive, but to elect a certain number of representatives who, until the next election, would discharge with greater continuity the functions which, according to the first alternative, the popular assembly would have performed directly. This is representative government. All these three forms of government existed side by side in the British Constitution at the beginning of the 19th century.

Direct government of the people by the people is adapted only to the very elementary needs of very small communities. We are not, therefore, surprised to find this form of government persisting in the meeting, whose president was a meadsman, a common herd, a fieldsman or an overseer, and whose function it was to regulate the cultivation of the common land of the parish.[1] The meeting was perhaps the final relic of a constitution of society anterior to the feudal system. It was, moreover, a survival which lost constantly in importance, as the organization of society became more complicated,

[1] Webb, *English Local Government*, vol. ii. pp. 128 sqq.

and was even on the way to vanish completely, since the avowed object of legislation was now to vest the ownership and cultivation of the soil entirely in the hands of individuals. But we are more surprised to discover that the constitution of the parishes themselves, those small units of local government into which the whole of England is divided, was also based on the principle of government by public meeting. The parish was administered by five officials, who together constituted the parochial executive—the churchwardens, the constable, the surveyor of highways, and the overseer of the poor—and by an assembly, the vestry meeting, a meeting of all those interested in the government of the parish. This assembly exercised a control over the actions and the expenditure of the executive, and in certain cases nominated these officials, or at least took part in their nomination. The vestry, which owed its name to the fact that it met regularly in the vestry of the parish church, naturally played a very important part in the choice of the churchwardens. These were partly secular, partly ecclesiastical officers, responsible both to the ordinary of the diocese and to the parochial meeting. While it was their duty to keep the church accounts, they also took part in the local police, and in the administration of the Poor Law. The vestry also drew up the list of substantial persons, from which the magistrates selected the surveyors of highways.

In the vast majority of rural or semi-rural parishes the line of cleavage between those who paid the local rates—the farmers and shopkeepers—and the agricultural labourers who did not pay them, was sufficiently distinct to make it easy to exclude the latter from the vestry meeting. Under those circumstances the parochial assembly would be composed of a small number of persons, who were usually, as tenants, dependent on the class from which the magistrates were taken. It is, nevertheless, highly significant of the limitations imposed upon the authority of the magistrates that these officials had always left to the small tenantry settled on their estates the right to share with themselves the administration of the local finances. In the large urban parishes one of two things happened. In some places the great mass of ratepayers took no interest in local affairs and left their entire management in the hands of the parish officers, who were appointed by cooptation under the control, more or less effective, of the magistrates. A primitive form of democracy had degenerated into oligarchy.[1] Elsewhere the inhabitants did not allow the rights of nomination and control, conferred upon them by immemorial custom, to fall thus into abeyance. Since, however, no written law or fixed precedent determined whether the right to take part in the vestry meeting belonged to all the inhabitants, or solely to the ratepayers, all attempts at distinction were abandoned when the ratepayers were counted by thousands and where class distinctions had been obliterated. During

1 Webb, *English Local Government*, vol. i. pp. 61 sqq.

the economic crisis which followed the restoration of peace in 1815, the inhabitants of several large towns were brought by skilful agitators to realize that it was in their power, by demanding a return to the traditional constitution of the vestry, to restore the annual control of the local budget to an assembly of all the inhabitants of the parish, perhaps even to invade prerogatives which the magistrates and their administrative subordinates had come to consider by every right their own.[1]   These petty local revolutions, which were now to take place here and there throughout the country, and against which the magistrates had no legal weapon, would so dismay the ruling class, that laws would be passed to facilitate the transformation of open into select vestries—that is to say, the substitution of a representative system for government by public meeting.

Like the direct government of the people by the people, government by rotation, in which each of the governed is called in turn to discharge the functions of legislator or executive official, would seem adapted only to societies of very small size and of rudimentary structure. Therefore we shall not be astonished to find this form of government in certain institutions, which were survivals from a primitive state of society.   Take, for instance, the organization of the parish and the choice of the parochial officers.   According to a very ancient tradition, which seems to have been regarded everywhere as possessing the force of law, in default of a special custom to the contrary, all the parishioners, or at least all the men of substance in the parish, discharged in rotation the functions of local government.[2]   Or take the ancient manorial institutions.   The essence alike of the court-baron and of the court-leet was a jury discharging functions at once legislative, executive and judicial.   This jury was composed of at least twelve men of substance, chosen either by rotation or by lot.[3]   Or again consider the organization of the counties.   The "Court of Quarter Sessions" was assisted by a "Grand Jury," and this not only in the performance of its strictly judicial functions but even in its administrative capacity. Without a presentment of the jury, the assembled justices were unable even to order the necessary expenditure for the repair of a prison or of a bridge.   England was a museum of constitutional archæology where the relics of past ages accumulated.   But the very mention of the word jury is sufficient to make us realize that in the British Constitution government by rotation was much more than a mere archæological

---

[1] Webb, *English Local Government*, vol. i. pp. 91 sqq.

[2] S. and B. Webb, *English Local Government*, vol. i. p. 16.   Cf. Toulmin Smith, *The Parish*, Preface : " The business of the Parish does not concern only the rates and taxes that every man has to pay.   It concerns the daily comfort, convenience and health of every man, rich as well as poor.   Moreover, every man is bound to serve Parish Offices in turn.   Nothing can, then, be more necessary than an accessible account of the Parish and its relations."

[3] Webb, *English Local Government*, vol. ii. pp. 15, 23 ; Gneist, *Verfassungs und Verwaltungsrecht*, vol. ii. p. 167.

curiosity. There was a jury at the Assizes alike in civil and in criminal cases. The jury system is, indeed, one of the fundamental institutions of English society. Historians derived its origin from the period of the Saxon Kings. And it was, they asserted, to be found clearly formulated in Magna Charta. Once universal throughout the Continent, it was only within the past century that it had been abolished in Sweden. In the near future it would be revived everywhere under the influence of the sole country which had been able to preserve its life and prestige unimpaired. In the eyes of Blackstone trial by jury was the palladium of British freedom, the guarantee of its imperishability. If Athens, Carthage and Rome had lost their liberty, it was due solely to the absence of the jury system.[1]

In civil cases the law provided that twelve jurors should be chosen by lot from a list made up for each session of the Assizes, and containing from forty-eight to seventy-two names. Very extensive rights of challenge were granted to the contending parties. Once constituted in due form, the twelve jurors heard the speeches of counsel, the evidence and the judge's summing-up. After this they retired into an adjoining room, where " in order to avoid intemperance and causeless delay " they were " kept without meat, drink, fire, or candle, unless by permission of the judge, till they were all unanimously agreed." [2]

In criminal cases the law almost always demanded that before this jury of twelve, the petty jury, entered upon its task, a grand jury of twenty-four members should have previously examined and preferred the indictment. And a further precaution was taken. The coroner, who inquired into cases of violent or sudden death, could only conduct his inquest as the president of a jury. The jurors were not, strictly speaking, judges; for here also the British Constitution was true to its mixed character, and gave one part of the decision to professional magistrates who determined the question of law, another part to the jurors who were called upon to determine the question of fact. But the line between fact and law was not always so easy to draw. A masterful judge would, in his summing-up, put the question of fact to the jurors in language so skilfully manipulated as to leave the jury no real share in the final decision. An indolent judge would, on the contrary, contrive so to confuse the questions of law and fact as to throw as far as possible upon the jury the entire responsibility for the verdict.[3] The war waged between the Crown and the Press throughout the latter half of the 18th century turned entirely on this difficulty. Was the question before the jury whether the article incriminated was, or was not, in fact, libellous ? Or were they merely asked to decide whether the journalist accused was, as a matter of fact, the author of

---

[1] 3 *Comm.* 379. Cf. Montesquieu, *Esprit des Lois*, Book II, chap. vi. ; 4 *Comm.* 343–4.
[2] Blackstone, 3 *Comm.* 375.
[3] Campbell, *Lives of the Chancellors*, vol. v. p. 443 (*Life of Lord Bathurst*).

the article incriminated, the further question of its libellous character being a question of law and therefore coming within the province of the judge ? Finally Parliament intervened and settled the doubt in the sense most favourable to the pretensions of the jury.[1] It is remarkable that throughout the debates the speakers of both parties vied with each other in their zeal for the maintenance of the rights of the jury. Even during the period of anti-Jacobin reaction which followed, these rights were never the object of serious attack. Although Lord Eldon had no love for juries, he found himself obliged in public to pronounce their panegyric.[2] Far from decaying, the institution spread. In 1815 it was extended to civil cases in Scotland.[3]

The jury system, and certain customs closely bound up with it, gave to English trials an appearance which shocked the foreign visitor, accustomed, as he was, to the formality of Continental courts. When the Westminster judges on circuit arrived at a county town, all the local society came to meet them. A season of festivities began for the county, in which the trials were an afternoon diversion. " Everything," wrote the Frenchman Cottu, " breathes a spirit of levity and mildness. The judge looks like a father in the midst of his family occupied in trying one of his children. His countenance has nothing threatening in it. According to an ancient custom, flowers are strewed upon his desk and upon the clerk's. The sheriff and officers of the court wear each a nosegay. By a condescension sufficiently extraordinary, the judge permits his Bench to be invaded by a throng of spectators, and thus finds himself surrounded by the prettiest women of the county—the sisters, wives or daughters of grand jurors. . . . They are attired in the most elegant *négligé* ; and it is a spectacle not a little curious to see the judge's venerable head loaded with a large wig, peering among the youthful female heads." [4] The English were not always so enthusiastic. Edgeworth relates in his *Memoirs* [5] that at Oxford, where it was the custom of the undergraduates to invade the court and create a scene of incredible uproar, he was compelled to intervene to save a prisoner who merely in consequence of the din was on the verge of an unjust and illegal condemnation. " It is," wrote another Englishman, " rather too much to see the ladies putting on their bonnets in the morning, to look at the judges and hear the prisoners condemned to death, and then take them off again to prepare for the dance at night. One would not expect that they should return home to eat no dinner ; but, without incurring the charge of any mawkish sentimentality, one may be permitted to feel something revolting in the very name of an assize-ball." [6] Objectionable

---

[1] 32 Geo. III, cap. 60.   [2] Campbell, *Lives of the Chancellors*, vol. v. pp. 66–7, 104.
[3] 55 Geo. III, cap. 42.   See Cockburn, *Life of Jeffrey*, vol. i. p. 240.
[4] Cottu, *Administration de la Justice Criminelle en Angleterre*, pp. 107–8, trans. Miller.
[5] *Memoirs of R. L. Edgeworth*, vol. i. pp. 95–7.
[6] R. Ayton, *Voyage round Great Britain*, vol. ii. p. 108.

or not, the custom reveals the real significance of the jury system, namely, that it is essentially trial *per patriam, per pais,* by the country, to use the traditional term. England desired the public to assist the judges in the administration of justice. Most certainly professional judges would know the law better than judges picked up for the occasion, but would they have the same interest in the protection of the rights of the subject? If they were permitted to dispense justice alone, what guarantees would the public possess against their cruelty, despotism or pedantry? Trial by jury carried out the principle underlying all popular government—control of efficiency by interest. Certainly we must not leave out of consideration the rules which determined the composition of the list out of which the jurors were chosen by lot. It was the sheriff, himself nominated by the King on the presentation of the magistrates, who drew up this list. Then was the time to eliminate all who did not belong to the governing aristocracy ; and although the law prescribed no pecuniary qualification for members of the Grand Jury at the Assizes, they were in reality always taken from the local gentry.[1] Now, if this is the case, must we not rank the jury system among the institutions employed by the aristocracy to defend their position against encroachments of the Crown officials, but unable to exercise any check on oppression by that aristocracy itself? Let us beware of exaggeration.

In the first place, what is true of the Grand Jury at the Assizes is not true of the Grand Jury at Quarter Sessions. In this latter case, while the aristocracy judged, the Grand Jury was taken from the middle class.[2] And, again, what is true of the provinces, especially those truly rural, is not true of the great urban centres. There the landed aristocracy took no interest in public life, and abandoned judicial functions to the middle, even to the lower middle class.[3] And, further, what is true of the Grand Jury is not true of the Petty Jury. From members of the Petty Jury the law demanded only the freehold property of land producing an annual income of at least £10 a year, or a life tenancy at a rent of at least £20. And since the work of a juryman made no small demand on time, and there existed many legal methods by which a man could have his name taken off the list, the gentry exempted themselves from jury service and representatives of the middle class sat on the petty juries, well-to-do merchants at the Assizes, small shopkeepers at Quarter Sessions. "Every new tribunal," wrote Blackstone, "erected for the decision of facts, without the intervention of a jury . . . is a step towards establishing aristocracy, the most oppres-

---

[1] This no doubt occasioned the attacks directed by advanced Liberals against the Grand Jury. See, for instance, *Edinburgh Review*, December 1828, No. 96, Art. 5, *Police of the Metropolis and Prevention of Crime* (vol. xlviii. pp. 415–16).

[2] Webb, *English Local Government*, vol. i. p. 447.

[3] *Ibid.*, vol. i. pp. 524–6.

sive of absolute governments. . . . In every country on the Continent,"
as trial by jury " has been gradually disused, so the nobles have increased
in power." ¹ The professional judges, both in their private correspondence and in conversation, displayed a sovereign contempt for the
democratic character of the juries : " petty juries, county assizes and
untutored mechanics " was the scornful exclamation of Thurlow.²
In the capital, where, as in all the large towns, there was nothing
aristocratic about the body of magistrates, the Prime Minister Perceval
complained in 1810 that the Under-Sheriff of Middlesex always
empanelled democratic juries to try political cases.³ When that same
year the Duke of Cumberland scandal occurred, it was a Charing
Cross tailor called Francis Place, the great leader of the local democrats,
who, in the capacity of foreman of the jury, made his way into
St. James' Palace and there carried out the inquest.⁴

There exists also a third form of popular government, namely
representative government. Far from being adapted, like government
by public meeting and government by rotation, solely to small and
rudimentary societies, representative government seemed to have been
devised for the express purpose of enabling a vast population to govern,
through the medium of elected representatives, a great civilized nation.
In the assemblage of institutions which composed together the government of Great Britain, the King constituted the monarchic element,
the Upper House the aristocratic element, and the Lower House, as
representing the people, the popular element. The members of the
House of Commons owed their seats to the working of a highly complex
and heterogeneous franchise. This " heterogeneity " was the object
of widely differing criticisms. Conservatives ⁵ saw in it a guarantee
for the representation in Parliament of all classes and interests. The
discontented, on the contrary, maintained that this heterogeneity was
sheer muddle, and a muddle which had deprived the vast majority of
the citizens of the means to make their will prevail, or even to make
their voice heard, in the counsels of the nation. We must, therefore,
undertake a detailed examination of the British representative system.
Only after such examination can we decide how far it really deserved
this appellation and to what extent the House of Commons in 1815
did really express the opinion of the country.

Complexity of the Franchise.   Scotland, Ireland, Wales.

The British system of representative government was, in the first
place, " heterogeneous," because the United Kingdom was composed

---

¹ 3 *Comm.* 380.   ² Campbell, *Lives of the Chancellors*, vol. v. p. 500.
³ *Diary of Lord Colchester*, April 15, 1810 (vol. ii. p. 361).
⁴ See Graham Wallas, *Life of Francis Place*, pp. 54–5.
⁵ Among these must be included many of the moderate reformers. See *Edinburgh Review*,
December 1818, No. 61, Art. 8, *Universal Suffrage* (vol. xxxi. p. 180).

of several distinct nations. Scarcely more than a century had passed since the union between Scotland and England. The parliamentary union between Ireland and England only dated from 1800. In the case of the Welsh principality, it is true that the English conquest had taken place in the very distant days of King Edward I, and that it had never possessed a separate constitution. It was, none the less, a real nation, with a distinctive culture and language of its own. It might even be said to possess also a distinctive religion of its own, since Calvinistic Methodism seemed destined to become the creed of the majority of the population. And the operation of the franchise differed in these three nations from its operation in England ; nor was it even the same in Ireland, in Scotland and in Wales.

With a population of two million inhabitants Scotland returned forty-five representatives ; but only by a legal fiction could these forty-five members be considered to represent two million Scotchmen. According to the principle obtaining throughout the United Kingdom they were divided into the representatives of the rural constituencies, the "counties," and the representatives of the urban constituencies, the "burghs." The thirty-six county representatives were returned to Parliament by a body of not more than 2,405 electors. In the counties the franchise was confined to freeholders whose land was liable to a tax of 45s. on lists drawn up at the close of the 13th or at the beginning of the 14th century. The electors might either be absolute proprietors, or tenants holding immediately of the Crown. And the number of county electors in Scotland would have been even more restricted had not the landlords devised means to create in their own interest a certain number of tenants who, while their nominal status was that of tenants-in-chief of the Crown, were in reality their dependents. The fifteen representatives of the Scottish burghs, the royal burghs, represented, on the other hand, a body of 1,220 electors. Of these, however, only thirty-three, the members of the corporation of Edinburgh, directly elected their representative. The other elections were indirect. The burghs were combined in groups of four or five, and each group sent a representative to Westminster.

An electorate so scanty was naturally at the mercy of the omnipotent influence of the local nobility. And what was the result of this ? Undoubtedly clan rivalries kept up a semblance of political life. The Whig, Sir James Mackintosh, had been returned for Nairnshire in 1813, owing to the support of the Thane of Cawdor. His election had caused a sensation and was regarded as the first sign of a new epoch.[1]

---

[1] At the elections of 1812, the fact that Sir John Dalrymple dared to stand as Whig candidate for the constituency of Midlothian, which was considered as the appanage of the Dundas family, had already appeared remarkable. See Cockburn, *Memorials*, pp. 273–4. For the Scottish elections of 1812, see *Morning Chronicle*, October 12, 1812 ; Smith, *Register of Contested Elections*, pp. 126 sqq. ; Porritt, *Unreformed Parliament*, vol. ii. p. 175.

But the very astonishment aroused by this episode helps us to realize what was the normal character of a Scottish election at the beginning of the 19th century. The great families sold their support for places and titles to the Government in office of whatever political complexion it might be. It was the rule that "the management of Scotland," as it was termed, should be entrusted to a particular member of the Cabinet. Under Tory government this task fell to the Dundas family, to the first[1] and second Lord Melville. It was universally taken for granted that Scotland always supported the Government. Nevertheless, Scotland—or at least lowland Scotland—was one of the most active centres of British civilization. Whether for agriculture or manufactures the Lowlands could bear comparison with any English county. The Universities of Glasgow, Edinburgh, Aberdeen and St. Andrews, organized on the Continental system, despised the lifeless routine of Oxford and Cambridge. At the Bar, in journalism, in letters, the Scottish had won the first places. How then could so progressive a nation endure, even provisionally, a system so oligarchic? It was because the system, as it had functioned during the last half-century, functioned in the national interest. The Scottish could do without the help of the Government when it was a question of establishing factories, or of making money by speech or writing; but they could not dispense with it when it was a question of obtaining posts in the public service. The "South Briton" endowed the "North Briton" with the attributes of audacity, obstinacy and freedom from prejudice, and therefore felt a deep-rooted distrust of him. How was this unpopularity to be overcome? The Scottish aristocracy undertook the task. The Ministry knew that it could count on forty Scottish votes, provided a fixed number of posts in the Army and the Civil Service were put at the disposal of Scotland. Never had the great Scottish families sold on other terms than these the seats which they controlled; never, or hardly ever, had they allowed anyone of English birth to represent one of their electoral fiefs.[2] The exclusiveness of their local patriotism explains, to a large extent, why Scotland endured a franchise so outrageous. The system was one of the means which she employed for the conquest of England.

Would the same thing happen in Ireland as in Scotland? The Opposition speakers expressed this fear when, in 1800, Pitt effected the parliamentary union of England and Ireland. Was it not, they asked, his intention to increase by this means his majority in Parlia-

---

[1] For his life, and the power of his family in Scotland, see an interesting notice in the *Annual Register*, 1801, pp. 133 sqq.

[2] No such case ever occurred, according to Wakefield (*Ireland*, vol. ii. p. 314). Nevertheless, Porritt (*Unreformed House of Commons*, vol. ii. p. 131) notices two exceptions: the *historic* instance of Fox, and that of George Damer, Lord Milton's eldest son, elected in 1775 for the Crail District of Scottish burghs. Some other instances were to occur in the 19th century before the Reform of 1832.

ment and to buy the votes of the Irish representatives who would sit henceforward at Westminster, as he already bought those of the Scottish representatives ? [1] Had not a member of the Cabinet been entrusted, almost officially, since 1800 with the management of the Irish members ? [2] Nevertheless, Ireland did not resemble Scotland. Her customs were different ; her traditions were different ; both the degree and the character of her civilization were different. An identical franchise would have operated differently in the two countries. And the franchise was not identical.

Thirty-six members of the House of Commons represented the thirty-four urban constituencies of Ireland, the " cities " or " boroughs." The Irish boroughs had not the same character as the Scottish. Like the English boroughs, with which we shall deal presently, they had constitutions differing in different places, either fixed by charter or statute, or determined by immemorial custom. In fact, only nine of these constituencies—ten, if we include the University of Dublin— were regarded in 1815 as " open " constituencies—that is, constituencies where the electorate was to some extent free and conscious of its power.[3] The remainder were divided into two unequal classes. There were eighteen boroughs,[4] where the franchise belonged to a close corporation, to twelve burgesses chosen by cooptation. In these cases the right to elect the member was the private property of the landlord, who had succeeded in making himself the " patron " of the corporation. In the six remaining boroughs[5] the franchise belonged either to the free-holders or to the members of the local corporation, the freemen, an indefinite number of whom could be created. Here also the influence of the great local landowner was supreme. The freeholders were at his beck and call ; and if he were their patron, the corporation bestowed the freedom of the borough on all his nominees.

Despite all this the electorate was more numerous than that of the Scottish boroughs, and the control of the aristocracy was perhaps somewhat less absolute. This aristocracy, moreover, possessed political traditions more ancient than those of the Scottish aristocracy, and was bound less strictly to the Government in office. But in other respects electoral conditions were worse than in Scotland ; for the

---

[1] H. of C., April 2, 1800, Grey's speech (*Parl. Hist.*, vol. xxxv. p. 71).

[2] See on this matter the advice given to Addington by Abbot in 1801 (*Diary of Lord Colchester*, vol. i. pp. 326 sqq.). Cf. *ibid.*, vol. i. p. 517, Wickham's letter to Abbot, May 21, 1804.

[3] Carrickfergus, Cork City, Drogheda, Dublin City, Londonderry, Dungarvan, Downpatrick, Newry, Waterford. This list is taken from Wakefield, *Ireland*, vol. ii. pp. 218 sqq., and Oldfield, *Representative History*, vol. vi. pp. 209 sqq., 297 sqq. Plowden, *Historical Review of . . . Ireland*, vol. ii. Appendix, pp. 227–8, makes out, for the period anterior to the Union, a list of twelve popular constituencies (including Dublin University). The borough of Swords (since abolished) and that of Lisburn (considered by Wakefield and Oldfield as under the patronage of the Marquis of Hertford) are added.

[4] Belfast, Armagh, Carlow, Ennis, Youghall, Bandon Bridge, Kinsale, Enniskillen, Tralee, Dundalk, Portarlington, Sligo, Clonmel, Cashel, Dungannon, Athlone, Wexford, New Ross.

[5] Lisburn, Mallow, Galway, Kilkenny, Limerick, Coleraine.

Irish aristocracy which controlled the borough representation was not, like the Scottish, a national aristocracy. Set up in Ireland by the right of conquest, it possessed nothing in common with the majority of the population. It was, moreover, Protestant, whereas the poorer classes of the country were Catholic ; and although, since 1792, Catholics had been eligible for membership of the borough corporations, since these were filled by cooptation, Catholics remained in practice excluded. A Protestant minority, therefore, exploited the country as if it had been a plantation, with no other aim in view save to draw from it as many advantages and as much revenue as possible.

In Ireland a borough seat was for sale and possessed a recognized market value which varied from time to time. When, in 1800, it was decided that certain boroughs which had been represented in the Dublin Parliament should have no separate representation at Westminster, it was actually found necessary to pass an Act of expropriation to indemnify those " whose property was bound up with the constituencies in question." Each seat suppressed had cost the Treasury £2,000. From a document contemporary with the election described we learn that in the general election of 1807 thirteen Irish boroughs sent an Englishman to represent them at Westminster. Of these thirteen some few had been chosen for political reasons by a patron acting in obedience to the orders of his party leaders. An instance of this was George Tierney elected for Bandon Bridge, a seat entirely in the hands of Lord Bandon, because he had been defeated in England and the Opposition could not dispense with his services. The rest— such men as Mr. Strahan, a London printer, elected for Carlow, and Mr. Wigram, a London merchant, elected for New Ross—were wealthy men who paid hard cash for the privilege of entering simultaneously Parliament and good society.[1] Such facts show that the Irish aristocracy employed their electoral patronage for ends very different from those of the Scottish nobility. In one way or another only English politics were concerned in the Irish borough, the interests of Ireland were ignored entirely.

The thirty-two Irish counties returned sixty-four members to the House of Commons, two members for each county. The county franchise belonged to all the forty-shilling freeholders. It was therefore identical with the franchise of the English counties. But forty-shilling freeholders were far more numerous in Ireland than in England. Curwen, who visited Ireland in 1813, was astonished to find the franchise in several Irish counties so wide as almost to approach universal

---

[1] In these two boroughs the electorate consisted of twelve burgesses chosen by cooptation. At Carlow the patron was Lord Charleville, at New Ross Mr. Tottenham and Mr. Lee exercised the patronage in turn (Wakefield, *Ireland*, vol. ii. pp. 302, 310). Cf. John O'Connell, *Life and Speeches of Daniel O'Connell*, vol. i. p. 52 ; O'Connell's speech at Dublin, September 18, 1810 : " What is the fact ? Why, that out of the 100, such as they are, that sit for this country, more than one-fifth know nothing of us, or are unknown to us."

suffrage.[1] The vast majority of these electors were bogus freeholders, the creation of the landlords, who regarded the exercise of the franchise as a sort of feudal due or *corvée* attached to the usufruct of the soil.[2] As a general rule they voted as their landlords directed. Nevertheless, the game played by the landlords when they multiplied the freeholders on their estates was by no means without its risks for themselves. During the opening years of the 19th century these risks were becoming visible.

Since 1800, and especially since 1807, public opinion had been faced with the problem whether or no Catholics should be allowed to sit in the House of Lords, and should be capable of holding posts in the Army and Civil Service, and of election to the House of Commons. It was not likely that the priests would fail to make the Irish peasants realize that they had both the power and the duty to take an active part in the solution of the problem. If all the tenants in a county agreed to return a candidate favourable to Catholic emancipation, the landlords would be defenceless against this universal movement of popular opinion. And there was nothing to prevent a tenant who had quarrelled with his landlord subdividing his tenure among a number of tenants for life, and thus creating a body of electors dependent on himself and hostile to the great landowner. When in 1805 Lord Castlereagh, a former supporter of emancipation who had subsequently deserted the cause, was defeated for County Down, Dublin welcomed the news of his defeat with every manifestation of popular rejoicing. Lord Henry Petty, who witnessed these rejoicings, predicted the rapid decline of Government influence. "There is in most counties," he wrote to Creevy, "a rising spirit of independence, and the weight of the Catholic interest will be strongly felt."[3] Some months later, when Lord Loftus succeeded to the title of Marquis of Ely and entered the House of Lords, the electors of the county of Wexford returned a man of obscure origin in opposition to the family of the new marquis.[4] On the whole, the Catholic agitation made constant progress, notably in Tipperary and Roscommon.[5] It was only in the boroughs that the nature of the franchise rendered the position of the great landowners impregnable. In the counties they owed their supremacy

---

[1] Curwen, *Ireland*, vol. ii. pp. 20–1. For the detailed statistics see the present work, Book II, chap. i

[2] For electoral purposes not only proprietors were deemed to be freeholders, but also tenants whose lease was at least for life. In determining the annual income derived from the land, the tenant's oath was always accepted in Ireland.

[3] *Creevy Papers*, vol. i. p. 43 (letter of October 24, 1805). Cf. *ibid.*, pp. 62–3. It must be admitted that Lord Castlereagh's defeat was by no means a typical case. County Down was Protestant. Lord Castlereagh failed because he was opposed by the powerful Marquis of Downshire. In 1812, with the Marquis' good-will, he was to secure his election (Henry Grattan, *Life and Times of Grattan*, vol. v. pp. 497–9).

[4] Wakefield, *Ireland*, vol. ii. p. 310.

[5] *Ibid.*, vol. ii. pp. 771–2.

not to the nature of the franchise, but to the disposition of the electors.[1] This disposition was changing, and it wanted but a few years for a universal revolt of freeholders to break out in all the rural constituencies of Ireland.

The principality of Wales does not require such lengthy treatment as Scotland or Ireland. It was a tiny country with primitive manners and a backward civilization, although the iron and coal mines were already beginning to enrich the southern half of the principality. With two exceptions, the boroughs possessed a franchise much more democratic than the franchise of Scottish or Irish boroughs. " The influence which prevails," wrote Oldfield, a severe critic of the established system, " is not the produce of corruption, but arises from the popularity and hospitality of men of considerable property. . . . An instance of bribery is very uncommon among them, nor are their morals debauched by frequent invitations to election treats, which are the parents of drunkenness, idleness and dissipation." [2]

It is evident, from what has been said, that we are not entitled to pronounce a wholesale condemnation upon the parliamentary franchise as it operated in Scotland, Ireland and Wales. It is indeed true that the forty-five representatives of Scotland, returned by an infinitesimal number of electors, had made it their regular practice to support the Government in office whatever its complexion. But of the hundred Irish constituencies, there were sixty-four where the rural electorate would be perfectly free, whenever they should desire to do so, to return Catholic and revolutionary members to Parliament. It would not even be true to say that the thirty-six remaining constituencies were, without exception, under the despotic power of the aristocracy ; and the electors who returned the twenty-four representatives of Wales were universally regarded as honest and independent, and public opinion approved their choice. Nevertheless, our study of the Scottish, Irish and Welsh franchise has but cleared the approaches to the problem. To discover the extent to which the House of Commons, taken as a whole, represented the will of the nation, we must analyse the laws and customs which regulated the election of the 489 representatives of England. Once more we are faced with a highly complex problem. The county franchise differed from the borough franchise, and the franchise of one borough differed from the franchise of another.

[1] Wakefield, *Ireland*, vol. ii. p. 308. See *Life and Speeches of Daniel O'Connell*, vol. i. pp. 223 sqq. for an interesting description, given by O'Connell in a speech of November 5, 1812, of the progress registered at the last elections by the cause of Catholic emancipation.

[2] Oldfield, *Representative History*, vol. vi. p. 1. With the exception of Walter Wilkins, the Member for Radnorshire, whose birth was obscure, and who had purchased an estate in Wales after making a fortune in India, all the Welsh members belonged to the gentry (W. R. Williams, *Parl. Hist. of Wales*). H. R. Smith registers six contested elections in 1812 (one of these a county election). This is certainly a considerable proportion (H. R. Smith, *Register of Contested Elections*, 120 sqq.).

The Franchise in England. The Counties.

The franchise was identical throughout the counties. It belonged to freeholders whose land brought in an annual revenue of forty shillings. But the elections by no means presented the same character in all counties alike. There were counties in which, owing to the presence of dockyards, naval ports or bonded warehouses, the influence of the Government was peculiarly strong. Such a county was Hampshire,[1] and to a lesser degree Kent. There were others which presented the character of great urban constituencies, and where influence of all kinds, whether of the Government or of the local aristocracy, was in consequence enfeebled. Such, for instance, were Warwickshire and Yorkshire. The remaining counties could be arranged in a scale. At one extreme would be found the counties in which a handful of great landowners exerted an irresistible pressure upon the electors. This was the case in Westmorland, which was dominated by the all-powerful influence of the Lowther family. At the other extreme would be found the counties where the small proprietors and those with estates of moderate size were very numerous, and where in consequence the aristocracy found it more difficult to assert their authority. This was the case, for instance, in Shropshire, where the haughty independence of the freeholders was proverbial. Nevertheless, critics of the established system were inclined to denounce as universal the excessive influence of the great landowners. Only six or seven of the forty English counties are classed by Oldfield as independent.[2] Possibly the decline of the rural industries and the increase of large estates had even increased the electoral influence wielded by the aristocracy. On the whole, despite the variety of conditions, it is possible to arrive at an average type of English county in which, although the influence of the aristocracy was very strong, it was not unlimited, and where the large landed proprietors to maintain their authority must incur very great trouble and expense. The poll was taken at one place only in each county. Thither the freeholders of the county came to give their vote in public on the hustings where the sheriff sat among the local landowners. The candidates were obliged to defray the electors' travelling expenses from their homes to the hustings. They had, moreover, to pay for their board and lodging during the election. The law allowed the polling to continue for a fortnight, and the great question was which of the rival candidates would abandon the contest first. There existed a regular system of electioneering tactics, an art of holding in reserve troops of electors or sending them into action as the circumstances demanded, and of overwhelming the enemy by a sudden display of forces at the right

---

[1] Oldfield, *Representative History*, vol. iii. pp. 494–5. Cf. Cobbett's *Political Register*, November 22, 1806.

[2] Oldfield, *Representative History*, vol. iv. p. 54.

moment. The following instances will enable us to form some idea of the expenses entailed by an electioneering campaign in the counties. Sir William Geary, returned unopposed for Kent in 1812, warned the freeholders that they were sending to Westminster a ruined man, since his contests in 1776 and in 1802 had cost him £22,000.[1] In 1807 the three candidates contesting the two Yorkshire seats spent almost £500,000.[2]

Sometimes the smaller gentry and independent freeholders revolted against the yoke of the great local families. In the elections of 1812 Sir Gilbert Heathcote, of Normanton Park in Rutland, stood for that county. He appeared at Oakham, the county town, with a following of 500 freeholders, mounted on horseback, and snatched from the Marquis of Exeter a seat which since 1747 his family had regarded as their hereditary fief.[3] As a general rule, however, candidates shrank from contests so costly. Only nine county elections were contested in 1807, only two in 1812.[4] There were two seats for each county. In the majority of counties[5] the great families found that their most prudent policy was to agree to divide the seats—one of the two being allotted to the Whigs, the other to the Tories. In Yorkshire an agreement of this nature had been concluded between the two great local families, the Whig House of Wentworth and the Tory House of Harewood. In 1807 Wilberforce defied the coalition, stood as an independent candidate, and won his seat from the Harewoods.[6] In 1812, however, he retired from the field. When another attempted to take his place, the Harewoods announced publicly that they were prepared to spend £30,000 on the contest. The candidate beat a retreat and the traditional system triumphed.[7] Bitter were the complaints of the reformers. How could such a system fail to deprive the majority of counties to all intents and purposes of their representation?

Nevertheless, the injustice was not so glaring as would appear at first sight. On a vast number of questions, economic, administrative and religious, there existed a natural solidarity between the county

---

[1] *Morning Chronicle*, October 14, 1812 ; Oldfield, *Representative History*, vol. v. p. 268.

[2] Oldfield, *Representative History*, vol. v. p. 268. Cf. Miss Edgeworth, *Patronage*, chap. xvi : " Sir James Harcourt . . . a courtier who, after having ruined his fortune by standing for Government two contested county elections, had dangled year after year at Court, living upon the hope and promise of a pension or a place, till his creditors warning him that they could wait no longer, he had fallen in love with Lady Angelica Headingham." Also Wordsworth, *The Excursion*, Book VI :

> " When he had crushed a plentiful estate
> By ruinous contest, to obtain a seat
> In Britain's senate."

[3] *Morning Chronicle*, October 20, 1812 ; Oldfield, *Representative History*, vol. iv p. 371

[4] Jephson, *The Platform*, vol. i. pp. 323, 346.

[5] In twenty-six of the forty (Oldfield, *Representative History*, vol. iv. p. 132).

[6] *Life of Wilberforce*, vol. iii. pp. 315 sqq.

[7] *Morning Chronicle*, October 10, 26, 27, 1812 ; *Leeds Mercury*, October 3, 14, 17, 24, 1812 ; *Newcastle Chronicle*, October 17, 1812.

electors and their representatives in Parliament, to whichever party the latter belonged. To take only one instance, both constituents and members in the English counties were convinced supporters of protection with a common interest to secure agriculture against foreign competition by the imposition of a heavy tariff. Even where the community of interest or sentiment was less perfect, the very nature of the franchise obliged the great landowners to respect the opinions of those who returned themselves, their relations or their clients to Parliament. If they wished to play a part in politics, they must prove accommodating in their dealings with the farmers, indeed with all their humbler neighbours. They must be prepared to spend lavishly on all occasions, to support local societies and to give public entertainments. All this was costly enough even in the intervals between elections, but popularity was not to be obtained at a cheaper rate. When in 1816 Brougham decided to defy the head of the Lowthers, the powerful Lord Lonsdale, in his own county of Westmorland, he was amused to see this great nobleman in preparation for the approaching contest, "bleeding at every pore—all the houses open—all the agents running up bills—all the manors shot over by anybody who pleases." [1] The great English landowner was not, like a great landowner in Ireland, a species of slave-owner, convinced that he had a right to the peasants' toil every day throughout the year and to his vote at an election. If he counted on the votes of his tenants, he treated them in return with a liberality which farmers—who were not downtrodden peasants but men of substance and standing—had come to consider their right.

To be sure, country gentlemen now took a larger share in city life than had formerly been the case. Admirers of the past regretted the days when they only visited London at rare intervals, when their departure was a local event and the bells of the parish church welcomed their return. But they still spent the greater part of the year on their estates; and even in town and in Parliament they remained, and were proud to remain, countrymen. The county members, the representatives of their class in the House of Commons, formed a distinct group with their peculiar traditions. By an unwritten law they alone had the right to wear spurs in the House. [2] They were symbols of the "old England," essentially aristocratic and rural, and voiced all the suspicion felt in the provinces for the Court and for officialdom.

"It is the subserviency of agriculture to the wants of mankind, connected perhaps with its sober and healthful pleasures, and the spirit of independence which it fosters, that has secured to it, in every age, the first rank among the useful arts, and obtained for it, in every country,

---

[1] *Creevy Papers*, vol. i. p. 254. Cf. Cottu, *Administration de la Justice Criminelle en Angleterre*, p. 161: "In England extensive tracts of land belonging to the chief noblemen of the realm are let by them for a rent of half their real value, solely in order to secure votes."

[2] *Diary of Lord Colchester*, March 18, 1796 (vol. i. p. 45).

the patronage of those most eminent for wisdom and virtue. The honours paid to it in China take their date from the remotest antiquity ; and through the purer ages of the Roman Republic it was held in the highest estimation. In our own country the name of Russell, so proudly distinguished in the annals of freedom, stands pre-eminent among those who have patronized this noble art ; and the great founder of American liberty, when the toils and dangers of warfare were ended, retired to the cultivation of that soil which his valour and his virtues had rendered free." This is the language of the *Edinburgh Review*,[1] the organ of advanced Liberalism ; and although that journal waged an unremitting campaign in favour of a reform of the franchise, no attacks were made upon the county franchise. The day was indeed not far off when the Liberal Party would be the party of the towns in opposition to a country party representative of the old social order. But in 1815 the Opposition was still disposed to admit that the county members, who represented the agricultural interest, formed the healthiest element of the House of Commons, since their constituents were beyond the reach of ministerial corruption.[2] At the general election of 1812, which had on the whole been favourable to the Government, the Opposition had gained four or five county seats.[3] Men such as Charles Western and Thomas Coke were at once county members and typical Whigs. The criticism of the advocates of reform was directed entirely against the borough franchise. But we must remember that as against eighty county members at Westminster there were, exclusive of the four representatives of the Universities of Oxford and Cambridge, 405 members representing the English cities and boroughs. Alone they formed four-sixths of the House of Commons. On our estimate of the borough representation of England must depend our estimate of the representative system of the United Kingdom.

[1] *Edinburgh Review*, January 1814, No. 44, Art. 1 ; Sir H. Davy's *Elements of Agricultural Chemistry* (vol. xxii. p. 251).

[2] H. of C., May 4, 1809, Curwen's speech : " The peculiar advantage of having a landed proprietor in this House is that each individual brings with him the affections and the confidence of a portion of the people. . . . The infallible consequence, sir, of increasing the numbers of our country gentlemen within these walls, would be to make us more pacifically disposed. . . . It would turn our efforts and our attention to domestic improvement, to the melioration of our internal resources and the happiness of our country" (*Parl. Deb.*, vol. xiv. pp. 362–3). The elections of 1780, Fitzmaurice, *Life of Lord Shelburne*, vol. ii. pp. 74–5. See also Lord Shelburne's letter to Lord Mahon, April 2, 1780 (Porritt, *Unreformed House of Commons*, vol. i. p. 280) : " It is acknowledged that the approaching election has a very great influence on the divisions now taking place in the House of Commons in favour of reform and redress of grievances. The county members have very generally voted on the public side, except a few who are likely to lose their seats for not doing so." The Elections of 1784, Moore, *Life of Sheridan*, p. 178 : " At length, however, the spirit of the people, that last and only resource against the venality of Parliaments and the obstinacy of Kings, was roused from its long and dangerous sleep by the unparalleled exertions of the Opposition leaders. . . . The effect of this popular feeling soon showed itself in the upper regions. The country gentlemen, those birds of political omen, whose migrations are so portentous of a change of weather, began to flock in numbers to the brightening quarter of Opposition."

[3] *Morning Chronicle*, November 5, 1812.

The English Franchise. Open Boroughs.

We will consider, first of all, the fifty-three boroughs where the franchise was extremely wide. In thirteen of these [1] it belonged to all the inhabitants not in receipt of poor relief and able to provide themselves with the necessities of life "to keep their pot boiling." Hence arose the term "potwallopers" or "potwallers" sometimes given to the electors of these boroughs where a system of practically universal suffrage prevailed. There was even one of these thirteen boroughs, namely Preston, where the franchise was given to all the inhabitants without exception. In thirty-six boroughs,[2] the franchise was granted only to those who paid the local imposts, scot and lot. To these thirteen potwallers' boroughs and thirty-six scot-and-lot boroughs must be added certain boroughs where the vote was possessed either by the forty-shilling freeholders, as in the counties, or by all the freeholders. But in nine of these the franchise was mixed and the freeholders were not in the majority. They must therefore be classed under other headings. There remain the double borough of Weymouth and Melcombe Regis where the freeholders, all of whom possessed the franchise, formed the majority of the electorate, and the three boroughs of New Shoreham, Cricklade and Aylesbury, where the area of the constituency had been enlarged by three Acts passed successively since the accession of George III, and where the suffrage had been granted, as in the counties, to all the forty-shilling freeholders.[3] Thus the parliamentary reformers who asked for an extension of the franchise found their ideal partially realized already in the electoral system of the country. If, with Major Cartwright,[4] they desired a system of universal suffrage such as obtained in America, they were demanding the extension to the whole of the United Kingdom of the system which obtained in the potwallers' boroughs. If with Horne Tooke [5] they were content to demand the grant of the franchise to those who occupied a house assessed for taxation, they found their ideal in the scot-and-lot boroughs.

[1] Bedford, Cirencester, Hertford, Hindon, Honiton, Ilchester, Minehead, Northampton, Pontefract, Taunton, Tregony, Wendover, also the borough of Preston. Porritt (*Unreformed House of Commons*, vol. i. p. 30) enumerates fifty-nine scot-and-lot boroughs. He probably included under this heading the fifty-three boroughs classified as such by us together with a certain number of boroughs with a mixed franchise which we have classified elsewhere.

[2] Abingdon, Aldborough (Yorkshire), Amersham, Arundel, Bridgwater, Bridport, Callington, Camelford, Chichester, Dorchester, Eye, Fowey, Gatton, Great Marlow, Leicester, Leominster, Lewes, Newark, Penryn, Peterborough, Reading, St. Ives, St. Michael's, Seaford, Shaftesbury, Southwark, Stamford, Steyning, Stockbridge, Tamworth, Wallingford, Wareham, Warwick, Westminster, Windsor, Wootton Bassett.

[3] 10 Geo. III, cap. 55 ; 22 Geo. III, cap. 31 ; 44 Geo. III, cap. 60.

[4] *Life and Correspondence of Major Cartwright*, vol. i. pp. 82 sqq. Cf. our *Formation du Radicalisme Philosophique*, vol. i. pp. 227 sqq.

[5] A. Stephens, *Life of Tooke*, vol. i. pp. 501 sqq. ; vol. ii. pp. 463, 479. *Formation du Radicalisme Philosophique*, vol. ii. pp. 198 sqq. This was the proposal which *in the years immediately preceding* 1815 was supported by Sir Francis Burdett, Bentham and Cartwright himself.

Indeed, if the system obtaining in the fifty-three boroughs of which we are now speaking had existed in all the English constituencies, they would have been democratic, or to use the traditional phrase "popular" constituencies. But this was far from being the case. The most important towns were not among the popular constituencies. When they had been granted the right to send representatives to Parliament, the intention of the Government had not been to bestow upon them the parliamentary representation to which they were entitled by their importance, but to extend its patronage, and to increase its influence at Westminster by falsifying at need the representation of the country.

Again, for more than a century the franchise had remained unaltered, although the distribution of the population throughout the entire kingdom had been profoundly modified. Great towns had grown up which had no parliamentary representation. Although many of the boroughs had grown in every direction, the boundaries of the constituency remained those of the old town. Taunton, for instance, would have counted 1,200 electors had all the quarters of the town taken part in elections. In reality the number of electors scarcely attained the third of this figure, for they were confined to one part of one of the town parishes.[1] Only half the district and population of Guildford actually possessed the scot-and-lot franchise.[2] At Southwark, the entire parish of Christ Church and half the parish of St. Saviour petitioned to be included in the parliamentary borough.[3] Elsewhere a decayed borough preserved its representation intact. The franchise was certainly democratic, but the electors were a mere handful. There were nine electors in the borough of Camelford, where the Duke of Bedford owned all the houses, and in 1812 had sold the borough and its representation for the sum of £32,000.[4] At Gatton there was only one elector. The six houses in the borough belonged to Sir Mark Wood, who occupied one himself, let the other five by the week, paid all the rates and taxes, and thus was the sole person in the borough entitled to exercise the scot-and-lot franchise.[5]

Moreover, the smaller the number of electors in a constituency the more easily was a majority changed by a slight alteration in the voting. The returning officer, who was a nominee of the local aristocracy, skilfully took advantage of the complexity of the franchise arbitrarily to allow or refuse a certain number of votes, and thus to turn the balance in the direction desired.[6] It is true that the candidate

---

[1] Oldfield, *Representative History*, vol. iv. pp. 436, 438.
[2] *Ibid.*, vol. iv. pp. 593-4.
[3] *Ibid.*, vol. iv. pp. 587-8.
[4] *Ibid.*, vol. iii. p. 236.
[5] *Ibid.*, vol. iv. p. 606.
[6] For instance, the law deprived public officials of the franchise. An official came forward to vote. The crowd protested. But the returning officer declared that the official in question had been appointed by the county, not by the central government, and accepted his vote (Oldfield, *Representative History*, vol. iii. p. 295). In another place the law granted the franchise

injured by such trickery could seek redress from Parliament. The electors whose vote had been illegally refused would be only too glad to come up and give evidence in his favour. But they would only do this if he paid the expenses of their journey to London and their board and lodging in the capital during the inquiry, which of course his opponent would take care to protract as long as possible. He had need be as wealthy as a " nabob " to support the expense of a " petition " of this kind before a parliamentary committee. Moreover, there was always the chance of an unfavourable result. Only too often the vanquished candidate found it more prudent to accept his defeat. Frequently the candidate who did not possess noble patronage retreated before the contest began. This was the reason why at every general election so many boroughs were uncontested.

From the foregoing considerations we see how difficult it is to estimate the resistance which the fifty-two boroughs possessing a democratic franchise were able to oppose to the influence of the aristocracy, to the pressure of the Government, to electoral corruption in all its forms. To arrive at even an approximate estimate we must classify them in distinct groups. We may leave out of account the two rotten boroughs of Camelford and Gatton, to which we may add the borough of Saint-Michael with its eighteen electors. The remaining boroughs fall naturally into three groups.

The first group comprises the constituencies—twenty-two in all —where the number of electors ranged from fifty to three hundred.[1] Poor men whose house and field were the property of a member of the ruling aristocracy, could not but feel themselves absolutely dependent upon him. Of such it may be affirmed without paradox that electoral corruption was their first instrument of emancipation. When the scot-and-lot elector shook off the landlord's yoke, put up his vote to auction, and sold it to a wealthy stranger, it meant that he had realized for the first time that at an election he could use his vote to make his landlord dependent upon himself, to oblige him " to

---

to potwallers who were not paupers in receipt of relief. Did those come under this category who received relief from charitable funds at the disposal of the borough, independently of the Poor Law ? The answer was " yes " or " no," as best suited the interest of the party to which the returning officer belonged (Oldfield, *Representative History*, vol. iv. pp. 435–6). Might prisoners vote ? or even lunatics ? It is related that once an elector, whose vote would have given a majority to one of the rival candidates, was arrested for debt at the entrance of the Town Hall and kept in gaol till the poll was concluded (Oldfield, *Representative History*, vol. iii. p. 367).

[1] Aldborough, Amersham, Arundel, Bridport, Callington, Dorchester, Eye, Fowey, Great Marlow, Hindon, Ilchester, Minehead, Penryn, St. Ives, Seaford, Steyning, Stockbridge, Wallingford, Wareham, Wendover, Wootton Bassett, with the borough of Weymouth and Melcombe Regis. In this last instance, indeed, the freeholders, to increase their electoral influence, had succeeded, by constant subdivision of their freeholds, in raising by degrees the number of electors from 200 to 2,000. But those 2,000 electors were merely men of straw, fictitious electors, and the wholesale corruption of the borough brings it past all dispute within the present category.

dance to his tenant's tune." This happened in the smallest constituencies of the group under consideration, even in those which scarcely contained above fifty electors. At Stockbridge the fifty-seven electors refused *en masse* to pay their rent and to give their vote unless they received £60 a head. At Ilchester the sixty electors successfully revolted in 1802 and sold their votes at £30 a head. At Tregony in 1812 the Treasury carried off the two seats from the noble family which regarded them as a secure possession. For it was not alone the *nouveaux riches* —"nabobs" returned from India, financiers, manufacturers — who profited by those conditions ; the Government itself took advantage of it. George III, in the long struggle which he had waged against the Whig aristocracy, had organized on a large scale the traffic in parliamentary seats. At every general election he regularly set aside £12,000 out of the Civil List to secure the success of Government candidates.[1] The local solicitors were the natural agents of corruption. They organized the revolt of the borough against the great landlord, formed the electors into a syndicate, and went up to London to negotiate in the name of the syndicate the sale of the seats. The general character of elections in these small constituencies, where the number of electors did not reach 300, is now plain. There was certainly no absence of contest, but a perpetual contest, sometimes open, sometimes concealed, between the old feudal servitude and the new boroughmongering, encouraged by the King and the Cabinet.

We now come to the nineteen constituencies where the number of electors ranged between three and eight hundred.[2] The demarcation between this group and the former must of necessity be arbitrary. We have drawn it where Oldfield begins to recognize the existence of "independent" constituencies. Only three of these boroughs are considered by him as being respectively the property of two noble families. Newark with its 700 electors belonged to the Duke of Newcastle, Stamford with its 640 electors to the Marquis of Exeter, Peterborough with its 400 electors to Lord Fitzwilliam. At Lichfield, where the electorate numbered 600, two noble families had made an agreement to share the two seats. An influence of another sort was dominant at Tamworth, where Sir Robert Peel purchased the borough from two families of the neighbourhood,[3] and at Taunton, which was in the hands of two local bankers.[4] Two constituencies sold them-

[1] When in 1806 the Government happened for once to be Whig, the Court found itself deprived of a portion of its resources. George III then hit upon a scheme by which seats were purchased at a low figure from families favourable to the Crown, the loss being made up by administrative favours, and then resold at a higher price to others, the profit thus made being spent on the purchase of other seats (Lord Holland, *Memoirs of the Whig Party*, vol. ii. pp. 93–4 ; Bulwer, *Life of Lord Palmerston*, vol. i. p. 52).

[2] Abingdon, Bedford, Bridgwater, Chichester, Hertford, Honiton, Leominster, Lewes, Newark, Peterborough, Pontefract, Reading, Shaftesbury, Stamford, Tamworth, Taunton, Warwick, Windsor.

[3] Oldfield, *Representative History*, vol. iv. p. 523.   [4] *Ibid.*, vol. iv. p. 437.

selves to the Treasury.[1] Twelve, however, are considered by Oldfield as being independent of any outside influence.[2] A memorandum drawn up by Abbot, the future Speaker of the House of Commons, when in 1796 he thought of standing for Abingdon, enables us to understand without any need of further comment the character which an electoral contest might assume in a borough of this group. " The electors at Abingdon," he wrote, " are 240 scot and lot ; about 70 of them take money. About half of the 240 go with the corporation. The Dissenters, headed by the Tomkisses and Fletchers, are the next best interest. Child, the brewer, and his friends have also considerable weight. If all three sets can agree, they carry the place in defiance of all opposition. . . . The election (unopposed) would cost within £300, and annual subscriptions afterwards about £100 a year. Politics free." [3] Of the extent to which the influence of the Treasury and of the great landowners tended to diminish when the number of electors increased even slightly we can best judge from the example of Windsor, where at the very foot of the royal palace 300 electors returned in 1807 an independent candidate.[4]

We may now cross a considerable gulf to the third group. It consists of eight constituencies where not only was the franchise democratic but the number of electors exceeded a thousand. This was the case in the three boroughs of New Shoreham, Cricklade and Aylesbury. It was also the case in a certain number of large towns. Northampton had 1,300 electors, Leicester 2,000, Preston 2,100, Southwark 3,000, Westminster 17,000. There the elections presented practically the same character as the county elections, and were the field on which obstinate and ruinous contests were fought out between rival families. In these urban constituencies, however, a new class of society intervened in the contest—that of the manufacturers, who in the north of England had already begun to make enormous fortunes. They could rely on the assistance of the Treasury in a struggle against the great Opposition families. It was with the aid of Lord Liverpool and of the Church and King Club at Manchester that the Horrocks carried one of the Preston seats against the Stanley family.[5] The names of Horrocks, of Peel, of Arkwright—in fact the greatest names of the cotton industry—are to be found in 1815 among the supporters of the Government. The interference in politics of these *nouveaux riches* increased the corruption of political life and many of their contemporaries took alarm. Certain manufacturing towns, according to Thomas Gisborne, were so convinced of the gravity of

---

[1] Honiton, Bridgwater.
[2] Lewes, Shaftesbury, Windsor, Bedford, Chichester, Leominster, Cirencester, Hertford, Pontefract, Tewksbury, Warwick, Abingdon.
[3] *Diary of Lord Colchester*, May 30, 1796 (vol. i. p. 55).
[4] Oldfield, *Representative History*, vol. iii. p. 46.
[5] *Ibid.*, vol. iv. pp. 97–8. Baines, *Lancashire*, vol. iv. p. 346.

the evil that they regarded the grant of parliamentary representation as a calamity.[1] Wakefield deplored the facility with which business men purchased seats. According to him such men exerted an influence hostile alike to virtue and freedom, for they were the authors of a system of treating and bribery which was the disgrace of English elections.[2] But after all the evil, though it gave scandal from its very novelty, was not in reality so very grave.

In the first place, whatever the means they employed to get into Parliament, it is undeniable that the presence in the House of this new industrial aristocracy redressed the excessive preponderance of the great landowners. Nor could these new men from the factories, however greedy of titles and social importance, sacrifice their economic interests to their ambition. When the protectionist Corn Bill came under discussion and had obtained the approval of a large number of Whig landowners, Sir Robert Peel, a Tory member, energetically denounced the Measure and voted against a Ministry into which he was proud to have introduced his son. Moreover, as the number of electors multiplied, the cost of corruption became absolutely prohibitive. Thomas Babington, Member for Leicester, and Henry Thornton, Member for Southwark, were model members. Southwark had rejected Tierney the moment he accepted a lucrative sinecure. The gigantic constituency of Westminster had effected, during the last ten years, nothing short of a revolution in the history of English parliamentary representation. After a century of violent and often ruinous contests—in 1788 his election had cost Lord Townshend £50,000—the two parties had adopted the system of sharing the seats. Though this system was economical, since it suppressed electoral contests, it had the disadvantage of involving the political annihilation of the constituency. In 1807 the electors revolted against it and returned Sir Francis Burdett, the popular candidate who was independent of both the traditional parties, without the expenditure of a single penny on his part. In 1812 other democratic agitators, Hunt and Cartwright, came forward with the same programme as Burdett. Though unlike him they failed to secure their return, nevertheless the English electorate was attaining an ever clearer consciousness of their independence. Many symptoms justified the hope of a sensible improvement in the conduct of elections even under the existing system. The price of boroughs had been lowered.[3] Many candidates rejected propositions for the wholesale purchase of a majority.[4] The Opposition papers remarked with pleasure that less cynicism was now displayed

---

[1] Gisborne, *Duties of Man*, vol. i. p. 214 n.
[2] Wakefield, *Ireland*, vol. ii. pp. 64–5.
[3] To £2,000 and under. *Morning Chronicle*, October 2, 1812, Alderman Wood's speech (City of London).
[4] *Newcastle Chronicle*, October 19, 1812; *Morning Chronicle*, October 23, 1812,

in the preparations for an election, and more regard shown for decorum and respectability.

For all their defects the constituencies which we have just described were the remnants of a democratic system of representation. The majority of English boroughs, however, still remain to be examined. In all these we shall find that the enjoyment of the franchise was subjected either by law or custom to more rigorous conditions.

The English Franchise. Burgage Boroughs.

There were thirty-seven boroughs described as burgage or burgage tenure boroughs.[1] The burgage was a feudal tenure, which imposed on the tenant the performance of certain fixed services to the Lord of the Manor. In these burgage boroughs the number of voters was determined by the number of holdings, whether cultivated or uncultivated, occupied or unoccupied, whose tenure was a burgage tenure. If one single owner managed to gather into his hands all the burgage holdings, there was but one elector for the borough, which then became in the strictest sense of the term the property of an individual, a proprietary borough. No abuse of the English franchise was to be the object of such violent denunciation by the Radical reformers of 1832 as the proprietary borough. None had been treated so leniently in Parliament during the last years of the 18th century. The more the great families who dominated Parliament declaimed against the corruption of the constituencies, since this was a weapon too frequently employed at their expense by the Treasury or by the *nouveaux riches*, the more were they inclined to regard the burgage boroughs as the solid support alike of their own power and of the liberties of the nation. Nor must we forget that the number of these burgage boroughs, which it is tempting to regard as typical examples of the ancient system of representation, was extremely small. Moreover, before passing upon them an indiscriminate condemnation, we must first decide to what extent they really were the absolute property of an individual or family, and even when this was the case, what use was made of the property. Where the number of burgage holdings was very small, where they all belonged to a single owner, and where the law expressly gave the franchise not to the tenant but to the landlord of the burgage holding, the borough was in the most absolute sense a close borough,

---

[1] Oldfield reckons thirty-six of these (*Representative History*, vol. iii. pp. 298–338). Porritt, however, enumerates thirty-nine (*Unreformed House of Commons*, vol. i. p. 30). I make out thirty-seven: Appleby, Ashburnham, Berealston, Bletchingley, Boroughbridge, Bramber, Chippenham, Clitheroe, Cockermouth, Corfe Castle, Downton, East Grinstead, Great Bedwin, Haslemere, Heytesbury, Horsham, Knaresborough, Lichfield, Ludgershall, Malton, Midhurst, Milborn Port, Newport, Newton (Isle of Wight), Newton (Lancs), Northallerton, Old Sarum, Petersfield, Richmond (Yorks), Ripon, Reigate, Saltash, Tavistock, Thirsk, Westley, Westbury, Whitechurch. Oldfield probably omitted Lichfield when the franchise was of a mixed character, but which should, we believe, be included in this list.

and it was impossible to open it. Such was the proverbial borough of Old Sarum. The Earl of Caledon had bought from Lord Camelford the uninhabited estate on which had once stood a flourishing town. As owner of the seven burgage holdings he nominated two members at a general election.[1] Where, however, the number of burgage holdings was larger, where they were divided among several owners, and where the franchise belonged not to the landlord but to the occupier, the borough at once ceased to be the exclusive property of an individual. At Northallerton, in Yorkshire, the landlord of a large number of houses to which burgage tenures were attached could only preserve his right of nomination by granting the tenants a rebate of £100 on every long lease.[2] At Haslemere, the first Lord Lonsdale, the owner of forty freeholds carrying with them the franchise, actually brought forty of his Northumberland miners to Surrey, lodged them and paid them at the rate of 10s. 6d. a week without exacting any service in return save a vote for his candidates. When in 1812 the second Lord Lonsdale, finding this procedure too costly, dismissed his professional electors, the seat was at once threatened.[3] At Malton the proprietor, or rather the would-be proprietor, of the borough at one election actually lost one of the seats.[4] The landlords had invented a number of fraudulent or semi-fraudulent devices to defend what they deemed their property. One of these was the creation of electors for the occasion, whose lease was purely fictitious, valid only for the period of the election. Another was the splitting of the freeholds to multiply the number of votes at the disposal of the proprietor.[5] This gave rise to grievances and lawsuits, which might cost the parties concerned as much as £40,000 or even £60,000. Thus even in the burgage boroughs the political privileges of the aristocracy were threatened.

Let us suppose, however, that in one of these boroughs the proprietor exercised in perfect security the right conferred upon him by custom. In what way, in what spirit, would he employ his parliamentary fief? Possibly as a source of pecuniary profit. For the last forty years the honour of membership of the House of Commons had been more coveted than in the past, and it was now more common for the proprietors of boroughs to sell them to the highest bidder. This practice, however reprehensible, presented certain advantages. It might guarantee the independence of the new member against the interference of the proprietor. It was for this reason that Sir Francis Burdett, the democrat, bought in 1796 one of the seats for Boroughbridge from the Duke of Newcastle. But it is most important to bear in mind that in England this boroughmongering was quite

---

[1] Oldfield, *Representative History*, vol. v. p. 217.
[2] *Ibid.*, vol. v. p. 341.   [3] *Ibid.*, vol. v. pp. 599 sqq.
[4] *Ibid.*, vol. v. p. 346.
[5] *Ibid.*, vol. iii. pp. 323, 570; vol. iv. p. 599; vol. v. p. 214.

the exception. Wakefield, an impartial critic, witnesses to a great difference in this respect beween England and Ireland. The proprietors of boroughs were, indeed, he tells us, " only too often disposed to this traffic, but such boroughmongers were held in very slight esteem and occupied a very low position in society." [1] In the majority of cases the proprietors of boroughs used their property for the profit of their family. Their political morality was the morality not of a merchant but of the chief of a clan. Each member of one of the great families who governed the English provinces regarded his intellect, his energy and the influence at his disposal as due in the first instance to his family, and after that to the party to which his family belonged. Though the system was one of pure oligarchy, it contained, nevertheless, representative and even democratic elements. At the opening of the 19th century a theory was evolved by the apologists of the existing system, according to which a Member of Parliament did not represent his own constituency, but joined with his fellow members to constitute the indivisible representation of the kingdom as a whole. [2] This was the theory of virtual representation which maintained that virtually, if not actually, the members who sat for Gatton or Old Sarum represented not only the phantom electors of these two boroughs, but also the scot-and-lot electors of Southwark and Westminster and the freeholders of the counties. Nor was this paradoxical plea on behalf of an unequal franchise without an element of truth. The representative of a close borough belonged from the day of his election to an aristocratic party which comprised not only the representatives of other close boroughs, but also members elected either by open boroughs or by counties. One with his party in all things, and under the control of a party leader, he yielded indirectly or " virtually " to the pressure exerted upon these by a wider electorate. Suppose him, for instance, a Tory, an advocate of war at any price, an opponent of Catholic emancipation. When he gave his vote on this side, he knew that he was not merely obeying the commands of a patron, but that he also voiced the opinion of a very large section both of the borough and of the county electorate. Suppose him, on the contrary, a nominee of the Duke of Bedford or of the Duke of Norfolk. He would then vote with the Opposition, and would demand a peace policy and even the reform of the representative system to which he owed his seat. In 1832 two proprietors of boroughs, Lord Fitzwilliam and Lord Radnor, were to form, with their clientele in the House of Commons, the backbone of the majority in favour of reform.

Not only their relations, but also their dependents, were sent to Parliament by the proprietors of boroughs. After the 1812 elections

[1] Wakefield, *Ireland*, vol. ii. p. 315.
[2] *Edinburgh Review*, November 1820, No. 68, Art. 12, *Parliamentary Reform* (vol. xxxiv. pp. 475-7).

the great Whig families enabled the intellectuals of the party, defeated in the open boroughs, to re-enter Parliament by offering them the seats at their disposal. Pocket boroughs had at all times provided for clever youths who had left the Universities and had begun to show their capacity at the Bar a means of entering Parliament without the risk or expense of an electoral campaign. For such men their first years in Parliament were often very difficult.[1] Gratitude and self-interest alike kept them under the strict control of their political patrons. If they dared to speak or vote without orders from their patron they might lose their seats; but their independence increased with the increase of their personal importance. In 1795 and in 1797 Abbot, the nominee of the Duke of Leeds, twice voted in support of important Measures of which his patron disapproved. After a correspondence the Duke withdrew his censure of Abbot's conduct.[2] In 1815 Francis Horner, although he owed his seat to Lord Grenville, dissociated himself from Lord Grenville's more conservative and bellicose party and voted with Lord Grey and Whitbread. He felt obliged to excuse himself and to offer to resign his seat. The offer, however, was not accepted and the hope was expressed that Horner would still adorn the group of Lord Grenville's friends with the prestige of his name.[3] What is true of Abbot and of Horner is naturally even more true of a great man like Wilberforce. In 1811 Lord Calthorpe offered Wilberforce, who was tired of representing Yorkshire and in search of a "quiet borough," his burgage borough of Bramber.[4] Obviously he would not have dreamed of giving orders to Wilberforce; but Wilberforce was related to him, they belonged to the same party, and it would be alike to his honour and to his credit to have Wilberforce as the representative of his borough.

The English Franchise. Corporation and Freemen Boroughs.

In the burgage boroughs the franchise was attached to the soil. In the boroughs, whose constitution remains to be studied, it was the privilege of a corporate body. Among these were boroughs in which the franchise was the sole property of the members of the "corporation," the membership of which was recruited by cooptation. Elsewhere it was wider, and belonged to all the freemen of the borough—that is to say, to all the members of the guilds or "companies." We find, there-fore, two distinct bodies of electors. Certain practices, however, tended to blur the distinction between them. Wherever the freemen possessed the franchise, it would appear to have belonged equally, whether by

---

[1] On their position, whose difficulties were often permanent, see Gisborne, *Duties of Man*, vol. i. pp. 217–18.
[2] *Diary of Lord Colchester*, vol. i. pp. 17, 124 sqq.
[3] *Court of England during the Regency*, vol. ii. pp. 124 sqq.
[4] *Life of Wilberforce*, vol. iii. pp. 534 sqq.; *Diary of Lord Colchester*, vol. ii. p. 345.

express statute or by immemorial custom, to the corporation, and where the practice was not expressly prohibited by law, the corporation possessed the right to create an indefinite number of honorary freemen, and was able by this means to acquire a preponderating influence even in boroughs where all the freemen voted. The majority of English boroughs were either corporation or freemen boroughs. There were thirty-six of the former, seventy-seven of the latter. Taken as a whole these boroughs illustrate perfectly the complex character of the unreformed franchise in England ; for in them we discover a host of divergent influences at work—the influence of the great landowner, the influence of the wealthy merchant or manufacturer, the influence of the Treasury, and finally the influence of independent public opinion.

The thirty-six corporation boroughs [1] were obviously those in which the independence of the electorate was at the minimum. These tiny constituencies, where the electorate often did not exceed ten and very rarely rose above a hundred, were inevitably exposed to illicit pressure, and the poorer the electors, the more incapable they would be of resisting the pressure. Among the thousand inhabitants of the small borough of Malmesbury were bankers, solicitors and merchants, who would have conferred the desirable respectability on the corporation, had they been members of it. On the contrary, of the thirteen members of the corporation there had been quite recently ten incapable of signing an official document. [2] For these illiterates, the franchise was not a weapon for the defence of reputable interests, but simply a means of gaining money at intervals without having to do any work for it. The electorate of these corporation boroughs, like that of the smaller scot-and-lot boroughs, was subject to the influence of the landed aristocracy, for the electors were, as a general rule, tenants of the great landowners of the district. They were not, however, prepared to give their vote for nothing. A solicitor, as at Andover, Bewdley and Devizes,[3] or a chemist as at Malmesbury,[4] acted as their agent and in their name offered the two borough seats at a fixed price to anyone willing to conclude the bargain. The Government did not fail to take advantage of this traffic, and it is perhaps in this group that we find the greatest number of those boroughs which were termed Treasury or Admiralty boroughs, because the Government had

---

[1] Andover, Banbury, Bath, Bewdley, Bodmin, Brackley, Buckingham, Bury St. Edmunds, Calne, Christchurch, Dartmouth, Devizes, Droitwich, Harwich, Helston, Launceston, Liskeard, Lostwithiel, Lyme Regis, Lymington, Malmesbury, Marlborough, Newport (Isle of Wight), Plymouth, Portsmouth, Salisbury, Scarborough, Thetford, Tiverton, Truro, West Looe, East Looe, Wigan, Wilton, Winchester, Yarmouth. Porritt (*Unreformed House of Commons*, vol. i. p. 30) places forty-three boroughs in this class. The discrepancy is doubtless to be explained by the existence of many boroughs with a mixed franchise. Porritt does not, however, give the names of his forty-three corporation boroughs, which makes it difficult to control his estimate.

[2] Oldfield, *Representative History*, vol. v. p. 179.

[3] *Ibid.*, vol. iii. p. 545 ; vol. v. p. 256 ; vol. v. p. 157.

[4] *Ibid.*, vol. v. p. 180.

either bought the votes of the corporation or had filled the corporation itself with its paid clients. It was in vain that the law forbade public officials to vote. Their fathers, brothers and sons could always exercise the franchise, and they might themselves be members of the corporation, and would then take care that vacancies among the members were filled by men agreeable to the Government.

Where, on the other hand, the corporation was composed not of an ignorant and irresponsible rabble but of the leading men of the neighbourhood, this was often in itself sufficient to emancipate the corporation borough from servitude of any kind, whether to the aristocracy or to the Government. The borough of Calne in Wiltshire did not possess above seventeen electors, all members of the corporation, and for forty years the patronage of Lord Lansdowne had been accepted without demur. But in 1807 Lord Lansdowne had tried in vain to compel the corporation to get rid of Mr. Jekyll, one of the retiring members. The corporation had stood firm and Mr. Jekyll had been re-elected free of cost in opposition to Lord Lansdowne's wishes.[1] The borough of Portsmouth contained, with the suburb of Portsea, 33,000 inhabitants, of whom 3,000 were employed in the Admiralty dockyards. Only the members of the corporation—the mayor, the aldermen and the burgesses—110 in all, were electors. During the greater part of the 18th century the borough had been an Admiralty borough. In 1780, however, the corporation had rebelled. For a long time the numerical strength of the parties remained almost equal. Finally the Government was defeated in the first naval port of the realm.[2]

The seventy-seven boroughs[3] where the franchise belonged to the freemen presented a greater diversity of character and it would seem at first sight, from the extreme variability in the number of the electorate—in some places insignificant, in others considerable—that they must have resembled very closely the scot-and-lot boroughs. Their constitution was not, however, quite the same, and the part played by corruption was probably somewhat greater.

In these boroughs the enjoyment of the franchise was determined

---

[1] Oldfield, *Representative History*, vol. v. p. 152.   [2] *Ibid.*, vol. iii. pp. 504 sqq.

[3] Aldborough, Barnstaple, Berwick-on-Tweed, Beverley, Bishop's Castle, Boston, Bridgenorth, Cambridge, Canterbury, Carlisle, Castle Rising, Chester, Colchester, Wycombe, Coventry, Derby, Dover, Dunwich, Durham, East Retford, Evesham, Gloucester, Grampound, Grantham, Great Grimsby, Hastings, Hereford, Heydon, Higham Ferrers, Hull, Huntingdon, Hythe, Ipswich, Lancaster, Lincoln, Liverpool, City of London, Ludlow, King's Lynn, Maidstone, Maldon, Monmouth, Morpeth, Newcastle-under-Lyme, Newcastle-upon-Tyne, New Romney, Orford, Oxford, Plympton Earle, Poole, Queenborough, Rochester, Rye, St. Albans, St. Germans, St. Mawes, Sandwich, Shrewsbury, Southampton, Stafford, Sudbury, Totnes, Wells, Wenlock, Woodstock, Worcester, Yarmouth. York. To these sixty-eight constituencies we must add the nine following constituencies where the franchise belonged conjointly to the freemen and to the freeholders or to the forty-shilling freeholders : Bossiney, Bristol, Exeter, Guildford, Norwich, Nottingham, Oakhampton, Tewkesbury, Winchelsea. Porritt gives sixty-two freemen boroughs (vol. i. p. 30).

not by a property qualification—either high or low—but by the accident of an ancient municipal constitution. It might happen, as at Liverpool [1] and in the City of London,[2] that the franchise belonged to the poor, to the exclusion of the rich. Such a plebeian electorate often lacked the necessary independence. The Opposition complained, for instance, in 1812 that Brougham's defeat at Liverpool had been caused by the labourers voting in gangs in obedience to the orders of the important electors of the locality. Again, the electors were not necessarily denizens of the place. Hereditary freemen did not lose their franchise by living away from the borough. The candidate in need of their votes had therefore to seek them out and to convey them to the poll at his expense. He had to pay them 6s. a day for their travelling expenses, 7s. 6d. for their maintenance, 10s. 6d. to cover any losses incurred. It would therefore cost £10 to bring a voter from London to Colchester, £15 to bring him from London to Bristol, £20 from London to Exeter, £30 from London to Newcastle-on-Tyne.[3] A contested election at Barnstaple, in Devonshire, cost from £10,000 to £13,000,[4] since the voters were scattered throughout the entire realm. And finally the power possessed by the corporation to create honorary freemen also falsified the conditions of an election. A candidate who felt doubtful of his popularity among the freemen, and did not consider himself in a position to spend the sums necessary to secure it, would betake himself to the corporation and obtain from that body the creation of a sufficient number of honorary freemen to swamp the hostile majority. At Carlisle there were 700 electors, and the popular candidates were the nominees of the Duke of Norfolk. But Lord Lonsdale was master of the corporation. At his instance the corporation conferred the honorary freedom upon 14,000 of his coal miners and on three occasions his candidates thus secured election.[5]

We have found the same abuses universally prevalent, though perhaps graver in these boroughs than elsewhere. Everywhere, on the other hand, we remark the same variety, perhaps more accentuated in freemen boroughs than in others. If there were nine of these with less than twenty electors,[6] there were twenty in which the electorate ranged from 500 to 1,000,[7] and twenty-two in which

[1] Oldfield, *Representative History*, vol. iv. p. 195.

[2] *Ibid.*, vol. iv. p. 195 ; *Morning Chronicle*, October 29, 1812.

[3] *State of Representation*, 1793, p. 12.

[4] Oldfield, *Representative History*, vol. iii. p. 300.

[5] *Ibid.*, vol. iii. pp. 264, 265. Ordinarily the two seats had been shared between the two parties (*ibid.*, p. 255). If in 1812 both seats were secured by Lord Lonsdale's party, it must be added that the defeat of Curwen, the popular candidate, was ascribed by Curwen himself to causes into which fraud does not enter (Curwen, *Observations . . . on Ireland*, vol. i. pp. 6, 7, 15). Cf. R. S. Ferguson, *The Cumberland and Westmorland M.P.s*, p. 222.

[6] Bossiney, Dunwich, Hastings, New Romney, Orford, Rye, St. Germans, St. Mawes, Winchelsea.

[7] Berwick-on-Tweed, Bridgenorth, Carlisle, Derby, Evesham, Grantham, Ludlow,

it exceeded 1,000.[1] Bristol counted 6,000 electors, the City of London 17,000. The nine boroughs where the number of electors was infinitesimal are instances of degeneration from the normal type. In these, to the advantage of the local patrons, the franchise was in practice confined to the members of the corporation ; but immediately the number of electors ceased to be absolutely insignificant the influence of the aristocracy was weakened. At Chipping Wycombe there were only fifty electors. Nevertheless, twenty years before our period, Sir John Dashwood had won from Lord Lansdowne the seat which he had been accustomed to regard as his property.[2] When the number of electors exceeded 500, and a fortiori 1,000, the electorate began to assert its independence.

If even in the large towns the ancient families still retained much of their influence, it was because they were prepared to make the necessary concessions to popular demands, or to discover points on which their political feelings were identical with those of the electors. Thus the Duke of Norfolk remained the patron of the borough of Gloucester, where 3,000 freemen exercised the franchise, because he had succeeded in winning the confidence of the people by his constant largesses and by the firmness of his political conduct. The scandals which took place at a Bristol election were doubtless disgraceful, but these scandals cannot be ascribed to corruption by the Government or by wealthy individuals. Bristol was governed by two clubs—two caucuses we should call them to-day—one Whig, the other Tory. Sometimes these agreed to divide the seats amicably,[3] sometimes they contested them with a bitter animosity, which knew no scruples in the choice of weapons. In other words, Bristol was already, under the unreformed franchise, a demagogue-ridden city and the growth of democracy by no means tended to cure the evils from which it was suffering. In London Waithman, a draper, the shopkeepers' candidate, when defeated in the 1812 elections, complained, and his complaint was echoed by the Opposition journals, that the establishment of the Excise offices and of the Bank of England in the heart of the City, the introduction of an armed force for their protection, and the growing importance of the offices of the Customs and of the East India Com-

Maidstone, Maldon, Monmouth, Newcastle-under-Lyme, Rochester, Sandwich, Shrewsbury, Southampton, Stafford, Sudbury, St. Albans, Tewkesbury, Yarmouth.

[1] Beverley, Bristol, Canterbury, Chester, Colchester, Coventry, Dover, Durham, Exeter, Gloucester, Hereford, Hull, Lancaster, Lincoln, Liverpool, City of London, Newcastle-on-Tyne, Norwich, Nottingham, Oxford, Worcester, York.

[2] Oldfield, *Representative History*, vol. iii. p. 85. Cf. Lord Lansdowne's complaints as given in Fitzmaurice, *Life of Lord Shelburne*, vol. ii. pp. 362-3 : " And after all, when the crisis comes, you are likely to be outbid by a nabob or adventurer, and you must expect all that you have done to go for nothing, and the most you can look for is a preference. What can you say to a blacksmith, who has seven children, or to a common labourer who is offered £700 for his vote, or to two misers who are offered £2,000, which are all instances distinctly upon record at Wycombe since Mr. Dashwood's election."

[3] Oldfield, *Representative History*, vol. iv. pp. 416 sqq.

pany, had increased the influence of the Government.[1] But obviously no extension of the suffrage could abolish an influence which took this form. Like Nottingham, where the artizans ruled the constituency,[2] Norwich, Newcastle and Coventry, both Bristol and the City of London were "independent" and "popular" constituencies.

Defects and Merits of the Unreformed Franchise.

The abuses of the English system of representation were undoubtedly many and grave ; but it is surely impossible to pass a general judgment upon a system so extremely complicated. Are we in a position to estimate the exact degree in which the nature of the parliamentary franchise stultified the operation of the representative principle and prevented public opinion from finding expression in Parliament ? In 1817 Oldfield attempted to compile statistics on this point.[3] According to his estimate, of the 405 representatives of the English boroughs fourteen were returned to Westminster not by the free choice of the electorate of their respective constituencies, but because their seats were in the patronage of the Government.[4] This figure is in our opinion too high, but even were it correct, it is obvious that the interference of the executive in the English representative system was after all very trifling. It was by no means the same with the aristocratic influences. According to Oldfield 197 representatives, or rather so-called representatives, of the English boroughs were the arbitrary choice of a certain number of local "patrons," themselves members of the House of Lords or the House of Commons, and belonging as a general rule to the governing aristocracy. In the case of another 119 boroughs, although there was no nomination by a patron in the strict sense of the term, the influence of a patron was the decisive factor in determining elections.[5] But

---

[1] *Morning Chronicle*, October 15, 1812.

[2] Brentano, *Guilds and Trade Unions*, p. 117.

[3] Oldfield, *Representative History*, vol. vi. pp. 280 sqq., Appendix, containing correct tables of parliamentary patronage in England, Wales, Scotland, and Ireland.

[4] According to Oldfield the patronage of the Government was exercised over sixteen seats, including the two Hampshire seats. These two subtracted, we are left with fourteen seats for the boroughs. But Oldfield means that in the 1812 elections fourteen candidates in ten boroughs had been returned owing to Government pressure. But in only one borough, Queenborough, did the nomination of the two members belong permanently and incontestably to the Government. Elsewhere it was only a matter of influence, an influence constantly threatened by opposing influences. The two seats for Plymouth had been lost since 1792. One of the two Windsor seats had been lost since 1804. It was only by a fortunate chance that the Government had been able to recover the two seats for Sandwich.

[5] From Oldfield's table of the parliamentary patronage in England and Wales we have removed the Welsh and county seats. It is instructive to compare this table with the table drawn up in 1793 on the same plan by the "Society of the People's Friends" (see *State of the Representation*, pp. 30 sqq.). Oldfield's figures are higher than those of the Society of the Friends of the People. According to the latter list there were 168 boroughs in which there was nomination by a patron, 108 in which the influence of a patron was predominant. We must not, however, conclude that the system of parliamentary patronage had been aggravated during

we have still to ask what is the real worth of this division of the English boroughs into three watertight compartments? Surely the division rests upon a false principle. From the nomination borough to that in which there was nothing more than a dominant influence, and from that again to a popular borough, there was an imperceptible transition. Even the boroughs classified by Oldfield as nomination boroughs were by no means always a property of which the assured possession passed down in a family from father to son without need of effort for its preservation. In very many cases constant attention and almost infinite outlay were essential, if the electoral fief were not to be lost. A great rival family, a "nabob" returned from India with an enormous fortune, a local banker, a wealthy manufacturer, might at any time, if the proprietor were not willing to sell his electoral interest for ready money, declare war upon him, buy the voters and outbid the patron, until the day came when the new patron would be threatened in his turn by the operation of the same causes. Thus the very corruption of the electorate corrected to some extent the vices of the system, and afforded a means by which new classes of society could obtain seats in Parliament and the representation of their interests in the House. Over fifty bankers, merchants and business men of all kinds, were members of the House of Commons in 1818.[1] Some of these had already founded

the last twenty-five years. It is always difficult to arrive at a clear and objective definition of "patronage" or "influence." Oldfield, for instance, ascribes to Lord Darlington the nomination of the two members for Tregony. In 1812, however, his candidates had been defeated by the Government candidates (*Representative History*, vol. iii. pp. 197–8). The borough is a case not of nomination but of influence. Oldfield also ascribes to the Marquis of Lansdowne the nomination of the two Members for Calne. But elsewhere he tells us that in 1807 the electors had returned in opposition to the Marquis an independent candidate (*Representative History*, vol. v. p. 152). Johnstone expressly asserts as an unquestionable fact (H. of C., May 19, 1809, *Parl. Deb.*, vol. xiv. p. 658) that " if 275 members were returned to Parliament by individual interests, as was stated in the Petition for Reform in 1797, the proportion is now greatly diminished. No one can deny the sentiment that now pervades every town and city in the empire ; nor is it to be doubted that, in a very few years, their independence will be exerted in such a degree, that no returns will be made by individuals, but those who are possessed of burgage tenures."

[1] There were twenty-three bankers, of whom fifteen were from London : James Cocks, G. H. Drummond, William Heygate, Sir J. W. Lubbock, John Martin, Sir John Perring, John Ramsbottam, Abraham Robarts, Rob. Shaw, Abel Smith, George Smith (Wendover), George Smith (Midhurst), Samuel Smith, Henry Thornton, Robert Williams ; and eight from the provinces : R. A. Crickitt, R. H. Davies, John Latouche, Sir John Newport, Joseph Pitt, M. W. Ridley, Robert Morris, Thomas Thompson. Four sat for nomination boroughs, nine for boroughs of a mixed character, eight for open constituencies, two for counties, one Scotch and one Irish county. There were thirty-five representatives of mercantile interests of all kinds. Among these we notice six manufacturers (Kirkman Finlay, John Hodson, Sir Robert Peel, George Philips, Sam. Horrocks, Richard Arkwright), three directors of the Bank of England (Alexander Baring, William Mellish, Thomas Whitmore), two directors of the East India Company (Sir Thomas Baring and John Jackson), twelve merchants (William Manning, Edward Protheroe, Samuel Thornton, J. Marryat, N. Sneyd, W. Smith, J. Irving, J. Bollard, Sam. Scott, Richard Sharp, John Staniforth, Robert Wigram), four brewers (Charles Barclay, Whitbread, the two Calverts), one director of an insurance company (Ch. E. Wilsoun), one manager of a private post (Palmer), one printer (A. Strahan), one bookseller (Joseph Butterworth), and the four members for the City of London. Fourteen of these represented nomination boroughs, six boroughs of a mixed character, twelve

parliamentary families. Sir Robert Peel had begun the purchase of the patronage of the borough of Tamworth, one of whose seats he occupied. For his two sons he bought two other seats.[1] The banker Robert Smith, now Lord Carrington, had become the proprietor of two nomination boroughs. Of the four seats for these two boroughs, three were occupied by his near relatives. But even electoral corruption had its limits. In 1806 Major Cartwright had asked the electors of Boston what guarantee they possessed with a House of Commons elected under such scandalous conditions that Bonaparte would not purchase seats and obtain agents at Westminster.[2] In reality no such thing ever happened. The days of Louis XIV and the Stuarts had passed and English electioneering agents could be bought only with English money. And again, no sooner did the electors exceed a mere handful than aspirations after independence, hard to repress, began to show themselves.

Certainly the electorate comprised but a very small fraction of the nation. The "Society of the Friends of the People," founded to promote parliamentary reform, estimated in 1793 that fifty-one English and Welsh boroughs, whose total electorate was under 1,500, sent 100 representatives to Westminster, and that 11,075 English and Welsh electors, who belonged to a certain number of boroughs carefully chosen, elected 257 members of the House of Commons. Nevertheless, the representation of the counties was undoubtedly of a very popular character. Anyone prepared to buy a forty-shilling freehold could obtain a vote. In the boroughs the system was not so democratic, but several disadvantages attaching to a system of pecuniary qualification were absent. The law fixed no definite sum to qualify for the franchise, thus disfranchising all whose wealth fell below that figure. The borough electorate consisted of 100,000 individuals, the haphazard selection of customs varying in different localities, and drawn indiscriminately from every class in the nation—aristocrats and men of the people, rich and poor, members of the middle class and the proletariat. In 1815 many European nations were considering the adoption of the British parliamentary system. Not a single one

---

open boroughs, three counties (Surrey, Middlesex, and the Irish county of Cavan). To form a complete idea of the representation of the mercantile and industrial interest we should add to the above the names of the great landowners who owned and worked mines. The foregoing statistics, doubtless incomplete, are based on the *Return of the Names of Members of Parliament* where the professions of members are sometimes given, and on the list of the Members of Parliament in 1818, which is to be found with mention of their professions in the Black Book for 1818. The information thus obtained has been supplemented by numerous details mentioned incidentally elsewhere.

[1] He had sat as one of the two members for Tamworth since 1790. In 1818 both seats belonged to him, as the result of a transaction which cost him £132,000, and his son Robert was sitting for the borough of Chippenham. In 1817, his son, William Yates, had been returned for the borough of Bossiney.

[2] Cobbett's *Political Register*, November 15, 1806 (vol. x. p. 777).

would have dared to admit so wide an electorate. Considerable time and peculiarly favourable circumstances would be needed before the principles of representative government could become in Continental countries what they were in the England of 1815—a hallowed tradition, part and parcel of the national heritage.

"All civilized Governments," wrote the *Edinburgh Review* in 1807, "may be divided into free and arbitrary : or, more accurately, . . . into the Government of England, and the other European Governments." [1] These words of the *Edinburgh Review* in 1807 could still have been written in 1815, even after the fall of Napoleon's empire. Obviously the system was in need of reform, and public opinion had already begun to press for reform. The south of England was over-represented, while the north lacked adequate representation. The agricultural interest was too strongly entrenched, while the manufacturing interest was very insufficiently safeguarded. The list of boroughs needed revision and the number of electors might very well have been increased. The important question, however, was whether the electorate as constituted in the opening years of the 19th century would oppose an obstinate resistance to the demands of a new era and a transformed civilization. Fifteen years hence would come the decisive test. Twice in succession a House of Commons, elected under the system described above, would vote the reform of that very system and would force that reform upon the House of Lords. This proves that, unlike the House of Lords, the unreformed House of Commons already represented to a large extent the opinion of the country. It proves also that normally and constantly it was subject to the pressure of certain external forces whose character must now be defined.

POPULAR LIBERTIES.

The Right to Rebellion.

The first of these forces was rebellion—whether actual or merely potential, effectively carried out or simply threatened. Throughout the 18th century England, the sole European country where the reigning dynasty had been set up as the result of a successful rebellion, had been the home of insurrection. There had been an outbreak of anti-Jewish rioting in 1753, when the Government had decided to grant the right of naturalization to the Jews domiciled in England. The Cabinet had yielded and repealed the statute. Extremely characteristic of English conditions was the speech in which Lord Hardwicke defended the policy of the Cabinet, as the only possible policy where a nation is governed by public opinion. "However much," he had said, "the people may be misled, yet in a free country I do not think

[1] *Edinburgh Review*, April 1807, No. 19, Art. 1, *The Dangers of the Country* (vol. x. p. 11).

an unpopular Measure ought to be obstinately persisted in. We should treat the people as a skilful and humane physician would treat his patient ; if they nauseate the salutary draught we have prescribed, we should think of some other remedy, or we should delay administering the prescription till time or change of circumstances has removed the nausea." [1] In 1768 there were riots against the Government. The popular hero Wilkes triumphed in the end over the opposition of Court and Cabinet. In 1780 an anti-Catholic riot broke out ; during four entire days the centre of London was given up to pillage. A Government without a police force was powerless either to prevent these outrages or to repress them promptly. The right to riot, or as it was termed by the lawyers " the right of resistance," was an integral part of the national traditions. In vain does Blackstone, in one of the most embarrassed passages of his *Commentaries*, do his best to get rid of this right. He affirms that " the King is, and ought to be, absolute," but he adds " in the exertion of lawful prerogative," and he explains this to mean " so far absolute that there is no legal authority that can either delay or resist him." He denounces the " over-zealous republicans " who would grant " to every individual the right of determining " whether or no it is necessary to have recourse to resistance and " of employing private force to resist even private oppression." He does not, however, contest that there were " extraordinary " cases, where the first principles of society must be directly applied. Such would arise inevitably " when the contracts of society are in danger of dissolution, and the law proves too weak a defence against the violence of fraud or oppression." [2] But the current of history had changed its course during the last twenty years. It was now no longer England as in the 17th century, but France which had witnessed a popular revolution, the decapitation of a King, a military dictatorship, a Royalist restoration. In Western Europe France had succeeded England as the typical country of rebellion. Nevertheless, despite the anxiety aroused by the events in France, the English remained faithful to their traditional creed. The orators and writers of the Opposition continued to maintain that the English people possessed a right of resistance in the last resort. Fox, Grey and Sheridan insisted upon this, even at the very height of the Jacobin scare. The *Edinburgh Review* was never weary of harping on this theme. " The *sole* check," declared this organ, " to the encroachments of power, and the oppressions of inceptive tyranny, is the spirit, the intelligence, the vigilance, the prepared *resistance*, of the people." [3] . . . " The great and ultimate barrier against

[1] Lord Campbell, *Lives of the Chancellors*, vol. v. p. 124 n.
[2] 1 *Comm.* 250–1. Cf. Gisborne, *Duties of Man*, vol. i. pp. 97 sqq. In the same way Blackstone (1 *Comm.* 143–4) considers the right to " bear arms in self-defence " as " a public allowance, under due restrictions, of the natural right of resistance and self-preservation when the sanctions of society and laws are found insufficient to restrain the violence of oppression."
[3] *Edinburgh Review*, July 1809, No. 28, Art. 1, *Parliamentary Reform* (vol. xiv. p . 3 0 5)

corruption, oppression and arbitrary power must always be raised on public opinion—and on opinion so valued and so asserted as to point resolutely to *resistance*, if it be once insulted or set at defiance." [1] Nor should we regard this merely as the assertion of an abstract and theoretical right. From 1810 to 1815 both in London and in the provinces rioting had been the order of the day. In 1810 we find a riot directed against Parliament itself. It had been found necessary for the maintenance of order to bring up in haste to the capital an army of 50,000 men. In 1812 a regular Jacquerie broke out, which spread over the manufacturing districts of the Midlands, Yorkshire and Lancashire. Again, the February of 1815 witnessed a grave outbreak of rioting, directed against the Act of agrarian protection, whose clauses were being hastily passed through Parliament. The riots of 1812 had been merely the revolt of misery and want, the incoherent rising of a disorganized and leaderless rabble, which immediately united against it all the wealthy and ruling classes. The riots of 1815, on the other hand, were tolerated, encouraged, even perhaps directed, by leaders of industry, bankers and stockbrokers, who were bitterly hostile to the policy of the landowners and the agriculturalists. Parliament was besieged by the crowd, and the houses of the principal leaders of the party in office were pillaged. We may wonder what would have been the result of this popular agitation had not the return of Napoleon from Elba suddenly changed the current of feeling and saved the cause of order. But even this did not put an end to the manifestations against the Government and the open-air meetings. On June 16th, on the very eve of Waterloo, Lord Castlereagh, riding through Whitehall, encountered a meeting unauthorized by the local authorities in which the leaders of the popular party were haranguing the crowd. He was recognized, insulted and followed through the Horse Guards to St. James' Park. That evening he thought it prudent to guard his house with troops.[2] In a few days' time, the peace of Europe was re-established ; but the misery and discontent which had occasioned the risings of 1812 and 1815 did not disappear. Every one in Government circles foresaw a general insurrection—all the more dangerous that it could no longer be diverted by foreign warfare. Nor were even these sporadic manifestations of popular opinion required to keep the ruling classes constantly sensible of the possibility and danger of a popular rising. The proceedings at an election were a periodical reminder both to the newly elected members and to their noble patrons that riot formed part of the political traditions of the English people. In virtue of an unwritten law which enjoyed universal respect, the mass of inhabitants, voters and non-voters alike, played a very active part on polling days, when the rival candidates met face to face. The

[1] *Edinburgh Review*, February 1811, No. 34, Art. 1, *Parliamentary Reform* (vol. xvii. p. 278).
[2] *Examiner*, June 18, 1815.

nomination day was equally a day of popular demonstrations. The candidates owed their constituents a speech, a declaration of their political principles, and the crowd flocked to hear them, to approve or disapprove, according to circumstances. In boroughs where the franchise was the monopoly of a small number of burgage holders or burgesses, and where the remainder of the inhabitants considered themselves robbed of their ancient civic rights by the tiny group of electors, they would often seize the opportunity of an election to pave the way by a noisy manifestation for a petition demanding from Parliament the enlargement of the franchise in their constituency. When, however, an election was contested, popular excitement knew no bounds. A French writer who visited England in 1818 and was present at an election declared himself unable to understand these " Westminster mountebanks . . . addressing a worthless rabble of whom not a man would vote for them." " There is," he wrote, " an entire absence of dignity and greatness." It was all " mean parody and wretched farce." On the following page he describes the riot which broke out on the defeat of the popular candidate. The successful candidates were obliged by custom to ride in procession. They were immediately " pelted with filth, greeted with a shower of thick and black mud. . . . I saw Lord Nugent with one side all black. Lord Molyneux's face resembled a pug's. Lord John Russell attempted with difficulty to wipe off the stinking patches of dirt which continually bespattered his cheeks. . . . One of the servants received so violent a blow on the head with a stick that he fell from his horse unconscious. . . . Some had their windows broken and their furniture damaged. The houses of Lord Castlereagh and several others met with the same fate." The constables were insufficient to restore order, and the troops had to be called out. Such scenes shocked a visitor from the Continent, but they had long been familiar to the English public.

This tradition of rowdyism, however, did not lack its English critics. Even numbers of the Whig Opposition complained of it as enabling a wealthy candidate, who distributed money by handfuls and treated on a large scale, to acquire a low popularity which corrupted the public morals. Romilly, the typical Whig theorist, only consented with great difficulty to prepare for his candidature in 1812 by an electioneering campaign of the customary type, and openly showed the disgust he felt at the reception, though of a triumphal nature, accorded to him by the populace of Bristol.[1] On the other hand these rowdy customs found defenders in the Tory ranks. A Tory speaker protested in Parliament against the desire shown by certain reformers for " a filtering stone to clear away all the mud of poverty, vulgar mirth, etc., from popular elections." " Cockades," he con-

[1] *Memoirs*, vol. ii. pp. 424 sqq. ; vol. iii. pp. 8, 21-2.

tinued, "and the liberty of huzzaing, were things which every Englishman admired ; they contributed to give him an idea of the rights he enjoyed, and on the possession of which he prized himself." [1]   This right of noisy and disorderly demonstration during an election was an integral part of the old English system.   The seat was being contested by two candidates who both belonged to the same class of society. The electors would vote for the candidate who had managed to make himself the more popular, who had displayed the greater activity in organizing those periodical saturnalia of which Johnston speaks, [2] the great political carnival which the common people regarded as their right. Even if we take into consideration the material advantages which the candidates might derive from victory at the polls, the enormous sums swallowed up in one election often exceeded all reasonable bounds. They are only explicable, if we regard the electoral contests in the light of a national sport, as popular, indeed more popular than horse-racing. [3]   The rich incurred the expense for their own pleasure and for the pleasure of the people, and the passion which they put into the contest was a form of the gambling mania.   Though the system was illogical and anarchic, it was free and popular.   Just as the democratic nature of the constituencies with an extended franchise compensated for the oligarchy of the burgage and corporation boroughs, so the licence enjoyed by the populace at elections balanced the aristocratic composition of the House of Commons.   The members of the aristocracy were compelled to come into personal contact with the masses, to solicit their favour, possibly to incur their anger.   After the repeated reforms to be effected in the British franchise in the course of the 19th century, this counterpoise would no longer be so necessary, and the part played in elections by the mob was destined to vanish, as Parliament became more truly representative of the people.

The Rights of Petition, of Public Meeting, of Association.

The threat of rebellion was the first weapon wielded by public opinion to overawe the Government in office and even the House of Commons itself.   And the popular electioneering demonstrations may be considered an attenuated form of rebellion.   But by the British Constitution the public possessed other and more legal methods by

---

[1] H. of C., March 21, 1806, Courtenay's speech (*Parl. Deb.*, vol. vi. pp. 516–17).

[2] Quoted by Jephson, *The Platform*, vol. i. p. 86.

[3] A good instance of this feeling is to be found in a letter in the *Morning Post* of November 13, 1812, from a correspondent who, writing on December 4th, describes the scene at Clonmel on an election day : " All the neighbouring windows are stuck thick with company—elegant ladies, fashionable youths, the gay and the grave, quakers and soldiers, the politicians and the fribble—all partake of the pleasure, all own the zealous emotions." The article is headed *Election Sports*. In another notice (*Morning Post*, October 21, 1812) a correspondent, who writes from Galway, on October 15th, employs the language of the turf : " The election for this county will commence on Monday next.   Five candidates will start, etc."

which to remind the ruling classes of its existence and to intervene in parliamentary disputes. Blackstone lays down that in cases where a right has been violated, and the regular course of justice is powerless to redress the violation, a further right was possessed by every subject, the right to address a petition to the King, or to one or other of the two Houses, for the redress of the wrong inflicted on the petitioner. But this right to petition involved the right of private persons to meet for the joint preparation and signature of the statement of their grievances. It involved, moreover, the right to meet for deliberation on the opportune moment to present a petition. Thus were the people brought by degrees to the belief that they had a right to form permanent associations to maintain the defence of their interests. The right of petition, the right of public meeting, the right of association (though to be sure this last expression is absent from the legal terminology of the United Kingdom) were rights of the subject, recognized as such by the executive and by the legislature.

This recognition was, however, by no means unconditional. The eighteenth-century Whigs, to protect themselves against a Tory reaction, had put serious restrictions upon the right of meeting. The Riot Act passed in 1714 as the permanent law of the land, conferred upon a single justice of the peace authority to disperse after a delay of one hour any meeting of at least twelve persons " unlawfully assembled together, to the disturbance of the public peace." [1] And this statute indemnified the magistrate in advance, if his efforts to disperse the crowd involved any deaths. Blackstone considered this statute as of sufficient gravity to counterbalance, in conjunction with the establishment of a standing army and the increase of the national debt, all the measures adopted in 1688 to limit the Royal Prerogative.[2] Nevertheless, individuals arrested by order of a magistrate in execution of the Riot Act were secured from the possibility of arbitrary imprisonment or condemnation. In virtue of the Habeas Corpus Act they were entitled to demand an immediate trial in a regular court, where the judge was assisted by a jury. But during the last twenty years the right of meeting and the right of association had been the object of more serious attacks.

The French Revolution had been echoed in England by a democratic agitation in 1792. The ruling classes had taken fright and had passed a series of very severe statutes to repress the movement. Repeated statutes had suspended temporarily the operation of the Habeas Corpus Act.[3] In 1795 a statute had been passed dealing

---

[1] " Being unlawfully, riotously and tumultuously assembled together, to the disturbance of the public peace." (1 Geo. I, st. 2, cap. 5).

[2] 4 Comm. 433–4.

[3] 34 Geo. III, cap. 54 (May 23, 1794) ; 35 Geo. III, cap. 3 (February 5, 1795) ; 38 Geo. III, cap. 36 (April 21, 1798) ; 39 Geo. III, cap. 15, 44 (January 9, May 20, 1799) ;

with seditious meetings and assemblies, to have effect for the three following years.[1] For any meeting of more than fifty persons notice had first to be given to three justices of the peace. Every magistrate was empowered to break up with the help of the troops any meeting which had not complied with this formality ; and even when a meeting was itself in order, a magistrate might break it up, if in his opinion the speeches were tending to arouse among the people hatred or contempt of the King, the Government or the Constitution. Any breach of these provisions was punishable with death. By this statute the right of public meeting was made subject to the discretion of the local Bench of magistrates, and further provisions of this Act restricted even the freedom of association. All premises not open to the general public, where societies held regular political discussions, henceforth required the preliminary authorization of the magistrates and were submitted to their constant supervision. When the Act of 1795 expired in 1799 a new Act imposed fresh restrictions upon the freedom of association.[2] Five important societies were suppressed, and all societies which required their members to take an oath unrecognized by the law were declared to be *ipso facto* illegal, as also were all federations of societies. The penalty imposed for breach of these provisions was transportation for seven years. And to this Act directed against political associations, another was added against combinations of workmen and trade unions. This statute prohibited unions formed for the purpose of obtaining higher wages, and empowered the magistrates to condemn summarily all infractions of the Act. This Combination Act, originally passed in 1799 as a temporary measure, was made permanent in 1800 under a slightly modified form.[3] Thus at the very time, when on the other side of the Channel the Jacobin Republic was nearing its close, in England an entire code was being drawn up against the right of public meeting and the right of association.

What measure of success attended this legislation ? It would certainly appear that the law against trade unions remained largely inoperative, and that in default of an efficient police English statesmen were, as a rule, indisposed to embark on a contest with these unions, a contest whose issue might have been humiliating for the Government. We must also remember that the freedom of religious associations remained unimpaired and that the penal laws formerly enacted against Catholics were either repealed or applied with an ever increasing laxity. The Methodist sects prospered, their open-air meetings multiplied,

39 and 40 Geo. III, cap. 20 (February 28, 1800) ; 41 Geo. III, cap. 32 (December 31, 1800) ; 41 Geo. III (United Kingdom), cap. 26 (April 18, 1801).

[1] 36 Geo. III, cap. 8. Renewed (41 Geo. III, cap. 26) " until six weeks after the commencement of the next session of Parliament."

[2] 39 Geo. III, cap. 79 (July 12, 1799). We must add to this a statute against the administration of illegal oaths (37 Geo. III, cap. 123, 1797).

[3] 39 Geo. III, cap. 81 ; 40 Geo. III, cap. 106.

and their organization received the explicit sanction of law. But our present concern is neither with the religious nor with the economic life of the nation. The question at present before us is to ascertain the extent to which the political life of the country had suffered from the three statutes above enumerated. Though it is true that the propaganda of the democratic associations underwent a temporary decline, it is equally true that it had given proof of renewed vitality during the last decade. Towards the close of 1806 the Middlesex Club had been founded in London, whose members, numbering about 300, paid an entrance fee of one guinea and an annual subscription of half a guinea. The object of this club was to purify political life, to emancipate it from the two-fold influence of wealth and social rank, and to secure the return of democratic candidates, without the labour and ruinous expense of an electoral campaign.[1] Societies similar in character were formed at Bristol and at Westminster.[2] In these societies—to which the provisions of the law did not apply, as they were neither secret nor combined into a wider group—we see the germ of the future democratic organization of the great political parties. About the same date the aged Major Cartwright revived the propaganda on behalf of universal suffrage, and under his influence were founded throughout the country the Society of " The Friends of Parliamentary Reform," the Hampden Club and the Union Society.[3] From 1812 to 1814 the "Luddite" associations were spreading disorder through the manufacturing districts of Yorkshire, Cheshire and Lancashire. The Cabinet, not content with employing against them the existing statutes, obtained from Parliament a further statute of repression. No doubt the societies for political propaganda organized by Cartwright were as peaceable and as harmless as their head. No doubt the Luddite associations were rather unions of workmen than political associations. Without political creed or programme, their aim was the destruction of machinery and factories, not a political revolution. It was, nevertheless, impossible to regard the future without apprehension, and it was easy to foresee the day when the two forms of

[1] Cobbett's *Political Register*, October 25, 1806 (vol. x. pp. 662 sqq.).

[2] For the Patriotic and Constitutional Association of Bristol, see Cobbett's *Political Register*, August 8, 1807 (vol. xii. pp. 210 sqq.). For the Westminster Club for promoting Parliamentary Reform, see *Examiner*, November 8, 1812. The latter Club was more democratic than the Middlesex Club, founded in 1806. The entrance fee was only 6d., and there was also a weekly subscription of 2d. (in place of an annual subscription, which it was found more difficult to secure).

[3] *Life and Correspondence of Cartwright*, vol. ii. p. 377 (Rules of the " Union for Parliamentary Reform," June 10, 1812), p. 380 (Rules and list of members of the Hampden Club). Nor should we fail to remark the increasing reluctance shown by Parliament during the years preceding 1815 to adopt legislation hostile to political liberty. When the Act of 1795 expired in 1809 the Ministry asked that the Act of 1799 should be in consequence revised and rendered more stringent. Parliament refused to accede to the desire of the Cabinet and the Government deemed it useless to insist. H. of C., May 18, June 9, 1809 (*Parl. Deb.*, vol. xiv. p. 615). Cf. H. of C., February 24, 1817, speeches of Lord Castlereagh, of Romilly, of the Solicitor-General (*Parl. Deb.*, vol. xxxv. pp. 590 sqq.).

agitation would unite, and the Government would be faced with a revolutionary movement far more dangerous than the Jacobin movement of 1795. Against the venerable English tradition of popular disorder, the Tory reaction was helpless.

It was, in fact, impossible to abolish freedom of association without at the same time abolishing freedom of meeting. But King George's ministers had never been able to effect the complete abolition of the latter. The county meetings were a regular institution, in many respects conservative, enjoying the consecration of tradition. These meetings were specially exempted by the Act of 1795 from the operation of the new statute. The summons to attend was issued by the sheriff. It was the custom that only the freehold electors of the county took part in the meeting. It was concluded by the adoption of an address drawn up by the local authorities in accordance with a solemn and traditional formula. The matter of the address was regularly an expression of loyalty to the Sovereign.[1] But although the presence of the sheriff and the exclusion from the meeting of all the inhabitants of the county not on the list of voters were considered obligatory, these restrictions were not based on any written law. In 1780 the Duke of Richmond in Sussex had neglected to observe the former.[2] And more recently the independent gentlemen of Cornwall had violated both.[3] Certain counties, for instance Middlesex, were vast urban democracies, where a county aristocracy did not even exist. In other places the aristocracy was split into rival factions which at times did not shrink from imparting an almost revolutionary character to their quarrels. In 1805 and in 1807 county meetings had denounced the scandals in high places, had demanded the impeachment of Lord Melville, and the retirement of the Duke of York. In 1815 they called upon the Ministry to abolish the property tax. It is clearly impossible to draw any clear line of demarcation between the county meeting held according to legal forms and the popular meeting which the Tory legislator desired to prohibit. During the last few years the English had been making a constantly increasing use of the right of meeting, as also of the right of petition inseparable from it.

The right of petition had been affirmed by the Bill of Rights of 1688. In virtue of this statute every British subject possessed the right to address a petition to the King and to the two Houses. It is true that a statute of the Restoration[4] had submitted the exercise of this right to certain restrictions, had made the presentation of a

---

[1] For the procedure, see Jephson, *The Platform*, vol. i. pp. 16–17. Cf. the opinion expressed by the radical agitator, Cartwright, on the subject of these county meetings (*Life and Correspondence*, vol. i. p. 327) : " I must confess I have seen too much not to be thoroughly sick of the old dull road of meetings of freeholders convened by the aristocracy."

[2] Jephson, *The Platform*, vol. i. p. 103.

[3] Oldfield, *Representative History*, vol. iii. p. 135.

[4] 13 Car. II, st. 1, cap. 5.

petition by a gathering of more than ten persons illegal, and had laid down that every petition signed by more than twenty persons whose object was an alteration of the established institutions must have received the signature either of three magistrates or of the majority of a grand jury. But although Blackstone considered the statute as still in force, and expressed his approval of it,[1] no one thought of applying it except in one exceptionally troublous year, namely during the anti-Catholic riots of 1780. When in 1795 William Pitt introduced his Bill to repress seditious meetings he expressly disclaimed any intention of interfering with the right of petition.[2] This right, therefore, throughout the whole period of the Tory reaction remained at the disposition of the public, a means of bringing peaceful pressure from without to bear upon the legislature, and of preventing Parliament from passing statutes without regard to public opinion. A Member of Parliament considered himself obliged to present to the House of Commons any petition signed in his constituency, even when he disagreed with its object.[3] Those who did not possess the franchise could sign a petition, and could thus take an indirect part in public life and warn the Government that if no regard were paid to their wishes, a discontent would be aroused which might easily assume a form dangerous to the public peace. The opponents of the slave trade were first to make a systematic use of the right of petition. Their magnificently organized agitation had obtained a decisive victory in 1806. Collective petitions were henceforward the order of the day. In 1812 Brougham had secured the revocation of the Orders in Council by organizing petitions on a large scale, and the agitation of 1814 which followed immediately the restoration of peace, and whose object was to protest against the obstacles which Parliament desired to impose upon the importation of foreign corn, also took this form. Petitions to this effect had already been circulated in Glasgow in 1813, and it was in Glasgow that the movement was renewed in the following year. Thence it reached Lancashire and quickly spread throughout the length and breadth of England. Mr. Protheroe, a Whig member for Bristol, collected 22,445 signatures in his constituency. In five days 20,000 were brought to Leeds. All, or almost all, the large towns of the kingdom sent up petitions. A few months of truce followed. It was the parliamentary vacation, the plans of the Cabinet were still uncertain and the petitioners hoped that they had succeeded in alarming the Government. It was, however, plain by the winter that the policy of dear bread had won a decided victory in the Cabinet, and the Corn

---

[1] 1 *Comm.* 143. Cf. 4 *Comm.* 147.

[2] H. of C., November 10, 1795, Pitt's speech (*Parl. Hist.*, vol. xxxii. pp. 274–5).

[3] H. of C., May 17, 1813, Canning's speech; April 27, 1814, speech of W. Smith. H. of L., March 6, 1815, Lord Derby's speech (*Parl. Deb.*, vol. xxvi. p. 216; vol. xxvii. p. 574; vol. xxx, p. 2).

Bill was introduced. The agitation was renewed immediately. On February 7, 1815, forty-two petitions were presented to Parliament. On March 4th a mass meeting was held in London, at which city men of every shade of political opinion were represented. On this occasion 40,571 signatures were collected within ten hours. The petition from Manchester bore 52,000 names. Undismayed by these demonstrations the Cabinet and its majority in Parliament persisted in their intentions, the protectionist Corn Bill was passed and the meetings degenerated into riots. But in spite of its ultimate failure, the monster agitation had made a deep impression. " It is the first time," remarked the *Morning Chronicle*, " when a majority of the adult male population of England has petitioned the two Houses of Parliament on any subject." [1]

Freedom of the Press.

Employment of the right of meeting and of the right of petition merely enabled the governed to exert a somewhat spasmodic pressure on the Government at exceptionally critical periods. But we must not, therefore, imagine that the British public at this period was without any means of exercising a permanent control over the policy of Parliament. On the contrary, for a century past, and especially during the last fifty years, there had been in existence a powerful instrument of public control, an instrument which came to be regarded as part of the unwritten Constitution of the Realm, namely the political Press. The English maintained that in their country the Press was free. By this they did not mean that no expression of opinion was criminal or that a journalist could without fear of prosecution hold up to hatred or contempt either the Constitution or an individual statesman, but that since the closing years of the 17th century the Government had lost the right of preliminary censorship over printed matter. England was the sole country in Europe where liberty of the Press in this sense existed. All political parties willingly or unwillingly agreed to declare this liberty inviolable. The opponents of the Court party saw in it their surest guarantee against a despotic reaction. " Give me," exclaimed Sheridan in 1810, " but the liberty of the Press, and I will give to the minister a venal House of Peers—I will give him a corrupt and servile House of Commons—I will give him the full swing of the patronage of office . . . armed with the liberty of the Press I will go forth to meet him undismayed." [2] Indeed, the classic toast of Whig banquets was " The liberty of the Press—'tis like the air we breathe—while we have it we cannot die." [3]

[1] *Morning Chronicle*, March 15, 1815.
[2] H. of C., February 6, 1810, Sheridan's speech (*Parl. Deb.*, vol. xv. p. 341).
[3] F. K. Hunt, *Fourth Estate*, p. 276. Cf. letters of the Earl of Dudley to the Bishop of Llandaff, pp. 57–8, August 9, 1814 : " Every Englishman, from Johnny Grotes' House to

We should hardly expect, however, to find that the liberty of the Press had been immune from attack throughout the last half-century. During the first half of the reign before the war with France it had gained more ground than it lost. It was in vain that Parliament had attempted by means of antiquated legal decisions, originally intended to protect the House of Commons against the abuse of the Royal Prerogative, to prevent the publication of their debates in the newspapers. A protracted and stormy conflict had ended in the capitulation of the Tories. The extension in 1792 of the powers of the jury in libel cases furnished yet another guarantee for the liberty of journalists. With the anti-Jacobin scare, however, a new epoch opened, and the party of reaction attempted to take its revenge.

A royal proclamation of May 21, 1792, against "criminal and seditious writings" was the Government's declaration of war upon the journalists. Legislation of a novel kind followed. An Act of 1795 punished persons found guilty of having incited by speech or writing to hatred or contempt of the King or the Government, with penalties amounting to seven years' transportation in the case of a second offence.[1] An Act of 1798 prohibited the anonymous publication of newspapers.[2] Six clauses of the Act of 1799 against seditious societies imposed a system of registration upon the printers of books and newspapers, also upon the owners and even the makers of presses and type.[3] Moreover, even apart from special legislation, the Government possessed a number of indirect means to fetter the freedom of the Press. The custom was established with ever-increasing stringency that those prosecuted by the Government for libel might not prove the facts alleged. The procedure by "ex-officio informations" enabled the Attorney-General to dispense in the prosecution of journalists with the complicated formalities of a presentation by the grand jury. He could, moreover, bring journalists before a court where the judge was assisted not by the "common jury," the assize jury, but by a "special jury," which was selected according to different principles, and could be summoned whenever the Government pleased. Journalists and their counsel complained, with or without justification, that a special jury was too often biased in favour of the prosecution.[4] The Attorney-

---

the Land's End, is certain that he knows the worst—that nothing is concealed—that all the materials for judgment are before him—and that by reading and comparing the newspapers and journals, he may be just as wise as if he lived within the sound of Bow-bells."

[1] 36 Geo. III, cap. 7, § 2.   [2] 38 Geo. III, cap. 78.

[3] 39 Geo. III, cap. 79, sec. 23–9.

[4] For denunciations of the special jury system, see Cobbett's *Political Register*, February 27, 1811; Bentham, *Elements of the Art of Packing* (*Works*, vol. v. pp. 61 sqq.). Blackstone, on the other hand (3 *Comm.* 357–8), depicts the institution as a favour granted to the accused. Cf. the Attorney-General's speech (H. of C., March 28, 1811, *Parl. Deb.*, vol. xiv. p. 572). We may add that Lord Holland, in a speech delivered in the House of Lords in support of relaxation of the Press laws, does not express himself at all decidedly on this point (H. of C., March 4, 1811, *Parl. Deb.*, vol. xix. p. 143).

General could also protract at pleasure the interval between the information and the trial. During this interval he had the right to reverse
his original decision and abandon the prosecution. Even so the
journalist had been submitted to the threat of a prosecution, and
this intimidation necessarily diminished his freedom. And in any
case, even if the verdict were one of acquittal or if the trial were
abandoned, the accused had to pay the costs.[1] The Government
also took advantage of the financial difficulties with which it was
confronted to raise the stamp duty from time to time.[2] The
existence of the newspapers was thus made increasingly difficult.

The zeal displayed by the Government in the repression of excesses
on the part of the Press was very considerable till the Peace of Amiens,[3]
but was undoubtedly relaxed during the years immediately following.
Between 1801 and 1807 the average yearly number of prosecutions
did not exceed two ; only one such trial took place during the Ministry
of Fox and Lord Grenville. Then the prosecutions were renewed.

In 1808 the adoption of new regulations hostile to the freedom
of the Press rendered the existing legislation even more severe. All
distinction was abolished between the procedure of ex-officio informations and the procedure of ordinary prosecutions.[4] The number
of prosecutions increased. Between 1808 and 1810 there were
forty-two ex-officio informations, and eighteen trials of journalists.[5]
An attack was made on important journalists such as Cobbett,
whose *Political Register* was notorious for its attacks upon leading
politicians, and Perry, the universally respected proprietor of the
Morning Chronicle. And this period also witnessed a final attempt
to restrict the right claimed by the Press to report parliamentary
debates. This right was not legally theirs. A standing order forbade
the publication of debates. Since this order prevented any official
account of the sessions, debaters in both Houses were obliged to
endure the publication of their speeches in an imperfect and often
deliberately garbled report. This led to frequent complaints and
the prosecution of journalists.[6] It was only by favour of the

---

[1] On the whole question see H. of L., March 9, 1811, Lord Holland's speech (*Par . Deb.*,
vol. xix. p. 129). Cf. C. Jephson, *The Platform*, vol. i. p. 183).

[2] In 1776 Lord North raised it from 1d. to 1½d. Pitt in 1789 raised it to 2d., in 1797
to 2½d., in 1804 to 3½d. In 1815 it was raised to 4d. (Grant, *Newspaper Press*, vol. i. pp.
221–3). Lecky, *History of England*, vol. iii. p. 470, corrects a mistake of date made by Grant.

[3] In 1795 the Attorney-General, Sir William Scott, afterwards Lord Eldon, expressed his
satisfaction " that in the last two years there had been more prosecutions for libels than in
any twenty years before " (Campbell, *Lives of the Chancellors*, vol. vii. p. 120).

[4] 38 Geo. III, cap. 58. For the bearings of this Law see Lord Erskine's speech (H. of L.,
May 24, 1808, *Parl. Deb.*, vol. ii. p. 541).

[5] H. of C., March 28, 1811, Lord Folkestone's speech (*Parl. Deb.*, vol. xix. p. 549).
Also *Return of the Ex-Officio Informations filed for Political Libel and Seditious Conduct . .
since 1807, 1821*.

[6] See particularly H. of C., December 27, and Dec. 31, 1798 (*Parl. Hist.*, vol. xxxiv. pp.
148 sqq.). H. of C., February 15, 1813 (*Parl. Deb.*, vol. xxiv. p. 518).

House that the public was permitted to be present at the sessions of Parliament. Each member had the power to call attention at will to the illegal presence of "strangers," and the "gallery" must then be cleared immediately. This actually happened in 1810. When the House of Commons began the discussion of a disastrous military expedition, a member successfully demanded that the House should expel the public and constitute itself a secret committee. Windham, who had made himself famous in Parliament for his unwearied protests against the impudence of the Press, seized the opportunity to utter once more his hatred of the reporters who listened to his speech and took it down, a vile set, "bankrupts, lottery-office keepers, footmen and decayed tradesmen." [1] An obscure City politician, an old Jacobin of 1792 named John Gale Jones, procured the adoption by a small democratic club of an order of the day protesting against this exclusion of the public. He was arrested without any legal formality by order of the Commons for breach of privilege and brought before the Bar of the House. Sir Francis Burdett, the representative of democracy in Parliament, published in Cobbett's *Political Register* [2] a lengthy address to his constituents, in which he protested against this procedure. Thereupon he was himself imprisoned.

It was an unskilful and useless attempt at reaction. For we must regard it not as an energetic attack on the Press by the Government, but as a desperate effort of self-defence against journalists, whose independence and audacity were constantly increasing. The Duke of York scandal implicated the War Office and affected the honour of the Royal Family. The newspapers loudly voiced the popular indignation. Burdett had been in prison for seven weeks, and six weeks would pass before the condemnation of Cobbet, when the Duke of Cumberland scandal occurred on May 30 1810. The ministers called upon to deal with events so disastrous to the prestige of the Government were men of mean abilities and personally unpopular. It availed them little to multiply prosecutions. Every case must go before a jury and the Government had therefore to consider, before undertaking a prosecution, whether or no it could count on the desired condemnation. The indefinite postponement of so many trials was not perhaps due to a Machiavellian scheme, as the Opposition journalists would have us believe. The Attorney-General hesitated and temporized, because he dared not face a jury. Though Cobbett had been found guilty, Perry had been acquitted. Not only did the jury often acquit those whom the Government required it to condemn. The foes of the Government, when libelled by the official Press, could appeal to it in their turn and obtain damages. This course was adopted, for instance, in 1810 by Roger O'Connor, a friend of Sir

---

[1] H. of C., February 6, 1810 (*Parl. Deb.*, vol. xv. p. 330).

[2] Cobbett's *Political Register*, March 24, 1810 (vol. xvii. pp. 421 sqq.) H. of C., March 27, 1812 (*Parl. Deb.*, vol xvi. p. 27).

Francis Burdett.[1]

Even if the condemnation of the journalist were secured, the Government could scarcely be said to have gained much by the trial. The publicity of the article incriminated was at once increased tenfold. The Attorney-General was obliged to reproduce in his pleading the text of the article, and on the following day the entire Press was authorized to reproduce with impunity, as part of the Attorney-General's accusation, a writing judged by the Government libellous or seditious. In 1809 an article by Cobbett on the question of corporal punishment in the Army had been held to compromise military discipline and the safety of the realm. But as a result of the prosecution the question of flogging in the Army was discussed in every newspaper. Fresh trials were commenced, which of course served only to bring the matter before an even wider public. In 1811 the Government promised reforms. A condemned journalist was not subject in prison to the treatment of criminals and ordinary offenders. When Cobbett was imprisoned in Newgate, he spent his mornings editing his paper, his afternoons receiving his political friends.[2] He employed his two years' imprisonment in conducting a campaign on behalf of the freedom of the Press. The contest between the House of Commons and Sir Francis Burdett provoked a riot in the London streets. Only the timidity of Sir Francis, who avoided the manifestations prepared in his honour, deprived the popular triumph of its final crown. And even so the Government was obliged to yield. Already in 1809 journalists had secured certain reductions in the stamp duty.[3] The Act of 1808, empowering the Attorney-General to imprison accused journalists as a precautionary measure, was applied on one single occasion, and fell thenceforward into disuse.[4] In 1811 the Government relaxed the provisions of the penal statutes of 1798 and 1799,[5] and during the four years following the number of trials for expressions of opinion once more became insignificant.[6]

---

[1] Cobbett's *Political Register*, December 22, 1810 (vol. xviii. pp. 1249 sqq.). The *Morning Post*, a Government organ, was sentenced to pay £500 damages.

[2] See Cobbett's letter to Creevy, Newgate, September 24, 1810 (*Creevy Papers*, vol. i. p. 134). It is only fair to add that this lenient treatment gave rise to suspicions on the part of some of Cobbett's colleagues. Leigh Hunt, in the *Examiner* of July 12, 1812, accused Cobbett of having entered into negotiations with the Government and of having offered to suspend the publication of his paper if he were not condemned, and during his imprisonment accused him of systematic toadying to the Duke of York and the Prince of Wales.

[3] The rebate of 16 per cent. granted since 1797 to newspapers whose price did not exceed 6d. was extended to all newspapers without exception. 49 Geo. III, cap. 50. See H. of C., April 27, 1809 (*Parl. Deb.*, vol. xiv. p. 266).

[4] H. of L., March 4, 1811, Lord Ellenborough's speech (*Parl. Deb.*, vol. xix. p. 148).

[5] 51 Geo. III, cap. 65.

[6] *Return of the Ex-Officio Informations . . . 1821.* Prosecutions for Libel, Blasphemy and Sedition 1813–22. 1823 also Prosecutions for Libel, etc. . . . during the reigns of Geo. III and Geo. IV . . . 1830.

Modern Journalism.

The empire of the Press was in process of foundation. To be sure, a large and important Press was already in existence at the close of the 18th century, and the numbers of newspapers had scarcely increased since that date. The progressive increase of the stamp duty, the enhanced cost of paper, the rise of salaries, had necessitated an increase in the price of newspapers. In 1815 a big daily paper cost 7d.[1] But twenty-five years of dramatic events, of revolutions, of battles had aroused in the public both of London and the provinces an insatiable appetite for news, which had enabled journalism to develop in the face of all obstacles and had increased the circulation of the papers already in existence.

In London there were daily papers, both morning and evening, of which several editions appeared on days when any event of importance occurred.[2] There were papers appearing thrice weekly, and weekly papers which summed up every Sunday the events of the week, and flourished in spite of all the efforts made by the Puritan party to prevent this violation of the Sabbath. Many of these papers, edited by adventurers and banned by the police, endured a highly precarious existence, always on the look-out for some scandal which would enable them to enjoy a few weeks of ephemeral popularity. Far above such miserable rags five or six leading newspapers stood out—the *Times*, the *Morning Chronicle*, the *Morning Post*, the *Courier* and the *Morning Herald*. These consisted of four pages of small print. The first and fourth of these pages were devoted to advertisements. On the second page were two columns of extracts from the Parisian newspapers. Then followed advertisements of theatres and the news of the day, chiefly concerning the internal politics of the country. Sometimes, though by no means every day, one of the items of news was accompanied by a lengthy comment which already constituted a leading article. The third page contained foreign news, sporting and society news, law reports, and an occasional article of dramatic criticism. When Parliament was sitting, the whole of the second page was occupied by a report of the proceedings in the House, a report which would often take up, in addition, a part of the third page and might even, if a matter of great importance were under discussion, fill almost the

---

[1] Interesting information as to the financial aspect of the production of an English newspaper at this period is to be found in Cobbett's *Political Register* for March 4, 1809. Cf. J. Grant, *Newspaper Press*, vol. i. pp. 223–4, on the rise of prices—3d. till 1775, 3½d. till 1789, 4d. till 1797, 6d. till 1815, and in 1815 7d.

[2] *Examiner*, March 19, 1815 : " One of the evening papers (the *Star*) had no less than five editions yesterday, altogether containing the following assertions : That Marseilles had offered a reward of two millions for the head of Bonaparte—that Ney had taken an oath to bring him alive or dead to Paris—that the Parisians begin to manifest some enthusiasm for the Bourbons—that the Minister of Marine had been displaced—that Bonaparte had retreated with 4,000 men into the mountains—that Lefebvre was taken—that Victor, Dupont and Ney were advancing against Bonaparte—and that he was, in fact, surrounded."

entire paper. We find already, on a smaller scale, the arrangement of a leading English newspaper of our own time. The *Times*, which had been printed for a year past by steam,[1] enjoyed a daily circulation of 5,000, the *Courier* sometimes reached a circulation of 10,000.[2] The proprietors of leading newspapers, such as John Walter of the *Times*, Daniel Stuart of the *Morning Post*, Perry of the *Morning Chronicle*, were persons of no slight importance, and the magnificent appointments of their offices, their "rosewood tables and silver inkstands," awed and dazzled poor editors.[3] Among the weeklies Cobbett's *Political Register* was undeniably in the very front rank—a paper always violent, often scurrilous in its attacks not only upon the party in office but also upon the moderate Opposition, but excellently informed all the same. An equally high position was held by Leigh Hunt's *Examiner* —a paper as "radical" in its political complexion as the *Register*, but first of the London journals for literary merit.

In the provinces each county town possessed its weekly paper, often two papers—one supporting the Government, the other the Opposition. These papers were modelled on the London papers. But the news from the Continent was not so recent, and the local news was more detailed. An excellent system of distribution enabled the proprietors to sell their paper the moment almost it was printed, in all the market towns of the district, sometimes even to dispatch copies to other country towns, there to compete with the local Press. These proprietors prided themselves on an unimpeachable respectability, and their papers were serious in tone, independent and well supplied with information. Their readers were the local gentry, shopkeepers and farmers—a fairly extensive and extremely constant and reliable public. The total number of newspapers published in London and in the provinces was about 250. In 1753 the stamp duty was paid on 7,411,757 copies, in 1792 on 15,005,760 : that is on more than double. In 1801 it was paid on 16,000,000 : the number had hardly increased a million during the previous decade. Then progress began afresh : in 1821 duty would be paid on 25,000,000 copies.[4]

The commercial invention on which modern English journalism was based was the combination of the newspaper with the advertiser. This combination dated from the decade between 1770 and 1780,

---

[1] F. K. Hunt, *Fourth Estate*, vol. ii. pp. 171–2.

[2] Grant, *Newspaper Press*, vol. i. pp. 355–6 ; vol. ii. p. 4. On some occasions the circulation of the *Courier* had reached 16,500. With the restoration of peace its circulation began to decline.

[3] Charles Lamb, *Essays of Elia, Newspapers Thirty-five Years Ago.*

[4] See *Stamps issued for Newspapers* where we find the official figures for the years 1801 and 1821, published in 1822. (They are reproduced in the *Annual Register* for 1822, pp. 350–2.) In 1821 the total number of newspapers was 278 : London dailies = 16, London papers appearing thrice weekly = 8, London weeklies = 32, English local papers = 16, Scotch d. = 31, Irish d. = 56. The sale of London papers = 16,254,534 copies ; the sale of local papers = 8,525,252.

when George III was engaged in a stubborn contest with the London Press. The Press, though formidable through the savagery of its attacks, had nevertheless fallen very low in public opinion. It was no longer conducted, as during the earlier half of the century, by eminent men of letters, by men of high birth, by statesmen, men such as Steele and Addison, Bolingbroke and Pulteney ; it had fallen into the hands of literary adventurers, of sharpers, of rogues of every description. Little by little it was to raise its head once more by adapting itself to the novel needs of the period and by becoming an industry. No longer, as of old, was it to be literary and witty ; henceforth it would be serious, commercial, practical. It is true that the profession of a journalist was still regarded as barely respectable ; but a few years had passed since the attempt of the Bar to prevent barristers from engaging in journalism. In 1825 Walter Scott was to refuse for his son-in-law the post of chief editor of a leading London paper, as being in his opinion unworthy of his social position.[1] Nevertheless, the proprietor of a newspaper was scaling the social ladder and was conquering by degrees the position naturally taken in a mercantile society by men of commerce and business men of all kinds. Usually a group representative of a particular interest—for example, a syndicate of coachbuilders, of auctioneers, of booksellers, or of brewers—advanced the necessary capital for the foundation of a new paper to obtain thus the free use of the advertisement columns. Once the paper had achieved success, the editor would often find the control of the syndicate burdensome and would attempt to shake it off. The syndicate would then avenge itself by the foundation of an Opposition paper. It was under these circumstances that a syndicate of booksellers founded the *British Press*, a morning paper, in opposition to the *Morning Post*, and the *Globe*, an evening paper, in opposition to the *Courier*.[2] But even when the syndicate maintained its control over the editor, his very dependence on the syndicate emancipated him from the control which political groups, the Court, the party organizations sought to exercise over him in other directions. Regarded from this point of view, the growing independence of the Press will appear as another form of the plutocracy which marks the 19th century.

The Government, feeling itself powerless to destroy the freedom of the Press, sought to utilize the newspapers for the support of its policy. What, however, could it offer the newspaper proprietor as the price of his services ? A pecuniary bribe was out of the question. The advertisements brought far more than the Government was in a position to offer and were paying better every day. Moreover, the

---

[1] Smiles, *Life of Murray*, vol. ii. pp. 180 sqq. Cf. Moneypenny, *Life of Disraeli*, vol. i. pp. 81 sqq.

[2] F. K. Hunt, *The Fourth Estate*, vol. ii. pp. 90 sqq. Cf. H. of C., April 27, 1809 (*Parl. Deb.*, vol. xiv. p. 267).

wider the circulation of the paper, the more profitable were the advertisements, and to attract the public the paper must bow not to the orders of the Cabinet, but to the popular taste. In 1815 the proprietor of the *Times* would not have agreed, as his father had agreed twenty years earlier, to support the policy of the Government in return for a pension of £600. Nor was it of any use for the Government to offer official announcements. On the contrary, the Government had more need of the papers to publish its announcements than they of the Government. Nor had it news to offer. The time was gone by when the Government was better informed of passing events than the Press. Although the proprietors of the London papers did not as yet employ regular correspondents stationed permanently in the great capitals of the world, or attached, almost officially, to the staff of warring armies, it was nevertheless common knowledge that they were prepared to pay handsomely for news brought secretly from Continental ports. They made a skilful use of private correspondence. They had devised a host of methods by which the British Press had become a focus for the rumours of Europe. The Government had indeed attempted, as a last resource, to intercept the couriers employed by the newspapers, and to oblige the Press to purchase as a favour the services of the official post. But these attempts had failed. Five years of conflict with the *Times* had resulted in the victory of that paper, which had foiled the tricks and illegal practices of the Government.[1]

On the whole, then, it would appear that the accusations of servility and venality brought by the Opposition organs against the papers supporting the Government credited the Government with much more influence than in reality it possessed. Even the ministerial organs depended rather on the public than on the Cabinet. In 1809 the *Courier* had turned against the Government in the matter of the Duke of York. In 1814 and 1815 all the Government papers deserted the Ministry on the questions of the Property Tax and the Corn Bill. "No paper that has any character," Lord Liverpool wrote to Lord Castlereagh, "and consequently an established sale, will accept money from Government; and indeed their profits are so enormous in all critical times, when their support is the most necessary, that no pecuniary assistance that Government could offer would really be worth their acceptance. . . . The truth is, they look only to their sale. They make their way like sycophants with the public, by finding out the prejudices and prepossessions of the moment, and then flattering them; and the number of *soi-disant* Government or Opposition papers abound just as the Government is generally popular or unpopular."[2]

---

[1] *The Times*, February 11, 1807. Grant, *Newspaper Press*, vol. i. pp. 436 sqq. For the relations between the proprietor of *The Times* and the Government, see also *Croker Papers*, vol. i. pp. 36 sqq.

[2] *Letters and Memoirs of Lord Castlereagh*, vol. xi. pp. 16–17, Lord Liverpool to Lord Castlereagh, September 5, 1815.

In the House of Commons Windham was wont to defend the thesis that the British Constitution would be altered, and that England would become a democracy if the newspapers were free to report and to criticize at their pleasure the parliamentary debates. His contention was not altogether unfounded. In the 18th century writers on Constitutional Law had been accustomed to discuss the problem whether or no democracy were practicable in a large State, and whether it was possible to conceive of democracies of a different type from those which had obtained in the city States of the ancient world, and which were being held up by Rousseau as a model for modern imitation. When the United States of America had been founded, it was thought that the solution of the problem had been furnished by federalism, and that it was possible to construct a large democratic State by the federation of a number of petty republics ; but the new development taken by the political Press had rendered federalism unnecessary. Thanks to the progress of printing, and the improvement of the means of transport, it had become possible for the parliamentary orator, for the editor of a leading newspaper, daily to lay his view of the political events of the day before every citizen of a great nation. And in this way the newspaper editors performed the part played by the demagogue in the petty republics of antiquity. Naturally the effect produced by the newspaper politician was less immediate and did not provoke so violent a response as the speech of a demagogue. The scattered readers of a newspaper were a public, not a mob. There was, however, exactly the same sensationalism, the same appeal to the emotions of the multitude. Thus has the modern newspaper reduced the dimensions of an entire country to those of an ancient agora or forum.

PARLIAMENT AND PUBLIC OPINION. THE STATE OF PARTIES IN 1815.

The Parliamentary Parties Discredited.

We have seen that rebellion, or the menace of rebellion, or milder forms of rebellion, popular demonstrations, public meetings, general petitions, political associations, newspapers, were weapons employed by the Englishman as his traditional right for the defence of his liberty. But the very necessity for their employment is proof that the Constitution, understood in the strict sense of the term, was an insufficient safeguard. According to the theory of the Constitution, which regarded it as a mixture in three equal parts of three distinct principles, the House of Commons, as opposed to the Crown and the Upper House, represented the democratic principle. But the guarantees which the people should have found in the House of Commons for the security of their liberty and interests, they were, in fact, obliged to seek elsewhere against the House of Commons itself. That is to say, the interests of the Crown and those of both Houses of Parliament had now become identical. No longer did a conflict of interests render each a check upon the two others, securing thus a balance of political forces. The Constitution had been stultified.

This was the belief of all who demanded " a reform of Parliament," and of those especially who wished this reform to be "radical," and who were therefore shortly to receive the nickname of "radicals." [1] In their opinion, the House of Commons could never represent truly the will of the people, could never perform the function assigned to it by the Constitution, until it was elected by all the taxpayers or even by all adult males without exception. William Cobbett, a former anti-Jacobin writer who had broken with the Tories, was the journalistic exponent of the new group. Sunday by Sunday, in his *Register*, he fulminated wholesale denunciations of the self-seeking and absence of political conscience displayed equally by both the great parliamentary parties. Henry Hunt, " the man with the white hat," a violent demagogue, Major Cartwright, an old dotard termed in mockery the "mother of parliamentary reform," [2] founded societies to carry on the propaganda and addressed public meetings. The group began to display its activity during the general elections of 1806 and 1807. In 1809 Sir Francis Burdett, Member for Westminster, brought forward a motion in favour of the extension of the franchise to all taxpayers. The same year the party gained a more important adherent in the person of Bentham. He had been known previously in England as a prison reformer, on the Continent as a penologist. His political opinions had been conservative and sceptical. His *Catechism of Parliamentary Reform*, which appeared in 1810, announced his conversion to the cause of radical reform. He now became the philosopher of the party. Near him at Westminster lived his secretary, James Mill, who recruited for Bentham the intellectual youth of the nation. Francis Place meanwhile was organizing the electors. It was in truth a motley group, and counted but a small number of adherents. Its prestige was due to the fact that it brought forward with untiring zeal arguments in justification of the growing feeling of dissatisfaction with the parliamentary machine which had been felt for some years past by the British public.

Pitt and Fox were both in their graves, and no first-rate statesman was left in Parliament. The English—not merely those who were eager for reform and took a keen interest in politics, but the indifferent and fickle masses—were disgusted by the mediocrity of their politicians. Democratic orators and publicists but echoed their own secret suspicions, when they called the leaders of both parties to account

---

[1] For the origin of the term, see our *Formation du Radicalisme philosophique*, vol. ii. pp. 206–7.
[2] *Memoirs, Journal and Correspondence of Thomas Moore*, September 7, 1818 (vol. ii. p. 157).

for the courtesy and consideration with which they treated their opponents. What, they asked, was the meaning of this courtesy, of this consideration, if the two parties really stood for ideas, were radically divided from each other by a difference of principle ? But in reality the two parties did not represent ideas. They were merely two rival factions disputing the possession of power, the ins and the outs ; and since the outs knew that some day or other the turn of the political wheel would put them into office, they were very guarded in their attacks on abuses by which sooner or later they would themselves profit. And, again, why did every Member of Parliament defend so obstinately the antiquated constitutional dogma which taught that immediately on his election he became independent of his constituents, and that the House of Commons would be no longer a free and deliberative assembly, if the members took orders from those who had sent them to Parliament ? [1] Nor was this thesis maintained only by the Tories. Romilly, the typical Whig theorist, and an advocate of administrative and parliamentary reform, had made it a point of honour for the past three years not to enter into any engagement with the Bristol electorate to support either of these reforms. [2] It is not surprising that the electors would have none of him and that the democrats were committed to an implacable feud with this Liberal pedant. More recently, in the course of the debates on the Corn Bill, Western had actually boasted of his indifference to the opinion of his constituents ; and William Smith even thought it necessary to apologize for deferring to the opinion of his constituency. [3] Nevertheless, the radical reformers were not justified in ascribing this divorce between Parliament and public opinion wholly to the defective franchise. We should be forming altogether too high an estimate of the value of democratic institutions, did we believe that the adoption of manhood suffrage or of any other very broad franchise would of itself secure immediately an absolute identity of interest and a complete harmony of sentiment between the electorate and their representatives. Moreover, the unpopularity of the Commons, of the parties who composed it, of the statesmen who led it, was but a recent and a passing phenomenon

[1] See the speeches of Lord North and of Jenkinson (the future Lord Liverpool), given in Jephson, *The Platform*, vol. i. pp. 149, 207. Cf. H. of C., February 20, 1815, Vansittart's speech : " He could not conceive any such thing as a contract between the Commons in Parliament assembled, and the Commons at large, by which the former stipulated that they would not, under any circumstances, resort to a particular measure. Whatever might be the situation of Parliament, they could not enter into a contract or bargain with the subjects of the realm at large, whose representatives they were, and whose interests were identified with their own " (*Parl. Deb.*, vol. xxix. p. 854).

[2] *Memoirs*, vol. iii. pp. 23 sqq. : " The merit " (of my speech) " consisted more in what I omitted than in what I said. I touched upon no topics calculated to court popular favour. I said nothing of a reform of Parliament, of pensions, of sinecures, of economy in the public expenditure, of peace, or of any other of the subjects which are at the present moment generally so favourably received in public assemblies." Of what, then, did he speak ?

[3] H. of C., March 6, 1815 (*Parl. Deb.*, vol. xxx. pp. 24, 27).

The days of Pitt were not long past, the days of Canning were in the near future. We must take a sufficiently long period into consideration, if we would form a just estimate of the working of the British Parliament during the latter half of the reign of George III, an estimate which will, indeed, account for the temporary discredit into which both parties had fallen, but will not fail to recognize that all the while both parties had been laying insensibly the foundations of the future democracy.

The Whigs. The Policy of a Self-seeking Faction.

We will study first the Whig Opposition, now become so weak and so unpopular. How shall we account for the profound discredit into which had fallen the party once the incarnation of the soul of England ? The Whigs had not really been vanquished, as they alleged, by the gold of King George and his friends. The true cause of their downfall was that public opinion had repudiated a policy too obviously oligarchic. The downfall dated from the year 1784, the year which had witnessed a reconciliation between Fox, the bitter opponent of the American War, and Lord North, who as Prime Minister had been responsible for that war. The two statesmen, as the result of a joint intrigue, had formed a coalition Cabinet and had succeeded in obtaining a chance majority in Parliament. They fell together when they attempted by their East India Bill to subject the entire Indian empire to the control of a committee sitting in London, whose nine original members were to be the nominees of Parliament. This meant the open and direct annexation of the colonial government by the great parliamentary families. George III rebelled against the scheme, secured the rejection of the East India Bill by a small majority of the House of Lords, dismissed Fox and Lord North, and appointed as Prime Minister the youthful William Pitt, a son of Lord Chatham, who had resisted pressing solicitations to enter the coalition Cabinet, and had constituted himself the advocate in Parliament of an extensive reform of the franchise. The country declared in favour of Pitt against Fox and Lord North. In other words, the nation repudiated the Whigs the moment they ceased to represent a principle—the defence, namely, of the liberties of the people—and degenerated into a mere coalition of selfish factions. Within a few months the Whigs had lost the fruits of a century of prestige and power.[1]

[1] A letter from Pitt to Addington, written in 1800, proves that the popularity of Parliament as an institution was then intact. " I see nothing so likely to prevent the progress of discontent and internal mischief as what we have more than once found effectual, and cannot too much accustom the public to look up to—a speedy meeting of Parliament. Even if no important legislative measure could be taken, the result of Parliamentary inquiry and discussion would go further than anything towards quieting men's minds, and checking erroneous opinions." (Pellew, Life of Lord Sidmouth, vol. i. p. 264.)

This had been the cause of the fall of the Whigs in 1784, and still in 1815 it remained one of the causes of their weakness. For the last fifteen years, the Tory party had been tending to split, and the Whigs had attempted to utilize the split to rally to their standard the greatest possible number of deserters and to attempt once more that policy of coalition which in 1784 had served them so ill. Even the old epithets of Whig and Tory, hallowed by tradition and implying a policy of definite principles, had fallen into disuse. Men now spoke only of the Opposition and the party in office.[1] The effect of these tactics upon the country at large we know already. Popular opinion regarded with the same indifference and contempt all the groups which disputed in Parliament the possession of power. Nor had the new tactics of the Whigs met with better success in the House of Commons itself. By their policy of compromise the Whigs had not captured a sufficient number of votes to compensate for their loss of popularity. On this point, at least, there existed no divergence between the House of Commons and the nation. The days of political oligarchy were past. During the first fifteen years of the new century the characteristic feature of English parliamentary life had been the decline of the system of aristocratic groups and the speedy disintegration of any such group that showed signs of formation.

Of these groups Addington's group had been the earliest. It is remarkable that the leader of this new clique did not belong to a noble family of established political importance, nor even to an old county family. He was merely the son of an eminent physician who had had the good fortune to number Lord Chatham among his patients. His sisters had made good matches, and he owed his entry into Parliament to the patronage of his brother-in-law, James Sutton. Pitt had then taken him up, had made him Speaker of the Commons, and had designated him his successor, if ever circumstances should compel his resignation. Addington found himself Prime Minister. Pitt was always willing to be his friend, provided he were content to remain the obedient agent of his policy, ready to re-enter the ranks, should his patron ever take it into his head to return to office. Addington, however, had come to believe in his own greatness; and since the conclusion of the Treaty of Amiens the Foxites flattered his vanity by their laudation of his policy of peace. When hostilities broke out afresh, Pitt tried in vain to resume the direction of affairs. He failed to win Addington's consent by the offer of an important post in his Cabinet. Whereupon, yielding to the solicitations of his friends, he led a direct attack upon the Cabinet and rendered its existence so precarious that Addington

---

[1] Cobbett's *Political Register*, March 1, 1809, vol. xv. p. 355: "There are men who are in place, and others who, upon all occasions, whether right or wrong, censure the measures of Ministers, with the sole view of supplanting them. But, in any other sense, the word party has now no more meaning than has the word *Tory*, which no man has any longer the impudence to use."

was compelled to resign. Nevertheless, Pitt's former lieutenant was now in command of an independent group. He was followed by a small company, numbering in all some forty or sixty members of the House of Commons, and including his brother John Hiley Addington, his brother-in-law James Adams, Lord Hobart, Bond, Bathurst, Vansittart, and Lord Powis.[1] It was in vain that Pitt effected a reconciliation with Addington and gave him a seat in his Cabinet with the title of Lord Sidmouth. Addington knew perfectly well that his credit with the King stood as high as that of the Prime Minister.[2] And by his unbending Toryism he had made himself popular with the country gentlemen. He acted, therefore, just as he pleased, voted at times against Pitt, and even as a member of the Cabinet continued to behave as the leader of an independent faction.

His position in Parliament was still further strengthened, and Pitt's party rendered even weaker, by the secession of another group. Lord Grenville, who for many years had been Pitt's faithful subordinate, now came forward to advocate a " junction of all the parties," or as it was termed, " of all the talents," and the admission of Fox into the Cabinet. King George, however, rejected the proposed coalition and Lord Grenville was compelled to retire. Henceforward the Opposition possessed two heads—Fox, representing the old, and Lord Grenville, representing the new, Opposition. This " cooperation," to use the expression which the allied groups loved to employ, in order to avoid the discredited term " coalition," strengthened by some thirty votes the Opposition in the Commons.[3] Lord Grenville, Lord Temple, Lord Nugent, and Admiral Fremantle led this new group of aristocrats After the death of Pitt, in the early days of 1806, the King resigned himself to accept a Cabinet formed by the alliance of the groups led respectively by Fox, by Lord Grenville and by Lord Sidmouth. The new Ministry failed, however, to gain the confidence of the country. Fox died in September, and the men of the " old Opposition," now led by Grey, lost their influence in the Cabinet. The Grenville faction received an accession of strength, and Lord Sidmouth's party was also strengthened.

From these groups the nation could scarcely expect a war against aristocratic privilege and administrative abuses. Moreover, in the February of 1807 the King quarrelled with his Ministers on the

[1] Sixty-eight members in 1804, according to Rose (*Diaries and Correspondence*, vol. ii. p. 119); forty-three members in 1805, according to the estimate of Abbot (*Diary of Lord Colchester*, June 12, 1805, vol. ii. p. 9). For the composition of the group, see *ibid.*, December 1804 (vol. i. pp. 532–3). Forty to fifty members in 1806, according to Pellew (*Life of Lord Sidmouth*, vol. ii. p. 412).

[2] Addington's relation, Sutton, Bishop of Norwich, was appointed Archbishop of Canterbury in preference to the candidate favoured by Pitt, Prettyman, Bishop of Lincoln (Cobbett, *Political Register*, January 26th and February 16th, vol. viii. pp. 105, 246).

[3] Thirty-four votes in 1803 (Pellew, *Life of Lord Sidmouth*, vol. ii. pp. 141–2); twenty-three votes in 1804 (Rose, *Diaries and Correspondence*, vol. ii. p. 119).

question of Catholic emancipation. The Cabinet resigned, and the orthodox disciples of Pitt returned to power. Once more the policy of coalition had brought disaster upon the Whigs.

Nevertheless, the disintegration of the party in office still continued. In 1809 Canning, Foreign Secretary in the Duke of Portland's Cabinet, provoked by his intemperate ambition a Cabinet crisis. Although the son of an actress, a political pamphleteer of no particular standing, and without noble connexions of any kind, he had entertained since Pitt's death the dream of taking his place as the great national statesman. In his impatience to attain the first rank he engineered an intrigue against his colleague, Lord Castlereagh, the Secretary for War. Lord Castlereagh, who, like Canning, was an orthodox disciple of Pitt, had planned a disembarkation of English troops on the island of Walcheren. Canning immediately took exception both to the general idea and the detailed plan of the expedition. He told the Duke of Portland that he did not wish to form part of a Cabinet containing the organizer of this disastrous campaign, and he obtained from the weakness of his chief a secret promise to compel the resignation of Lord Castlereagh, as soon as the expedition had been concluded and the folly of the scheme demonstrated. Perhaps the plot would have succeeded if Lord Castlereagh had not discovered it. Then England presented to the astonished gaze of Europe the spectacle of a duel between the Foreign Secretary and the Secretary for War. The Cabinet could not survive so grave a scandal, and resigned *en bloc*. Perceval then reconstructed a Tory Cabinet in which neither Canning nor Lord Castlereagh found a place. Canning, at once the most ambitious and the most eloquent of the members of the Lower House, was henceforward the leader of a new group, united not by the influence of a noble family, but by the personal genius of its leader. The group comprised some fifteen members of the House of Commons.[1] Among these were Sturge Bourne, Robert Smith, James William Ward, and, most important of all, Huskisson, a man, to be sure, of obscure origin—a retired banker according to some, a retired chemist according to others—but a great financier whose merit had already won the recognition of Pitt.

In 1812 occurred a further split, whose effect was to strengthen the Canning group. The Marquis of Wellesley, Canning's successor at the Foreign Office, resigned, alleging as his reason for the step " that he had not the weight in the Government which he expected when he accepted office." [2] Inspired by the memory of his viceroyalty of India, and the victories now being won in Spain and Portugal by his brother Wellington, the ambition of the Marquis knew no bounds. His " connexion," an aristocratic " connexion " of the old

---

[1] Twelve in September 1812 (*Court of England under the Prince Regent*, vol. i. pp. 404–5).

[2] Lord Liverpool to Wellington, February 1812 (Yonge, *Life of Lord Liverpool*, vol. i. pp. 377–8).

style,[1] entered into close relations with the group led by Canning. What, then, was there to prevent the two statesmen from undertaking the leadership of a new Cabinet—the former in the Lords, the latter in the Commons? Such a Cabinet would surely enjoy a prestige to which Perceval's Ministry of dullards could never aspire. The proposed Cabinet was, if possible, to consist only of Tories. If necessary, however, the cooperation of the Whigs was to be invited ; for the Whigs possessed no candidate whom they could seriously put forward in opposition to Canning as the representative of the Government in the House of Commons. Wellesley and Canning also counted on the support of the Prince Regent, for the Marquis was his intimate friend. Moreover, the Regent possessed devoted servants among the Whigs—Lord Moira in the Lords, Sheridan in the Commons. Never had the coalition of groups which constituted the Opposition been stronger than in these opening months of 1812. When Perceval was assassinated in May, the House demanded by a majority of four a radical alteration of the Government policy.[2] But although everything appeared to conspire to the triumph of the Opposition, it continued to suffer from the same defect of internal organization. It was, after all, only a coalition of groups and the day of groups was over.

The Prince Regent proved false. He took advantage of the differences of opinion which manifested themselves between the leaders of the coalition to procure the failure of the negotiations. Lord Grey and Lord Grenville were in favour of a policy as pacific as circumstances would permit ; Wellesley and Canning, on the other hand, were denouncing the slackness with which the Tories were carrying on the war. The two groups were unable to agree upon a common foreign policy, and the Regent formed a strictly Tory Cabinet. Lord Liverpool was Prime Minister, Lord Castlereagh Foreign Secretary. Lord Sidmouth's group was bought with the most important posts in the Government, and was henceforth merged in the main body of orthodox Toryism.[3] Wellington meanwhile entered Madrid, and Napoleon retreated from Moscow. The despairing forecasts of Grey and Grenville, for whom victory over Napoleon was an absolute im-

---

[1] Eleven members in September 1812 (*Court of England under the Prince Regent*, vol. i. pp. 404–5) ; seventeen members in November after the general election (*ibid.*, vol. i. p. 411).

[2] H. of C., May 21, 1812 (*Parl. Deb.*, vol. xxiii. p. 249).

[3] For several years past Lord Sidmouth had been paving the way for his reunion with the Tories. Immediately after the downfall of the Ministry of all the talents, he had expressly reasserted his independence of the groups of Grey and Grenville (Pellew, *Life of Lord Sidmouth*, vol. ii. p. 470, letter to Lord Dunstanville, April 5, 1807), and had given to his own group the distinctive feature of theoretic conservatism. ("The doctrinal party," Canning termed them.—*Diary of Lord Colchester*, May 11, 1809, vol. ii. p. 185.) In 1809 he permitted his client, Lord Bathurst, to enter Perceval's Cabinet. He now secured for himself and his friends in Lord Liverpool's Cabinet the Home Office, the War Office, the Board of Trade, the Exchequer, and the India Office.

possibility, were thus refuted ; as was also the contention of Wellesley and Canning, that victory could never be obtained until they were permitted to infuse fresh vigour into the prosecution of the war. Lord Liverpool seized his opportunity, dissolved Parliament in September and strengthened his majority. The disintegration of the Tories was suddenly arrested, and it was now the Opposition that fell to pieces.

Canning realized his impotence. The great families which composed the Whig aristocracy had always regarded him as a dangerous upstart, the orthodox disciples of Pitt were irretrievably committed against him. Even before the election of 1812 Wellesley and Canning had entered into negotiations with the Cabinet.[1] After the election their position was worse than ever. Disavowed by Wellington,[2] Wellesley abandoned the ambitions of the past two years. Never might he hope to be Prime Minister. Indeed, he no longer possessed even a following in Parliament. In 1813 Canning flatly refused an offer to become the recognized Leader of the Opposition in the House of Commons.[3] The following year he solemnly discharged his group of supporters, and declared his followers free to act and vote according to their individual judgment. His cousin, Stratford Canning, accepted from the Government a special diplomatic mission to the Swiss cantons ; Thomas Sydenham, a former member of Wellesley's group, accepted a similar mission to the Court of Lisbon ; Wellesley Pole became Director of the Mint. To furnish Huskisson with a place in the Cabinet, the new post of Chief Commissioner of Woods and Forests and Land Revenues was created expressly for him. Canning himself accepted from Lord Castlereagh a splendid and purposeless mission to the Court of Portugal. " It was like the last lottery," exclaimed Tierney, " where there were no blanks, but all prizes." [4] But in reality Canning, like Wellesley, had failed. Had he but served his party faithfully, the superiority of his personal merit would have given him in due time the uncontested leadership. And if his ambition had not led him into intrigues which strengthened the position of their intended victim, perhaps Lord Castlereagh, instead of being the arbiter of European politics, would have buried his political reputation in Walcheren.

Thus of all the groups which had successively seceded from the

---

[1] Who took the initiative in these negotiations ? Who was responsible for breaking them off ? Our accounts conflict. See Twiss, *Life of Lord Eldon*, vol. ii. pp. 211–12 ; *Court of England under the Prince Regent*, vol. i. pp. 404–5 ; *Life of Wilberforce*, vol. iv. pp. 37 sqq. See also the *Morning Chronicle* of September 26, 1812 for the current rumours about the negotiations and their failure. See also Wellesley Pole's address to the freeholders of Queen's County, to be found in the *Morning Chronicle* of October 26, 1812.

[2] *Court of England under the Prince Regent*, vol. i. p. 411.

[3] *Diary of Lord Colchester*, February 30, 1813.

[4] H. of C., November 15, 1814 (*Parl. Deb.*, vol. xxix. p. 218). For the discharge of Canning's group, see *Court of England under the Prince Regent*, vol. ii. pp. 36–7 : Francis Horner to Lord Grenville, July 22, 1813. *Letters to Ivy*, pp. 213, 216. *Creevy Papers*, vol. i. p. 151.

Tory ranks since the beginning of the century, one alone, Lord Grenville's group, still remained faithful to the Opposition ; but its self-seeking and greed rendered it wholly unreliable.   In 1813 the Grenvilles had already begun to detach themselves from active politics, leaving their clients, Fremantle, Wynne, Horner, and Plunkett, the Irishman, to uphold their standard in the field of debate.   And they would shortly betray their followers.   After their departure what elements, or rather what remnants, were left to compose the Opposition in Parliament ?   " A few Whig families," Mackintosh told Thomas Moore in 1819, " are our only security for the Con-stitution." [1]

In the foremost rank were the great families of the Revolution— the Percys, the Cavendishes, the Russells, the Howards.   The Duke of Bedford, head of the Russell family and owner of immense estates in Bedfordshire, in Devonshire and in the heart of London, was an influential politician.   Samuel Whitbread, the democrat, was his intimate friend.   His eldest son, the Marquis of Tavistock, took an active part in the debates in the House of Commons.   But of his three other sons, one, Lord George, was on active service ; another, Lord William, was plunged so deeply in debt that he dared not show his face at Westminster ; and the third, Lord John, who was hereafter to confer such honour on the family, had scarcely attained his majority and entered Parliament.   The glory of the family had been under eclipse since the death in 1802 of the fifth Duke of Bedford, a great agriculturalist, who had taken part in public life and had been honoured by the invective of Burke and a funeral panegyric by Fox.   Alone among the heads of noble families, Charles Howard, Duke of Norfolk, who died in 1815, had preserved throughout all the long years of the war the great political traditions of the old English aristocracy.   His love of racing was so intense that he was commonly nicknamed the " Jockey."   Boon companion of the Prince of Wales, a hard drinker, a gambler, proverbially dirty and untidy, but a man of culture and a splendid conversationalist, he had been deprived by Pitt of his Lord-Lieutenancy for having toasted at a public banquet " Our Sovereign, the People."   An ardent politician, around his Sussex castle at Arundel he had enlarged his electoral fief.   At Hereford, Gloucester and Carlisle he led the popular party.   In Gloucester-shire in 1811, alone of all the local aristocracy, he had supported, and

[1] *Memoirs, Journal and Correspondence of Thomas Moore*, May 30, 1819, vol. ii. p. 316). It is possible to reconstruct the list of the Whig remnant by means of the debates on the Six Acts of 1817.   See particularly the list of the ninety-eight members who voted against the Habeas Corpus Suspension Bill at its First Reading on February 26, 1817 (*Parl. Deb.*, vol. xxxv. pp. 758–9).   But on that occasion only 371 members voted.   The list may be completed from other divisions.   See particularly the division of March 14th on the Seditious Meetings Bill, where eight new names appear ; and that of March 28th, where we find eight further names (*Parl. Deb.*, vol. xxxv. pp. 1131, 1302).

supported successfully, an independent candidate. He gave Romilly a seat, when he had failed to secure his election at Bristol. Among his clients was Creevey, the democrat. The Duke of Norfolk was indeed the typical Whig, an aristocratic republican, who passed his entire life provoking by his insolence the pride of King and Ministers.

Other families grouped themselves around these great houses. George Ponsonby, chosen in 1808 as Leader of the Opposition in the Commons in preference to the irresolute Tierney and the violent Whitbread, represented one of the three great families who disputed the empire of rural Ireland. The Ponsonbys were allies of the Fitz-williams, a powerful Yorkshire family ; and Lord Fitzwilliam's son, Lord Milton, was in 1815 among the hopes of the Whig party. In the Upper House the Opposition was led by Lord Grey in conjunction with Lord Grenville. Lord Grosvenor and Lord Folkestone played a very active part in politics—the former in the Lords, the latter in the Commons. But there is no need to enumerate all the Whig families who together marshalled 100 or 130 members of the House of Commons. We need only mention two noble families whose intellectual and literary activities surpassed even their political action, and who occupied a place apart in the ranks of the Opposition.

The prestige of Lansdowne House was due to Lord Shelburne, first Marquis of Lansdowne, the friend of Adam Smith, a patron of Bentham, a correspondent of the French encyclopædists. His second son, now heir to the title, had made a brilliant appearance in the House of Commons. When he passed to the Upper House he fell into the background of political life ; but this rendered it all the easier for him to continue the traditions of his father both in London and at Bowood. Mackintosh, Romilly, Dumont of Geneva, and Madame de Staël gathered under his roof. Nevertheless, Lansdowne House was in its decline. Holland House, on the contrary, was at the height of its fame. It was there that Fox had died in 1806 in the presence of his nephew and niece, Lord and Lady Holland. Lord Holland was an ardent Whig and a clever politician. Lady Holland was the deity of the shrine. Although neither a beauty nor a woman of high intellectual gifts, she was a born ruler. Owing to the irregular circumstances of her marriage with Lord Holland she was not received at the strict Court of George III. She took her revenge by establishing a court of her own, by opening a *salon*, where she received, commanded and bullied every Englishman of eminence in the Opposition ranks—men of letters, philosophers and publicists. Lord Holland and his wife were too independent not to make many enemies. They were charged with an affectation of cosmopolitanism, and their zeal for the cause of Spanish independence offended the advocates of peace at any price.[1] Both Lansdowne House and Holland House regarded

[1] In Spain a political party had been formed which bore the novel designation of "Liberal."

the great Opposition review, the *Edinburgh Review*, as their appanage. Thus the two houses kept the Whig aristocracy in touch with the thought of the day, and prevented the Whigs from degenerating into a group of great country families. This was no slight service.

Lord Grenville, commenting in the July of 1813 on the dissolution of the Canning group, expressed himself in the following terms : "What I most lament in it is the discredit which it throws on all party connexion, the upholding which, on its true foundation of public principle, I take to be essential to the benefit of a parliamentary Constitution. The mere fact of a party being thus dissolved shows abundantly it could exist to no good purpose." [1] What, however, did Lord Grenville understand by this party system which he regarded as the very essence of parliamentary government ? Did he mean that in every free country parties would necessarily be formed divided from each other either by philosophic or religious tenets or by the economic interests of their members ? If so he merely stated a truism ; though, of course, the spirit of party might overpass the limits essential for the maintenance of national unity, and party strife degenerate into a civil war in which the combatants, though members of the same social organism, no longer recognized any common principles of political conduct. But Lord Grenville meant perhaps to endorse Burke's doctrine that the contending parties, if they were not to become two hostile societies, two nations in one, must entrust the care of their interests, sentiments and convictions to an oligarchy of noble families, who, because they belonged to the same class, would be able to observe in their warfare a rigorous code of behaviour, and would obey common principles. The great work to be achieved by English politics in the 19th century would indeed be the perpetuation of parliamentary aristocracy. Such a feat, however, could only be accomplished by a constant and careful adaptation of this aristocratic policy to the changing needs of a society which was becoming industrial and democratic. During the first years of the 19th century, however, the mass of the population found this process of adaptation too slow. The nation regarded the intrigue of Lord Wellesley and Canning as a survival of the system of oligarchic groups. Nor was Burke's interpretation of the system accepted by public opinion. For the past thirty years the parties had been regarded not as patriarchal groups, fixed immovably in their ancestral principles, but as shifting cliques, the offspring of intrigue, and formed to exploit the emoluments of office. The memory of the coalition of 1784 hung heavily, as was indeed simple justice, over the repeated attempts of the Opposition to get together a majority

---

It was perhaps through the channel of Holland House that the term found its way into the political vocabulary of England.

[1] *Court of England under the Prince Regent*, vol. ii. p. 38. Lord Grenville to Francis Horner, July 25, 1813.

in Parliament hostile to the Tories. The party in office was a homogeneous whole, the Opposition a federation of independent groups. Viewed from this standpoint it is intelligible that the victory of the Tories, supported, as it was, by the opinion of the country, was favourable to the progress of political morality.

The Whigs and Political Reform.

Nevertheless, extenuating circumstances may be pleaded in favour of the Opposition. Never during the past half-century of adverse fortune had the party, as its accusers alleged, wholly betrayed the cause of reform. Even the partial betrayal of which it was in fact guilty, was only too often due to the knowledge that it lacked the support of the country.

During the opening years of the reign prior to the disastrous coalition of 1784, the Whigs had relied on the people to support their resistance to King George. The legislation of the period witnesses to the energy with which, when in office, they had themselves initiated reforms, and when in Opposition had successfully put pressure on their opponents to yield to their demands. We have already seen how the English Government undertook the reform of the administration, and regulated the exercise of the Royal Prerogative of pensions, reducing thus the means of parliamentary corruption at the disposal of the Crown. At the same time a beginning was made with the reform of the franchise. The Grenville Act of 1770 [1] limited the right claimed by the majority of the House of Commons to decide contested returns at their arbitrary pleasure. The new Act referred the hearing of election petitions to a select committee chosen by lot. Another Act, passed in 1782, forbade Government contractors to sit in the House, especially contractors to the War Office and the Admiralty. [2] And simultaneously the composition of the electorate was modified. Statutes were passed restricting the franchise, which would reduce the influence of the Crown and the *nouveaux riches*. An Act of 1782 deprived tax collectors and Customs officers of the vote. [3] An Act of 1763 provided that honorary freeholders might not exercise the borough franchise unless they had received the freedom at least twelve months before the election. [4] An Act of 1786 exacted from scot-and-lot electors a residence of at least six months to qualify for a vote. [5] An Act of 1788 provided that the county electors must have been on the register at least a month before they were entitled to vote. [6] Other Measures, on the contrary, enlarged the franchise to

---

[1] 10 Geo. III, cap. 16 ; 11 Geo. III, cap. 42.   Rendered permanent, 14 Geo. III, cap. 15. This legislation was modified by 25 Geo. III, cap. 84 ; 28 Geo. III, cap. 52.

[2] 22 Geo. III, cap. 45.

[3] 22 Geo. III, cap. 41.

[4] 3 Geo. III, cap. 15.

[5] 26 Geo. III, cap. 100.

[6] 28 Geo. III, cap. 36, 57.

punish the electors of certain small boroughs who had too openly put up their votes to auction. This was done to New Shoreham in 1771, to Cricklade in 1782. Finally, in 1788, Parliament repealed a statute of 1729 which had stereotyped the franchise in each constituency, as it had been fixed by the last decision of the House of Commons.[1] The right to revise its former decisions was thus restored to Parliament.[2] The House of Commons had now at its disposal an instrument by which, if necessary, the entire franchise might be reformed piecemeal, constituency by constituency.

Great reforms are, however, but rarely effected by a series of petty changes. Public opinion towards the close of the 18th century became too strongly democratic to be content with so slow and so complicated a procedure. Democratic republics were founded in America and in France. The doctrines now professed at Paris, such as the theories of the social contract, of the rights of man, of the sovereignty of the people, were old ideas in England. Fox, the Leader of the Opposition, recognized in the principles of 1789 the Whig principles of 1688, and advocated peace with democratic France. Among his supporters Lord Grey was devoting himself to the cause of parliamentary reform. A small number of great families, with whom rebellion was a tradition and who were ready to go any lengths rather than yield to the Court, adopted the same line of policy. Nevertheless, these "new Whigs," Jacobins as they were termed, were but a handful. Clergy, gentry, financiers, merchants, manufacturers even (except during the months of famine), the proletariate, in short all classes of society, united to oppose them. The indignation excited by the savage excesses of the French Terror produced in England by reaction an "anti-Jacobin" terror. Fear of a French invasion enlisted on behalf of the Tories the warlike and patriotic sentiments formerly exploited by the Whigs in the days of Louis XIV and Louis XV. The vast majority of the Whigs deserted the Opposition and entered the Tory ranks. In the person of Burke, a Whig became the philosopher of the counter-revolution in Europe. Evidently misfortune dogged the steps of Fox and his friends. In 1784 public opinion had repudiated them because their policy was too oligarchic; in 1792 it repudiated them because their policy was too democratic. Finally, in 1797, weary of protests which fell on deaf ears, Fox and his followers ceased even to attend the sessions of Parliament. The years pass: we approach 1815: we witness a return on the part of the Whigs to the policy of coalition. But the great Opposition families never abandoned entirely the cause of reform. In 1808 Whitbread, indignant that he had been given no place two years earlier in the Fox-Grenville Cabinet, and still more indignant that after the fall of the Ministry he had not been designated Leader of the Opposition in the Commons, marshalled

[1] 2 Geo. II, cap. 24.   [2] 28 Geo. III, cap. 52, § 31.

under his banner some fifty members, who, regardless of the political
strategy adopted by their party, called loudly for peace at any price
and the suppression of abuses.   But the members of this group, termed
sometimes the " Mountain "—men such as Lord Cochrane, Lord
Folkestone, Creevey, and Peter Moore—were attached to the great
aristocratic connexions.[1] Whitbread himself was a wealthy brewer
and Grey's brother-in-law.   At Bedford, which he represented, he
was in alliance with the Russells and their clients.   So little did the
violence of his policy involve him in strife with the other Opposition
groups that in 1812, when the defeat of the Tory Government was
expected, he was promised the Home Office in the new Cabinet.   We
have already had occasion to notice the progress of administrative
reform during this period, and sinecures and offices in reversion were
on the eve of abolition.   Even as regards the reform of the franchise,
matters were not at an utter standstill.

In 1804 the borough of Aylesbury underwent the same treatment
that had been meted out thirty years previously to Shoreham and
Cricklade.[2] And in 1815 only the action of the House of Lords
saved Helston from the same fate.[3] To be sure, two attempts to
obtain an amendment of the Treating Act which would render corruption at elections more difficult, were unsuccessful.[4] Nevertheless, in
1809 an important step was taken.   The affair of the Duke of York
led to the revelation of another scandal, the barter, namely, of a seat
in Parliament for a post in the Government service.   A few days
later a member, who owed his election in 1807 to the support of the
Government, voted against the Government on the Duke of York
scandal.   Lord Castlereagh demanded and obtained his resignation,
as though he had been guilty of a breach of contract.   Public opinion
was strongly excited, and the Whig Curwen took advantage of this
favourable opportunity to secure the passage of a Bill against corruption
at elections.[5] This statute provided that whether the bribe offered
were money or a place, both the giver and the recipient should be liable
to a heavy fine.

[1] Of great assistance in arriving at the list of the members who, about 1815, composed
the " Mountain," are the lists of the members who voted on February 29, 1808, for Whitbread's
motion in favour of peace ; on June 15, 1809, for Sir Francis Burdett's motion (reform of the
franchise), and on June 30, 1813, that a petition in favour of a reformed franchise should be
taken into consideration.   The figures are respectively 58, 15 and 13 (*Parl. Deb.*, vol. x.
p. 869 ; vol. xiv. p. 1070 ; vol. xxvi. p. 997).   Cf. Harris, *Radical Party*, p. 112, and *Creevy
Papers*, vol. i. p. 216, letter of G. Bennett to Creevey, May 31, 1815.

[2] 44 Geo. III, cap. 60.

[3] See the debates H. of C., November 8, 10, 22, 24, 26, 1813 ; H. of C., March 14, 1816 ;
H. of L., May 9, 1816.   (*Parl. Deb.*, vol. xxvii. pp. 49, 75, 179, 195 ; vol. xxxiii. pp. 296, 408).

[4] Election Treating Bill, passed and introduced by Tierney, H. of C., March 10, April 29,
May 22, June 9, 1806 (*Parl. Deb.*, vol. vi. pp. 371, 955 ; vol. vii. pp. 336, 571).   See on
this Bill an interesting article in Cobbett's *Political Register* for April 19, 1806 (vol. ix. pp.
597 sqq.).   Election Expenses Bill, H. of C., March 29, May 9, 16, 1814 (*Parl. Deb.*, vol.
xxvii. pp. 377, 546, 888).

[5] 49 Geo. III, cap. 118.

Opposition grumblers complained that this measure was doomed to remain inoperative.[1] Was this complaint justified? One thing at least is certain. The traffic in seats was no longer carried on openly by means of advertisements in the newspapers. There is even some contemporary evidence for the belief that the reform initiated by Curwen went deeper than this. In 1812 Romilly resigned himself to enter Parliament as the client of an aristocratic connexion, because, as he said, Curwen's Act had made it impossible for him to purchase his seat with hard cash, as he would otherwise have done.[2] At the same moment Lord Liverpool was deploring, in a private letter, the novel difficulties encountered by the Government in preparing elections as the result of this statute. "Mr. Curwen's Bill," he wrote to Sir William Scott, "has put an end to all money transactions between Government and the supposed proprietors of boroughs. Our friends, therefore, who look for the assistance of Government must be ready to start for open boroughs, where the general influence of Government, combined with a reasonable expense on their own part, may afford them a fair chance of success."[3] If, nevertheless, we are still of the opinion—an opinion fully justified by the facts—that during the period with which we are dealing the efforts of the Opposition on behalf of reform were wanting both in zeal and in efficacy, extenuating circumstances may be pleaded in favour of the Whigs, and the timidity which they displayed need not be ascribed wholly to calculations of self-interest. In countries where there exists either universal or almost universal suffrage, it happens constantly that democratic parties hesitate to bring forward measures apparently demanded by the immediate interests of the masses, and this not from selfish calculation but because the measures in question are opposed to the prejudices of the people themselves. Man is not governed by interest, but by beliefs and passions; and about 1815 the beliefs and passions prevalent among the people were favourable to the party in office.

Why, it may be asked, had not the Opposition persisted since 1809 in a unanimous demand for a reform of the franchise, and why from 1815 onwards did it fail to conduct a campaign in favour of free trade? To ask such a question is to confuse 1809 and 1815 with 1832 and 1846. Radicalism was not yet a popular creed, and some years had yet to elapse before the small group of "radical reformers" in the metropolis could effect a junction with the crowd of workmen who were smashing looms and machinery in Lancashire and Yorkshire.

---

[1] See Romilly's criticisms in *Memoirs*, vol. ii. p. 287; vol. iii. p. 34. Also those of Cobbett in *Political Register*, May 13, 1809 (vol. xv. pp. 721 sqq.).

[2] *Memoirs*, vol. ii. p. 72.

[3] Yonge, *Life of Lord Liverpool*, vol. i. p. 444, letter to Sir William Scott, September 23, 1812.

When Parliament raised the duty on corn and tried to establish a monopoly of the national market in favour of the English farmers, the entire population were in arms against the measure. It was, indeed, a flagrant instance of the betrayal of the electorate by the majority in Parliament. We must not, however, forget that this movement of public opinion was extremely sudden, so sudden that both parties were taken unawares ; and the Commons took the lesson to heart and would never dare to repeat the mistake then made. Again, there were two important questions demanding solution, on which politicians were obliged to come to a definite decision, before any other question could be dealt with. The first of these was the question of the war. So long as Napoleon had been Emperor of the French, peace, however desirable, had been out of the question. Therefore the Tories, who were essentially the war party, were supported by the nation. Now that peace was restored and Napoleon vanquished, the Tories were certainly deprived of this appeal. But the other question remained, the question of Catholic emancipation. Brought forward in a most clear and definite form fifteen years earlier, it had been confronting politicians ever since ; and ever since it had remained a cardinal point of difference between the two parties. All the different groups composing the Opposition—Wellesleyites, Canningites, Greyites, Grenvilleites—though they disagreed on so many points, were at one in demanding the entire emancipation of the Catholics. But until the final settlement of the question the Whigs were to be confronted in this matter with the combined opposition of the Court and the country at large. The year 1829, when the Whigs were at length to gain the support of the nation on this important issue, and when, therefore, Catholics would be admitted to Parliament and to the public service, would prove fatal to the old Tory Party. For the moment, however, the Tories did not owe their majority solely to the exercise of pressure on Government officials or to bribes of money and place. It was with the No Popery cry that they intimidated the Opposition and secured, together with the confidence of the Regent, the support of the electorate and of public opinion.

These, then, were the causes whose operation maintained in power the small group of mediocrities who at this period shaped the policy of the country. On a host of questions, whose solution was daily more urgent, the country was growing ever more and more dissatisfied with the party in office, but on two fundamental questions it remained the popular party. Moreover, although in 1815 the Ministers were men of indifferent ability and personally unpopular, they were, nevertheless, the heirs of a great statesman and still profited by the prestige attaching to his name. Personally they were narrow-minded reactionaries. But in 1784 William Pitt had succeeded in infusing fresh life into the party, because he had been able to make it for a time the popular party and he had strengthened the Crown and the established institutions of the realm by imparting indirectly to both a more democratic character.

The Tory Policy and the Inheritance of Pitt.

Pitt's first step, when chosen by King George to succeed Lord North as Prime Minister, had been to dissolve Parliament and to make, as he termed it, "an appeal to the people," [1] who were thus called upon to decide between the policy of the Crown and that of the great aristocratic connexions. Twice already, in 1774 and in 1780, the King and his Ministers had dissolved Parliament in defiance of custom before the period had expired for which it had been elected. But on both these occasions the Government had possessed a majority in the Parliament thus dissolved. Now, however, the innovation was made of dissolving a Parliament where the majority was opposed to the policy of the Government that dissolved it. Henceforward dissolution under these circumstances became customary. Between 1784 and 1815 no Parliament lasted longer than six years out of the seven for which it was legally entitled to continue. The Parliament elected in 1802 was dissolved four years later, this time by a Coalition Ministry of Whigs. The Parliament of 1806 lasted only a few months, and that of 1807 was dissolved at the end of five years. Dissolution after an important Government defeat was indeed destined to become, during the 19th century, a maxim of the Constitution. Nevertheless, towards the close of the 18th century the use made by George III of this novel procedure gave rise to complaints. Suppose, it was urged, an executive able to exert sufficient pressure on the country to secure a strong and obedient majority in the new Parliament, suppose also a servile but influential body of officials and a narrow and venal electorate. Under such circumstances was there not a considerable danger that the pretended "appeal to the people" would be no more than an instrument with which the Government enforced its will ? Nor was it, it would be added, necessary to imagine conditions so unfavourable to realize the evils which might result from the practice of dissolution. Even if the result of a general election did truly represent the will of the people, and even if at the actual moment of election the will of the people was at one with the will of the Ministry on the particular question then before the public, it would be easy for a clever statesman to watch his opportunity, dissolve, obtain a majority and thenceforward govern the country, with or without public support,

---

[1] See the Speech from the Throne, May 19, 1784: "I have the greatest satisfaction in meeting you in Parliament at this time after recurring, in so important a moment, to the sense of the people" (*Parl. Hist.*, vol. xxiv. p. 804). Pitt's speech, April 21, 1800: "There may be occasions, but they will ever be few, when an appeal to the people is the just mode of proceeding on important subjects" (*Parl. Hist.*, vol. xxxv. pp. 83–4).

till the legal duration of Parliament had expired.[1] These observations were well founded; but it is nevertheless undeniable that the adoption of this method by George III and his Ministers towards the close of the 18th century marks a democratic development of parliamentary government.

As we have seen already, according to the accepted constitutional theory, the representatives returned every seven years constituted from the moment of election " the legal country." On every question which presented itself while their mandate lasted, their votes were to be determined not by the wishes of their constituents but by their own judgment. This fiction of a Parliament independent of public opinion during the interval between elections was undoubtedly minimized, as we have already seen, by the exercise of the rights of meeting and association, and by the freedom of the Press. It was, moreover, expressly contradicted by the practice of dissolution. The moment a Prime Minister, who was opposed to a Measure approved by the majority in Parliament—as, for example, the India Bill of 1784 and Catholic Emancipation in 1807—appealed to the judgment of the country, he recognized that the electors had the right, indeed the duty, to exercise a constant control not only over the choice but also over the votes of their representatives. George III went even further. He called upon the country to decide between the policy which he personally favoured and the policy of the majority in Parliament. By this step the fiction of royal irresponsibility was greatly diminished. The policy adopted by the Tories during the closing years of the 18th century transformed the constitutional monarchy into a popular monarchy, in which the King assumed the power to resort at pleasure to a species of plebiscite. In 1784 and in 1807 the result of the plebiscite had been favourable to the Crown. Sometimes the parliamentary majority yielded to the demands of the Sovereign to save him the necessity of dissolving Parliament, and provoking a constitutional crisis when the country was passing through a period of stress and danger. Thus in 1800 Pitt's party had yielded, with Pitt's consent, on the question of Catholic emancipation.

Nor was it only by making Parliament more closely dependent upon the electorate that the action of Toryism in this reign had been

---

[1] See H. of C., April 20, 1809 (*Parl. Deb.*, vol. xiv. pp. 116, 120). Creevey maintained that " to talk of a dissolution of Parliament as an ' appeal to the people ' was mere mockery and imposition. . . . (It was) not an appeal to the people but to the Treasury." Whitbread thus qualified Creevey's contention : " He believed the Treasury did possess a most preponderating influence, but at the same time he knew that the people had a voice which would be used. The infringement, therefore, of the elective right of the people was not so great, if they were not first driven mad and then appealed to ; if they were not first driven into a state of frenzy and then desired to make use of their senses." For an exposition of the Whig objections to the practice of dissolution, see *Edinburgh Review*, November 1812, No. 40, Art. 8, *Rights and Duties of the People* (vol. xx. pp. 405 sqq.).

of a revolutionary character. Its action in modifying the composition of the Commons and the Lords had been even more revolutionary.

Since 1792 fear of Jacobinism had driven a certain number of noble families into alliance with the Court. The Dukes of Portland, Newcastle and Rutland supported the royal policy, and thus counterbalanced the influence of the Dukes of Bedford, Norfolk and Devonshire. Nevertheless, when George III first ascended the throne, he could scarcely have counted on disunion among the great families to overcome their opposition. Even the Tory gentry of the provinces were not sufficiently pliable to be always subservient to his wishes. He turned accordingly to the *nouveaux riches*, who wished to improve their social position by a seat in Parliament. These he found prepared, as the price of his favours, to play the Tory on every occasion. The most zealous members of the party, now known as the party of the King's friends, were the nabobs, adventurers who, having made their fortunes in India, had returned home to enjoy the fruits of commercial or administrative robbery. Warren Hastings was the typical representative of this class, and his great accuser, Burke, who represented Whig aristocracy, probably detested in Hastings not so much the oppressor of the Hindus as the agent of the Tories. When in 1784 Pitt became head of the Government, he but developed a tradition which already possessed the sanction of twenty years' practice. Addington, Huskisson, Canning—who, as his biographer tells us, had in 1792 wavered between the two parties until he was forced into the Tory ranks by the insolence of the leading Whigs—Charles Long, George Rose, all these great men of humble origin owed their political career to Pitt. All were young when the century opened. In 1815, when all the leaders of the party once led by Fox were dead or dying, they were still active politicians—in many instances full of ambition and with a great future before them. Innovators love the young, and Pitt was an innovator. When, fifteen years before the close of the 18th century, the royal policy triumphed with Pitt's advent to power, the Tory Party thus renovated found itself in sympathy, in more decided sympathy than the old Whigs, with the new currents of public opinion.

We have reached the period when economics first became a science, and when the teachings of industrial and commercial Liberalism were being widely accepted. Pitt adopted the ideas of the new school. He put into practice the sinking fund system preached by the economist, Richard Price. He concluded a commercial treaty with France in accordance with the doctrines of Adam Smith. It was only natural that he sought recruits for his party among the men whose interests were expressed by the new dogmas, among those who represented classes of growing importance—the new families of finance, of commerce, of manufacture. Cobbett in 1802 protested against the invasion of the governing class by these new-comers. "The ancient nobility and gentry of the kingdom," he said, " have, with a very few exceptions, been thrust out of all public employments. . . . A race of merchants and manufacturers and bankers and loan jobbers and contractors have usurped their place." [1]   And this was the period when the evangelical revival began to influence the English middle class, the very class in which these new fortunes were made and from which Pitt's party drew so many followers.   Pitt was himself in sympathy with the movement.   Wilberforce, the leader of the evangelical group in Parliament, was his friend and supporter.   The four Thorntons, the Christian bankers, belonged both to the group over which Wilberforce presided and to the party of Pitt.   This combination of business and Christianity, of trade and asceticism, lent itself to satire. "There always was," wrote Cobbett, "amongst the creature and close adherents of Mr. Pitt, a strange mixture of profligacy and cant : jobbers all the morning and Methodists in the afternoon." [2]   Such, nevertheless, was the new spirit.   Against this youthful ardour, this intense commercial and philanthropic activity, of what avail were the classical tirades of Fox, who read the *Æneid* on his death-bed,[3] but admitted that he had never read the *Wealth of Nations* ? [4]

During the ten years since Pitt's death, the Tories had, it is true, been visibly degenerating.   They were on the way to become once more a party narrowly conservative, rural, out of touch with the progressive forces of the nation.   The Industrialists had already begun to leave their ranks.   In the Corn Bill debates Sir Robert Peel adopted an attitude of energetic opposition to the Cabinet.   Pitt's former lieutenant, George Rose, earned several months' popularity by an important speech delivered against the policy of agrarian protection, a speech drawn from him by the disgust which he experienced at the unfaithfulness of the Tories to his master's ideas.   As the result of all these factors the year 1815 found at Westminster a discredited Opposition facing a discredited Government ; this state of affairs was,

[1] Cobbett's *Political Register*, July 10, 17, 1802 (vol. ii. p. 56).   Cf. vol. iii. p. 159, January 29th.   February 5, 1803 : " Yes, good honest men, plain men, men in the middle classes of life, as Mr. Wilberforce said, may be excellent judges of public measures ; but, unfortunately, in searching after these men in the middle classes of life, we have gone too far, and have taken them out of the *lower* classes of life.   But then comes the question *who* was it that stirred up these lees ?   It was Mr. Pitt."   Cf. *Examiner*, October 30, 1814 : " If a Whig and a Tory of the days of George the First could take a peep into our modern House of Commons, how they would stare to see a fox hunter (Mr. Ponsonby) at the head of the Whigs, and the merchants, almost to a man, supporting the party of the Tories."

[2] Cobbett's *Political Register*, June 30, 1804 (vol. v. p. 1024).

[3] Lord Holland, *Memoirs of the Whig Party*, vol. i. pp. 264–5.

[4] *Butler's Reminiscences*, vol. i. pp. 187–8 ; Chalmers, *An Inquiry* . . . 1805, p. 245. Cf. *Diary of Lord Colchester*, June 19, 1806 (vol. ii. p. 71) : " In talking of books upon political economy, he said (as I often heard him say in debates) that he had but little faith in Adam Smith or any of them, their reasons were so plausible but so inconclusive.   That . . . in Greece, arts and arms engrossed the whole efforts of the human mind, and their progress and eminence in those pursuits had probably been the greater for their abandonment of all other pursuits, such as engaged modern nations in commerce, manufactures, etc."

however, of but a few years' standing. Just as, at the opening of the 18th century the Whig Party had consisted of an alliance of great landed families and merchants against the Tory gentry, in the same way a hundred years later the Tory Party as reconstituted by William Pitt was an alliance of the gentry and the industrialists against the great Whig families.

The revolutionary activity displayed by the Tories since the accession of George III was not confined to the Commons. It embraced the Lords also. Till 1760 the number of Peers had remained almost stationary. In 1688 there had been 150 Temporal Peers, in 1719 there were 178, and in 1760 there were only 174. These 174 Peers represented the *élite* of the old English families. In almost every case their titles were older than the reigning dynasty. The Whig spirit inspired this small circle. To extend the sphere of his influence George III decided to employ a method which would be strictly constitutional. By creating a sufficient number of Peers to swamp the Whig majority in the Upper House, while making these creations the reward for services done to himself in the Commons by the clients of the new Peers, he would strengthen simultaneously his position in both Houses. Few years passed without the creation of new Peers. Seven were created in 1776, eleven in 1780, eight in 1780. Between 1760 and 1784 forty-three Peers were created in all, exclusive of fifty-nine new Irish peerages, which did not carry with them a seat in the House of Lords. William Pitt continued on a grander scale the system inaugurated by King George. Unfettered by aristocratic prejudice, unmoved by personal sympathies, he was swayed only by his ambition. His supremacy in the Commons was uncontested ; and his intention to exercise the same authority over the Lords was evident, when in the course of a single session he made his intimate friend and colleague Grenville first a Peer, then Leader of the Upper House.[1]

During the seventeen years of his first Ministry, William Pitt created ninety-five new peerages, exclusive of seventy-seven Irish peerages.[2] Among them were lawyers, sailors, soldiers, and a few diplomatists. But in the majority of cases the new creations were due to electoral considerations. Already in 1792 it was calculated that nine of the Peers recently created, directly or indirectly, nominated through their influence twenty-four members of the House of Commons. As a rule, titles were conferred on members of old families. Thus the second son of the Duke of Northumberland was created

---

[1] Yonge, *Life of Lord Liverpool*, vol. i. pp. 14–15 ; Stanhope, *Life of Pitt*, vol. ii. pp. 73–77.

[2] Well-nigh the entire marquisate dates from Pitt's administration. There had been but one English Marquis in 1784, in 1801 there were ten. There had not been a single Irish Marquis at the former date, in 1801 there were nine (John Hampden, jun., *The Aristocracy of England : a History for the People*, 1846). Cf. *Life of Wilberforce*, vol. iii. p. 412, letter to Hannah More, July 15, 1809 : " Do you know that far more than half of the nobility both of England and Ireland has been raised to their present elevation since I came into public life ? "

Earl of Beverley, Sir James Lowther, Baron Lonsdale, and Mr. Henry Lascelles, Baron Harewood. The British aristocracy could further accept with equanimity the grant of an Irish peerage to Robert Clive, the military adventurer, famous for his conquest of India ; nor need they feel dishonoured when a peerage of Great Britain with the title of Earl of Powis was bestowed on Clive's son, the patron of five seats in Shropshire and Montgomeryshire. Other creations, however, creations sufficiently numerous to excite contemporary indignation, had been frankly purchased with hard cash, or political services by men devoid of merit or birth.[1] The great creation of 1797, when sixteen peerages were conferred, excited particular scandal. There was an illusive air of antiquity about some of these titles, which served to dissimulate the novelty of the patent. When, for instance, the Duke of Bolton died without heirs, a Mr. Thomas Orde, who had wedded his natural daughter, adopted the title. Although there would no longer be a Duke of Bolton, there would be a Baron Bolton. Mr. Robert Smith, a London banker, discovered that in the 17th century the patronymic of the Lords Carrington had been Smith ; therefore when he was raised to the peerage by Pitt he took the title of Baron Carrington.

This multiplication of peerages continued under Addington's Ministry, under Pitt's second Ministry, and under the Ministry of All the Talents. Five years witnessed the creation of twenty-eight English peerages and one Irish peerage. The number of Peers had been almost doubled since the accession of George III. After this the rate of creations diminished. Ministers of indifferent ability, timid and conservative, ceased to turn out Peers in batches. In 1810 a speaker belonging to the party in office stated that during the last three years, apart from the military peerages, themselves few in number, the Cabinet had only created two Peers.[2] From 1810 to 1812 the Regent was

---

[1] We subject a list, no doubt incomplete (the pedigrees of noble families are often difficult to unravel), of the *nouveaux riches* ennobled under George III. *Irish Peerages* : 1762, Baron Waltham of Philiptown (John Olmius) ; 1789, Baron Eardley of Spalding (Sir Sampson Eardley, formerly Gideon) ; 1789, Baron Cloncurry (Sir Nicholas Lawless, Bart.) ; 1790, Baron Caledon (James Alexander) ; 1792, Baron Oxmantoun (Laurence Harman Parsons) ; 1796, Baron Huntingfield (Sir Joshua Vanneck, Bart.) ; 1796, Baron Carrington (Robert Smith) ; 1797, Baron Teignmouth (Sir John Shore, Bart.) ; 1800, Baron de Blaquiere (John Blaquiere) ; 1800, Baron Henniker (Sir John Henniker, Bart.) ; 1806, Baron Rendlesham (Peter Isaac Thellusson). *English Peerages* : 1761, Baron Melcombe (George Bull, son of Bubb Dodington) ; 1796, Baron Gwydyr (Peter Burrell) ; 1797, Baron Carrington (Robert Smith) ; 1797, Baron Bolton (Thomas Orde-Powlett). Strictly speaking, we should not reckon among these the Irish peerage of Baron Teignmouth, which was of the same nature as that conferred on Clive. Sir John Shore, though of very humble origin, had won his position by his services in the office of the East India Company. See *Annual Register*, 1820 ; *Chronicle*, pp. 291–95. *Peerage of England . . . at the Accession of George the Fourth.* The account there given includes a reference to the particular grounds of the promotion of such as were ennobled or advanced in the reign of the late King. Seventy-one promotions are attributed to the wealth of the new Peer.

[2] H. of C., December 31, 1810 (*Parl. Deb.*, vol. xviii. p. 487).

legally incapable of creating Peers.[1] But the years 1814 and 1815 witnessed once more the creation of peerages on a lavish scale.[2] These, however, had, strictly speaking, no political significance. The Government was obliged to find a reward for victorious generals—hence the majority of the new peerages.

Nevertheless, even for our present purpose we cannot afford to treat these military peerages as of no account. Still less can we leave out of consideration the legal peerages, now increasingly numerous. Both classes of peerage tended to change radically the character of the House of Lords. It was now no longer a close, or all but close, caste, but had become, to employ the phrase current in Napoleonic France, "open to talent." Significant of this change was the custom which had become common since the accession of George III of allowing admirals and generals on their elevation to the peerage to take their title not from an English locality but from the name of a victory. Napoleon took this English custom as his model. We must, of course, beware of pressing too far the parallel between the peerage of King George and the peerage of Napoleon. According to Pitt's system the peerage was open even more to intrigue than to merit, and in so far as it was open to merit, that merit was confined to the Government service. Scholars, men of letters and artists were still excluded. Nevertheless, the English conception of aristocracy was undoubtedly being modified. "God Almighty," Selden had written in the 17th century, "cannot make a gentleman," and Bailey, in the 1707 edition of his dictionary, did but develop Selden's paradox, when he defined a gentleman as a man who has received his nobility from his ancestors, not from the munificence of a Prince or a State.[3] At the beginning of the 18th century it was by no means uncommon for a gentleman to refuse to change the old family name which he derived from his ancestors for a title which he would owe to the favour of the Sovereign.[4] The House of Lords was becoming more and more a house of noblemen, less and less a house of gentlemen.

---

[1] 51 Geo. III, cap. 1 (Regency Act), § 8.

[2] 1814 : eight new peerages, of which six were military, two diplomatic ; 1815 : twelve new peerages, of which three were military, two diplomatic.

[3] See Sir James Laurence, *Of the Nobility of the British Gentry*, Paris, 1825.

[4] An expression of this feeling may be found in Miss Burney's novel, *Cecilia*, where an old family refuses to buy a peerage at the cost of its name (Book VIII, chap. iv., ed. 1784, vol. iv. p. 220) : " Mr. Delvile angrily declared that though such a scheme might do very well for . . . a Peer of twenty years, his own noble ancestors should never, by his consent, forfeit a name which so many centuries had rendered honourable." Cf. *Diary of Miss Burney*. Miss Burney to Miss Crisp, April 6, 1782 : " The people I have ever met with who have been fond of blood and family, have all scouted *title* when put in any competition with it. How, then, should these proud Delviles think a new-created peerage any equivalent for calling their sons' sons for future generations by the name of Beverley ? " (ed. 1854, vol. ii. p. 107). Cf. *Memoirs and Correspondence . . . of Lord Combermere*, vol. i. pp. 19–20 : " Sir, Robert Cotton was offered a peerage by Lord Shelburne, which he without hesitation declined, declaring that he preferred being a county member to taking his place at the bottom of the peerage."

Not only titles of nobility, orders of knighthood also were at the disposal of the executive, to reward services to the State, or the party, and to arrange English society in nicely graded ranks. In 1807 one of his friends on a visit to London wrote as follows to Constable the publisher. " On the whole, it is impossible not to admire the Peers ; so truly noble-looking and finely dressed, with their stars, garters, etc., etc. They looked so much better than the other classes of mankind— the Commons even appeared to me like *trash* compared with them." 1 But these orders did not serve merely to augment the prestige of Peers ; they provided a means of compensation for those who desired a peerage and whom it was impossible to satisfy. The Tories, therefore, while multiplying peerages, increased simultaneously the number and importance of the orders of knighthood. In 1783 George III founded the Irish order of St. Patrick as a counterpart to the English Garter and the Scottish Thistle.2 When in 1786 his sons were invested with the Garter, he enlarged the order, and prescribed that it should henceforward consist of twenty-five knights, exclusive of the King and his sons.3 That the restoration of peace might be celebrated by a lavish distribution of honours, the Order of the Bath was reorganized, the number of knights considerably increased, and within the order itself was established a hierarchy of Grand Crosses, Commanders and Companions.4 The reform aroused great opposition, not only among the great aristocratic families, but generally throughout the gentry. It was denounced as an imitation of the decorations distributed on the Continent, and a plagiarism of Napoleon's methods. The reformed order received the nickname of the " New Legion of Honour." 5 The imitation was undeniable. Nevertheless, it was hardly to be expected that popular opinion would share these prejudices of the aristocracy, or would take offence when to the hereditary hierarchy of peerages the Government added another and a strictly personal hierarchy of honours. If the Cabinet had entertained for a moment the idea of confining the new order to the nobility, the idea was immediately abandoned.6 The primary object, nay the very *raison d'être* of the order, as of the Legion of Honour, was to reward meritorious service in the Army and Navy.7 Nevertheless, the innovation was made of

1 A. G. Hunter to A. Constable, March 15, 1807 (*Archibald Constable*, vol. i. p. 110).

2 *Nicolas History of . . . Orders of Knighthood*, vol. iv. pp. 3 sqq.

3 *Ibid.*, vol. ii. pp. 291 sqq.

4 *Ibid.*, vol. iii. pp. 124 sqq., and *Annual Register*, 1815, *Appendix to Chronicle* (p. 134). The increase of feats of arms meriting reward has necessitated, since 1792, the creation of a great number of " supernumerary companions " (Nicolas, *ibid.*, pp. 89 sqq.).

5 For this attack see *Morning Post*, January 6, 10, 1815 ; *Examiner*, January 15, 22, 29, 1815.

6 *Letters and Dispatches of Lord Castlereagh*, vol. iv. pp. 167–8—Edward Thornton to Lord Liverpool, Kiel, January 18, 1814.

7 The maximum number of Grand Crosses was seventy-two, of whom not more than twelve might be chosen " in consideration of eminent services rendered to the State by British subjects in civil and diplomatic employments."

including in the first list of Companions of the Bath, Sir Joseph Banks, the President of the Royal Society, whose title to distinction was neither military nor political, but purely intellectual.

One final question remains. To what extent were the political colour and influence of the Upper House modified by these changes in its composition? For 1815 the question is difficult to answer. Only a conflict with the Commons could have settled the question decisively; but for the moment both Houses were agreed on all important points. The same class and the same party were dominant in both alike. It is, nevertheless, a fact worth remark that as a general rule the House of Lords defended established abuses with greater obstinacy than the Commons. The majority of its members owed their rank to the Crown, and were more closely attached to the reigning dynasty than in the days when the British aristocracy despised the Royal Family as a line of foreign intruders. And the self-made man is always the worst reactionary. The day was even now in sight when the House of Commons would yield more readily to the pressure of the nation's will; the Lords, on the other hand, would accomplish the prediction made by Wilkes when Pitt began to multiply his new peerages, and become the " dead weight " of the Constitution.[1]

We have yet to discover the effect on the national destiny of this conservatism of the Lords. The Commons would always possess the effective control of government. An ambitious statesman would have as little desire, as in the 18th century, to be promoted to the Upper House, and would regard such promotion as a restraint, indeed a sign that his active career had come to an end. The House of Lords was at most a check upon the Commons. It did not attempt to extend its right of revision in matters of finance, which had been extraordinarily curtailed in the course of the last century. Everything, in fact, points to the conclusion that not only had the prestige of the Upper House not increased, it had positively diminished. Its pomp was, indeed, still impressive. Nevertheless, at the time of the Revolution of 1688, when a peerage was a privilege confined to a very small number, a title was held in greater esteem than at present. If ever a conflict should arise between the two Houses, on any matter of importance, the Upper House would be adopting an extremely hazardous course if it should attempt, in conjunction with the Crown, the defence of laws condemned by the popular chamber. It was now sixty years since the House of Lords had ceased to be an inviolable and immutable institution.

[1] Butler, *Reminiscences*, ed. 3, vol. i. p. 78 : " While the relation between the Minister and the new-made Peers shall subsist, their subserviency to his measures will continue ; but when this relation ceases, the probability is that, as succeeding Ministers will not have the means of attacking them, they will form a silent sulky Opposition, a dead weight on every administration. Will it not then be found that the descendants of Mr. Pitt's Peers will be mutes to strangle his successors ? "

The Real Insignificance of the Tory Reaction.

It must now be evident that the Tory reaction amounted, after all, to very little. The political passions exploited by the Tory leaders, the catchwords so dear to their lips, differed in no essential point from the mass of sentiments and commonplaces which had composed the Whiggery of sixty years earlier. In 1815, as in 1760, the party in office—though Whig then and Tory now—was the party of war, and moreover of war with France, and the Protestant party resolved to maintain the penal laws enacted against Catholics. The Tories of 1815, in their struggle against the Jacobin Revolution and the Empire, posed, as the Whigs had done formerly in their struggle against the Bourbons, as the defenders of the freedom of Europe, threatened with French domination. It was Burke—a Whig who had gone over to Pitt's party, a great orator, a great writer, and, we must add, a great thinker—who developed, in opposition now to the new theories of democracy, as earlier in opposition to attempted encroachments of the Crown, the theory of a system inseparably liberal and aristocratic. The Tories, moreover, were supported, or rather had been supported during the greater part of the war, by the same combination of interests which had formerly supported the Whigs—by the world of finance, of commerce, of industry—that is by the most enterprising and innovating elements in the country. Nor is it true that the increase of the standing army was a danger to public liberty. The British Army possessed none of the characters of an army which could accomplish a *coup d'état.* Moreover, peace had scarcely been concluded before Parliament began to insist on the reduction of the military forces.

In fact, the reform of the public services had already been taken in hand, and attempts had even been made towards the reform of the franchise. And these were assuredly but the first symptoms of a mighty movement of reform. No doubt in 1815 the Cabinet and its supporters were obstinate defenders of every existing institution. The policy then predominant was essentially one of legislative stagnation. Nevertheless, a reform of the traditional body of legislation had already begun, and the stagnation had been far more complete in the period of Whig rule, when Walpole or Lord Chatham governed the country.

Nor had the system of government changed. There was still the same "mixed" Constitution of which we may say with Montesquieu that it was based on the "separation of powers," provided we do not understand thereby a separation rigidly defined by express statutes. It was a Constitution in which the lines of demarcation between the different powers were blurred and confused to the detriment indeed of the executive, but to the advantage of the legislature and public opinion. The Government was systematically weakened, always a prey to internal strife, and deprived by the Constitution itself of the necessary means to repress economic or religious disorders, the war of classes and of creeds. Nevertheless, in the course of the coming century the British Government was destined to give proof of greater stability than any other Government in Europe. How are we to explain the apparent paradox ? We might point to a certain number of accidental circumstances as affording the solution of the problem. It might be said that England, as an insular State, could endure an anarchic Constitution, such as no continental State could accept, if it would not lie at the mercy of a foreign invader. It might also be said that it would be difficult for a revolution to alter the form of government in a country where, owing to the weakness and inertia of the executive, there existed no central authority of which an active minority might take possession to impart thus a new direction to the body politic. These explanations are not wholly worthless, but they are insufficient. What actually took place in England was this. The elements of disorder and anarchy inherent in the political tradition of the country, lost their character and submitted insensibly to the organization of a discipline freely accepted. Though sects multiplied, sectarian animosities died down. Riot was softened into peaceable demonstration, and civil war became a party strife, waged in accordance with rules freely admitted on either side. We must, therefore, seek elsewhere, in the character either of the economic organization or of the religious life of the nation, the secret of this progressive regulation of liberty.

BOOK II

ECONOMIC LIFE

ECONOMIC LIFE

Is it not perilous for a nation to sacrifice its agriculture to the development of its industries, and thereby to become dependent upon the foreigner for the satisfaction of its most elementary needs ? In the course of the 19th century England deliberately made the experiment, and it was in 1815 that the problem for the first time came definitely before public opinion. Although fifty years had already gone by since the days when England exported corn and imported manufactured articles, the methods of agriculture had been so greatly improved, and the state of universal war had made the regular importation of cattle and corn so difficult, that, until the advent of peace, agriculture had remained very prosperous, despite the enormous growth of industry. The farmers had kept, so to speak, the monopoly of the national market. It was only to supply a slight excess of demand over supply—amounting, according to some estimates to a twenty-fifth, according to others to a fortieth of the consumption of corn [1]—that it had been necessary during the preceding ten years to import foreign corn. In 1812 and 1813 exports once more exceeded imports.[2] It was, nevertheless, undeniable that the equilibrium of the English economic system had been completely destroyed. It was in vain that the orators attached to the agricultural interests persisted in claiming that half of the population was engaged in agriculture. For some years past statistics had given them the lie.[3] According to the census returns for 1811, there were only 6,129,142 persons employed in agriculture and mining, as against 7,071,989 persons in commerce, navigation and manufacture. Agriculture and mining produced a revenue of £107,246,795 ; commerce, navigation and manufactures a revenue

---

[1] It is difficult to obtain exact statistics. Sir Henry Parnell (H. of C., May 5, 1814, *Parl. Deb.*, vol. xxvii. p. 713) estimated the average annual import of corn at 700,000 quarters, amounting, according to him, to a twenty-fifth of the total consumption, which would therefore have amounted to 17,500,000 quarters. Western, however (H. of C., May 16, 1814, *Parl. Deb.*, vol. xxvii. p. 903), estimated the average annual import at 1,000,000 quarters, the total consumption at 35,000,000 quarters. According to Gascoyne (H. of C., February 22, 1818, *Parl. Deb.*, vol. xxix. p. 962), who, however, does not give any figures, the import amounted to a fortieth of the consumption. On what basis should the total consumption be calculated ? Baring (February 22, 1815, *Parl. Deb.*, vol. xxix. p. 967), following Adam Smith, proposed to reckon a quarter for each inhabitant. We should obtain from this a figure closely approximating to that of Sir Henry Parnell.

[2] *Corn Trade Report*, 1813, p. 7. Export of corn in 1812 = £1,498,229 ; import = £1,213,850.

[3] H. of C., February 17, 1818, Brand's speech (*Parl. Deb.*, vol. xxix. p. 833).

of £183,908,352.[1] What would be the effect of this destruction of equilibrium now that the restoration of peace had made the relations between England and the outside world once more peaceful and normal ? It was a grave problem ; and all Englishmen realized its gravity.

Nor was the anxiety which led to the introduction into Parliament of a new tariff policy confined to the landed proprietors who were directly threatened. Even among the exponents of the new political economy, free-traders by principle, there were many who were unwilling to see England become, like ancient Tyre or mediæval Venice, a purely commercial or industrial State, compelled to purchase her bread and meat of the foreigner. Malthus was opposed to the free importation of corn, if it involved this consequence. Ricardo and his disciples, in order to recommend their policy of free trade to the country, struggled to prove by arguments of somewhat dubious validity, that it would not produce any such effect. Whatever the correct answer, the country was faced by an economic problem which, during the interval between the Treaty of Paris and the Hundred Days, took precedence over all problems of constitutional reform and of foreign policy, formed the burden of all debates in Parliament and of all the Press polemics, and which finally, in the spring of 1815, led to street riots. Landowners and manufacturers after long years of fairly cordial agreement suddenly realized that their interests were opposed. They formed two powerful economic parties somewhat similar in their internal organization. To the large estate corresponded the large factory. In both were found the same spirit of enterprise, the same improvement of machinery, the same recourse to banking credit, the same growth of output, the same concentration of capital. We must, therefore, investigate both in British agriculture and British industry what was the grading of activities and incomes, what deference and respect existed between the different classes, and whether the two societies, now ranged in hostile camps, were internally united or disunited. In no country of Europe did the new capitalism, whether agricultural or industrial, owe less to Government assistance. How, on the other hand, had this financial development affected the development of political institutions ? Had it been an element of order or of anarchy in English society ? Had it made for stability or for revolution ?

[1] Colquhoun, *Wealth . . . of the British Empire*, p. 109. For other statistics bearing on this point see pp. 55, 89. We must not forget that these figures are conjectural. For a period slightly anterior, see Gentz, *Essai sur l'état actuel de . . . la Grande-Bretagne*, 1800, especially pp. 30, 82, and Arthur Young's estimates, greatly exaggerated in favour of the landed interests (Sinclair, *History of Public Revenue*, 3rd ed., 1803, vol. iii. p. 339). Moreau de Jonnès (*Statistique de la Grande-Bretagne*, vol. i. pp. 301 sqq.) criticizes several attempted estimates of the national wealth, and of the revenues of different classes made since the opening of the 18th century.

CHAPTER I

AGRICULTURE

THE GREAT LANDLORDS IN IRELAND.

The Landlord System. Ireland.

IT is impossible to understand the organization, in a given country, of the section of society devoted to the cultivation of the soil without knowing first what is the established system of land-ownership. The obvious tendency of British legislation and juris-prudence was to maintain intact great landed estates. Real property was not subject to the same rules of law as personal property. Its rules must, it would seem, have been devised by lawyers in collusion with a Parliament dominated by an aristocracy of great landowners for the express purpose of rendering impossible either the subdivision or the transfer of land.

Except in Scotland, there was no registration of land. For anything that concerned the transfer of land it was necessary to have recourse to the complicated agency of trustees—that is, if it was desired to apply the contractual system to land, and to subject an estate to the equitable jurisdiction of the Court of Chancery. It was, however, doubtful whether the responsibility of the trustees could be enforced. Hence the purchaser of a property could never be certain that the trustee with whom he had concluded the purchase had not exceeded his legal powers, and that the whole transaction might not be set aside on the appeal of the legal owner. If a landowner died intestate, his personal estate was divided among his children, but the land went entirely to the eldest son. A father possessed, moreover, the power to leave everything to the eldest—both land and capital. He might do even more. The law of entail enabled him to tie up his real estate in the possession of a series of his descendants ; each of the succeeding generations having only a life interest under the strict control of trustees. Everywhere throughout the United Kingdom was to be found this system of great landed estates. Such a statement expresses but the truth—a truth universally admitted. Nevertheless, a statement so general needs qualification. In the first place, to speak without further explanation of a great landed estate, is to speak somewhat vaguely. Great, very great, enormous, are measures impossible of accurate determination. In the second place, a great estate does not necessarily involve large farms—cultivation on a big scale. But the extent of the cultivation is at least as important a factor as the extent of the estate. In the third place, what was true of England and Scotland might not be true of Ireland. What was true of one English or Scottish county was not true of another. Thus our subject becomes complicated and requires subdivision.

Let us first of all take Ireland. Nowhere in the United Kingdom was landlordism so absolute. English economists envied a country where landed property, being rooted in conquest, was free from all manorial obligations and common land existed no longer.[1] Nowhere was partition more difficult. Entails were so common that an estate very rarely came into the market. Nowhere had the formation of big estates been carried so far. The land had been divided among a small number of conquerors of English origin and Protestant religion. The class of small landlords with incomes ranging from £200 to a £1,000 was represented only by a few instances to be found scattered over the counties of Leinster,[2] and in certain districts on the east coast of Ulster[3] and of Munster.[4] In Co. Monaghan there still lingered a handful of small proprietors of the Protestant faith, descendants either of Scottish colonists, or of Cromwellian soldiers, to whom the Government had once granted land.[5] Though a few members of the old Catholic gentry were still to be found among the landlords, many of these apostatized in order to belong to the religion of their class.[6] In Ireland there was a great gulf between the English and Protestant landlords, and the Irish and Catholic tenantry.

Ireland. Landlords, Agents, Tenants.

Too few in number to organize in the country any social life worthy of the name, the landlords did not live on their estates. They spent as much time as possible, sometimes their entire life, in Dublin or London, at watering-places, or perhaps on a country estate they might happen to possess in England. This absenteeism, which had been increasing since the opening years of the century, led to very great

[1] Wakefield, *Ireland*, vol. i. pp. 242 and 307.

[2] Co. Dublin (where the exception is explicable by the neighbourhood of the capital). Wakefield, *Ireland*, vol. i. p. 258. Co. Wexford (*ibid.*, vol. i. p. 282).

[3] Co. Down (*ibid.*, vol. i. p. 255).

[4] Co. Cork (*ibid.*, vol. i. pp. 250–1).

[5] *Ibid.*, vol. i. p. 270. Many of the descendants of these Protestant colonists did not derive above £20 annual income from their lands.

[6] Bonn (*Englische Kolonisation in Irland*, vol. ii. p. 174) reckons 4,800 apostacies between 1703 and 1788, most of these among the upper classes. Cf. Wakefield's statistics for the number of Catholic proprietors (*Ireland*, vol. ii. pp. 630–1).

evil. The machinery of local government was rendered almost un-workable. There were counties in which it was only just possible to scrape together sufficient proprietors to form a grand jury. With-out any attachment to the soil, the landlords' one thought was to extract with a minimum of trouble the maximum amount of money from a population as widely separated from themselves in their ways of life as Jamaica negroes from the slave owners who exploited their labour. Accordingly they put the management of their estates into the hands of men of business, small local solicitors, "agents" as they were termed. The agents, who received a certain percentage of revenue from the estate, oppressed, in the name of their employer, the cultivators of the soil. At the period with which we are now dealing, owing to the rise in price of all foodstuffs, and owing also to Sir John Newport's Act of 1806 permitting the free export of Irish corn to England and Scotland,[1] rents had been growing constantly higher.[2] This sufficed to persuade the landlord that Irish agriculture was progressing and that the country was prosperous. Trusting to the increase in the revenue yielded by his estate he borrowed from his agent. The landlord was henceforth at the mercy of the very man who was supposed to look after his interests, and it was made impossible for the tenantry to appeal from the latter to the former. The tenantry was, therefore, compelled to satisfy all the agent's demands, and to buy his good-will with presents to himself, his wife, his daughters or his mistress. Such was the custom of the country ; and it shocked no one. Certainly it mattered nothing to the landlord, so long as he pocketed his rents, and those rents went on increasing. Only it sometimes happened that his debt to the agent increased even quicker. One day the agent would put down his foot, and would either compel the landlord to grant him a lease of the estate on his own terms, or would simply inform him that the whole or part of the estate had now passed into his ownership.[3] This was one of the methods employed by the Catholics to repossess themselves of their native soil. To protect the landlords a statute was passed by which it was made illegal for them to grant leases to their agents.

If the tenant devoted himself to cattle breeding, he was said to occupy a grazing farm ; if to agriculture in the strict sense, he was said to occupy a tillage farm. The graziers were by far the wealthier

---

[1] 46 Geo. III, cap. 97.

[2] "In about fifty years . . . from 1676 the rental of Ireland appears to have doubled. In the next fifty years, it appears to have also doubled. But in the last thirty years, it appears to have increased so as to double in about nineteen years " (Newenham, *View . . . of Ireland*, 1809, p. 232). Arthur Young estimated in 1778 the total rental of Ireland at about £6,000,000, Newenham in 1805 at £15,000,000 (see Young, *Tour*, Part II, pp. 4 sqq. ; Newenham, *View*, p. 232). Wakefield, in 1814, was content to point out the difficulty of arriving at an exact estimate and shirked the task (*Ireland*, vol. i. pp. 245–6).

[3] See Miss Edgeworth's *Castle Rackrent*.

of the two classes. They occupied great farms in the centre of Ireland in the counties of Limerick, Tipperary, Clare, Meath, and Waterford. Their numbers were few by reason of the extent of the land which they farmed. Sometimes they paid a rent of from £3,000 to £10,000.[1] Well might Arthur Young call them "the greatest graziers and cow-raisers in the world."[2] They dressed like gentry, or at least did so to the best of their ability. Sometimes they took an old Irish name, and spread a report that they belonged to an ancient family robbed formerly of its possessions by the English invader. The furniture of their houses was absurdly luxurious, but pigs and hens ran about the kitchen. Their intense ignorance made it impossible for them to improve their stock ; and their sole method of enrichment was to speculate on a rise in the price of cattle. The aristocracy despised them ; the peasantry loathed them.[3] They formed a class apart, and were, so to speak, the half-castes of Irish society. In the period under review, the grazing industry, after a continuous increase throughout the 18th century, had begun to give way to tillage. But this change was not in any way a sign of real progress in Irish agriculture or of the substitution of intensive for extensive cultivation.

Irish leases were usually long, for twenty-one years, thirty-one years, a life and twenty-one years, a life and thirty-one years, a life and sixty-one years.[4] We might, therefore, be inclined at first sight to believe that the reason for the substitution of tillage for grazing was that the farmer whose long lease gave him an interest in the improvement of his farm deliberately chose the most intelligent method of cultivation. But before we accept this explanation we must first know both the terms and the actual working of these long leases.

They were always reduced to the simplest possible form. The landlord erected no building on his property, spent nothing to keep it in good condition ; it was naked soil, or very little more, that he let to the tenant.[5] When the lease expired, no account was taken, in the majority of the Irish counties, of any rights which the outgoing tenant might have acquired. No amicable negotiations took place. The farm was simply put up to auction and the lease granted to the highest bidder. At first sight this seemed to be to the landlord's advantage, because his rent increased. But in reality he lost by it in the long run because the farmer had no inducement to refrain from exhausting the soil as the end of the lease drew near. On the contrary, he knew that the better his cultivation had been the more certain he was to lose the land, which by his efforts had become more attractive to would-be purchasers.

---

[1] Wakefield, *Ireland*, vol. i. pp. 319 sqq.
[2] Arthur Young, *Tour in Ireland*, Part II, p. 30.
[3] Wakefield, *Ireland*, vol. ii. pp. 545–6, 754–5.
[4] *Ibid.*, vol. i. p. 285.   [5] *Ibid.*, vol. i. p. 244.

The terms of the lease did not even leave the farmer free to devote himself entirely to the cultivation of the land which he had rented. The landlord seemed to be determined to make the farmer into a labourer —a labourer, moreover, at a reduced wage. By a written or verbal agreement, or sometimes in virtue of a tacit understanding, the tenant bound himself to work, at the landlord's demand, for a very low wage or even without payment.[1] As we have seen already, beside the demands of the landlord, there were also those of the agent to be satisfied. Both landlords and agents were wont to call attention with pride to this voluntary service of the natives whenever they did the honours of an estate to some foreign visitor. But English agriculturists who came to Ireland were far from admiring this quasi-slavery. Often indeed, to avoid the stamp duty, or even out of sheer indolence and dread of legal complications, the tenants made no written agreement. "If your Honour," the tenant would say to his landlord, "would make a note of the transaction in your book, that will be sufficient." [2]

In such cases it is obvious how insecure was the tenant's position in relation to his landlord or agent. Everything which had to do with Ireland bore the stamp of carelessness and greed.

An Irish farm was a disgusting sight.[3] There was no vestige of a garden—only a bare, muddy yard, surrounded by a low wall of loose stones. There was neither gate nor bar. The entrance was closed by placing there a cart, shafts in air. The house consisted of a single room, without flooring or pavement, where the farmer and his family ate, slept and did their cooking surrounded by pigs and fowls. The grain was threshed on the bare earth. The agricultural implements rusted from exposure to the rain. They were, moreover, very rudimentary. The plough was of wood, and in many districts was still attached for use to the tail of a horse or cow. Of scientific cultivation there was none. The fallow was succeeded by as many crops as could possibly be got out of the soil—sometimes ten or twelve in succession—and then the land was allowed to lie fallow once more. For many years past England and Scotland had been obliged to seek abroad a fifth part of the corn consumed by their large population, now so greatly increased by the growth of industrialism. Ireland, however, despite the fact that the great majority of her population was engaged in agriculture, was unable to supply the deficit. Only in the south-west had the cultivation of wheat made some progress. Elsewhere the lack of roads and transport hindered the carriage of grain to the ports, and thus discouraged the cultivation of wheat. Often the most profitable use of corn was to take it to an illicit still, where it was made into the native whisky, *poteen*.[4] In the north wheat was giving way to

---

[1] Wakefield, *Ireland*, vol. i. pp. 245, 366; Arthur Young, *Tour in Ireland*, p. 51.
[2] *Ibid.*, vol. i. p. 276. [3] *Ibid.*, vol. i. p. 468, 470; Tigh, *Kilkenny*, pp. 411 sqq.
[4] *Ibid.*, vol. i. pp. 246 sqq.

potatoes, the food of the common people in Ireland. Everywhere farms were small and were being more and more subdivided. When Arthur Young visited Ireland in 1778, farms of 500 to 1,500 or 2,000 acres had been far from uncommon. They were now of very rare occurrence. On the other hand farms of forty, thirty, twenty and fifteen acres were greatly increasing in number and had, indeed, become the normal unit of cultivation.[1] Even if we do not share the systematic prejudice of English agriculturists in favour of cultivation on a large scale, we cannot surely deny that this shrinkage of the Irish farm was, under the circumstances which occasioned it, a sign that the agriculture of the country was in a bad condition.

The Disappearance of the large Farm.   Middlemen and Cotters.

The splitting up of farms was due to different causes, which contributed in different degrees towards this result. First among these was the Act of 1793 restoring the suffrage to Catholics. Before 1793 it had been to the landlords' political interest to settle on their estates Protestant farmers who would vote under their orders. Since, however, few Protestant farmers were available, and since they were exacting in proportion to their scarcity, it had been necessary to expel several Catholic tenants to satisfy one Protestant. The effect, therefore, of the anti-Catholic legislation had been to increase the average size of farms. Now, however, the political interest of the landlords was altogether different. To increase the number of their electors they divided their estates amongst a number of Catholic forty-shilling freeholders. Such division was practically without limit, since the landlords made up the voters' register themselves, and put down as forty-shilling freeholders, where it suited them, even those whose land brought in less than forty shillings. In 1795 there were 40,768 freeholders, a year later there were 64,752, and by 1821 the figure was to reach 184,229.[2]

A second cause of subdivision, deeper rooted and more permanent in its operation, was the scarcity, one might almost say the non-existence, of wage labour, in the Irish country districts. Not only was the Irish farmer poor, and therefore without the spare cash necessary to advance the wages of labour, but also—and this was probably the graver difficulty—he had to encounter tenacious prejudices in his search for workers.

To work, to receive a wage, and to purchase with the money so

[1] Curwen, *Observations . . . on Ireland*, vol. i. pp. 104–5, 250 ; vol. ii. p. 38. He remarks as something very exceptional a district near Londonderry, where farms were generally more than 100 acres in extent.

[2] Bonn, *Englische Kolonisation in Irland*, vol. ii. pp. 201–4. For the sources see the parliamentary papers cited in our bibliography, which are, however, incomplete and even at times contradictory.

earned the necessaries of life, formed a series of operations too complicated for the understanding of an Irishman of the lower classes.[1] In his view the normal method of obtaining a livelihood was to obtain directly from his own fields a sufficient quantity of potatoes and dairy produce to feed himself and his family.[2] This explains the survival of village partnership, in Ireland, and especially along the whole of the west coast.[3] The land was not rented by an individual, who then worked it by means of paid labourers, but it was farmed in common by a group of heads of families. The arable land was divided among the partners. The cattle pastured in common. Each partner had the right to a certain amount of pasturage, which was reckoned in units known as "collops." This unit varied slightly in different districts, but was everywhere determined by a perfectly definite tradition. Usually the horse was the unit of calculation, and was the equivalent of so many goats, calves or geese.[4] "It was an abominable system, which prevented, so long as it remained in force, any emulation among the farmers in the matter of drainage, enclosure, liming, or, in short, as regards any operations undertaken to increase the productivity of the soil. An individual, here and there, might perhaps be disposed to improve the soil, but one or all his neighbours would immediately oppose his schemes, and so the entire plan for improving the farm would go by the board."[5] Nevertheless, the system continued in force and even assumed, it would seem, a more and more aggravated form, for according to the old Celtic customary law the goods of the deceased were divided equally among his sons and daughters.[6] When, therefore, a member of a village community died, his fellow partners would never dare to deprive his children of their lawful heritage. Hence the number of partners must needs go on increasing indefinitely. Even where the village community did not exist, customs similar to this entailed similar consequences. When a farmer's sons attained their majority, or when his daughters married, custom required him to divide up his farm for their benefit. On his death custom required the equal division of the farm among his heirs. The result of this was that twenty, thirty or perhaps even forty families were now settled on a farm of 150 acres, occupied forty years earlier by a single tenant. The traditional moral code of the country, together with the quasi-legal institutions which expressed that code, confined the individual's

[1] According to Wakefield (*Ireland*, vol. i. p. 511) the Irish peasants were even inclined to regard wage labour as dishonourable.

[2] "In England complaints rise even to riot when the rates of provisions are high, but in Ireland the poor have nothing to do with prices; they depend not on prices, but on crops of a vegetable very regular in its produce" (Arthur Young, *Tour in Ireland*, Part II, pp. 22–3).

[3] Wakefield, *Ireland*, vol. i. pp. 255, 260, 271, 275, 278; vol. ii. pp. 308–9, 372.

[4] *Ibid.*, vol, i. pp. 309, 316, 349.

[5] *Ibid.*, vol. i. p. 278. See also on the system of village partnership, Tighe, *Kilkenny*, pp. 418–20.

[6] *Ibid.*, vol. i. p. 251.

means of livelihood to a small plot of ground to which he was personally attached, which he cultivated himself, and on which he was dependent for subsistence.

Even if a farmer did still possess more land than he could cultivate by himself, he was obliged to satisfy his labourers' demands and establish them on the soil. The landlord had himself set the example. By imposing upon the tenant the obligation to furnish a certain amount of labour at a reduced wage, he had made him a hired labourer as well as a tenant. The farmer would therefore erect on his farm "*dry cots*," dwellings to which sometimes no land was attached, but which usually carried with them a plot of ground on which the dry cotter could grow oats or potatoes.[1] In return for this the cotter undertook to work for the farmer at the rate of 5d. a day. Moreover, it generally happened that at the end of the year the cotter was in the farmer's debt. Accordingly the final reckoning between them was made according to what was termed the system of conveniences, that is without the medium of coin, by a simple exchange of services.[2] The richer party granted a piece of land to the poorer in exchange for his labour. The poorer was practically the serf of the richer.

Nevertheless, the quality of the work done by these cotters was far from satisfactory. Obliged to divide their time between their own plot of ground and their employer's farm, they worked for their master in a half-hearted and spasmodic fashion. Then the farmer devised a new method. He reduced to a minimum the area of the land which he cultivated directly, and thus was able to dispense almost completely with wage labour. The remainder of his land he divided into "*corn acres*," which he leased for an annual rent of six to ten guineas an acre. He thus became as it were a secondary landlord, and from the greater part of his farm received income for which he did no work. His sole concern was, how best to obtain more rent for these pieces of land than he himself owed for them to the landlord. He had ceased to be the head of a big farm and had become instead a middleman—the middleman of ill-repute.

The landlord and his agent did not regard with disfavour this transformation of the farmer into the middleman. Certainly the land lost by it. Formerly it had been a case of the substitution of cultivation on a small scale for cultivation on a large or moderately large scale ; now it was the substitution for cultivation on a small scale of cultivation on an infinitesimal scale. Every year the miserable peasant who dug his patch of oats and his patch of potatoes left the soil more impoverished. For that, however, Irish improvi-

---

[1] For these cotters see Wakefield, *Ireland*, vol. ii. p. 740. Cf. Arthur Young, *Tour in Ireland*, pp. 304, 357, 373, and Part II, p. 20 ; also Curwen, *Observations . . . on Ireland*, vol. i. pp. 220, 251-2.

[2] Wakefield, *Ireland*, vol. i. pp. 507 sqq., p. 599.

dence cared nothing. The landlord ran no risk. If the middleman failed to pay his rent, the landlord had the right to seize the
cattle of the subtenants even when they had paid their rent to the
middleman. The latter, however, seldom failed to pay in full. Since
the price of corn was constantly rising, circumstances favoured him.
He had obtained a long lease from the landlord and concluded short
leases with the subtenants.[1] While the half-yearly rent due from him
to the landlord remained the same, he kept on raising the amount due
from the subtenants. Sometimes the landlord, remarking this, would
put into his leases a stipulation that the rent should be raised if part
of the farm were sublet. Even so this rise in the rent never equalled
the increase of the middleman's receipts. Landlord and middleman
alike grew richer. That was all.

The landlord found this new system so profitable that often in
place of letting his land directly to small tenants, he would himself
appoint a middleman. By this method both he and his agent were
spared the irksome task of collecting one by one a number of small
debts. The middleman was better acquainted than the landlord or
his solicitor with the feelings and manner of life of the peasantry, who
were willing to accept from him terms which they would have rejected
in direct negotiations with the landlord.[2] Moreover, they were now
compelled to pay regularly, for their new master watched them from
their very midst and knew all their tricks. The sole resource of the
more prudent of these subtenants, who wished to rise in the social
scale, was to repeat the procedure which had been carried out at their
expense and to become the middleman's middlemen. These men
constituted the middle class in the country districts of Ireland, a class
equally destitute of culture and morality. They swarmed in the
small towns, drinking hard, seducing young girls and loafing from
morning till night, or even went so far afield as Dublin, Bath and
London to squander on their pleasures the fruits of their extortion.[3]

Thus in Ireland, while the estates were excessively large, the units
of cultivation were on the other hand excessively small. At once
farmer and wage-earner, the Irish cotter obtained from his patch of
land an amount of produce barely sufficient to nourish his family.
Beyond this bare minimum all his toil went in the shape of rent or of
forced labour to enrich a long chain of exploiters, the middleman of
the first, of the second, and sometimes even of the third degree, the
agent, and after the agent the landlord. He had, moreover, to satisfy
the claims of the tax collector, of the Catholic priest, and of the clergyman of the Established Church into the bargain. The revenues
received by the landlords were not earned by the management of their
estates—for they did not reside. Nor did these revenues represent

[1] Bonn, *Englische Kolonisation in Irland*, vol. ii. p. 201.
[2] Wakefield, *Ireland*, vol. i. p. 288.   [3] *Ibid.*, vol. i. p. 288.

the profit of capital laid out upon the land, for the system adopted by the landlords was not to enrich the soil, but simply to exhaust it.   The connecting links of the chain—the middleman, the agent and the grazier—did not constitute a middle class which could assure, by its universally admitted respectability, the stability of the social fabric. Despised by the landlords for the vulgarity of their manners and also as belonging to a conquered race, and at the same time hated by the cotters whom they bullied and oppressed, they were but a new element of instability in a society already chaotic.   How could the enormous army of peasants in which they were the subalterns, or rather the slave drivers, fail to revolt against the miserable lot to which they were condemned ?   Was it not inevitable that the barbarism to which the peasants were reduced should invest these outbreaks of fury with a character of peculiar atrocity ?

The Agrarian Anarchy.

For some time past English travellers making a journey of inspection in Ireland had been astonished at the infrequency and sporadic character of agrarian disturbances.   About 1780 Arthur Young had been much shocked to observe that in Ireland a " gentleman " could cane or flog a peasant for insolent carriage or disrespectful language without exciting fury by such treatment.   It aroused his indignation to witness " whole strings of cars whipt into a ditch by a gentleman's footman, to make way for his carriage " without a thought of protest on the part of the poor wretches.[1]   Thirty years later Wakefield was equally astonished. The resignation, nay the good humour, with which the Catholic cotter accepted his degraded position was incomprehensible to him.[2]   He noticed that the gentry preferred Catholic to Protestant servants, because they found the former the most docile " slaves." [3]   Nevertheless, a movement of revolt was taking shape.   During the last half-century very few years had been entirely free from crimes committed in one district or another by bands of malcontents called in succession Peep-o'-Day Boys, Steelboys, Oakboys, Defenders, Ribbonmen, Whiteboys, Rightboys, Caravats, Shanavests, Thrashers, and Carders.[4]   Some of these associations possessed a religious character.   The Defenders and the Ribbonmen had been organized to oppose the Protestant Peep-o'-Day Boys and Orangemen.   The others had been formed to defend the economic interests of their members.   Sometimes the object of

---

[1] Arthur Young, *Tour in Ireland*, Part II, p. 54.

[2] Wakefield, *Ireland*, vol. ii. pp. 773–4.   [3] *Ibid.*, vol. ii. p. 613.

[4] For these associations see Wakefield, *Ireland*, vol. ii. pp. 9 sqq., 486, 562, 568, 763–4, 769 sqq., 781.   Cf. for the first beginning of these disturbances and an account of the Whiteboys 1760–70, Arthur Young, *Tour in Ireland*, pp. 75–7, also Part II, p. 30.   For the Peep-o'-Day Boys and Defenders of the same period, and the Rightboys of 1785, see Newenham, *A View* . . . pp. 262–5, 258 ; also, for the entire movement, a long and important speech of O'Connell's, December 31, 1813 (*Life and Speeches*, vol. ii. pp. 112–22).

attack was the local dues, the county cess, the equivalent of the English rates. More often, however, it was the tithe, which was particularly odious to the Irish peasantry, since it was not paid to the clergy of their own cult, and also a peculiarly heavy burden upon the cotters, because in Ireland it was exclusively a charge upon the tillage farms, and the rich graziers were therefore exempt.[1] But the contest was coming more and more to turn upon the relations between landlord and tenant. The conspirators sought to fix the leasehold value of the corn acre, to forbid the landlords to put up these allotments to auction, and to secure for the cotter a right to a lease of his land in perpetuity. If the Irish lower classes began to interest themselves in the cause of Catholic emancipation, this was not because they cared much for the knowledge that henceforward a Catholic might be returned to Parliament, and would be eligible for any employment civil or military. It was rather that in Catholic emancipation they foresaw vaguely the satisfaction of many desires, the expropriation of the Protestant landlords, and the division of the land among themselves—in a word, the restitution to the Catholics of the soil that had belonged to their ancestors.[2]

Wakefield travelled through Kerry and Tipperary in 1808 when disorder was universal there.[3] He saw a farm burnt, after warning given to the occupant by an anonymous letter ; he saw thousands of men assemble to prevent the distraint of a cotter's cattle ; he saw landlords unable to leave their house without the protection of armed guards. In 1813, after a few months of calm, disturbances broke out afresh in the southern counties—Waterford, Tipperary, Meath, West Meath, King's County, and Limerick—nor by 1815 had order been yet restored. In 1814 Parliament was obliged to pass two special statutes to repress the campaign of outrage.[4] When a landlord evicted a cotter who refused to pay a higher rent, and found another peasant to take the farm of the evicted cotter, both landlord and peasant incurred the vengeance of " Captain Thrash " and his deputies the Thrashers. Bands of men masked and wearing a disguise went from house to house in quest of arms. Shortly afterwards came the news of the public execution of a condemned landlord or farmer under the eyes of the peasantry and with the connivance of the entire population.[5] These

[1] Wakefield, *Ireland*, vol. ii. pp. 485 sqq. The Carders' Association would even seem to have been formed originally to resist the pecuniary demands of the Catholic priesthood. (Curwen, *Observations . . . on Ireland* vol. ii. p. 183. Cf. Wakefield, *Ireland*, vol. ii. p. 562).

[2] *Report of the Select Committee of the House of Lords appointed to inquire into the State of Ireland*, 1825 (*Minutes of Evidence*, p. 214).

[3] Wakefield, *Ireland*, vol. ii. pp. 764, 769-70.

[4] 54 Geo. III, cap. 180-1.

[5] For the grave disturbances in Ireland at this period, see *Copy of a Dispatch from his Excellency the Lord-Lieutenant of Ireland to Lord Viscount Sidmouth, dated June 5, 1816, viz. : A Statement of the Nature and Extent of the Disturbances which have recently prevailed in Ireland and the Measures which have been adopted by the Government of that Country in consequence thereof*, reproduced in the *Annual Register*, 1816, pp. 402 sqq. See also H. of C., June 23,

outbreaks were as yet but slave risings, outbursts of savagery,[1] spasmodic, incoherent and badly organized. In 1798 a general movement of insurrection had only been rendered possible by the co-operation of the Presbyterian farmers of the north-east. The Catholic peasantry was still scarcely capable of general views, and the judges who condemned members of their secret societies sometimes remarked with astonishment that these different associations were rival clans implacably hostile one to another.[2] Nevertheless, war had begun between the landlords and the cultivators of the soil. A century of agrarian strife was dawning on Ireland.

THE SYSTEM OF LARGE ESTATES IN ENGLAND AND SCOTLAND.

The Distribution of Landed Property. The Enclosures.

As in Ireland, so also in England and Scotland, the system of large landed estates prevailed. In the 15th century the disbanding of feudal retainers had driven to the towns a crowd of small landowners, vassals of the great lords. The latter then became absolute proprietors of vast estates drained of their population. They converted these into sheepwalks. The dissolution of the monasteries in the 16th century did not involve the division of the great ecclesiastical domains. All that took place was the substitution of aristocratic for clerical mortmain. In the 18th century, owing to new causes, this movement of concentration recommenced. The districts which had escaped the enclosures of the 15th century were now in their turn invaded.

Sometimes the waste of the manor, common land lying continually fallow on which every one had the right to pasture his cow, to cut a little wood, and dig some turf, became, by virtue of an Enclosure Act, the private property of an individual owner. It was then systematically improved and transformed into a meadow for pasture or into a field of arable land. Sometimes such an Enclosure Act dealt with the open field, which was cultivated every year in common by a number of smallholders, to each of whom belonged one or more of the narrow strips into which the field was divided. These they cultivated collectively according to a fixed plan ; and the produce was divided among them in proportion to the size and value of their allotments. Such lands

---

1814, Mr. Peel's Bill for the better execution of the Laws in Ireland (*Parl. Deb.*, vol. xxviii. pp. 162 sqq.). Also, for supplementary details, June 27 and July 4, 1814 ; H. of L., July 21, 27, 28 ; H. of C., November 18, 21, 23 ; H. of L., November 21, 24, 26, 1814 (*Parl. Deb.*, vol. xxviii. pp. 822, 853, 862 ; vol. xxix. pp. 335, 387, 492—366, 497, 593).

[1] The Carders were so called because they tore the bodies of their victims with carding-combs.

[2] " In 1816 at Ballyvourney two rival clans came to mortal combat " (*Annual Register*, 1816, *Chronicle*, p. 107).

were now redistributed by law, and grouped into allotments of which the cultivation as well as the ownership was henceforth individual. But inevitably those who owned larger allotments were in a better position to make them pay. The others whose allotments were of poorer value sold their land and emigrated. In this fashion the cultivation of the soil of England passed into the hands of men with large capital. Thus disappeared, or tended to disappear, the small-holder of whom England had formerly been so proud, for in him she had seen the born defender of her national independence and political liberties. This concentration of landed property in a few hands tended to produce to a certain extent the same effects in Great Britain as in Ireland. On the landed estates of England and Scotland, as on those of Ireland, we find two hostile classes facing each other—the capitalists and the proletariat. But the resemblance was, after all, but partial. The differences between the two countries were numerous and profound.

We must distinguish at the outset between the two systems of law which favoured the existence of large estates—between the laws of feudal origin which prevented such estates from breaking up when once formed, and the modern laws of enclosure which tended to create new estates. The movement of enclosure had been growing constantly stronger during the last century and especially during the last half-century. Never had it been so rapid as during the last ten years of the war.[1] The same, however, cannot be said of the system of entail, which far from progressing was actually declining. Even in Scotland, where about a third of the landed property was entailed,[2] the pro-prietary rights possessed by an heir of entail over his land had been on several occasions extended by statute.[3] In England, where entailed estates were fewer, the institution had been, from the time of Charles II, subjected to certain restrictions. It had been provided, as a universal rule, that, after a fairly short lapse of time, the entail, unless expressly renewed, would cease to exist.[4] The economists, zealous advocates of the policy of enclosures, were far from favouring entails. They preached the system of agricultural capitalism, not of landed feudalism. Agricultural undertakings on a huge scale, in which large investments of capital intensified production, were dear to their hearts. It was, however, far from their wish that the capital necessary for cultivation should be tied up by lawyers' devices in the interest of the perhaps

---

[1] From 1809 onwards there were over 100 enclosures a year (Tooke, *History of Prices*, vol. i. p. 326).

[2] Sinclair, *Scotland*, vol. i. pp. 105–22.

[3] *Ibid.*, vol. i. pp. 102–4. He cites these statutes—20 Geo. II, cap. 50, 51; 10 Geo. III, cap. 51.

[4] For a life or lives in being at the creation of the entail and for a further period of twenty-one years (Charles Butler, *Reminiscences*, 3rd ed., vol. i. p. 61). Cf. Humphreys, *Observations on . . . English Laws of Real Property*, 1826, pp. 28 sqq.

incompetent heir of an old family. They demanded that land should pass from one owner to another as easily as did any other form of capital, so that it might always be at the disposition of the wealthiest and ablest. Romilly had made himself their mouthpiece when in 1807 he had begun his parliamentary career by the introduction of a Bill rendering land equally liable to seizure for debt as were movables.[1] The growth of the system of large estates was the result of the development of modern capitalism. It was but natural that this growth should be at least partially counterbalanced by the decline of feudal institutions. The decline was extremely slow—a Parliament of Landowners did everything possible to retard it—but it was nevertheless a fact, which the success of the policy of enclosures could but disguise.

The class of small independent cultivators, or yeomen, were slowly vanishing. A radical separation was taking place in England and Scotland alike, between those who owned the soil and those who cultivated it. In the open market with its rapid fluctuations of value the small cultivator who lacked capital was powerless to resist for long a fall of prices. The great landowner, on the other hand, and the big farmer, were able to resist, and would then buy up, at the first good harvest, the land of the small cultivator who had been brought to ruin. Or they might even possess sufficient capital to buy at once, without having to wait for a good season.[2] This does not mean, however, that landed property tended in Great Britain, as in Ireland, to become concentrated in the hands of an extremely restricted number of owners. The 25,620 square miles of Scottish soil were owned by 7,800 proprietors.[3] This is obviously a small number. But if we would form

---

[1] The Bill was thrown out, but a second Bill, not so drastic, was passed (47 Geo. III, sess. 2, cap. 74). See *Diary*, January 10, 28, February 18, March 11, 18, also April 20 and August 14, 1807 (*Memoirs of Romilly*, vol. ii. pp. 173, 177, 180, 184–6, 198, 222). H. of C., January 28, February 18, 1807 (*Parl. Deb.*, vol. viii. pp. 561–851). Cf. H. of C., April 29, 1814 (*Parl. Deb.*, vol. xxvii. pp. 592 sqq.).

[2] Nevertheless, this statement, though on the whole true, requires qualification. The decline of the yeoman class, rapid during the 18th century, was apparently checked during the years of agricultural prosperity that terminated precisely in the year 1815. After 1815 it proceeded with headlong rapidity; but in 1815 small landowners were still numerous, not only in the north-east and the south-west, but in Suffolk and Cambridgeshire, and in the neighbourhood of the Metropolis. In Kent they had suffered no diminution (Cf. Defoe, *Tour*, ed. 1724, vol. i. p. 38, and Boys, *Kent*, 1796, p. 26). They occupied a third of the soil of Berkshire (Mavor, *Berkshire*, 1813, p. 112). According to A. Young their numbers were actually increasing in Essex (*Essex*, 1802, p. 23). Cf. Hasbach, *History of the Agricultural Labourer*, pp. 73 sqq. n., 106, and especially A. H. Johnson, *The Disappearance of the Small Landowner*, chap. viii., who from the evidence afforded by the assessment lists of the Land Tax, distinguishes three stages in the history of the disappearance of the class of small landowners : (1) 18th century till 1785. Decrease in the number of yeomen ; (2) 1785–1802. No decrease but a tendency to increase except in Lancashire, where the cotton industry attracted the yeomen ; (3) 1802–1832, decrease. It is, however, questionable whether the dates are well chosen. Not 1802 but 1815 was the turning-point in the history of British agriculture.

[3] Sinclair, *Scotland*, vol. i. p. 89. Large properties, or estates above £2,000 of valued rent, 386 ; middling properties or estates from £2,000 to £2,500 of valued rent, 1,077 ; small

a fair estimate of the average size of a Scottish estate we must remember that it is impossible to include in the same category the fertile lowlands where the ownership of the soil was divided among a fairly large number, and the uncultivated wastes of the Highlands, where the formation of immense *latifundia* involved no injury to agricultural production. In England the land was more divided than in Scotland. There were, it is true, some enormous estates, either feudal survivals or monastic spoils. The Dukes of Bedford, Devonshire and Norfolk were the absolute rulers of territories which, if put together, would have extended over entire counties. In Oxfordshire,[1] Warwickshire,[2] and Derbyshire[3] were estates whose area reached 25,000 acres, and which produced an income of £25,000. But in most counties estates with a rental exceeding £12,000, £10,000 or even £8,000 were rare. And there was a fairly even distribution of smaller estates. Gilbert Wakefield fitly characterized the distribution of landed property in England when he deplored the absence in Ireland of " the minor proprietors, so common in England, who owned land producing an income of from £200 to £1,000." [4] Indeed, there is nothing strange in the fact that in England landed property was, by comparison with Ireland, distributed among many owners. On the contrary, it was the natural result of the nature of British aristocracy.

This aristocracy controlled all the machinery of government. It was supreme in both Houses of Parliament and disposed at pleasure of every Government office. All the local administration of the country was in its hands. Nevertheless, this aristocracy was not closed to new-comers. Since 1688 financiers, bankers, merchants, and manufacturers had constantly exerted a decisive influence on the affairs of the nation. It was the acquisition of land which enabled these new men to insinuate themselves into the ranks of the old aristocracy, and thus to bring their influence to bear upon the governing classes, not from without, but from within, through a number of secret channels. Our study of the political institutions of the realm has shown us already how the more ambitious of these men, by marrying their daughters into the nobility or gentry, by becoming justices of the peace and sheriffs, or by obtaining the patronage of an electoral borough, might themselves attain to the peerage. Others, whose aspirations were not so lofty, were content if they might emerge from the vulgar and illiterate circles in which they had grown up, and enter the ranks of the local gentry. There came into being in the neighbourhood of all the large towns an increasing number of estates on which manufacturers and

---

properties or estates under £500 of valued rent, 6,181 ; estates belonging to corporate bodies, 144. This gives a total of 7,798.

[1] Davis, *Oxfordshire*, p. 11 ; Young, *Oxfordshire*, p. 16.

[2] Murray, *Warwickshire*, p. 25.   [3] Brown, *Derbyshire*, p. 12.

[4] Wakefield, *Ireland*, vol. i. pp. 254–5.

business men lived during part of the year. These manufacturing centres had multiplied and developed to an enormous extent in England during the last twenty years—a development which operated with an ever-increasing force to prevent an excessive concentration of landed property. When an estate was put up to sale the *nouveaux riches*, who were invading the English country districts, were in a position to outbid the greatest landowner of the neighbourhood. It might even be to the latter's advantage to sell a portion of his estate to one of these new-comers. Already, at the opening of the 18th century, Daniel Defoe had remarked that in the neighbourhood of London families belonging to the local gentry were frequently replaced by families enriched in business.[1] In a few years from our date Cobbett was to journey on horseback through all the southern and south-western counties, to compile with indignation a list of the " mansions " and " lodges " which he would find in the occupation of financial and commercial parvenus, the " Squires of Change Alley."[2] A sociologist of fantastic views, he even regarded this invasion of *nouveaux riches* as the fundamental cause of the expropriation of the peasant proprietors.

The Landowners.

The landowners, whether heirs of old families or recent purchasers, resided on their estates. This had been for a long time past the taste of the leaders of fashion. During the war the bonds which attached the landowners to the soil had been drawn still tighter. There were no more journeys possible in France, Switzerland and Italy. The leisured classes had now to be content with the peaceful landscapes and humdrum recreations afforded by the English countryside. England was not a country in which the capital had proved the social death of the provinces. There was no absolute monarch in England, with his court and centralized administration. London was no more than a huge business centre where the representatives of the nation assembled yearly for a limited number of months, and that rather to dictate to the capital the wishes of the country than to issue orders to the provinces in the name of the central government. Nor was England a country where the town had proved the social death of the country. Even less than London were the provincial towns centres of a complete civilization. They were too ugly, too gloomy, too exclusively organized for the production of wealth. The result was that, despite cold and fog, the modern Englishman regarded the country as the place in which to live if you would lead a life happy and worthy of a gentleman. The rigour of the climate encouraged violent forms

---

[1] *Tour through the whole Island of Great Britain*, ed. 1724, vol. i. pp. 17–18.
[2] *Rural Rides*, October 11, 1822. Cf. November 2, 1821 ; January 4, June 24, September 25, 28, November 17, 1822 ; August 1, 2, 7, 31, October 30, 31, 1823 ; November 9, 13, 1825 ; August 30, September 4, 12, 25, 29, October 18, 1826.

of exercise, such as hunting and games played in the open air ; and the practice of these games, whose organization was daily being brought to greater perfection, gave rise to a new moral code. In addition to the religious, civic and industrial codes, arose the code of athleticism, or to employ a term which English custom was to render universally popular, the morality of sport. The growth of this rustic virtue exerted a decisive influence upon the agrarian economy of the realm.

When the landlord does not reside, but is content to receive through an agent the rents due from his tenants, and considers that the more he receives the better he is served, landlords and tenants form two classes hopelessly at strife. There is an avowed warfare between them. When, however, the landlord resides on his estate, a human relationship is inevitably established between himself and the local inhabitants of the place. They were, indeed, his dependants, and his tributaries. He was the spoilt child of the legislature. But despite all, landlord and tenant led the same life and met daily. In England, it often happened that the tenant was an elector whose vote was sought by the landlord. Even if a resident landlord cared nothing for popularity and showed himself harsh and greedy, the very fact of his residence among his tenantry obliged him to spend a portion of his rents in the locality whence they were obtained. This portion was thus restored, indirectly, to those who had paid it. He took, moreover, a personal interest in the cultivation of his land. He would either improve it himself or would watch his tenant closely. Sometimes when a lease expired he took over temporarily the management of the farm, put in it order, erected more spacious and healthier buildings, renewed the stock, and radically altered the methods of cultivation. After this he would lease the farm to new tenants, who, being better provided than their predecessors, could pay a higher rent. Sometimes he was content to reserve one of his farms, which he transformed into an " experimental farm." Perhaps this farm would cost him more than the profits he derived from it, but it served as a model to all the tenants on the estate. Agriculture was at once the great source of revenue and the great luxury of the English aristocracy. The King, and the heads of the great families who so bitterly opposed him, agreed in their zeal for agriculture. The King raised a famous breed of sheep on his farm at Windsor, and delighted in his nickname of " Farmer George." The annual festivity given by the Duke of Bedford on his Woburn estate, when he displayed a magnificence incredibly lavish, was given to celebrate the shearing of his flocks.

The Government also showed its interest in the progress of agriculture. In 1793 it had founded an important institution, which enabled landowners to deliberate in common upon their economic interests. This was the Board of Agriculture, whose president and secretary were two eminent agriculturists—Sir John Sinclair and

Arthur Young Its membership included, in addition to the high officials of the State, all the leading English agriculturists without distinction of party. The Duke of Bedford sat side by side with Lord Lonsdale ; Thomas Coke of Holkham side by side with Pulteney. The Board was not a department of Government charged with the administration of laws. English public opinion had no liking for bureaucracy. It was a sort of corporation, subsidized by the State, whose legal character jurists found it difficult to define. It was empowered by the State to carry on with the funds at its disposal—funds derived from Government subsidies and public subscription—a semi-official propaganda on behalf of particular methods of cultivation and of stock breeding, and of a particular agrarian policy. It incurred the hostility of the Anglican clergy by its demand for the commutation of the tithe, of the lawyers by its demand for the simplification of the legal formalities to be observed in making enclosures,[1] and since 1813 of public opinion by its campaign begun in that year in favour of an increase in the Corn Duties. As a result the Board of Agriculture was in its decline, and was to be abolished in 1818.[2] Nevertheless, its twenty-five years of existence corresponded to a period of great prosperity for British agriculture. It brought together and coordinated the countless experiments that were being made by individual landowners.

It was the private initiative of these landowners which had made England, at the opening of the 19th century, the leading agricultural state in the world. They had increased the fertility of the soil by continuous rotation of crops and by manures, and the produce of cattle by the constant creation of new breeds, both of cattle and of sheep. They had formed and moulded the animals, obtaining every year from their sheep either more meat to satisfy the ever-increasing demand for food, or more wool to render the national manufacture independent

---

[1] The Board had obtained from Parliament in 1801 the passage of a statute " for consolidating in one Act certain provisions usually inserted in Acts of Enclosure, and for facilitating the mode of proving the several facts usually required on the passing of such Acts."—41 Geo. III (U.K.), cap. 109. This Act, however, failed to satisfy the Board, which vainly demanded its amendment. See, A Bill to amend the general Enclosure Act, February 27, 1811 ; A Bill to explain and amend the general Enclosure Act, May 1, 1812 ; A Bill (as amended by Committee) to repeal the Forty-First of George the Third, Chapter one hundred and nine, and to make provisions for facilitating the inclosure of waste and commonable lands, March 22, 1813. Cf. *Memoirs of Sir John Sinclair*, vol. ii. pp. 104 sqq.

[2] For the part taken in the creation of the Board by the agriculturists John Marshall, Sir John Sinclair and Arthur Young, for Marshall's attack—after his expulsion from the Board—upon the administration of Sinclair and Young, for the rivalry between Sinclair and Young, for Sinclair's intrigues against Pitt and Pitt's intrigues against Sinclair ; in short, for all that concerns the inner history of the Board, see *Memoirs of Sir John Sinclair*, vol. i. pp. 252 sqq., vol. ii. pp. 45 sqq. ; Marshall, *A Review of the Reports of the Board of Agriculture*, 1808 (Introduction) ; Arthur Young, *Autobiography*, pp. 219 sqq. The published " reports " dealing with the condition of agriculture in each of the English counties, though often charged with superficiality, constitute a valuable document for the historian of the first years of the 19th century.

of the import of Spanish wool.[1] The originators of all these improvements had been enthusiasts, in some respects even cranks, but men
possessed of a genius equal to that of the inventors of new manufacturing
processes. They were men such as Jethro Tull and Lord Townshend,
or such as Bakewell, who lived like a peasant without a single friend
save his shepherd, and received in his kitchen the statesmen and crowned
heads, to whom he did the honours of his estate. These innovators
were frequently ruined by rash experiments, nor would their efforts
have proved as successful as they did, had they not received the support
of the entire class to which they belonged. Societies were formed
by the landowners of a particular district for the joint search of markets,
encouragement of experiments, and popularization of discoveries ;
in contrast with the world of manufacture, the world of agriculture
was characterized by a strong sense of solidarity among producers.
The inventors of new processes, and the creators of new breeds, were
by no means scientific workers ; they learnt by practice without any
theoretical preparation. Nevertheless, the technical progress accomplished by them assisted the progress of scientific knowledge. Cross-
breeding, together with selection of the individuals most fitted to
produce fine varieties, tended more and more to become the subject-
matter of a special science. On all the great estates of England and
Scotland was created thus an atmosphere which would favour the birth
and success of Darwinism. Nevertheless, the members of the Board
viewed with anxiety the undue contempt for pure science and for
theory displayed by the British agriculturists. They sought to counteract this tendency and to convince them that knowledge of the laws of
chemistry and biology was not without practical use. It was at the
invitation of the Board that Erasmus Darwin wrote his *Phytologia*,
and that Davy gave in London, from 1803 to 1813, a series of courses
on vegetable chemistry.[2]

The attempts of the innovators were directed to another object
also : they were on the high road to transform all the implements of
farming. Take, for example, the preparation of the soil in order to
facilitate cultivation in a climate always rainy. The old method of
drainage—according to which the fields were cut by a series of small
parallel valleys, sometimes over three feet in depth—was abominable.
The better part of the soil was carried away by every shower and the
bottom of each little valley remained a muddy swamp. Elkington,
and after him Smith, introduced the modern system of drainage.[3] Or
again to take the matter of ploughing. The plough on wheels was
just coming into use, but had still many enemies, who denounced it

[1] For the active propaganda carried on in this matter by the *Society for Improving Wool*,
also a creation of Sir John Sinclair, see *Memoirs of Sir John Sinclair*, vol. i. pp. 217 sqq.
[2] *Memoirs of . . . Sir John Sinclair*, vol. ii. pp. 82 sqq.
[3] Prothero, *Pioneers . . . of English Farming*, p. 96.

as too costly, as unworkable where the ground was uneven or stony, and useless where it was even.[1]   Once more to take the question of sowing.   The use of the drill machine for sowing, not indeed corn, but beans, peas and turnips, had been already discovered.   This drill scattered the seed in the furrows, at first in one only and then, a few years before our date, in several furrows at the same time.   An English farmer who left his fields to themselves after the sowing would have been considered very negligent.   They required to be rolled to break up the clods, to be submitted to the horse hoe to eradicate the weeds which sprang up between the furrows.   Then would come the time of harvest ; and for this no machines had as yet been invented.   Experiments had, indeed, been made with harvesting machines, but so far in vain.   The *Farming Club* of Dalkeith in Scotland had offered a prize of £500 to the inventor of a really practicable apparatus.[2]   On the other hand, the threshing machine invented in 1758, and since greatly improved, had been installed by 1815 on all good farms.[3]   It had rendered threshing at once far easier, far quicker and far more economical.   Before the introduction of the threshing mill, as much, if not double, the amount of corn as was necessary for next year's sowing had been wasted.   Oxen were employed at first to turn the machine Later, in imitation of the method in use in cotton spinning, a water mill was employed.   It then became the rule to establish farms, like factories, on the banks of streams.   But already, for some years past, steam power had replaced water power in districts where coal was cheap.   The Duke of Bedford had ordered for the Woburn estate from Cartwright the engineer a steam engine to thresh and grind corn, which cost him £700.[4]

The effect of all these technical inventions was to increase the amount of capital sunk in each farm.[5]   Despite the profound differences still separating, as they always will separate, agriculture from manufacture, agriculture was taking more and more the appearance of a manufacture.   To realize this, we have but to consider Arthur Young's description of the offices of the Reevesby estate in Lincolnshire farmed by Sir Joseph Banks.[6]   They consisted of two rooms, divided from each other by a brick wall and a double door of iron, so that if a fire broke out in one it might not spread to the other.   In these,

[1] Sinclair, *Scotland*, vol. i. p. 217.

[2] *Ibid.*, vol. i. pp. 223, 231.   Cf. *Farmers' Magazine*, February 12, 1816 (vol. xvii. pp. 1 sqq.) ; *Corn Law Report*, 1814 (*Minutes of Evidence*, p. 25).

[3] Brown, *West Riding*, 1799, p. 57 ; Bailey, *Durham*, 1810, p. 80 ; Sinclair, *Scotland*, vol. i. p. 227.

[4] Arthur Young, *Autobiography*, p. 396.   Arthur Young disapproves of the experiment.

[5] *Corn Law Report*, 1814 (*Minutes of Evidence*, p. 30) : " Suppose you had had a farm of 300 acres to let twenty years ago, what would be the capital a man would have required to cultivate that land ?—About £2,000.   What do you think he would require now ?—He ought to have £4,000 to do it properly."

[6] A. Young, *Lincolnshire*, 1799, pp. 20-1.

all papers relating to men and stock—agents, tenants, labourers, drains, fences, arable land, and woods—were accumulated, classified, and catalogued in 156 drawers. You could not tell whether you were on a farm or in the heart of a large factory.

The progress which was being made in British agriculture had two centres. There was, in the first place, old England, the eastern counties Essex, Suffolk and Norfolk, to which should be added Hertfordshire and Leicestershire, among the Midland counties. In the 17th century, Hertfordshire had taken the first place, but this pre-eminence now belonged to Norfolk. Between 1730 and 1760, Lord Townshend had introduced into that county the improved methods of cultivation which he had observed in Hanover. Since 1790, Thomas Coke of Holkham had given a fresh impulse to Norfolk agriculture. The second centre was formed by the Lowlands of Scotland. The large farms of the region which extended from Edinburgh on the north to the border of Northumberland on the south, and especially the farms of East Lothian, were the best·managed farms in Great Britain—indeed in the entire world. It was there that new machines and new methods of breeding and cultivation had been first adopted, often indeed invented.[1]

From these two centres a fostering influence had been diffused on all sides. To the north of the Scottish centre the Highlands had been improved systematically by Lord Caithness, the Lord-Lieutenant ; Mr. Trail, the Sheriff, and Sir John Sinclair, the President of the Board of Agriculture.[2] To the south the situation of Northumberland was most favourable to the imitation of any novelty introduced into the south-eastern counties of Scotland. Even the vast wilderness which in the 18th century still divided the south from the north of England was now being brought under cultivation. In former days cattle sent from Scotland to the London market had been obliged to pass through extensive tracts of barren fen in Yorkshire, Lincolnshire and Cambridgeshire. A line of posts driven into the peat and, in the middle of Lincolnshire, a beacon lit every night, saved them from the danger of straying into the bog. In the 17th century the first attempt had been made to enclose and drain the fens, but the undertaking had been stopped by the Civil War. After the Restoration the attempt had been renewed, but the inhabitants of the district, who saw themselves deprived of their rights of pasture and believed themselves threatened with expropriation, had risen in revolt. Now at last the work of reclamation was being accomplished. There was no longer a gulf fixed between the two districts in which the new agricultural methods had been first invented.

[1] For the causes which made these two districts the centres of the new agriculture, see an interesting theory in G. Slater's *English Peasantry*, pp. 78 sqq. It had long been customary in both districts to cultivate the land continuously without an interval of fallow. It was necessarily, therefore, the farmers' chief care to find means to avoid the exhaustion of the soil.

[2] *Memoirs of . . . Sir John Sinclair*, vol. i. pp. 334 sqq.

Everywhere forests were being cut down. Use was made of every kind of soil. On the mountains of the north and middle of Scotland, throughout the greater part of Cumberland, and Westmorland and in North Wales, where the lack of coal prevented manufactures, and where there was neither sufficient sun nor sufficient soil for the cultivation of corn, immense flocks of sheep were raised. There also, during the first two or three years of their existence, were grazed the cattle who would be taken later to fatten on the richer pastures of the south. In the plains large farms were given up at the same time to corn growing and to cattle raising. The heavy land along the banks of streams was transformed into pasture. If there were a town in the neighbourhood this pasture land would serve on small farms, not to fatten cattle, but to feed the cows from which were derived milk, butter and cheese. At this epoch every year witnessed fresh conquests by the plough on hillsides, and on the top of tablelands and cliffs. The profits of agriculture had increased enormously. In 1814 all witnesses agreed in estimating that rent had risen 100 per cent., perhaps even 150 per cent. during the last twenty or twenty-five years.[1] The extent of land under cultivation had increased in an equally high ratio. 1883 Enclosure Acts passed in the course of the twenty years following the foundation of the Board of Agriculture had brought into cultivation 2,260,000 acres. But even this was very little in comparison to the 22,000,000 acres uncultivated, though capable of cultivation, which appeared in the statistics drawn up by the Board for 1795. "We have begun," exclaimed Lord Sinclair in 1803, "another campaign against the foreign enemies of the country. . . . Why should we not attempt a campaign also against our great domestic foe, I mean the hitherto unconquered sterility of so large a proportion of the surface of the kingdom ? . . . let us not be satisfied with the liberation of Egypt, or the subjugation of Malta, but let us subdue Finchley Common ; let us conquer Hounslow Heath ; let us compel Epping Forest to submit to the yoke of improvement."[2] This invincible enthusiasm which animated both the members of the Board of Agriculture and the British landowners, who as a body followed their guidance, formed the true justification of modern capitalism.

The Farmers.

To erect buildings, to make roads, to drain the fields, to put up fences : all this was the business of the landlord. It was the farmer's

---

[1] 100 per cent. (*Corn Law Report*, 1814, *Minutes of Evidence*, pp. 4, 10, 16) ; over 100 per cent. (*ibid.*, pp. 17 sqq.) ; 150 per cent. in Surrey, in twenty-one years, on Mr. Birkbeck's farm (*ibid.*, pp. 95–6). Arthur Young, for a farm of 300 acres, chosen as typical, gives the three following figures : 1790, £88 6s. 3¼d. ; 1803, £121 2s. 7¼d. ; 1813, £160 12s. 7¼d. (*ibid.*, p. 81). Sir John Sinclair (*Scotland*, 1814, vol. i. p. 197) estimated that the total rental of Scotland twenty years earlier did not exceed £2,000,000, had attained £5,000,000 at the moment of writing, and was increasing at a yearly rate of about £100,000 or £200,000.

[2] *Memoirs of . . . Sir John Sinclair*, vol. ii. p. 111.

business to supervise the ploughing and manuring of the land, to select the seeds, and to decide what rotation of crops he should best adopt. This was a difficult task which required intelligence, experience and technical knowledge. If we would form an accurate idea of the agricultural system which obtained in Great Britain we must know first the average size of the farms cultivated by each farmer. Such an average is certainly difficult to strike, for it is hard to find a common measure for the tiny farms of south-western England and the enormous sheep farms of Northumberland. It is, nevertheless, certain that the English farm was universally considered large by comparison with those of the Continent, and that it tended constantly to become larger with the improvement of agricultural machinery. Moreover, the Reports of the Board of Agriculture enable us to determine the size and the profits of arable farms, which, in the more fertile and better-culti-vated districts, are defined by the Board as medium-sized or large. They generally regarded as " medium-sized " a farm of 300 acres ; [1] as " large," a farm exceeding 500 acres. [2] The average rental of an acre in the more fertile districts of England was from £1 to £2, in similar districts of Scotland it reached or exceeded £4. [3] This meant on a farm of 300 acres a rental of £450, or on a farm of 500 acres a rental of £750. The farmer's profits were exactly equal to the rent. [4] They represented, therefore, if we capitalize them at 10 per cent. (the percentage universally reckoned by contemporary witnesses) [5] a capital of £4,500 on the medium-sized farms of 300 acres, [6] of £7,500 on the farms whose 500 acres entitled them to the appellation of large. This was the average wealth of the farmers truly representative of their class, the middle class of rural England.

It is, of course, impossible to sketch this class in a few general out-lines, without of necessity omitting many subtler shades of the portrait. There were certain remote country districts of England—the Peak of Derbyshire, Shropshire and Cornwall—where the old traditions sur-vived intact. In the farmhouse were to be found a floor paved with flags, a bare table, a tin dinner service, and straw mattresses instead of beds—in the fields antiquated wooden yokes, straw collars of an equally venerable antiquity, and ploughs of the type in use 500 years ago. [7] Even in the neighbourhood of London, in Surrey, the Board

[1] Sinclair, *Scotland*, vol. iii. p. 273 ; Young, *Essex*, vol. i. p. 58.

[2] Young, *Lincolnshire*, p. 37 ; *Hertfordshire*, p. 23.

[3] *Corn Law Report*, 1814, *Minutes of Evidence*, pp. 56, 106–7. For Scotland, see *Corn Law Report*, 1814, *Minutes of Evidence*, pp. 103, 108.

[4] *Ibid.*, pp. 4, 32, 41 ; Tuke, *North Riding*, 1800, p. 76. In Scotland the farmer's profits were equal to half the rent (Sinclair, *Scotland*, vol. i. p. 113) ; but this was due to the fact that the Scottish farmer paid neither tithe nor poor rate.

[5] Sinclair, *Scotland*, vol. iii. p. 207 ; Young, *Suffolk*, 1797, p. 25. Cf. *Corn Law Report*, 1814, pp. 74 (Essex), 103 (East and Mid Lothian), 108 (Near Dunbar).

[6] *Corn Law Report*, *Minutes of Evidence*, p. 16.

[7] Howitt, *Rural Life of England*, 1840, p. 100.

of Agriculture denounced the farmers, all too numerous for its liking, who still wore the round frock of their ancestors, determined foes alike of agricultural progress and ·the growth of refinement, men with so little business capacity that they preferred to sell their corn cheap to old customers than to accept better offers from persons with whom they were unaccustomed to deal.[1] But, after all, these were but survivals of the past. The new generation were of quite another style.

Of all the farmers of Europe the English were most foreign to the spirit of toilsome, severe and sometimes sordid routine. They were intelligent capitalists—on the alert for any new method of making money, for every opportunity of acquiring knowledge. In Lincolnshire and Durham it was the regular custom for a good farmer to make from time to time a tour on horseback through England in order to keep in touch with the progress which was being made in other counties.[2] With the landlord's connivance the tenants became professional speculators as well as capitalists. The disappearance of the small farms, which made way for agricultural enterprises on a large scale, rendered it easier for certain large farmers to unite to raise the price of corn. The increased wealth of these large farmers, which left greater cash reserves at their disposal, freed them more and more from the necessity for immediate sale of their crops, and thus enabled them to wait for the most favourable moment to dispose of the corn which had accumulated in their barns. It was useless for an old-fashioned demagogue like Cobbett to denounce the speculators of the London Stock Exchange, the Mark Lane Quakers, worthy confederates of the Change Alley Jews. All the legislation against the engrossing of corn, against forestalling and regrating, had been rendered worthless during the last forty years by the simple fact that the farmers were no longer the victims but the accomplices of any engrossing that took place.[3] In this way

[1] James, Surrey, 1794, p. 88.

[2] A. Young, Lincolnshire, 1799, p. 40 ; Bailey, Durham, pp. 67–8.

[3] An Act of 1772 (12 Geo. III, cap. 71) had repealed the old legislation against Badgers, Engrossers, Forestallers and Regraters in view, as the preamble declared, of the fact " that the restraints laid by several statutes upon dealing in corn, meal, flour, cattle, and sundry other sorts of victuals, by preventing a free trade in the same commodities, have a tendency to discourage the growth and to enhance the price of the same." Nevertheless, prosecutions were still possible, and monopolists and speculators were once more the object of sharp attacks during the years of dearth about 1800. (See the facts cited in Smart, Economic Annals, pp. 5–6.) Since then, however, public opinion on the subject had undergone a rapid change. See Whitbread's typical speech (H. of C., February 22, 1815) : " When the price of bread was high, the popular feelings blinded the judgment ; and he could remember when it was the fashion of the times, countenanced too by the then Lord Chief Justice of England, to attribute it all to the acts and practices of forestallers, regraters and middlemen. It was now, however, a time when the people might be told that the forestallers, the regraters and middlemen were doing more good in their private dealings than could be done by all the plans for public granaries and warehouses. The middleman was always the friend of the people. He collected corn during a time of cheapness, to sell it out during a time of dearness ; and if in his speculations he sometimes went beyond the mark, he required no other punishment than what his avarice received from being disappointed in its calculations (Parl. Deb., vol. xxix, p. 995). Cf. H. of C., May 5, 1814, George Rose's speech (Parl. Deb., vol. xxvii. p. 698).

the interests of the agriculturists came to coincide with the conclusions which were being reached by the new school of political economists. Burke was the mouthpiece of the great landowners and of the farmers when, in his *Thoughts on Scarcity*, he plainly pronounced in accordance with the doctrines of Adam Smith against any restriction upon free trade in corn.[1] We should also remember that of the classes which made up English economic society the agricultural class had during the last fifty years made the least appeal for State assistance.

In 1773 [2] an Act had been passed to render the export of corn more difficult and its import easier. Such was the liberalism displayed at that time in commercial matters by the agriculturists who were predominant in Parliament. Adam Smith [3] delighted to hold them up as a model to the manufacturers, who were so eager for protective measures. It is indisputable that the landed proprietors had since become more protectionist. To satisfy their demands Pitt had raised from 48s. to 54s. in 1791,[4] and from 54s. to 66s. in 1804,[5] the price above which imported corn was free of duty, while the price below which its export was allowed was raised at the same time from 44s. to 46s. and then to 48s. Circumstances, however, made this protective legislation useless. The Act of 1804 never came into actual operation.[6] During the following decade the average price of wheat was upwards of 100s. In 1812 it had been almost double the price at which import began to be free. It was only in 1815, when prices had fallen, that the farmers succeeded in obtaining a really efficacious protective tariff. The price required for free import was raised from 66s. to 80s., though in 1814 the farmers had asked for 84s., 95s., and even 105s. Throughout the debates, however, which preceded the passage of the Corn Bill they did not fail to insist on the fact that they were merely asking to be placed on an equal footing with the manufacturers as regards the customs tariff.[7] Unlike the latter, they had accepted during the entire war a system of practical free trade.

For all their enterprise the big farmers were, nevertheless, fully aware that they could never make as large fortunes as were made by the manufacturers of the towns. Even during this period of exceptional

---

[1] *Thoughts and Details on Scarcity* (*Works*, vol. vii. pp. 397 sqq.).

[2] 13 Geo. III, cap. 43.

[3] Adam Smith, *Wealth of Nations*, Book IV, chap. ii. (ed. Thorold Rogers, vol. ii. pp. 34–5). Cf. C. Bosanquet, *Thoughts on the Value . . . of Commmerce in General*, 1808, pp. 2–3: " Though Dr. Adam Smith may not, generally, be considered as hostile to commerce . . . yet will the young student not rise from the perusal of his work without strong prejudices against merchants and mercantile pursuits. The class is abused, degraded and vilified."

[4] 31 Geo. III, cap. 30. The price given is that of the quarter.

[5] 44 Geo. III, cap. 109.

[6] For all the Acts passed on this subject previous to 1814, see especially George Rose's important speech, H. of C., May 5, 1814, with Western's reply, H. of C., May 16, 1814 (*Parl. Deb.*, vol. xxvii, pp. 666 sqq., 898 sqq.).

[7] H. of C., June 15, 1813, Sir Henry Parnell's speech, vol. xxvi. pp. 651–2; May 16, 1814, Huskisson's speech (*Parl. Deb.*, vol. xxvii. p. 920).

agricultural prosperity it was the summit of their pecuniary ambitions to treble or quadruple their capital and to place each of their children in as good a position as that from which they had themselves started.[1] They might, however, indulge other ambitions. Without ceasing to farm, a farmer might assimilate by insensible degrees his social position to that of a landowner. An aristocrat did not consider it below his dignity to cultivate his lands personally. Nor did his son regard it as a humiliation to be sent as a boarder at £100 a year to one of the large Northumberland farmers in order to learn there the new methods.[2] Suppose a gentleman who managed an estate of 1,000 to 2,000 acres, and near him a farmer cultivating an estate of double the size, of 2,000 or 4,000 acres. The former, when once the rates and taxes on the land had been paid, was free to spend the remainer of his income as he pleased. The latter had to pay in addition half of that remainder to the owner of the farm which he cultivated. If his labour was greater, his farm and capital were larger and his implements more perfect. In the end the landowner and farmer were equally rich. Both shared the same toils, the same cares, the same pleasures, the same ways of life and of thought. We hear of a large number of farmers in Essex who, having taken over several farms, did not attempt to unite these into a single centralized farm, but installed an overseer on each and contented themselves with the work of supervising their whole estate.[3] Surely there was no great difference between the economic position of the landlord in the strict sense and these sub-landlords who no more farmed their land directly than did he. When the size of the farm exceeded 400 or 500 acres the farmer required an area of 200 square feet on which to build his house and its outbuildings. He must have two reception rooms, two kitchens, an office and at least four bedrooms.[4] Less than this had been sufficient a century earlier for the dwelling of a country gentleman. The parlour must contain a sofa, bookshelves, and engravings on the walls.[5] There he would give dinners when in one afternoon £10 or £12 would be spent on entertaining his fellow farmers at table[6] The English farmer was a gentleman of secondary rank. His wife and daughters would have blushed to

---

[1] Boys, *Kent*, 1796, p. 32 : " The smaller farmers are in general a very industrious and sober set of men, fare hard, and live with great frugality. The great occupiers, who have property in stock from 1 to 2 or £3,000, live, as they ought, more at their ease ; but as to making of fortunes by farming, there is no such thing that ever came to my knowledge." Tuke, *North Riding*, 1800, p. 177 : " Should a farmer make . . . a fortune it is in general in consequence of his uniting some other profession with his farm. He is a land surveyor, a steward, a corn factor, or has some other pursuit ; instances of fortunes acquired by such an union may frequently be found ; without it the industrious, the orderly, the persevering farmer, the man peculiarly the pride and boast of England, is not often enabled to quit the path on which he first entered."

[2] Bailey and Culley, *Northumberland*, pp. 29–30.

[3] Vancouver, *Essex*, 1795, p. 167.   [4] Sinclair, *Scotland*, vol. i. p. 138.

[5] Cobbett, *Rural Rides*, October 20, 1825.

[6] *Thoughts on Enclosure*, by a Country Farmer, 1785, p. 21.

be seen in the dairy, the poultry house or the kitchen. They bought their clothes in the neighbouring town, and aped the dresses of the squire's wife and daughters. If a farmer gave his son an education that was just passable and that son obtained a commission in the militia, ceased to farm in person and lived in the country on the income of the capital amassed by his father, he would have enough wealth, the necessary country tastes and sufficient culture to take his position in local society.[1]

Doubtless the harmony of interests between landowners and farmers was far from being complete. Whenever their mutual contracts expired, their demands came at once into conflict. While the lease continued, the rent had remained at the sum originally fixed, whereas the farmer's profits had risen with the rise in the price of foodstuffs derived from agriculture. Now, however, the landowner attempted, in drawing up the new lease, to obtain a higher rent, and thus to reduce the farmer's profits to their former amount. Ricardo was shortly to write an enormous volume in order to combine against the landlords all the rest of the nation—heads of industries, workmen and farmers alike. According to him there existed an iron law in virtue of which rent was always rising while wages remained stationary, and the profits of the manufacturer and farmer, kept at the same level by the competition of capital, were constantly declining. The farmers, however, turned a deaf ear to the appeal of the economists. So long as their rent remained fixed, it was as much to their interest as to that of the proprietors that the market price of meat and corn should rise. And when the rise was artificial and due to the depreciation of the coinage they still profited. Those who suffered were the fundholders and officials—all, in fact, who were in receipt of a fixed income in cash. Creators of their own wealth, greedy of gain, and men who had always lived on and by the soil, the farmers felt themselves perfectly capable of holding their own against the landlords or their agents when a lease had to be renewed. The agents, indeed, were often solicitors more skilled in matters of legal procedure than in questions of farming. We have also seen how the class of landowners had contributed by many experiments to the progress of English agriculture. The relationship between the two classes was still up to a certain point one of collaboration, and the rent paid was not regarded as merely unearned increment. Part of the rent represented a salary earned by the work of supervision

[1] See the beginning of Miss Burney's *Cecilia* : " Her ancestors " (Cecilia's) " had been rich farmers in the county of Suffolk, though her father, in whom a spirit of elegance had supplanted the rapacity of wealth, had spent his time as a private country gentleman. . . ." He left Cecilia a fortune of £10,000, and when she fell in love with young Delvile, who belonged to a very old county family, the authoress informs us that " his situation in life was just what she wished, more elevated than her own, yet not so exalted as to humble her with a sense of inferiority." Boys, *Kent*, 1796, p. 32 : " Those of the higher class, the large occupiers and principal yeomanry, are a very respectable class of society, and have a great weight in the political scale of the country."

and direction. Part represented the profits of the extensive capital laid out on land and buildings.

There is no doubt that the general conditions regulating leases according to the law of England were extraordinarily onerous for the farmer. The law of distress or distraint empowered the landlord whose tenant failed to pay his rent to take the matter into his own hands, to seize through a bailiff and to sell the farmer's cattle or indeed all his movable effects. By the law of fixtures the farmer was left only a very limited and very dubious right to indemnification when the lease expired for any improvements which he had made in the farm. We must, however, inquire how rigorously this system of agrarian legislation was actually carried out. The English landlord claimed very commonly, if not always, to manage his estate in a spirit of liberality and consideration, not as a business man, but as a kind master. Under the old military feudalism the lord had required of the cultivators not so much to make him wealthy as to make him powerful by furnishing him with a large number of men. Even so, in modern times, there had been organized throughout the country districts of England a species of peaceful feudalism, in which the great aim of the landowners was to form an army of faithful voters, a band of political retainers. But to effect this he was obliged to make himself popular. The greatest landowners were also those who granted their tenants the most generous conditions and made every effort to deal with them in a friendly spirit.[1] Agrarian reformers were, as a general rule, in favour of extending the system of long leases as being the most favourable to good cultivation by the farmer, and as being their surest protection against exactions on the part of the landlord. But the opposite system of leases renewed annually, also found its advocates on the Board of Agriculture. They called attention to the fact that the districts in which this system prevailed—Bedfordshire, Cambridgeshire, and the North Riding of Yorkshire[2]—were those in which farms remained perhaps the longest in the same hands, passing generally from father to son and often changing ownership without a change of occupancy.[3] This was due to the fact that annual contracts establish the closest and most human relations between the two parties concerned—a matter of no slight importance in a country possessing free institutions where the landowner could not govern unless supported by the public opinion of the county.

There were also certain other laws and institutions which seemed calculated to menace the peace of the country districts and to foster a revolutionary spirit among the class of farmers. Miss Burney, the novelist, noted in her *Diary* for November 1789, a conversation with

[1] *Corn Laws Report*, 1814, p. 25.   [2] *Ibid.*, 1814, p. 25.
[3] Batchelor, *Bedfordshire*, p. 43 ; Vancouver, *Cambridgeshire*, p. 181 ; Tuke, *North Riding*, 1800, p. 329.

Lord Mountmorres in which the latter predicted that revolutionary feeling would soon cross the Channel. " In what," asked Miss Burney, " could be its pretence ?—The game laws, he answered, and the tithes." [1] By the game laws the crops were exposed throughout the whole year to the depredations of hares and pheasants, and during the hunting season to the damage inflicted by hunters and hounds. These laws were, moreover, being constantly made more stringent. The cost of a licence became ever dearer.[2] The crime of poaching was defined with increasing rigour ; and the penalties enacted against it were made heavier. An Act of 1816 actually allowed even the mildest cases to be punished with seven years' transportation.[3] Moreover, sporting rights were confined by law to landowners the annual value of whose lands exceeded £100, to tenants whose leases were for life and who paid a rent of at least £150 a year. The magistrates who administered the law, namely the justices of the peace, were the very landowners whose pleasures it was designed to protect. As for the tithe, it was levied not on the clear profits but on the total produce. Hence the greater the cost of cultivation the heavier was the burden of the tithe on the cultivator who had to pay it to the Anglican clergy.[4] Nevertheless, the conflict of interests aroused by the game laws and the tithe was not so acute as the foregoing observations might lead us to believe.

The game laws did not set class against class, all the landowners against all the farmers. They forbade sporting rights to some land-owners and gave them to some tenants. The severity of the penalties enacted was no anomaly in English criminal law. All the penalties prescribed by it were equally extravagant, and in default of an efficient police equally ill-applied. Moreover, whenever a poaching case assumed any importance it had to be tried at Quarter Sessions, where the magis-trates were assisted by a jury. It would often happen that this jury, which was composed of poorer folk, succeeded by skilfully organized

[1] Diary of Miss Burney, November 18, 1789 (ed. 1854, vol. v. p. 62).

[2] See for a list of increases in the cost of licences, Dowell, History of Taxation, vol. iii. p. 240 sqq.

[3] The fundamental statute was 22 and 23 Car. II, cap. 25. This had been rendered more stringent during the war by 39 and 40 Geo. III, cap. 50 (1800), and its severity was soon to be further increased by 56 Geo. III, cap. 130 (1816), amended the following year (57 Geo. III, cap. 50). The mere fact of being caught during the night with implements implying the intention to poach was treated as actual poaching, and the duration of this legal night was successively extended in 1800, 1816 and 1817. The Act of 1800 prescribed a maximum penalty of one month's hard labour in a house of correction, the Act of 1816 a maximum penalty of seven years' transportation. Throughout this period only one statute was passed (36 Geo. III, cap. 39, 54), showing an intention on the part of the legislature to soften the rigour of the game laws in the interest of the cultivator. This Act postponed the commence-ment of partridge shooting fifteen days. It was passed before a general election and repealed after it (39 Geo. III, cap. 34). See the debates, H. of C., April 16 and 18, 1799 (Parliamentary Register, vol. lxx. pp. 447, 453).

[4] On the tithe question in 1815, see Edinburgh Review, August 1820, No. 67, Art. 3, Plan for a Commutation of Tithes (vol. xxxiv. pp. 61 sqq.).

obstruction in preventing the execution of the law.[1] It was the same with the tithe. The tithe caused an immediate conflict of interests between the cultivators and the local representative of the Established Church. But however close the ties attaching the landowners to the Anglican Church, they had no love for an institution which discouraged farmers from improving their farms. It would not, indeed, be altogether untrue to assert that the landowners ultimately bore the burden of the tithe. Rent in Scotland was almost double what it was in England. Nevertheless, the Scottish farmers were no poorer than the English. That the English landlord received less than the Scottish landlord was due in part to the fact that the English farmer, unlike the Scottish, paid the tithe in kind. Accordingly the landowners composing the Board of Agriculture supported their tenants' demand for the reform of the tithe.

We cannot, in short, deny the existence of serious divergences of interest alike in England and Scotland between the landowners and the farmers. Inhabitants of other countries, men of a more levelling humour and brought up in different intellectual and religious traditions, would have refused perhaps to tolerate oppressive and humiliating institutions, even as a practical compromise. It is, however, indubitable that the state of English society rendered such a compromise possible and that the English farmers accepted it. They turned a deaf ear to the entreaties of the economists and Radicals. In a few years Cobbett would bear angry witness to the persistence of this sense of solidarity between the tenants and those whom, in his opinion, they ought to regard as their exploiters. Ruined by the restoration of peace and the fall in the price of corn, they saw no other remedy for their ills than a new war, and read nothing beyond the local papers, the inspired organs of their landlords. "The farmers," he wrote, "are cowed down : the poorer they get, the more cowardly they are. . . . They hang on, like sailors to the masts or hull of a wreck."[2]

Farmers and landlords formed a solid body of opinion. The two classes united were the governing class of the country districts. They had forwarded with extreme activity the cause of agricultural progress. At what cost had this been effected ? The system of large farms was accused of having been a direct cause of the formation of an agricultural proletariat, a wretched and discontented class entirely without community of interests or feeling with the block of rural capitalists.[3] The system

---

[1] *Edinburgh Review*, March 1829, No. 97, Art. 3, *The Game Laws* (vol. xlix. pp. 70, 73-4). Landowners even complained that if the case came to assizes the judges favoured the poachers as against themselves (see Lord Milton's letter to Lord Kenyon, July 5, 1791, *Life of Lord Kenyon*, p. 267).

[2] *Rural Rides*, October 30, 1821, October 11, 1822, May 18, 1830.

[3] Tooke, *History of Prices*, vol. i. p. 14 n. : " By agricultural interests, I mean exclusively farmers and landlords and owners of tithes, who are alone benefited by an advance of price resulting from scarcity." Landlords and farmers had come to assume such importance as

was also charged with rural depopulation and the influx into the towns of the hands needed by manufacturers. It had thus, it was alleged, contributed indirectly to the formation of a revolutionary proletariate of the great industries. Both these grievances must now be examined in turn.

The Agricultural Proletariate.

According to the old system the labourers on the fields were farm servants boarded and lodged by the farmers who employed them. Once yearly, usually at Michaelmas, the Statute Fair was held at some town in the district. Thither the farmers flocked from all sides to hire the necessary servants for the following year. These occasions were the saturnalia of the country folk. For eight days the young men and girls found themselves free from the contract which had bound them to a master during the past year. The farmers were also away at the fair, and their wives had bolted themselves in the empty farmhouses, terrified by the crowds of tramps and drunkards passing on the roads. When the actual fair day came the labourers took their station in the market-place. The shepherd wore a tuft of wool in his hat, the milkmaid a tuft of cow's hair, the carter a piece of whip-cord, and the stable-man a bit of sponge. By the evening all the agreements had been concluded. Every youth could now spend his last day of freedom amusing himself with his girl. Then for a year to come, perhaps for a longer period, if he had so arranged with his master, he would share the life of the latter, dining at the lower end of the great oak table where the farmer presided in person, said the grace, carved the bacon, poured out the beer, and distributed the potatoes. Here was indeed a patriarchal régime [1] which for this very reason tended to disappear with the introduction into farming of the methods of modern capitalism.

It was always necessary to keep a certain number of servants who lodged at the farm to look after the sheep, the cattle and the horses. But as the farms increased in size, the farmers adopted more and more the ways of middle-class mercantile life, and strove to emphasize more clearly the distance dividing them from their hired servants. They ceased to dine at the same table with them. They made the number of labourers living at the farm as few as possible.[2] They had now

apparently to constitute by themselves the entire agricultural world. The existence of the poor was forgotten. See the following characteristic anecdote related by Butler, *Reminiscences*, p. 69 : " Mr. Pitt, being on a visit in Essex, descanted with great satisfaction on the prosperous state of the poor. His host let the discourse drop, but contrived that, on the following day, Mr. Pitt should walk in the adjoining town of Halsted. It presented a state of the utmost poverty and wretchedness. He surveyed it for some time in wonder and silence ; and then declared that he had no conception that England presented, in any part of it, such a scene. He made a liberal donation to its distressed inhabitants, and soon afterwards brought into Parliament a Bill for the relief of the poor."

[1] Howitt, *Rural Life of England*, 1840, p. 493.

[2] Mavor, *Berkshire*, 1813, p. 416 ; Young, *Norfolk*, 1804, p. 484 ; Batchelor, *Bedfordshire*, 1808, p. 580.

every possible motive for paying their servants no longer by the year, but either by the job or by a very short period of time, by the month, the week or even the day.[1] The disappearance of the small farms involved the disappearance of skilled labourers, who were, moreover, rendered less valuable by the improvement of agricultural machinery. The Poor Law system gave the right to relief to every pauper who had lived at least a year in the parish. It was, therefore, to the interest of the farmers who had to pay the cost of this relief to prevent the labourers passing twelve months in the same place.[2] Moreover, farm servants were exacting about their food. They demanded in the morning cold meat, cheese, bread and beer ; in the middle of the day roast or boiled meat and pudding, and in the evening meat again.[3] In one of his short rural poems Crabbe depicts a farmer's daughter who had been brought up in the town, terrified and disgusted by their swinish gluttony. It was both simpler and cheaper to pay the labourer who worked daily on the fields a wage on which he must get his own living as best he might. " Why," asked Cobbett, " do not farmers now *feed* and *lodge* their work-people, as they did formerly ? Because they cannot keep them *upon so little* as they give them in wages. This is the real cause of the change." [4]

Agricultural labourers were not equally in demand throughout the whole year. There were certain important seasons—the hay and wheat harvests—when the farmer found himself in sudden and immediate need of an abundant supply of labour for a few weeks or perhaps only for a few days. To meet these intermittent demands for hands regular migrations of labour had come into existence throughout the United Kingdom. Bedfordshire sent haymakers to the neighbourhood of London, and in turn sought its harvesters from Northamptonshire and Buckinghamshire.[5] Every year seven or eight thousand harvesters from Dorsetshire and Somersetshire landed in the Isle of Wight ; as the Isle of Wight was close to the great naval harbour of Portsmouth, the landowners and farmers took all necessary precautions

[1] For piece work see Tuke, *North Riding*, 1800, p. 285. For a comparison between piece and time work in agriculture, see Sinclair, *Scotland*, vol. iii. pp. 247–8 n. For work by the day, see Bailey, *Durham*, 1810, p. 262. For the harvest, labourers were hired every morning, by a kind of auction in every village, one farmer bidding against another, and very often (either from necessity or pique) to very extravagant lengths. In Devonshire and Cornwall the farmers often availed themselves of the parish apprentices (Worgan, *Cornwall*, 1815 p. 159 ; Vancouver, *Devonshire*, 1813, pp. 359–361). For the parish apprentices, see below p. 264.

[2] Eden, *State of the Poor*, vol. i. p. 347. He quotes Dr. Burn, *History of the Poor Laws*, 1764. Cf. Stevenson, *Dorset*, 1812, p. 454 : " It is said to be prevalent to hire servants for only eleven months, for the purpose of avoiding additional encumbrances on the parishes. See also *Poor Laws Report*, 1817, *Minutes of Evidence*, pp. 69, 88–9.

[3] See Donaldson, *Northamptonshire*, 1794, p. 45. Cf. Parkinson, *Huntingdonshire*, 1813, p. 285 ; Middleton, *Middlesex*, 1798, pp. 388, 285 ; Driver, *Hampshire*, 1794, p. 27 ; Vancouver, *Hampshire*, 1813, p. 383. Servants were worse fed in the north than in the south.

[4] *Rural Rides*, October 20, 1825.

[5] Batchelor, *Bedfordshire*, 1808, p. 598.

in war-time to secure their harvesters from the press gang.[1] The workmen of the towns knew that in case of unemployment they could find work on farms in the neighbourhood of the great manufacturing centres. Hence the price of labour rose or fell in the country as industry prospered or languished in the towns.[2] The poorer and more backward regions of the kingdom sent workmen every year to seek good wages in the richer and better-cultivated districts. The Highlands of western Scotland furnished labourers to the farms of the east and south. The poverty-stricken inhabitants of the Welsh mountains, and especially of Cardiganshire, flocked down in bands into the West of England, where they were known as the *Companies of Ancient Britons*.[3] A horse without bridle or saddle accompanied each band. He was ridden by each in turn, and the fatigue of the journey was thus lessoned for all. One of the band knew sufficient English to act as guide and interpreter. Their ignorance was exploited. A foreman usually treated with the farmer and then engaged the necessary hands at a lower rate. These Welshmen were temperate, industrious and naturally grateful, easily irritated but easily satisfied. For some years past they had come in smaller numbers. The Irish, on the other hand, had been pouring into England. They were unpopular both because they lowered wages and also because they were noisy and quarrelsome. Brawls, often bloody, were constantly breaking out between them and the natives.

The large farmer, however, could not cultivate his farm with no other assistance than this floating mass of labourers. He needed a certain number of settled labourers who would always be at his disposal. These he found in the neighbouring village or borough. Unfortunately the more industrious and intelligent men yielded to the attractions of the large factories and of the large towns. Those who remained behind were the more indolent and the more careless. The result was that the authors of the large farm system, after they had helped on the disappearance of the petty landowners, of the small tenants and of the servants living in the farmhouse, now began to ask themselves whether their interest did not force them to take action against certain natural consequences of the new method of farming. In the North of England and the South of Scotland a contract of service prevailed in virtue of which the agricultural labourer, the *hind* as he was called, not only received part of his wages in cash but was in addition lodged in a cottage of his own, given a piece of land, and supplied with a certain amount of fuel and oats. In return for these advantages the hind entered into an obligation to work for his master the whole

---

[1] Warner, *Isle of Wight*, 1794, p. 65.
[2] Wedge, *Warwickshire*, 1794, p. 295.
[3] J. Clark, *Herefordshire*, 1794, p. 29 ; J. Duncomb, *Herefordshire*, 1805, p. 64.

year round.[1] This bondage system was perhaps simply an attenuated form of the ancient serfdom. The cottage system, however, which resembled it in several respects and which was becoming general in England, was a new invention, begotten by the necessities of modern capitalism.

The philanthropists, led by Lord Winchelsea, and supported by the Board of Agriculture, advocated the plan of letting to the labourer at a low rent a cottage and a little ground close to the farm on which he worked.[2] Arthur Young, on his journey through Lincolnshire, remarked with admiration on the comfortable dwellings and pretty gardens which Sir John Sheffield and Lord Carrington had established on their estates for the accommodation of the agricultural labourers. " Population increases so," wrote Young, " that pigs and children fill every quarter."[3] The landowners realized the danger to which their hayricks and cornstacks, their farm buildings and their houses, would be exposed in a time of dearth, from a poverty-stricken and barbarous proletariate. They knew how much it cost to feed the proletariate at the public expense in order to prevent such hunger riots. The cost of erecting these small labourers' cottages was considered by many competent witnesses more than repaid to the landlord by the decrease effected in the charges of poor relief. The amount of the poor rate, they maintained, varied enormously—from 4 per cent. to 36 per cent. of the total sum chargeable upon the parish—according as it contained a larger or a smaller number of these cottages built by philanthropic enterprise.[4]

This poor rate was levied not only on the owners of land but also on all those who occupied it on any sort of title. It was, therefore, as much to the farmer's interest as to the landlord's to introduce this cottage system. The farmers, therefore, followed the example of the landowners and began to let cottages to their labourers. Sometimes they defrayed the cost of erection themselves. In other instances the landlord built the cottages and alloted the adjoining ground. Then the farmers obtained from the agent a general lease of the cottages and took upon themselves the task of subletting them one by one, and of

[1] Bailey and Culley, *Northumberland*, 1794, p. 53 ; Pringle, *Westmorland*, p. 29 ; Howitt, *Rural Life of England*, p. 119.

[2] See *Reports of Society for Bettering the Condition of the People*, vol. i. p. 116 (1797) ; extract from an account of three cottagers keeping cows, and renting land in Rutlandshire, by the Bishop of Durham ; also *ibid.*, p. 129, extract from an account of the advantages of cottagers renting land, by the Earl of Winchelsea. Cf. G. Slater, *English Peasantry*, pp. 132 sqq. The same author mentions (pp. 127–8) thirteen statutes passed between 1757 and 1812, all except one Acts of Enclosure, designed to protect the cottagers' rights. In 1775 a statute of Elizabeth was repealed, which prohibited the erection of cottages to which less than four acres of ground were attached. (See Eden, *State of the Poor*, vol. i. p. 361.)

[3] Young, *Lincolnshire*, 1799, pp. 412 sqq.

[4] De Montveran, *Situation de l'Angleterre*, vol. i. pp. 295–6, who quotes the *Report of the Board of Agriculture* for 1816.

collecting a number of small rents. By this they got the labourers well into their power.

What motive, indeed, had the farmer to deal generously? He was a business man, with his fortune to make—not a fine gentleman for whom the art of good living consisted in knowing how to spend freely money earned by the toil of others. He would not hear of any useless luxury. He saw no need for the elegant cottages, built pretentiously in Gothic—such as were to be seen on the estates of some great landowners. A mud hovel, dark and badly ventilated, was quite sufficient. There must be no field whose cultivation would take up some of the labourer's time. A tiny kitchen garden was enough. Every day the labourer must be at his employer's disposal. There must not be a meadow to pasture a cow—since that would require too much care—but merely sufficient land to keep a pig. The lease of the cottage and garden became thus a new and additional means of exploiting the labourer—a means of paying him partly in kind and thereby of lowering his wages, an indirect and elaborate form of the truck system. £1 a rood or £4 an acre was a fair rent. We cannot say the same of a rent of 1s. a rod, or £8 an acre, which Cobbett remarked in Wiltshire in 1826. "Still," added Cobbett, "the poor creatures like to have land : they work in it at their spare hours, and on Sunday mornings early." [1] The cottage system became a device to tie the labourer to the soil under an ostensible system of free contract and to oppress him more thoroughly. A system of petty cultivation had grown up by an inevitable reaction, as it were an offshoot of the large farm system.

How then did the agricultural labourer live? For the last fifty years, and more particularly for the last twenty-five, their wages had been constantly rising. About 1793, at the outbreak of the great war, the average wage—so far as it is possible to arrive at an average for all the counties of England—did not exceed 1s. a day during the winter months, 1s 6d. during the summer months. About 1800 we find an increase of 20 to 25 per cent. After 1807 the upward movement became more rapid. 2s. became the average wage, even the minimum winter wage. In summer wages rose in some counties to 3s. in 1810, to 3s. 6d. in 1813. The farmer raised loud protests and attributed to over-payment the growing drunkenness, idleness and insolence of the labourers. The agriculturists, and among them the members of the Board of Agriculture, echoed their complaints. "Farmers, like manufacturers . . . require *constant labourers*—men who have no other

---

[1] Cobbett, *Rural Rides*, Highworth (Wiltshire), September 4, 1826. Cf. Cirencester, November 7, 1821. The rent of £4 per acre was that asked by Sir John Sheffield in Lincolnshire (Young, *Lincolnshire*, 1799, pp. 412–13). Parkinson (*Rutlandshire*, 1808, p. 101) gives the same rent. Those who drew up the surveys of the Board of Agriculture were agreed that in the lease of cottages the farmer must not be allowed to come between the landlord and the labourers, as otherwise the latter would infallibly be oppressed.

means of support than their daily labour.[1] . . . The greatest of evils
to agriculture would be to place the labourer in a state of independence,
and thus destroy the indispensable gradations of society." [2] We must,
however, ask how much truth there was in these complaints.   Certainly
the nominal wage had risen during the last twenty-five years ; but
was it the same with the real wage ?   The labourer kept on receiving
more and more money.   But would this larger sum purchase him a
proportionally greater amount of food and other necessaries of life ?

The contemporary economists answered unhesitatingly in the negative—indeed they maintained that such a thing was in itself impossible.
According to the laws enunciated by Malthus, population was always
pressing upon the means of subsistence.   If in any part of the world
it happened by accident that the number of inhabitants was larger
than could be supported by the amount of foodstuffs at their disposal,
famine, disease and war would soon remedy the disproportion by ex-
terminating the surplus population.   If, conversely, the rate of production exceeded the growth of the population, an increase in the
birth rate would soon restore equilibrium.   According to Ricardo, wages
should be regarded as a fixed quantity, unalterable by economic progress,
temporary oscillations about a constant mean being, of course, negligible.
Nominal wages might, indeed, rise, but it would be found in the long
run that the rise was but apparent—the result of a decrease in the
purchasing power of money—and that the increased wage would after
all go no further than the old wage had done.   Whether this is really
a law of nature, as Ricardo maintained, and whether or no the Malthusian explanation be satisfactory, are questions of very little importance.
The fact remains that Ricardo could never have framed such a law,
had it not represented more or less exactly an economic phenomenon
whose reality was admitted by all observers at the time when he wrote.

1815 and 1816 were the years during which he worked out his
famous *Principles*.   That is to say, he undertook his great work at the
very moment when the agrarian problem was occupying the attention
of the public, of Parliament and of the Press.   It is extremely probable
that his iron law was first suggested by the course of agricultural wages
during the preceding half-century.   About 1770 Arthur Young estimated the weekly wage of an agricultural labourer at about 7s. 4d.

---

[1] Marshall, *Western Department*, p. 115.

[2] Rudge, *Gloucestershire*, p. 48.   He concludes thus : " The great body of mankind, being
obliged to live with, and by each other, must necessarily consist of proprietors and workmen."
Donaldson, *Northamptonshire*, 1794, p. 45 : " The luxury in which this class of people live,
accounts in a great measure for the necessity of levying such immense sums annually for the
support of the poor in England."   Young, *Lincolnshire*, 1799, pp. 397–8 n. (High Wages in
the Fens) : " The consequences of such high prices are very baneful.   The workmen get drunk,
work not above four days out of the six ; dissipate their money, hurt their constitutions,
contract indolence and vicious dispositions, and are lost to the community for at least one-third
of their time in this important crisis.   It is a pity—but the legislature could interfere."   Cf.
ibid., pp. 420–1.

About the same date the price of wheat was about 42s. 4d. a quarter. In 1810 and 1811, as the result of very careful investigation, he estimated the average weekly wage of a labourer at 14s. 4d. Wages had, therefore, almost doubled. Wheat, however, now stood at 105s. 4d. a quarter. The rise of wages had almost corresponded to the rise in the price of wheat. Ricardo's law had been verified. But according to Arthur Young the rise in the prices of meat, butter and cheese had exceeded the rise in the price of bread.[1] Ricardo's theory would thus be too optimistic. The real wage of the labourer would have fallen, since according to Young the increase of his nominal wage had been less rapid than the rise in the price of his necessary food.

Suppose, however, that we admit the exact verification of Ricardo's law, and affirm that the real average wage had remained the same during the last fifty years. We have still to discover the actual value of this constant wage—whether it allowed the labourer to live in decent comfort or was but a starvation wage. The landowners and farmers who gave evidence before the Corn Law Committee of 1814 expressed their conviction that a labourer and his family could live well on a wage equivalent to the cost of a bushel of wheat—the standard to which in practice the average wage of an agricultural labourer tended to approximate. Can we, however, put faith in such interested testimony? What, moreover, are we to understand by a sufficient wage? The witnesses defined it as a wage sufficient to feed, clothe and lodge a family consisting of the husband, the wife and two children. But there might well be more than two children.[2] Sir Frederic Morton Eden, the statistician, made an inquiry in 1795, about the commencement of the war, into the annual wages and expenditure of fifty families of the country labourer class, taken from the most diverse districts of England. He found, almost without exception, a deficit which in one instance exceeded £20.[3] Apart from such statistics, the significance

---

[1] Arthur Young, *Inquiry into the Rise of Prices*, 1815, pp. 201–2. It would be interesting to compare prices for the exact period covered by the great war, 1792–1814. Several surveys of the Board of Agriculture were repeated at different dates for the same county and allow of comparison. See especially Maxwell, *Huntingdonshire*, 1793, p. 18, and Parkinson, *Huntingdonshire*, 1813, p. 268; also Granger, *Durham*, 1794, p. 44, and Bailey, *Durham*, 1810, p. 262. Their evidence confirms the results reached by Young. For the difficulty of reaching a decided conclusion, see Hasback, *History of the Agricultural Labourer*, pp. 125–6.

[2] *Corn Laws Report*, 1814, *Minutes of Evidence*, p. 59: "Will a bushel suffice for the maintenance of a man, his wife and two children, including all his necessary expenses? Yes, certainly, it is what we calculate; we calculate that every person in a labourer's family should have per week the price of a gallon loaf, and 3d. over for feeding and clothing, exclusive of house rent, sickness and casual expenses" (p. 16). This wage is regarded as sufficient to satisfy somewhat larger needs: "Do you believe that anywhere a labouring man maintains himself and his wife and the four children upon 15s. a week? Where they have three children, I think they do; but when they have larger families they generally revert to the parish." Cf. Ricardo, *Principles*, chap. v. (ed. MacCulloch, p. 50): "The natural price of labour is that price which is necessary to enable the labourers, one with another, to subsist and to perpetuate their race, without either increase or diminution."

[3] Eden, *State of the Poor*, vol. iii. Appendix, pp. cccxxxix sqq.

of which is always disputable, the history of the Poor Law affords a striking proof of the inadequacy of the wages received by agricultural labourers during the past twenty-five years. In 1795 the Buckinghamshire, Berkshire and Hampshire magistrates had admitted the insufficiency of wages, had determined once for all what the normal labourer's wage should be in proportion to the price of wheat, and had decided that henceforward the landowners and farmers must pay in the shape of poor rates the difference between this normal wage and the wage actually paid. So pressing was the need met by this novel measure that it was inevitably adopted by degrees in all the southern counties of England.

This, then, was the expedient devised by the governing classes to give some satisfaction to the labouring population of the country districts, lest driven by want and infected by the contagion of French ideas it should plunge into revolutionary excesses. The expedient proved ruinous, and was by no means always efficacious. The extremely sudden and violent fluctuations in the price of wheat baffled calculation and rendered useless the administration of relief. From 61s. 8d. in May 1797, the price of the quarter rose to 134s. 5d. in June 1800, and 156s. 2d. in March 1801. In August 1812 it was once more at a figure practically identical with that of June 1800. Then a fall began. In August 1813 the price of the quarter was 112s., in December it was 75s. 6d., in July 1814 66s. 5d., and in January 1816 it was to reach the minimum figure of 52s. 6d.[1] This meant a time of prosperity for the labourers, and of severe loss for the landowner and farmer. The landowners made their grievances heard in Parliament and attempted to keep up prices by raising the tariff. The farmers entered into conflict with the labourers and attempted to reduce their wages. Then the quarter rose suddenly to 74s. in May, to 117s. in June. The result was an outbreak of rioting throughout the country districts.

In the eastern counties—Essex, Suffolk, Norfolk, Cambridgeshire, and Huntingdonshire—stacks and houses were burnt and agricultural machinery broken.[2] In the district around Ely nothing short of an armed rebellion was organized, and its repression by the Government was marked by several executions. The labourers demanded a rise of wages, and the enactment of a fixed maximum price for bread and flour.[3] They even formulated more daring demands. It was under an agrarian form that revolutionary Socialism made its first appearance

---

[1] Tooke, *History of Prices*, vol. i. pp. 212, 216, 224, 323, 341 ; vol. ii. pp. 2, 4.

[2] *Annual Register*, 1816, *Chronicle*, pp. 61–2, 65, 76, 191. Incendiarism was not confined to the eastern counties, but occurred also in Surrey in the neighbourhood of Godalming (June 29th), in Wiltshire, around Chippenham (December 1st), and in Devonshire, around Honiton and Exeter (June 11th and 22nd).

[3] *Annual Register*, 1816, p. 93, and 1817, p. 9 (*Report of the Secret Committee of the House of Lords appointed to inquire into certain Meetings and Combinations endangering the Public Tranquillity*). For the revolutionary spirit predominant among the agricultural labourers of the Cambridgeshire fens, see Vancouver, *Cambridgeshire*, 1794, p. 176.

in England immediately after 1815. Spence and his disciples demanded the expropriation of the landholders, the restoration of collective ownership of the land, and the establishment in each parish of a system of common cultivation. In short, the system of landed property had led in Great Britain to results similar in certain respects to the results of the system in Ireland. It had formed two separate classes whose interests were totally distinct and discordant—on one side the landowners and farmers who wanted their produce to be dear and wages cheap ; on the other the labourers who wanted high wages and cheap bread. When the labourers prospered, the capitalists complained. When the capitalists grew wealthy, the labourers suffered. There had grown up in the country districts of England and Scotland, as in those of Ireland, a proletariat ripe for revolt.

The Problem of Rural Depopulation.

We have still to examine the second accusation brought against the agrarian changes introduced by the English and Scottish landowners and their farmers. What truth underlay the contention that those changes had disturbed the equilibrium of the national economy, had emptied the countryside of its inhabitants, and had led in consequence to the formation of vast urban centres ? It is impossible to return to this second question an answer so categorical as we did to the first.

It would hardly be true to assert generally that, as the landowners and farmers increased their estates and farms, they tended to substitute for arable land which demanded constant care and many labourers, pastures on which a handful of shepherds sufficed to take care of enormous flocks. This had, indeed, happened in the 15th and 16th centuries in Tudor England, when the first enclosures were made, and when a mass of small cultivators, condemned to vagrancy and cast upon the towns, complained that England had been transformed into one enormous sheepwalk. This was, moreover, what was taking place in 1800 in the Highlands of Scotland, or, to speak more accurately, in one part of the Highlands.[1] A species of feudal system had survived there down to 1745, when the expedition of Charles Edward and the final Scottish rebellion took place. The clan chiefs let their territory to the greatest possible number of tenants ; for their farmers were their soldiers, and the more numerous they were, the greater was the military and social importance of the chief. The same thing took place among those tenants who had leased the more fertile lands, and who were called *tacksmen*. These installed in turn on their farms small cultivators or *cotters*, who paid for this grant of a strip of land by furnishing a fixed amount of labour on the estate retained by the tacksman for

[1] For all the following see Lord Selkirk's admirable work, *Observations on the present State of the Highlands of Scotland* . . . 1805.

himself. The relative importance of each tacksman in the chief's army was determined by the number of cotters whom he could produce in the field. As soon as the rebellion had been crushed, this savage country was rapidly civilized by the energetic efforts of the English Government, aided by the active cooperation of the Scotch themselves. The disappearance of these last relics of feudalism involved the same consequences as the disappearance of English feudalism had involved two centuries earlier.

Peace reigned throughout the entire country. The great land-owner and the tacksman were no longer leaders of an armed band anxious to support the largest possible number of retainers. They had been transformed into capitalists eager to grow rich by the receipt of high rents. In this cold and mountainous country the cultivation of cereals barely sufficed to provide food for the cultivator. The High-lands were, on the other hand, adapted perfectly to the raising of cattle —oxen and especially sheep. Breeders from the Lowlands established themselves in the Highlands as large tenants to raise their cattle on the tablelands of the north. The tacksmen followed their example, threw their land into pasture, and got rid of the cotters. The value of land rose enormously. We hear of one estate sold in 1764 for £3,800, which brought in an income of £800 in 1801, and of another bought in 1736 for £16, which was sold by auction in 1794 for £3,620.[1] What, then, was the fate of the small cultivators who had been expelled ? The poorer among them settled in the Lowlands and constituted the proletariat of the important industrial centre which was coming into existence on the banks of the Clyde. Those who had a little capital at their disposal went down to the port of Greenock and thence em-barked for America. Public opinion took alarm at this emigration. It was a pure loss of capital and men—men, moreover, with the most valuable qualities, good farmers, excellent soldiers. Attempts were made to keep the Highlanders in the country by employing them on great public works. Immediately, however, certain works of urgent necessity had been carried out—the construction of harbours, roads and canals—the emigration began once more.[2] The public alarm con-tinued unallayed.

---

[1] A. Irvine, *Inquiry*, pp. 24–5.

[2] It may be asked to what extent did this movement of emigration during the opening years of the century involve an actual decrease of population. The answer is supplied by the following statistics for the districts affected, taken from the three first census returns : *Caithness*, 1801, 22,609 inhabitants ; 1811, 23,419 ; 1821, 30,238. (Increase, 1801–11, 4 per cent. ; 1811–21, 29 per cent. A decrease of population occurred only in 3 out of 10 parishes.) *Sutherland*, 1801, 23,117 ; 1811, 23,629 ; 1821, 23,840. (Increase, 1801–11, 2 per cent. ; 1811–21, 0 per cent. A decrease occurred in 7 out of 14 parishes.) *Inverness*, 1801, 74,292 ; 1811, 78,356 ; 1821, 90,174. (Increase, 1801–11, 5 per cent. ; 1811–21, 15 per cent. A decrease occurred in 3 out of 36 parishes.) *Ross and Cromarty*, 1801, 55,343 ; 1811, 60,853 ; 1821, 68,828. (Increase, 1801–11, 10 per cent. ; 1811–21, 13 per cent. A decrease occurred in 7 out of 34 parishes.) It must be admitted, therefore, either that the emigration only

The sufferings attendant upon the revolution which took place in the rural economy of the North-West of Scotland at the opening of the 19th century were perhaps inevitable. It is hard to conceive that so profound a social change could be effected without a time of distress and crisis. In any case the difficulties which four or five Scottish counties had to face were peculiar to themselves. Nothing at all similar took place in England or even in the South of Scotland. There a certain amount of land was undoubtedly thrown into pasture ; but it consisted either of mountain-sides naturally barren, which were usually nothing but desolate wastes before they were employed to pasture sheep, or more fertile tracts, plains in the Midland and alluvial valleys, where cattle were fattened for some months for the butchers, on farms far smaller than the vast estates of the north. Hence the pasture system entailed in England far less depopulation than was the case in the Highlands. But the characteristic feature of the period which concluded about 1815 was not the extension of pasture. Wool was cheap, corn was dear. The cultivation of cereals was, therefore, more lucrative than the raising of sheep. Every year fresh meadows came under the plough. The agriculturists even attempted to grow corn on the high plateaux where the cost of cultivation was very high and where the attempt was only justified by the equally high prices of corn at that time. It may perhaps be maintained that the new methods of agriculture now being employed in England had contributed to the depopulation of the country districts. To determine this point we must answer the question whether or no the system of large arable farms necessarily involved a decrease in the rural population.

Take, for instance, the case of a Hampshire farmer who sowed 1,400 acres of corn and 2,000 acres of rye. The total area of the farm was 8,000 acres. It covered the ground formerly occupied by forty small farms. Was it to be wondered at, asked Cobbett, that in such circumstances the number of paupers was increasing ? [1] Or again, take the case of Highclere, where the common land was divided and cultivated at great expense by a handful of farmers in the attempt to grow corn. What, asked Cobbett, was to become of the poor folk who used to turn their geese and their donkey out to graze upon it, and cut turf for their fuel on the waste ? [2] Nevertheless, however plausible

carried off surplus population (Selkirk, *Observations*, pp. 112 sqq.), or that even in the district concerned there was no actual decrease of population but simply a change in its distribution ; and that even in the most distant counties, small towns had grown up large enough to compensate for the rural depopulation. We must not fail to notice that at any rate the small tenants and cotters were not expelled at this period, as they were to be later, in order to transform the land which they occupied into pleasure estates, into enormous deer forests. Sir John Sinclair remarked in 1814 (*Scotland*, vol. i. pp. 171–2) that the Highland deer forests had lost much of their original extent, and that a large number had been devoted to sheep farming.

[1] *Rural Rides*, Bollitre (Herefordshire), November 14, 1821.
Ibid., Burghclere, November 20, 1821.

such charges may sound, we should hesitate to decide in what measure they were well founded. Undoubtedly when an Enclosure Act had divided a common among several owners, it usually happened that many, perhaps the majority of these, ceded their right and went away. But we have still to ask whether or no this decrease in the number of owners was compensated by the increase in the number of wage-earning labourers; and, if it was so compensated, what proportion of these labourers lived permanently on the spot, either at the farm itself or near it, as opposed to those who came from a distance to work for a few weeks and then disappeared leaving the country uninhabited. The complexity of the problem is obvious.

It would certainly appear that the years immediately following the execution of an Enclosure Act always witnessed an increase of the population at the place where the enclosure was made. There were fences and hedges to be made, the land to be divided and drained. All this required labourers at work during the entire year. A witness giving evidence in 1817 before a parliamentary committee affirmed that the population of his parish had increased 6 or 7 per cent. since the census of 1811. When asked to explain the increase he attributed it unreservedly, as if the fact were self-evident, to the enclosure which had taken place "eight or nine years back." "We have," he said, "more work in the parish." [1] The census returns of 1801, 1811 and 1821 prove that in every county of England without exception —both in those whose population was mainly industrial and in those where it was mainly agricultural—the population had increased. The rate of increase exceeded 10 per cent. in every county save twelve [2] during the first decade of the century, in every county save two [3] during the second decade. We have obviously to do with a conflict between two sets of causes—the one set tending to increase, the other to diminish, the population. The causes promoting increase operated by far the most strongly in the industrial districts, but even in the agricultural districts they still about 1815 tended to prevail more or less decidedly over the causes of depopulation.

[1] *Poor Laws Report*, 1817, *Minutes of Evidence*, p. 114. Cf. Vancouver, *Cambridgeshire*, 1794, p. 175: "Inclosures appear to increase population. . . . The additional employment seems to attract more than additional assistance, some part of which becomes stationary and thus the population is increased."

[2] (1) An entire group of adjoining counties, namely—to proceed from south to north—Dorsetshire (8 per cent. increase), Wiltshire (5 per cent.), Berkshire (8 per cent.), Oxfordshire (9 per cent.), Buckinghamshire (9 per cent.), Northamptonshire (7 per cent.), Warwickshire (10 per cent.); (2) the two northern counties of Northumberland (9 per cent.), and Westmorland (10 per cent.); (3) Herefordshire (9 per cent.), Norfolk (7 per cent.), Rutlandshire (0 per cent.). In the North Riding of Yorkshire the increase during this period was only 7 per cent.

[3] Shropshire (increase 6 per cent.), Herefordshire (10 per cent.). From 1821 to 1831 the rate of increase in 14 counties did not exceed 10 per cent. These are the same counties as those mentioned above for 1801–11 and 1811–21, with the exception of Warwickshire and Northumberland, and with the addition of Cumberland, Suffolk, Huntingdonshire, and Hertfordshire.

Even in so far as the country was losing population by the movement of the poorer class to the towns, it remains doubtful whether the extension of the large farm system is the true explanation of the fact. Two phenomena appeared simultaneously in England during the 18th century—cultivation on a large scale, and the rise of the great industries. It is hard to say how far either of these phenomena was the cause or the effect of the other. Did the example of the first great manufacturers fire the emulation of landowners and incite them to transform their farms into these rural factories ? Or was it rather the general adoption of the policy of enclosures, and the expropriation of the yeomen, that drove into the towns a sufficient number of men to furnish the manufacturers with the hands necessary to work their improved looms and to watch their steam engines ? Or again had the large manufactures, like some vast suction pump, begun to draw into the towns all the floating population of the countryside, and thus compelled the landowner to introduce machinery into his farms to meet the dearness and scantiness of agricultural labour ? It was probably a case of action and reaction. According to the period under consideration we should find that one or the other of these alternating causes was the predominant factor. Probably, also, the later the period and the nearer to 1815, the more decisive was the influence exercised by the progress of industry over that of agriculture.

At the beginning of the 18th century a large number of poor people, scattered up and down the country districts, lived in part by the cultivation of the soil, in part by the spinning and weaving of flax and wool. But when the separation between agriculture and manufacture had taken place, how was it possible for these small cultivators deprived of half their livelihood to live in decent comfort ? [1] The more intelligent and more well-to-do among them took to manufacturing, and became the organizers of the new world of industry.[2] The others, less quickwitted and lacking the requisite capital, fell into the ranks of the proletariat, and obtained work as labourers either on the large farms or more commonly in the large factories.[3] Here we have a cause whose action, every year more marked, singularly facilitated the concentration of the farms, and explains, moreover, why the protests raised in England against the enclosures became fainter every year.

[1] Worgan, *Cornwall*, 1815, p. 33 ; Vancouver, *Devonshire*, 1808, p. 387 ; Cobbett, *Rural Rides*, Horsham, July 31, 1823.

[2] Holt, *Lancashire*, 1794, p. 13 : " Not only the yeomanry but almost all the farmers who have raised fortunes by agriculture, place their children in the manufacturing line." " The farmers in this country mostly spring from the industrious class of labourers." Cf. Mantoux, *Révolution Industrielle*, p. 381.

[3] Holland, *Cheshire*, 1808, p. 296 : " In the neighbourhood of Macclesfield, Stockport and the manufacturing parts of the county . . . such high wages are occasionally obtained by children . . . that few are now brought up to husbandry, and it is there as difficult to get a boy to drive the plough as a man to hold it." Brown, *Derbyshire*, 1794, p. 38 ; William Pitt, *Staffordshire*, 1808, p. 218.

It was easy for Cobbett on his rides through the south and south-west of England about 1825 to paint a picture of silent and deserted landscapes, of countless steeples without a village at their feet.[1] But the reason was that there had once been iron mines and smelting works in Surrey and Wiltshire. Once Wiltshire and Somersetshire had been like an enormous manufacturing town scattered over a wide area ; but now the iron industry had been transferred to the centre and the west, and the woollen manufacture was deserting the south for Yorkshire. The growth of large-scale farming was not the direct cause of rural depopulation ; it was rather that the new manufactures, now being developed on such a vast scale, were attracting the country population to the new urban centres and facilitating thereby the enlargement of estates and farms.

[1] *Rural Rides*, November 11, 1825 (Petersfield), September 11, 1826 (Malmesbury), October 11, 1826 (Uphusband).

CHAPTER II

INDUSTRY

COAL, METALS: THEIR EXTRACTION AND PREPARATION.

The Industrial Revolution.

A NEW era was dawning for the industries of England, and indeed, owing to the impulse given by England, for those of the entire world. Every year new technical processes were increasing the productivity of human labour. Every year witnessed the employment of larger numbers. The equilibrium of society was overthrown to the detriment of the country districts, and to the advantage of the towns which were rapidly increasing both in number and in size. The population of London, which was only 864,000 at the opening of the century, had exceeded the million by 1811. To the north-west of the City an entire town had sprung up devoted to amusement and luxury, had crossed the Oxford road, and encroached upon the estate which had recently been laid out by the Duke of Bedford. To the south of the Thames a large and busy town was coming into being, free from the regulations enforced by the corporation in the City. In the east, Spitalfields was no longer an isolated group of houses and workshops. An enormous workman's quarter had arisen around the new docks. Apart from London there had been nine towns in the first year of the century with a population of over 50,000. Of these nine, only two—Dublin and Manchester—had a population of over 100,000. Ten years later eleven towns had reached the 50,000 figure, and four of these—Edinburgh and Glasgow as well as Dublin and Manchester—counted over 100,000 inhabitants. In 1821 the United Kingdom would contain fifteen towns with a population of over 50,000 and six with a population of over 100,000, Liverpool and Birmingham being now added to the four above mentioned.[1]

In these vast urban masses and in the manufacturing districts surrounding them the established social fabric was completely shattered.

For footnote see next page.]

The epoch of the "Industrial Revolution," to employ the term sanctioned by general usage, deserves this appellation on two grounds— in the first place because the great manufacturers to whose initiative it was due were daring innovators, "revolutionaries" in the proper sense of the term ; and in the second place because the workmen were in revolt against the novel conditions of labour which it was being sought to impose on them. The new industrial society was, however, too complex to admit of summary definition. We must enter into details. The transformation of technical processes and the introduction of machinery were not effected with equal rapidity and did not follow the same course in different manufactures. Neither was there any direct ratio between the spirit of revolt among the workmen and the progress accomplished by modern machinery in any particular manufacture.

The Mines.

The new type of manufacture presupposed a twofold material— coal and iron. It substituted an iron machine for the wooden loom, and had employed coal since the middle of the 18th century to smelt the iron ore at the pit mouth, to fashion it afterwards into tools or machinery, and to supply the motive power to these machines when constructed. Manufacture, therefore, like agriculture had its roots deep in the soil. Great Britain was rich in mines. There were tin and copper mines in Cornwall, which had been worked from the remotest antiquity. There were copper mines in Anglesey also, and lead mines in Derbyshire, Flintshire and Cumberland. Coal mines and iron mines were the most abundant of all. There were the coal mines of Durham

				1801	1811	1821
Manchester	...	...	...	109,218	137,201	155,707
Glasgow	...	...	...	84,124	112,330	150,818
Edinburgh	...	...	...	81,147	102,147	138,235
Liverpool	...	...	...	77,653	94,376	118,972
Birmingham	...	...	...	73,670	85,755	106,722
Bristol ...	...	...	...	63,645	76,433	97,779
Halifax	...	...	...	62,425	73,315	91,930
Leeds ...	...	...	...	54,162	62,534	83,758
Plymouth	...	...	...		56,000	61,112
Sheffield	...	...	...		53,231	62,275
Blackburn	...	...	...			53,330
Bradford	...	...	...			52,954
Oldham	...	...	...			52,510
Norwich	...	...	...			51,188
Dublin *	...	...	...			185,881

* Wakefield gives 167,899 for 1804 (*Ireland*, vol. ii. p. 702).

and Northumberland, situated to the north and south of the estuaries of the Tyne and Wear. For a long while past these coalfields had supplied the capital by sea with the fuel necessary for its fires. There were also the coalfields of the Scottish Lowlands between Edinburgh and Glasgow, and the coal mines of Cumberland around Whitehaven, the source whence the Lowther and Curwen families drew their wealth. The Lancashire coalfields extended over a vast quadrangular area to the north of Liverpool and Manchester and to the west of the Pennines, and stretching on the south into Staffordshire. Parallel to these ran the coalfields of Yorkshire. South Wales also had its coalfields. In Scotland, Staffordshire and Wales iron was found in the vicinity of the coal. In 1754 Sir John Dalrymple pointed out that "among all the known countries on the surface of the globe it was in Great Britain alone that the coal beds, the iron ore and limestone, which constituted the three raw materials of the iron manufacture, were frequently found together and moreover in close proximity to the sea."[1]

We have here an essential condition, if not a sufficient cause, of the extraordinary development of British industry during the 18th century. The coalfields were worked with an activity so relentless that many Englishmen were already asking with alarm how many centuries—ten or five, or perhaps only two or three—it would take to exhaust the mines.[2] Among this crowd of new industries, all strictly interdependent, those really fundamental were concerned with mining. How, then, were these organized? What was the distribution in them of functional activities and economic rewards? How far do we find the features universally regarded as characteristic of the industrial revolution?

It is admitted on all hands that the first and chief feature distinctive of this revolution was the appearance of a new class—the captains of industry. The modern capitalist was no longer a member of a corporation, binding him by its strict regulations. He was no longer content merely to supply the demands of trade. He had won his independence, and was himself his own merchant. He systematically forced the rate of production, anticipated the demand for his goods, and was aiming at the conquest not only of the national markets but of the markets of the entire world. It is, however, only in a small number of mining centres that capitalism will present itself to us as a novelty peculiar to the 19th century. In Cornwall, for example, we witness a conflict in progress between capitalism and an older industrial system. From time immemorial the Cornish mines had been worked by syndicates of adventurers,[3] men of no great wealth and lacking both in initiative

---

[1] *Address . . . on . . . the Coal, Tar and Iron Branches of Trade*, p. 8.

[2] J. H. H. Holmes, *A Treatise on the Coal Mines of Durham and Northumberland*, 1816, pp. 35–6. The opinions of Bakewell, Millar, Thompson, see Thomas Chalmers, *An Inquiry . . . 1805*, pp. 25–6.

[3] For the organization of labour in the Cornish mines see the copious details given in

and in the capacity for organization. They were exposed to the exactions alike of the owners of the subsoil whose tenants they were and of the traders who intervened between them and the consumer.[1] Little by little the revolution was accomplished, and capitalism took the place of these old-time forms of mining. In 1785 Thomas Williams, a Welshman, and John Vivian, a Cornishman, founded the large *Cornish Metal Society* for the mining of copper. Certain manufacturers now took into their own hands the mining of the ore which provided the raw material for their factories. The Birmingham manufacturers, headed by Bolton, founded the *Birmingham Mining and Copper Company* and the *Crown Copper Company* for the exploitation of the Cornish mines.[2] But normally things happened otherwise ; and no disturbance was caused in 1815 by the introduction of the capitalist system into mining, for the sufficient reason that this system had to some extent always existed there.

Mines were subject to a system of a quasi-feudal character, according to which the subsoil was the absolute property of the Lord of the Manor. And it was not until a very recent date that some legal restriction had been placed upon the exercise of this right by requiring, prior to the opening of a mine, the consent of the freeholders and copyholders who occupied the surface.[3] The Lord of the Manor was therefore inclined, naturally enough, to undertake himself the working of the mines which he owned. The heads of certain old families such as the Lowthers in Westmorland, the Curwens in Cumberland and the Percys in Northumberland were the hereditary rulers of a realm of collieries. In a word, industrial feudalism blended here with agrarian feudalism. A system of ancient standing, it did nothing to disturb the existing relations between classes. It had no revolutionary significance.

We now come to another distinctive feature of the industrial revolution—a feature which was in truth inseparable from the former.

W. Pryce's *Mineralogia Cornubiensis*, London 1778. (This work was written thirty-seven years before 1815, but the organization of the mines would seem to have undergone no practical alteration in the interval.) See also *Report on the State of the Copper Mines and Copper Trade*, 1799. (This contains a complete list of the adventurers of the Cornish mines.) Cf. for the Newcastle district, *Report on the State of the Coal Trade*, 1800, p. 640 *a* ; R. Warner, *Northern Tour*, vol. i. pp. 303 sqq.

[1] For this exploitation by the middleman see, as regards the Newcastle collieries, the *Report on the State of the Coal Trade*, 1800. These middlemen were the *fitters* who transported the coal on their barges from the pit to the collier, the *shippers* who brought it from Newcastle and Sunderland to London, and the *merchants* who bought it wholesale in the capital to retail it afterwards to the consumer. Two syndicates, the *Factors* and the *Coal Budgers*, defrauded alike the producer, the consumer and the treasury. For the Cornish mines see *An Address to the Gentlemen of the County of Cornwall* . . . 1772, also *British Mining : A Treatise* . . . by Robert Hunt, 1887.

[2] *Report on* . . . *Copper Mines and Copper Trade*, May 1799, pp. 654 sqq., 659 and *passim.* Pye, *A Description of Modern Birmingham*, pp. 44–5.

[3] J. H. H. Holmes, *Coal Mines of Durham and Northumberland*, 1816, pp. 69–70.

Capitalism was tending to concentrate an enormous number of work-men in a small number of large factories. It compelled them to an intense productivity under the strict supervision of the manufacturer and his subordinates. This sudden herding together of wretched and oppressed workmen generated a discontent that was perilous to public order. In this respect, however, the conditions of labour in the mines had undergone no practical change. Perhaps mining was now a harder task than it had been a century earlier. It had become necessary to attack the more difficult seams, to invest more capital in the undertaking, and therefore to require more work from the miners in order to maintain profits. Formerly in Cornwall the miner, on his descent into the mine, had begun by sleeping as long as it takes a candle to burn down. He had then worked for two or three hours, at the conclusion of which he rested for half an hour to smoke a pipe before recommencing work. Half the day had been spent in sleeping and lounging about.[1] Certainly such a thing was no longer possible in 1815. It is, however, scarcely credible that it had ever been possible, even in the 18th century, outside the tin mines of the south-west. It could never, we may be sure, have been possible in the coal mines of the north. We should remember, moreover, that the ever-increasing demand of the new manufacturers for iron and coal necessitated a constant increase in the number of miners. Every time, therefore, that an industrial crisis occurred as the result of over-production, it affected a greater number of miners and was consequently more serious. It was, however, only in this indirect manner that the industrial revolution reacted upon the mining industries.

Steam engines had, however, been introduced into mining. It would surely seem that here at any rate the industrial revolution exercised a direct effect upon mining. The first of these to be introduced was the steam pump employed to clear the mines of water. It had been used first in Cornwall, and long before the end of the 18th century its employment had become universal. Savery's "steam engine," and Newcomen's, as also Watt's first engine, had been steam pumps. When in 1767 Bolton added to his Soho workshops a factory for the construction of machines, he was thinking only of the suction pump. The use of these pumps had made it possible to reopen flooded mines which their owners had abandoned,[2] and also to extend further the workings of mines already in existence. The invention of the railroad marked a further progress. Originally of wood, iron rails soon came into use. Many travellers have left description of the enormous *staiths* in use on the banks of the Tyne and Wear. The rails were laid on a slope so that the heavy trucks loaded with coal might run of themselves. By a system of pulleys every full truck pulled up an empty truck, which was

---

[1] W. Pryce, *Mineralogia Cornubiensis* . . . 1778, pp. 178–9.
[2] Galloway, *Papers relating to . . . the Coal Trade . . . and Steam Engine*, pp. 9, 25 sqq.

then loaded afresh and in its turn pulled up the last truck unloaded.[1] Experiments had even been made in the course of the last few years with the object of working simultaneously on the staiths, by means of a fixed steam engine, trains consisting of six or even twelve trucks. Surely the employment of these engines must have altered in some way or other the condition of the workmen ? The question requires careful examination and discrimination between different cases.

The workman complained that machinery lessened the number of men required. One workman was now sufficient where perhaps two, four or more even had been necessary hitherto. He also complained that it cheapened his labour, since all the skill and precision of his eye or hand was now the property of the machine. The workman had ceased to be an artisan to become the guardian of an engine, and therefore women and children could take the places of grown-up men. But nothing, or almost nothing, of the sort had taken place in the mines.

Certainly we must except from this denial all the machinery employed on the banks of the Tyne and Wear for the transport of coal from stack to ship. The total destruction in March 1815 by the *keelmen* and *casters* of Bishop's Wearmouth of a bridge, of the staiths, and indeed of the entire apparatus set up by the Nesham Company for the automatic transport of coal,[2] was an instance of these essentially futile but wholly natural labour riots which are always aroused by the first introduction of machinery. But within the mine itself the introduction of machinery had neither decreased nor cheapened manual labour. Indeed pumps, by making it possible to extend the working of mines, involved immediately the employment of a greater number of miners. The extraction of coal must always require duly qualified miners—sturdy, experienced and skilful. No machine under the charge of women or children could take their place. Not, of course, that there was no employment for women and children in the mines. Women led the horses which drew the trucks, children opened the gates to let them pass. The children began work at the age of seven or eight. Throughout the entire winter they never beheld the daylight. We are told that they could work for thirteen hours on end without dying of exhaustion. But the labour of these women and children did not compete with that of the grown-up men, since they were employed to work under the orders of the latter. The management of the mine left the payment of the women and children to the miners, together with full liberty to use them at pleasure for the gratification of their bestial and filthy desires. In 1815 their sufferings were but beginning to make themselves heard in Parliament. The miners

[1] See especially *Coal Mines of Durham and Northumberland*, pp. 37–8 ; also Dupin, *Force Commerciale*, pp. 82 sqq.

[2] *Annual Register*, 1815, March 20th, Chron., p. 26 ; *Newcastle Chronicle*, March 20, 1815.

had never rioted against the employment of women and children in the mines.[1]

The miners lived like utter savages absolutely cut off not merely from the middle class, but also from the other sections of the labouring classes.[2] Their underground labour was unlike any other ; it was hard, gloomy and exceedingly dangerous. The further the working of a bed of coal was pushed the more frequent and the more serious became the explosions of fire damp. After many unsuccessful experiments the *Society for Preventing Accidents in Coal Mines* which had been founded in 1813 under the patronage of the Duke of Northumberland, succeeded in obtaining the discovery of Davy's safety lamp.[3] But it required constant effort to overcome the obstinate carelessness of the miners. Savages are always careless, and the miners lived, as we said above, like absolute savages both in the dirty and ruined villages in which they spent the night and in the subterranean galleries where of necessity there was less supervision than in the workshops of a factory. A traveller who visited the mines at Whitehaven relates the terror he felt on meeting "at a place of rendezvous . . . a party of men and girls " with " haggard faces and ruffian-like figures." " These gloomy and loathsome caverns," he continues, "are made the scenes of the most bestial debauchery. If a man and woman meet in them, and are excited by passion at the moment, they indulge it."[4] The sole influence to counteract such degradation was to be found in sudden outbursts of religious enthusiasm. It was in the collieries around Bristol and Newcastle that the preaching of Whitefield and Wesley obtained its first triumphs. For sixty years before our date Methodism had been the one really civilizing influence at work among the miners whether in Durham or in Cornwall.

When, however, we seek for exact information as to the miners' wages, food and lodging, we have to do without the help of any inquiry either official or unofficial made at this time. We can only bring

[1] *First Report of Commissioners . . . as to the Employment of Children in Factories*, 1833, p. 60. Children worse treated in collieries than in factories. See also, *The Literary Life of William Brownrigg, M.P., F.R.S.*, by Joshua Dixon, London 1800, for an estimate of the proportion of adult to child labour in a Cumberland mine : " Number of persons . . . necessary for the purpose of raising 160 baskets of coal in 9 hours at 100 fathoms deep : eight men to hew the coal, i.e. to cut it out of the solid mine, and to break it to a proper size, in order that it may be conveniently taken into the baskets ; two persons to lift the coal into the baskets, each filling ten baskets in one hour ; eight boys to drive eight horses from the workings to the bottom of the pit ; one person, at the bottom of the pit, to hook the full basket to the rope, and take off the empty basket ; one man at the top of the pit, to empty the basket ; two boys to drive the gin horses, which are yoked to the vertical wheel." In the Newcastle district, the employment of women had apparently ceased with the close of the 18th century (Galloway, *Annals of Coal Mining*, vol. i. p. 305).

[2] R. Nelson Boy, *Coal Pits and Pitmen*, 1892, p. 14, who quotes a contemporary witness.

[3] J. H. H. Holmes, *Coal Mines of Durham and Northumberland*, 1818, pp. 83–91.

[4] R. Ayton, *Voyage around Great Britain*, vol. ii, 1815, pp. 156, 159.

together as well as possible the very scanty evidence and thus gather something of their miserable lot.

We catch a glimpse of the miners employed in the Yorkshire and Derbyshire lead mines, paid at the rate of about 10s. a week, obliged to walk a great distance over the mountains twice a day between their village and the mine, sleeping five or six together—father, mother and children on a single mattress—and often subsisting for weeks at a time on raw and unsalted oatmeal. " They were, notwithstanding, one of the most quiet, peaceable, well-intentioned descriptions of men in the Kingdom."[1]   In Scotland the miners were only just emancipated from a state of legal serfdom.   For three-quarters of the 18th century they had been tied for life to the soil.   As the demand for coal increased there arose an urgent need for a larger number of colliers, and an Act was therefore passed in 1775 abolishing this serfdom in the case of anyone who should in future take employment in these mines. But it was not till the last year of the century that the measure was made universal, and all the colliers of Scotland without exception were emancipated by an express statute.[2]   Moreover, in all the collieries of the north there prevailed a system of contract intermediate between this antiquated serfdom and wage labour in the strict sense.   Labour was hired for the year, the miners engaging to work throughout that period without strikes, combinations or absences. The men so bound by a yearly bond do not seem to have been badly paid.   At the close of the 18th century they earned on an average 16s. a week—that is to say appreciably more than an agricultural labourer earned at that date.   In the years immediately following their wages rose in almost equal proportion to the rise in the price of foodstuffs. In 1804, the rise was as much as 30 to 40 per cent.[3]   But the money

[1] Fred. Hall, *An Appeal to the Poor Miner*, 1818, p. 7.   Their wages had remained the same since 1795, in spite of the general rise in prices (see for 1795 the figures given in Eden's *State of the Poor*, vol. ii. p. 130).

[2] 15 Geo. III, cap. 28 ; 39 Geo. III, cap. 56.   It is true that the Act of 1775 gave all the miners, without exception, the power to emancipate themselves gradually.   The provisions of the Act, however, on this point were undoubtedly too complicated to be efficacious.   Cf. Cockburn, *Memorials*, pp. 78–9.

[3] When the yearly bond was signed the miner received a premium, which seems to have been about 6d. in 1763 (Galloway, *Annals of Coal Mining*, vol. i. pp. 269, 270).   In 1804 in the same district it had risen to the extravagant figure of twelve or fourteen guineas on the Tyne, of eighteen guineas on the Wear.   In 1809–10 it was only after a year's struggle that the coalowners succeeded in reducing the premium to five guineas on the Tyne, to 10s. 6d. on the Wear (*ibid.*, 440–1).   The account of the strike in Fynes' *Miners of Durham and Northumberland*, pp. 12 sqq., partially conceals this defeat of the miners.   Cf. Bailey, *Durham*, 1810, p. 22.   The earnings of pitmen are on an average about 21s. a week ; sometimes the hewers make from 30s. to 40s.   The wages of agricultural labour in the same district for the same period (*id. ibtd.*, p. 262) were 2s. to 2s. 6d. a day in winter, 2s. 6d. to 3s. in summer.   Eden, *State of the Poor*, 1796, vol. ii. pp. 169–70, gives some information as to the standard of life of the Durham miners : " Many miners keep a cow, which makes land let so high.   They use much oatmeal made into crowdie, and milk and barley bread.   The women spin jersey, and can earn 3d. or 4d. a day ; many of them manufacture their own woollen and linen apparel.   The lead miners are generally less profligate than those who work in the coal mines, are better clothed

earned was rapidly and ill spent. The miner was paid by the piece. Hence it chiefly depended on the character of the ground on which he happened to be working whether his labour would be well or ill paid at the end of the week. The result of this was that he developed the gambler's temperament. When he was well paid he spent every penny of his wages; when he had earned less, he counted on a return of luck and ran into debt.[1]

He had neither the capacity nor the desire to save, or indeed for any premeditated or concerted actions. The English or Scottish miners had up to the present scarcely ever formed unions. Unlike the workmen in many other industries, they had no ancient corporate privileges to defend. Many years had yet to elapse before they would come to realize their numbers and the power which those numbers gave them. Occasionally riots broke out, in years of industrial crisis, in which houses and machinery were destroyed. These were, however, purely impulsive and irresponsible outbreaks, and hence without any permanent result. The depression which followed the restoration of peace, and which affected the whole of British industry, spread in the winter of 1815–16 to the mines. Wages fell, men were thrown out of employment, and strikes occurred in Staffordshire, Cardiganshire and Durham.[2] These strikes were, however, no sign that the revolutionary spirit had been awakened among the miners. In Staffordshire the employers hit upon an ingenious device for getting rid of the malcontents at slight cost to themselves. They gave them a few tons of coal and trucks in which to cart it, and sent them in bands throughout England pushing their coal along and appealing to the people to take pity on their destitution. The miners carried notices bearing the inscription *Willing to work but none of us will beg*, and whenever they passed through a new town or district they applied to the magistrates before leaving for a certificate of good conduct.[3]

Metals.

When ore had been extracted from the earth it required to be wrought into a fit state for industrial use. If lead, copper or tin mines were situated at a distance from a coalfield, either the necessary coal was

---

and mostly better informed." See also, for the prosperous condition of the Durham miners, the testimony of Cobbett for a period somewhat later than ours (*Rural Rides*, October 4, 1832). Gisborne, *A General View of the Situation of the Mining Poor, compared with that of some other Classes of the Poor*, 1798 (see the *Reports of the Society for Bettering the Condition of the Poor*, vol. i. pp. 36–9), who drew his information from Durham and Cornwall, affirmed that "the earnings . . . of the miner are on an average great; and in many instances far exceed all prospects of gain, which a labourer in husbandry can propose to himself."

[1] Rev. Thomas Gisborne, *A General View*, etc., 1798, in the *Reports of the Society for Bettering the Condition of the Poor*, vol. i. pp. 368–9.

[2] *Annual Register*, 1816, Chron., p. 13, January 22nd; p. 73, May 28th.

[3] *Annual Register*, 1816, Chron., pp. 95–6, 99–100.

brought thither and the foundry was set up near the mine—this was done, for instance, in the case of the Cornish tin mines—or the ore was sent either to a colliery district or to the neighbourhood of the factories where the smelted and refined metal was used as the raw material of the manufacture—as happened in the case of the Cornish copper, which on leaving the mine was sent by sea to Welsh or Warwickshire foundries. In some areas the metalliferous strata were mixed up with the coal beds, e.g. in Glamorganshire, Monmouth, Staffordshire, and Shropshire. In such areas the extraction and preparation of the ore were parts of one and the same industry. Immediately on leaving the pit the ore was thrown into the blast furnace, melted down with coke fuel mixed with quick-lime. Every twelve hours the fire doors at the foot of the furnace were opened and the molten iron flowed out. Ingots were formed which, when laid around the furnace, resembled so many little pigs being suckled by their mother. This was the pig iron, in which iron was still mixed with dross of various sorts. To change molten iron into iron, the English manufacturers and workmen, who lacked the least rudiments of scientific knowledge, had arrived empirically at the discovery of a host of new processes. They had begun very early to employ first water and then steam power to move the hammer which beat the iron into bars, and the bellows which kept up a blast of air in the furnace. In 1783 and 1784 Cort had taken out two patents—one for the process of puddling, the other for that of flattening. Or again, in the transformation of iron into steel, more than half a century had already passed since Sheffield steel had been rendered famous by Huntsman's experiments. And fifteen years before Musket had invented a process by which steel could be made directly from pig iron or even from untreated ore.

As the result of all these inventions British metallurgy had made rapid strides. In Wales, which was the most important centre of the industry, in Staffordshire, in the Newcastle district, and in Stirlingshire, not only had the number of blast furnaces been greatly multiplied but the yield of each furnace had also increased. The average yield in 1740 had been 294 tons a furnace, in 1788 it was 545 tons, in 1796 1,048 tons and in 1807 1,546 tons.[1] At this last date the total annual production was estimated at 250,000 tons, the capital engaged at £5,000,000, the number of workmen employed at 200,000. It would seem at first sight that no manufacture had been more affected by the industrial revolution than this. In reality, however, the improvement of technical processes had altered the economic condition of these foundries as little as it had altered that of the mines.

Even the size of the foundries underwent no appreciable change. In iron works of the old type, before the substitution of coal for charcoal in the treatment of the ore, the average number of workmen employed

[1] Scrivenor, *History of the Iron Trade*, 1841, pp. 35, 86-7, 95-6.

had been 2,500 for every three furnaces.[1] Manufacture on a large scale had evidently preceded in this field the introduction of the new processes. Moreover, the improvement of machinery had scarcely affected the character of the work to be done, and had by no means rendered useless the strength and skill of the workmen. Women and children were employed very little.[2] The keeper of the blast furnace was paid by the piece as were also his assistants—the fillers, cokers, limestone-breakers, and mine-burners ; but the object of this system of payment by the piece was to increase neither the amount nor the intensity of a purely mechanical task. It was left to the workman to raise his earnings by displaying such conscientiousness, intelligence and skill as would result in an increase in the amount of cast iron produced at the end of the day. We may add that a system prevailed of subletting piece work. It was only the principal workmen with whom the ironmaster treated directly. These were bound by contract to provide the necessary hands for the accomplishment under their direction of a particular piece of work. The keepers and puddlers formed a species of aristocracy among the workmen which took care to sell its productive capacities to the capitalist as dear as possible. Their wages, accordingly, represented so large a portion of the cost of production that the ironmaster's chief anxiety was the constant struggle with his workmen regarding rates of pay.[3]

Moreover, iron had been rising in price during the last twenty-five years, and the constant demands of the Army and Navy for iron had put the manufacture beyond the reach of the crises which afflicted the other branches of English manufacture. Wages had risen,[4] and the workmen

---

[1] Scrivenor, *History of the Iron Trade*, 1841, pp. 64–5. He is dealing with Sir Charles Coote's works in Ireland. He divides the workmen into the following classes : " Woodcutters, Sawyers, Carpenters, Smiths, Masons and Bellow-makers, Water-leaders or Water-course Keepers ; Basket-makers ; Boatmen and Boatwrights ; Diggers, Carriers ; Colliers ; Corders ; Fillers ; Keepers of the Furnace ; Finers ; Hammerers ; besides several other labourers who, having no particular task, must help to put their hands to everything."

[2] See the work in the *Library of Useful Knowledge*, entitled *Manufacture of Iron*, 1831, p. 30, for the statistics of a foundry consisting of five blast furnaces, and furnishing a weekly yield of 200 tons of iron in bars.

	Men	Women	Boys
Colliers	280	0	27
Miners	395	40	73
Furnaces	257	39	3
Forge and Mill	145	5	55
Agents, Overlookers, etc.	31	0	0
	1,108	84	158

[3] *Manufacture of Iron*, 1831 (in *Library of Useful Knowledge*), p. 9.

[4] Eden, *State of the Poor*, vol. ii. p. 109, gives the wages of the workmen in the Chesterfield foundries (Derbyshire) in May 1795. They were about 15s. a week. Towards the end of

had enjoyed a period of continuous prosperity. An eyewitness describes the pleasing aspect of their villages in Staffordshire; the rows of cottages whose doors were all open, thus allowing the passer-by to remark the cleanliness of their interiors; the strong and healthy inhabitants; the groups of well-kept children romping and playing in the streets.[1]

It was only after the restoration of peace that the foundries experienced a period of acute depression, and passed through a crisis of extreme gravity. In Staffordshire the stoppage of work reduced thousands of workmen to destitution. No riot, however, broke out, and there was but little plundering.[2] In Wales the factory owners lowered the men's wages, whereupon they declared a strike. They formed themselves into a procession and traversed the country, leading away any workmen they met and extinguishing the furnaces. But after a fray, in which several of the strikers were wounded and one killed, the agitation lost its riotous character, although the number of those taking part in it continued constantly to increase : in the end the strikers constituted a regular army of ten or twelve thousand men. When an employer offered them bread, cheese and beer, they refused the beer, saying " that if they should get intoxicated they might be guilty of what they might afterwards be sorry for." [3] This first crisis of 1816 took, so to speak, by surprise, the proletariat of the affected districts. Neither in Wales nor in the Midlands were the ironworkers ready for revolt

The Manufacture of Machinery and Tools.

Wales did not merely make iron bars; it also manufactured iron goods. Glamorganshire had become, in the last quarter of the 18th century, a centre of iron manufacture. The larger portion, nevertheless, of the iron bars produced around Merthyr Tydvil and Pontypool was sent on board ship from Cardiff and Newport, up the Severn to Stourport on the borders of Shropshire and Staffordshire, where the iron of Wales, of Lancashire and of Cumberland was brought together to be used in the factories of the Midlands. In this district, which itself was rich in iron and coal, the manufacturers, united more closely than was common with English manufacturers,[4] had set up a number of

1816, at the time of Merthyr Tydvil strike, a local official in Wales denied in a public statement that there had been an undue lowering of wages. " None had less, he states, than 10s. a week ; and the miners and colliers, who form the great body of workmen, had at least 15s. per week. The wages of the firemen, who also form a considerable body, average from 21s. to 25s. per week (*Annual Register*, 1816, Chron., p. 167).

[1] *Annual Register*, 1816, Chron., pp. 110–12.

[2] Except for a day of fairly serious disturbances at Wolverhampton (*Annual Register*, 1815, Chron., pp. 89–90, November 15th).

[3] *Annual Register*, 1816, Chron., pp. 165 sqq., October 22nd.

[4] John Hall, *The Iron Trade*, 1843, p. 7. Although the date of the work is far later than 1815, we can, nevertheless, make use of it. John Hall depicts the organization of the ironmaster of this district as of very long standing.

factories which already competed seriously with those of Wales. There were factories in which the metal—iron, tin, lead, or zinc—went through a series of different stages from its arrival from the mine till the moment when it was put upon the market in the shape of shoe buckles, nails, hardware, ploughshares, and the pistons and cylinders of steam engines. The labour required in these factories was necessarily skilled labour. No women or children were employed. The workmen exacted good wages. It would seem, moreover, that these factories involved two distinct types of manufacture to which there corresponded two methods of labour organization.

On the one hand complicated and costly machinery was required to divide the iron bars into small pieces, and this involved the sinking of capital on a large scale. In 1785 a Shropshire society consumed 500 tons of coal daily, and their buildings represented a capital of £100,000,[1] and during the thirty years following such operations were carried out on an increasing scale. On the other hand, the final stages of the manufacture of small articles required specialization of manual dexterity rather than intricate machinery : to prove the advantages of a division of labour Adam Smith took the instance of the pin manufacture.[2] Sheffield manufactured not only steel but knives as well ; Birmingham not only machinery but a host of small articles, toys and hardware. The result was that Sheffield and Birmingham were towns not of large factories but of small workshops, where small manufacturers turned out small articles. The undertakers obtained the necessary raw material from the master manufacturers and brought back to them the finished article. Nor were the master manufacturers themselves large capitalists.[3] The largest factories in Birmingham represented a capital of £6,000 to £7,000, the majority a capital of less than £100.[4]

---

[1] William Gibbons, *A Reply to Sir Lucius O'Brien*, p. 22.

[2] *Wealth of Nations*, Book I, chap. i. (ed. Thorold Rogers, vol. i. p. 6).

[3] *First Report of Commissioners . . . as to Employment of Children in Factories*, 1833, Mr. Horner's report, p. ii. The existence of these small workshops caused a marked difference between the conditions of labour in Birmingham and those which obtained in domestic industry in the strict sense. See *Memoirs of Richard Lovell Edgeworth*, vol. ii. p. 278 : " He became acquainted with some of the working mechanics in Paris (in 1802), and had an opportunity of observing how differently work of this kind is carried on there and in Birmingham. Instead of the assemblage of artificers in manufactories, such as we see in Birmingham, each artisan in Paris, working out his own purposes in his own domicile, must in his time ' play many parts,' . . . so that in fact, even supposing French artisans to be of equal ability and industry with English competitors, they are left at least a century behind, by thus being precluded from all the miraculous advantages of the division of labour." But he is thinking throughout only of manufactures based on the division of labour, not of factories where machinery was employed.

[4] *Report . . . on the Copper Trade*, 1799, pp. 662b–663a. In manufactures of this kind wages do not seem to have risen during the great war, as far as we can judge from the scanty and insufficient evidence. Real wages must, therefore, have greatly fallen while remaining sensibly higher by about a third than the wages of the agricultural labourer. See Eden, *State of the Poor*, vol. ii. p. 655 (Wolverhampton) : " The wages in the different manufactures vary from 9s. to £2 a week ; men, in full employment, earn, on an average, from 15s. to £1 5s. a week, The manufactures are the heaviest sorts of hardware : such as axes, shovels, etc. ; buckles, watch-chains, toys, spectacle-cases, etc." *Report . . . on . . . State of Children*, 1816, *Minutes of*

With the manufacture of cutlery, toys and hardware we may, it would seem, compare in many respects the manufacture of pottery which, largely as the result of the initiative of the important Wedgwood family, employed thousands of workmen in Staffordshire. The vases and plates of every description which issued from the workshops of Burslem and Etruria were famous throughout the entire world for the perfection of their make and the good taste of their decoration. But here also, when once the raw material had been broken up, the technical manufacture was based on the principle of the division of labour.[1]

If the growth of the revolutionary spirit among the workmen had been due solely to the progress of machinery, we should have expected to find it very little developed among the small handicraftsmen who made practically no use of machinery, not even of a loom. Josiah Wedgwood, indeed, in 1816, depicted the population of the Staffordshire Potteries as extremely peaceable, and was, he said, the recruiting ground for the best disciplined troops.[2] Sheffield was a manufacturing town whose industries were controlled by a company of Hallamshire cutlers, a body enjoying corporate privileges which had been granted originally in the 17th century and renewed in 1791.[3] Their secrets had been jealously guarded and the number of their apprenticeships was limited. The spirit of the place was extremely conservative. On the other hand, the hardware country, despite the similarity of the conditions of labour, afforded a totally different spectacle. Although the population of Birmingham, like that of Sheffield, consisted of artisans and not of the proletariat attached to large factories, that city was destined in a few years' time to be one of the headquarters of revolution in England. How are we to account for this difference?

Evidence, p. 301. Mr. J. Dutton, a Liverpool ironmonger, supplies the following information as to the conditions of labour: No child labour, piecework; an 8-, 10-, sometimes a 12-hours' day (but the workmen often wasted working days drinking); very good wages, 25s. to 30s. a week, 4s. 6d. to 5s. a day; the work was, in his opinion, not so hard, though demanding more strength, as in the cotton industry, and there was also less heat and dust. H. of C., April 17, 1812 (Brougham's speech): "The hardware manufactures were carried on by about 70,000 persons; not persons brought from the field but men of skill, who had undergone a regular apprenticeship. . . . At present the master manufacturers kept them working a little at the reduced wages of 12s. a week, instead of from 25s. to 35s." (*Parl. Deb.*, vol. xxii. p. 437). At Sheffield, in the latter part of the 18th century, the great merchants concentrated in their hands the articles produced by the small workshops, and undertook the task of finding markets for them. The independence, however, of the small manufacturers was not yet touched. (Hunter, *Hallamshire*, p. 121.) At Birmingham machinery had made its appearance. The owners of the machinery did not, however, become themselves the employers of labour. They supplied the small workshops with motive power, letting the use of it to the undertakers.

[1] *Report . . . on . . . State of Children*, 1816, *Minutes of Evidence*, pp. 60 sqq. (Josiah Wedgwood's evidence, p. 61): ". . . I think I should also add that our people do not work so regularly as I suppose they do in manufactories, where a considerable expense is incurred in providing power by machinery; our people, I think, on an average lose one day a week, and of course the children have the same relaxation as the men." And *Reports from Commissioners*, 1833. *First Report . . . as to the Employment of Children in Factories*, 1833, Mr. Spencer's report, pp. 78 sqq. We find here some additional information as to the conditions of labour in the "Potteries" at a somewhat later period.

[2] *Report . . . on . . . State of Children*, 1816, *Minutes of Evidence*, p. 63.

[3] Webb, *History of Trade Unionism*, pp. 14, 33.

Was it entirely due to the fact that the local industry was passing through a period of depression, because metal buttons and buckles were no longer the fashion, and war had diminished the export of articles of local manufacture? These were doubtless partial causes, but the chief cause was that the established traditions of Birmingham were Liberal, indeed almost Republican, and hence promoted active discontent among the citizens. In a town as new as Birmingham industry had never been subjected to old corporative rules possessing the force of law. It had become in consequence, during the 17th century, an asylum for the dissenters who were the object of persecution in the corporate towns. After a temporary outbreak of anti-Jacobin feeling, the workmen returned to their former democratic spirit, and revolted in the beginning of the 19th century for the same reasons which would have roused them to revolt at the time of the Cromwellian republic or the Revolution of 1688. London was even less than Birmingham a city of large factories. The workmen of Westminster could not be said to have any wide experience of the direct competition of machinery. Nevertheless, there was perpetual discontent among these workmen, who were for the most part cobblers, tailors or bricklayers. Strike followed strike. The reason was that, like Birmingham, London was a city of revolutionary traditions. The time-honoured custom of political agitation explains why the London workman adopted the attitude of a rebel even in the field of his strictly economic interests.

We have now determined the main characteristics of the industries with which we have been dealing above. What, then, are the conclusions which have resulted from this analysis? In the first place we have found that, in this field at any rate, the introduction of machinery had not, as is commonly supposed, fostered directly a spirit of revolution. Neither in the mines nor even in the foundries had technical improvements sensibly affected either the size of the undertaking or the organization of labour. We have found, in the second place, that in many industries the introduction of machinery had not even begun, and that the system of division of labour and of the small workshop survived in its integrity. It is, of course, true that all these industries had suffered indirectly from the economic crises through which the industrial and financial world had been passing almost continuously during the last twenty years. But the really important point is the attitude adopted by the workmen towards the causes of their sufferings. The revolutionary spirit which animated the Birmingham artisan was due rather to ethical and political than to strictly economic causes. On the contrary, despite the disturbances which broke out in the mines and foundries in 1815 and 1816, no Englishman, at the date of the restoration of peace, would have been inclined to regard the mining and ironworking districts as hotbeds of industrial discontent. By the year 1815 the entire series of phenomena characteristic of the industrial revolution had as yet appeared only in certain manufactures of a particular type—manufactures few in number but important owing to the quantity of labour employed. These phenomena consisted in the entire transformation of the mechanism of manufacture, a sudden alteration of the relations previously existing between masters and men, and popular risings caused directly by the break-up of the old economic order.

TEXTILE AND SIMILAR INDUSTRIES.

Machinery in the Textile Industries. Cotton Manufacture.

The leading feature of the industrial revolution was undoubtedly the establishment of large factories in which all the motive power was supplied by a single mechanism installed in the centre of the factory, and looked after by a large number of hands working under the supervision of one man. It was in the silk manufacture that the first signs of this revolution had appeared. Three-quarters of a century had already passed since the day when a traveller, on a tour through England, had seen near Derby, on an island in the Derwent, an enormous building, 500 feet in length, six stories high, and lit by 460 windows, in which the brothers Lombe were throwing silk. The machine, whose parts were set in action by one large wheel, turned by the power of the stream, contained, he tells us, " 26,586 Wheels, and 97,746 Movements, which work 73,726 Yards of Silk-Thread every time the Water-Wheel goes round, which is three times in one minute." [1] Nevertheless, the manufacture of silk had not prospered in England. Not only was it obliged to obtain its raw material from abroad (this was also the case with the cotton manufacture, which enjoyed great prosperity), but it had, moreover, to obtain it from France and Italy, where the inhabitants spun and wove raw silk themselves. It was in vain that the English manufacturers had attempted to secure their profits by lowering wages. The Spitalfields weavers had risen in revolt, and had secured in 1773 the passage of statutes which gave the old corporate customs the force of law, and thereby affirmed the principle of a fixed wage determined by the public authorities.[2] In the north, where the new towns were strangers to the guild system, and where waterfalls supplied the mills with motive power, silk manufacture had been ousted by the manufacture of cotton.

This latter industry was, indeed, better adapted to the new conditions of manufacture, which consisted in the production and sale, in very large quantities, of cheap goods of everyday use. It had therefore grown with truly fabulous rapidity. The weight of raw

---

[1] Defoe, *A Tour through . . . Great Britain . . .*, ed. 1742, vol. iii. p. 67.
[2] 13 Geo. III, cap. 68. Completed by 32 Geo. III, cap. 44 and 51 ; Geo. III, cap. 7. For the " Spitalfields Acts," see L. Brentano, *History . . . of Guilds*, p. 127.

cotton employed in the manufacture had exceeded 30,000,000 pounds in 1790, and 50,000,000 in 1801. In 1805 it exceeded 90,000,00 pounds,[1] and in 1810 the figure of 123,701,826 pounds had been reached The total value of woven fabrics exported had risen from £5,407,000 in 1800 to £18,426,000 in 1809, and in 1815 had reached the sum of £21,480,792.[2] In former times the woollen manufacture had been the principal source of England's industrial wealth, but the manufacture of cotton goods now held the first place. In 1814, Colquhoun estimated the wealth produced annually by the cotton manufacturers at £23,000,000, the wealth produced by the woollen manufacturers at £18,000,000.[3] Lancashire, the seat of cotton manufacture, became the classic ground of the new industrial capitalism.

The raw cotton was unloaded at Liverpool and sold by local brokers to Manchester manufacturers.[4] Business was transacted very quickly, and scrupulous honesty prevailed in the market. The cotton was bought after the inspection of a sample, frauds were of very rare occurrence, and disputes between vendor and purchaser were settled immediately by impartial arbitrators. The raw cotton was brought to Manchester by water, and then underwent in the mills the series of operations which made it into thread suitable for weaving. The fibres were opened and cleaned by the scratching machine, spread out and rolled by the spreading machine, drawn and combed by the carding machine and the roving frame, and finally dealt with by Crompton's mule—a machine whose invention, forty years earlier, had marked the turning-point in the history of the manufacture.[5]

After the abortive experiments of Wyatt and Paul, there had followed a series of decisive inventions, all comprised within the short period of a single decade, namely the years between 1766 and 1775. The common feature of the processes invented by Hargreaves, Arkwright and Crompton was the production, by means of a rotatory movement, of the series of movements required to draw and twist the cotton. This rotatory movement could be obtained by the use of a machine, a "mill," for which the motive power was furnished either by horses,[6] or dogs turning a wheel,[7] or by the current of a stream. "In the year, I think, 1796," wrote a traveller, "being particularly captivated with the romantic scenery of Matlock, we stayed a week or ten days there. In the course of a forenoon's ride, I discovered, in a romantic valley, a palace of a

[1] These figures were obtained by Porter, *Progerss of the Nation*, p. 347, by deducting from the amount of raw cotton imported the amount that was again exported.

[2] Baines, *History of Cotton Manufacture*, p. 350. As he takes the " official value " which was fixed for a given weight, his statistics furnish us with reliable information as to the variations in the quantity exported.

[3] Colquhoun, *Wealth . . . of British Empire*, p. 91.

[4] Baines, *History of Cotton Manufacture*, pp. 318–19.

[5] For the entire series of operations see Baines, *History of Cotton Manufacture*, pp. 241 sqq.

[6] Kennedy, *Rise and Progress*, p. 121.

[7] Baines, *Lancashire*, vol. ii. p. 554 ; Mantoux, *Revolution Industrie!le*, p. 238.

most enormous size, having, at least, a score of windows of a row, and five or six stories in height. This was Sir Richard Arkwright's (then Mr. Arkwright) cotton mills " [1] Arkwright had fled from the hostility displayed by the Lancashire workmen towards the new processes, and had established himself in that very county of Derbyshire in which formerly another traveller had contemplated with amazement the silk factory of the Lombe brothers. We may add that Arkwright's example was followed shortly afterwards by Hargreaves. Derbyshire was a country of steep inclines and abundant water power. Nottingham, the centre of the hosiery manufacture, was conveniently near, and needed cotton thread. However, Lancashire itself and the western slopes of the Scottish Lowlands presented to an even greater extent the advantages afforded by the banks of the Derwent for the establishment of spinning mills. Not only were rivers plentiful, but these districts were also close to the ports where the raw cotton arrived from America. The mill owners gradually triumphed over the opposition of the workmen. On the model of the Derbyshire spinning mills, and often with Arkwright's financial assistance, spinning mills sprang up on the banks of the Clyde around Glasgow, and around Manchester on the banks of the Irwell, " the hardest worked river in the universe." [2]

The time soon came when manufacturers were no longer satisfied with water power. The amount of water in a river varied in different years, and at different seasons of the year. Moreover, the number of mills had so multiplied that in order to increase and to equalize the pressure of water, every mill captured the stream in a reservoir, letting the water out again after it had done its work. This made it impossible in any establishment to work for more than a certain number of hours a day—namely, the hours during which the water was flowing in from the reservoir upstream. Every day the need of a more constant power was being felt with greater intensity. In 1781 Watt invented at Birmingham a method of employing steam to produce a circular motion. Four years later the first spinning mill driven by steam was set up in the county of Nottingham ; and from 1790 onwards the invention spread rapidly throughout the two cotton-weaving districts, Lanarkshire and Lancashire. The geological conditions were favourable. In both counties coal was so cheap that it had been for a long time past in daily use among the poor, both for cooking their food and warming their cottages. If we consider what was the exact area in Lancashire which was being occupied by cotton manufactures, we shall find that it coincided almost exactly with the colliery district.[3] By 1815 the trans-

---

[1] *Correspondence of Sir John Sinclair*, vol. i. p. 361, Geo. Dempster's letter, January 21, 1800.
[2] W. Cooke Taylor, *Handbook* . . ., 1843, p. 156.
[3] Preston formed the almost solitary exception. See Baines, *Lancashire*, vol. iv. p. 366 : " A combination of causes has doubtless conspired to produce this effect, but the principal are probably to be found in the central situation of the town, in the united advantages of river and canal navigation, and in the skill, capital and enterprise of the principal manufacturers."

formation of the plant employed in cotton manufacture was practically complete. Machinery, driven either by water or by steam, had replaced the hand loom.[1]

The number and size of the factories were increasing at the same time. Before the introduction of machinery there had only been forty-one spinning mills in the whole of Lancashire,[2] in 1816 there were over sixty in the Manchester district alone.[3] Two of these employed over a 1,000 men, the sixty together about 24,000.[4] According to an estimate made a little later every workman implied a previous expenditure on machinery of some £100.[5] Therefore a total capital of over £20,000,000 must have been sunk in the mills of this district. According to another contemporary estimate, made in 1817, 110,000,000 pounds of raw cotton were converted annually into 99,687,500 pounds of cotton thread. It was calculated that this output required 300 working days in the year, 6,645,833 spindles, 110,763 workmen and 20,768 horse power.[6]

Robert Owen's *Memoirs* present us with a vivid picture of this epoch of feverish activity.[7] His account of Manchester between 1790 and 1800 reminds us of a newly founded colony, into which a stream of immigrants is constantly pouring. Here the immigrants consisted of the most enterprising and most adventurous elements of the population of England. The founders of factories were almost all men of humble origin—yeomen or farmers of the neighbourhood, small shopkeepers or artisans, sometimes ordinary workmen.[8] For wealth, while it civilizes, softens and enervates. A man who was not of the common people would not have had sufficient energy—brutality, if you prefer it—to triumph over the violent resistance opposed by the mass of the local population, to the execution of his designs. When the factory had been built it was always in danger of being burnt or looted on the first industrial crisis by the workmen of the neighbourhood. On such occasions the manufacturer must turn it into a citadel and spend days

---

Baines, however, adds that the harbour was by no means good (*ibid.*, p. 361). The town chiefly owed its prosperity (the number of inhabitants was doubled between 1801 and 1821) to Horrocks and others like him.

[1] *Report . . . on . . . State of Children*, 1816, *Minutes of Evidence*, p. 207. The evidence given by Kinder Wood, an Oldham surgeon : " Are there any spinners who work in their own houses ?—They do in some cases use a small machine, which they call a Twining Jenny, in their own houses ; but I am not acquainted with the peculiar mechanism of this business."

[2] Baines, *History of Lancashire*, vol. ii. p. 462.

[3] *Report . . . on . . . State of Children*, 1816. In Manchester, Salford, Hulme and Charlton there were sixty-four, according to Mr. G. A. Lee (p. 357 [fifty-two in 1802]) ; seventy according to another witness, Mr. Nathaniel Gould.

[4] *Ibid.*, pp. 372–3.

[5] Holland Hoole, *Letter to Lord Althorp, in Defence of Cotton Factories*, p. 5, quoted in Baines, *Lancashire*, vol. ii. p. 154.

[6] J. Kennedy, *Rise and Progress*, p. 154.

[7] *Life of Robert Owen*, pp. 21 sqq.

[8] P. Gaskell, *Artisans and Machinery*, p. 33 : " Few of the men who entered the trade rich were successful."

and nights under arms. Sometimes he was obliged to yield, and built another factory in a district not yet industrialized, where he had not to fear the hostility of artisans, the artisans of an old-established manufacture. Power, however, and wealth were the reward of final success. Two hundred, 500, even 1,000 workmen would be employed by the successful manufacturer. By the side of his factory would soon rise a mansion, whose magnificent façade and ostentatious furniture hurled defiance at the old families, who were being swamped by the rising flood of this new civilization.

The magistrates and squires, who were the natural rulers of the districts, and their dependents and allies the farmers, complained that the multiplication of factories filled the country with paupers, and thus increased the poor rate at their expense. Whenever a riot broke out, in which the factories and houses of these parvenus were threatened, the secret sympathies of the landowners were often with the rioters, and the magistrate, though refusing to afford direct encouragement to the rioters, would at least shut his eyes, parade his powerlessness to act, and let things take their course.[1] Nevertheless, throughout all this period of crises and riots the manufacture of cotton was constantly spreading. The landed gentry had no choice but to vanish from the district or come to terms with their conquerors.

Life in the Spinning Mills. Masters and Men.

The factories contained vast masses of workmen working under the orders of the great manufacturers. It would be inaccurate to term them indiscriminately a proletariat, in the Marxian and revolutionary sense of the word. On the contrary, one effect of the introduction into the mills of machinery driven either by water or steam power had been to divide the workers into two distinct classes. There were a certain number of highly paid workmen who needed to understand the machinery employed in the manufacture of cotton thread— a machinery which was becoming every day more complicated. The weekly wage of a spinner ranged from £1 10s. to £1 17s.[2] Thus the foundations were already laid in the Lancashire mills of the future trade unions of this district, which were to be the admiration, fifty or sixty years later, of all the conservative economists of England and the Continent. There were also a mass of workers to whom the progress of mechanism had left no other work than that of watching a machine

---

[1] The reason put forward by the Government for the exclusive selection of the magistrates from the landowners was that, if taken from the trade, they could not act as impartial judges in disputes between employers and men. H. of C., May 12, 1813, Romilly's question and Bathurst's reply (*Parl. Deb.*, vol. xxvi. pp. 100–1).

[2] Baines, *History of Lancashire*, vol. ii. p. 510. G. Wood (*History of Wages in the Cotton Trade . . .*, 1910) gives a higher rate of wages for those who spun the thread of specially fine quality (1804, 32s. 6d.–36s. 6d. ; 1810, 42s. 6d. ; 1814, 44s. 6d.–60s.).

—a " mechanical " task indeed.[1] To place the cotton in the machine, to take off the thread when ready, to bind it together when it broke : occupations such as these required but little strength or intelligence. Women and children could be employed in such work. They were naturally more timid and easier to rule ; their slender and more pliant fingers were better adapted to the tasks required of them ; their shorter stature made it possible to place them in corners, and underneath machines where a man neither could nor would consent to be placed. Moreover, their wages were lower. For these reasons female and child labour was gradually substituted to an enormous extent for the labour of adult males. Of 10,000 hands employed in 1816 by forty-one Scottish mills, only 3,146 were males and 6,854 were females—4,581 were children, male or female, below the age of eighteen. For forty-eight Manchester mills an estimate of the same period gives the practically identical pro-portion of 6,687 adults to 6,253 children.[2] That is to say, there were twice as many women as men, and almost as many children as adults.

The wretched condition to which these women and children had been reduced was made public by the parliamentary inquiry of 1816, as also by the more detailed and thorough inquiries of 1832 and 1833. The children of the district were not enough, and others, were, therefore brought in from outside. They came from distant counties and from Ireland—sold by their parents. The workhouses of the large towns, even of London, sent their pauper children to the Lancashire work-houses. They were put to work in the mills, where the employer had only to provide them with food and clothing. On entering a mill, these children became exposed to a twofold exploitation by the employer and by the adult workman, better paid than themselves, under whose orders they worked. The day was long, interminably long. Children under ten years of age, often only six or even only four or five years old, had to work twelve, sixteen, seventeen, even eighteen hours a day. If the supply of water happened to fail, or something went wrong with the steam engine, the employer made up afterwards for the lost time. He gave the hands their choice between a reduction of their wages to correspond with the days of enforced idleness, and overtime work to compensate for the time lost. The millhand could scarcely refuse the latter alternative. The wage for this overtime work was offered to the children themselves, not to their parents, and of course proved an irresistible attraction. The overseers of the workhouses, whose duty it was to lodge the children during the night, deposed that they were obliged to keep them under lock and key to prevent them from running away, and obliged also, when work was over for the

---

[1] " No labour . . . watching " (*Report . . . on . . . State of Children*, 1816, p. 9). This passage deals, indeed, with weaving—not with spinning.

[2] P. Gaskell, *Artisans and Machinery*, p. 142 ; *Report . . . on State of Children*, 1816, pp. 240 sqq.

day, to make the round of the mills to collect those who had fallen asleep in corners, worn out by sheer fatigue. They slept at their work, upright beside the dangerous machines, which were constantly injuring and maiming them. They could scarcely snatch the time to devour a meal abominably cooked on the boiler itself. Sometimes in the worst managed factories the millhand was obliged to eat as best he could while he worked. The atmosphere of the workshops had to be kept moist—to prevent the cotton threads, stretched on the machines, from breaking. The workers were soaked to the skin ; and in cold weather their garments froze to their backs, as they were returning home.

Men, women and children of both sexes were herded together in the factories, at work in an overheated atmosphere which excited the sexual instinct. It was not to be expected that the women, who lived promiscuously like beasts with their male companions, would offer much resistance to the desires of the foreman, or of the factory owner himself, or of his sons, who from the age of fifteen or sixteen were placed in the mill with full authority to command and punish. In 1828 Francis Place told d'Eichthal, the Saint Simonian, that when a friend of his visited a Lancashire mill, the owner had bid him take his choice among the mill girls.[1] At night the streets of Manchester presented a disgusting spectacle. It was quite common for the mill girls, with their husbands' connivance, to eke out their scanty wages by prostitution.[2]

One would naturally have expected, as the result of all this misery and degradation, that the race would rapidly degenerate and that the population of England would be destroyed by the development of the factory system, as the aborigines of Australia and New Zealand are being destroyed by contact with European civilization. This, however, was by no means the case. About 1775 it was still possible to find economists who maintained that the population was decreasing. Twenty years later, however, when Malthus wrote his famous *Essay on the Principle of Population*, the marvellous success of his book proves that the surplusage of the population was a phenomenon patent to all observers. Shortly afterwards, with the new century, began the series of decennial censuses ; and every ten years Malthus could appeal to the official statistics as an experimental proof of his thesis.

Undoubtedly this growth of population could be explained in two different ways. It might be explained by an increase in the birth rate, in which case a temporary growth of population would have harmonized

---

[1] *Condition de la Class ouvrière en Angleterre* (1828), *Notes de Voyage de Gustave d'Eichthal* (*Revue Historique*, vol. lxxiv. 1902).

[2] J. T. Barber, *A Tour throughout South Wales*, p. 140 n. : " In Manchester . . . an almost promiscuous intercourse prevails in the great mass of the people ; insomuch that the magistrates attempt to check the increase of bastard children by inflicting stripes and imprisonment on the women who bear above a certain number."

perfectly with an enfeeblement of the race. The conditions of life for the worker in a great industry, with no possessions and no care for the morrow ; a Poor Law which compelled society to keep the children of an indigent workman ; factories, larger and more numerous every day, which demanded thousands of children : all these were causes directly favourable to the growth of population. But this growth could be explained equally well by the lowering of the death rate. According to trustworthy statistics, gathered in a manufacturing district, the death rate in 1780 amounted to a fortieth of the population. It was only a fifty-fourth in 1810, and was to fall to a sixtieth by 1830.[1] Surely this was the result of an improvement of the public health. When all is said and done, we can hardly deny that the conditions of life among the poorer classes were even worse before the establishment of the factories than they were in 1815. We must beware of regarding a paler colour, less developed muscles and a greater precocity as infallible signs of racial decadence.   For a purely rural healthiness was substituted a new type of healthiness, in harmony with the new environment which was being created by industrialism for an ever-increasing number of Englishmen.   Undoubtedly new and deep-seated causes of misery had come into being.   Nevertheless, if the factory system tended to revolu- tion this was mainly because it concentrated the misery of the lower classes in a few large towns, where it was exposed to the universal gaze and became a public scandal.   Already in 1815 English society had begun to seek and to devise remedies for the evils for which it felt itself responsible.

The progress of machinery was of itself a remedy. We shall soon see what the life of the common artisan had become in the period im- mediately preceding the introduction of the factory system.   At present we will simply point out certain features of the new technical inventions which rendered possible an improvement in the hygienic conditions of those engaged in manufacture. The wooden houses which were soon saturated with oil and became perfect hotbeds of infection were replaced by an enormous iron building, whose very structure was healthier.[2] The system of overtime was one of the worst methods by which the employer could exploit his men, though practised with their apparent consent. It was, however, chiefly in the factories where water power was employed that this was in a certain sense in- evitable. Where steam took the place of water the millhands could, and to a certain extent did, escape this oppression. Where a stream drove the mill wheel, every manufacturer was obliged to wait till the factories further upstream let the water escape. Hence there were periods of enforced idleness, which varied in length according to the

[1] *Statement of Progress under the Population Act*, pp. 14–15.   For the period between 1780 and 1800, cf. Porter, *Progress of the Nation*, ed. 1851, pp. 20 sqq.

[2] P. Gaskell, *Artisans and Machinery*, 1836, p. 141.

amount of water in the stream at a particular time.[1] Then the water poured in, and while it was flowing, to leave it unemployed was to lose money. There was, therefore, a time of forced labour, during which the millhand worked as many hours as the factory owner demanded, in order thus to regain the money lost in the hours of inaction. When the steam engine was introduced, it could work day and night almost without intermission. It was, of course, impossible to demand from the millhands twenty hours' work every day. Henceforward two relays would divide the day and night between them, each relay working eleven hours. It appeared from every inquiry that the sweating was worse in the small factories than in those of considerable size. The small manufacturer could only maintain his position if he compensated for the inadequacy of his plant by lowering wages. The large manufacturer, on the other hand, scorned, and paraded his scorn of these paltry economies. He knew that well-paid hands, debarred from intemperance, and over whom a certain moral supervision was exercised, produced more in the long run than a rabble of drunken slaves.[2] He knew that on the whole the best advertisement for the products of his factory was a large mill, airy and well built, where he could display to visitors the ingenious devices which he had adopted for the ventilation of the workshops. He also knew that, as the importance of a business increases, more money must be spent on advertising. The large manufacturer was, therefore, induced to play the philanthropist by motives which we may well regard as strictly economic.[3] But there were further motives which conspired with these to produce the same effects.

There was, in the first place, social snobbery. The manufacturer who had made his fortune sought admission into the ranks of the local gentry, to whom he felt himself an object of suspicion. The constitution of English society opposed no insuperable barrier to the realization of his ambition. The landowners could not, after all, be quite hostile to an industry which was enriching the district so rapidly. The rise of the poor rate was certainly vexatious, but was compensated by the rise of land values. A farm of 100 acres counted for very little, but when this insignificant piece of land became the site of an entire suburb of some large town, the owner found his property better worth having.[4] The landowners were, moreover, in need of wealthy men to fill certain honourable but extremely costly posts, and to perform certain

---

[1] *Report . . . on . . . State of Children*, 1816, p. 116.

[2] *First Report of Commissioners . . . as to Employment of Children in Factories*, 1833, p. 200 : "It appears that in Scotland and in the eastern districts of England, where the harshest treatment of children has taken place, the greatest number of bad cases occur in the small obscure mills belonging to the smallest proprietors."

[3] See the characteristic evidence given by Richard Arkwright before the Parliamentary Committee of 1816 (*Report . . . on . . . State of Children*, 1816, pp. 277 sqq.), as also his letter to the Committee, June 10, 1816 (*ibid.*, p. 306).

[4] J. Kennedy, *Rise and Progress*, pp. 121-3.

obligatory functions both judicial and administrative—to become "sheriffs" in the counties, magistrates in the large towns. They were also divided politically into two opposing parties. We have already seen how, during the last thirty years, the Tories had sometimes profited by utilizing industrial parvenus to destroy the preponderance of the great Whig families. But the manufacturer desirous of being smuggled in among the members of the ruling aristocracy must be prepared to make some pecuniary sacrifices to obtain his ambition. The sight of an ill-kept factory, full of debauched and drunken hands, was offensive to the beholder and occasioned slanderous reports. If the factory had been set up at a distance from the towns the factory owner would be well advised to make his factory a model factory, to erect decent-looking cottages for his workmen, and to appear as a patriarch ruling peacefully over his tribe, or a great landowner administering his estate. The ability which had made him his fortune would now be directed to the skilful expenditure of that fortune in the interests of a social and political career. If he wished to pass as a leader of society, he had to learn to spend lavishly the wealth which he had made, in order thereby to cast a veil of oblivion over the methods, often dishonourable enough, which he had originally employed in order to make it.

Besides this snobbery another motive influenced the ideas and actions of the large manufacturers—a motive which also made for the improvement of the conditions under which the workers lived and toiled. This was evangelical zeal. An important religious revival, which has exercised a profound influence over the whole of modern England, had been spreading a rejuvenated Protestantism, a new Puritanism, throughout the manufacturing districts of the north-west. No Church, however, can be successful except by coming to terms with the Devil. The evangelicalism of Wesley and Whitefield, in many respects remorselessly fanatical, had learnt to adapt itself to the economic requirements of North-west England, and displayed the greatest indulgence towards all the business methods of the speculative financier or promoter. Here also a fusion took place between two opposed tendencies. There came into existence a class of austere men, hard workers and greedy of gain, who considered it their twofold duty to make a fortune in business and to preach Christ crucified. This class had its hypocrites, but it had also its saints—zealous philanthropists, who were, moreover, possessed of the practical turn of mind which enabled them to effect their schemes of benevolence without self-impoverishment.

The Strutts of Belper in Derbyshire,[1] the Ashtons of Hyde in Cheshire, and the Dales of Lanark on the Clyde enjoyed universal respect. Dale, who was soon assisted by his son-in-law, Robert Owen, employed 1,700 hands in his spinning mill, which was, indeed, the liveli-

[1] For the Strutts, see *Memoirs, Journal and Correspondence of Thomas Moore*, vol. ii. p. 315, Thomas Moore to Miss Dalby Mayfield, 1814.

hood of all the 3,000 inhabitants of the village of Lanark. They were lodged in cottages specially built for them at Dale's expense, and bought their food from a shop where he sold at cost price provisions of good quality. No children were put to work before the age of ten, and even then their working day did not exceed ten hours. A school was opened, attendance at which was optional for little children, compulsory for children over the age of ten.[1] Perhaps, however, all this tutelage was found galling by some workmen. They were well treated but felt the lack of liberty, and regretted their original savagery. In 1816, in the course of a parliamentary inquiry, a large manufacturer of the neighbourhood was asked whether many workpeople left the New Lanark factory to take work in his employment. He replied in the affirmative. When asked the reason of this, he answered, on the authority of a workwoman who had just arrived from New Lanark, "There had been," she had informed the witness, "a number of new regulations introduced. They had got a number of dancing-masters, a fiddler, a band of music, there were drills and exercises, and they were dancing together till they were more fatigued than if they were working." [2] It cannot, however, be denied that the factory system, for the very reason that it was despotic, did in some instances lead to the establishment of a discipline organized in the interest of philanthropy.

The combined influence of all these motives is visible in the campaign which had been carried on since the closing years of the 18th century against the ill-usage to which children were subject in factories. Manufacturers who had improved the conditions of labour in their own establishments were indisposed to tolerate in the factories of their neighbours the abuses suppressed by themselves.[3] A full thirty years before the first appearance of modern Socialism they realized that the factory system lent itself to legal interference, and to a systematic inspection which had been impossible under the system of handloom and home industry. They demanded accordingly the intervention of the State to equalize the conditions of the economic struggle between themselves and their competitors. Moreover, when, in 1802, Sir Robert Peel, a big manufacturer of cotton goods and a member of the House of Commons, introduced and secured the passage of the first Act for the regulation of child labour, he was conscious, more or less distinctly, that his initiative was strengthening his position in Parlia-

---

[1] *Reports of the Society for Bettering the Condition of the People*, vol. ii. pp. 367 sqq. Extract from an account of Mr. Dale's cotton mills at New Lanark, in Scotland, by Thomas Bernard, Esq.

[2] *Report . . . on . . . State of Children*, 1816, p. 167, Mr. Adam Bogle's evidence.

[3] *Reports of the Society for Bettering the Condition of the Poor*, vol. iv. Appendix, No. I. Report of a Select Committee of the Society upon some Observations on the late Act respecting Cotton Mills . . . p. 9 : " It has not been alleged that grievances do exist in *all* Cotton Mills. The Committee has a pleasure in stating that many are now worked in conformity to the principles of the late Act of Parliament. . . . From the practical experience of those Mills the regulations of the late Act were framed."

ment.   His influence was proved by the passage of his Bill.   He won the respect and approval of Wilberforce and his " Evangelical " followers, who possessed at that time considerable authority with the Government.   For they were the philanthropists who had created the movement of public opinion, of which he now made himself the mouthpiece in Parliament—Manchester doctors anxious for the public health, pious Christians scandalized by the gross immorality to be witnessed in the mills.[1]

Sir Robert Peel's Bill [2] fixed at twelve hours the maximum working day for child apprentices sent into the mills by workhouses.   Night work was prohibited.   They were to receive daily a certain rudimentary instruction, for which the necessary time was to be deducted from the hours of work.   We have been warned by certain historians not to exaggerate the importance of a statute which was simply an amendment of the Poor Law.   The Report, however, of the debates which preceded its adoption is ample proof that the legislators were fully aware how important was the step they were taking.[3]   Why not have recourse, demanded certain opponents of the measure, to the old methods of regulating labour, and limit the number of apprentices ?   The objection clearly shows, replied Sir Robert, that the objectors knew nothing of the new industrial conditions.   That the cotton manufacture was superior to the woollen manufacture was owing precisely to the fact that it was not trammelled by the old regulations limiting the number of apprentices.   Other opponents, over-zealous for the new policy—Evangelicals such as Wilberforce and Lord Belgrave—asked why the operation of the new statute should be confined to the cotton manufacture and not extended to other manufactures, or why pauper children alone should be protected and not all children employed in cotton mills.   It would not do, replied Sir Robert, to compromise the safety of the Bill by attempting too much.   As it was, the leading manufacturers in the North were beginning to agitate against it.

Finally the Bill became law.   Was the Law carried into execution ? Only too often the magistrates neglected their duty, or were actually ignorant of the obligations imposed upon them by the new statute. The overseers, elected annually in each parish to secure the proper

---

[1] Hutchins and Harrison, *History of Factory Legislation*, pp. 7 sqq.   *Report . . . on . . . State of Children*, 1816, *Minutes of Evidence*, p. 135, Sir Robert Peel's evidence : " I was the first person that was employed in bringing (the general regulation of cotton work) under the attention of Parliament, but the subject had been discussed for years before, at Manchester, at London and at other places."

[2] 42 Geo. III, cap. 73.

[3] H. of C., April 6, May 4, 18, June 2, 1802 (*Parliamentary Register*, vol. lxxix. p. 446 ; vol. lxxx. pp. 183, 457, 590).   See also, in the Report of the Sitting of March 15, 1802, a *Bill* brought in by Mr. Wilbraham Bootle, " that the overseers of the different parishes should be compelled to keep registers of the names of the persons to whom parish children were appriticed, the names of the parishes whither they were sent, etc., under certain penalties " (*Parliamentary Register*, vol. lxxix. p. 199).

administration of the Poor Law, had neither the time nor the capacity, often not even the desire to enforce the execution of this special statute.[1] It is true that the abuses condemned by the Act of 1802 tended to some extent to disappear. This was, however, due to the fact that the introduction of the steam engine was concentrating the spinning mills in the large towns, where child labour was plentiful, and where there was consequently no need to obtain it from the workhouses of the entire land.[2] These children, however, of the large manufacturing towns were surely no less worthy of public attention because they were not actually the wards of the parishes and the State.[3] It was, indeed, impossible to neglect for long the objection raised in 1802 by Wilberforce and Lord Belgrave. Another philanthropic factory owner, Robert Owen, persuaded Sir Robert Peel to complete his Act of 1802,[4] by introducing in the Commons on June 6, 1815, a new Bill, which applied to all children employed in any factory, where the raw material of the manufacture was either cotton, wool or flax. The employment of children below the age of ten was absolutely prohibited, and a working day of ten hours and a half was fixed for all workers under eighteen years of age. Half an hour of compulsory instruction was to be given daily. A body of paid visitors was to be appointed to secure the execution of these provisions. Such was the character of the project. It was not to be adopted definitely till 1819 and then only in a very mutilated form.[5] This, however, mattered little. The foundations were being laid of a new code of industrial legislation, adapted to the needs of the factory system. The originators, moreover, of this legislation, which was being gradually built up, were the leading manufacturers themselves.

We have perhaps somewhat over-emphasized the attempts made since the opening of the century by philanthropists and Members of Parliament to introduce some measure of legal protection of labour in the cotton mills. Certainly up to 1815 such efforts had borne very little fruit. Nevertheless, something had been done, and it was thereby

---

[1] *Report . . . on . . . State of Children*, 1816, pp. 178 sqq. The evidence of John Moss, governor of the Preston workhouse : " Do you know of an Act of Parliament prohibiting the employment of apprentices in cotton work above twelve hours a day ?—No, I never heard anything of that " (*ibid.*, p. 329). Evidence of William David Evans, Esq., J.P. : " Are you aware that the Act of Parliament, generally called by the name of Sir Robert Peel's Act, directs the appointment of certain inspectors by the magistrates, one of them to be a magistrate and the other a clergyman ?—Yes. Has that provision been put in force in Manchester ?— I have only been aware of that provision since reading the Act yesterday." In 1804 Wilberforce had introduced, at the request of fifty " respectable and experienced magistrates of the county of York," a Bill to increase the powers of control enjoyed by the Bench (H. of C., May 8, 1804, *Parl. Deb.*, vol. ii. p. 397).

[2] *Report . . . on . . . State of Children*, 1816, pp. 132, 137, 141. Sir Robert Peel's evidence.

[3] A further Act was passed in 1816, imposing stricter conditions on the apprenticing of pauper children (56 Geo. III, cap. 139).

[4] *Life of Robert Owen*, pp. 115 sqq.   [5] 59 Geo. III, cap. 66.

proved that something could be done. There were more difficult problems to be solved, the position of the workman was more unfortunate, and his spirit more revolutionary, in those branches of the cotton manufacture in which machinery, in the proper sense of the term, had either not been introduced at all or was as yet in its infancy.

Cotton Weaving.

Cotton was combed, carded, slubbed, and spun in large factories. It was also in large factories that the cotton fabrics, once woven, were bleached, dyed and colour-printed. But in 1815 the actual weaving was still done almost entirely by hand. How are we to account for this solitary survival of hand-loom weaving when, in all other branches of the same industry, machinery had successfully ousted the handicraftsman ? We have already had occasion to notice that the universal employment of women and children in spinning mills was throwing out of work an ever-increasing number of adult male workmen. They had to obtain a living somehow or other, and their very destitution kept hand-weaving in existence. The scantiness of the wage with which they were content enabled them to compete with machinery.[1] Nevertheless, although we may well admit that this cause was operative, we can hardly believe that it was preponderant. A further cause was that the number of weavers bore too large a proportion to the number of spinners. In 1811 it was calculated by one witness that in the town and suburbs of Manchester there were 12,000 weavers as against only 9,000 spinners.[2] The poverty-stricken weavers of Lancashire were not even indirectly the victims of machinery. It would, on the contrary, be nearer the truth to say that the fear inspired by their threats and numbers was the real cause why machinery was not introduced earlier into this department.[3] If we would understand how it was

---

[1] P. Gaskell, *Artisans and Machinery*, 1836, p. 33.

[2] *Report . . . on . . . Petitions of several Weavers*, 1811, p. 2, Joseph Hanson's evidence. Cf. *Report . . . on Petitions of several Cotton Manufacturers and Journeymen Cotton Weavers*, 1808. Evidence of James Atherton, a Bolton weaver, p. 24 : " Would you wish to turn manufacturer yourself ?—I would not, to injure the weavers ; they are the greatest bodies in Yorkshire, Cheshire, Cumberland, Lancashire, and some other counties." Cf. the figures given by G. H. Wood, *The Statistics of Wages . . . the Cotton Industry*, in the *Journal of Royal Statistical Society*, 1910, p. 596.

[3] Other reasons have been adduced to explain the long survival of hand-weaving. Attempt have been made to explain it in the same way as the sweating system of our own time is explained. The progress of machinery led to such lowering of wages, that the artisans were able to maintain a struggle against the competition of machinery only by working for a starvation wage (Mantoux, *Révolution Industrielle*, pp. 239, 240). But, in the first place, the progress made by machinery up to 1815 was insufficient to permit of this theory. Why, moreover, do we find this phenomenon in cotton weaving and not also in cotton spinning ? It is also alleged that the growth of the large-farm system in rural districts caused an influx into the manufacturing towns of workers compelled by poverty to accept any pittance rather than die of starvation (*Report . . . on Petitions of several Cotton Manufacturers and Journeymen Cotton Weavers*, 1808, p. 25, evidence of James Atherton, a Bolton weaver. *Report . . . on*

that in cotton weaving the hand loom stood out so long against machinery, we must consider the history of the technical inventions which gave rise to the English cotton manufacture, the order in which the several inventions took place, and the intervals between them.

In spinning, the rate of production had been accelerated by two distinct classes of inventions. To speak accurately, the machines were either looms set in motion by the human hand or automatic devices driven by water or steam power. Hargreaves' jenny was a loom, Arkwright's water-frame a machine in the stricter sense, Crompton's mule a loom. These inventions of equal ingenuity, but of a different nature, took place almost simultaneously. In the spinning mills the introduction of the perfected loom was contemporaneous with the introduction of the power machine. Only three years separated Hargreaves' invention from that of Arkwright ; Arkwright's invention took place eleven years before Crompton's. Moreover, both Hargreaves' jenny and Crompton's mule were so constructed as to admit of easy adaptation to machinery driven by water or steam. Eleven years after Crompton's invention Kelly invented a means of making the mule automatic.[1] In weaving, however, inventions followed an entirely different course. In 1733 John Kay had patented his fly-shuttle, which enabled a weaver to turn out with his loom larger and more numerous pieces of cloth than before. It was not until 1785—fifty-two years later, that Edmund Cartwright patented his machine for the automatic weaving of cloth. In the interval a powerful industry had grown up, based on the employment of the fly-shuttle. The result was that when, towards the close of the 18th century, attempts were made to introduce machinery, the problem was not the same for the weaver as for the spinner. In the spinning mills it was simply a matter of constructing a new plant. For the weavers, however, the change involved the complete sacrifice of the old plant, in which much capital had been sunk. It was surely but natural that the forces of resistance should be much stronger in this department and that the critical period of change should be far longer and should entail far greater suffering.

It was in 1785 that Cartwright invented his weaving machine, his power loom. In 1787 he attempted to establish a factory at Doncaster, in Yorkshire, but, not being a good man of business, he failed. In 1791, in concert with the Grimshaw firm, he set up a large factory in Manchester. The weavers of the district rioted, and one night the mill was burned. It was now out of the question to face the popular indignation in Manchester, and the Grimshaws sought

---

Petitions of several Weavers, . . . 1811, p. 6, evidence of Thomas Smith, of Glasgow). It must not, however, be forgotten that at this very period agriculturists were bewailing the increasing dearness of agricultural labour, which they ascribed to the emigration of labourers into the towns.

[1] P. Gaskell, *Artisans and Machinery*, 1836, p. 30.

in vain throughout the whole of Lancashire for a favourable locality
to make a new attempt. In 1803 Horrocks took out a patent for
a machine which marked a slight advance on Cartwright's—a machine
made entirely of iron, and taking up so little room that several hundreds
could be employed in a single workshop. He won the first victory
obtained in Lancashire over the weavers' opposition. About the
same date Radcliffe invented a dress machine which accomplished
automatically an operation which had hitherto demanded, with Cartwright's machine, the constant presence of a workman, and the frequent
stoppage of the machinery. On the whole, however, the power loom
made its way very slowly. In 1808 Radcliffe calculated that it was
only employed in some twenty-eight or thirty mills.[1] In 1813 there
were not above a thousand or two thousand looms driven by steam.[2]
Ten or twenty years had yet to elapse before the new process of manufacture was in general use. In 1812 an outbreak of disorder among
the workmen whose centre was Nottinghamshire spread to Lancashire ;
and in that county it was the weavers who rose against the introduction of machinery. Riots occurred ; the soldiery were employed
to repress them, and sanguinary conflicts followed between the troops
and the rioters.

The industrial system which prevailed among the weavers of cotton
cloth was not the factory system ; neither was it the system of domestic
industry, in the strict sense of the term. It was a system intermediate
between both, which, in the history of modern capitalism, was the
immediate precursor of the factory system. So far the capitalist only
appeared under the aspect of the merchant. He bought the cotton
thread which he required from the large mills of Manchester and the
banks of the Irwell, and distributed it among a scattered host of domestic
weavers[3] to be made into cloth. He then resold the cloth to the
factory owners to be bleached, dyed and printed. The weavers, to
whom he supplied the raw material, were to all appearance independent
producers. They owned their looms. They did not work directly
for a wage. They were given a certain quantity of thread to weave,
and the price which they would receive on delivery of the cloth to
the capitalist who had supplied the thread was fixed by bargaining.

---

[1] Report . . . on Dr. Cartwright's Petition respecting his Weaving Machine, 1808, pp. 8–9,
Radcliffe's evidence.

[2] W. Cooke Taylor, Modern Factory System, p. 94 : 1,000 ; Baines, Lancashire, vol. ii.
p. 471 : 2,400 ; W. Cooke Taylor, Handbook of Silk, Cotton and Woollen Manufactory, p. 127 :
2,500.

[3] These usually worked without any assistance outside the members of their family. Report
. . on Petitions of several Cotton Manufacturers and Journeymen Cotton Weavers, 1808, p. 29,
evidence of John Sharpe, a cotton weaver of Stockport : " I only employ my own children,
sometimes three and sometimes four." Sometimes, however, they employed a small number
of paid workmen. See the above-mentioned report, p. 27, evidence of John Honeyford, a cotton
weaver at Bolton. He owned four looms worked by " John Wilson a journeyman, John Haley
a journeyman, and the third is worked by an apprentice, Sarah Needham. I always wrought
myself ; John Haley is working my loom till I return."

The resemblance was, however, only apparent between this system of manufacture and the old village industries, where cottage workers divided their time between the cultivation of the soil and the manufacture of flax, wool or cotton.

The weavers were no longer peasant workmen, but workmen alone ; and they were exploited by the merchant who supplied the thread. The merchant had no means of profiting by improvement of the plant ; and since in Lancashire the looms were the property of the workmen, he would scarcely trouble to inquire how they did their work.[1] For this reason, and also because the rate of a loom's production was regarded as a constant factor, his only way of increasing the rate of production was to prolong and render more intense the labour of the weavers. The feverish over-production, which we are usually inclined to consider as characteristic of the factory system and of the use of machinery, was already a marked feature of the hand-loom system, in the period immediately preceding the introduction of machinery. Already the capitalist had realized that in this field also he could force the demand and increase it almost boundlessly, by simply increasing the rate of production. Every day witnessed the appearance of new employers—ex-workmen who bought cotton thread with borrowed capital and offered work to an ever-increasing number of weavers. They attempted, by reducing the sale price of cloth to an absurdly cheap figure, to rob the old-established firms of their custom.[2] By an equally excessive lowering of the price paid to the weavers, they sought to escape the ruin with which they were threatened in consequence of their daring methods of business. If we were to construct a curve showing the fluctuations in the weavers' profits during the twenty-five years of war, we should find that this curve, though extremely irregular, was on the whole descending from beginning to end.[3] About

[1] Report . . . on Petitions of several Cotton Manufacturers and Journeymen Cotton Weavers, 1808, p. 4, evidence of J. Bury of Stockport : " State what part of these charges vary with the rate of wages which the workman receives and what part are independent of the variation ?— I am not a practical weaver and therefore cannot answer so precisely as a workman."

[2] Report . . . on Petitions of several Cotton Manufacturers and Journeymen Cotton Weavers, 1808, p. 191, evidence of Mr. Thomas Helps, City of London, a wholesale dealer in cotton goods : " We employ persons to manufacture for us whose goods we take nearly exclusively— some of them the whole ; but in consequence of the great number of jobs, as we term it in the trade, we have not been able to dispose of goods, manufactured by persons who purchase their materials in the cheapest and best way. What is meant by jobs ?—It means a lot of goods to be sold under their actual value." See the entire report with the evidence attached, for a view of the state of the weaving industry at this period.

[3] Report . . . on State of Children, 1818, p. 7, evidence of Mr. A. Buchanan, of Glasgow : " Do you find that where manual labour is used the wages fluctuate more than in your manufactory ?—The hand-weaving fluctuates very much. Is your employment more uniform than in other trades when there is less machinery ?—Of course." For the fluctuations in weavers' wages during the war see the copious details given in the Report . . . on Petitions of several Cotton Manufacturers and Journeymen Cotton Weavers, 1808, especially pp. 9, 21-2, 26, 27, 28, 29. Cf. G. H. Wood, The Statistics of Wages . . . the Cotton Industry, in the Journal of Royal Statistical Society, 1910, pp. 428, 434.

1792 the cotton weavers were better paid than the majority of British workmen. In 1811 a weaver could no longer earn more than 11s. a week ; and the frequent periods of unemployment reduced his real average wage for a week to 7s. At the same date an agricultural labourer of the neighbourhood would be earning, without any fear of unemployment, his 12s. to 14s. a week.[1] Unbridled competition, over-production, periods of crisis, merciless sweating of the handicrafts-man—all existed in this industry before the appearance of the factory. Yet these evils are universally considered as inseparable from the modern organization of commerce and manufacture.

The weavers raised an outcry, and their grievances were ventilated in Parliament. Sometimes they blamed the spinning mills for their destitution, complained that cotton thread was too dear, and demanded that obstacles should be placed in the way of its export, that its price might be thus lowered in the home market. These complaints were sheer absurdity ; for now that cotton thread was spun by machinery, it was only too plentiful. Or again they would demand the legal protection of employers and men against their mutual competition, to be effected by a scale of prices determined by the magistrates and enforceable at law. In making this demand they doubtless recalled the time, not so long past, when they were prosperous members of the lower middle class, and formed enormous and powerful associations for the defence of their corporate customs. But the day of corporations had gone by. The evils under which they suffered admitted of no remedy until the technical processes of the industry were revolutionized and the hand loom replaced by the machine. Then perhaps legal in-terference would be more practicable, since the industry would not be so scattered. Then, perhaps, the employer would be able to obtain greater profits, not by lowering wages, but by improving plant. Such a change, however, could only be brought about at great cost, both of old habits broken and of small accumulations of capital lost.

The weavers clung desperately to the semblance of home life and to the semblance of liberty. To keep these they were ready to accept an ever smaller price for their work ; and their employers, therefore, had but little inducement to employ machinery. The change was not worth the risk of a riot, in which a factory might be burned and an entire fortune lost. The weavers worked " at home," that is to say, in an apartment that was not their own—a kennel in which the looms took up all the available room, a dark hovel, almost a cellar : weaving had to be done in a damp place to keep the thread supple.[2] They were,

---

[1] *Report . . . on Petition of several Weavers*, 1811, pp. 2–3, Joseph Hanson's evidence : " The spinners can get three times the wages we can," deposed a weaver in his evidence given before the Commission of 1808 (p. 24).

[2] *Report . . . on . . . State of Children*, 1816, p. 202, evidence of Kinder Wood, Esq., Oldham : " Do they (the handweavers) work in small damp workshops ?—They like a damp

indeed, property owners because the looms at which they worked were their property—the looms which they refused to give up although they were the means of their exploitation. They felt that they were still to some extent free. Although the conditions of their labour were in reality dictated by those who supplied the thread, they were not subjected to daily supervision. They could work at a strain for several days in succession, toiling for longer hours than they would have been willing to do in a factory, and then indulge in two or three days of idleness and drinking.[1] The military discipline of the factories was their bugbear. When they smashed the power looms they were revolting by anticipation against the orderly and regular habits which modern civilization was to impose upon them.

To sum up, the cotton manufacture in England at the beginning of the 19th century presented a double aspect. In certain departments the system of machinery, of factory work and of wage labour was already in full swing and producing all its effects. In other departments, on the contrary, there prevailed a system of actual wage-labour but of apparent liberty, where the workman working in his room was keenly attached, despite his extreme and ever-increasing destitution, to his old habits of work, and to the loom which was his own property, and struggled desperately against the introduction of the factory system. It was in these departments that the labour unrest presented its gravest aspect. The examination which has been made of the cotton industry will greatly facilitate our understanding of the other textile industries. Although machinery had nowhere else made such rapid progress as in the cotton manufacture, and although there were important differences between one industry and another, we shall find everywhere phenomena closely akin to those which we have just been studying.

Linen : Woollens : Hosiery.

The state of the linen trade was far from flourishing. The use of cotton spread from day to day, for the contest between the two industries was by no means even. And it would have been still more uneven had not the landowners done their best for the last century to encourage the manufacture of linen. They had obtained protective measures from Parliament.[2] In the three kingdoms they formed societies for the distribution of prizes and bounties.[3] What, then, was

workshop." See also the evidence of Mr. Thomas Whitelegg, *ibid.*, p. 148 : " Those cellars that the weavers work in have not the means of thorough ventilation in the same way that the factories have ?—They have thorough ventilation, for very often the windows are broken."

[1] *Report . . . on . . . State of Children*, 1816, p. 120 (Skipton, evidence of William Singwick). Cf. pp. 234–5 (suburbs of Glasgow), H. Houldsworth's evidence.

[2] 7 Geo. III, cap. 58. This statute imposed a duty on the import of foreign linen and deducted from the proceeds of this duty a sum of £15,000 to distribute in the shape of bounties to the cultivators of hemp and flax.

[3] There was founded in Ireland *A Board of Trustees of the Linen and Hempen Manufactures*

the reason of all this interest? It was partly because the cultivation of flax was a source of wealth to the landowners and their tenant farmers. It was partly also due to the fact that the farmers and agricultural labourers could add to their income or wages by spinning and weaving in their spare time. It was, therefore, to the interest of the patrons of the linen trade to perpetuate the system of village and domestic manufacture, and to hinder the transference of the industry from the country to the towns. It should be added that the greater proportion of British linen was woven in Ireland in and around Belfast. Shortly after the revolution of 1688 a species of industrial compact had been concluded between the two kingdoms. England, which had systematically ruined the woollen manufacture in Ireland, consented, in the interest of the Protestant farmers of Ulster, to tolerate the Irish linen manufacture. In Ireland, however, there existed neither factories nor machinery; the system of work was purely and simply domestic. Small farmers and cottagers cultivated the flax, spun it and wove it with the assistance of their families, and took the linen to market, where agents of the Dublin *Board of Trustees* verified the alleged measurements, guaranteed the quality and then dispatched the goods, marked with their stamp, to England and the Continent.[1]

We have already seen how wretched was the existence led by the Irish cultivator. He was therefore content, when he wove linen, with a remuneration so scanty, that it wholly prevented in Ireland, and retarded even in England, the introduction of machinery. After thirty years of experimenting, alike in England and in Scotland, with the earliest machines for spinning flax,[2] and despite the establishment around Leeds and Dundee of two important centres of flax spinning by machinery, it was only some three years before our date that one solitary factory in London had introduced machinery for the manu-

---

(A. J. Warden, *Linen Trade*, p. 393). The *English Linen Company* was incorporated in 1764 (*ibid.*, p. 371). In Scotland there was the *British Linen Company* (*ibid.*, p. 442). This last was turned later into a bank.

[1] For the organization of the linen manufacture in Ireland see A. J. Warden, *Linen Trade*, pp. 395 sqq.; Arthur Young, *A Tour in Ireland*, Part II, pp. 104 sqq.; Wakefield, *Ireland*, vol. i. pp. 684 sqq., vol. ii. p. 740. See in Arthur Young's *Tour in Ireland*, p. 194, some interesting reflexions upon the prudential motives which at the close of the 18th century deterred the merchant manufacturer from becoming a manufacturer in the strict sense of the term. " The drapers who are bleachers, purchase the linen, do not weave it on their own account; and here lies probably much of their profit. They take advantage of the variation of *times*, to use a commercial term, and often get the linen under its fair value; they have the advantage of all temporary necessities among the weavers; but at all events they know to a farthing the value they can give, and they do not buy a piece more than suits them. But if the weaving was done on their account, they would be obliged to make the linen, however, dead the market, or else have their men idle. Another observation which goes generally to all undertakings of this sort is, that the uniting in one person several branches of manufacture, will rarely be found advantageous. If every step is a distinct trade, alone occupying capital and attention, the fabric is the more like to thrive. . . . I question whether the most sagacious draper in Ireland would make considerably, if he wove the cloth as well as bleached it."

[2] Warden, *Linen Trade*, pp. 381, 690.

facture of coarse sail cloth.[1] In 1815 the weaving of linen cloth was still a village handicraft.

The woollen manufacture was one of the oldest English industries. It had always been the object of parliamentary solicitude, being regarded as the chief source of British wealth. About 1750 the export of woollens accounted for a third of the entire value of English exports. As long as the war with revolutionary and imperial France continued, the constant demand for woollen cloth for the Army had rendered less acute the crises of this industry. And wages had even risen. Since the opening of the 19th century the manufacturers had been accustomed to ascribe the victory which they enjoyed over their French or Flemish competitors to the superiority of their plant.[2] Nevertheless, the progress of machinery, though more rapid than in the linen manufacture, was slower than in the cotton manufacture. What was said above of cotton weaving in Lancashire may be applied to the woollen manufacture as a whole. The manufacture of cotton was a new industry which had been obliged to create within a century its entire plant. The woollen manufacture, on the other hand, being based on long-established traditions, offered more opposition to technical innovations. Whatever desire they might feel to force the rate of production, the capitalists were obliged to consider the attachment shown by the workmen for their old organization and old plant. The discontent and the turbulence of the wool workers never ceased to engage the attention of Parliament during the first fifteen years of the century. There are, therefore, at our disposal numerous official documents informing us as to the state of the wool trade in the two districts where it had centred since the economic decline of Norfolk had been completed—namely certain counties in the south-west, Gloucestershire, Somersetshire, and Wiltshire ; and the West Riding of Yorkshire.

Machinery had already made its appearance in the south-western district, but the opposition of the workmen rendered its introduction difficult. Moreover, the machinery was confined to the preparatory and to the final stages of the manufacture—the carding and spinning, the dressing and dyeing. The gig-mill, whose use was destined to render one of the dressing operations speedier and more perfect and against which the workers rose in revolt, was not even a machine, but merely an improved frame.[3] Water power was used, not steam power as yet. At the very time when the Lancashire mills were abandoning the rivers and were being concentrated in the large towns, the woollen manu-

---

[1] Warden, *Linen Trade*, p. 710.

[2] *Minutes of Evidence . . . respecting . . . Laws relating to Woollen Trade*, 1803, p. 347, evidence of Mr. Edward Austin, merchant in London : " We have . . . thrown them (the French and Flemish drapers) entirely out (of the London market) by means of machinery. The machines have been the means of ameliorating the cloth and of keeping down the price."

[3] *Minutes of Evidence . . . respecting the Laws relating to the Woollen Trade*, 1803, pp. 345, 361.

facture in Gloucestershire was being dispersed throughout the country-side in the search for waterfalls.[1] Weaving was still done entirely by hand. In this department the backwardness of the woollen as compared with the cotton manufacture is obvious. Nearly a century earlier John Kay had invented his fly-shuttle for use in the manufacture of woollen cloth. The cotton weavers had appropriated it ; and when now the fly-shuttle was at last being introduced, in the face of many obstacles, into the houses of the weavers of wool in the south-west, in the cotton districts it was being superseded by the power loom.[2]

The organization of labour was, however, much the same as that which obtained among the cotton weavers.[3] For many years the town merchant had successfully controlled the artisans of the countryside, the manufacturers, whose goods he sold ; he had become in fact, to employ the current term, a merchant manufacturer. He furnished the artisans with the raw material, and received back from them the manufactured article. The price paid for their work was contested between himself and them under conditions almost identical with those of the labour disputes of our own time. Certain of the merchant manufacturers, in order to obtain more absolute control over the processes of production, even attempted to introduce the factory system, by collecting a large number of fly-shuttles in one single place, to be worked under their direction. But popular hostility usually compelled them to close their establishments ; and they would then sell the looms which they had acquired to the artisans of the neighbourhood. It was in this way that John Kay's already antiquated fly-shuttle spread throughout the country districts of the south-west.[4] It is, nevertheless, indisputable that before the first appearance of machinery and the factory system there had grown up in this district a system closely akin to that of capitalism.

The West Riding of Yorkshire had remained more faithful than Gloucestershire to the old system of domestic industry. Every year the small handicraftsman mounted his horse and rode off to buy raw wool from the farmers. He had it picked, carded and combed. Then he returned home and wove it with the help of his family. He would, moreover, give out work among his neighbours.[5] Leeds and Bradford

[1] *Report . . . on Woollen Clothiers' Petition*, 1803, p. 14; *Minutes of Evidence . . . respecting the Laws relating to the Woollen Trade*, 1803, pp. 335-6.

[2] It seems to have made its first appearance, as an importation from the North, about 1801 (*Report . . . on Woollen Clothiers' Petition*, 1803, pp. 8-9).

[3] *Minutes of Evidence . . . respecting the Laws relating to the Woollen Trade*, 1803, p. 383. Mantoux, *Révolution Industrielle*, pp. 40 sqq. Cf. the author's article entitled *La Naissance du Méthodisme en Angleterre*, *Revue de Paris*, August 15, 1906.

[4] *Report on . . . Woollen Clothiers' Petition*, 1803, p. 15; *Minutes of Evidence . . . respecting . . . Laws relating to . . . Woollen Trade*, 1803, p. 266.

[5] *Report . . . on . . . Woollen Manufactories*, 1806, p. 8. The report was drawn up by Wilberforce (see *Life*, vol. iii. pp. 265, 267, 530). Cf. R. Warner, *Northern Tour*, 1802, vol. i. p. 245 The domestic system was destined to hold out for a long time to come, in certain

in the north in the Aire valley, Wakefield, Huddersfield and Halifax in the south in the Calder valley, were the centres of the woollen industry. The wool market was held at Wakefield and the cloth market at Leeds, while Bradford was the emporium for combed wool. In these towns large halls had been erected either by public subscription, or at the cost of a society, in which to hold a weekly market. Whenever cloth was to be sold, the artisans were drawn up in rows, each behind a counter, and the merchant passed along the rows selecting and purchasing their goods. In the West Riding the control of the artisans' labour had not fallen, as in Gloucestershire, into the hands of the merchants.

Nevertheless, certain manufacturers were already setting up spinning mills where machinery was employed. They were copying the example of the processes employed in Lancashire for spinning cotton—had perhaps come themselves from Lancashire. These mills were, however, at first, what were termed locally public mills—that is mills open in a sense to all comers where the small manufacturers, instead of being obliged, as before, to make long journeys across the hills, could bring their parcels of wool to be carded or their carded wool to be spun. It would appear, in short, that in Yorkshire machinery only came into employment with the express approval of the weavers, and in a form which endangered their economic independence as little as possible. For example, an attempt, made in Bradford in 1794, to introduce an excellent combing machine of Cartwright's invention, had proved a failure on account of the invincible hostility of the workmen. More recently the merchants had begun to open dressing shops or dressing mills in which certain operations necessary for finishing the cloth before it was put on the market were performed under their control by men working together for wages. An improved frame, known as the shearing frame, was introduced into these mills. The shearers declared war against the new machine and appealed to the weavers for support. The weavers responded to the appeal, for they also had begun to feel themselves threatened by the competition of machinery. Certain merchants, not satisfied with establishing workshops for the final processes of the cloth manufacture, had attempted, in Halifax, in Huddersfield and in Leeds, to open weaving mills. When the cloth workers espoused the cause of the shearers, they were defending their own cause. Their numbers were large and they extended over a district, twelve to fifteen miles wide, and twenty to thirty miles long. They were members of the lower middle class, men who owned a house, a few acres of land, a horse and its stable. They formed the bulk of the West Riding

parts of Yorkshire, against the introduction of the factory system. Howitt (*Rural Life of England*, 1840, p. 242) can still speak of dales where the inhabitants " won't work in a factory. The experiment was tried in this dale ; but the people, like the French, would only work just when they pleased, and soon would not work at all. . . . The scheme failed ; the factory stands a ruinous monument of the attempt, and these beautiful dales are yet free from the factory system."

electorate, and could put pressure on their representatives. It was, therefore, a very difficult matter to overcome their opposition to the factory system. Out of 466,000 pieces of cloth manufactured in Yorkshire in 1805, only 8,000 were made in the factories, which were confined to the production of a small number of fancy goods.[1] In 1812, the Yorkshire artisans, like those of Lancashire, destroyed power looms. The West Riding affords the sole instance of a direct transition from the domestic system to the system of machinery and factories, without that intermediate stage which we found existing among the cotton weavers and the wool weavers of Gloucestershire. In 1815 this transition had not yet been accomplished.

There were, therefore, labour riots in Lancashire, and also in Yorkshire. But in both districts alike the disorders of 1812 were but the backwash of an agitation whose centre was the neighbouring county of Nottingham. The special industry of Nottinghamshire—namely hosiery—dated from the opening years of the 17th century. It was then that the knitting frame had been invented—a frame composed of 2,000 pieces of wood or iron, in which the enormous number of needles at work simultaneously had made it possible to knit 100 stitches in the time formerly required to knit one.[2] It was a machine quite as ingenious, more ingenious indeed, and more difficult for an outsider to understand than the fly-shuttle, the jenny, the water-frame or the mule. Since the 17th century the knitting frame had already undergone a certain number of improvements. From 1750 onwards there had been numerous inventions for knitting ribbed stockings,[3] and fancy patterns,[4] and for making tulle and lace.[5] In 1812[6] there were in England 29,582 knitting frames, of which the vast majority were either at Nottingham, where the raw material was cotton, at Leicester, where it was wool, or at Derby, where it was silk. England enjoyed in this industry the same preeminence as in the textile industries. As against her 30,000 frames the entire Continent only possessed a little over 13,000.[7] Machinery in the strict sense, however, had not made its appearance as yet, and the large factory was unknown. There was instead a system similar to that which we have remarked among the wool

[1] Report . . . on . . . Woollen Manufactories, 1806, p. 12. The sole grievance of the discontented in 1806 was that the progress accomplished by the domestic industry, which they admitted to be real, had not been sufficiently rapid. Report . . . on . . . Woollen Manufactories, 1806 (Minutes of Evidence, p. 16, James Ellis' evidence): " . . . there generally has been an increase in the domestic manufactory till lately : lately the trade has increased, but the trade of the Domestic Manufacturer has not increased in proportion to the increase of the trade. That, I consider, is owing to factories. Cf. ibid., pp. 89 (Samuel Waterhouse's evidence), 173 (evidence of two merchants, Jeremiah Taylor and John Oxley).

[2] See the text of the petition to Cromwell given in Felkin, Hosiery and Lace, pp. 63–5.

[3] Felkin, Hosiery and Lace, pp. 87 sqq.   [4] Ibid., pp. 102 sqq.

[5] Ibid., pp. 133 sqq.

[6] Ibid., pp. 437–8 (quoting Blackner). See also for an account of the various processes of the local manufacture, J. Blackner, History of Nottingham, pp. 213 sqq.

[7] Felkin, Hosiery and Lace, pp. 87 sqq.

weavers of Gloucestershire. Here, however, the system involved more intolerable abuses and led to popular outbreaks of a graver character. Middlemen, who did no manual work, had acquired control over the industry, were forcing the rate of produce, and sweating the workers, who were for all intents and purposes a proletariat in their employ.

Around Nottingham, Leicester and Derby the social edifice was constructed as follows. At the summit were the real capitalists, the hosiers, who bought the raw material and finally received back the finished produce to put upon the market.[1] They never came into direct contact with the actual workers, the framework knitters. Between the two classes came those known as master stockingers, or bag hosiers—people of no great wealth or importance, usually local shopkeepers.[2] The hosiers paid them by the job to give out work and to collect it when finished. It is obvious that these middlemen could only make a profit at the cost of the artisan. They robbed him by payment in kind.[3] They robbed him by estimating too low the amount of work supplied, and by opposing, for this reason, the adoption of certain machines which would have rendered possible the automatic measurement of the goods delivered.[4] They robbed him by refusing to pay for work of whose quality they disapproved, while keeping the goods in question. The Nottinghamshire hosiers were subject to a further form of exploitation from which the Lancashire and Gloucestershire weavers were free. They did not own their frames. The knitting frames, whose cost was beyond an artisan's purse, were regarded in the district as one of the most profitable investments that a capitalist could make. In nine years he could get back the price he paid for one. It was a common thing for gentlemen of independent means who lived in the neighbourhood to invest sums of £100, £500, even £1,000 in the purchase of frames, although they were themselves utter strangers to the industry. About 1810 some two-fifths of the frames were in their possession.[5] Usually the hosiers themselves owned the frames and deducted a frame rent every week from the wages of every knitter.[6] The wages of the knitters, who were so mercilessly sweated in these various ways, had sensibly

---

[1] The fusion of the functions of merchant and manufacturer was less complete here than elsewhere. See *Report on the Framework Knitters' Petition*, 1812, *Minutes of Evidence*, p. 44 : ". . . There are four descriptions of persons concerned in the stocking-making business : first, the merchant who buys from the hosier and sells to the shopkeepers ; the next is the hosier—he is the person who employs the workmen and finds the material," etc. Cf. Felkin, *Hosiery and Lace*, p. 552 : " Forty years ago, the machinery of the bobbin net trade was to a large extent in the hands of more than 1,000 small owners, chiefly handicraftsmen, most of whom were unused to business. . . . These employed some hundreds of agents in the disposal of the produce of their machines. Many of these were not much in advance of their employers ; they carried their goods in large packs daily for sale at the warehouses and in the main were paid weekly."

[2] *Report . . . on . . . Framework Knitters' Petition*, 1812, *Minutes of Evidence*, pp. 30, 44.
[3] *Ibid.*, pp. 31–2.   [4] *Ibid.*, p. 15 ; Felkin, *Hosiery and Lace*, p. 170–1.
[5] Felkin, *Hosiery and Lace*, p. 454.
[6] *Report . . . on . . . Framework Knitters' Petition*, 1812, p. 6, *Minutes of Evidence*, p. 16.

fallen during the last twenty-five years. At the outbreak of the war the average wage had been close on 13s. a week. In 1811, despite the enormous rise in the cost of foodstuffs, it had fallen almost to 12s.[1]

When the hosier was the owner of the frames at which the artisans worked, he was for all intents and purposes the owner of a dispersed factory, where everything belonged to him—both the raw material and the plant. Furthermore, an artisan would sometimes hire several frames at once, and put several men to work with these, collected in a single workshop under his supervision. Such a "shop of frames" or "shop of machines," as it was termed at Nottingham, was of course simply a factory in embryo.[2] Only in embryo, however : many years were yet to elapse before the establishment here of large factories where the power was supplied by engines. The bobbin net machine invented by Heathcote in 1809 for the manufacture of lace was not a machine in the strict sense in which we have been employing the term. It was a frame which required a man to work it. It was not until in 1816, when the artisans had wrecked his lace-making frames, and compelled him to remove to Tiverton in Somersetshire, that Heathcote was to invent a process whereby the frame could be driven by water or steam power, and to set up in that district a real lace factory.[3]

Here again was an industry without factories or machinery, in which, nevertheless, the condition of the workers resembled very closely that of factory hands. During the years immediately preceding 1815, Nottinghamshire was the hotbed of acute discontent among the proletariat. The artisans of the hosiery manufacture were in loud protest against the remorseless competition which prevailed among the hosiers, against the bad quality of the raw material, against the low wages they were receiving, against over-production. Illogically enough, they complained simultaneously that the number of looms was excessive, and their rent too high. A movement of insurrection on a large scale was organized in 1811. For two years the Luddites, as these revolted workmen were called, smashed frames by the hundred, pillaged houses, and assaulted or killed obnoxious persons. The agitation spread to the neighbouring districts and caused panic throughout the length and breadth of England. Cobbett extolled the Radicalism of Nottingham ; Byron sang the praises of the Luddites.

[1] *Report . . . on . . . Framework Knitters' Petitions*, 1812, pp. 59–61 : November 1792, 12s. 7d. ; May 7, 1796, 12s. 7½d. ; November 1811, 13s. 3¼d. (we must deduct from this a frame rent of 1s.). In the interval the hosiery industry had experienced, about 1808, a period of extraordinary prosperity, and the weekly wage had risen to 18s. and 21s. (*Report . . .* pp. 23–30). Immediately afterwards, about 1810, they fell as low as 7s. (Felkin, *Hosiery and Lace*, pp. 230–1). We have neglected this abnormal rise and fall.

[2] *First Report of Commissioners . . . as to Employment of Children in Factories*, 1833, North-Eastern District, p. 34 : " There are only four or five factories, properly so called, in Nottingham, where twist machines are worked ; when assembled in small numbers, as ten or twelve, or lower, the term used is a shop of machines, as in the hosiery trade a shop of frames."

[3] Felkin, *Hosiery and Lace*, pp. 171 sqq., 240 sqq. ; *Annual Register*, 1816, Chron., p. 100.

THE MEANS OF TRANSPORT.

The Transport Industry.   Internal Communications.

In order to secure the transport of raw material to the places where it was manufactured, to dispatch the manufactured articles to the places where they would be used, to send out on all sides a host of commercial travellers, to receive the news of the entire globe, the manufacturers and merchants demanded plentiful and speedy means of communication. Nevertheless, the transport industry about 1815 was lagging behind the rest of the British industries.   Urgent need was indeed spurring on inventors to discover new contrivances for the purpose ; but the decisive inventions had not yet been made, or rather, to speak more accurately, although made, they had not yet come into practical use.

To take first internal communications.   As far back as the 17th century the English had begun to improve these.   They had established the system of turnpike roads, according to which the sums necessary for the repair of roads was levied from those who used them.   They had rendered more navigable the small and shallow streams that intersected the English country districts.   More recently Telford, famous for the roads which he made in Scotland, had inaugurated a new era by following Thomas Paine's advice and employing iron in the construction of bridges.   In 1815 John Macadam was appointed Surveyor-General of British Roads, and could henceforth apply on a large scale the results of sixteen years of study.   The various transport services had also been sensibly improved.   About the middle of the 18th century it had been a source of general congratulation that the journey from London to Edinburgh could be accomplished henceforward in ten to twelve days instead of requiring three weeks.   In 1784 the service of mail coaches organized by Palmer for the conveyance of letters and passengers had suddenly shortened distances.   Henceforward Edinburgh was now only sixty hours' journey from London.   Then the speed of the mail coaches was itself surpassed.   During the years immediately preceding 1815 a perfect mania for speed possessed the rival coach services.   The diatribes of the Press against the races between the drivers of stage coaches only provided the proprietors with an excellent advertisement.   A stage coach performed the journey between London and Leeds in twenty-one hours—that is twelve hours less than the mail coach.[1]   Nevertheless, when all is said and done, both roads and vehicles resembled very much the roads and vehicles at the service of a contemporary of the Stuarts or Tudors, perhaps even of a contemporary of Alfred the Great or Julius Caesar.   All the progress accomplished amounted only to this—that a speed which was formerly the exception

[1] *Leeds Mercury*, May 6, 1815.

was now the normal speed, available at all times and in all seasons, on certain fixed days and at fixed hours. Moreover, as the speed increased so also did the cost of travelling. Outside the metropolitan district, where the postage of a letter was only 2d., the rates of postages had been growing constantly dearer. The postage of a letter from London to Chester, which had been only 4d. at the commencement of the 18th century, cost 6d. after 1784, 8d. after 1786 and 10d. after 1812.[1]

One single technical invention, copied from seventeenth-century France, had effected in the transport industry an unquestionable economy of time, labour and cost. A canal was in all truth a labour-saving machine, " roads of a certain kind on which one horse will draw as much as thirty horses on ordinary turnpike roads, or on which one man alone will transport as many goods as three men and eighteen horses usually do on common roads."[2]   Even had the construction of a canal been twenty times as costly as the construction of a road, there would still have been good reasons for making the canal rather than the road.   In many cases, however, it was actually less expensive to make a canal than a road. Great landowners followed the example set by the Duke of Bridgewater and supplied skilful engineers such as Brindley, Telford and Rennie with the necessary capital to cover England with canals.   From 1815 onwards the Port of Liverpool was connected by a network of waterways with all the manufacturing centres of Lancashire, with Kendal in Westmorland, with the manufacturing centres of Yorkshire and Staffordshire and beyond these with the Midlands, the ports on the south coast, and the estuaries of the Thames and Severn.   In the course of fifty years 2,600 miles of canal had been constructed in England, 276 miles in Ireland and 225 in Scotland.   Locks enabled the canals to cross hills, aqueducts took them over valleys.   The construction of canals was to be continued with feverish activity until the competition of railways began.   To all appearances this competition was imminent, for the need to which railways ministered was pressing, and the canals that intersected England were far from satisfying it.   Railroads existed already in every coal mine, and in several places Parliament had already sanctioned the construction of actual tramway lines.[3]   We have seen already how the fixed engines which pumped water from mines were sometimes used to draw wagons along rails.   It was in 1815 that George Stephenson, a miner's son and a miner himself, patented, as the result of experiments carried out at the instigation and with the assistance

---

[1] On the successive rises in postal rates, some due to a desire to improve the Services, others to a desire to increase the revenue obtained from the Post Office, see Joyce, *History of the Post Office*, pp. 216, 318, 330–1, 356.

[2] S. Philipps, *General History of Inland Navigation*, ed. 1792, p. ix.

[3] Porter, *Progress of the Nation*, 1851, p. 327, gives a list of these Acts, sixteen of which were passed between 1801 and 1815.   The Hay railway (between Brecon and Parton Cross), 1811, was twenty-four miles long ; the Severn and Wye Railway (between Lidbrook and Newern with branches), 1809, was twenty-six miles long.

of his employer, the first locomotive that can be regarded as really practicable. Nevertheless, some ten to fifteen years had yet to elapse before the invention came into actual use.

External Communications.

After the foregoing sketch of the internal communications of England, we must now turn to the means at her disposal for the exchange of her products for those of foreign countries. In this department also progress had undoubtedly been made, but nothing of any great moment had been accomplished. In Scotland the Government had appointed in 1786, in pursuance of a concerted plan, a commission to inquire into the lighthouses of the North of Scotland,[1] and in 1806 had devoted [2] the residue of the sums confiscated sixty years before, after the rebellion, to the improvement of commercial ports. In England the intervention of the State was more indirect and was confined to the passage of a series of statutes authorizing the foundation of societies due to private initiative. The lighthouse on the Bell Rock, erected by Rennie in the open sea at the entrance of the Firths of Forth and Tay, was an object of world-wide admiration. A century had already passed since Liverpool, by the construction of docks, had delivered shipowners from the extortions of the quay owners, had put an end to the activity of the bands of thieves who used formerly to loot merchantmen, and had enabled the loading and unloading of merchandise to be organized on a business footing. Liverpool had ruined in the north-west the old ports of Lancaster and Chester, and had taken the place once occupied by Bristol in the trade between England and America.[3] London followed the example set by Liverpool. In the first decade of the century alone, three mercantile bodies had constructed, in accordance with Rennie's designs, the London Dock, the West India Dock and the East India Dock. These docks covered some twenty to thirty acres, employed thousands of officials and labourers, and were surrounded by warehouses, whose construction had been the first experiment in iron architecture.[4] When, however, we leave the work accomplished on the coast and in the ports, and consider the construction of the vessels themselves, we are again struck by the universal backwardness of the industries of transport as compared with the directly productive industries.

From 1801 to 1809 the yearly tonnage of the vessels entering

---

[1] 26 Geo. III, cap. 101.   [2] 46 Geo. III, cap. 154, 155, 156.

[3] Dupin, *Force Commerciale*, vol. ii. p. 210; R. Ayton, *Voyage Round Great Britain*, vol. ii. (1815), pp. 80 sqq.; Baines, *Lancashire*, vol. iv. p. 149 sqq. By 1815, however, the Liverpool docks were already inadequate to the needs of navigation.

[4] See an excellent description of the London docks in Dupin, *Force Commerciale*, vol. ii. pp. 18 sqq.

British ports, as of the vessels leaving those ports, had been on an average about 1,700,000 tons. In 1810 it had reached 2,000,000 tons and did not exceed this figure during the following decade.[1] The number and tonnage of British vessels entering and leaving the ports certainly did increase, but not the total number and tonnage of vessels of every description.[2] It is, indeed, quite likely that the crises of over-production which were afflicting British manufacture were in part explicable by the insufficiency of the means of transport. It is true that inventors were engaged in the search for methods of navigation which were shortly to revolutionize the entire art. Already their efforts were being crowned with success. In 1801 Lord Dundas had employed a small steamboat for touring on a Scottish canal.[3] In 1807 Boulton and Watt constructed, on Fulton's model, another steamboat, intended for use on the Hudson. Since 1811 two or three small steamboats had plied regularly on the Clyde between Glasgow and Greenock, and in fine weather performed the journey quicker than the mail coach.[4] Two other steamships, built like the former at Glasgow, were in use on the Thames—one between London and Gravesend, the other between

[1] The exact figures are as follows :—

Date.	Tonnage of Vessels Entering.	Tonnage of Vessels Leaving.
1801	1,702,749	1,634,804
1809	1,697,962	1,650,315
[Between 1801 and 1809 no sensible fluctuations occurred.]		
1810	2,072,244	1,999,159
1820	2,115,671	1,982,515
[Between 1810 and 1820 no sensible fluctuations occurred.]		
1815	2,119,093	2,150,065

In these statistics the coasting trade and vessels trading between England and Ireland are left out of account (Porter, *Progress of the Nation*, 1815, pp. 397–8).

[2]

Year.	No. of British Vessels Entering.	No. of British Vessels Leaving.	No. of Foreign Vessels Entering.	No. of Foreign Vessels Leaving.
1810	5,154	3,969	6,876	6,641
1815	8,880	8,892	5,314	4,701
1820	11,285	10,102	3,472	2,969

Porter, *ibid*. On the other hand, Porter's estimate does not give so striking an increase for the entire Merchant Fleet of Great Britain (United Kingdom, European Possessions, Colonies) for the same period : 23,703 vessels in 1810, 24,860 in 1815, 25,374 in 1820 (*ibid*., p. 168). We can only conclude that each vessel made a larger number of voyages.

[3] Galloway, *Annals of the Steam Engine*, p. 233.

[4] W. Daniell, *Voyage round Great Britain*, vol. iii. (1818), p. 17 ; Porter, *Progress of the Nation*, 1851, p. 315.

London and Margate. This latter ship reached London by sea, and the newspapers celebrated as a magnificent feat her voyage of 1,500 miles, rounding Land's End.[1] Nevertheless, the idea of steam navigation on the open sea still seemed Utopian. No one thought that the steamship could ever come into general use except as a means of carrying passengers on the English estuaries between deep water and the landing stages.

Shipowners profited on the whole by this insufficiency of the means of transport, and were in a position to dictate their own terms to the merchants who competed for the privilege of shipping goods on their vessels.[2] For them the opening years of the century had been years of uninterrupted prosperity.[3] The sailors of the Merchant Service benefited by the favourable condition of affairs as well as their employers. We possess exact statistics enabling us to follow the fluctuations in rates of pay on the colliers at Shields and Sunderland. Before the war the pay for each voyage to London had been from £2 10s. to £3. By 1800 it had risen to £10, £11, and even to £11 11s. The rise ought not to surprise us, if we remember the general rise of prices, the demand for sailors for the Navy, and the risk of navigation in time of war. It was inevitable that the rate of pay should fall with the restoration of peace, but it did not fall so low as the shipowners desired. The Newcastle and Sunderland sailors obtained by a skilful and methodical opposition, without any resort to violence, a collective contract, fixing their pay at £4 10s., and determining the number of men and boys required to man each ship, according to the size of the vessel. The industry of marine transport was as yet free from that over-production which invariably accompanies the progress of technical invention. In this department the era of iron and coal had not yet opened.[4]

INDIVIDUALISM AND FREE TRADE.

Industrial Anarchy.

In the period about 1815 British industry was in the throes of transformation. The entire revolution in technical processes was causing grave social disorders. It is true that the crisis was not

[1] *Tilloch's Philosophical Magazine*, June 1815, vol. xlv. p. 472.

[2] H. of C., March 3, 1812, Rose's speech : " In the year 1807, when the Orders in Council were originally issued, the rate was 19s. per ton ; but at present it was not less than 25s. per ton—a clear proof . . . that the great body of the shipping of the country was constantly employed " (*Parl. Deb.*, vol. xxi. p. 1119).

[3] Porter, *Progress of the Nation*, p. 392.

[4] *Report on . . . the Coal Trade*, May 1800, Appendix, p. 569b ; *Annual Register*, 1815, Chron., pp. 76–7, October 14th–28th. The statistics are hard to interpret. Sometimes the pay for a *London voyage*, or for a *voyage*, is intended, at others the monthly pay. It would appear that the voyage from Sunderland to London and back was estimated to last longer than a month (*Annual Register*, *loc. cit.*) : " The shipowners of Shields have offered the men £5 per London voyage, or £4 per month on foreign voyages."

equally violent in all branches of manufacture. Machinery did not make equally rapid progress in all alike. In several the system of capitalism had preceded the introduction of machinery. The condition of the workmen was not everywhere equally miserable, and even where the destitution of the men was the same, the spirit of rebellion was not equally aroused within them. The hotbeds of proletarian revolt were the districts where the system of domestic industry still prevailed, and where the artisans were rising either against the imminent introduction of machinery and factories or against the sweating to which they were subject, even before the appearance of the machine and the factory, at the hands of the merchants for whose profit they worked. It remains true, however, despite the various character of the phenomena produced, that we are witnessing a cleavage, and a cleavage growing ever sharper, between two classes. One of these consisted of the wealthy capitalists, who aimed at increasing the productivity of the workmen's labour, either by obtaining a more absolute control in workshops and factories or by the adoption of improved plant and more powerful machinery. The other consisted of the manual workers, reduced to the state of living machines, and completely under the thumb of the capitalist who interposed between themselves and the consumer. These two confronting classes bore no sort of resemblance to two properly constituted nations, each conscious of its unity, and capable of declaring war according to certain juridical rules, and of concluding treaties which it felt bound to observe. Neither the new class of employers nor the new class of workmen had yet learnt to organize. Not only was there open war between Capital and Labour, but also, in the ranks of Capital and of Labour alike, confusion and anarchy prevailed.

Competition, Over-production. The Struggle for Markets.

The capitalists, the owners of factories and heads of manufacturing and commercial undertakings, moved forward like a disorderly mob to the conquest of markets. Combinations and syndicates of any kind were unknown. The producers had come to no understanding for the assignment to each producer of a particular market to be supplied with his goods, or for a fixed quantity of articles to be made at his factory. The combination of capital under any form played a very insignificant part in British manufacture. It is true that joint stock companies had made considerable progress since the early years of the 18th century, when they had been prohibited by a statute passed expressly for that purpose.[1]

[1] 6 Geo. I, cap. 18. Section 18 of this Act prohibits " the acting or presuming to act as a corporate body or bodies, the raising or pretending to raise transferrable stock or stocks, the transferring or pretending to transfer or assign any share or shares in such stock or stocks, without the authority, either by Act of Parliament or by any charter from the Crown, to warrant such acting as a body corporate, or to raise such transferrable stock or stocks, or to transfer shares therein."

Adam Smith was only registering the progress accomplished despite this legal prohibition, when he recognized the useful part played by joint stock companies in all undertakings which could be reduced to "what is called a routine or to such a uniformity of method as admits of little or no variation."[1] Such undertakings were banking, insurance, the construction of canals, the water supply of large towns. These companies had made further progress during the opening years of the 19th century and had won an important victory at law when the Court of King's Bench refused to apply to one of them the antiquated statute of George I.[2] They continued, nevertheless, to occupy an anomalous position in the organization of British industry. Lawyers were embarrassed, and public opinion outraged by the difficulty of fixing the financial responsibility of the shareholders in case of bankruptcy.[3] Joint stock companies were unknown in the branches of manufacture really representative of the industrial revolution such as the manufacture of cloth, metal working and mining.[4] Any companies that did exist in these departments consisted of a mere handful of individuals, who shared not only the stock but also the control of the business.[5] Individualism was the general rule. Each manufacturer founded his own fortune, and desired to remain, and did remain, sole master thereof.

The immediate result of this individualism was irregularity of production. Every individual capitalist had seen that there was a market for an ever-increasing yearly output. He concluded from this that he could force on the market, without any agreement with his fellow manufacturers, all the articles he could produce in his workshops or factory. The inevitable result, however, of the fact that all were making simultaneously the same calculation, was that the increase in

---

[1] *Wealth of Nations*, Book V, chap. i. Part III, ed. Thorold Rogers, vol. ii. p. 340.

[2] See *Report of the Arguments upon the Application to the Court of King's Bench*, 1808. Judgment was given on May 30, 1808.

[3] See the Parliamentary Debates, H. of C., June 16, 1800. Lord Hawkesbury's motion "for the Second Reading of the Bill for incorporating certain individuals into a society, under the name of the ' London Incorporated Society ' for the manufacture of flour, bread, etc.," and Tierney's speech thereupon (*Parliamentary Register*, vol. lxxiv. pp. 118 sqq.).

[4] Tooke (*History of Prices*, vol. i. p. 278 n.) gives a list, taken from a contemporary newspaper, of forty-two joint stock companies founded in 1807, nearly all of which were stillborn, and perished in the crisis immediately consequent upon this feverish outburst of speculation. Of these five were insurances companies, seven breweries, four distilleries, seven companies for the sale of wine and spirits, two companies for the sale of foodstuffs, one for the sale of drugs, three banks, one a company for the sale and transfer of land, one agency. This leaves eleven companies (coal, light and heat, cloth, wool, linen, copper and paper) more nearly connected with manufacture. In many instances, however, the title hardly enables us to decide whether the company was concerned with the actual manufacture (or extraction) of the articles in question, or merely with the trade in these articles when already manufactured. There can be no doubt in the case of the *London Clothing Company*, whose title informs us that it was founded "for supplying the Army, Navy and Public with clothes."

[5] Schmoller, *Die geschichliche Entwickelung der Unternehmung*, in *Yahrbuch für Gesetzgebung Verwaltung, und Volkswirtschaft im Deutschen Reich*, 17th year, 1893, p. 1014.

the rate of production was in excess of the increase in the rate of consumption. This meant over-production and consequent crisis. The credit even of old-established firms was shaken and thousands of workpeople thrown upon the streets. Then, as the actual result of the crisis, the correct ratio between production and consumption was restored. The goods offered for sale at very low prices were finally sold out. The ruined employers disappeared. The workmen thrown out of employment found work again either in new establishments or in the old, carried on now on an even larger scale ; for no sooner was a crisis over, than the producers resumed once more their feverish toil. Had the manufacturers been prudent they would have sought to protect themselves against the excesses and dangers attendant upon competition either by demanding Government interference or by the conclusion of voluntary agreements among themselves. But their systematic optimism and their manufacturing and mercantile enthusiasm blinded them to every difficulty. They counted on the discovery of new markets to absorb an ever-increasing production. They demanded the abolition of all restrictions on the freedom of production and exchange, and especially the abolition of the tariff wall between different countries. Their programme was one of universal brotherhood of a sort : Free Trade was to abolish war. We must remember, however, that for the collective rivalries of nations, they would have substituted competition between all the individual members of those nations. Moreover, the manufacturers had only recently begun to take up this Free Trade propaganda. Adam Smith, in his classical work, had still to censure their obstinate adherence to Protection. We can even follow, during the years preceding 1815, the stages of their conversion to the cause of Free Trade.

After the annihilation of French sea-power at Trafalgar, Napoleon had adopted other tactics in a second attempt to destroy the industrial and commercial supremacy of Great Britain. He tried to take his revenge on land, by using his dominion over Europe to organize an economic blockade of the two islands composing the United Kingdom ; to starve England into submission by depriving her of the foodstuffs of which her own soil no longer furnished a sufficiency, and to ruin her by refusing her the raw material which her manufacturers obtained from the Continent, and by closing the principal markets to her manufactured goods. In 1806 the Decree of Berlin had prohibited all commerce or intercourse of any kind with England, had ordered the arrest of all British subjects found on French soil, and the confiscation of all vessels and cargoes of English origin. In 1807 the Decree of Milan had declared as denationalized and lawful prize any vessel which had submitted to be searched or taken into an English port by an English cruiser. In 1810 the Fontainebleau decrees had ordered that any articles of English manufacture found in the countries subject to Napoleon should be confiscated and publicly burnt. A quantity of goods actually were burnt to a value exceeding £40,000,000.

The English response to this policy of systematic boycott was an attempt to break through the circle which enclosed them. Since Napoleon had excluded them from Europe they sought new markets beyond the ocean. The hemp, and the timber needed for building, which they could no longer obtain from Russia and Denmark, was now procured from Bengal and from the North American colonies. Since corn could not be obtained from the Baltic, its cultivation in Ireland was fostered, and in 1806 Ireland was allowed for the first time to import corn into England free of duty. In another dirction the English attempted to force their way into the Spanish and Portuguese colonies in America, which for centuries had been closed to foreign commerce. As the result of an understanding with the London merchants, but without the approval of the Government, Sir Home Popham and General Beresford ventured in 1806 to make a regular raid on Buenos Ayres and Montvideo. The raid failed. Shortly afterwards, however, the French armies invaded the Spanish peninsula, and immediately, not only the whole of South America but also Oporto, Lisbon and Cadiz, in revolt against the French occupation, opened their markets to the products of English manufacture.

The total value of English exports to America (exclusive of the United States) rose from £7,771,418 in 1805, to ten and eleven million in 1806 and 1807, to £16,591,871 in 1808 and to £18,014,219 in 1809. The value of exports to Portugal rose from £426,122 in 1808, to £804,022 in 1809, to £1,308,216 in 1810, and to £4,650,703 in 1811.[1] Nor was Portugal the sole European market for British goods. British goods found their way even into the parts of Europe subject to the dominion or influence of Napoleon. The elasticity of commerce, as an English orator termed it, proved strong enough to overcome all the obstacles piled up by Continental Governments. The goods would be landed in some Baltic port, and no system of police, however well organized, could then prevent them from reaching any point in Europe. Napoleon himself, who was always short of money, tolerated infractions of his own system. His troops needed to be clothed and shod, and for that purpose he permitted the import of English cloth and leather by way of Hamburg " in perfect safety and at half-price." English goods had accumulated in Denmark ready to be smuggled over the frontier. The importers must have paid an insurance premium of 33 per cent. Napoleon decided to permit the open importation of the goods on payment of a duty equal to that percentage. By this step his treasury benefited to the extent of thirty

[1] For the figures see *An Account of the Real Value of Exports* . . . 1805-11 and 1812. For the difficulty of interpreting the statistics of imports and exports, see Brougham's interesting observations (H. of C., March 3. 1812, *Parl. Deb.*, vol. xxi. pp. 103-4).

million francs in one year.[1] In 1810 the harvest in England failed, famine was imminent and the blockade might perhaps have proved successful. But Napoleon, in order to obtain English gold for France, and to increase his revenues, authorized the export of corn on a large scale into England on payment of an export duty. Thanks to his action, England was supplied with bread and the famine was averted.

So far we have observed no traces of any opposition between the policy of the British Government and the interests of the manufacturing and mercantile classes. The aim of both was the same—namely to discover new markets, to recover markets which had been closed, and in every way possible to render nugatory the measures taken to boycott British commerce. Pitt's party was at once the war party and the commercial party. In 1803 the City had manifested its warlike spirit by the foundation, at an enormous public meeting attended by 5,000 people, of Lloyd's Patriotic Fund. £150,000 were subscribed in the space of a month ; and six years later the society's funds had reached the sum of £425,000. Out of this fund relief and pensions, the latter often larger than those given by the Government, were distributed by a committee of business men to officers, soldiers and sailors, and to their wives and children.

> If the world ever saw a magnificent act
> That time might on adamant write,
> Sons of Commerce, 'tis yours.

Thus wrote Dibdin, the popular ballad-monger. But as time went on far-reaching differences of opinion revealed themselves between the Cabinet and the City.

The Struggle against the Orders in Council.

To the measures taken by Napoleon the British Government replied by a tariff policy resembling, on the whole, very closely that adopted by the Emperor. To Napoleon's decrees corresponded the Orders in Council opposing an English blockade to the French.[2] It is, indeed, hard to say which of the two Governments, during the struggle which had been going on throughout the past decade, had been the first to strike. Napoleon had issued the Berlin Decree as an answer to an Order in Council of April 1806, declaring the entire Continental coast

---

[1] Bourrienne, *Memoirs*, vol iv. ; chaps. xv. and xx. (ed. Lacroix, vol. iv. pp. 169–70, 210–11).

[2] A list of the Orders in Council will be found in the *Cambridge Modern History*, vol. ix., Napoleon, chap. xiii. The Continental System, by J. Holland Rose. The list is, however incomplete. Cf. Twenty-four Orders in Council (H. of C., February 28, 1813, Lord Holland's speech, *Parl. Deb.*, vol. xxi. p. 1058). Mr. Holland Rose only gives eleven.

from Brest to the Elbe in a state of blockade. Similarly the Decree of Milan was the direct reply to an Order in Council of January 7, 1807, and to seven Orders in Council of November 1807. The substance of these Orders may be summed up as follows. The entire coast of the countries subject to French domination or in alliance with France was declared to be in a state of blockade. All commerce was prohibited between one French or allied port and another, or between any such port and a neutral port. One resource was, however, offered to neutrals desirous of trading with a French or allied port. Greater facilities than were formerly given were now accorded to neutral vessels importing foreign goods into England. They were even permitted to re-export these goods or export others. They were allowed to carry on this import or export trade with any part of the coast of France or of her allies, which was not at the time actually blockaded by English vessels. The sole condition imposed was that the neutral vessels should have touched at an English port, declared and unloaded their cargo, and paid a duty on it.[1]

In short, Napoleon issued a prohibition of all commerce between England and the countries subject to his authority or influence. The English Government replied by a prohibition of all commerce between neutrals and France, unless the neutral ships put in at an English port on their way and paid a duty to the English exchequer. Napoleon defied England to dispense with the Continental market and the British Government in return defied the French Empire to dispense with all goods which were either of English manufacture or had passed through the English customs. The two nations, to employ the illustration of a Minister, George Rose,[2] were in the position of two men who had both put their heads in a bucket, and were trying to see who could keep his head under the longer.

The manufacturers, however, far from accepting this policy, rose up against the restrictions placed by Cabinet and Parliament on the export of their goods. It was in vain that William Spence, the economist, in a work which reached a fifth edition within two years, reaffirmed the old physiocratic doctrine that land was the sole source of wealth ; that commerce, being merely an exchange of equal values, was barren, and that therefore a great nation, and England above all others, would lose nothing by the sacrifice of her trade.[3] James Mill began his career as a writer by a defence of Commerce, which enjoyed an equally great

---

[1] The text of the Order in Council of January 7, 1807, of the three Orders in Council of November 11th, and of the four Orders in Council of November 25th, will be found in the *Annual Register* for 1807, pp. 671, 746, 749, 750, 754, 755, 757, 759. Other Orders in Council are mentioned in the *Annual Register* for that year, bearing date August 19th, September 2nd, November 4th, December 9th and 18th.

[2] This illustration was, according to Tierney, employed by Rose in a conference with the Birmingham manufacturers. H. of C., April 27, 1812 (*Parl. Deb.*, vol. xxii. p. 1063).

[3] *Britain Independent of Commerce*, 1st ed., 1807.

success.[1] He contrived to prove that commerce was the creator of utility and wealth, that universal over-production was an impossibility, and that the supply was, of its nature, always equal to the demand, since all products were exchanged against all products, and partial gluts of the market were due solely and entirely to the clumsy interference of Government, which paralysed exchange. This was undoubtedly the first work, explicitly and dogmatically preaching Free Trade, which had appeared in England since the beginning of the war. It reflected the opinions of the manufacturers and merchants. From 1807 onwards Liverpool was in open protest against the Orders in Council. As the years went by all the seaports and manufacturing towns joined the movement of protest.

Eventually the movement became so strong that the Cabinet beat a hasty retreat. An Order in Council of April 26, 1809, opened to free trade all the German ports beyond the Ems, and the Italian ports between Pesaro and Orbetello. It is true that the blockade, while restricted in scope, was apparently rendered more stringent. The Order in Council of 1809 discontinued the facilities granted in 1807 to neutrals willing to trade with the blockaded coast on condition of first touching at an English port. But this discontinuance was merely formal. Since 1806 the British Government had assumed the authority to grant licences authorizing individual merchants, in direct contravention of the Orders in Council, to import a determined quantity of certain kinds of foreign merchandise, on condition that the importing vessel re-exported English merchandise to the value of £5 or more for every ton of cargo capacity. These licences were the object of the most reckless speculation, both in the City and in all the ports of the Continent and their number went on constantly increasing ; 1,600 in 1806, they exceeded 18,000 in 1810.[2] Nevertheless, the system was still far from giving satisfaction to merchants and manufacturers.

The licensed vessel was usually a neutral, owned by a foreigner and manned by a foreign crew. This aroused the complaints of English shipbuilders and shipowners. The interests of the Merchant Service were, they alleged, being sacrificed to those of commerce. The Baltic Powers, henchmen, whether voluntary or involuntary, of Napoleon, were being assisted to build fleets and to train sailors. Between 1806 and 1809 the number of ships built in England fell by more than a half.[3] During the same period the proportion of foreign to British

---

[1] Commerce Defended : An Answer to Arguments by which Mr. Spence, Mr. Cobbett and others have attempted to prove that Commerce is not a Source of National Wealth, 1st. ed. 1807, 2nd ed. 1808.

[2] H. of C., March 3, 1812, Brougham's speech (Parl. Deb., vol. xxi. p. 1105). For the licence system see Brougham's entire speech, with useful corrections by Rose (ibid., p. 1118). See also William Herbert's speech (H. of C., April 16, 1812, Parl. Deb., vol. xxii. pp. 410 sqq.), and A. Baring's speech (H. of C., August 17, 1812, ibid., pp. 425 sqq.).

[3] H. of C., March 3, 1812, Brougham's speech (Parl. Deb., vol. xxi. p. 1106).

vessels in the ports of the United Kingdom was constantly increasing,[1] and in 1810 had reached 13·127 per cent. The merchants themselves complained. They charged the licence system with favouring the Port of London to the detriment of other ports, since the London merchants were nearer the Cabinet and therefore in a better position to obtain all the licences they wished. They also charged the system with extending unduly the influence of the Executive. How, they asked, could the Cabinet refuse a licence to a merchant who was an influential Member of Parliament or who possessed a strong electoral interest in a borough ? Even if the working of the system could be kept free from abuses, the Board of Trade was, according to them, undertaking a task wholly beyond its power in thus claiming to act as the Providence of the economic world, and to know better than the parties interested what sorts of goods were in demand, and at what time and in what quantity these goods were wanted. The irregularities observable in the distribution of goods, the repeated crises and the constant gluts of the market were due perhaps to the mistakes of the Board of Trade. Opposition to the licensing of trade strengthened among manufacturers and merchants their distrust of all Governmental interference with the economic machinery of the country. The dispute which broke out in 1812 between the British Government and the United States formed the occasion of a decisive conflict.

The economic interests of the United States had been injuriously affected by the Franco-British war. To defend themselves against the effects of the Decrees and Orders in Council, they had adopted in their turn a policy of retaliation. By the Non-Intercourse Act of 1809 all commerce, whether of import or export, between the United States, France and England was rendered impossible. When in 1810 the Non-Intercourse Act expired, the American Government adopted a subtler policy, and put up its favour, as it were, to auction between the two rival Powers. It declared the Non-Intercourse Act would be suspended until March 1811, and would then only come into force against whichever of the two nations had failed during the interval to modify its decrees so as to free the neutral commerce of the United States. Napoleon's diplomacy did not fail to turn to profit the deep-rooted ill-feeling which existed between the English and their former colonists. At little cost to himself he gave full satisfaction to the American demands. It was, therefore, against England alone that the Non-Intercourse Act came back into operation on February 2, 1811. Notwithstanding negotiations continued between the Cabinets of St. James and Washington. They concerned several matters ; fictitious blockade ; the right claimed by England to recapture, without any form of trial, English sailors, or those presumed to be such, found on board American vessels ; and the Orders in Concil. It was this

[1] Porter *Progress of the Nation*, 1851, p. 392.

last matter that affected the manufacturers and merchants. Throughout the winter of 1811–12 they were engaged in a campaign to force the hand of the Cabinet, and to compel it to grant the demands of the American diplomatists by revoking completely the Orders in Council.

Licences were granted freely to Baltic shipowners, but refused to Americans. This was, maintained the Opposition speakers, an absurd policy. North America was the sole Power in the world beyond the reach of Napoleon, and its Navy could never be incorporated in the enemy's fleet.[1] It was, therefore, to the political interest of Great Britain to conciliate the United States instead of constantly provoking them and driving them into war. Moreover, England's economic interest coincided with her political. In Warwickshire men were everywhere being thrown out of work : the reason was that North America had ceased to buy her hardware.[2] In Lancashire also there was similar unemployment, because raw cotton could no longer be obtained from North America. It was by no means unlikely that if America could no longer exchange her agricultural produce for English manufactured articles, she would become herself a manufacturing State. The report spread that the United States were already beginning to manufacture their own nails and horseshoes, and that in certain Baltic ports American cotton thread had already made its appearance.[3] The speakers on the side of the Government made a very poor defence. They confined themselves to casting upon the Opposition leaders the responsibility of having inaugurated in 1806 and 1807 the policy of Orders in Council. They pretended to be in doubt whether the Orders themselves were being attacked or the licensing system which was a departure from the Orders. They urged their opponents not to compromise the freedom of action of the English diplomatists by unseasonable debates, while the negotiations with the United States were in progress. When a motion was made for the institution of an inquiry into the operation of the Orders in Council and the Licensing System they secured its rejection in both Houses.[4] Nevertheless, their majority in the Commons was only seventy-two.

Very significant defections occurred among the supporters of the Government, among them being Canning, a member for Liverpool,[5] and Wilberforce, a Yorkshire member.[6] A widespread agitation was

---

[1] H. of C., March 3, 1812, Brougham's speech (*Parl. Deb.*, vol. xxi. p. 1105).

[2] *Ibid.*, April 17, 1812, speeches of Rose and Brougham (*Parl. Deb.*, vol. xxii. pp. 430, 437).

[3] H. of L., February 18, 1812, Lord Lansdowne's speech ; H. of C., March 13, 1812, A. Baring's speech (*Parl. Deb.*, vol. xxi. pp. 1043, 1128). Cf. Charles Lyne, *A Letter . . . to Lord Castlereagh . . . on the North American Export Trade during the War . . .* 1813.

[4] By 135 votes to 71 in the Lords, by 216 to 144 in the Commons.

[5] H. of C., March 3, 1812 (*Parl. Deb.*, vol. xxi. pp. 1139 sqq.). In justification of this apparent abandonment of a policy that he had once warmly defended he argued that the supporters of the Orders in Council had nothing to fear from the inquiry.

[6] H. of C., March 3, 1812 (*Parl. Deb.*, vol. xxi. pp. 1150–1). He denounced the systematic fraud and perjury inseparably bound up with the grant of licences.

organized. The Leicestershire framework knitters, the Staffordshire potters, the clothiers of the West Riding, the workers engaged in the cotton industry at Kendal, and in the Birmingham hardware manufacture, the shipowners of London, Liverpool, Glasgow, and North and South Shields united to demand the revocation of the Orders in Council. At Liverpool a petition was signed by three-fourths of the shipowners.[1] The petition from Birmingham bore 14,000 signatures.[2] After Perceval's assassination, the Cabinet, reconstructed only with the greatest difficulty and in confused disorder, was forced to yield. On June 23rd there appeared a proclamation by the Prince Regent revoking the Orders in Council of April 26, 1809, so far as concerned American vessels and their cargoes.[3] Rejoicing took place in the manufacturing districts. At Birmingham the *Committee of Artisans* prepared a triumphal reception for the delegates who had carried their petition to London. A crowd of 50,000 took part in the celebrations.[4] When a general election was held a few months later Brougham, who had led the entire campaign, stood for election at Liverpool against the Tory candidates Canning and General Gascoyne. Though he failed to win the seat, his opponents' majority was very small indeed ; and the result of this election was generally regarded as a sign that on the question of freedom of commerce the business world was at issue with the party in office. But since 1688 the party in power had always enjoyed the support of the business world.

The Progress of Free Trade Propaganda (1813–1815).

The victory gained in 1812 by the supporters of freedom of commerce was in reality no victory at all ; or rather, to speak more accurately, it was a victory won a few days too late. Five days before the revocation of the Orders in Council on the 23rd of June, the Government of the United States had declared war on England. Two years were to pass before peaceful relations were reestablished between the two nations. The South American market was insufficient to compensate for the loss of the market afforded by the United States to English merchandise, and was glutted by the goods profusely and indiscriminately thrown upon it. Where was a new market to be found ? In Asia perhaps, did not the monopoly of the East India Company stand in the way. The advocates of freedom of commerce pressed for its abolition.

There existed formerly in England several large trading companies, privileged with rights of monopoly, which organized trade with foreign countries and established permanent factories abroad. As the power

---

[1] H. of C., May 13, 1812 (*Parl. Deb.*, vol. xxiii. p. 183).
[2] H. of C., April 17, 1812 (*Parl. Deb.*, vol. xxii. p. 427).
[3] See the full text of the proclamation (*Parl. Deb.*, vol. xxiii. pp. 716–18 n.).
[4] *Leeds Mercury*, July 11, 1812.

of the State grew, and the Government was enabled to afford direct protection, by its consuls, sailors and soldiers, to Englishmen residing abroad, these privileged companies had all disappeared with the exception of one, which continued to occupy a position of peculiar importance. This was the East India Company, the *United Company of Merchants of England trading to the East Indies*. It is true that its sovereign rights had been restricted. The meeting of shareholders, the *Court of Proprietors*, and the *Council of Directors*, had been made subject in 1785 to a *Board of Control*, composed of six members which were nominated by the Government, the President of the Board being ex-officio a member of the Cabinet. Nevertheless, the Company retained the right, subject to the control of the Board, to build forts, to appoint governors, to coin money, to hold courts of law, and to raise and maintain an army. It is also true that the economic privileges of the Company had been curtailed.[1] In 1793 a statute had been passed to compel the Company to ship every year on board its vessels 3,000 tons of goods belonging to private merchants. But the Company still retained the monopoly of navigation between the United Kingdom and India and China, and all the imports from the Far East had to be deposited in the Company's warehouses and there sold publicly. The Company owned a fleet of 115 vessels, manned by some 10,000 sailors, and maintained, around its docks and warehouses between London Bridge and Blackwall, a population of 50,000. In India it governed a territory of 380,000 square miles, a population of 60,000,000 and an army of 150,000 men. It was considered to represent a total capital, in stocks, land and buildings, docks, vessels, and the private means of its 2,000 shareholders and of all its employés, of £21,000,000.[2] In the economic conditions of the time the existence of the East India Company constituted a glaring anomaly.

The Company's charter expired at the beginning of 1814. Ever since 1808 negotiations had been in progress between the Court of Directors and the President of the Board of Control to settle the conditions under which the contract should be renewed between the Company and the nation. The Company's political rights were not even the object of serious discussion. Had the Government attempted to exercise a more direct control over the administration of British India, the Opposition would have protested against this dangerous increase of the patronage and influence of the Crown. But, on the other hand, public opinion demanded the abolition of the economic monopoly. This was actually effected in 1813, after eighteen months of heated debate. The Company still retained the monopoly of navigation and trading with China. But trade with India was thrown open to the merchants and shipowners of every British port.

---

[1] 33 Geo. III, cap. 52.
[2] *Quarterly Review*, December 1812, Art. 1, papers respecting the E.I. Company's charter (vol. viii. p. 245).

It would, however, be untrue to say without considerable reservations that the entire business world was in arms against the sole surviving trading company. The East India Company had managed to create a group of supporters among the merchants. To grant to all the British ports the right to trade with India was to deprive not only the Company but the Port of London of the monopoly of commerce with the East. The London merchants, therefore, sided with the Company, and we find Alexander Baring in 1813 defending the Company's monopoly as zealously as he had denounced the Orders in Council the year before. The opposing forces were, on the one side, these kings of British commerce, who lived in London and prided themselves on their culture, their connexions with the gentry and their respectability of long standing ; on the other side, the *nouveaux riches* of the North and Midlands, of whom only a mere handful were beginning to make their way into the ranks of good society, a rabble of upstarts, as the Londoners were pleased to consider them, without commercial morality, without traditions and without manners. The old mercantile society of London was defeated by a combination of interests whose power was perhaps now realized for the first time. Their opponents had, moreover, won their victory under the banner of novel principles, which since 1792 had never been explicitly avowed.

The revocation in 1812 of the Orders in Council had sought the resumption of normal economic relations with a foreign nation whose attitude threatened war. Military as well as commercial interests had been involved. Had the advocates of commercial freedom invoked too openly the doctrines laid down by Adam Smith in his *Wealth of Nations*, they would have been denounced as unpatriotic cosmopolitans, and would thus have endangered the success of their cause. No difficulty of this sort existed in 1813. When the East India Company's monopoly came up for discussion, the question concerned Englishmen alone. Hence the debates assumed an entirely different tone. The opponents of the monopoly openly adopted the language of the new school of political economy, and demanded the recognition of their right to an open trade, an unlimited trade, a " free trade " with the British possessions in India : [1] " the natural state of things was free trade." [2] This was the first appearance of a formula destined in a few years' time to become, in a somewhat wider acceptation, a popular catchword. The public discussion in 1813 of the renewal of the

[1] See the text of the petitions presented to the House between March 19 and July 1, 1812 (*Parl. Deb.*, vol. xxii. pp. 89–90 sqq.).

[2] H. of C., June 3, 1813, Th. Courtenay's speech (*Parl. Deb.*, vol. xxvi. p. 543). See also p. 462 (Geo. Phillip's speech), pp. 516–17 (Richard's speech), p. 683 (Sir John Newport's speech), p. 695 (Canning's speech) ; and H. of L., June 21st, p. 788 (Lord Lansdowne's speech), July 16th (Lord Lauderdale's speech). Several months later, during a discussion on a connected Bill, Lord Castlereagh himself, though narrow in his views and badly informed regarding industrial and commercial matters, began to speak the language of Adam Smith (H. of C., December 9, 1813, discussion of the East India Circuitous Trade Bill, *Parl. Deb.*, vol. xxvi. pp. 272–3).

East India Company's charter was the starting-point of that wide campaign in favour of the economic dogma of Free Trade which spread ever more and more rapidly in commercial and political circles.

The victors of 1813 suddenly found themselves in the following year thrown upon the defensive. Two good harvests in succession, and the renewed importation of foreign corn consequent upon the restoration of peace, had lowered the price of cereals. This was a source of rejoicing to the manufacturers ; for they considered that the rate of wages and hence the cost of manufacture was determined by the price of bread, and it was therefore to the manufacturer's interest that bread should be cheap. But the landowners and farmers saw ruin staring them in the face, and demanded the imposition of higher duties to protect agriculture. It was in vain that the manufacturers organized an agitation even more powerful than the agitation of two years before against the Orders in Council. The Cabinet paid no heed to it and brought in a Bill in conformity with the demands of the agriculturists. It was in vain that the manufacturers invited the populace to riot. In spite of rioting the Bill became law. The defeat of the manufacturers was unquestionable. We submit, nevertheless, that the defeat actually helped forward the cause of Free Trade.

The debates on the Corn Bill compelled the manufacturers to reconsider their own position. "Why," urged the agriculturists, "would you prevent us protecting ourselves against foreign competition ? Are you not protected yourselves ? " British industry had, indeed, grown up during the past two centuries under a system of strict protection. Merchant shipping was subject to the Navigation Acts which only permitted the import of foreign goods on ships of the country from which they came or on English ships, built in England and manned by a crew three-quarters English. If the goods were imported on ships of their own country they paid higher duties. During the war the Navigation Acts had been applied with greater laxity. Nevertheless, they remained on the Statute Book, and it was only in 1814 and 1815 that their provisions were slightly relaxed in the case of the Indian and American trade.[1] The recruitment of English labour for works abroad or the export of machinery were offences punishable with heavy penalties. Moreover, additional legislation on these points had been placed from time to time on the Statute Book, as new industries had arisen.[2] The import duties imposed by Pitt's great Consolidation Act of 1787 had been increased in 1797, 1798 and 1803.[3] In 1809 the duty on merchandise of a kind not specified particularly elsewhere, and wholly or partially manufactured, had been raised to $37\frac{1}{2}$ per cent.,

---

[1] 53 Geo. III, cap. 155 ; 54 Geo. III, cap. 35, 134. See H. of C., December 9, 1813 (Parl. Deb., vol. xxvii. pp. 268 sqq.) ; also the treaty of peace with the United States, 1815.

[2] 22 Geo. III. cap. 60 (calico, cotton, muslin) ; 25 Geo. III, cap. 67 (metal-working).
7 Geo. III. cap. 15 ; 38 Geo. III. cap. 76 ; 43 Geo. III. cap. 68 (Consolidating Act.)

with a special war duty in addition, amounting to a third of the permanent duties.[1] In 1813 the permanent duties were increased by a quarter on all imports ; by two-thirds, while the war should last, on all goods coming from France or countries under French supremacy.[2] Iron paid a duty of £7 18s. 4d. a ton, tin a duty of £114. The duty on earthenware exceeded 79 per cent., on cotton goods it amounted to 85 per cent., on cloth to 90 per cent., and on glass to 114 per cent. The importation of silk was absolutely prohibited. If the manufacturers wished to escape from the force of this *ad hominem* argument of the agriculturists, they had to be prepared to give up the benefit of these duties.

But there was really no reason why they should not do so. For many years past the agriculturists had enjoyed under a system of low duties a most effective protection, thanks to the difficulties of importation in time of war. The manufacturers, on the other hand, had built around manufactures a lofty and skilfully constructed tariff wall, which had proved totally unnecessary. The preeminence of England in manufacture was too great. Goods of foreign origin were simply unable to compete in England with the home-made articles. The manufacturers would surely be well advised to set the example of free trade by the abolition of duties in the vast majority of cases perfectly useless, even at the risk of sacrificing a small number of industries in a weaker position. Prudence equally dictated the abolition of certain duties whose sole purpose was to produce revenue. The duties, for instance, on French wine were very heavy, and had been made still heavier in 1815 ; but in so far as the French were prevented from selling their wines in England, they were prevented from buying British cotton and woollen goods. The petitions of 1814 and the riots of 1815 proved that on the question of Free Trade the manufacturers had working-class opinion on their side, despite the conflict of interests between employers and employed, and could therefore organize against a small group of agriculturists a large popular Opposition party truly representative of the will of the nation. The hour of triumph for Free Trade had not yet come, but it was drawing near. Cobbett and Burdett, at once landowners and demagogues, tried in vain to stem the rising tide which swept them before it. In February Ricardo published his *Essay on the Influence of a low Price of Corn on the Profits of Stock*," to demonstrate, as the title proceeds to tell us, " the Inexpediency of Restrictions on Importations." In him the Free Traders had found the classical exponent of their doctrines.

The Disorganization of Labour.   The Combination Act.

We have seen that in the new class of employers there was a total lack of organization or even of the desire for organization. When

[2] 49 Geo. III, cap. 98 (Consolidating Act).   [2] 53 Geo. III, cap. 33.

the leading manufacturers acted in concert it was not to demand measures of protection, but, on the contrary, the removal of all legal restraints upon their absolute freedom to contest among themselves the markets of the world. They demanded the reduction of tariffs and the abolition of monopolies. They also demanded the prohibition of workmen's unions and the repeal of statutes regulating the conditions of labour in the interest of the worker. On these two last points they obtained satisfaction, with the result that the disorganization of labour corresponded to the disorganization of the employers. There was, however, this important difference—that the disorganization of the employers was the deliberate choice of the employers themselves, whereas the disorganization of labour was forced on the workmen against their will. It was in part the work of the employers and the legislature, in part the inevitable result of circumstances.

The progress of the system of wage-labour, and the opposition which was becoming ever more and more acute between Capital and Labour, tended to increase the number of associations formed by the workmen to defend themselves against their masters' exactions. Throughout the whole of the 18th century these associations had been the object of a series of prohibitory statutes. An Act of 1749 prohibited workmen's unions in all branches of the textile industry enumerated severally, in the principal departments of metal-working, in the manufacture of felt and hats, and in certain other specified industries.[1] In 1799, when a Member of Parliament brought in a Bill to prohibit combinations in a particular industry, Wilberforce intervened to demand a general statute applying to any and every combination of workmen.[2] The war, the financial crises, the rise in the price of food, the revolt of the workers against machinery, and of the sailors against discipline, the Irish rebellion, all combined to fill the ruling classes with alarm. It was in 1799 that the statute was passed prohibiting political associations. The moment was, therefore, favourable. Wilberforce was at once the mouthpiece of the party of order and of the business world. Within a month the Bill for which he asked had been introduced,[3] passed, and had received the royal sanction.[4]

In 1800, as the result of a motion by Gascoyne, supported by Sheridan, a second Act amended and to a certain extent relaxed the first.[5] The Act of 1800 extended to combinations of employers the penalties enacted by the Act of 1799 against combinations of work-

[1] 22 Geo. II, cap. 27.   See a summary of the Act in Held, *Zwei Bücher* . . . p. 560.

[2] H. of C., April 9, 1799.   Sir John Anderson's motion (*Parl. Reg.* vol. lxx. p. 323).

[3] Who introduced the Bill does not clearly appear from the account given in the *Parliamentary Register*.   Certainly not Pitt.   (H. of C., June 30, 1800, vol. lxxiv. p. 219.)   Perhaps it was introduced by Wilberforce, but more probably by one of the Ministers.

[4] July 12th.   39 Geo. III, cap. 81.

[5] 39 and 40 Geo. III, cap. 106.   Another Act (41 Geo. III, cap. 38) is without significance ; it merely corrected one or two mistakes in the drafting of the former Act.

men. It forbade any magistrate, who as an employer had a direct interest in the struggle, to take part as a magistrate in enforcing the Act. It organized an entire system of compulsory arbitration by the magistrates in contests between employers and workmen. But despite these modifications, introduced in deference to Opposition criticisms, the spirit of the new Act was identical with that of the Act of 1799. It remained a criminal offence for workmen to form a combination with the object of securing an improvement in the conditions of their labour, of compelling the choice of certain workmen in preference to certain others, or of exercising any sort of control over the management of a business enterprise. It was a criminal offence to attempt to take a man from his work by bribery, persuasion, solicitation, intimidation or any other means whatever. It was a criminal offence to take part in a meeting, or to collect funds on behalf of any of the above-mentioned purposes. Three months' imprisonment with two months' hard labour, was the penalty prescribed. Any money illegally collected was liable to confiscation—half being forfeit to the Treasury, half to the informer. Nor was this enough. Despite the criticism raised by Hobhouse and Lord Holland,[1] a summary process was instituted to punish breaches of the Act. One single magistrate by himself received power to condemn and sentence offenders. The power of appeal to Quarter Sessions was a mere farce ; for the appellant had to deposit £20 as caution money, and no workman possessed £20 to deposit.

Such was the nature of the Act to whose provisions labour was subject for fifteen years. We must now inquire how it was applied in practice. The British Government possessed no efficient police, and therefore had scant weapons at its disposal to repress breaches of the law. The employers asked the Government to take the initiative in prosecuting illegal combinations, but the Attorney-General refused. They, on the other hand, were loath to take the first step, as this would

---

[1] For the Opposition criticisms see (a) on the first Bill, H. of C., June 26, 1799 (*Parliamentary Register*, vol. lxxi. p. 65 ; H. of C., July 9, 1799, *Parliamentary Register*, vol. lxxi. pp. 562 sqq.), cf. *Journal of Lady Holland*, vol. ii. pp. 101–2. (b) On the second Bill, H. of C., June 13 and 30, July 22, 1800 (*Parliamentary Register*, vol. lxxiv. pp. 110 sqq., 218 sqq., 459 sqq.). No mention of these debates is to be found in Cobbett's *Parliamentary History*. Stephen was therefore correct in his assertion (*History of Criminal Law*, vol. iii. p. 208) that " in the Parliamentary History for 1799 and 1800 there is no account of any debate on these Acts." We receive, nevertheless, a false impression when we read into his pages or learn on his authority in Mr. and Mrs. Webb's *History of Trade Unionism* (p. 63 n.) that the two Combination Acts were not discussed in Parliament. This mistake is probably the source of the all too frequent misstatements about the legislation of 1799–1800. Mr. George Howell (*Labour Leaders and Labour Movements*, p. 23) tells us that the Act of 1800 was an aggravation of the Act of 1799, whereas the exact contrary is the truth. Mr. Dicey (*Law and Opinion in England*, p. 99) writes : " The men who passed the great Combination Acts were not despots. . . . The Parliament of 1800 . . . contained among its members Fox." But in reality Fox and the entire body of his followers vigorously opposed the new legislation. So ran the note to our first edition, 1913. We think it may be interesting to let it stand as it was ; but Mr. and Mrs. Hammond, following our lines, have since told the same story, only more fully (*The Town Labourer*, 1760–1832, 1918, pp. 123 sqq.) ; and Mr. and Mrs. Webb have accordingly modified the sentence here quoted (*History of Trade Unionism*, revised ed., 1920, pp. 69 sqq.).

provoke reprisals on the part of the workmen, who would combine to cease working—the very thing the employers were most anxious to prevent.[1] The workmen's combinations, therefore, were not prosecuted systematically. The employers waited till a strike occurred (the term " strike " was coming into use at this period).[2] Then they did not spare severity. The strike leaders were imprisoned and the funds confiscated. But in ordinary times the workmen's combinations were tolerated, and in some exceptional cases the toleration was open and quasi-legal.

An instance of this was the foundation in 1803 at Leeds of the *Clothiers' Community*, a body governed by an elected committee which claimed to limit the number of apprentices, and collected funds for the relief of sick members and the widows of deceased members. A parliamentary commission, appointed in 1806 to investigate the conditions of labour in the woollen industry, never entertained a serious thought of disputing the legality of this association.[3] Here we are dealing with one of those industries in which the transformation of the system of production was still far from complete. Domestic labour still continued side by side with factory labour. The workmen's combinations still possessed somewhat of the character of guilds, while already possessing certain of the characteristics of a trade union. They contained both employers and men, who agreed in an effort to uphold the old industrial system against the factory system. This made it difficult to regard them as illegal combinations in the sense of the Act of 1800.[4] Similarly in the silk industry at Spitalfields near the City, the workmen on the one hand, and the employers on the other, constituted respectively two associations which collected funds, elected officers, and assumed the discussion of all questions respecting the prices which according to law were to be fixed by the magistrates. Both societies were illegal, and both would have been suppressed had any complaint been made. But because the employers and the men were in agreement no complaint was made, and the system of collective contract prevailed at Spitalfields,

[1] For the difficulties of applying the Act of 1800, see a letter from Perceval, then Attorney-General, to Lord Hawkesbury (the future Lord Liverpool), October 5, 1804 (Yonge, *Life of Lord Liverpool*, vol. i. pp. 166 sqq.). Cf. John Blackner, *History of Nottingham*, p. 235.

[2] In 1797 Eden (*State of the Poor*, vol. i. p. 382) found it necessary to explain the term to his readers : " A paper-maker . . . entered into a combination with his fellow workmen to ' strike,' as it is called, or leave off working." We find the word still written in italics in a cutting from a newspaper of November 1810, which is to be found among F. Place's papers (Add. Brit. Mus., 27, 799. f. 93, 4). The usual expression was " to turn out " (*Report . . . on the Woollen Manufacture*, 1806, *Minutes of Evidence*, p. 369). *Minutes of Evidence on the Calico Printers' Petition*, 1804, pp. 7, 8, 17.

[3] *Report . . . on . . . Woollen Manufactories*, 1806, pp. 16 sqq., also *Minutes of Evidence*, p. 40 : " Are you aware of the existence of any law which authorizes the seizure of funds belonging to such societies ?—No, I am not aware of it. Are you not aware that by the Combination Act, passed in 1799, these funds become tangible if kept together after a certain period ?—I do not consider it as a combination ; I do not know that I ever read the Combination Act in my life."

[4] S. and B. Webb, *History of Trade Unionism*. p. 58.

as a matter of public knowledge and with the toleration of the law.[1]

The law itself left open to the workmen a means of securing their funds from danger of confiscation. They could have their associations registered as friendly societies.[2] The oldest friendly societies dated from the beginning of the 18th century, but they had only become numerous during the last sixty years. Certain statistics drawn up in 1803 enumerate 9,672 societies with a total membership of 704,350.[3] The governing classes beheld them with mixed feelings, with anxiety but also with sympathy. The village inn was usually the headquarters of the friendly society, and it was also at the inn that unemployed workmen in search of a job found lodging.[4] The publican acted as treasurer, and the members of the society paid into his hands a weekly subscription of twopence or threepence. In case of illness they received six or seven shillings a week relief. Once a month, sometimes once a week, the societies held a meeting, when they played games and drank far into the night. What might not pass, what language might not be held at the banquets which formed part of the compulsory rites of a friendly society? What was a friendly society but a popular club, likely, during a time of political agitation, to become a centre of " Jacobin" propaganda? But on the other hand the relief, distributed by these societies, reduced the number of paupers thrown upon the parish, and in this way prevented the poor rates from becoming too heavy a burden on the ratepayers. How to keep these advantages, while guarding against the danger of revolution, was the problem which Cabinet and Parliament tried in vain for thirty years to resolve. To compete with the friendly societies other societies were founded, called Savings Banks, which were managed by aristocratic committees of patronage.[5] But they met with very indifferent success.[6] Unavailing attempts were made to place the friendly societies under Government control. The Act of 1793,[7] the first legal recognition of friendly societies, which gave them the right to prosecute defaulting treasurers before the courts, also allowed them, if they desired it, to put themselves under the control of the magistrates, but it also expressly permitted them to refrain from so doing. The workmen were, therefore, at once protected and emancipated by this Act of 1793. They founded an ever-increasing number

[1] Brentano, History and Development of Gilds, and Origin of Trade Unions, pp. 126–7.

[2] Parliamentary Register, vol. xv. p. 162, Report of the Committee of the House of Lords. Also H. of C., July 21, 1812, Hume's speech (Parl. Deb., vol. xxiii. pp. 1176–7).

[3] P. Colquhoun, A Treatise on Indigence . . . 1806, p. 116.

[4] Eden, State of the Poor, vol. i. p. 545 n.

[5] George Rose, Observations on Banks for Savings, 1816. Cf. Edinburgh Review, June 1815, No. 49, Art. 6, Parish or Savings Banks (vol. xxv. pp. 135 sqq.).

[6] As is apparent from the Report . . . on the Poor Laws, 1817. See especially Minutes of Evidence, pp. 42, 52, 64, 71, 79.

[7] 33 Geo. III, cap. 54 (see a summary of this Act in Nicholls, History of the English Poor Law, vol. ii. pp. 116–17). Later statutes, 35 Geo. III, cap. 111; 43 Geo. III, cap. 111; 49 Geo. III, cap. 145.

of nominal friendly societies, whose real purpose was to improve the conditions of labour.

We must not, however, exaggerate the opportunities offered to workmen by the friendly societies for the defence of their economic interests. The magistrates would always be disposed to apply to them the provisions of the Act of 1799 prohibiting any federation of political associations. The friendly societies would, therefore, be well advised, if they would safeguard their funds, to remain isolated one from another. But in that case any joint action by the workmen belonging to these societies would be rendered impossible and the organization of the working class would be broken up into a vast number of small and scattered fragments. It was, moreover, dangerous to attempt the utilization of a friendly society as a trade union for resisting the employers. So long as the members of a friendly society confined themselves to the administration of sick pay they kept clear of all conflict with the Law. But the moment the authorities suspected that they were helping unemployed members,[1] whose unemployment was demonstrably due to a strike, the funds were immediately confiscated.[2] We find, accordingly, that from 1800 onwards workmen's unions of a different type were founded. There was no subscription, either compulsory or voluntary, to a common fund. Every member received a ticket, and at any place in the United Kingdom he was entitled, on the presentation of his ticket, to receive a definitely fixed payment from his fellows. The trial at Edinburgh in January 1815 of four calico printers revealed the existence in that industry of such an association.[3] A local newspaper, the *Glasgow Herald*, denounced the organization as " more a case of sedition than combination, and, in fact, an attempt made by the journeymen calico printers in the three kingdoms to form a sort of Parliament of their own, and by that means to dictate the price of labour." [4] Associations of this nature were the more dangerous to public order, because they were free from financial considerations of any kind, neither having nor desiring to have any accumulated funds. They were not even organized in view of a strike, a demonstration on the whole peaceable, and during which the workmen need a reserve fund on which to subsist. They were rather organized for violent demonstration, for intimidation by armed force, for the destruction of looms and machinery.

The Luddite Rising. The Repeal of the Statute of Elizabeth.

The Luddite outbreaks of 1812 were the development of a form

---

[1] *Minutes of Evidence . . . respecting Laws relating to Woollen Trade*, 1803, pp. 23, 27, 227.

[2] See Gascoyne's criticisms, H. of C., June 30, 1800 (*Parliamentary Register*, vol. lxxiv. p. 221).

[3] The society was already in existence in 1804. See *Minutes of Evidence on the Calico Printers' Petition*, 1804, pp. 7–8, 18.

[4] Quoted in *The Times* for January 10, 1815.

of revolutionary association directly caused by an oppressive legal code aggravated by new legislation equally oppressive. This popular rising occasioned at the time diverse opinions as to its causes. The journalists and speakers who supported the Government hinted that the rising bore a political character, that the rebels dreamt of a restoration of the Cromwellian republic, and that the outbreak had its instigators in high position.[1] These insinuations were scarcely serious and often insincere. As far as Nottinghamshire was concerned their object was apparently to injure the position of the Lord-Lieutenant, Lord Fitzwilliam, who belonged to the Opposition.[2] As a matter of fact the aristocratic leaders of the Whig Party had been the first to take alarm for the safety of their properties. In 1812 the rumour spread that Lord Derby's seat in Lancashire and the Duke of Devonshire's seat in Derbyshire had been burnt.[3] The ministerialists also charged the manufacturers with inciting the working classes to riot in order to intimidate the Cabinet into abolishing the Orders in Council. This was an equally absurd accusation. It was against the manufacturers that the rioting was immediately directed, and, if they redoubled their exertions to obtain markets abroad, it was in the hope that, by alleviating the widespread destitution, they might avert the urgent danger which threatened their private houses and factories. The Luddite rising was the rising of a class, due exclusively to economic causes, to questions of wages and labour organization.

For a whole year, from March 1811 till the second half of January 1812, the movement was confined to Nottinghamshire, where the glutting of the market by the cheap manufacture of articles of an inferior quality had lowered wages and reduced 50,000 families to starvation.[4] In this county a secret society was formed, concerning which, in the absence of official documents, we can only gather scattered scraps of information and doubtful rumours. Irish immigrants were plentiful in the manufacturing districts of the North ;[5] and a military organization was there descernible, probably copied from the United Irishmen of 1799. Its object was the destruction of frames, which was accomplished in accordance with a general plan.[6] Four companies divided among them, in 1811, four districts of the county. Frames

---

[1] *Nottingham Journal*, July 11, September 12, 1812 ; *Leeds Mercury*, September 19, 1812 ; *Report of the Committee of Secrecy*, July 8, 1812 (*Parl. Deb.*, vol. xxiii. p. 954) ; H. of C., July 10, 1812, Wilberforce's speech (*Parl. Deb.*, vol. xxiii. p. 978). Cf. *Quarterly Review*, vol. xv. pp. 569–70 (July 1816), and vol. xvi. p. 257 (October 1816).

[2] *Leeds Mercury*, May 18, 1812.

[3] Thomas Grenville's letter to Lord Buckingham, March 14, 1812 (*Court of England under the Prince Regent*, vol. i. p. 294). *Leeds Mercury*, quotation in the *Star*, May 18, 1812.

[4] *Examiner*, September 20, 1812, *History of the Luddites*. Felkin, *Hosiery and Lace*, pp. 230 sqq.

[5] For these Irish influences see *Nottingham Journal*, May 16, 1812. Cf. H. of C., July 10, 1812, Wilberforce's speech (*Parl. Deb.*, vol. xxiii. pp. 977–8).

[6] Felkin, *Hosiery and Lace*, pp. 231–2.

would be smashed systematically on the same night at a distance of twelve miles one from another. Operations were controlled by a rigid discipline. An eyewitness has depicted the insurgent forces walking in groups of not more than fifty, some keeping guard armed with swords, pistols and guns, other entrusted with the actual destruction of the frames, armed with axes and hammers. Immediately the task of destruction was accomplished, the leader of the band called over the names, every man being designated and called by a number. Then, on the firing of a pistol, the band dispersed, and the authorities never succeeded in discovering the culprits. The smashing of frames was no novelty in the district, and for a long time past the proverbial expression had been current that when frames were destroyed, "Ned Ludd had passed that way." A rumour grew up in consequence that the movement was directed by a mythical personage "King Ludd" or "General Ludd," and it would appear that several of the leaders of bands adopted that name.[1]

In February 1812, the Cabinet decided to take action. Over 3,000 troops had already been assembled at Nottingham. Two Acts were passed—one making the destruction of knitting frames a capital offence,[2] the other conferring on the magistrates of the county exceptionally wide police powers.[3] But at this very moment the troubles spread to the woollen district in the West Riding of Yorkshire, to the cotton district of Lancashire and Cheshire, and even reached the Lowlands of Scotland, where a general strike broke out among the weavers.[4] Everywhere the working classes were suffering from the same evil, and the crisis of over-production was universal. The ruling classes were stricken with panic. A rumour spread that there existed a huge conspiracy, reaching from Glasgow to London, and controlled by the same leaders, whose object was first to stir up a rebellion in the North which would draw off the troops of the capital, and then, as soon as London was left without a garrison, to give the signal for a general rebellion throughout the entire kingdom.[5] Napoleon was making preparations to invade Russia, war with America was imminent, the Prime Minister had been assassinated, and the news of his death had been greeted with demonstrations of popular rejoicing. Southey, who was engaged on an article upon the French Revolution for the *Quarterly Review*, confided to a correspondent his opinion that the subject was

---

[1] *Leeds Mercury*, May 9, 1812, August 22, 1812. Felkin, *Lace and Hosiery*, p. 231.

[2] 52 Geo. III, cap. 16 (deportation had been the penalty prescribed by a former Act, 28 Geo. III, cap. 16). By the end of 1813 order had been sufficiently restored for the passage of a new Act replacing the death penalty by deportation (54 Geo. III, cap. 42).

[3] 52 Geo. III, cap. 17. A temporary Act to expire on March 1, 1814.

[4] S. and B. Webb, *History of Trade Unionism*, p. 52.

[5] Pellew, *Life of Lord Sidmouth*, vol. iii. p. 84, letter from Major Seale to Lord Sidmouth, June 30, 1812. *Court of England under the Prince Regent*, vol. i. pp. 284–5, W. H. Fremantle's letter to the Marquis of Buckingham, May 2, 1812.

"most mournfully well timed. At this moment nothing but the Army preserves us from the most dreadful of all calamities, an insurrection of the poor against the rich, and how long the Army may be depended upon is a question which I scarcely dare to ask myself." [1]   "You are quite right in apprehending a Jacquerie," wrote Walter Scott to Southey, "the country is mined below our feet."[2]   Once more the Cabinet sought from Parliament new weapons for the repression of the riots, now becoming general, and obtained in July an Act "for the preservation of the public peace in certain disturbed counties in England.[3]

In reality, however, civil war, chronic in England, had lost its more atrocious features.   The extraordinary horror, aroused towards the end of April by the isolated assassination near Huddersfield of a manufacturer named Horsfall, proves how free from bloodshed the outbreaks of 1812 had on the whole been.   By January 1813, when the judges, in virtue of a special commission, passed their last sentences on the Yorkshire rioters, order may be regarded as universally restored. Napoleon had evacuated Russia, markets had been found for British industry, and the price of corn had fallen.   It is the recovery of employment, rather than the measures of repression, which explains the cessation of the disturbances which had all along been due simply to hunger. Nevertheless, the great manufacturers were anxious, now that the disturbances were over, to strengthen their position for the future. They wished to win a last crowning victory over the workmen's associations.

The discontented artisans of Nottinghamshire, at the same time that they were organizing a conspiracy for the destruction of frames, had addressed a petition to Parliament in which they demanded, since the old corporate regulations had fallen into disuse, legal intervention to protect both themselves and the public against fraud and bad work. They asked for a statute guaranteeing to the workers the correct measurement of work done, forbidding payments in kind, and compelling the employers either to pay a legally fixed wage or at least to advertise publicly the wages offered, that any unfair bargaining might be rendered impossible.[4]   Nothing could have been more regular than this action of theirs, nothing more in conformity with the spirit of industrial legislation of the 18th century.   The State forbade workmen to form combinations, but intervened, on the other hand, as an impartial arbiter, between employers and employed, and regulated their relations.   Indeed, the reason why the State was opposed to the formation of workmen's

---

[1] Smiles, *Memoir of John Murray*, vol. i. p. 202, letter from Southey to Murray, May 19, 1812.

[2] Lockart, *Life of Sir Walter Scott*, vol. iii. pp. 352–3, letter from Scott to Southey June 4, 1812.

[3] 52 Geo. III, cap. 162.

[4] *Report from the Committee on the Framework Knitters' Petitions*, 1812, pp. 5 sqq.

combinations was not because their objects were regarded as, in themselves, unlawful, but because in thus attempting to obtain justice for themselves the workmen were considered to be usurping the functions proper to the State.[1] Furthermore, there were a certain number of old statutes which had never been repealed. Among these was the celebrated Statute of Elizabeth, an enormous code of labour legislation in forty-eight articles, which fixed the length of apprenticeship and provided for the fixing of wages by the magistrates. The workmen had, therefore, no need to demand, like the Nottinghamshire hosiers in 1812, a new statute for their protection. They used frequently to club together and pay a lawyer to prosecute employers for a breach of the provisions of the old statute. The Act of 1800 gave the great manufacturers no handle against these temporary associations whose object was so strictly legal. In the contest between themselves and their men they were in a false position. The workmen were obeying the law ; the employers were the revolutionaries.

But just because it was a period of revolution circumstances favoured them. The introduction of new mechanical processes was overturning daily in every workshop and factory the order of rank and importance which obtained formerly among the various operations of any manufacture. In such conditions it was impossible to fix a definite scale of wages. The magistrates were simply incompetent to estimate the alterations which must of necessity be made in such a scale from day to day. The new machinery suddenly simplified certain processes which had required special skill, and substituted unskilled for skilled labour. It was out of the question to enforce the seven years' apprenticeship prescribed by the statute, when the use of a frame or loom could be learnt in a year or two, sometimes even in a month or two. It was equally out of the question to enforce the limitation in the number of apprentices imposed by certain provisions of the statute, now that one skilled workman, assisted by a large number of children, sufficed to accomplish a task which had formerly demanded several adults. It may be admitted that the workmen's combinations had been in some cases rendered impossible by judicial prosecutions, but on the whole it is truer to say that they had been rendered impotent by the rapid transformation of the methods of manufacture.

At the very time that a few philanthropic employers were laying the foundations of a new code of legislation, adapted to the conditions of the new factories, the old legislation regarding labour was on its deathbed. The magistrates often refused to apply it. It was the boast of the lawyers that there was not a single statute through which

[1] The Act of 1799 seems at first sight an exception to this rule, since it forbade combinations without providing for arbitration. But, as we saw above, this omission was supplied the following year in deference to the criticisms of the Opposition (H. of C., July 22, 1800, *Parliamentary Register*, vol. lxxiv. pp. 459 sqq.).

they could not drive a coach-and-six.[1] Sometimes defeated employers refused to obey the injunctions of the Bench ; and the magistrates did not possess the necessary powers to enforce obedience to their decisions. Moreover, the Statute of Elizabeth applied to England alone, and neither to Ireland nor to Scotland, which had become so important a manufacturing centre. Nor did it apply to the women who were employed in such multitudes in the factories. It had been legally decided that it did not apply to any industry which could be proved not to have existed at the time when the statute was passed.[2] The statute had thus been rendered practically inoperative, and from the close of the 18th century its repeal had been expected as the recognition of an accomplished fact. From 1800 onwards all petitions sent up by associations of workmen to demand new regulations—such as those of the calico printers in 1804, and the cotton weavers in 1808, 1809 and 1811—had been rejected. In 1802 the clothmakers committed the imprudence of petitioning for the enforcement of the old regulations. The only result was a temporary Act passed in 1803, and made perpetual in 1809, repealing the Statute of Apprenticeship so far as concerned the woollen manufacture.[3] Then came the disturbances of 1811 and 1812. The House of Commons, while passing special legislation to repress the rising, also adopted, to give some satisfaction to the malcontents, a Bill regulating the conditions of labour in the manufacture of hosiery.[4] But the Bill was thrown out by the Lords and abandoned by the Commons. This was the last occasion on which Parliament attempted anything of the kind. In 1813 an Act was passed repealing those sections of the Elizabethan statute which gave the magistrates power to fix wages.[5] Another Act, passed the following year, repealed the articles regulating apprenticeship.[6]

It was in vain that the workmen sent up petition after petition against the repeal of the old legislation. While the supporters of free commerce were triumphing in the repeal of the Orders in Council and the abolition of the East India Company's monopoly, the supporters of free industry won an equal triumph by the repeal of the Statute of Elizabeth, which they maintained to be contrary to the natural rights of man.[7] It

---

1 *Report on Petitions of Several Weavers*, 1811, *Minutes of Evidence*, p. 18.   For the failure to apply the statutes protecting labour in the hosiery trade (as regards payment in kind), see *Report . . . on Petitions of Framework Knitters*, 1812, pp. 5–6, and *Minutes of Evidence*, p. 32. In the cotton manufacture (Arbitration Act of 1808), see *Report . . . on Cotton Weavers' Petition*, 1808, p. 23.

2 For all these anomalies, see H. of C., April 27, 1814 (*Parl. Deb.*, vol. xxvii. pp. 563 sqq.).

3 43 Geo. III, cap. 136 ; 49 Geo. III, cap. 109.

4 See, in the course of the debates in the House, Hume's characteristic protests, based on what he held to be axioms of sound political science, approved by the most competent economists (H. of C., July 21, 1812, *Parl. Deb.*, vol. xxiii. pp. 1162 sqq.).

5 53 Geo. III, cap. 40.

6 54 Geo. III, cap. 96.

7 Lord Mansfield's opinion quoted by Thompson, H. of C., May 13, 1814 (*Parl. Deb.*, vol. xxvii. p. 881).

was a triumph by no means making for social peace. The workmen, deprived first of their right of association and then of their legal right to State protection, were driven to the formation of secret societies, to conspiracy and to riot. It is true that the Luddite disturbances had subsided, and that employers and men alike took part in the rising of 1815 ; but two years were not to elapse before a renewal of Luddite outrages. Never before had the existence of workmen's associations in England been so precarious ; never had their character been so revolutionary.

CHAPTER III

CREDIT AND TAXATION

BANKS AND FINANCIAL CRISES.

The Bankers of London and of the Provinces. The Bank of England.

THE entire edifice of the new economic system was based on the ability of every head of a manufacturing enterprise to run the risk of temporary crises, to turn out every year a larger quantity of goods than he had turned out the year before, and to increase every year the numbers and demands of his clientele by forcing the supply of the articles which he produced. Moreover, in his efforts to force the rate of production, the manufacturer was not confined to the use of the capital which he actually possessed. As a matter of course he borrowed regularly. He therefore needed the services of a banker to advance him the necessary sums. And a vast banking system, already over a century old, regulated, or should have regulated, the industrial organization of the country.

On the outer edge of the system were the country banks, whose numbers Adam Smith had already considered excessive, but which multiplied still further during the period following the War of American Independence. A merchant, a manufacturer or a shopkeeper would begin by merely dabbling in finance, accepting deposits and discounting bills of exchange. His sole stipulation was that he need not return deposits immediately. In the meanwhile he used them to discount bills. Very soon he would discover that this class of business demanded too much time to be compatible with other occupations, and he would then become a banker pure and simple—a specialist in the art of making payments and recovering debts on behalf of manufacturers and merchants, and endeavouring to render these proceedings as economical and as expeditious as possible.[1] Here, as in all other departments of English commerce, individualism reigned supreme. It would appear from some statistics of 1819 that out of twenty-eight or thirty joint stock companies engaged in banking in Scotland there were twenty whose

[1] For an account of the beginnings of banking, see Thornton, *Enquiry*, chap. vii. Cf. Sir William Forbes, *Memoirs of a Banking House*, 1860 (history of Coutts' bank at Edinburgh).

shareholders were below fifteen in number, and some which only had two or three.[1] In England the foundation of joint stock banks was illegal, and the banks that were only too plentiful were private banks controlled by isolated individuals.[2] Despite the crises which compelled periodically the liquidation of a large number of banking houses, banks continued to multiply. There were 353 banks before the crisis of 1797, 386 in 1800.[2] In 1810, after a further crisis, the banks numbered 646,[3] and there were 761 in 1813 after a third crisis.[4] A further period of difficulty opened in 1814 and continued till 1817. Eighty-nine banks failed in the course of these three years.[5] But past experience was calculated to inspire bankers with confidence. In spite of so many disasters the system went on constantly spreading.

The custom of accumulating gold and silver pieces at home was dying out in the country districts of England. The moment the coin had been received it was deposited in a bank, which found it ever easier, as commerce and manufactures developed, to obtain profitable investments for the money. In Scotland, where the law was more favourable to banks than in England, the system of cash accounts had become general.[6] The bank opened for a client a credit account for a certain sum—say £2,000 or £3,000—on the guarantee of two persons of known solvency. The Scottish banks had, moreover, acquired the reputation of affording their creditors exceptional facilities for repayment. In England this practice was unknown. At the most a few bankers were willing to make advances on a mortgage or on the security of capital sunk in a business.[7] It was by discounting bills that the banks supplied the capital necessary for the advancement of trade and manufacture. In Lancashire this method of business had been carried so far that bills drawn upon London at two or three months' date had replaced banknotes as the fiduciary currency employed in conducting

---

[1] *Appendix to Lords' Report on the Resumption of Cash Payments*, April 25, 1819, quoted in the *Edinburgh Review*, February 1826, No. 86, Art. 1, *Thoughts on Banking* (vol. xliii. pp. 282–3).

[2] *An Account of the Number of Country Banks in England and Wales . . . distinguishing . . . the Number of Partners concerned in the Banks of each County*, 1819.

In January 1811 there were 649 banks in which 1,947 persons had an interest.

,,	1812	,,	625	,, ,,	1,812	,, ,,
,,	1813	,,	643	,, ,,	1,967	,, ,,
,,	1814	,,	689	,, ,,	2,069	,, ,,
,,	1815	,,	696	,, ,,	2,164	,, ,,

[3] G. Chalmers, *Considerations on Commerce, Bullion and Coin*, ed. 1819, pp. 227 sqq. See his criticisms of the official figures.

[4] *An Account of the Number of Country Banks in England and Wales . . .* 1819.

[5] Twenty-seven in 1814, 25 in 1815, 37 in 1816. Marshall, *Digest*, vol. ii. p. 172; Pebrer, *Taxation*, p. 284.

[6] Hume, *Balance of Trade, Essays*, ed. Green and Grose, vol. i. pp. 339–40; Adam Smith, *Wealth of Nations*, Book II, chap ii., ed. Thorold Rogers, vol. i. pp. 297–8.

[7] *Gold Bullion Committee, Minutes of Evidence*, p. 76. The majority of bankers disapproved of the practice.

important business transactions.[1] As bills of exchange came into general use coin became less necessary. The bankers began to realize that it was not necessary, in order to meet withdrawals of deposits, to keep a cash reserve equal to the amount deposited. What, then, prevented them from extending their clientele, and increasing the circulation by discounting bills not in cash but in their own notes, in their own paper money, payable by them on demand ? It was estimated that between the years 1810–1815 the private banks of the provinces issued notes to the value of some £20,000,000.[2] In 1810 one bank alone issued to its clients notes to the value of £70,000.[3] Bank of England notes were largely driven out of use by the paper issues of the private banks, and their circulation became confined to the district within a radius of fifty to sixty miles from London.[4] A little further from the capital than this the farmers and shopkeepers actually refused Bank of England notes, so unfamiliar was their appearance. We hear of half-guinea notes in 1802.[5] In 1810 Cobbett declared that he had seen notes for 7s.[6] Notes for such tiny sums served for almost every purpose of currency.

Having the control of credit, the bankers throughout England formed a very influential body. Cobbett used to reckon up the country seats, bought, to his knowledge, by these squires of a novel type—country rag merchants as he called them, as indeed they really were, seeing that they had acquired their wealth by flooding the country with paper money.[7] Besides possessing great influence, the bankers, despite the increase in their numbers, were as a class extremely respectable.[8] Although the English bankers, forming part of a system shaken by

1 Thornton, *Inquiry*, pp. 43–4 n. ; *Gold Bullion Committee, Minutes of Evidence*, p. 178.

2 *Edinburgh Review*, February 1826, No. 86, Art. 1, *Thoughts on Bankings* (vol. xliii. pp. 272–3), gives the following figures taken from statistics compiled by Mr. Sedgwick, the Chairman of the Board of Stamps, from the number of stamps distributed among the country banks : 1810, £21,819,000 ; 1811, £21,453,000 ; 1812, £19,944,000 ; 1813, £22,597,000 ; 1814, £22,709,000 ; 1815, £19,011,000.

3 *Gold Bullion Committee, Minutes of Evidence*, pp. 330–1.   4 *Ibid.*, p. 165.

5 *Utility of Country Banks considered*, 1802, pp. 33–4.

6 *Political Register*, September 1, 1810 (*Paper against Gold*, letter 1, vol. xviii. p. 262). These small notes, though tolerated by the authorities, were in strictness illegal, being contrary to a statute (15 Geo. III, cap. 51), which prohibited the issue in England of notes whose value was below £1.

7 *Rural Rides*, November 5 and 23, 1821. November 23rd : " Hard by (Whitchurch) is a pretty park and house belonging to ' Squire ' Portal, the *paper-maker*. The country people, who seldom want for sarcastic shrewdness, call it *Rag Hall*."

8 *Gold Bullion Committee, Minutes of Evidence*, p. 214 (J. H. Tritton's evidence) : " Can you state whether the new country banks are as respectable a class of people as the old ones ?—I should consider that several of those which have lately been established consist of respectable persons." Cf. *Utility of Country Banks considered*, 1802, p. 44 : " . . . Whilst the law protects, as it now does, the claims of the Country Bank Notes, and whilst gentlemen of great property and well-known integrity engage in these concerns. . . . The country is much indebted to gentlemen of large landed property for emerging from the indolence of their forefathers, and entering into the commercial concerns of a bank. They have given a degree of respectability to those undertakings, at the same time that they have added to the confidence and security of the people."

repeated crises, conducted a highly speculative business in which a huge fiduciary circulation rested upon a cash reserve of very small dimensions, they continued, notwithstanding, to take a position far above that occupied by traders and manufacturers.

They presided over the progress of the industries of the nation. It was their profession to pass judgment upon the credit of the businesses whose paper was brought to them for discount and to decide whether they would accept it, and so suffer the business in question to continue in existence, or refuse it and thus condemn that business to extinction. It was, moreover, easy for them, as part of their professional practice, to make opportune advances of cash to county families. It was by such methods that Mortlock, the Cambridge banker, had acquired great popularity and had made himself the most influential personage in the town. In return for electioneering services rendered to the Duke of Rutland's clique he had obtained lucrative posts under Government.[1] He had sat in one parliament. Gloucester, Newcastle-on-Tyne and Bristol returned local bankers as their representatives. At Ipswich Crickett, the banker, successfully opposed with Government support the aristocracy of the neighbourhood. At Rochester another banker, James Hulkes, triumphed over the influence of the Government. A seat in Parliament was by no means injurious to a banker's professional interests. He would take into partnership the clerk who had shown the greatest industry and honesty and would entrust the routine work to him. Meanwhile he was living at the centre whither the news of the entire world converged. If he made himself serviceable to the Cabinet, he would be rewarded by useful pieces of information and by financial services of all kinds.[2] In a large city such as Liverpool the banking interest assumed a different shape. The bankers and the merchants together constituted the aristocracy of a purely mercantile city, and were divided by a wide social gulf from the cotton manufacturers. Among them was Roscoe, who collected a magnificent library, wrote the history of Lorenzo de Medici, and entertained the chimerical dream of making Liverpool a modern Venice or Florence renowned at once for her commerce and for her culture. It would be an exaggeration to regard him as typical of his class. Nevertheless, he was the pride of his native city.[3]

The banks were like reservoirs into which flowed all the capital accumulated by saving, and from which it flowed out again to stimulate production anew. But some banks received more money than they could dispose of among their local clients. Others, on the contrary, found that the demand for cash exceeded the contents of their

---

[1] Oldfield, *Representative History*, vol. ii. pp. 125–6. Cf. Grenning, *Reminiscences of Cambridge*, vol. i. pp. 139 sqq.

[2] Gisborne, *Duties of Man*, vol. ii. pp. 318–19.

[3] See the chapter on Roscoe in Washington Irving's *Sketch Book of Geoffrey Crayon*.

coffers. The banks of agricultural districts belonged to the former category. The agriculturists lent more than they borrowed, and the difficulty experienced by the landlords in collecting their rents was due in part to the farmers' and bailiffs' habit of keeping their money as long as possible at interest in the local banks.[1] Money left the agricultural districts of the south-east and went to assist the development of the manufactures of Lancashire and Yorkshire. London served as a sort of natural balance to establish an equilibrium of supply and demand between the banks of the agricultural and those of the manufacturing districts.

The provincial bankers had begun by keeping paid agents in the capital. They had come, however, to realize that this was an unprofitable expense. For purposes of discount with other parts of the kingdom they made use of the independent banks which had been established in London to supply the local needs of the capital. They deposited, moreover, with the private banks of London their Government securities and investments of all kinds, which they were obliged to keep available for realization so as to be ready to meet demands for cash. The superior importance of London as compared with the provinces was the measure of the preeminence in dignity and influence of the sixty to seventy Lombard Street bankers who controlled the financial organization of the nation as compared with the thousand or so country bankers. Not only did they obtain seats in the House of Commons; it was not altogether unknown that one of their number should be raised to the peerage.[2] They prided themselves on their culture and knowledge of literature. They were, in the true sense of the word, an aristocracy. The banker Bagehot, writing at a period when joint stock banking was on the increase and when the golden age of private banks had passed away, speaks of the " charmed value " possessed by the name " London banker " in the opening years of the 19th century. " The calling is hereditary ; the credit of the bank descends from father to son ; this inherited wealth soon brings inherited refinement. . . . There has probably very rarely ever been so happy a position as that of a London private banker ; and never perhaps a happier."[3] To satisfy more perfectly the economic needs of the country, the London bankers were

[1] See some reflexions on this matter by Lord Shelburne (*Life*, by Fitzmaurice, vol. ii. pp. 337–8) : " To obviate this," concludes Lord Shelburne, " so far as regards your particular interest, it will be prudent on no account to receive or pay the notes of any country bank, but both to receive and pay in current coin."

[2] It is true, however, that the case of Robert Smith raised to the English peerage with the title of Lord Carrington remained an isolated exception. The creation gave scandal, and the scandal was increased twofold in 1810, when the report spread that Lord Carrington's barony was to be made into a viscounty (see Wraxall, *Posthumous Memoirs*, vol. i. pp. 65–88, also Lord Carrington's reply to Wraxall's defamatory statements, *Quarterly Review*, vol. lvii. p. 456). Cf. Arthur Young, *Autobiography*, p. 370, letter from T. Symonds to Arthur Young, March 20, 1801.

[3] Bagehot, *Lombard Street*, pp. 268–9.

untiring in their efforts to improve the machinery of their banking operations. They began by fostering the growth of a new profession, which served to bring them into closer connexion with the country bankers. The bill brokers devoted themselves exclusively to the task of becoming acquainted with the credit of their country clients. They brought the London bankers bills to cash, and cash for which they received bills. They were simple go-betweens who did not need capital, nor did they guarantee the value of the bills they brought to be discounted. But the large number of their clients, and their financial prosperity, were of themselves a sufficient proof of the soundness of their judgment to warrant the London bankers to trust them almost blindly. £7,000,000 passed annually through the hands of Thomas Richardson, the greatest of these brokers. A London banker knew that he had only to apply to Richardson or to one of his fellow-brokers to obtain at any moment as much money as he needed on the security of commercial bills.[1] He was thus enabled to carry on more business than before with a smaller cash reserve. The circulation of capital thus became brisker. It was rendered brisker still by the institution of the Lombard Street clearing house, forty years before our date. It became the general custom in the banking world of London to settle the daily accounts by striking a balance of reciprocal indebtedness. Every day at four o'clock drafts and cheques were taken to the clearing house ; and when reciprocal debts had been cancelled between the banks concerned, only a small number of bank-notes were required to pay the difference and thus settle the entire account. In 1810 forty-six bankers made use of the clearing house. The cheques and drafts brought in daily represented a sum of close on £5,000,000. To settle these debts some £220,000 to £250,000 worth of notes was found sufficient.[2]

Thus was accomplished spontaneously, first in the mutual relations of country banks, and then in the mutual relations of the London banks, a process of centralization. The centralization was completed, however, by an institution due not to private initiative, but to the intervention of the Government, namely the Bank of England, which formed the apex of the entire system. The enormous edifice in the classical style of architecture between Threadneedle Street and the Poultry, known as Grocers' Hall, harboured a host of 700 persons, exclusive of those engaged in menial offices, working under the orders of the Governor, the monarch of the place, and twenty-four directors, who were in theory elected by the shareholders of the Bank, but were chosen in practice by a species of cooptation. Since bankers were legally ineligible, the directors of the Bank of England were London merchants, highly respectable and tolerably cautious, as was only fitting in view of the

[1] *Gold Bullion Committee, Minutes of Evidence*, pp. 177 sqq., 228.
[2] *Ibid.*, pp. 230 sqq.

manner of their choice. The Bank was, practically speaking, contemporary with the " glorious Revolution " of 1688. The newly established Government had allowed a group of merchants who were prepared to advance them a loan of £1,200,000 at 8 per cent. to form a corporation authorized to engage in banking, in London. The society, thus formed, took advantage of the constantly recurring pecuniary embarrassments of the Government to make their position ever stronger and stronger. An Act of 1713,[1] confirmed and explained in 1742,[2] granted the Bank the sole right to carry on in England the operations in which it was engaged. Without the express grant of any statute, the Bank had acquired a monopoly of the issue of banknotes in the capital. Later, in return for advances of money made to the Government, it obtained on several occasions the renewal of its privilege. It had been agreed in 1781[3] that the monopoly was to expire in 1812. It had been agreed since 1800[4] that it was not to expire till 1833. In 1815 the Bank was paying an interest of 10 per cent. on a capital of £11,642,400.[5]

The country banks deposited the bulk of their reserves with the London banks. The London banks used the Bank of England as a deposit bank. The funds thus placed at the disposal of the Bank were employed to discount commercial bills. It was for the governor and the directors to display the necessary shrewdness and to make advances on such a scale as to ensure a satisfactory dividend to the shareholders, while not advancing enough to diminish unduly the reserve of the Bank. For this reserve—a reserve of metal in normal times, of banknotes in the exceptional periods when the Bank was dispensed from the necessity of making payments in specie—was the final reserve, on which alone the entire currency of the nation was based. Among the clients of the Bank was one whose debt exceeded out of all proportion the debts of all the others. This was the State, which owed the Bank in perpetuity the interest on a capital not only equal to, but larger than, that on which a dividend was paid to the shareholders. The State made use of the Bank to discount the bills issued by the Treasury—Navy Bills bearing interest after six months, Exchequer Bills from the day of issue. Sometimes the Bank would take bonds from the Government at par and then issue them to the public at a profit. In the discussions which took place on such occasions between the Bank and the Treasury, that is between the largest borrower and the largest lender in the Kingdom, it was the duty of the Bank to display the necessary independence, and to take care, while allowing the State freely to increase the national debt, that public credit was not endangered or the fiduciary currency depreciated. The Government rewarded the services thus rendered

1 12 Anne, St. 1, cap. 11.   2 15 Geo. II, cap. 13.
3 21 Geo. III, cap. 60.   4 40 Geo. III, cap. 28, § 15.
5 Hamilton, *Inquiry*, 2nd ed., 1814, pp. 230-1.

by depositing its balances with the Bank. The entire Consolidated Fund accumulated in the coffers of the Bank, from the time when it was collected from the taxpayer till the time when it was spent by the State. In the interval the Bank was free to put out to interest the enormous capital that was temporarily at its disposal, on the sole condition that there was always sufficient ready money to pay the creditors and officials of the State.

In 1694 the foundation of the Bank of England had been a daring innovation. Countless had been the protests raised against it. The Bank had been regarded either as incompatible with the conditions requisite for the existence of a healthy economic society, or else as dangerous to the liberties of the subject, if not to the Crown itself. Now it had on its side the force of long prescription. The Bank of England, like the Hanoverian dynasty, was an institution clothed with all the majesty of law. Contemporary with the system of government so dear to England, it shared the prestige of the system. "The stability of the Bank of England is equal to that of the British Government. . . . It acts not only as an ordinary bank, but as a great engine of State."[1] This panegyric, coming from the determined foe of every kind of State interference in economics, is truly astonishing, and justifies the irony of Cobbett. "Some people suppose that paper *always* made a part of the currency or common money of England. They seem to regard the Bank of England as being as old as the Church of England at least, and some of them appear to have full as much veneration for it."[2]

The Banking System. Financial and Industrial Crises.

The institutions above described were calculated, if they functioned normally, to exert a steadying influence on national industry and commerce. The country bankers, the London bankers and the Bank of England advanced capital to every individual according to his credit and his ability to make profitable employment of the sums advanced. But were the bankers good judges of this credit, of this ability? For many years past economic crises in England had been increasing in number and gravity. While the bills and acceptances of the banks were increasing beyond all bounds, coin grew scarce and the price of the precious metals rose abnormally. The rate of exchange on Hamburg rose 15 to 17 per cent. above par. Manufacturing and commercial crises occurred simultaneously with banking crises. How were these simultaneous phenomena related? Which was the cause, which the effect?

Fluctuations of foreign exchange are due to two different causes,

---

[1] *Wealth of Nations*, Book II, chap. ii., ed. Thorold Rogers, vol. i. p. 320.
[2] *Political Register*, September 1, 1810 (vol. 18, p. 264)

which will sometimes be mutually exclusive, but will at other times work together. One cause is the favourable or unfavourable balance of trade. Let us suppose, for example, that a manufacturing country like England obtains raw materials from some foreign country, say from Sweden, and in return supplies Sweden with manufactured articles. As far as possible the English and Swedish buyers try to pay their respective debts by means of bills of exchange, and in so far as this can be done actual transport of the precious metals is avoided. If, however, the debt of one of the two countries exceed the debt owing from the other country, a certain amount of precious metal must be transported from one country to the other. Bills of exchange drawn by the first country on the second will bear a premium, which will exactly correspond to the cost of transporting the precious metals—that is the freight, the merchant's profit and the risks of transmission. This is the first and most general explanation of the course of exchange. But there are factors of another sort to take into account which may at times outweigh in importance the factors above mentioned, and even in some degree conceal their operation. Let us suppose the coinage of a particular country to consist entirely of worn or clipped pieces, and that in consequence of this, while their face value remains the same, their real value has depreciated in comparison with the coins current in a neighbouring country. In exchanging sums reckoned in the currency of the former country against sums reckoned in the currency of the latter there will be a loss corresponding to the difference of intrinsic value between the two coinages. Or again, let us suppose that the Government of a particular country issues a paper currency and enforces its circulation. In relation to specie this paper money will suffer a depreciation wholly comparable to the depreciation of worn or clipped coinage. Hence any country whose currency is depreciated in either fashion is obliged, when paying any debt contracted abroad, to pay a sum larger than the nominal amount of the debt as calculated in its own coinage. Here we have the other cause of a rise in the rate of exchange to the disadvantage of the country in question.

To which of these two causes, then, are we to ascribe the unfavourable position of England as regards exchange ? Apparently to the second. For we must remember that for almost twenty years past the banking system had been in an abnormal condition, owing to the suspension of cash payments. This step had been taken by the Government in 1797 in order to avert a financial crisis and to prevent the exhaustion of the Bank's metallic reserve. Cash payments should have recommenced with the conclusion of the war. At the time, however, of the Peace of Amiens it was considered necessary to continue the suspension. When, as the result of the artificial system thus established by law, the foreign exchanges became ever more and more unfavourable to England, public opinion naturally began to connect the two facts. In 1809

Ricardo began his literary career by an article in the *Morning Chronicle* in support of the doctrine of the so-called bullionists, namely, that the cause of the rise in the price of gold was the depreciation of the bank-note. A few months later his conclusions were endorsed by a committee of the House of Commons, and the bullionists seemed on the point of obtaining from the Cabinet the repeal of the Act of 1797, and a return, if not forthwith, at least as speedily as possible, to the system of cash payments. Nevertheless in 1811 the acceptance of banknotes at their face value was practically made compulsory. In 1815 Napoleon's return from exile, and the resumption of hostilities with France, enabled the Government once more to postpone the return to cash payments. It was, nevertheless, undeniable that Ricardo's doctrine was gaining wider acceptance every day and that public opinion was becoming constantly more accustomed to regard the resumption of cash payments as the remedy for the almost chronic troubles which afflicted the finance, the manufactures and the trade of the country.

An unfavourable balance of trade failed, according to the bullionists, to account adequately for the enormous fall in the exchanges. In the first place, it required to be shown that the balance of trade really was unfavourable. But in truth, during the very years when cash payments were suspended, England had acquired a monopoly of manufactures for the entire world. The report of the Parliamentary Committee of 1810 showed that between 1807 and 1809, while the exchanges were becoming more and more unfavourable to England, the balance of trade had become more and more favourable to her. The excess of exports over imports had passed from £5,866,000 in 1807 to £12,481,000 in 1808, and £14,834,000 in 1809.[1] Even if it were granted that the balance of trade was unfavourable and so caused a fall of the exchanges on Hamburg, Paris and Amsterdam, accompanied by an export of the precious metals, these phenomena would only have been temporary. It was impossible to account in this way for the persistence of a low exchange for many years before 1815. For gold is a commodity like any other, and if it is exported in preference to other commodities, it is because it is worth less than the others. But the more it is exported the rarer it becomes, its price goes up, and its exportation will be more difficult. It becomes, therefore, more profitable to export other commodities and the balance of trade is reestablished automatically, as the necessary consequence of the export of specie. Finally, it was argued, not only was the persistence of the phenomenon inexplicable by an unfavourable balance of trade, but the extent of the fall in the exchanges was equally inexplicable on this hypothesis. The

---

[1] *Report of the Gold Bullion Committee*, p. 28. Cf. Appendix No. 73, p. 110. Official statistics of 1812 (*Accounts relating to Imports and Exports*, February 18, 1812) give different figures. But exports always exceeded imports; by £4,251,048 in 1808, by £6,166,360 in 1809.

cost of the transport of gold in 1797 did not exceed $3\frac{1}{2}$ per cent. of its value. Even the growing difficulty of communication between England and the Continent, and the corresponding increase in the risks of navigation, could not possibly have raised the cost above 5 or 6 per cent. of the value. If, then, the rate of exchange was 15 to 20 per cent. below par, such an enormous fall could only be explained by causes of an entirely different order.[1]

The true reason why the rate of exchange was so extremely unfavourable, and that for so long a period, was the excessive issue of paper money ; so that banknotes, being the sole currency in England, had undergone a depreciation, corresponding to the excess in their issue, by comparison with the coinage current in the North of Germany and in France. That the economic condition of the country was so unhealthy was the fault of the Government which took advantage of its control of the Bank of England to deal arbitrarily with the currency. The economists of Ricardo's school were opposed in principle to any kind of legislative interference. If they could once succeed in demonstrating that the present evil was actually due to State interference, and that the financial and commercial equilibrium of the entire world would be speedily reestablished if the Bank of England would only leave the economic machine to work by itself, they would gain new converts to their social creed. The Opposition meanwhile was making use of the opportunity, thus presented, to attack the policy of the Tory Cabinet, the dictatorial policy of Pitt and his followers. The Opposition saw that the Tory Government obtained from the Bank all the money it asked for, and remembered that the Bank had refused to make the advances required by Lord Henry Petty when he was Chancellor of the Exchequer in the Grenville-Fox Cabinet.[2] "In the latter end of 1795, when the Bank . . . appear to have resigned all prudence in the management of their concerns and to have constituted Mr. Pitt sole director." [3] The use of such language by Ricardo in a pamphlet apparently theoretic and abstract shows that he did not disdain to appeal to the political passions of his readers. The pamphleteers who carried on a literary warfare as free-lances, independently of party organizations, went even further than the economists and the parliamentary orators. Cobbett said that the Government was no better than a coiner of false money, since it was attempting to pay with scraps of paper the enormous debt accumulated from year to year as the result of its warlike policy.

The supporters of the Bank of England and the Government attempted to meet the contention of the bullionists by counter arguments. These counter arguments are of widely differing weight, and

[1] Ricardo, *High Price of Bullion* (*Works*, ed. MacCulloch, p. 280).
[2] H. of C., March 2, 1815 (*Parl. Deb.*, vol. xxix. pp. 1195, 1197).
[3] Ricardo, *High Price o Bullion* (*Works*, ed. MacCulloch, p. 297 n.)

we should make a distinction between them. Only too frequently they were dictated by the desire to justify at any cost the policy of the Cabinet. But some it will be worth our while to consider; for when the bullionists claimed that the mischief was due entirely and solely to an excessive issue of notes by the Bank of England, they were obviously under a misapprehension both as to the real gravity of the evil and as to the remedies required.

The anti-bullionists asked whether the statistics of imports and exports were really as conclusive as the bullionists suggested. These statistics showed what had been the value of the goods brought to English ports during a given period, and also what had been the value of the goods sent from these ports during the same period. But if it was desired to find out exactly at the end of the year, not what had been the balance of trade, but what had been the balance of payments, it was necessary to notice with what country and under what conditions of settlement the trading had been effected.[1] Suppose then, as was actually the case, that the Continent, owing to a state of blockade, took less than the normal quantity and value of English goods, and that, on the other hand, in consequence of a bad harvest, England imported a large quantity of corn from France or Germany. Thus the balance of trade *with the Continent* would be, for the time, unfavourable to England. But supposing that this excess of imports were compensated, and more than compensated, by the sudden opening of the American market to English manufactures, the balance of trade would as a whole be in favour of England. But goods from the Continent arrived in England in a few hours and were paid for in cash; whereas goods going from England to Caracas or to Buenos Ayres took a long time in transit and were sold on credit; they were not finally paid for, as a general rule, in less than eighteen months. And for this period of a year and a half the balance of payments might be unfavourable, though the balance of trade, as shown by statistics, might be quite favourable. Moreover, the expenditure of the British Government on its Peninsular army, and its subsidies to such Continental sovereigns as were willing to declare war upon Napoleon, added still more to the unfavourable balance of payments. Here were wide-open cavities through which gold could constantly escape without affecting in any way the statistics of foreign trade.

Again it was wrong to conclude that exchanges were not governed by the balance of payments, merely because they rose at times to rates higher than could be justified by the cost of shipping gold. Ricardo and his disciples were wrong in considering men in general, and business men in particular, as expert calculators, acting always with a full know-

---

[1] *Gold Bullion Committee, Minutes of Evidence*, p. 76 (J. L. Greffulhe's evidence), p. 99 (evidence of Mr. ———, a Continental merchant). Cf. p. 52 (communication from Mr. Lyne) and *passim*.

ledge of all the possible consequences of their actions. In the money market, as in all other markets, sentiment, and not reason, was supreme. Every day in the region of Lombard Street and Leadenhall Street there gathered a busy and excitable crowd. And if it were heard that the export of coin was leading to a tightness in the money market, every individual of such a crowd, always intent upon learning the latest news, might well be seized with an unreasonable fear of finding himself short of cash. Thus a panic would arise ; and the exchanges would go beyond the point at which, normally, they should have stopped. It was, therefore, useless to ascribe the fluctuations of exchange to causes of another kind, such as an excessive issue of notes. Bankers know that in their treatment of the money market they must take account of mob psychology. Their experience of the 18th century, before the suspension of specie payments, had taught the directors of the Bank of England that the truest wisdom often lay in flouting counsels of prudence and in continuing to discount bills even when the metallic reserve had been reduced to very small dimensions. To husband the reserve would have resulted in telling the public too suddenly of their peril, in provoking a panic instead of merely giving a danger signal, and in destroying confidence by the very act which to all appearance was the wisest course for its preservation.

Moreover, if an excessive issue of paper, and a consequent depreciation of banknotes, causes a rise in the price of gold, then all prices should rise at the same time and to the same extent, since they are all measured by the same standard, which for the time being is paper money. But the immediate cause of the crisis of 1809 was the rapid fluctuation of all prices in different directions and degrees. During the course of this crisis, which subsequently resulted in the appointment of a Parliamentary Commission and the publication of its report, the price of all manufactured goods fell, in spite of issues of paper money which were supposed to be excessive. There was, in fact, over-production. The South American markets, just opened to English trade, were glutted with goods. At the same time the price of grain went up, not because the banknote was depreciated, but because the harvest was bad. The price of gold rose also ; but why seek to attribute this rise to the depreciation of the currency, instead of, as in the case of all other goods, to the operation of commercial causes which have no direct connexion with the issues of the Bank of England ?

There was no close correspondence from one year to another between the issues of notes and the price of gold. At the time when Ricardo was writing his letters to the *Morning Chronicle* and Horner was writing the report of the Bullion Committee it might seem perhaps that the bullionist theory was supported by the events of the previous year. There had been a large increase in the note circulation accompanied by a large rise in the price of gold, which at the beginning of 1810 reached £4 5s. an ounce. The two figures, however, did not continue to follow the same course ; and no sooner had the Committee's report been published than the bullionist theory was disproved by the course of events.[1] In 1810 the Bank of England issued notes to the value of £4,500,000 ; [2] but the price of gold fell to £4 4s. 6d. From 1811 to 1813 issues were less, but the price of gold rose to £5 5s.[3] During the first half-year of 1814 the circulation of Bank of England notes rose from £24,801,080 to £28,368,290, but in spite of this great rise the price of gold fell from £5 8s. to £4 11s.[4] Subsequently the price of gold underwent sudden variations ; but on the whole tended to fall slowly, though the note circulation now remained at much the same level, never being below £27,000,000.[5] And in 1816 gold and paper were almost on an equality. At a price of £3 18s. 6d per ounce the premium on gold was only 7½d.

At first sight the bullionists seemed to be right in their arguments, since it was hard to deny that a suspension of cash payments should have produced in England the same effects as the issue of *assignats* had produced in France at the end of the 18th century. But the defenders of the Bank denied that there was any similarity between the policy of the French Government at the time of the *assignats* and the methods of the Bank of England during the period of the restriction of specie payments. The Bank of England, however closely attached to the Government, was none the less an independent corporation. It was free to resist, and did sometimes resist, the demands of the Government. And it boasted that throughout all the troubles and disturbances of the time it had never wavered from those traditional principles of wise administration which it had observed during the whole of the past century.

The directors of the Bank argued—not without some foundation— that their note issues had always been regulated by the normal demands

[1] Nor were the bullionists justified by the events of the previous period, 1796–1809. Bosanquet, *Practical Observations*, p. 9–10.

[2] Tooke, *History of Prices*, vol. i., p. 362.

[3] *Ibid.*, pp. 367–8.

[4] *Weekly Account of the Market Prices of Gold, First and Second Reports of the Lords' Committee,* 1819, Appendix, p. 350 : February 18th, £5 8s. ; August 23rd, £4 11s.

[5] The average note circulation was as follows : 1815—1st quarter, £27,298,290 ; 2nd quarter, £27,103,440 ; 3rd quarter, £27,171,430 ; 4th quarter, £26,074,570. 1816—1st quarter, £26,573,280 ; 2nd quarter, £26,363,240 ; 3rd quarter, £27,233,700 ; 4th quarter, £26,129,040 (Pebrer, *Taxation*, p. 251). From the end of 1815 the price of gold was falling steadily, as follows : 1815, September 15th, £4 9s. ; October 13th, £4 3s. ; December 15th, £4 2s. 1816, April 9th, £4 1s. ; April 23rd, £4 ; July 9th, £3 19s. ; October 8th, £3 18s. 6d. (*Weekly Account of the Market Prices . . . ibid.*, p. 350). To evade the difficulty the bullionists said that the issues of private banks ought to be taken into account. But as these private banknotes were redeemable, the bullionists tried to show that the quantity of such notes was governed by the quantity of irredeemable notes. (Ricardo, *High Price of Bullion, Works*, pp. 282–3 ; *Report of Bullion Committee*, pp. 67 sqq. ; King, *Thoughts . . .* 2nd ed. 1804, pp. 106 sqq See, in reply, Bosanquet, *Practical Observations*, 2nd ed., 1810, pp. 72 sqq.). According to our own theory it would be more exact to say that the country banks, by excessive issues of notes, compelled the Bank of England to follow their example.

of the discount market.[1] They insisted that when the public interest was at stake they subjected all applications for discount to a scrutiny more careful than that generally made by private banks.[2] But the debaters of 1810, occupied almost exclusively with the problems of note circulation, neglected altogether to investigate the really important question, namely whether the discount policy of the Bank of England and of the private banks was based on wisdom as well as on long custom, and whether it was such as to prevent crises both when notes were convertible and when they were not. There had been a crisis in 1797 before the suspension of specie payments; indeed, it was this very crisis which brought the suspension into being. And crises still continued to occur after 1819, at which date the bullionists had brought their remedy into effect.[3] We must seek the explanation of these repeated crises, and indeed of the excessive note issue itself, in the manner in which the national production was organized under the control of the great discounting institutions, the banks.

All modern production rests on a basis of credit. The great manufacturers buy on credit the raw materials of their industry; the wholesalers buy on credit the goods which they wish to retail. On receiving delivery of these raw materials or goods they give to the person who supplies them a promise to pay, good for a date by which they expect to have completed the process of manufacture and sale. This promise to pay becomes itself an object of commerce, a means by which the holder can pay his debts before the time of maturity has arrived. A, a shipbuilder on the Clyde, buys wood on credit from B, the owner of forests in Sweden. C, a Stockholm shipowner, buys ships on credit from the Clyde builder. A bill of exchange enables A to transfer to C the debt which he owes to B, and thus obviates a double transfer of gold, from England to Sweden, and from Sweden to England. The bankers, who collect such bills and act as agents for their transfer, have the special function, by means of a kind of brokerage, of reducing to a minimum the use of cash in business transactions, and of reestablishing in a more complicated form the primitive truck system whereby goods are exchanged directly for goods. Or rather, such would be the working of the credit system and such would be the function of the banker, in a world where existed only independent producers or groups of individuals associated on a footing of equality in the work of production.

---

[1] *Gold Bullion Report, Minutes of Evidence*, p. 131, evidence of J. L. Greffulhe: "The bank paper of this country is issued when called for, in exchange for valuable securities, in which respect it is essentially distinct from what I call a forced paper, which may be issued without limits and without any security whatever." This opinion has all the more force in that it came from a merchant who had himself nothing to do with the administration of the Bank (Bosanquet, *Practical Observations*, 1810, 2nd ed., pp. 49 sqq.).

[2] *Ibid.*, p. 189, evidence of Mr. Whitmore, Governor of the Bank. Cf. H. of C., March 2, 1815, Baring's speech (*Parl. Deb.*, vol. xxix. p. 1,198).

[3] *Memoirs of Sir John Sinclair*, vol. ii. p. 271: "If the panic of 1825 had occurred in our struggle with Napoleon, Great Britain would now be a province of France."

In such a world there could only be partial crises, local disturbances due to a bad harvest or to some mistake in production. A general crisis of over-production would be inconceivable. Supply and demand would always be in equilibrium. One service would be exchanged for another.

But the new industrial society, which at the beginning of the 19th century asked for the assistance of the banks, was based on different principles. The chief users of credit were the captains of industry superintending the labour of workmen who were wage-earners, and therefore not independent. These employers could not unload upon the home market all the goods which they produced, unless the workers were paid enough to be able to buy the whole output of the factories where they worked; in which case the employers could have made no profits. It was necessary, then, that the capitalist should proceed to the conquest of foreign markets, should sell more than he bought, or, to speak more exactly, should exchange goods for gold. The whole series of loans proceeded in one direction—from the first seller to the last—and the last seller sought to pay his debt by obtaining gold from abroad against the goods which he supplied. But an exchange of goods against gold cannot be continued indefinitely either by two individuals or by two countries. Sooner or later the buyer will have no gold left to pay for the goods which are sent to him. He becomes an insolvent debtor; the goods which arrive for him are thrown upon the market; and there is a general fall of prices.

What will happen, then, to those who, in a country of large-scale industry and commerce, continue for months and years to sell goods on credit? So long as prosperity lasts, production will increase, prices will rise, and bills of exchange, easily negotiable, will appear a safe medium for the reciprocal liquidation of all debts. But, once creditors take alarm at the prospect of debtors becoming gradually unable to meet their engagements, everyone will be anxious to get rid of the bills which he holds, and to obtain cash in exchange. If the currency is convertible the banks will see their portfolios grow fat with bills, whilst their metallic reserves dwindle alarmingly. If there is a currency of inconvertible paper the central bank will be able to discount, by the mere issue of notes, all bills that may be brought to it. But such issues will have been the effect, not the cause, of the crisis. Moreover, paper money could only be used for the payment of internal debts. To satisfy creditors abroad gold would have to be exported; and such exports would not be caused by the excessive issues of paper. Both exports of gold and issues of notes would be effects due to the same cause.

The fact that notes have only been issued in the discount of bills based on genuine transactions by reputable firms, does not prevent the issue being excessive in conditions where there is a general crisis and the whole capitalist system is threatened with insolvency. If the notes were convertible, bankers would be warned of the approaching crisis by a fall in their reserves. But would they pay attention to such a fall, and what measures would they take? The bankers of our period did not possess the necessary outlook or even the technical knowledge. It was many years before they thought of warding off a crisis, or at least of diminishing its dangers, by raising the rate of discount. And not only did they lack the necessary knowledge, but the law, by prescribing a maximum rate of interest, prevented them even from contemplating such a system. Moreover, the same spirit of the time which induced the manufacturers to produce without limit, induced the bankers to lend without prudence. They were not sufficiently alert to distinguish the keen demand for discounts which arises from a normal development of business—an increase of reciprocal indebtedness between one part of England and another, or between England and the Continent—from that demand which shows that business is waning, that men are finding it difficult to pay their debts, and that a crisis is in view. A crisis is essentially a crisis of over-production combined with a crisis of inflation. In this matter the bankers are the accomplices of all those who direct in any way the activities of the economic world.

PUBLIC DEBT AND BURDEN OF TAXATION.

Public Debt.

If our analysis has been correct, the economic crises which occurred in England during the years leading up to 1814 were caused ultimately, not by the financial imprudences of the Government, but by the very system on which commerce and industry were organized. It is true that the financial necessities of the Government were such as to aggravate the disorder. Gold was scarce in England, for every year it was exported in increasing quantities—£15,182,000 in 1811, £18,533,000 in 1812, £22,931,000 in 1813, £31,284,000 in 1814 [1]—and this export was due in large measure to the policy of the Cabinet in granting subsidies to all countries hostile to France and in maintaining a great army in Portugal and in Spain. England was crushed by taxation ; the Budget—to use a term which was now current [2]—became every year more oppressive. There was not much expenditure under civil heads—nothing for poor relief or for education, nothing even for local

[1] H. of C., March 2, 1815, Vansittart's speech (Parl. Deb., vol. xxix. p. 1185).

[2] H. of C., November 1814, Vansittart's speech : " . . . the right hon. gentleman (Mr. Ponsonby) has expressed a wish . . . that he would previously enter into a general statement of the finances of the country. If, by that expression, the right hon. gentleman meant that general winding-up of the financial accounts which was familiarly termed the Budget . . ." (Parl. Deb., vol. xxix. p. 147). The Annual Register for 1797 quotes the term as a neologism : " On the 7th of December (1796) the Chancellor of the Exchequer produced his annual estimate of the public revenue and expenditure, with a demand for supplies, or what is barbarously called

administration and justice or for local police. Administrative expenditure amounted to little more than £4,000,000.[1] But the Navy in 1814 required over £20,000,000, the Army and Ordnance just under £40,000,000.[2] And finally, in addition to meeting all these charges and granting more than £10,000,000 to the Allied Powers,[3] the State had to pay its creditors—the interest on the public debt being over £37,500,000.[4] The resources of the State were eaten up by these payments of interest. Peace might come ; naval and military expenditure might be reduced ; but how was the burden of this dead weight to be relieved ? All the financial difficulties of the time were summed up in this question of the Public Debt.

The Debt " this vile paper-money and funding system, this system of Dutch descent, begotten by Bishop Burnet and born in Hell," [5] dated from the Revolution of 1688. From that time onward the Government, engaged in a long series of wars with France, had taken to raising loans for military expenditure, so as to relieve the taxpayer, who had now only to meet the interest charges of the debt so contracted. And it was said by Sheridan [6] that one-half of the English national debt was incurred in putting down, and the other half in restoring, the House of Bourbon. In order to raise from the public large and ever-increasing loans the English Treasury never ceased to improve their methods of borrowing. They tried tontines, annuities for one or more lives, or for a fixed number of years, loans from big corporations in return

---

his bag, or budget " (p. 131, cf. p. 14). In 1808 the term was not yet current. See *Annual Register*, p. 95, H. of C., April 11th : " The Chancellor of the Exchequer rose, pursuant to notice, to bring forward the Budget." (A note explains this as " A budget of papers relative to the public income and expenditure.")

[1] Civil List, Courts of Justice, Mint, allowances to the Royal Family, salaries and allowances, bounties, £1,561,121 ; Civil Government of Scotland, £114,032 ; miscellaneous services at home and abroad, £2,384,591. Total, £4,059,745. See *Public Income of Great Britain for the year ending fifth January*, 1815. An Account of the Ordinary Revenues and Extraordinary Resources of the Public Income of Great Britain (*Parl. Deb.*, vol. xxv. Appendix, pp. 1 sqq.).

[2] Navy, £21,961,567 ; Ordnance, £4,480,792 ; Army, £33,795,556.

[3] Exact figure, £10,024,624.

[4] See below, pp. 351 sqq., for a statement of the Budget of 1815. The financial position of France at the first Treaty of Paris, was much stronger than that of the victor. See H. of C., February 22, 1815, Lord Binning's speech : " France had a population of 26 or 27 millions, a revenue of about 35 millions, and a debt of 70 millions. In Great Britain (he should not speak of Ireland at present) the population was 12 millions and a half, the taxes 60 millions a year, and the debt between 800 and 900 millions. It therefore appeared that the people of France were taxed at the rate of less than £1 for each individual, while the people of this country were taxed at the rate of £5 for each " (*Parl. Deb.*, vol. xxix. p. 982). The armies of Napoleon lived on the conquered countries ; so that his policy of militarism, though it exhausted France of men and paralysed her industry and commerce, imposed no burden on the Treasury so long as a state of war continued. In short, a state of continuous war was necessary to France for financial as well as administrative reasons. (For the economic policy of France under Napoleon, see a letter from Wellington to Baron Constant, Gallegos, January 13, 1812, *Dispatches*, vol. v. pp. 494 sqq.) In England exactly the opposite conditions prevailed. The war did not exhaust the country of men or improve directly her industry and commerce ; but it was terribly expensive. Only the economic activity of the country enabled her to support the burden of taxation.

[5] Cobbett, *Rural Rides*, August 7, 1823.

[6] Quoted by the *Leeds Mercury*, April 6, 1815.

for the grant of financial or commercial concessions ; but the most common, and finally the only method, was to raise loans by public subscription. The State asked for a certain sum and promised to pay a certain rate of interest. The bankers of London acted as agents between the Treasury and the public ; they were called into consultation by the Chancellor of the Exchequer, and they made their proposals—each banker present acting as the agent of a group of lenders, bankers or merchants. And finally the public took up the securities—annuities redeemable at the option of the State but not at the option of the investor, or perpetual annuities which the investor could transfer freely by means of entries in the books of the Bank of England. So there arose in the English economic system a new class of investors in the public funds, "stockholders" or "fundholders." It was a thrifty class with whom the taste for saving became a passion. Sir John Sinclair in 1803 estimated that a fifth of the interest paid out annually by the State to its creditors was re-invested in the public funds.[1] It was a class which became more and more numerous. Hume at the middle of the 18th century estimated that there were 17,000 [2] fundholders. In 1829 official statistics gave their number as 275,839, of whom 250,816 received an annual interest of £200 or less.[3]

The investor in public funds had this unique advantage, that he could at any time sell his investment without any of the difficulties which confront the owner of land or of a business enterprise. He had only to go to the "stockbrokers," who, in return for a brokerage fee, undertook all the formalities of transfer in the offices of the Bank.[4] Professional stockbrokers had no legal monopoly, but in practice they were employed by all. They formed a sort of corporation governed by an elected committee, and they received a licence from the Lord Mayor. From 1804 onwards they met in a special building, the Stock Exchange, erected by them close to the Bank of England out of funds raised by subscription from the profession. They had won a position of such importance and influence that for twenty years before our date they had been competing with the bankers in negotiations with the Treasury for the issue of loans. Stockbrokers had married their daughters to members of the House of Lords. Amongst the members of the Stock Exchange were the great economist Ricardo, and the eminent scientists Francis Bailey and Benjamin Gompertz. Moreover, just because they considered themselves to be the aristocrats of the

---

[1] *History of Public Revenue*, 3rd ed., 1803, vol. iii. p. 139.

[2] *Of Public Credit* (Essays, ed. Greene and Grose, vol. i. p. 373 n.), including foreign holders of British funds.

[3] Doubleday, *Financial . . . History of England*, 1847, p. 264, who quotes Cobbett. The complete statistics give 250,816 fundholders receiving interest of £200 or less ; 22,934 receiving between £1,000 and £200 ; 1,937 receiving between £4,000 and £1,000 ; and 152 receiving more than £4,000.

[4] For this organization, see Hamilton, *Inquiry*, 3rd ed., 1818, pp. 313 sqq.

London Stock Exchange, the brokers did not wish to be concerned with bringing together buyers and sellers. They left this work to the stockjobbers, another class of intermediaries between Government and public, who also made a living from dealings in the funds. These stockjobbers did not only act as agents for the public ; they bought for their own account with a view to selling later at a higher price and thus making a profit by the double operation. Or they engaged in operations which were essentially in the nature of betting upon the price of Government stock at some future date. On that date some would win and others lose. Some, perhaps, might be ruined. By a statute still in force, operations in futures had been deprived of all legal sanction, and by another statute they had been expressly prohibited,[1] but nevertheless such operations were carried through on the Stock Exchange, and the name of stockjobber was given to all, whether professionals or not, who speculated in investment values. Thus there arose amongst the prudent and thrifty investors in Government funds an inner circle of speculators and gamblers. At one time Quakers were numerous in both the stockbroking and the jobbing professions ; but later they seem to have diminished in number and to have devoted themselves specially to the finance of the corn trade which was localized in the neighbourhood of Mark Lane. They were replaced by Jews, who now acted in large numbers as stockjobbers and penetrated even into the ranks of the brokers. A rule of 1772 limited to twelve the number of Jews who might exercise the latter profession.[2]

The great fortunes made by speculating in the public funds were regarded with dislike and distrust by public opinion. Such fortunes were not based on any increase of real wealth, and they were rendered conspicuous by being made in London at the very centre of the political life of the nation. Fortunes were succeeded swiftly by failures ; the business of Change Alley in the City was marked by constant scandals. In 1810 Abraham Goldsmid, the King of the Stock Exchange, committed suicide ; the King and the Prince of Wales were informed by special messenger, and the price of securities fell 3 per cent. In 1811 the stockbroker Benjamin Walsh was excluded from Parliament for having defrauded Sir Thomas Plomer of £16,000. The same punishment was inflicted in 1814 on Lord Cochrane, the great sailor and popular politician, on the charge of having, with several others, made a *coup* on the Stock Exchange by circulating a false rumour regarding the death of Napoleon. The amount involved was some £826,000. Both speculators and fundholders[3] were abhorred by the public. They were said to have prolonged the war so that their activities

[1] 7 Geo. II, cap. 8 ; 10 Geo. II, cap. 8.
[2] Francis, *Chronicles and Characters of the Stock Exchange*, p. 113.
[3] " Tax-eaters." Cobbett, *Rural Rides*, December 4, 1821, January 8, 1822, May 5, 1823, and *passim*.

might be given a wider field by the increase of the National Debt. They were held responsible for the great residential area around the City of London which was now being developed for the accommodation of business men or idle fundholders, a veritable " wen " [1] on the body politic attracting to itself an undue proportion of the population. They were charged with causing the depopulation of the countryside by buying land and forming large estates, buying out the yeomen and turning away the small farmers. [2]   Cobbett, who was essentially an inhabitant of Southern England, expressed no doubt the view of many of·his contemporaries when he charged the stockjobbers with being responsible for this new phenomenon, the concentration of wealth. The manufacturers, according to him, did but follow the example of those who speculated in the public funds. " A national debt and all the taxation and gambling belonging to it have a natural tendency to *draw wealth into great masses.* These masses produce a power of congregating manufactures and of making the many work at them for the gain of a few." [3]

For more than a century, indeed, the increase of the National Debt had been a cause of alarm to competent observers. Certainly the borrowing system had brought certain political advantages during the 18th century, for it had given rise to a growing class of fundholders keenly interested in national solvency and therefore in safeguarding from revolution the system of government which dated from 1688. Moreover, the system had not prevented an enormous increase of wealth in England ; and thanks to this increase, which resulted in the debt being held almost entirely by its own nationals, the State was able to avoid paying a tribute of interest to the foreigner.   In 1762, shortly after the accession of George III, it was calculated that only one-seventh of the total debt was held abroad.   The external debt increased afterwards, but only to a slight extent, whilst the total debt expanded much more quickly.   In 1815 it seems that only one-twenty-fifth

---

[1] " The Wen, the great Wen."   Cobbett, *Rural Rides*, December 4, 1821, January 8, 1822, May 5, 1823, and *passim*.

[2] H. of C., December 3, 1798, Tierney's speech (*Parl. Hist.*, vol. xxxiv. pp. 23–4).

[3] *Rural Rides*, August 1, 1823.   Cf. H. of C., December 3, 1798, Tierney's speech : " Such, indeed, is the operation of all great capitals of credit, which enable the capitalist by means of banks to multiply the natural power of his stock even three or fourfold ; to grasp, monopolize and control everything. . . .   Large capitals and credits . . . have a tendency to monopolization, and to form a kind of bourgeois and upstart aristocracy, with all the faults of the former, without any of its virtues " (*Annual Register*, 1799, pp. 177–8).   Wm. Morgan (*A Comparative View of the Public Finances* . . . London, 1801, pp. 40–1) says that the war encouraged speculation in the public funds ; and in consequence, " by rendering the division of property more unequal, it has also increased the number of great capitalists."   See also de Montveran, *Situation de l'Angleterre* . . ., vol. i. p. 155.   The system of public borrowing seems to tend (where, on the advent of peace, the debt is not or cannot be paid off) to increase the number of big fortunes and to diminish the number of moderate fortunes, which are the source of public prosperity and which give a larger measure of individual ease and happiness.

of the debt was held by foreigners.[1] But even so the danger of insolvency remained.

In the 18th century it was a source of anxiety to Hume, Price and Adam Smith ; [2] and, after the American War of Independence, statesmen also began to be infected by the fears of the economists. All their efforts, however, were powerless to relieve the burden of indebtedness. They wished to redeem ; but payments to the sinking fund were constantly suspended. They wished to convert ; but the rate of interest, which had fallen from 8 to 3 per cent. during the first half of the century, began to rise again after the Seven Years' War. They even invented the plan of creating debt with a face value greater than the sums actually lent, so that whilst borrowing nominally at 3 or 4 per cent., they paid in fact more than 5 per cent. At the end of the American War the debt had risen to the enormous figure of £238,231,248.[3] Of the normal revenue of £12,000,000 more than three-quarters—£9,139,000—were absorbed by the service of the debt. It was at this crisis that Pitt, now Prime Minister, was to inaugurate a new era in the history of English finance.

The Policy of Redemption of Debt (1786–1813).

In 1786 William Pitt applied an annual sum of £1,000,000 [4]—derived in part from economies in various services, in part from new taxation—to the constitution of a sinking fund based on a new principle. Instead of redeeming and cancelling a portion of the debt every year, thus lessening the burden of interest payments, be applied to the redemption of debt the system of compound interest. The taxpayer was to continue to pay interest on the amount of debt annually redeemed, until, by the accumulation of this interest, the income of the sinking

[1] Sir John Sinclair (*History of the Public Revenue*, 3rd ed., 1804, vol. iii. Appendix, pp. 160 sqq.) gives figures for 1762 showing foreign holdings of the funds as £14,970,671 2s. 4d., bearing interest £576,613 8s. 10d. Adding South Sea stock and East India stock not included in these amounts, he gets a total holding of £17,000,000 bearing interest to the extent of £770,000. Total foreign holdings were thus less than a seventh of the National Debt. For the year 1804, he arrives, by very conjectural calculations, at a total foreign holding of £24,435,478 9s. 11d., bearing interest £954,123 16s. 10d. Hamilton (*Inquiry*, 3rd ed., 1818, p. 260), calculating foreign holdings in 1806 from the applications for exemption from property tax, obtains the figure of £18,598,666, together with £17,147 of life annuities. As these figures took no account of bank shares of which some £3,000,000 were held abroad, especially in Holland, he puts his final total at £22,000,000 ; that is, $\frac{1}{35}$th of the National Debt. The *Edinburgh Review* in April 1808 (No. 23, Art. 13, *Baring and others on the Orders in Council*, vol. xii. p. 238) estimates that England was paying £700,000 a year to its foreign creditors. All these estimates made for the first ten years of the century are more or less similar. See, however, for the uncertainty which prevailed upon this point, de Montveran, *Situation de l'Angleterre*, vol. i. p. 118.

[2] For a series of contemporary opinions announcing the imminent ruin of England, 1688–1783, see Sir John Sinclair, *History of Public Revenue*, Appendix, vol. ii. p. 51.

[3] These figures, and the figures which follow, are taken from Rob. Hamilton (*Inquiry . . . Concerning the National Debt*, 1st ed., 1813 ; 2nd ed., 1814 ; 3rd ed., 1818), whom we have always found very precise and accurate.

[4] 26 Geo. III, cap. 26.

fund should reach the total of £4,000,000. In 1792 further measures were taken. A sum of £400,000 was made a prior charge upon the Budget to be used for the purpose of the sinking fund,[1] and it was settled that in subsequent years a sum of £200,000 should be applied annually under the same conditions. These payments were to be a net addition to the sinking fund and did not relieve the taxpayer from his obligation, under the original scheme, to enlarge the annual sum of £1,000,000 by the gradual accumulation of interest, until it should reach £4,000,000. Moreover, it was decided as a precautionary measure that whenever, in the future, it became necessary to raise a loan from the public, a fresh sinking fund equivalent to 1 per cent. of the loan should be constituted which, with its interest, should be devoted to the redemption of the new loan.[2] Thus it was said every new loan would be automatically redeemed within a maximum period of forty-five years.

Pitt's scheme was based in all its details on the work of the economist Richard Price. Political economy was now fashionable ; and the scheme had a scientific aspect which made it attractive. But, regarding the problem from a purely financial standpoint, calculation will show that the new method of redemption did not differ from the old. The redemption of a debt will proceed at exactly the same rate, whether it be affected by setting aside every year a definite sum to purchase and cancel so much of the stock, or whether, every year, the same sum be used to purchase stock and thereby to constitute a fund which, with its interest, shall finally become equal to the total debt originally contracted. Nevertheless, if it becomes necessary to raise a fresh loan whilst the process of redeeming a previous loan is still being continued, we cannot regard the two operations as cancelling each other and leaving the situation unchanged ; for to borrow with one hand and to redeem with the other involves at any rate the expenses of conducting these two series of operations.[3] In what, then, lay the superiority of the new method ? It may be found in the constitutional rather than in the financial aspects of the problem.

If a State is redeeming its debt solely by devoting a specified sum every year to this purpose it may be tempted in times of financial stress to divert this sum to other purposes and so to suspend the task of redemption entirely until conditions become more favourable. If, on the other hand, a State relies, for the redemption of its debt, not only upon a contribution made annually for this object but also upon the interest of a sinking fund already accumulated, though the State will then have the power, in periods of difficulty, to divert to current expenditure both these sources of income, yet in practice it would probably fear to arouse opposition by so sweeping a measure, and would perhaps rest content with only a partial raid upon the money which should

---

[1] 32 Geo. III, cap. 12. [2] 32 Geo. III, cap. 55.
[3] Hamilton, *Inquiry*, 2nd ed., 1814, pp. 52 sqq., 129 sqq., 175 sqq.

have been devoted to redeeming debt. It would continue, for instance, to pay its annual contribution to the sinking fund, but would cease to pay interest on the fund already accumulated. The sinking fund would continue to grow, though its rate of growth would be lessened. In short, because the new method was more complicated than the old it offered more resistance to the depredations of the Government.

But that was not all. In 1786 Pitt set up a body of "commissioners" appointed from amongst the highest officials of the realm, the "Commissioners for the reduction of the National Debt," in whose name was inscribed all the stock annually redeemed, to whose account was paid every three months the sums devoted to redemption, and who, at similar intervals, employed these sums, as well as the accumulated interest of the fund, to the purchase of stock. In this way the money voted annually by Parliament was utilized every quarter. It never remained as an idle balance into which a Minister at times of financial stress might be tempted to dip his hand. Moreover, Parliament, after having created this imposing body of commissioners, bound itself in respect of them by a sort of perpetual undertaking. Students of the English Constitution, at the end of the 18th century, regarded it as composed of certain constituent bodies—Parliament and Magistracy—House of Lords and House of Commons—Crown and Cabinet—which had learnt by custom to respect each other's rights. Pitt wished to add to the political, or rather to the financial system, a new body and to endow that body with some of the prestige enjoyed by those of older establishment. In this way he hoped to give to his method of redemption a permanence and a stability which had been lacking in the methods hitherto tried. "A Minister could not have the confidence to come to this House and desire the repeal of so beneficial a law which tended so directly to relieve the people from their burthens. . . . It was the essence of his plan to keep that (sinking fund) sacred, and most effectually so in time of war."[1] But the question remained whether it was possible to bind Parliament, by means of a sort of incantation, to respect an undertaking given to another body which had been recently established and which rested, as all the world knew, upon the authority of Parliament itself.

War was declared with France; and repeated loans were required to provide for the expenses of the Army, Navy, and for subsidies to Allied Powers. In the four years from 1793 to 1797 a new debt of more than £130,000,000 was contracted on very onerous terms. In 1825, to obtain the sum of £18,000,000 the State was obliged to issue a loan to the face value of £24,000,000; and in 1796, to obtain the same sum, debt was incurred to the face value of £26,000,000. It is calculated that the effective rate of interest on the *Loyalty Loan* of December 1796 was 11½ per cent. However, that very rise in the rate of interest,

---

[1] H. of C., March 29, 1786, Pitt's speech (*Parl. Hist.*, vol. xxv. pp. 1309, 1321).

which was needed to attract money from the public, facilitated the work of the sinking fund. When the Government 3 per cents., which were at par in January 1792, fell by the end of December to 76, in January 1796 to 70, in January 1797 to 55⅛, and in May of the same year to 47⅞, a price even lower than that reached during the American War, the Debt Commissioners were able, with the same expenditure, to redeem twice as much debt. Until the election of 1796, Parliament held to the undertakings which it had given in 1786 and 1792. The working of the sinking fund, which had hitherto been maintained at its normal activity, was now relaxed.

In 1798, 1799 and 1800 loans were raised to a total of £56,445,000 without the provision of a 1 per cent. sinking fund ; and the interest on these loans, which could not longer be met from the Consolidated Fund, was provided by means of new taxes. At the Peace of Amiens the total debt was £567,008,978 ; and if from this is deducted the £67,225,915 redeemed by the operation of the sinking fund, the total becomes £499,783,063, showing a net increase of over £260,000,000. The work of the sinking fund was not expressly forbidden, but the Commissioners were not provided with funds sufficient to comply altogether with the provisions of the laws of 1786 and 1792. The Consolidated Fund was no longer able to support the burden of interest payments. The debt controversy, which for the time had ceased, now began once more ; and it became entangled in the disputes which raged between political writers of reactionary and of Jacobin tendencies. The human race, declared Thomas Paine, is composed of successive generations which are independent of each other. A perpetual debt destroys this independence by imposing upon future generations the burden of paying the debts of their ancestors. It is an absurd and unnatural system.[1] On the contrary, it is an admirable system, replied Gentz, the recognized advocate of the Counter-Revolution ; for it makes men feel that society is something more than the mere aggregate of individuals who happen to be alive at the time, and that it is the duty of the State to bind together the generations which, passing imperceptibly one into the other, constitute the human race.[2]

In 1802 Addington, who had become Prime Minister, issued a loan of £30,350,375 without providing the 1 per cent. sinking fund prescribed by the law of 1792. He endeavoured, however, to regularize the position of the Treasury by a comprehensive measure, which had the full approbation of Pitt. In place of the temporary war taxes he levied permanent taxes to meet the interest charges in respect of debt incurred since 1798. He merged into a single sinking fund all the funds set up since 1786—the funds of 1786 and 1792, and the special funds of 1 per cent. for each loan—this single fund to be used for the redemption

[1] *Decline and Fall of the English System of Finance*, p. 21.
[2] *Administration des Finances . . . de la Grande-Bretagne*, pp. 137 sqq.

of all debt without distinction, and even of those loans, amounting in all to £86,796,375, to which a 1 per cent. fund had not been attached. Towards the redemption of this amount of £86,796,375 were applied monies which had not been destined to that end ; and the rate of redemption of other loans was thereby diminished. On the other hand, Addington abolished the limit of £4,000,000 which had been imposed by the Act of 1786 on the growth of the original annual sum of £1,000,000. Interest was now to accumulate until the whole debt had been redeemed. For such redemption a period of forty-five years would be sufficient.[1]

But again war broke out ; and from 1803 to 1806 a fresh debt of £98,480,000 was incurred. As, during this period, debt to the amount of £46,604,601 was redeemed, the net addition was £51,875,399. There seemed no hope of an early end of war and continued borrowing. In 1807 Lord Henry Petty, Chancellor of the Exchequer in the Grenville Ministry, proposed a new scheme of redemption.[2] He suggested a series of loans, spread in gradually increasing amounts over fourteen years, and reaching a total of £210,000,000. The charges for interest and redemption in respect of these loans were to be met from war taxes ; every year the country was to pay 10 per cent. of the total debt incurred. To make up the deficit created by diverting war taxes to the payment of interest on these future loans Lord Henry Petty suggested supplementary loans, to each of which should be attached a 1 per cent. fund, as in Pitt's scheme. But in one point he departed deliberately from Pitt's principles ; for he provided that, when the income of the sinking fund existing in 1807 should exceed the interest on the debt still unredeemed, the excess should in times of peace be at the disposition of Parliament. And in criticizing this measure the speakers of the Opposition proposed an alternative which was equally an abandonment—temporarily at least—of the principles of Pitt and of Addington. They suggested that, whenever a loan did not exceed the total income of the sinking fund, the interest on the loan should be paid from the interest on the debt redeemed in that year by the Commissioners.[3] Both parties, indeed, seemed to agree that it was permissible to violate, partially or temporarily, the undertaking made in 1786. Lord Henry Petty's scheme did not, however, constitute a grave default from the principles laid down by Pitt. Certainly he foresaw that it would be possible eventually to apply a part of the original sinking fund to the redemption of fresh loans, and

[1] H. of C., April 14, May 17, June 3, June 17, June 25, 1802 (*Parl. Hist.*, vol. xxxvi. pp. 889 sqq.). 42 Geo. III, cap. 71.

[2] H. of C., January 29, 1807 (*Parl. Deb.*, vol. viii. pp. 565 sqq. ; resolutions, pp. 593 sqq.). 47 Geo. III, sess. 1, cap. 55.

[3] H. of C., February 12, 1807, Lord Castlereagh's resolutions (*Parl. Deb.*, vol. vii. pp. 725 sqq., and particularly pp. 743–4).

he planned systematically to use extraordinary revenues for the service of such loans. But on the other hand his scheme of redemption for such loans was much more rapid than that adopted for the loans of the first war. He calculated that each successive loan would be redeemed in fourteen years ; so that, fifteen years after the last war loan, fifteen years after the establishment of peace, the country would find itself relieved of the whole burden of debt incurred since 1807.

Lord Henry Petty's scheme was approved, but the accession to power of the Tories in the following year led to its abandonment. The new Ministry redeemed with one hand and borrowed with the other. In 1809, Perceval raised a loan without imposing additional taxes to meet the payment of interest ; he used for this purpose part of the proceeds of the war taxes.[1] From the beginning of the war to 1813 debt had been incurred to the amount of £245,004,157. Deducting redemptions of £143,205,441 the net additional burden of debt was £101,798,716. The war, however, seemed now to be nearing its end. Vansittart proposed and procured the acceptance of a new scheme to replace that of Addington.[2]

The sinking fund set up by Pitt in 1786 was to cease working when the whole of the outstanding debt had been redeemed. In 1786 the debt amounted to £238,231,248 ; and by 1813 the sinking fund had redeemed £238,350,144, being an excess of £118,895 over the debt of 1786. Vansittart then argued that according to the statute of 1786 a part of the National Debt amounting to £238,231,248 should be cancelled and the public relieved from paying interest on this amount to the Commissioners of the Debt. This proposal was open to argument ; for the sinking fund which by 1813 had redeemed more than £238,231,248 was not the fund which Pitt had created in 1786. It dated from 1802, and resulted from the merger of the fund of 1786 with various other funds set up by Pitt at subsequent dates. Moreover, it had been increased, since 1802, by a series of special funds created for the redemption of fresh loans. So that the cancellation of all debt incurred before 1786 was rendered possible only because there had been borrowing on a large scale since that date. Vansittart further arranged that all debts incurred by borrowing since 1792 and since 1802 should be successively redeemed out of a common fund ; and that, whenever debt had been redeemed to the amount of one of these loans, that amount of debt should be cancelled. Thus Vansittart departed once again from the system devised by Pitt. He used the sinking fund, which had been attached to the loan of a particular year, to redeem the loans of previous years ; whereas Pitt had wished that

[1] H. of C., May 12, 1809, Perceval's speech (Parl. Deb., vol. xiv. p. 535). 49 Geo. III, cap. 92.
[2] H. of C., March 3, 1809 (Parl. Deb., vol. xxiv. p. 1078, and Appendix). 53 Geo. III, cap. 35.

each loan should be accompanied by the provisions for its own redemption. But though Vansittart, on the one hand, relieved the taxpayer of the payment of interest on a debt of £238,231,248, on the other he arranged, by certain subsidiary measures, that the scope of the new sinking fund should be enlarged. He established a sinking fund of 1 per cent. for the £86,796,375 which had been borrowed between 1798 and 1802 without provisions for redemption. He established a sinking fund of 1 per cent. for floating debt not redeemed in the course of the year during which it was incurred. And finally he promised to redeem the National Debt more quickly than would have been possible under Addington's scheme. His calculations were to be strongly disputed ; [1] but without such a promise he would not have been able to gain for his proposals the assent of a Parliament which sincerely wished to carry out the undertaking of 1786.

The policy which had been devised thirty years before had now undergone considerable changes. The partisans of Pitt declared that Vansittart had altogether abandoned the financial canons laid down by his predecessor.[2] But we have seen that the changes made by Vansittart were circumspect, indeed almost timid. The British Parliament clung religiously—one is almost tempted to say superstitiously—to the practice of redemption, even at times when it was obliged to borrow more rapidly than it redeemed. From 1792 to 1802, £60,483,565 had been redeemed, but new indebtedness amounted to £328,777,730. From 1803 to 1813 redemptions were £143,205,441, as against new indebtedness of £245,004,063. There was fresh borrowing in 1813 and 1814. In 1815 the total debt of Great Britain was £678,847,661. If to this amount are added the Irish debt [3] and the debts incurred on behalf of the Empire and of Portugal [4] the total becomes £832,197,004 without including a floating debt of £68,580,524. The taxpayer hoped, now peace had come, that the cessation of borrowing and the rapid extinction of the debt would reward him for his fidelity to the principle of redemption. But would it really be possible, even in time of peace, to abstain from fresh borrowing ? And if the Government, whilst redeeming with one hand, continued, with the other hand, to borrow more rapidly than it redeemed, was not the policy of sinking funds a mere deception ?

Taxation. The Income Tax.

In order to understand the critical situation of the English Treasury,

---

[1] Hamilton, *Inquiry*, pp. 220 sqq. Ricardo, *Essay on the Funding System* (*Works*, ed. MacCulloch, pp. 525–6).

[2] Alison, *History of Europe*, vol. ix, pp. 268 sqq. ; vol. xvi. pp. 296 sqq.

[3] Irish debt, interest payable in London, £133,677,146 ; interest payable in Dublin, £32,142,520. Total debt, £145,819,666.

[4] Loans on behalf of the Emperor of Germany, 1795 and 1797, £7,502,633 ; on behalf of Portugal, 1809, £27,044.

and the financial problems in general which were being discussed in London during the early months of 1815, let us essay to unravel the complications of the Budget and to resolve into their essential elements the main resources of the Government.

The first class of resources composed what had been known since 1787 as the Consolidated Fund—a fund which was allotted, in the first instance and before any other payments were made, to meeting debt charges, the Civil List and a few other civil expenses. The civil expenditure charged to this fund was only about £1,500,000 as against £41,000,000 for interest on the funded debt and £2,500,000 for interest on the floating debt.   All the permanent taxes, in other words those which did not have to be annually renewed by the House of Commons, were paid into the Consolidated Fund.

Of these *Customs* brought in about £5,000,000 and *Excise* about £18,000,000.   These were taxes upon consumption imposed upon manufacturers, upon wholesalers and retailers, and upon importers of dutiable articles.   Beverages of all kinds were taxed—beer, ale, cider, wine, vinegar, spirits—and also hops and malt, used in the manufacture of beer and ale.   There were taxes on coffee, tea and cocoa, and also upon a large number of other articles which could not be classed as luxuries ; tobacco, brass wire, candles, tiles and bricks, cloth and paper. *Stamp Duties* brought to the Consolidated Fund a sum of £5,500,000, of which a third was derived from judicial stamps and a sixth from succession duties.[1] The *Post Office* contributed £1,500,000.   The *Land Tax* was intended to be a tax on all income, whether derived from real or personal property.   But so far as movables were concerned the tax had always been of limited application and, after a time, was allowed to lapse almost entirely.   So far as other property was concerned Pitt, in 1798, limited the demand to a fixed amount for the whole of Great Britain, and allowed the assessees to redeem all future dues by a single capital payment made in Government funds at the price of the day. Consequently the yield from this tax could never increase ; it could only diminish ; and it amounted to hardly more than £1,000,000.   *Assessed Taxes*, on the other hand, were of ever-increasing importance in the English Budget.[2]   These were, in essence, sumptuary taxes, on male

---

[1] Stamp Duties were regulated at the beginning of 1815 by two Acts : 44 Geo. III, cap. 98, " An Act to repeal the several duties upon stamped vellum, parchment and paper, in Great Britain, and to grant new and additional duties in lieu thereof "—modified, in the whole of one part, by the important law 48 Geo. III, cap. 149, " An Act for repealing the Stamp Duties on deeds, law proceedings, and other written or printed instruments, and the duties on legacies and successions to personal estate upon intestacies, now payable in Great Britain ; and for granting new duties in lieu thereof."   These two Acts were amended and recast in 1815 by 55 Geo. III, cap. 184 (deeds, law proceedings . . . and duties on fire insurance), and cap. 185 (advertisements, newspapers, gold and silver plate, stage coaches, licences for keeping stage coaches).

[2] For a statement of the *Assessed Taxes*, see the Consolidating Acts, 25 Geo. III, cap. 47, 48 Geo. III, cap. 55, and Dowell, *History of Taxation*, vol. ii. pp. 189-90, vol. iii. pp. 155 sqq.

domestic servants, on dogs, on the licences of coach-builders and horse-dealers, on hair powder, on carriages and on armorial bearings ; but they were imposed also upon houses and windows, constituting, in this class, a heavy burden on the mass of the population. The number and the rate of the Assessed Taxes had been increased from year to year and they now produced more than £6,000,000. Then came a series of taxes on pensions and salaries, on hackney carriages and hawkers. In all the total receipts of the Consolidated Fund were about £38,000,000. All this was required to meet the first charges on the fund. Current expenditure had to be met from other sources.

Such sources were found in the so-called "annual" taxes. According to constitutional usage the House of Commons affirmed their right of control over the public finances by reserving to themselves the power, every year, to grant or to refuse to the Government at least a part of the revenue required to meet the annual expenditure. In the 18th century the land tax and the duty on malt came under this head. But in 1797, when William Pitt allowed the redemption of the land tax [1] and fixed for ever its maximum yield, he changed its character from that of an annual to a permanent tax. In order, however, to preserve the constitutional safeguards, he placed in the category of annual taxes the new duties upon sugar, malt and tobacco. These duties yielded much more than the land tax ; moreover, the duty on sugar was raised after 1797, and an annual tax was imposed upon pensions and salaries. But the whole yield of these taxes was not placed freely at the disposal of the Chancellor of the Exchequer. It was devoted to the amount of £3,000,000 to the repayment of Treasury Bonds ; and the surplus, which for the year 1814 exceeded £2,000,000, was paid, in case of deficit, into the Consolidated Fund. To meet the normal expenses of Army and Navy it was manifestly impossible either to be content with, or to do without, the "extraordinary" resources yielded by the war taxes which had been imposed for the past eighteen years. But these taxes expired by law a year after the establishment of peace. Would public opinion sanction their continuance ? And if not, how was financial equilibrium to be attained ?

The war taxes were derived, in the first place, to the amount of £3,500,000, from enhancements of customs duties ; and there was no organized agitation for the reduction or the discontinuance of these duties. The Cabinet retained them after the establishment of peace by three successive Acts passed without opposition in 1814, 1815 and 1816,[2] and finally made them permanent. On the other hand, opposition was aroused by the proposal to raise the import duties on cereals. But the Cabinet, in proposing this measure, had regarded it as a protection

---

[1] Or rather of the greater part of the land tax. The part concerned with movables remained in the category of annual taxes.

[2] 54 Geo. III, cap. 64 ; 55 Geo. III, cap. 33 ; 56 Geo. III, cap. 29.

to agriculture against foreign competition rather than as a fiscal expedient. And the riot which occurred in London in February 1815 was not, in the strict sense, a protest by taxpayers against measures of taxation : it was rather a protest by manufacturers and workmen against the dominance of the landed interests.

Extraordinary taxation under the heading of *Excise* yielded £6,500,000. Now, throughout the 18th century excise had been the most unpopular form of taxation, not because of the objects on which it was levied, but because of the methods of collection and the annoyance caused to the taxpayer. If a brewer bought casks without telling the exciseman he could be fined or his plant subjected to confiscation. The distiller's casks had to be kept under lock and key by the exciseman. Similar control was exercised over the manufacture of glass, and over the preparation and marketing of tea, coffee and cocoa. It was not permissible without leave of the exciseman to make cocoa for personal use or to move tea from one shop to another.[1] It was illegal to move more than six pounds of tea after dark, except in a postchaise or in a licensed public vehicle. We have had occasion to explain why this bureaucratic interference was specially intolerable to the Englishman of 1815 ; yet it was not against the extraordinary excise duties that the displeasure of the taxpayer at that time was directed. One of these duties indeed, the extraordinary duty of 2s. 4d. on malt, offended the agriculturist, and had soon to be abolished. But the other duties— that on spirits, equal to half the ordinary duty ; that on wine, adding 12s. to the ordinary duty of £32 11s. per cask ; the extra 18s. superimposed upon the duty on French wines of £48 6s. per cask—were not of serious weight and were, moreover, of a sumptuary nature. Serious agitation, both in the country and in Parliament, was directed for the time towards another war tax, a tax inquisitorial in the same manner as the excise duties, a new tax more productive and therefore more disagreeable than any of the others—the *Property Tax* or tax on income.

It was in 1798 that Pitt realized, for the first time after six years of war, that it was impossible to rely upon loans for all the resources necessary for a continuance of military operations. First he greatly increased the Assessed Taxes. In 1799, dissatisfied with the results so obtained, he decided to alter his system and to tax income instead of expenditure.[2] His *Income Tax*, which did not extend to incomes below £60, became gradually heavier on incomes between £60 and £200. From £200 upwards it was at the rate of 10 per cent. In its first form the *Income Tax* did not fulfil expectations. Pitt had estimated a yield of £10,000,000 ; but in 1801 he obtained hardly

---

[1] For administrative details see de Ranmer, *Exposé du Système de Contributions*, French trans. (from the German), pp. 152 sqq.

[2] 39 Geo III, cap. 13, § 8 ; 39 Geo. III, cap. 22.

more than £5,500,000.[1] The tax was abolished by Addington
after the Peace of Amiens, but was re-established in 1803 under
the name of *Property and Income Tax*.[2] As in 1799, it did not extend
to incomes below £60. Between £60 and £150 relief was given
to the extent of one shilling on every pound by which the income fell
short of £150, where the income arose from the exercise of a profession,
from a salary or stipend, or was in any way the reward of personal
labour. Above £150 the rate of tax was 5 per cent. Pitt raised it
to 6¼ per cent. in 1805,[3] and Lord Henry Petty to 10 per cent. in 1806.[4]
In 1814 the *Property Tax*, established on this basis, brought in nearly
£16,000,000,[5] more than one-third of all the war taxes put together.

The Government made every effort to avoid inquisitorial methods.
From 1803 the tax was not imposed on the total income of the individual,
but was assessed separately on incomes derived from different sources.
The commissioners charged with the task of assessment were not,
like excisemen or customs officials, paid by the central government.
Chosen by the Commissioners of the Land Tax, who were appointed
by a process of cooption from amongst the justices of the peace for
each county, the income tax commissioners were themselves justices
of the peace, landowners or large tax-payers who gave their services
without reward. In 1803 [6] it was even enacted that in certain cases
the taxpayer should himself make his own return, and that if this return
were questioned by the commissioners, the matter should be settled, not
by them, but by arbitrators chosen by them and the taxpayer in agreement. And finally, after a decision had been given, the taxpayer was
allowed, by special rules, to pay his contribution into the Bank without
disclosing his name. These provisions were subsequently abandoned
because they were too complicated and because very little use was made
of them. But in 1808 and in 1810,[7] after the fairly drastic income
tax reforms of Lord Henry Petty, laws were enacted to protect assessees,
especially the owners of land and houses, against the inquisitorial methods
of the tax collector. In spite of all precautions, however, the income
tax was in universal disfavour.

Merchants, manufacturers and business men all complained of it ;
for though vexatious inquiries might be unnecessary for the assessment
of incomes derived from real property or from the funds, they seem to
have been unavoidable when estimating the financial position of a

---

[1] Dowell, *History of Taxation*, vol. iii. p. 95.

[2] 43 Geo. III, cap. 122.   [3] 45 Geo. III, cap. 15.

[4] 46 Geo. III, cap. 65. At the same time the taxable minimum was lowered from £60
to £50 ; and exemption was confined to the incomes of salaried workers. The relief given by
Addington to assessees having more than two children was abolished ; and incomes derived from
real property were more strictly taxed.

[5] *Gross and Net Assessments of Property Tax*, April 24, 1815. Gross yield £15,795,961
10s. 8d., net yield £14,502,398 4s. 4¼d.

[6] 43 Geo III, cap. 122, §§ 110 sqq.

[7] 48 Geo. III, cap. 141 ; 50 Geo. III, cap. 106.

commercial house, of a factory, or of a bank. Baring, the banker, declared
before the House of Commons that " for his own part he would much
rather be summoned before the bench of bishops to give an account of
his religious beliefs than appear before the commissioners under the
property tax to answer their questions as to the exact amount of his
worldly goods and chattels."[1] It would have been most unwise, therefore, to arouse the enmity of the business world by maintaining this tax
at the very time that the price of corn was being artificially raised in
compliance with the demands of the agriculturists.

The agriculturists, on their side, protested against the Property
Tax. They argued that, of all classes of taxpayers, they were least
able to hide their true financial position,[2] and, moreover, that the method
adopted for estimating their income was unfair. Incomes from the
occupation of land were estimated at the average of the rent paid by the
farmer to the landowner during the previous seven years.[3] When,
as in 1815, rents were falling rapidly and continuously, the farmers
suffered ; for their tax decreased less quickly than their income. Thus
it was not only the business men of the City and the manufacturers
of the big towns, but also the country gentlemen supported by their
tenant farmers, who held meetings and signed petitions demanding the
abolition of a tax which, like the excise duties of the past, was denounced
as contrary to the principles of a free Constitution.

After four months of shuffling the Ministry at last capitulated in
February 1815 ;[4] and Vansittart, the Chancellor of the Exchequer,
introduced a Budget which contained no reference to a tax on incomes.[5]
He estimated that the Consolidated Fund, together with the amount
earmarked from war taxes for the service of debt, would reach the total
of £40,962,000, whilst the charges on that fund amounted to
£37,543,000. There was thus a surplus of £3,419,000 ; to which
might be added the annual duties imposed for repaying Exchequer
Bills—perhaps £3,000,000—giving a total surplus of £6,500,000.
On these estimates it was not possible to abolish the property tax
and at the same time to assure financial equilibrium. Garrisons had
to be maintained in the new Colonies ; the Fleet required repairs on
a large scale ; the enormous increase of persons in receipt of half-

---

[1] H. of C., February 20, 1815 (Parl. Deb., vol. xxix. p. 885).

[2] For the year 1814–15 the income derived from land under schedule A was estimated at
£53,500,000 for England, and at £6,600,000 for Scotland. Professional incomes of all kinds,
taxed under schedule D, yielded only £34,280,000 for England, and £2,770,000 for Scotland
(Dowell, History of Taxation, vol. iii. pp. 104–5). But the disproportion is partly explained by
the classification in schedule A of incomes from mines and metal works.

[3] 43 Geo. III, cap. 122, § 31.

[4] See Yonge, Life of Lord Liverpool, vol. ii. pp. 73, 77, 91–2 ; letters from Lord Liverpool
to Lord Castlereagh, November 18, 1814 ; to Canning, December 28, 1814 ; to Castlereagh,
January, 1815. For the efforts of the Cabinet to retain the tax, see also H. of C., February 9,
1815, Gascoyne's speech ; H. of C., February 20, 1815, Tierney's speech (Parl. Deb., vol.
xxix. pp. 695, 875–6).

[5] H. of C., February 20, 1815 (Parl. Deb., vol. xxix. pp. 854 sqq.).

pay or pension prevented the reduction of military expenditure below
£19,000,000. Deducting £2,000,000 chargeable to the Irish Budget,
£17,000,000 remained due, as against resources of only £6,500,000.
There was a deficit of £10,500,000. It would have been possible
to cover this by suspending the sinking fund—a solution which had
been mentioned by the Press.[1] But Vansittart refused to adopt it.
In proposing a whole series of taxes to meet the deficit—the retention
of the war duties under Customs and Excise, new customs duties, an
almost general increase of Assessed Taxes, higher postal rates, higher
stamp duties—he declared that, by the abolition of the income tax and
the retention of the sinking fund payments, the financial position would
be daily improved. This would have been true had it been possible
to avoid further borrowing. But a large loan was at once necessary to
provide for the arrears of the year 1814. Then Napoleon returned
from Elba ; and Parliament was obliged to meet the war expenditure
by continuing the Property Tax.[2] After Waterloo and the second entry
of the Allies into Paris the Cabinet was obliged to contend with the
same problems which it had faced six months before. It had to decide
upon the possibility of retaining the income tax or of finding some
other source of revenue.

Local Rates. The Poor Rate.

We have already seen that the burden of taxation in England was
heavy ; but it was rendered still heavier by items which do not appear
in the Budget. Besides the *taxes* levied by the central government
there were *rates* levied by the local authorities. The *County Rate*,
the amount of which was fixed by the justices at Quarter Sessions,
provided partly for the upkeep of the county bridges, partly for various
expenses connected with justice and police. The *Highway Rate*,
levied in each parish by the surveyor of highways, provided for the
upkeep of roads. The *Church Rate* was levied by the churchwardens
for the maintenance of the church, for the expenses of public worship
and also for other items of parish expenditure. The *Militia Rate*
supplied the pay of militiamen who agreed to replace those who had
been chosen by lot. And finally the *Poor Rate* gave assistance to the
poor of each parish. It was levied by the overseer of the poor in
accordance with the celebrated Poor Law of Elizabeth, which had
ever since been in process of amendment and expansion by new legislation. Ireland had no Poor Law. Scotland had one ; but it was very
strictly administered. In England alone was it considered that the
poor, merely by reason of their poverty, had a right to parish relief.

[1] *Morning Chronicle*, February 1, February 13, 1815.
[2] 55 Geo. III, cap. 53, with an amendment intended to protect taxpayers' returns from
publicity. (See § 5, for the words of the oath to be taken by Commissioners of Taxes.) Cf.
H. of C., May 1, 1815 (*Parl. Deb.*, vol. xxx. pp. 1022–4).

The Poor Rate was much the heaviest of the local rates, and indeed it served as a basis for all the others. A *rate*, as its derivation implies, means a proportion ; so many pounds, shillings and pence per pound of assessable income. And the overseer, when assessing the Poor Rate, assessed, as subsidiary thereto, the Highway Rate, the Church Rate, the Militia Rate and the County Rate, on behalf of the competent authorities of the parish or the county. The rates, which had increased since the accession of George III, rose still more rapidly after 1792. Prison reform and the increasing need for transport facilities had led to a rise of the County Rate. The Militia Rate had been imposed in 1802 when the militia was reorganized. As for the alarming increase of the Poor Rate, it was due to various causes.

In each parish the administration of the Poor Law devolved upon the overseers. They were assisted by the churchwardens, who were, generally speaking, elected by the rate-payers assembled at a vestry meeting. This assembly of rate-payers had even obtained, in an increasing number of parishes, the right to take part in the election of the overseers and to control their expenditure. But as a rule the power of the vestry meeting to control the work of the overseer was very limited ; and it was the justices who directed the general policy to be observed in the administration of the Poor Law. The justices to whom had always belonged the power to appoint overseers, had also the statutory right and obligation to check their accounts. And to the justices came appeals from poor persons who considered themselves to be unjustly treated by the overseers or the churchwardens of the parish,[1] or from rate-payers who were dissatisfied with the assessment of the rate or the distribution of the proceeds.[2]

Since the accession of George III the justices had been given still greater powers. They and their salaried subordinates controlled the workhouses and the poorhouses in which were lodged the persons in receipt of relief.[3] And besides the power of supervision entrusted to them by the legislation of the reigns of George I and George II, the justices were now given by new legislation the right to direct the details of administration. They could grant relief themselves, even where application had not been made in the first instance to the parish officials.[4] At first a justice could not give relief in this way for longer than a month ; after which the relief might be continued from month to month by two justices. But an Act of 1815 extended the first period of relief to three months : after which two justices might prolong it for six months.[5] Thus by the trend of legislation the justices were gradually empowered to direct the whole administration of the Poor

[1] 9 Geo. I, cap. 7.
[2] 17 Geo. II, cap. 3 ; 17 Geo. II, cap. 38.
[3] 22 Geo. III, cap. 83 (Gilbert's Act) ; 30 Geo. III, cap. 49 ; 50 Geo. III, cap. 50.
[4] 36 Geo. III, cap. 23.   [5] 55 Geo. III, cap. 137.

Law. They fixed the number of persons who might be assisted and the manner in which asistance should be given, whilst the overseers became reduced to the status of mere rate collectors. It will be interesting to trace the effects of this administrative revolution which had been so slowly and gradually accomplished.

The Poor Rate was assessable on income ; and the law under which it was levied seemed to imply that every sort of income might be assessed. This interpretation had indeed been confirmed by judicial decisions ; but in practice no attempt was made to assess income derived from movables. Such income was of a fugitive character, which rendered it difficult of determination by the ill-educated persons who were appointed as overseers ; [1] and in consequence the Poor Rate was assessed almost entirely on landed property. For this reason it would seem that the justices, who were necessarily, in view of the conditions of their appointment, wealthy landowners of the county, would have administered the Law with economy. But in practice they had good reasons for not doing so. In the first place the Poor Rate was not levied upon the owners, but upon the occupiers of the properties in question ; and these occupiers, though sometimes owners, were generally tenants. The justices only paid rates, therefore, in respect of the estates which they occupied themselves ; and, in respect of the large number of properties which were occupied by tenants, they were not affected by an increase of rates, except, indirectly and after some lapse of time, through the consequent fall of rents. In the second place, since the war, the justices and the landlords, the governing classes in general, and in particular those who administered the Poor Law, were obsessed by the fear that an agrarian revolution might occur in England as in France ; not to speak of an industrial upheaval which France had been spared in 1792. In their opinion the Poor Rate was an insurance against unrest ; and they were prepared to pay an enormous premium to safeguard themselves against this terrible danger.

Thus may be explained the historical paradox that at the very time the new economic theorists were denouncing all systems of State charity as demoralizing and useless, at the time when the works of Malthus were being largely sold, the administration of the Poor Law was becoming every year more slack and more extravagant. What might be called the administrative socialism of bygone England was contained in two great Acts—the Statute of Apprentices and the Poor Law. The first had been repealed ; but the second had never been so widely interpreted in favour of the poor.

The legislation of the war period contributed directly to the burden of poor relief. By a law of 1803, whenever a militiaman was called

---

[1] H. of C., February 21, 1817, Curwen's speech (Parl. Deb., vol. xxxv. p. 520) ; Report from the Select Committee on the Poor Laws, 1817, p. 6 ; Adolphus, British Empire, vol. iii. pp. 569 sqq.

upon for service, the parish had to give to his wife and each of his children a weekly allowance equal to the current wage for one day's agricultural labour—such allowance not to be less than one shilling.[1]   Indirectly a number of new measures tended to the same result. A series of Acts passed in 1795,[2] in 1809,[3] in 1811,[4] and in 1814,[5] made it more difficult for the local authorities to obtain relief from their burdens by expelling and returning to their native parishes poor persons who had but recently settled in the district.   And this was not all ; in the last years of the 18th century the whole spirit of the law had changed.   The original statute of 1601 did not provide for assistance to the able-bodied poor except in return for work, and gave no right to relief except through the right to work.   In pursuance of the same policy the law of 1722[6] empowered parishes, either singly or in groups, to set up workhouses, where the poor could either work for payment or if they declined this test, could be refused any assistance from the parish.   But as soon as war had been declared with revolutionary France[7] the administration of the Poor Law began to be animated by a new spirit. We have already seen how, in 1795, the justices of Berkshire, whose example was followed more or less closely by their colleagues in the neighbouring counties,[8] decided that henceforth the Poor Law should be used indirectly to fix the level of wages.   A minimum wage was to be calculated from the price of corn ; and every worker whose wage fell below this amount was to receive from the parish relief sufficient to raise his income to the prescribed minimum.   Next year Parliament passed two Acts to put the administrative decisions of the justices on a legal basis.   On the one hand, as the Poor Rate was no longer sufficient to meet the expenses of relief, the local authorities were empowered, in certain conditions, to vary the amount of the rate according to the price of corn.[9]   On the other hand, since the Poor Law, as interpreted by the justices, was no longer limited to providing work but had been extended to providing a normal wage for all, it was absurd to retain the old law under which applicants for relief had to seek work at a work-house.   These provisions of the law of 1722 were therefore repealed ; and the principle of relief at the home of the applicant was legalized.[10] From this moment it was inevitable that the burden of public assistance should soon be past bearing.

From the scanty statistics available it may be estimated that the annual cost of poor relief from the end of the American war to the

---

[1] 43 Geo. III, cap. 47.   [2] 35 Geo. III, cap. 101.
[3] 49 Geo. III, cap. 124.   [4] 51 Geo. III, cap. 80.
[5] 54 Geo. III, cap. 107.   [6] 9 Geo. I, cap. 7.
[7] The Act known as " Gilbert's Act " (22 Geo. III, cap. 83), had already relaxed, though it had not abolished, the principle of relief in return for work done.   It did not oblige the applicant for assistance to seek work in a workhouse.
[8] S. and B. Webb, *English Local Government*, vol. i. pp. 545 sqq.
[9] 36 Geo. III, cap. 10.   [10] 36 Geo. III, cap. 23.

beginning of the war with France was about £2,000,000 ; and that all other expenditure met by the local authorities did not exceed £200,000.[1] After the Peace of Amiens local taxation amounted to £5,348,205, out of which £4,267,915 was devoted to the relief of the poor. In 1813 the total was £8,646,841 and poor relief cost a little over £7,000,000. In 1814, in 1815 and in 1816 the two figures fell progressively. But the fall was only temporary ; and parish relief continued to absorb an amount greater than had been sufficient in 1803 to provide for all the expenses of local administration. In 1817 it returned again to the figure of £7,000,000, and in 1818 it rose to £8,000,000, whilst local administration as a whole cost £9,320,000. And to realize the burden imposed upon the rate-payer it must be remembered that the assessments, made on a parochial basis, were extremely unequal, the rate in some parishes rising to forty or fifty shillings to the pound of assessable income.[2]

Economic Anarchy in England.

Leaving out of account the £8,000,000 paid for poor relief and also the £8,500,000 paid by Ireland,[3] we find the English Budget amounting to £83,000,000.[4] Income tax brought in £15,000,000, representing, at 10 per cent., a total income of £150,000,000 for England, Scotland and Wales.[5] It would seem, then, that every year more than half the income of the nation was taken from the working classes and given to idle fundholders and to civil or military officials.[6] A great increase in the productivity of the nation rendered possible this almost extravagant rise in State expenditure. But the increase in national

---

[1] Poor Rate, average for years 1783, 1784, 1785, £2,167,750 ; County Rate, 1792, £218,185. See *Local Taxation*, 1839, p. 50.

[2] *Report from the Select Committee on the Poor Laws*, 1817, *Minutes of Evidence*, p. 86.

[3] The Irish Budget, even after 1800, was kept separate from the English Budget. It was only in 1816 that financial unity was added to political unity.

[4] Gross income, £83,436,765 ; net income, £75,324,084. The difference—£8,112,681 —must not be regarded as representing only the cost of collection. It consists in part of money repaid by the customs authorities in the form of drawbacks.

[5] See especially *Edinburgh Review*, February 1822, No. 72, Art. 4, *State of the Nation* (vol. xxxvi. pp. 375–6), de Montveran (*Situation de l'Angleterre*, 1819, vol. i. p. 437), suggests for 1813 the figure of £159,584,500 ; but Colquhoun, in 1814 (*Wealth of the British Empire*, p. 126), gives an estimate of £430,521,372 (in which, however, Irish incomes are included). Fifteen years earlier we find the same uncertainties. In 1798 Pitt estimated the annual income of the nation at £102,000,000, after making a deduction of one-fifth in respect of certain sources of income so as to allow for persons who paid no taxation (*Parl. Hist.*, vol. xxxiv. p. 18). But a contemporary (*Three Essays on Taxation of Income*, etc., London, 1799, pp. 63 sqq.) disputes the accuracy of these figures and suggests the sum of £236,000,000.

[6] Robert Wilson, *An Inquiry into the Causes of the High Prices of Corn and Labour* (*Farmers' Magazine*, February 1816, vol. xvii. pp. 79–80). Cf. Cobbett's *Political Register*, September 12, 1810 (vol. xvii. p. 330) : " If by the grips of taxation every grain of the surplus of a country be taken from the lowest class of those who labour, they will have the means of *bare existence* left . . . that surplus produce which should go to the making of an addition to their meal, or to the creating of things for their use, will be *annihilated* by those who do nothing but eat. . . . Such is the way in which *taxes* operate."

wealth was not continuous. It was subject to violent fluctuations and to sudden crises ; and at such times the burden of taxation became intolerable.

There were crises in 1793, in 1797, in 1800, in 1803, in 1810—the most serious of all—and finally in 1815. We have described how these disturbances originated. The banks were always ready to lend to manufacturers who asked for money ; the manufacturers produced more than the markets could absorb ; and, when the demand for goods became insufficient, factories closed, banks failed, and labourers died of hunger. The working classes, imbued with revolutionary ideas and spurred by misery, revolted in town and country. And to complicate matters there was open war between the Free Traders of the towns and the Protectionists of the country districts. The crushing weight of taxation only aggravated disorders which were inherent in the economic structure.

Sismondi visited England in 1817. He was a conservative, terrified by the spectacle of industrial revolution, and he predicted that, unless Governments could succeed in returning to a system of slow production and limited consumption, society would pass inevitably through crisis after crisis to the final upheaval in which a mob of angry workers would put an end to civilization. Thirty years later Karl Marx studied the British industrial system, and availed himself, but as it were in a contrary sense, of the pessimistic conclusions to which Sismondi had come. He hailed the industrial revolution as the prelude to a social revolution which would, before the end of the century, free the masses, abolish the State and transform the conscience of the human race. It is hardly necessary to say that all economists did not agree with the conclusions of Sismondi and Karl Marx. In England, indeed, there arose an optimistic school which maintained that the unfettered growth of productive forces, unlimited competition, free industry and free commerce, would lead inevitably and without the occurrence of crises, to a complete economic harmony. But Ricardo was one of the leaders of this school ; and the doctrines of Ricardo, elaborated in the years around 1815, were not so optimistic as would be thought from a perusal of the works of his followers. Everywhere he saw class wars ; and it was from him that the theorists of Socialism were to borrow many of their formulas. The difference between him and the Socialists who utilized his writings was that he saw in these struggles the inevitable result of the working of nature's laws, and that he believed it was not possible for a Government to remedy such evils by legislation. The same economic facts aroused in every mind the same conclusions : that in the world of agriculture, of industry and of finance there was everywhere over-production, inequality in the distribution of wealth, liberty without law or restraint, a state of ceaseless revolution.

If the materialistic interpretation of history is to be trusted, if economic facts explain the course taken by the human race in its progress, the England of the 19th century was surely, above all other countries, destined to revolution, both political and religious. But it was not to be so. In no other country of Europe have social changes been accomplished with such a marked and gradual continuity. The source of such continuity and comparative stability is, as we have seen, not to be found in the economic organization of the country. We have seen, also, that it cannot be found in the political institutions of England, which were essentially unstable and wanting in order. To find it we must pass on to another category of social phenomena—to beliefs, emotions and opinions, as well as to the institutions and sects in which these beliefs, emotions and opinions take a form suitable for scientific inquiry.

BOOK III

RELIGION AND CULTURE

RELIGION AND CULTURE

The religious institutions of the United Kingdom were no less intricate and confused than the political. The Established Church in England and Ireland was Episcopal, in Scotland Presbyterian. Of the subjects of the British Crown the majority were Protestant, but there were 4,000,000 Irish Catholics. Of the Protestants the majority were adherents of the Established Churches, but 2,000,000 belonged to free groups, whose organization was more or less republican. In the 17th century this diversity had been a source of disorder, even of anarchy. Was it the same during our period? Or amid so many conflicting currents was one influence predominant, and did it make for peace? If so, what was that influence?

England was not only remarkable for its intense religious life. It was also a country which could boast a high level of culture—artistic, literary, philosophic. It possessed a school of first-rate painters, and the greatest poets the age produced anywhere in the world. Dalton, Davy and the Herschells were scientists of world-wide renown. The English philosophers and economists amazed Europe by the boldness with which they applied to the study of Man the accepted methods of the Natural Sciences. Did this development of culture take place in the teeth of the dominant religion? Or here, too, can we discover a conciliatory influence at work? Had the opposing forces concluded a compact of peace, tacit or express; and if so, on what terms?

During the 18th century England had been the scene of a great religious movement, unparalleled on the Continent—the last Protestant movement which has given birth to permanent institutions. This was the " Methodist " or " Evangelical " revival. To this movement, in combination on the one hand with the old Whig political traditions, on the other with the new *ethos* produced by the industrial revolution, British Liberalism of the opening 19th century owed its distinctive character. We shall witness Methodism bring under its influence, first the dissenting sects, then the establishment, finally secular opinion. We shall attempt to find here the key to the problem whose solution has hitherto escaped us; for we shall explain by this movement the extraordinary stability which English Society was destined to enjoy throughout a period of revolutions and crises; what we may truly term the miracle of modern England, anarchist but orderly, practical and businesslike, but religious, and even pietist.

CHAPTER I

RELIGION

THE TWO FUNDAMENTAL FORMS OF ENGLISH PRO-
TESTANTISM: THE CHURCH AND THE SECTS.

The Methodist Revival.

IT was in the year 1739 that John Wesley and George Whitefield began to preach Methodism. It was a period of general
disturbance. A political was aggravated by an economic crisis.
On all sides there were strikes and riots. Similar conditions a
half-century later must have given rise to a general movement
of political and social revolution. In 1739 the revolt assumed a
different form. The discontented workmen flocked to the sermons
of three clergymen and their disciples. The popular ferment took
shape as an outburst of enthusiastic Christianity. But what doctrinal
novelty did the two Wesleys and Whitefield proclaim to the English
people? Anglican clergymen deeply attached to the Established
Church, their sole aim was her defence and regeneration. This they
sought to attain by reviving the venerable Protestant dogma of justification by faith. Despite the radical depravity of his nature, man was
capable, since his Saviour's death, of sudden illumination by grace.
It was for the Christian preacher by his eloquence to make himself
the instrument of the Divine Will, to stimulate " conversions " in the
sense that Protestant theology understands the term, to procure for
his hearers an immediate sense of holiness, a certainty of salvation.
At first the founders of Methodism preached in the churches, at Bristol,
at Newcastle, in London. Later, when the clergy alarmed by their
eccentric style of preaching and by their doctrinal extravagance forbade
them the use of their churches, they preached in market-places and in
the open fields. Their audiences numbered ten, fifty, even eighty
thousand. Driven from the Anglican Church, and carried away by
the very enthusiasm which they had excited, they drifted almost unconsciously into the sphere of the dissenting sects. It was on
the frontier of the Church of England that Wesley founded the vast

organization of Methodism.[1]   Thus the old establishment and the existing Free Churches constituted the double environment in which the new spirit was developed.   And it is only when we are acquainted with this environment that we can understand the character and estimate the importance of the Methodist revival.

The Church of England.

The Church of England, or, to call it by its official title, the " United Church of England and Ireland," was a complex institution, a patchwork.   Her apologists might say of the Church what Bishop Jebb said of her liturgy—that it " is not the work of one man, of one society, or of one age : it is like the British Constitution, a precious result of accumulative and collective wisdom."[2]   The ritual of the Church of England had retained many features of Catholic ritual ; but in obedience to long-established prejudices her unwritten constitution prescribed for the national worship the nakedness of Lutheranism or Calvinism.   Moreover, her creed as formulated in the thirty-nine articles is to all appearance unadulterated Protestantism.   At first sight the organization of the Church conformed to the Catholic type. In England there were two archbishops and twenty-six bishops, in Ireland four archbishops and twenty-seven bishops.   But these princes of the hierarchy and their subordinates had alike discarded celibacy Monasteries and convents had disappeared, as it seemed, for ever. Archbishops and bishops were direct nominees of the Crown : capitular election was a legal fiction, a mere registration of the royal choice.   The ordinary clergymen, the parochial representatives of the archbishops or bishops, were for the most part nominated, not by the episcopate, but by the Crown or lay patrons.   Convocation, a species of ecclesiastical parliament, with an archiepiscopal president, an Upper House of bishops, a Lower House of representatives of the inferior clergy, after losing under Henry VIII the right to revise the canons of the Church, under Charles II the right to fix clerical taxation, for a century had ceased altogether to meet.   The King, acting on the advice of Parliament, was the supreme head of a religion in which, to employ the accepted terminology, the " Erastian " principle, was scrupulously respected, a religion essentially national, whose source was the will of the secular government.

Of what character should we expect to find a clerical body thus constituted ?   England was probably the sole country in Christendom where no proof of theological knowledge was exacted from candidates for Ordination.   These were all drawn from the Universities of Oxford and Cambridge ; and neither of these Universities possessed a special

    [1] For the causes of the success of Wesley's preaching in 1739, see the author's study, *La Naissance du Méthodisme en Angleterre, Revue de Paris*, 15 Août–1 Septembre, 1906.
    [2] *Thirty Years' Correspondence between John Jebb and Alexander Knox*, vol. i, p. 368.

organization for the teaching of Christian doctrine. At Oxford theology was reduced to one single question asked of all candidates for examination. At Cambridge no theology whatsoever entered into any of the examinations for a degree. The entrance examination once passed, and it was elementary in the extreme, not to say childish, students, who were not the eldest sons of gentle families, and did not possess sufficient industry or capacity to face more difficult examinations, could proceed without further delay to the clerical status. It is true that to hold any benefice, episcopal ordination was indispensable, and that ordination involved a preliminary examination by the bishop or his chaplain, whose object was, or was supposed to be, to discover the candidate's intellectual and moral endowments. But, as all the world knew, this examination was a mere formality. "A few minutes' conversation or examination, which either good nature or pity or interest or carelessness, or all together, may render very slight, can never make the diocesan thoroughly acquainted with the literary, much less with the moral, character of the intended minister." [1]

It is, therefore, no matter for surprise that the clergy of the national Church of England were intellectually inferior to the clergy of the Established Churches of Protestant Germany. How could any serious criticism of the Scripture text be expected from men who did not even know their Bible? At the beginning of the 19th century Marsh brought back from Leipzig some results of the German Higher Criticism, a theory of the composition of the Gospels, namely the hypothesis of a lost Protevangelium, from which our Four Gospels have been derived. Jebb was contemporaneously engaged in the study of Hebrew prosody, discovered as a result new rules of rhythm, and utilized his knowledge of these to elucidate a few obscure passages in the New Testament. And this was all, or almost all.

If, however, the Anglican clergymen lacked scientific curiosity, neither were they possessed by a fanatic zeal for orthodoxy. In the 18th century the High Church party was far more a political than a theological party. The High Churchmen were Tories who supported the Royal Prerogative and denounced rebellion as sinful. To be sure they inclined to Arminianism, to the doctrines of free will and justification by works, but this was due to their abhorrence of the republican opinions held by the Calvinists. For their part, the Low Churchmen, in their antipathy to the Church of Rome, might oppose to the Catholic doctrine an orthodox Calvinism. But in the 18th century the Low Church tradition, which dated from William of Orange and his Whig bishops Burnet, Tillotson and Stillingfleet, was latitudinarian. Throughout the century the sermons of Anglican preachers, whatever their party, though most markedly among the Whigs, kept the miraculous character of Christianity as far as possible in the background. Their religion

[1] Cockburn, *Strictures on Clerical Education*, 1809, pp. 14–15.

was a liberal and rationalistic Christianity, a system of humanitarian ethics in which the supernatural was left out of sight. The goal of this direction of Anglican opinion was the book published by Paley in 1785 in which he identified Christian with utilitarian ethics, and presented Jesus Christ as the first teacher of the greatest happiness principle. Nevertheless, the members of the Church continued with little scruple to subscribe the thirty-nine articles which formulated the fundamental articles of Anglican belief. Those who in 1772 petitioned Parliament for release from this obligation merely betrayed a doctrinal scrupulosity of very doubtful taste. The attempt failed ; and why regret its failure ? The material point was that nobody was obliged to believe the thirty-nine articles or even to read them.[1]

The remedy that should have been applied was to reform, or more truly to organize, the theological education of the clergy. But Anglican opinion was opposed to this step. In 1809 Cockburn proposed the introduction of Christian theology into the Cambridge course of studies. But he was content to ask for the adoption of the system in force at Oxford, namely a theological question in every examination. For, he adds, "that divinity should not be the exclusive, nor perhaps the principal, employment of such young persons is reasonable, because men of all professions and ranks are at that period educated together ; future Peers, future senators, lawyers, physicians, clergymen, etc., are all fellow students at the same lecture ; and, as it would be absurd to make them all study physic exclusively, so it would be wrong to make divinity the sole object of their common attention."[2] As for making theology the special study of the minority of students destined for Orders, Cockburn does not even contemplate the idea. Above all things clergymen must be gentlemen ; and to secure this it was of the first importance that they should receive the education which all English gentlemen received. The Anglican clergy was, and was anxious to remain, a branch of the aristocracy.

Consider first the higher clergy. It was universally admitted that the choice of archbishops and bishops must be political. For the last thirty years the Tories had enjoyed an almost uninterrupted tenure of power. Consequently the two archbishops and almost all the bishops were Tories.[3] Eleven in 1815 were of noble birth, among them the

---

[1] Consider how Gisborne (*Duties of Man*, vol. ii. pp. 28–9) interprets the obligation to subscribe the articles : " In subscribing the thirty-nine articles the intention of the authority which prescribes subscription is to be satisfied. This authority is not the Legislature of the 13th Eliz. which passed the Act imposing subscription, but the existing Legislature of this country which, having the power of repealing that Act, and forbearing to exercise it, ratifies and, as it were, re-enacts the law. The point, therefore, which the candidate for Orders has to decide is the nature of the subscription which will satisfy the intention of the Legislature existing at the time ? [2] Cockburn, *Strictures on Clerical Education*, p. 17.

[3] Horsley was the only bishop who died during the Fox-Grenville Ministry ; but it was the Grenville group that designated his successor, a Tory (Lord Holland, *Memoirs of the Whig Party*, vol. ii. 90–1).

Archbishop of Canterbury, a Manners and a cousin of the Duke of
Rutland, and the Archbishop of York, a brother of Lord Vernon.
Ten had been tutors or schoolmasters of a prince, a duke or a statesman.
The Bishop of Lincoln, Tomline, successively tutor, secretary and
biographer of Pitt, is a typical representative of this category. Two
prelates, Thomas Burgess, Bishop of St. David's, and George Hunting-
ford, were personal friends of Lord Sidmouth. And the see of Sodor
and Man was actually a benefice in the hereditary patronage of the
Dukes of Athol. It was but the natural result that the present occupant,
George Murray, should be a member of the family. The Irish episcopate
was equally aristocratic. Three archbishops and eight bishops belonged
to influential families. One family alone, the family of Beresford,
occupied three sees.

Let us now turn to the lower clergy—the deans, the canons, the
archdeacons ; and the ordinary parish priests—the parsons. Wherever
their appointment was in the hands of the archbishop or the bishop, he
was careful to distribute his patronage among his clients and relatives.
And first among the latter, since the Anglican hierarchy was married,
were his sons and his sons-in-law. But the extent of the patronage
exercised by the episcopate was inconsiderable. Out of the 11,700
benefices of England and Wales, the patronage of scarcely 1,500
belonged to the bishops or cathedral chapters.[1] The English reformation found the religious orders predominant among the clergy, and in
the vast majority of parishes a religious order was perpetual rector, and
enjoyed the exclusive right to appoint the " vicar," who was the actual
parish priest. With the dissolution of the monasteries their parochial
patronage was transferred either to the colleges at Oxford and Cambridge, to the public schools of Eton and Winchester and to the
cathedral chapters, since all these bodies were the direct heirs of
former religious houses, or to the Crown, or to the families of the great
landowners. To this latter class belonged 5,700 benefices. Hence in one-
half of the parishes the appointment of the vicar was in the hands of the
landlord, his legal and incontestable right. And even when the appointment lay with the Crown the Government often found it difficult to
resist the pretensions of the gentry. The landowner of the parish
whose vicar was to be appointed demanded that the Crown should
give effect to his choice.[2]

Thus did the ecclesiastical constitution of the country harmonize
with the political. The landed gentry were masters equally of the
ecclesiastical as of the civil administration. Nepotism, the vice of

---

[1] *Black Book*, 1820, p. 311.

[2] Twiss, *Life of Lord Eldon*, vol. i. p. 390. In the same work are to be found a number of
letters by Lord Eldon, which throw an entertaining light on the manner in which ecclesiastical
appointments were made. See especially vol. i. pp. 388–9 (Lord Eldon to Reay, September 8,
1801), and vol. iii. pp. 465–6. See also a letter from Lord Eldon to Rose, 1801 (*Diaries
and Correspondence of . . . George Rose*, vol. i. pp. 376–7).

aristocracies, found full scope, and was aggravated by pecuniary interest. The sale of benefices by public auction was a normal occurrence. The highest bidder could purchase either the immediate enjoyment of the benefice, if there was then a vacancy, or the right to the next presentation. The sums offered were advertised in the newspapers, which informed the public of the value of the benefice and the age of its present occupant. For the older the clergyman in possession the higher was the sum that could be obtained for an advowson whose enjoyment could not be long delayed.[1]

Whether he owed his living to favour or had purchased it in the open market, there was nothing whatever of the "priest" about the English clergyman. Should a young man of good birth, or simply the son of a respectable or wealthy family, enter the Church or the Army? Circumstances, parental caprice, often chance decided his choice.[2] While the war lasted, the Army offered a better opening.[3] Peace came and the Church beheld once more a stream of candidates for Ordination. Crowds of military parsons, as Cobbett termed them, descended on the country parsonages, and combined the stipend of their living with the half-pay of retired officers.[4] Only too often, apparently, the scion of a good family regarded a vicarage as the means of closing an irregular youth. We hear, for instance, of a gentleman who on leaving the University squandered in town a considerable portion of his estate : he married a clergyman's daughter and took Orders. And we are told of another who, when plunged in debt, disembarrassed himself by a living in Suffolk. "Here he became a great favourite with the country gentlemen, by whom his society was much sought ; for he kept an excellent hunter, rode well up to the hounds, drank very hard. He sang an excellent song, danced remarkably well, so that the young ladies considered no party complete without him." After further vicissitudes and further pecuniary difficulties we find him possessed

[1] See the typical examples of these advertisements in T. Timpson, *British Ecclesiastical History*, pp. 500–1. R. Hodgson in his *Life of Porteus* (pp. 142–4) describes some curious devices current in the 18th century by which the advowson could be made to yield a maximum profit.

[2] Jane Austen, *Sense and Sensibility*, chap. xix : " We never could agree in our choice of a profession. I always preferred the Church, as I still do. But that was not smart enough for my family. They recommended the Army. That was a great deal too smart for me." *Pride and Prejudice*, p. 16 : " A military life is not what I was intended for, but circumstances have now made it eligible. The Church ought to have been my profession. I was brought up for the Church, and I should at this time have been in possession of a most valuable living had it pleased Mr. Darcy (the patron)."

[3] Overton (*English Church in the 19th Century*, p. 149) quotes from a charge of Bishop Kaye, of Lincoln : " In consequence of opportunities of employment in the Army and Navy afforded to young men during the war, the number of candidates for Holy Orders was not equal to the demand for curates. During the first ten years of this century the number of young men who annually graduated as B.A. in January at Cambridge averaged little more than a hundred ; it now (1852) averages more than three hundred."

[4] *Rural Rides*, September 23, 1826 ; October 11, 1826. For these ex-soldiers turned parsons, see Wakefield, *Ireland*, vol. ii. pp. 475–6.

of a substantial benefice—"by which he was enabled to launch again into the gay world."[1] The utmost that could be expected of clergymen thus recruited, was to avoid scandal and to behave as honourable gentlemen farmers. In any case, it was essential that they should be well paid. They belonged to good society, and usually possessed a wife and family. Even if their stipends were considerable, it was all they could do to support their social position. It is certain that the Anglican clergy were a heavy charge on the nation. But an exact estimate of their cost is difficult to reach. It is not easy to arrive at a fixed or an accurate valuation of incomes composed of the rental value of the parsonage, the rent of glebe land, and the tithe. In 1810 Cove estimated the total annual revenue of the Church as exceeding £2,900,000.[2] But the *Black Book* of 1820 estimates it at £5,000,000,[3] and later around 1832 there were critics of the system whose estimate was £9,000,000.[4] We may adopt the official figure reached in 1833 by a commission appointed for the purpose, the figure of £3,500,000, intermediate between Cove's estimate and the estimate of the *Black Book*. But no total estimate of this kind can give a sufficient idea of the stipends actually received by individual clergymen.

The Archbishops of England and Wales inclusive of the Bishop of Sodor and Man enjoyed a total income of £181,631. But whereas the income of the Archbishop of Canterbury and of the Bishop of Durham exceeded £19,000, and the income of the Bishop of London exceeded £15,000, the Bishop of Rochester had to be content with £1,500, and the Bishop of Landaff with a bare £900.[5] The total income of the parochial clergy was £3,250,000. But it would be of little use to attempt to form a notion of the English parson's income by simply dividing this figure by the number of livings. The average so attained would mean very little. For the income of 4,000 livings, over a third of the whole number, did not exceed £150, and of these 4,000 poor livings, there were 1,726 where the income ranged between £50 and £100, 1,061 where it did not exceed or fell below £50.[6] Must we draw the conclusion that the organization of the Anglican Church was chaotic, or even stigmatize it without qualification as a system that favoured some of the clergy at the expense of their fellows ? In reality, these official figures are often deceptive ; for the clergy, to eke out stipends admittedly insufficient, had built up an entire system, which custom had sanctioned, of accumulative benefices, or pluralities.

---

[1] Gunning, *Reminiscences of Cambridge*, vol. ii. pp. 62, 65 and 156.
[2] Cove, *An Essay on the Revenues of the Church of England*, 3rd ed., 1816, pp. 106, 109, 124. Incomes of bishops, £130,000 ; of deans and chapters, £276,000 ; of the parochial clergy, £2,557,202. Total, £2,962,202.   [3] *Black Book*, p. 310.
[4] H. of C., April 10, 1833, Lord Althorp's speech (*Parl. Deb.*, 3rd series, vol. xvii. p. 273).
[5] *Report of the Commissioners . . . into the Ecclesiastical Revenues*, 1835, pp. 6, 30, 95 † 40. Gross yearly income, £3,663,218 ; net yearly income, £3,373,389.
[6] Cove, *An Essay on the Revenues of the Church of England*, 3rd ed., 1816, p. 118.

One incumbent could hold simultaneously two, three, four, or even more benefices. There is an instance of a single ecclesiastic in possession of eight.[1] How, then, were these combined parishes served, since they were thus dependent on the spiritual care of a single man ? The rector or vicar (for the vicar of one parish could be rector of another and vice versa, and either, indeed, might even be a bishop or archbishop) appointed a curate at a low stipend, and took the rest of the income for himself. From the parishes of Wetherale and Warwick the Dean and Chapter of the see received tithe to the value of £1,000 per annum, and an equal sum in rents. They paid a curate £50. From Hesket in the Carlisle diocese the Dean and Chapter received annually between £1,000 and £1,500. They paid their curate £18 5s. or a shilling a day,[2] that is less than the pay of a workman paid by the day. These curates were in the true sense the inferior clergy of the Church of England—her plebs. To gain a livelihood for wife and family they were often obliged to become farmers,[3] and apologists of the system sought to console them for the extremity to which they were reduced by classical allusions and quotations from Cicero : *nihil agricultura homine libero dignius.*[4] Occasionally they sought their bread and butter from occupations even more " illiberal." A speaker in Parliament mentions in 1806 the case of a curate turned weaver.[5] Thus was reproduced in the administration of the Church an abuse we have already witnessed in the civil government of the Kingdom. Every position is regarded as its holder's sinecure. The actual duties are performed by a deputy—paid with a portion only of the emolument.

When the pluralist was not a corporation but an individual, and when the parishes from which he derived his income were not too far apart, he would not even appoint a curate. Alone he provided as best he could for the spiritual needs, to be sure extremely simple, of the faithful of his two or three parishes. Every Sunday morning he would gallop from church to church and hurry through a service shortened by himself for the purpose, and which he would make even shorter on days when he was more than usually pressed for time. If it was raining too hard he did not put in an appearance. No one was the least surprised. Dr. Drop, they said, was taking the service that Sunday. If he noticed that one of his churches lacked a congregation he shortened his Sunday round by omitting the service. But he did not omit the stipend. In country parishes Holy Communion was celebrated only three or four times a year—at Easter, Christmas and Michaelmas. In

---

[1] T. Timpson, *British Ecclesiastical History*, p. 506.

[2] *Ibid.*, p. 507.

[3] H. of L., June 18, 1810, Lord Harrowby's speech (*Parl. Deb.*, vol. xvii. pp. 752 sqq.). The entire speech is a very interesting picture of the condition of the clergy.

[4] Cf. *Edinburgh Review*, January 1805, No. 10, Art. 3, *Observations on the Residence of the Clergy* (vol. v. p. 301).

[5] H. of C. April 25, 1806, Wilberforce's speech (*Parl. Deb.*, vol. vi. p. 925).

the dilapidated churches, no better than empty barns, the children of the village played their marbles, the beadles hatched out their chickens.[1] Even the pocket boroughs of the political franchise were paralleled by pocket rectories. Cobbett, in the course of one of his rural rides, remarked a Wiltshire parish which was simply an ecclesiastical Old Sarum. The parson's income amounted to £300 a year. There was neither church nor parsonage. Whenever a new parson was to be inducted, a tent was erected on the site, where the parish church had once stood, and in that tent the ceremony of induction was performed.[2] So scandalous had the abuse of non-residence become, that public opinion was roused and a series of official inquiries were made which enable us to measure its extent. Out of 11,000 livings there were over 6,000 where the incumbent was non-resident.[3] Of the 3,998 livings whose income did not exceed £150 in 2,438 the incumbent was non-resident.[4] These inquiries, it must be remembered, were confined to England and Wales. In Ireland the vast majority of livings were obviously sinecures; for scarcely a sixteenth part of the population was Protestant, and by no means all Protestants were members of the Established Church. Nevertheless, that Church was established on precisely the same footing as if the entire population made use of its services. Here the scandal was not that the parsons neglected their flocks, but that the country was burdened by the expense of this enormous ecclesiastical establishment devoid of adherents.[5]

The churches actually in existence were empty; and a clergy devoid of conscientiousness or zeal had an interest in their remaining empty. Their work was the easier. But even had they been all filled, they would certainly have been insufficient to hold even a small minority of the population of England. Since 1688 neither bishops nor parsons had given a thought to the need of adapting the system to the increase of population and its altered distribution. Therefore the distribution of bishoprics and parishes was treated in the same fashion as the dis-

---

[1] For these abuses see Overton, *English Church in the 19th Century*, pp. 127 sqq. Also Gunning, *Reminiscences of Cambridge*, vol. ii. pp. 149–50.

[2] Cobbett, *Rural Rides*, September 29, 1826.

[3] 4,506 in 1804–5, 4,132 in 1805–6, 6,145 in 1806–7; but we are informed that the difference is due only to more accurate statistics. See *Abstract presented to the House of Commons of Returns relative to the Clergy*, 1808, 6,210 in 1807–8; see *Abstract of Returns respecting Residence and non-Residence for the Year ending March 25, 1808. 1809: 7,298 for 1808–9; see Abstract of the Number of Resident Incumbents and of the Number of Resident Incumbents according to the Diocesan Returns for the Year 1810. 1812: 6,311 in 1812; see Abstract of the Number of Resident and Licensed Curates, with the Amount of the Salaries of Curacies, according to the Diocesan Returns for the Year* 1811. 1813.

[4] An *Abstract of the Returns respecting non-Residence for the Year ending 25th of March*, 1808, including only Livings under the Value of £150 per Annum, 1810.

[5] H. of C., March 13, 1806, Grattan's speech (*Parl. Deb.*, vol. vi. p. 429). "In many parishes of Ireland there were no parishioners to whom the clergyman could minister; and therefore, it must be totally unnecessary to enforce the residence of an incumbent, so long as a parish continued to be so circumstanced."

tribution of constituencies. Formerly but half the province of York had been inhabited ; now great centres of industry were being rapidly multiplied. But it still counted only six bishops as against twenty in the province of Canterbury, and 2,000 parishes for 10,000 in the Southern Province. Bath, Chichester, Ely and Hereford possessed their bishops ; Manchester, Leeds, Birmingham, and Liverpool had none. The total church accommodation in Liverpool amounted to but 21,000 seats. The population was 94,000. In Manchester there was accommodation for 11,000 of the 79,000 inhabitants. In London the Established Church provided about 150,000 seats for a population that exceeded a million.[1]

An Act of Parliament had indeed been passed in the reign of Anne to provide for the erection of fifty churches in London ;[2] but its execution had been neglected. During the entire course of the century, despite the unexpected increase of the population, only ten churches were erected in the capital. To be sure any Englishman who chose might open a place of worship ; but the Anglican service must not be used. If he wished to erect an " episcopal " chapel, he was faced with endless difficulties. Tithe-payers were apprehensive of an increase in their burdens on the appearance of a new clergyman. The noble patrons of the existing churches had no desire for a new church which by its competition with the other livings would reduce their market value. The Duke of Portland compelled the parish of Marylebone, with a population of 40,000, to be content with a village church with accommodation at the utmost for 200.[3] But if the Church of England could neither obtain for her faithful a more diligent clergy nor a better provision of churches, what must be the inevitable result ? Either the population would be exposed to revolutionary influences, anti-clerical and hostile to religion (fear of this result was an increasing preoccupation in conservative circles towards the end of the 18th century : they could not fail to remark the rapid dissemination of Tom Paine's deistic and " Jacobin " writings in the poor quarters of the large towns) or the inertia of the Anglican clergy would be a valuable asset to the preachers of dissent. But from the professional standpoint of the Anglican clergy this latter prospect—a country religious indeed but alienated from the official worship, the established religion threatening to become the creed of a minority, the nation disposed to adopt the American system of free churches—was a prospect as little reassuring as the former.

---

[1] Overton, *English Church in the 19th Century*, pp. 144–5.

[2] 9 Anne, cap. 22.

[3] *British Review*, May 1803, Art. 21, *An Address to the Parishioners of St. Pancras, Middlesex, on the Subject of the intended Application to Parliament for a new Church*, by T. F. Middleton, D.D., London, 1812 (vol. iv. pp. 370 sqq.). Cf. September 1811, Art. 4, *The State of the Established Church in a Series of Letters to the Right Honourable Spencer Perceval, Chancellor of the Exchequer*, 2nd ed., 1810 (vol. ii. pp. 96 sqq.).

The abuses were crying. Yet public indignation was slow to awake. And even when in the opening years of the 19th century there grew up a powerful movement of democratic opposition directed against Governmental abuses, administrative scandals, the unfair system of parliamentary representation, the oppressive taxation, critics displayed an amazing forbearance towards the Church. Already for the past fifteen years the system of tithes had been the subject of severe criticism in Parliament. It was now a question freely discussed whether the tithes should not be " commuted " for a fixed money payment. But it was in Ireland, not in England, that the population revolted against the tithe. The Irish complained that their tithes were payable on arable land only, not on pasture, with the result that the entire burden rested on the poor cotter, while the wealthy cattle-breeder paid nothing. They complained that they were levied by middlemen, that the proctors who farmed the tithe paid the clergyman a lump sum and made their fortune by squeezing the peasants dry. And Catholics and Presbyterians complained of their obligation to support the episcopal worship.[1] In England these abuses did not exist. No doubt the farmers had reason to complain of an impost which discouraged agriculture, was levied solely on land, and bore indiscriminately on Anglicans and members of other religious bodies. But it was equally true that the vast majority of English farmers belonged to the Established Church, that in England every species of land was equally subject to tithe, and that the proctors were non-existent.[2] And as we have already seen, the English farmers were not, like the Irish tenantry, members of the proletariat. They were capitalists leagued with the landlord against the labourer, in a position, moreover, to dictate their terms to their landlord, and when the leases were renewed to shift the payment of tithe on to his shoulders.[3]

The other abuses, non-residence of vicars, the miserably inadequate stipends of curates, were already being remedied, not under the pressure of a party in arms against clerical oppression, but, as we shall see, to satisfy the demands of that section of the Church which under the influence of Methodism was seeking to strengthen the hold of the clergy on the masses. Take it all in all, the nation was tolerant of a clergy, apathetic indeed, and worldly, but little disposed to play the tyrant. Statesmen of both parties were agreed in their appreciation of a system under which the priests did not constitute an order marked off from the rest of the nation but were men of their own class, their relatives

[1] On the question of the Irish tithes, see especially a long and interesting debate in the Commons, April 13, 1810 (*Parl. Deb.*, vol. xvi. pp. 658 sqq.). It is noteworthy that throughout the discussion no mention is made of the English system unless to contrast it favourably with the Irish. See also Wakefield, *Ireland*, vol. ii. pp. 469 sqq.

[2] Cove, *An Inquiry into . . . a Commutation of Tithes*, 1800, pp. 23, 50, 51.

[3] It was therefore the landlords, united on the Board of Agriculture, who in England demanded the commutation of the tithe. See above, Book II, chap. i.

and friends, intimately bound up with the life of county society. Even a democrat like Cobbett, an avowed enemy alike of the Crown and the aristocracy, and a violent opponent of the Methodists, had not yet in 1815 declared war on the parish clergy.

The Dissenting Sects.

The Anglican Church found herself faced by the sects of Nonconformity. They were termed "Nonconformists" because their members refused to conform to the ritual and the discipline of the Establishment, "Dissenters," because of their doctrinal disagreement with the Church. Presbyterians, Independents, Baptists, the "three old denominations" agreed in pronouncing the hierarchical government of the State Church unscriptural. Their own constitutions were more democratic. The laity received a larger, sometimes even a preponderant, share in the government of the society. The fundamental doctrines of English Nonconformity were the theological principles of St. Paul, as revived by Luther and Calvin. Man is justified not by works but by faith ; and faith is regarded not as an activity of the soul, but as a state in which the soul is completely passive, a gratuitous gift, a work of grace, that is to say, of the Divine Will. That Will omnipotent, and inscrutable in its infinite excess of our understanding, has ordained everything in the universe, good and evil alike, and from all eternity has predestined a minute handful to salvation, the mass of mankind to damnation. Grace constitutes between the Creator and His creature an immediate and an intimate relationship, whose establishment does not require the mediation of a priest, who, if perhaps capable of pronouncing on works, is powerless to estimate the presence of faith. This theological individualism had constituted no small factor in the republicanism of the Cromwellians. How much of it survived among the eighteenth-century Dissenters in the period preceding the Methodist revival ?

Let us examine first their legal position. After a century of religious warfare in which the enemies of Anglicanism had been in turn the oppressor and the oppressed, even the Revolution of 1688 had failed to establish a system of complete religious toleration. The Episcopal Church continued to be the national Church, and those marriages alone were legal which had been solemnized by her ministers. The Corporation Act [1] and the Test Act [2] remained in force and continued, as under the Stuarts, to make communion according to the Anglican rite the indispensable preliminary to municipal honours or Government offices. And Acts even more oppressive, such as the Conventicle Act [3] and the Five Mile Act [4] continued on the Statute Book. The former of these Acts prohibited all gatherings of above five persons for the celebration

[1] 16 Car. II, cap. 1.   [2] 25 Car. II, cap. 2.
[3] 16 Car. II, cap. 4.   [4] 17 Car. II, cap. 21.

of any form of worship other than the Anglican. Infractions of the law were punishable by fines, imprisonment and deportation, even, for a second offence, by death. The latter forbade any clergyman who had failed to take certain oaths expressing his acceptance of the Anglican form of church government to reside within five miles of any borough or of any place in which he had formerly ministered. But a number of customs and legal enactments, without formally repealing these intolerant statutes, had rendered them inoperative.

The Toleration Act declared that the provisions of the Conventicle and Five Mile Acts should not apply to anyone who should repudiate papal authority by taking the oaths of "allegiance and supremacy," and should affirm his Protestantism by signing the declaration against Transubstantiation. Independent and Presbyterian ministers were required to subscribe thirty-five of the thirty-nine Anglican articles. They were not required to maintain that the Church has power to ordain rites and ceremonies, that the homilies contain a godly doctrine, that the ordination service is neither superstitious nor idolatrous. Baptist ministers were required to subscribe only thirty-four articles. They were not required to maintain that infant baptism is a laudable custom.[1] And means had been found to evade the Corporation Act. The Dissenters made use of a method termed "occasional conformity." Once and once only they received communion in accordance with the Anglican rite, and having thus rendered themselves capable of taking part in local government they returned to their Conventicles. Among the sects this custom gave occasion to scruples of conscience. On the other hand, it aroused the protests of the stricter Anglicans, protests which had even resulted in the passing in 1711 of an Act which rendered occasional conformity illegal. But in the end the practice was universally accepted, and every year Parliament passed an Indemnity Act which contained a collective pardon for all breaches of the Act of 1711 during the past year. And although about 1790 the Dissenters conducted a zealous propaganda for the repeal of the Corporation and Test Acts, they were, on the whole, well satisfied throughout the 18th century with the system of semi-legal toleration by which in practice they enjoyed absolute freedom.

But under this system of tolerance the primitive inspiration of Nonconformity began to evaporate. The cessation of religious persecution produced a decline both of uncompromising dogmatism and enthusiastic devotion. We have already remarked the extent to which the national Church displayed its indifference to questions of dogma. To this apathy the Dissenters responded by an equal indifference. Their activities became rather political than religious. They possessed in

[1] William and Mary, St. 1, cap. 18. To satisfy their conscientious scruples the oath demanded from dissenting ministers was further simplified in 1799 (19 Geo. III, cap. 49). See Bogue and Bennet, *History of Dissenters*, vol. iv. pp. 159 sqq.

London a general Committee, " the Committee of the Three Denominations," entrusted with the defence of their political interests and legal rights.[1] There were special coffee houses where the ministers and leading adherents of their different sects learned to know each other and to discover their affinities. All this was neither particularly theological nor particularly religious. But these political ministers were by no means ignorant men. On the contrary, they appear to have often excelled the higher Anglican clergy in intellectual capacity and in the extent of their erudition. Those among them who were attached by the bonds of Ordination, sometimes even by ties of kindred to the clergymen expelled in 1662, regarded themselves as a religious aristocracy. The " seminaries " or " Academies " which they founded, and which the High Church party vainly endeavoured to close, were famous for the solid education which they imparted. Even members of the Established Church sent their children to these Academies, in which Peers, even bishops, had received their education. But this attempt to attract to their schools pupils of every rank of society, made it a point of honour with the ministers to be free from fanaticism and narrow attachment to dogma. The orthodoxy of Dissent was in rapid decay.

It would seem that the eighteenth-century Dissenters, or those at least whose task was the guidance of consciences, were ashamed of the extravagant and savage features of the Calvinistic creed. Their theologians were increasingly less disposed to give an unreserved assent to the dogma of predestination, or to maintain man's absolute impotence to effect his salvation by his own free will. There was a universal rally to the doctrine of transaction defended by Baxter in the 17th century. But was Baxter's doctrine, strictly speaking, Calvinism ? At least it must be represented as such, unless the Dissenters were prepared to abandon their opposition to the philosophy of free will, to the " Arminianism " of the Catholics and the Anglican High Church party. And Dissenters were soon found who dared to go beyond even " the modified Calvinism " of a Watts and a Doddridge. The General Baptists separated from the Particular Baptists, because they maintained that Jesus died not for the elect alone, but for all men without exception.

Nor did this theological criticism confine its opposition to the doctrine of grace. It attacked the belief which seemed to be the fundamental doctrine of Christianity, the common faith of all Christians, the doctrine of the Trinity. Semi-Arianism, Arianism, naked Socinianism—such was the parallel development of thought in the Anglican Church and among the Dissenters. Two Anglicans, Whiston and Clarke, were the first to pronounce the symbol of Nicea untrue to the primitive Christian tradition. The Gospels, they maintained, teach us that there is but one God only, that the person of Jesus is not consubstantial

[1] Ivimey, *History of the English Baptists*, vol. iii. pp. 196, 198, 204.

with the person of the Father, that Christ is a created Divinity, no older than the universe of which He is the Saviour.[1] Outside the pale of the Establishment James Peirce put forward opinions scarcely less categorical. He was condemned by the assembly of Nonconformist ministers, as Whiston and Clarke had previously been condemned by Convocation.[2] But the heresy gained ground. At the close of the century the Anglican Lindsay, and the Presbyterians Price and Priestley, went even further than Whiston, Clarke and James Peirce. They refused to admit in Jesus even a divinity of subordinate rank. They regarded Him as no more than a man who enjoyed an intimate union with God, and was endowed with the gifts of prophecy and miracle-working. This revived Socinianism was known henceforward as Unitarianism, to distinguish it from the orthodox Trinitarianism, and the influence of Price and Priestley infected with the novel heresy well-nigh the entire Presbyterian body. But when the traditional creed had been thus stripped of every feature which in the religion of Israel had been a stumbling-block to reason, and at the same time of every speculation which had been elaborated by Greek theology to enrich the simplicity of the primitive monotheism, what was left of Christianity ?

We must not, however, imagine that these heterodox thinkers, Semi-Arminians, Arminians, Unitarians, were representative of the entire body of Dissent. The sects continued to contain a mass of adherents of the lower middle class attached to the old beliefs and ready to discover and denounce the doctrinal deficiencies of their ministers. But their "high Calvinism" which regarded the "low Arminianism" of their fellows as an error scarcely less abominable than Deism itself assumed forms which endangered the health of Dissent.

In the first place the Antinomian tendency continued in active operation and constituted for Dissenting ministers a cause of constantly recurring troubles. So long as Christianity has existed and will continue to exist sects have been and will be found to interpret its teaching in the sense of anarchy. Did not St. Paul say that " to the pure all things are pure " ? Good works, then, are evil, radically evil, and therefore of no avail for salvation. Those who have received the gift of grace, concluded the Antinomians, have received not the power to conform their actions more exactly to the moral law, but, on the contrary, a revelation that the moral law has no existence. The result of such doctrine was the open practice of free love, and a number of small disorders whose prevention, restraint and eradication required ceaseless labour.

---

[1] Hunt, *Religious Thought*, vol. iii. pp. 13 sqq.

[2] See especially *The Western Inquisition ; or a Relation of the Controversy which has been lately among the Dissenters in the West of England*, by James Peirce, London 1720. Cf. Ivimey, *History of the English Baptists*, vol. iii. pp. 160 sqq.

And the "hyper-Calvinism" of the sects assumed other forms which, if less scandalous, were more dangerous. If salvation is a gratuitous gift of God, and of God alone, it is not permitted to a man to convert his fellow-men. A minister named Brine developed this thesis,[1] and gave rise to long controversy on the point among the Independents and the Baptists.[1] "Christ and his apostles," exclaimed Fuller, an opponent of Brine and his followers, "without any hesitation, called on sinners to ' repent and believe the Gospel,' but we, considering them as poor, impotent and depraved creatures, have been disposed to drop this part of the Christian ministry. Some may have felt afraid of being accounted legal ; others have really thought it inconsistent. Considering such things as beyond the *power* of their hearers, they seem to have contented themselves with pressing on them things which they *could* perform, still continuing the enemies of Christ ; such as behaving decently in society, reading the Scriptures and attending the means of grace. Thus it is that hearers of this description sit at ease in our congregations. Having done their duty the minister has nothing more to say to them—unless, indeed, it be to tell them occasionally that something more is *necessary* to salvation."[2]

In any church where it established a footing this Quietism destroyed every species of missionary activity. It was, indeed, Moslem pride, not Christian zeal. The faithful were conscious of being the Saviour's elect. It was their privilege, perhaps also the privilege of their children, to whom the Redeemer had granted a peculiar opportunity of salvation by ordaining their birth in an elect family. All around them surged the mass of unbelievers and idolators. But this was only to be expected. For nature was corrupt and the elect few. Here and there a solitary individual would be saved not by human efforts but the incomprehensible operation of Divine Grace and would be added to the elect. All the rest we must pass over in disdain, and adore the Lord's Will. Thus while in one quarter the progress of criticism undermined the authority of the traditional dogmas, in another these dogmas assumed an increasing fixity. The Calvinism of the former party was undergoing decomposition, the Calvinism of the latter petrifaction.

But in both cases alike Dissent lost all capacity for propaganda. And there were further causes of weakness at work, due to the organization of the sects. The principle on which English Dissent was organized was the congregational or "independent." Every little group that chose to constitute itself a separate body enjoyed a strict autonomy. Once constituted the tiny community accepted no outside control, and any attempt to combine the groups of the same denomination in

---

[1] *A Refutation of Arminian Principles delivered in a Pamphlet intituled the Modern Question concerning Repentance and Faith, examined with candour . . . in a Letter to a Friend,* by John Brine, 1743. Cf. Ivimey, *History of the English Baptists,* vol. iii. pp. 270 sqq.

[2] Andrew Fuller, *The Gospel Worthy of all Acceptation* (1781), pp. 143 sqq.

a centralized organization was considered the initial admission of the principle of ecclesiastical authority, the first step towards Popery. In these little independent groups the pastor was not in the eyes of his flock the representative of any authority human or divine superior to themselves ; he was no more than their agent, their paid officer. In this Baptists and Independents were entirely agreed. They differed on one point only—the question of baptism which the Independent administered to infants by aspersion, the Baptist to adults by immersion. And although in principle the English Presbyterians accepted like their Scottish brethren a more hierarchical system, their common struggle with the Church of England had brought them into so intimate a connexion with the Independents and Baptists that they had inevitably been affected by their beliefs. Hence arose among these little religious communities, whose organization was thus democratic, even anarchic, a series of disputes and intrigues of which those brought up in the bureaucratic traditions of Roman Catholicism can scarcely form a conception.

If the pastor happens to incur the displeasure of a particular group among his congregation, a coterie or an influential family, he is at once the victim of a persecution. He is represented as an ignoramus— his sermons, it is declared, have been learnt by heart from some old collection of homilies. He is accused of immoral living, and indeed may perhaps have been guilty of some levity or imprudence, at the place where he preaches or in some remote village, eight days or ten years earlier. He is accused of heresy. Is he a Calvinist, an upholder of the Protestant dogma of justification by faith ? It is an easy matter to accuse him of teaching Antinomianism, corrupting youth, preaching free love. Are his opinions more temperate and is he inclined to "moderate Calvinism" ? Then he must certainly believe in free will and must be an Arminian—that is to say, a heathen. If he is a man of education and good family he may even in the end seek refuge in the Church of England, whose hierarchical constitution would remove him from the control of the laity. Or possibly a schism breaks out in the community. A section declares itself for the pastor denounced by the others and forms a separate congregation. In that case a flourishing community is replaced by two bodies, each miserably poor, and scarcely capable of supporting a pastor.

The result of all this was the wretched economic situation of the ministers which was the object of universal complaint among English Dissenters in the 18th century. Throughout this period the prices of all commodities had risen, salaries and wages were tending to a proportionate increase, but the stipends of ministers were sometimes even lowered. The congregations whose duty it was to support them were too small, and belonged to the lower middle class, were farmers or shopkeepers with the shopkeeper's parsimony. The average salary of a minister fell below £60 a year, often below £40, sometimes even £30.[1] But it was impossible on such an income to maintain respectably a wife and family, to insure against sickness and disablement, to provide for the support of widow and orphans in case of death. And the absence of any central fund compelled the individual minister of every congregation to settle these problems for himself and out of his own resources.

But the organization of the Dissenting communities was not after all quite so simple as it has been described above, and this fact gave rise to further complications and fresh intrigues.

There was a constant tendency for a division to be established within each local group between the " Church," namely those believers who were particularly zealous in the performance of their religious duties, who received Communion regularly, had been "converted," and had borne public testimony to their reception of grace ; and the "congregation," the lukewarm members who paid for their sittings in the chapel, and who, though not remarkable for religious zeal, wished nevertheless to hear a sermon every Sunday.[2] Thus the community was composed of two bodies compelled to establish a mutual *modus vivendi*. And the less fervent were often the wealthier whose help was indispensable for the payment of the minister, the repair of the buildings and the relief of the poor.

Yet another problem must be faced. The law obliged the congregations to put their places of worship into the hands of trustees. These trustees, chosen normally from the influential members of the congregation, became in quiet times rulers of the association of which they were the legal representatives. Thus the little religious democracy degenerated into a plutocracy. If difficulties arose between the pastor and a section of his flock, the pastor's safest policy would be an alliance with the trustees in opposition perhaps to the will of the majority. What could the malcontents do ? Go to law ? They were ignorant of the terms in which the deed of settlement had been drawn, and whether the trustees had not taken advantage of the obscurity of legal jargon to arrogate in correct legal form powers which those for whom they had acted had never intended to bestow. And even if their legal position were unassailable, they did not know how much time and expenditure a lawsuit would cost.[3] In very many instances they yielded or seceded. In the locality where the dispute had taken place Dissent was discredited. Its adherents lapsed either to Anglicanism or, what was practically the same thing, to religious indifference.

[1] *Protestant Dissenters' Magazine*, vol. iii. (1796), p. 68. Cf. vol. ii. (1795), pp. 119, 156, 292 ; vol. iii. (1796), p. 143.

[2] S. T. Porter, *Lectures on the Ecclesiastical System of the Independents*, p. 69.

[3] For a good example of these internal disputes, see *Statement of some late Proceedings relative to the General Baptist Church at Nottingham*, 1817. On the question of trustees see John Blackwell, *Life of Alexander Kilham*, 1818, p. 88 ; *Protestant Dissenters' Magazine*, vol. iii. (1796), pp. 110 sqq. ; S. T. Porter, *Lectures on the Ecclesiastical System of the Independents*, pp. 92, 101.

An Established Church apathetic, sceptical, lifeless ; sects weakened by rationalism, unorganized, their missionary spirit extinct. This was English Protestantism in the 18th century. And in 1815 it still presented in several respects the same spectacle although Methodism had been long at work and its action had changed profoundly the old order. On the Church of England the action of Methodism was late and slow, on Dissent it had been rapid and radical. The Wesleyan preaching had regenerated Nonconformity, creating new sects and transforming both the spirit and the organization of the "old denominations."

The Rise of Methodism : Its Influence on Engish Nonconformity. The New Methodist Sects.

John Wesley, whose genius for organization equalled his genius for preaching, had founded under his despotic rule a skilfully organized "society." This society did not propose to break with the Established Church, and had no objection of principle either to her doctrine or to her discipline. In its founder's intention it constituted a species of lay third order [1] whose mission was to complete the work of the clergy and to inspire the Church with the devotion of a genuine Christianity. Nevertheless, the Methodist societies found it an impracticable task to remain in the position Wesley had desired—persistent in fidelity to a Church which repudiated them. Methodism stimulated the growth of new sects, and the first of these was the Wesleyan body itself.

The Methodist preachers were conscious of the influential position they occupied in their local groups. Why should they resign themselves to accept a position of humiliating inferiority to the Anglican clergymen who ignored or insulted them ? Why should they not claim the same ecclesiastical privileges as were enjoyed by the Presbyterian, Independent and Baptist ministers around them ? Why should they bind themselves never to administer the Sacraments to the faithful, never to hold their meetings during the hours when the vicar was gabbling through the Anglican service in the parish church ? And around and beneath the preachers their lay adherents made their complaints heard. In the same village they saw Baptists or Independents treat their ministers as their agents and exercise a constant control over their acts and opinions. Why should they not claim similar rights over their ministers ? Why should they accept in the Methodist body the strictly subordinate position that had been imposed upon them

---

[1] Many Catholic religious orders (e.g. the Franciscans and Dominicans), beside their second order of nuns, possess a third order for men and women in the world, whose members are bound by rule to a higher standard of prayer and practice than is demanded of all Christians.—(TRANSLATOR'S NOTE.)

by John Wesley, who was personally inclined to the principle of authority and sincerely attached to the hierarchical tenets of Anglicanism ? The leaders of the movement hesitated. Disturbed by the violence and persistence of these demands they were nevertheless unable to arrive at an immediate conclusion as to the degree to which the interests of Methodism demanded concessions to the wishes whether of the ministers or of the laity.

To renounce their undecided attitude and to break openly with the Establishment was to sacrifice numerous advantages. The Wesleyan preacher did not demand from his convert a change of creed or church, but merely that he should learn under his spiritual direction a heartier love and a more faithful practice of the religion which he had professed from childhood. He did not, therefore, arouse at the outset of his work the suspicions which would have been excited had he been a minister of one of the old historic sects. But, on the other hand, to refuse the breach was to incur another danger. Nothing would then prevent Methodists determined to sever connexion with Anglicanism from leaving the Wesleyan body and joining the Independents or Baptists. Indeed this was actually happening, and if it became general would reduce Methodism to a recruiting ground for Dissent. First John Wesley himself, then his successors, were driven to adopt a policy of opportunism. They yielded to the advocates of rupture where concession was inevitable, in principle as little as possible, but every day more and more. The rules continued to lay down " that the Sacrament of the Supper shall not be administered in the chapels." But they admitted exceptions in cases where the central or local authorities of the " Society " should sanction it by a majority. It was only in certain cases clearly defined that the rules permitted the Methodist service during church hours, in direct rivalry with the service of the Establishment. But these cases were numerous. To render concurrent services licit it was enough that the parson was a man of notoriously immoral life, that he preached Arianism, Socinianism or any other doctrine equally pernicious, that the number of churches in the neighbourhood was insufficient for the population, that there was no church within a radius of two to three miles ; or even that the authorities of the local group had decided by a majority of votes that such was the will of the people and would not result in a split within the society.[1]

A constantly increasing number of societies availed themselves of the permissions granted by the rules. Wesleyan Methodism formed itself into a sect, and with this new sect a new principle of organization made its appearance in the history of English Dissent. The Wesleyans expressly rejected the congregational system. To employ the formula

---

[1] All those conditions, except the last, were laid down by Wesley in 1786 at a meeting at Bristol (*Minutes*, vol. i. p. 189). The last is contained in the *Articles of Agreement for General Pacification*, adopted at Manchester in 1795 (*Minutes*, vol. i. pp. 322–4).

of their own devising, they were connexionalists. They did not hold that each local society could be considered an independent church. All the local societies formed together one single "connexion" strongly centralized. Neither did they hold—for indeed the two principles are mutually inseparable—that the ministers are merely the elected servants of their congregations. The Wesleyan minister has received from God the gift of converting souls, and his preaching has proved his effective possession of that gift. The faithful cannot, therefore, by their votes for or against him confer or take away this miraculous endowment. And if, to discriminate between the truly inspired and the imposter, preachers must be subject to a controlling authority, that control can only be exercised by other inspired preachers, by those possessed of the mission to direct souls, not by those who have themselves need of direction.

The true unit of the Wesleyan organization was not the society but the circuit constituted by the union of a number of societies. At the head of the circuit were placed under the authority of a superintendent two or three travelling or itinerant preachers who within the circuit journeyed from one society to another, detached from any, supervising all and preaching as the representatives of a higher authority. They were not even allowed to remain attached for any length of time to the same circuit. They could be moved yearly, they must be moved at least every second year. Thus the foundation-stone of the Wesleyan organization was the systematic denial of local autonomy. To be sure, if a local society built a chapel, it must inevitably possess the appointment of the lay trustees. But every precaution was taken to preclude the possibility that these trustees would make themselves owners of the chapel and revolt against the corporation which had entrusted it to them. And further, every local society possessed its special preachers, the local preachers, laymen who after their Sunday sermons devoted the remainder of the week to their professional occupations in field, shop or factory. It possessed also its lay treasurers, the stewards. And it was divided into little groups for the mutual edification of their members called classes, and each class had its head, the leader. But the class leaders, stewards and local preachers were chosen not by the congregation but by the superintendent of the circuit, and only after a long series of tests could a local preacher be promoted to the rank of a professional preacher. When every three months the circuit meeting was held, only the stewards and the itinerant preachers took part in it. Neither class leaders nor local preachers were admitted. Nor was the individual congregation or circuit free to fix the stipend of the preacher. In virtue of his position as a preacher of the Methodist connexion, he had the right to £12 a year for himself, £12 for the support of his wife, £4 for each of his children, £6 for the board and wages of a servant. If a circuit were too poor to pay its preachers the connexion must make up the deficiency. To conclude, the entire system represented the sacrifice of freedom to organization.[1] Of all the Free Churches the Wesleyan was the least free.

Several circuits constituted a district, and the totality of districts was the connexion. How, then, was the central government of the sect organized? The central government was John Wesley himself, who, while he lived, exercised an undivided and despotic rule. He had thus created in the Methodist connexion a tradition of clerical authority not to be easily destroyed. He had even desired, when he established his first societies, to debar his lay helpers from preaching and from the administration of the Sacraments. The force of circumstances was too strong for these scruples of Anglican clericalism. In the end he had claimed for himself the episcopal power of Ordination. He had consecrated ministers to work in Scotland, in America, even in England itself. He had actually carried his pretensions so far as to consecrate Methodist bishops in America, though himself only a priest. But who after his death would succeed to his authority? In 1784 he drew up a list of a hundred preachers who became the legal representatives of the entire body, in whose name the trustees held the buildings of the sect. Henceforward these men constituted as of right the Conference summoned every year by Wesley to deliberate on Wesleyan affairs. After Wesley's death what form of government would this senate of preachers, the Legal Hundred, establish?

They could have replaced Wesley by the government of a few preachers permanently invested with superior authority, and thus have instituted a Methodist episcopate. Dr. Coke, an Anglican clergyman on whom Wesley had conferred authority to exercise episcopal functions in America, and Mather, whom Wesley had ordained priest, were advocates of this policy. It satisfied their personal ambition, for they hoped to become the heads of the new hierarchy. But the jealousy of their colleagues proved an insurmountable obstacle. Neither was chosen president of the Conference for the year following Wesley's death, and lest the president should degenerate into a dictator his office was made annual. On the proposal of Mather and Coke the Conference agreed to organize under the name of districts administrative areas comprising several circuits, but it refused to place these districts under superintendents. Methodism should have no bishops. At the same time loud protests were raised against the composition of the Conference. The choice of the original hundred members had already been a source of bitter resentment among the excluded preachers, although Conference

[1] *Methodist Magazine*, 1801, pp. 370, *The Design and Rules of a Society for the Casual Relief, when in Distress, of Itinerant Preachers and their Families, in the Connexion of the late Rev. John Wesley, London, Instituted* 1799. A notice of 1801, however, informs us that some societies had raised their preacher's stipend from £12 to £16. In 1818 the central fund to make up the deficits of poor circuits amounted to £11,193 14s. 6d. (*Free and Candid Strictures on Methodism and especially its Finances*, by Valentine Ward, 1818).

then exercised merely advisory functions, all authority being in the hands of Wesley. Now, however, when Conference had assumed all the power, executive and judicial, formerly exercised by Wesley their discontent came to a head. Concessions were made. Henceforward deceased members would no longer be replaced by cooptation, but vacant seats would belong of right to the older ministers in order of seniority. The year 1814 witnessed a further innovation. Election by the body of preachers would henceforward be a factor in the composition of the Conference.[1] To this extent the equalitarian principle of the collective pastorate triumphed over the principle of episcopacy or of government by a coopted assembly. But Conference continued to exercise an uncontrolled authority, and the laity were permanently excluded from all share either in its deliberations or in the choice of its members.

Thus the rude and fanatical preachers that Wesley had enlisted beneath his banner, not only continued to make converts after his death— there were 231,000 Wesleyan Methodists in 1813 [2]—but created a skilful organization whose hierarchic character was in some respects almost Anglican, and had been previously unknown among the Dissenting bodies. In matters of ritual also the Wesleyans were far less prejudiced against the practices of the Established Church than the members of the older denominations. They encouraged hymn singing against which the long-rooted prejudice of the Dissenters had persisted throughout the previous half-century. They would soon introduce organs into their chapels. Wesley had prescribed for use in their services either the Anglican liturgy or an abridgment of it drawn up by himself. In short, the Methodist connexion adopted a position intermediate between the Establishment and the older Nonconformist bodies. It thus constituted a transition between the former and the latter, which became the more insensible when new sects arose in turn from Wesleyanism and occupied the space between the Connexion and the original sects.

It was on doctrinal grounds that a section of the Methodists broke with the Wesleyan body. Wesley had adopted the paradoxical position of preaching justification by faith while rejecting the complementary

[1] The president and secretary were to be elected no longer by the Conference but by all preachers who had exercised their ministry for at least fourteen years. But at the same time, to prevent the Conference from becoming an assembly of greybeards, a return was made to the older method, and it was decided that one seat in four should be filled by cooptation (G. Smith, *History of Wesleyan Methodism*, vol. ii. p. 561).

[2] In 1815 the official figure for Great Britain, Ireland and the Colonies was 230,948. The increase for Great Britain and Ireland, which had been almost nil in 1803 and 1804, from 1806 onwards reached a yearly average of 8,000. In 1814, as the result of a great " revival " in Wales, it attained the exceptional figure of 12,009 (see George Smith, *History of Wesleyan Methodism*, vol. ii. p. 711). To arrive at the total of Wesleyan Methodists it would be necessary to include the Wesleyans in the United States, 211,129 in 1815 (George Smith, *History of Wesleyan Methodism*, vol. ii. p. 613).

doctrine of predestination. Whitefield had refused to divorce the two doctrines, and the Calvinism of his followers opposed the Arminianism of the Wesleyans. In 1811 in Wales Thomas Charles severed the last links connecting the Calvinistic Methodists with the Anglican Church. This secession possesses a peculiar importance in the religious history of Britain ; for it has been estimated that only one-third of the inhabitants of Wales remained in the Establishment.[1]

But more usually it was a question of organization that gave rise to quarrels among the Methodists. On Wesley's death a preacher named Alexander Kilham demanded a democratic reform of the Wesleyan constitution. Expelled from the society, he founded in 1797 the New Methodist Connexion, in which the lay members of the local congregations played an active part in the conduct of worship and in the choice of ministers. In all the assemblies of the sect—Circuit Meeting, District Meeting, Annual Conference—ministers and laymen sat in equal numbers.[2]

In 1806, and the years following, two Staffordshire local preachers—William Clowes, a potter, and Hugh Bourne, a carpenter—organized in imitation of the American Methodists large religious meetings in the open air, known as camp meetings. These lasted for several days and inflamed to the highest pitch the imagination of the pious crowds which frequented them. The new Wesleyan bureaucracy met these camp meetings with the same opposition which the Church of England had formerly displayed to the open-air preaching of Wesley and Whitefield. The "Cloweses" formed themselves into a separate sect which in 1812 adopted the official title of Primitive Methodists. It continued to be governed by a central Conference ; but the Conference was elected by the laity, and two-thirds of its members were laymen. Unlike the Wesleyan Conference, it did not assure a fixed stipend to all its ministers. Each circuit might fix what stipend it pleased. Nor did the conference hold itself responsible for debts contracted by a circuit for the construction of chapels. Yet another Methodist sect, the Bible Christians, was formed in 1818 on lines practically identical with Kilham's New Connexion.[3] These three new groups were examples of a type of constitution intermediate between the connexionalism of the Wesleyans and the congregationalism of the Independents and Baptists, and akin

[1] R. Ayton, *Voyage round Great Birtain*, vol. ii. (1815), p. 71. According to statistics compiled in 1812 (*Abstract of the Total Number of Parishes containing a Population of 1,000 Persons and upwards ; the Number of Churches and Chapels therein . . . and the Number of Dissenting Places of Worship therein*) there were in the diocese of Bangor 52 Anglican churches and chapels, 100 Nonconformist chapels ; in the diocese of Llandaff, 21 Anglican and 42 Nonconformist places of worship. Figures are wanting for the diocese of St. David's. Cf. Bogue and Bennett, *History of the Dissenters*, vol. iv. p. 339.

[2] [John Blackwell] *Life of Alexander Kilham*, pp. 227 sqq., 269 sqq.

[3] For these different sects see Crothers, Rider, Longbottom, Townshend, Packer, *The Centenary of the Methodist New Connexion*, 1797–1897.

to the federal and representative Presbyterian system, as it had been devised by Calvin.

The Influence of Methodism on the Old Denominations.

The very existence of these new Methodist sects is a proof that the influence of Wesleyan ideas was not confined to the 200,000 members of official Wesleyanism. Wesleyan influence spread, in fact, even further than these sects, and penetrated all the Dissenting bodies ; and everywhere it was a spirit of reaction against the rationalism and republicanism of the old Nonconformity. The dissenting sects of rationalistic tendency were decaying. When the French Revolution broke out, they were swamped by doctrines frankly anti-Christian. Paine, whose *Rights of Man* enjoyed an amazing popularity, was a Deist. The orthodox Utilitarian school, which from 1807 grew up in London around Bentham and James Mill, was radically irreligious, and endeavoured to prove that belief in God was not only a childish superstition but a dangerous error. Carlile and Hone had inaugurated, or were on the verge of inaugurating, an atheistic propaganda of a more popular and more vulgar type. Orthodox Protestants accused liberal Dissent, Wide Dissent as it was called, of paving the way to irreligion pure and simple ; and they regained lost ground among the sects.

The history of the Dissenting bodies at the opening of the 19th century is the relation of an uninterrupted series of victories won by the Independents and Baptists who had remained orthodox over the Presbyterians who had gone over to Unitarianism. A century earlier the Presbyterians had been the most important of the three old denominations. According to some calculations their numbers even equalled the combined total of Independents and Baptists. According to another reckoning they composed by themselves two-thirds of Dissent. Now they barely amounted to a twentieth part.[1] In every county the same spectacle was witnessed. The Arian or Socinian chapels are empty, often no longer used for worship ; then the Independents appear on the scene, obtain from the negligent trustees possession of the buildings, preach orthodox Christianity ; and once more large congregations fill the chapels. Thus it came about that in London where formerly the Presbyterians had been particularly numerous, in 1796 there were only fifteen Presbyterian congregations as against thirty-three Independent and eighteen Baptist, not to mention thirty Methodist congregations.[2] In Devonshire, the cradle of Arianism, twenty Presbyterian meeting-houses had been closed. In Hampshire, which had contained forty Presbyterian chapels in 1729, only two were left in 1812,

---

[1] Bogue and Bennett, *History of the Dissenters*, vol. iv. pp. 329-30.
[2] *Protestant Dissenters' Magazine*, vol. iii. (1796), p. 433.

and even these two were destined to disappear within the next fifteen years.[1]

The doom which befell the chapels where the liberal ministers preached befell also the seminaries, the Academies, which had been the boast of Latitudinarian Nonconformity. One by one they disappeared, and their place was taken by new schools of another type, orthodox and pietist. Two heterodox teachers, Dr. Kippis and Dr. Rees, taught at the Hoxton Academy. In consequence the school was compelled to close in 1785. It was united with the Academy at Daventry, where Belsham taught. But in 1789 Belsham went over to Unitarianism and resigned his position. Then the Daventry Academy was united with the Academy at Northampton, which the presence of Doddridge had once rendered famous. But this too was infected by Socinianism and in turn was closed in 1798 by the trustees. During these years Kippis and Rees were teaching at Hackney College, founded in 1786, where Belsham shortly joined them. After an existence of only ten years the College was closed. The unpopularity of French ideas, lack of discipline, financial mismanagement had combined to destroy it. The year 1811 witnessed a new attempt to found a Unitarian Academy. After seven years' existence the new school also disappeared. Meanwhile at Hoxton, Hackney and Hitchin liberal Academies were replaced by new foundations where the education was orthodox and Evangelical, and these flourished. The same thing happened in the South-West of England. The Arian Academies of Exeter and Taunton were closed. Rival schools, founded by the Independents at Ottery St. Mary, by the Baptists at Bristol, prospered. In the North the Warrington Academy founded by Priestley, after moving in succession to Manchester and York, was finally closed.

Meanwhile the Baptists founded in Bradford, in 1804, the Northern Baptist Education Society. In twenty years' time its premises needed to be enlarged. In Wales, when the Caermarthen Academy went over to Arianism, the Independents withdrew their support and founded an Academy at Abergavenny.[2] But the new impetus which was pushing Independents and Baptists into victory had been imparted to them by the Methodists. The Methodist sects sent them a constant flow of recruits, and if they did not, like Wesley, repudiate Calvinism, and if it was from Whitefield's Calvinist connexion that they drew the majority of their converts, nevertheless their Protestantism was as remote from the cut-and-dried Calvinism of old-fashioned orthodoxy as from the semi-rationalism of a Priestley. There was no systematical theology, no discussion of doctrinal niceties. The Dissenters drew their members from the lower classes of the population ; they were

[1] *Congregational Historical Society, Transactions*, January 1904, vol. i. Part 2, p. 297.

[2] For the details given in the text see Bogue and Bennett, *History of the Dissenters*, vol. iv. pp. 228 sqq.

small shopkeepers, small farmers, artisans, agricultural labourers. The example of Methodism had led to the growth of private religious gatherings for the mutual edification of their members. In these a young man could distinguish himself by the fervour of his exhortation, or by the charm of his eloquence. More often than the others he would be called upon to pray or to preach. Admirers and friends would urge him to abandon his trade and enter the professional ministry. He might perhaps scarcely know how to read or write, and would enter one of the Academies of his denomination. This pompous designation concealed a very modest reality. For a low fee a minister took a few boarders, and taught them in the intervals of his preaching. His pupils assisted him and went out to preach in the neighbourhood. In their spare time they learnt Grammar and Spelling. Greek, Hebrew and Theology were out of the question. Dissenters of the old school sorrowfully admitted the intellectual deterioration of their ministers and congregations. "Now, when a vacancy happens, the great object is to find a man of popular talents, who will bring an increase of hearers to their meeting houses" . . . "a man who can make the most noise, or tell the most entertaining stories, or talk the most fluently without notes and without study." [1]

The new preachers were illiterate enthusiasts, versed only in the methods of that popular oratory which was best fitted to awaken in the assembled crowd a "revival" of religious feeling, an emotional or "experimental" Christianity. Man bears in the depths of his soul a primitive superstition, which neither science nor abstract theology can satisfy. The notorious Joanna Southcott would be the talk of London for months, because she had promised at the age of sixty-five to become the mother of a son of God.[2] Evangelical Nonconformity provided this appetite for the marvellous with a more spiritual food. They had no desire to overawe their hearers by physical miracles. Their aim was to convert souls. Nevertheless, among the most ignorant classes and in the wilder districts their preaching often produced strange effects. In Wales the members of the sect of "Jumpers," an offspring of Methodist revivalism, threw themselves flat on the ground when the sermon began. Soon they felt themselves inspired from Above, rose to their feet and jumped in time. An outbreak of collective hysteria had begun which might continue for hours on end.[3]

The influence exerted by the religious revival of the 18th century

[1] *Protestant Dissenters' Magazine*, vol. i. pp. 502 sqq. Cf. pp. 351 sqq.

[2] For the riotous scenes that accompanied the post mortem on Joanna's body, see the *Morning Post*, January 2, 1815. For Joanna Southcott, see *Edinburgh Review*, Dec. 1815, Art. 11, *Publications respecting Joanna Southcott* (vol. xxiv. pp. 452 sqq.).

[3] R. Ayton, *Voyage round Great Britain*, vol. ii. (1815), p. 71, describes scenes of this kind witnessed by himself at a large religious gathering which comprised 20,000 persons, held at Carnarvon in the September of 1814. The sect is noticed for the first time in the *Gentleman's Magazine* for July 1799 (vol. lxix, p. 579).

on the outlook of the old Nonconformist sects was manifested in yet other ways. From the beginning the Independent churches had made attempts to form local asociations of greater or less extent without violating the principle of autonomy proper to their constitution. But these associations were loose in the extreme and never included all the churches of the denomination even in the district where they had been formed. They possessed no permanent character and amounted to nothing more than annual meetings for prayer in common and the exchange of religious "experiences" between the ministers. They had possessed no power to legislate for their constituent churches ; indeed the statutes of the associations expressly prohibited any attempt of this kind. And among the Congregationalists even these Associations had practically ceased to exist by the middle of the 18th century. Among the Baptists, where they had continued to be a regular feature of the organization of the sect, they were viewed with suspicion, even by those who consented to take part in them. Nor did their distrust tend to disappear.[1] "We confess, brethren, we entered this association with great jealousy and caution ; for although we clearly saw the practice of associating, consulting and mutually assisting in the purest ages of Christianity, yet we could not but recollect that such associations were in the end productive of the great anti-christian apostasy, an apostasy so fatal to the civil and religious liberties of mankind, and particularly to those of the brave old Puritans and Nonconformists, that the very words synod and session, council and canon, yet make both the ears of a sound Protestant Dissenter to tingle."[1]

But under the influence of Methodism this spirit of almost anarchic autonomy was soon to lose much of its primitive power. If Methodism made such rapid strides, if at each of their Annual Conferences the Wesleyans could publish statistics proving the enormous growth of their sects, this was obviously to a large extent the result of their superior organization. The itinerant preacher was obliged to a continual journey between the towns and villages of his circuit, and must visit not those places only in which congregations had already been established, but also, and indeed it was his first duty, those places where no Methodist had as yet preached. The Independent minister was, on the other hand, the representative of the congregation which had appointed him. To that congregation he belonged. Only with its authorization might he occasionally preach elsewhere. Thus the principle of absolute autonomy was a barrier to the progress of the sects which had adopted it. If missions were to be organized for the conversion of unbelievers, it was indispensable that the congregations should combine and send out the missionaries at their joint expense. And again, if the precarious financial position of the Nonconformist ministers was only too evident, here also the Methodist practice suggested the remedy. Why should

[1] Ivimey, *History of the Baptists*, vol. iv. p. 40.

not several congregations combine to form a common fund for the assistance of superannuated ministers, their widows and their children? Why should they not form associations which should do more than merely provide opportunities for mutual edification, which should centralize the finances of the sect?

The Congregationalists were the first to give way. In Lancashire in 1786 [1] they founded a county association whose objects were to organize a system of itinerant ministers, and to secure their local ministers against indigence. The association prospered, and its statutes served as a model to the associations which within a few years had sprung up in all or almost all the counties of England. The Baptists followed the example of the Congregationalists. In June 1796 they organized an itinerant tour in Cornwall, in September of the same year a permanent system of itinerancy in Essex, and in the following year they established in London a central society for the encouragement and support of itinerant preaching. [2] Already in 1784 they had created a central committee, the Baptist Case Committee, to assist the construction of chapels in every part of the kingdom. [3] In 1816 they would found a Beneficiary Society for the Relief of Superannuated Baptist Ministers. [4] A more momentous step followed in 1812. After a series of difficult negotiations sixty churches united to form a Baptist Union which embraced the entire kingdom, [5] and although eighteen years had yet to pass before the Congregationalists would form a similar federation, the preliminary negotiations had already been set on foot. [6] To be sure these associations preserved a voluntary character, individual churches were always free to join or to refuse adherence, and the Associations

---

[1] J. Waddington, *Congregational History*, 1800–50, pp. 110 sqq., and for the later history of the association, pp. 123 sqq. William Urwick, *Nonconformity in the County of . . . Cheshire*, p. 65, *Congregational Magazine*, 1841, *Supplement*, new series, vol. v. pp. 926 sqq.

[2] Ivimey, *History of the English Baptists*, vol. iv. pp. 67, 68. See the regulations of the society in the *Baptist Annual Register*, 1797, p. 465.

[3] *Ibid.*, p. 178.   [4] *Ibid*, pp. 122–3.

[5] J. Waddington, *Congregational History*, 1800–50, pp. 125–6. *Evangelical Magazine*, 1806, pp. 234, 334; 1807, p. 286; 1808, pp. 34, 140, 272; 1809, pp. 86, 169, 302; 1810, p. 253. S. T. Porter, *Lectures on the Ecclesiastical System of the Independents*, Lecture 3, pp. 129 sqq. A Scottish union had been in existence since 1806. The *Evangelical Magazine* for 1796, p. 119, describes a Societas Evangelica whose object was to spread "the blessings of the Gospel by Itinerant Preaching," and which since its foundation in 1776 had expended the sum of £8,000. The society offered to cooperate with ministers or county associations, apparently without distinction of sect.

[6] With the Unitarians the question of organization did not assume the same form, since they were sprung from the Presbyterian Church, whose organization had always been more hierarchic than that of the other two old denominations. A Western Unitarian Society governed the West of England, a Southern Society London and the Home Counties, a Northern Society the newly developed industrial districts. This organization had existed from the foundation of the sect. But in 1806, in spite of their dislike for the methods of the Wesleyan preachers, which they condemned as crude, they had so far yielded to their influence as to form a Unitarian Fund whose objects were the encouragement of popular preaching and the dispatch of itinerant missionary preachers throughout the country. For this movement and Belsham's opposition to it see Belsham, *Memoirs of Lindsey*, pp. 308–9, and the *Evangelical Magazine*, 1807, p. 68.

had no power to bind by their majority vote the local congregations. But this leaves unaffected the fact that the necessity of meeting Methodist competition had won Congregationalists and Baptists to the warm support of a systematic organization hitherto unknown among them. They were not, indeed, converted to the connexionalist type of organization which prevailed among the Wesleyans; but they were tending towards a system akin to the old Presbyterian or Calvinist model, and to the system of those dissident Wesleyan sects described above.

Finally, for the reasons already mentioned, the progress of Methodism was tending to render the Protestant Dissenters political conservatives. As their interest in theological polemics had cooled, they had lost their old taste for discussion, their former love of argument. And as their prejudices in favour of ecclesiastical autonomy weakened, their individualism in politics weakened simultaneously. Intermediate between the sects in the strict sense of the word and the Established Church, Methodism filled the gap between these rival bodies. The Methodists, and especially the Wesleyan Methodists, although in fact Nonconformists, refused to regard themselves as entirely cut off from the Anglican Church. The members of the connexion admitted an obligation to communicate according to the Anglican rite when unable to communicate in one of their chapels; and their ministry claimed to be not the enemy but the assistant or the locum tenens of a clergy which neglected its duties. And the other sects were infected with the same spirit. During the first fifteen years of the 19th century only isolated and eccentric individuals among the Nonconformists demanded either a reform of the constitution of the national Church in conformity with their ideas, or disestablishment and equal rights for all denominations.

But for all this the division was not less clearly marked than formerly between the social classes from which the Establishment and the sects respectively derived their adherents. In some respects we might even say that the line of demarcation was drawn more rigidly than ever before. From the beginning Nonconformity had been the religion of the middle class and particularly of the lower middle class. Nevertheless, in the 18th century Dissenters sat in the House of Lords, and on occasion boys of noble family had received their education in the seminaries conducted by Nonconformist ministers. Now both these things had become an impossibility. Nor was the number of wealthy Nonconformist merchants on the increase. In the normal course the more wealthy Dissenters went over to the Church of England. If a successful man of business wished to enter the governing class, to entertain at his country seat the clergy or the gentry of the neighbourhood, to obtain a title or a position in the Civil Service, he must not be a Dissenter. The wealthy Dissenter, therefore, was only too ready to yield to the entreaties of his wife, herself perhaps the daughter of an " episcopalian " family, or of his sons, who were eager to see the family enjoy a social position in keeping with its wealth and with the education they had received. He would seize the first opportunity to pick a quarrel with his pastor or with one of the influential members of the congregation. He thus escaped the moral supervision exercised by the fellow members of his congregation, and which he had so often found galling, and attended the worship of the Established Church where there was no obligation of religious zeal, and where the squire was his fellow worshipper. Puritan nonconformity thus tended to become a transitional creed, a stage in the history of an English family. The unskilled labourer becomes in turn a skilled workman, an artisan, the head of a small business, a business man possessed of a modest capital, and as he rises out of the barbarism in which the working class was plunged, he becomes a Nonconformist. If he himself rises still higher on the social ladder, or if his children rise after his death, he or they go over to the Church of England.

Nor was there the slightest difficulty in effecting the transition from one form of religion to another. The constitution of the Wesleyan body rendered the transition imperceptible. And what is most characteristic of the new spirit in Dissent is its acceptance of this subordinate position. The middle-class Nonconformist was content to be despised by the members of a Church which his own family might some day enter. He compensated himself by indulging an even deeper contempt for the common people of the fields or factories from whom his family had emerged.

Why was it that of all the countries of Europe England has been the most free from revolutions, violent crises and sudden changes? We have sought in vain to find the explanation by an analysis of her political institutions and economic organization. Her political institutions were such that society might easily have lapsed into anarchy had there existed in England a bourgeoisie animated by the spirit of revolution. And a system of economic production that was in fact totally without organization of any kind would have plunged the kingdom into violent revolution had the working classes found in the middle class leaders to provide it with a definite ideal, a creed, a practical programme. But the élite of the working class, the hard-working and capable bourgeois, had been imbued by the Evangelical movement with a spirit from which the established order had nothing to fear.

No doubt the English Nonconformists continued to oppose any movement towards bureaucracy. Without freedom of association they could not exist. But for all their freedom of theological difference the sects agreed among themselves and with the national authorities to impose on the nation a rigorous ethical conformity and at least an outward respect for the Christian social order. With their passion for liberty they united a devotion to order, and the latter finally predominated. Hence freedom of association proved in the end the restriction of individual freedom and the authority of custom replaced and almost superseded the authority of law. And this is modern England. On the Continent the leaders of the English labour movement are sometimes blamed for their middle-class morality and want of imagination, at others praised for their solid virtue and capacity for organization. Perhaps these qualities and defects are inseparable ; in any case they derive from a common origin. The majority of the leaders of the great trade-union movement that would arise in England within a few years of 1815 will belong to the Nonconformist sects. They will often be local preachers, that is practically speaking ministers. Their spiritual ancestors were the founders of Methodism. In the vast work of social organization which is one of the dominant character- istics of nineteenth-century England, it would be difficult to over- estimate the part played by the Wesleyan revival.

We can watch between 1792 and 1815 an uninterrupted decline of the revolutionary spirit among the sects. During the first years of the war the Dissenters of rationalist and republican leanings were loud in the utterance of their beliefs. In 1792, when Price and Priestley by their imprudent declarations of republicanism had compromised the sect of which they were the luminaries, the aristocracy and the populace combined against it. Chapels were sacked, congregations dared not meet. Tory politicians and Anglican bishops were not slow to exploit the unpopularity of the democratic Dissenters to the detriment of Nonconformity as a whole. Canning in his *Anti-Jacobin Magazine* was unwearied in his denunciations. In every revolutionary he saw either a Dissenter or a former Dissenter or a friend of Dissenters. In the associations recently formed by the Independents and Baptists to organize an itinerant ministry he saw a scheme plotted by political societies to preach under the disguise of Christianity, republicanism, Deism, perhaps even Atheism.[1] Bishop Horsley of Rochester, in a famous charge, attacked the Methodists as conscious or unconscious agents of the Atheistic and Jacobin propaganda. What, he asked, was the true character of these religious or apparently religious societies which met every evening in the towns and country villages ? of these fanatical and uneducated preachers ? of this federation of religious congregations at the very moment when the federation of political associations had been declared illegal ? " The Jacobins of this country, I very much fear, are at this moment making a tool of Methodism just as the illuminées of Bavaria make a tool of freemasonry ; while the real Methodist, like the real Free-Mason, is kept in utter ignorance of the wicked enterprise the counterfeit has in hand." [2]

[1] *Anti-Jacobin Review and Magazine*, July, November, December, 1798, vol. i. pp. 294, 590, 626, etc. Cf. *On the Welsh Nonconformists, Gentleman's Magazine*, September 1799, vol. lxix. p. 741.

[2] *Charge . . . to the Clergy of his Diocese . . .* 1800, p. 20.

When, however, we investigate what actually was taking place in the Nonconformist bodies, we discover that such denunciations are not to be taken very seriously. The only congregations in which republicanism was predominant were the Presbyterian, precisely the least numerous and the least prosperous, and their Jacobinism was hastening their decline. When in 1798 a Baptist pastor, the Rev. John Martin, declared in a sermon that, "should the French land, some, yea many, of these different and differing people" [the Dissenters] "would unite to encourage the French," the entire denomination was in arms. After a hasty inquiry Martin was expelled from the sect.[1] It is safe to say that the advocates of Revolution were the exception among the Baptists and Independents. Their most eloquent pastors denounced the political creed of Jacobinism. Robert Hall, Baptist preacher at Cambridge and a friend of Mackintosh, preached a famous sermon in 1800 attacking what he called Modern Infidelity. By this he understood the principles of the French Revolution.[2] The Congregationalist preacher William Bengo Collyer made himself famous in 1804 and 1805 by his patriotic sermons to the volunteers. The subscribers to his "Lectures on the Proofs of Scripture Truth" included Lord Grenville, Robert Southey and three Anglican bishops.[3] And all contemporary evidence agrees, that if the old Nonconformist denominations remained faithful to Whiggism, the vast majority of their members belonged to the right wing of the party.

When the anti-Jacobins made their charges universal and attacked the Methodist preachers, the injustice became scandalous, the calumny almost self-evident; for the sect was on principle conservative. At the time of the American War, when Price, Priestley and Wide Dissent as a body declared for the rebels, John Wesley had published two pamphlets, whose circulation extended to several thousands, to inculcate loyalty upon the colonists and the British public.[4] In 1792 the statutes of the Wesleyan body expressly demanded from their members loyalty and obedience to the King and his Government. "None of us," ran their declaration, "shall either in writing or in conversation speak lightly or irreverently of the Government. We are to observe that the oracles of God command us to be subject to the higher powers; and that honour to the King is there connected with the fear of God."[5]

---

[1] Ivimey, *History of the English Baptists*, vol. iv. p. 77.

[2] Gregory, *A Memoir of . . . Robert Hall*, 1833, p. 109. Again in 1805 he delivered a series of patriotic addresses (Stoughton, *Religion in England* . . . vol. i. pp. 11–12).

[3] J. Waddington, *Congregational History*, 1800–50, pp. 136 sqq.

[4] *A Calm Address to our American Colonies*, 1775 (*Works*, vol. xi. pp. 76 sqq.). *Some Observations on Liberty occasioned by a late Tract*, 1776 (*Works*, vol. xi. pp. 86 sqq.). This was a reply to Price's pamphlet, *Some Observations on the Nature of Public Liberty*, etc. Cf. *Journal*, November 27, 1775, for a copy of Wesley's open letter to the *Evening Post*.

[5] *Minutes*, vol. i. p. 270. Cf. *Strictures on Methodism by a careful Observer*, 1804, p. 115: "Their loyal principles, which make an essential part of their religious dogmas, render them loving and obedient subjects. . . . To the passive obedience of the Quakers in principle and

Such conduct ensured that in spite of the calumnies of writers and speakers among the supporters of the Government the unpopularity of Jacobin principles did not prejudice the Methodist propaganda. The new type of Nonconformity, evangelical and pietist, was gaining ground every year.

Progress of Nonconformity. The Act of 1812.

Nonconformity was making progress alike in the towns, the industrial districts, the country-side. It even made proselytes in the Army to the alarm of the officers.[1] Speaking in the House of Lords in 1810, Lord Harrowby prophesied the day when a majority of the nation would be Nonconformist.[2] There is no evidence available to determine the extent to which his prophecy was supported by facts. Neither the census of 1801 nor the census of 1811 included a religious census. In 1811, the Dissenters estimated themselves at only 2,000,000 out of a population of 10,000,000.[3] But according to an official inquiry of the same year in parishes of over 1,000 inhabitants the number of Nonconformist chapels considerably exceeded the number of Anglican churches, being 3,438 as against 2,533.[4] On the evidence we may conclude that while the nominal members of the Establishment still constituted an enormous majority, the Nonconformists already equalled, if they did not exceed, the Anglicans who practised their religion.

Naturally the ruling classes witnessed this flowing tide with dismay.[5] The squires had no love for the half-starved and shabbily-dressed preachers, and the parsons were annoyed to witness the peace of their parishes

---

[1] in practice, the Methodists as a body join active obedience, without the smallest scruple or reluctance. Hence several of them are found in the Army and Navy ; and not a few filling civil offices under Government." This spirit of loyalty inspired the other Methodist sects. See in John Petty's *History of the Primitive Methodist Connexion*, new ed., 1864, p. 21, the account of a camp meeting held in 1807 : "Many preachers were now upon the ground. . . . One . . . who had been in the field of war . . . showed the happiness of this land, and the gratitude we owed to God for being far from the seat of war. Another, who had seen the horrors of rebellion lately in Ireland, persuaded us to turn to righteousness, because we were exempt from such calamities."

[1] Wellington to Lieutenant-General Calvert, February 6, 1811 (*Dispatches*, vol. vii. p. 239) ; Wellington to Lord Eldon, November 13, 1820 (Twiss, *Life of Lord Eldon*, vol. ii. pp. 408–9).

[2] H. of L., June 18, 1810 (*Parl. Deb.*, vol. xvii. p. 762). Cf. *Zeal without Innovation*, 1808, pp. 16–17.

[3] "At least two millions. . . ." Resolutions adopted at a meeting of Nonconformists, May 15, 1811 (*Political Register*, May 22, 1811, vol. xix. p. 1264). In 1797 Robinson, a Baptist, estimated the three old denominations alone as a fifth of the nation (*A Plan of Lectures*, p. 48).

[4] *Abstract of the Total Number of Parishes in each Diocese of England and Wales, containing a Population of 1,000 Persons and upwards ; the Number of Churches and Chapels therein, and the Number of Dissenting Places of Worship therein*, May 20, 1812.

[5] See *Creevy Papers*, November 12, 1809 : "Warren the lawyer dines with us. . . . He predicts the present reign will end quietly from the popularity of the King, but that when it ends the profligacy and unpopularity of all the Princes, with the situation of the country as to financial difficulties, and the rapidly and widely extended growth of Methodism, will produce a storm " (vol. i. p. 113).

disturbed by their fanaticism. On the other hand, the Liberals and Democrats attacked the new type of Dissent with a violence at least equal to theirs. They were exasperated by the unexpected revival of unreasoning illuminism. Among these were Sydney Smith, the eccentric clergyman of the *Edinburgh Review*,[1] and Cobbett in his *Register*,[2] while Leigh Hunt in the *Examiner* surpassed the others in his angry attacks upon the popular evangelicalism.[3] But the leaders of the Whig party were obliged to show a greater circumspection ; for they needed Nonconformist support to obtain a majority in the boroughs. The Tories, on the other hand, and their attitude was altogether new, began to consider the susceptibilities of evangelical Nonconformity ; for they had remarked that, since the rise of Methodism, Dissent was not so strictly bound as of old to the Whigs. The Whigs were now the party of Catholic Emancipation, and at the general election of 1807 the Court party made a not unsuccessful appeal to the No-Popery prejudices of Dissent. Hence a series of measures administrative and judicial carried during the first decade of the century witnessed the greater tolerance now felt in Government circles towards the Nonconformists.

In 1802 the Duke of York, in his capacity as Commander-in-Chief, issued strict orders establishing absolute freedom of worship in the Army.[4] In 1809, the Dissenters obtained from the Government their veto on a law, passed in Jamaica, reserving to Anglican clergy the right to evangelize the slaves.[5] And in the same year a judicial decision granted them the right of burial in the churchyards, and equal freedom with Anglicans from the obligation to pay toll on their way to Sunday worship.[6] It was to satisfy Nonconformist complaints that in 1812, the inferior church courts were deprived of the power of excommunication.[7] And it was also in this year that after long months of struggle the Nonconformists won their most brilliant victory.

Throughout the 18th century it had been recognized that whoever possessed a preacher's license was exempt from the obligation of service

[1] *Edinburgh Review*, January 1806, No. 22, Art. 5, *Ingram on Methodism* (vol. vi. pp. 341 sqq.) ; April 1809, No. 27, Art. 3, *Styles on Methodists and Missions* (vol. xiv. pp. 10 sqq.).

[2] See especially *Political Register*, May 22, 1811, May 29, 1811, and a little later *Rural Rides*, November 14, 1821.

[3] See especially *An Attempt to show the Folly and Danger of Methodism* . . ., by the editor of the *Examiner* (Leigh Hunt), 1809. See also two articles in the *Examiner*, October 22, November 5, 1815.

[4] Bogue and Bennett, *History of the Dissenters*, vol. iv. p. 206.

[5] *Evangelical Magazine*, vol. xvii (1809), pp. 37, 262, 296 ; Ivimey, *History of the English Baptists*, vol. iv. pp. 85–7.

[6] *Evangelical Magazine*, vol. xvii. (1809), p. 565.

[7] 53 Geo. III, cap. 127. See H. of C., January 23, 1812, Sir William Scott's speech in defence of the existing legislation. "It appeared to him upon the whole that no case had been made out to call for so serious an inquiry ; and he rather feared that the facility of the noble Lord had been imposed upon by malignant representations from other quarters " (*Parl. Deb.*, vol. xxi. p. 309). Cf. *ibid.*, pp. 316–17, for an instance of persecution mentioned by William Smith.

in the militia ; and so long as Dissent retained its traditional organization the exemption gave rise to no difficulties. But the new system of itinerant and local preachers, inaugurated by Methodism and imitated by the other sects, made it possible for any labourer or farm-hand to escape military service by declaring his intention to preach without offering the least guarantee of education or even of good character. This was an obvious abuse, and in 1800 when political associations and trade unions had been made illegal, the Government had intended to take action. Since the Government was not in a position to make unnecessary enemies, nothing was done in the matter, and the question continued for the present undecided. But the Nonconformists felt their position threatened. In 1803 the Wesleyans organized a Committee of Privileges, modelled on the old Committee of the Three Denominations, to defend their interests in Parliament and in the courts.[1] At the same time Conference endeavoured to forestall State interference by regulating the legal status of its preachers. Members of local congregations were forbidden, under penalty of expulsion, to seek a license from the civil authorities without the previous approbation of the Conference of their circuit.[2] The decision was not calculated to satisfy the Government. It was precisely these missionaries, delegated by a distant authority and unattached to any particular congregation, whose activities alarmed the Anglican clergy. Nor, apparently, was it seriously carried out, since the Conference of 1810 judged it necessary to insist on obedience.[3] In 1811 the Cabinet returned to the design abandoned in 1800. Lord Sidmouth introduced in the House of Lords a Bill imposing a number of restrictions on the exemption from service hitherto granted to all Nonconformist preachers.[4] Immediately the entire Nonconformist body was in arms. For the first time an alliance was concluded between the old and the new Dissent. The Wesleyan Committee of Privileges joined the Committee of the Three Denominations ; and the Wesleyans, owing to their more perfect organization, directed the agitation. They launched a manifesto in which they called attention to the beneficent influence exercised by the Nonconformist sects during the previous half-century, "in raising the standard of public morals, and in promoting loyalty in the middle ranks, as well as subordination and industry in the lower orders of society." The war with France rendered national unanimity particularly urgent.

---

[1] *Life of Wilberforce*, vol. ii. pp. 355–6, 360 sqq. For these first attempts see *Zeal without Bigotry*, 1809, p. 44. R. A. Ingram, *Causes of Increase of Methodism*, 1807, pp. 144–6. At the end of his pamphlet he urged legal regulation of the status of the Nonconformist "teachers."

[2] *Minutes*, vol. iii. p. 93.　　　　　　[3] *Ibid.*, vol. iii. p. 93.

[4] For the history of the Bill see the abundant details given in Pellew's *Life of Lord Sidmouth*, vol. iii. pp. 38 sqq. Cf. *Life of Wilberforce*, vol. ii. pp. 507 sqq. The complete text of the Bill will be found printed after the proceedings in the House of Lords, May 9, 1811 (*Parl. Deb.*, vol. xix. pp. 1128 sqq.).

Why then revive old hostilities ?[1]   Two influential Nonconformists who played an active part in Parliament, William Smith and Thomas Thompson, approached Lord Sidmouth.   The Cabinet let the Bill drop before the Second Reading.

Nevertheless Anglican die-hards still possessed a weapon against their enemies.   What they could not obtain by legislation, they could obtain indirectly in the courts.   A Nonconformist preacher, who had failed to take the oath required by the Toleration Act, remained subject to the penal legislation of the Five Mile Act, and the Conventicle Act.   But the Toleration Act had not foreseen the new forms of organization which the Methodists had introduced into Nonconformity, especially the system of itinerant preachers.   The local justices began to take advantage of this to refuse the oaths of all preachers who could not prove their attachment to a particular congregation.[2]   And the decisions of the magistrates were confirmed on appeal by the Court of King's Bench.[3]   For the second time the world of Nonconformity was in an uproar. A new association was formed for the defence of Protestant liberty.[4] The Wesleyan Committee of Privileges called upon the ministers and preachers of the denomination to "suffer distress on their goods, or imprisonment of their persons, rather than pay any penalties for worshipping God agreeably to the dictates of their consciences."[5]   It would have been madness on the part of the Cabinet to antagonize the Nonconformists at a moment when the supporters of Catholic Emancipation were stronger than they had ever been.[6]   In 1811 Perceval had abandoned the attempt to alter the existing legislation to the prejudice of the Nonconformists.   In 1812 he altered it in their favour.   The Bill he had drawn up was passed after his death, in July.[7]   This Act,[8] popularly known as the New Toleration Act, repealed the Five Mile Act and the Conventicle Act, and only renewed their provisions with most important modifications.   Henceforward, religious meetings of under twenty persons were exempt from all control, as previously

---

[1] For the text of the resolutions adopted on May 14, 1811, see *Methodist Magazine*, vol. xxxiv. pp. 558–60.

[2] *Evangelical Magazine*, vol. xx. January 1812, p. 37 ; March 1812, p. 114.

[3] *Ibid.*, vol. xx. p. 116.

[4] Protestant Society for the Protection of Religious Liberty.   See Skeat, *History of the Free Churches*, p. 558.   It was this society which selected in 1812 three cases given against the preachers by the justices of the peace for decision on appeal by the King's Bench (*Evangelical Magazine*, vol. xx. p. 116).

[5] See the complete text of the circular in Richard Treffry, *Life of the Rev. Joseph Benson*, pp. 287–8, February 24, 1812.

[6] See Lord Liverpool's letter to Lord Sidmouth, May 20, 1811 (Pellew, *Life of Lord Sidmouth*, vol. iii. p. 62), and from Lord Eldon to Dr. Swire, September 22, 1812 (Twiss, *Life of Lord Eldon*, vol. ii. p. 225).   For the advantage taken by the Opposition of this tactical blunder of their opponents, see Lord Holland, *Further Memoirs of the Whig Party*, pp. 101–2.

[7] H. of C., July 10, 20, 1812 ;   H. of L., July 23, 24, 25, 1812 (*Parl. Deb.*, vol. xxiii. pp. 994, 1105, 1191, 1247, 1250).

[8] 50 Geo. III, cap. 155.

meetings of under five persons. This facilitated the prayer meetings of laymen held in private houses which the Methodist revival had brought into fashion. All exemptions which the law bestowed on clergymen, including exemption from military service, were expressly granted to the itinerant preachers.[1] An amendment introduced later in the House of Lords provided that the preacher must be a professional preacher and must not work at any other trade for his livelihood.[2] Thus the benefit of the Act, granted to the itinerant preachers, was refused to the local preachers. But this does not affect the fact that the new organization of the Nonconformist sects had received legal recognition by an Act passed unanimously and after the most cursory debates. And the victory won by the Evangelical Dissenters redounded to the advantage of their rationalist brethren.[3] In 1813 the Unitarians were able to advance from the practical toleration which they had hitherto enjoyed to legal recognition.[4]

THE INFLUENCE OF METHODISM ON THE CHURCH OF ENGLAND. THE EVANGELICAL MOVEMENT.

The Rise and the Present Position of the Evangelical Party in the Church.

Throughout the debates in Parliament during 1811 and 1812, on the degree of toleration to be granted to the sects, the Anglican prelates had either kept silence or adopted a conciliatory attitude. Not that there was much love lost between Anglicans and Nonconformists. No doubt the majority of the magistrates, who in 1812 refused licenses to the itinerant preachers, were parsons. But at the very time when Nonconformity was being remodelled, and by its growing alienation from democracy was winning Tory favour, the Church of England was the victim of a species of internal schism which enfeebled her power of resistance. In 1815 the *Quarterly Review* deplored the unhappy condition of the Church rent by the mutual antagonism of two powerful parties, " the breach daily widening, animosities daily inflamed, and charity almost extinguished by controversial rancour." [5] Here also Methodist influence was at work.

---

[1] Every person, it is stated in clause ix, who shall teach or preach in any such Congregation or Assembly, or *Congregations or Assemblies.* The plural met the case of the itinerant preachers.

[2] Accepted July 24th, in consequence of representations made by Lord Sidmouth on July 23rd (*Parl. Deb.*, vol. xxiii. pp. 1192–3, 1247).

[3] For the skirmishes that took place between the rationalist and evangelical advocates of religious toleration, see H. of L., July 3, 1812, Lord Stanhope's speech (*Parl. Deb.*, vol. xxiii. pp. 887 sqq.).

[4] 53 Geo. III, cap. 160.

[5] *Quarterly Review*, October 1815, Art. 12, *Lives of Melanchthon and Jeremy Taylor* (vol. xiv. p. 237). Cf. *Life of Hannah More*, vol. iii. p. 445, letter to Mr. Harford, February 22, 1816 : " Our church . . . is rent in pieces by the divisions of the High Church and the evangelical parties. O how I hate faction, divisions and controversy in religion ! "

To be sure John Wesley had been driven from the church of which he was an ordained priest. But he had left a rear-guard behind him which persisted in the attempt to realize his original dream, not the creation of a new sect, but the regeneration of the Church herself. Several clergymen, disciples of Wesley and Whitefield, without breaking with the Church, had founded in their parishes, on their individual initiative, little groups of laymen who met for mutual edification and the propagation of religious truth.[1] And laymen built chapels to supply the lack of churches, which they maintained at their own cost and under their private control, without consulting either the clergyman of the parish or the bishop of the diocese. Under their direction the old Low Church party was reorganized, no longer as of old liberal and rationalist, but pietist, or, as it was termed, evangelical. And this fact obliges us to complicate with an additional feature our picture of organized religion in England. If the Wesleyan sect, with its hierarchic constitution, and frank political conservatism, constituted the High Church of Nonconformity, the new Low Church or evangelical party was a species of Anglican Methodism. What had been the history of the movement? It originated with a number of clergymen who, if they did not break with the Church of which they were the accredited officers, did not display a scrupulous regard for her discipline. They continued to befriend Wesley and Whitefield, gave them hospitality when their preaching tours brought them to their parishes, even invited them to occupy their pulpits, and sometimes imitated their example by evangelizing neighbouring parishes, whose clergymen gave scandal by their lukewarmness. Among them were Walker, the Cornish revivalist ; Hervey, the author of *Meditations in a Churchyard* ; Grimshaw, the " mad parson " of the Yorkshire moors, who whipped his flock to church ; John Newton, who after a youth spent in the slave trade became parson of Olney, and boasted the " conversion " of the poet Cowper ; and others of a sterner and colder disposition, such as Venn and Romaine. All this generation had now passed away, and it was at the very moment of its gradual extinction, during the last years of the 18th century and the opening years of the 19th, that the Evangelicals organized themselves as a party with centres of propaganda, and methods peculiar to themselves, a party with no lack of friends proud to avow their friendship, yet attracting the implacable hostility of others.

The first centre of the Evangelical movement was the University of Cambridge, where the party possessed two great men, the leaders of Evangelicalism among the clergy. These were Isaac Milner and

[1] The indeterminate character of these groups was clearly marked in the debates of 1812 on the New Toleration Act. The Evangelicals took care that the word Nonconformist should not be used in the clause defining the legal status of preachers. Their object was to prevent the lay directors of their societies from being faced with the alternative of dissolving the societies or going over to Dissent. See *Life of Wilberforce*, vol. iii. pp. 507–8, 509 ; also *Correspondence between Jebb and Knox*, vol. ii. pp. 221–2 (*Letter from Jebb to Knox*, May 25, 1815).

Charles Simeon. Isaac Milner, a man of awe-inspiring and over-whelming personality—one of his admirers compared him to a sledge hammer—occupied the chair of Newton. At once president of Queen's College and Dean of Carlisle,[1] he was rather the professor than the scientist, and the preacher far more than the professor. Charles Simeon was vicar of Christ Church for thirty-two years. He received no stipend, performing his clerical functions purely for the love of God, and had even abandoned his share of his father's estate to his brother, lest excessive wealth should seduce him from his duty. Nevertheless he was still a rich man and lived as a gentleman.[2] For years he had to face the opposition of the fellows of his college, indeed of all the members of the university, graduates and undergraduates alike. The farmers of the neighbourhood and the poor of the town attended his sermons, which were interrupted by the jeers and booing of the undergraduates. But he possessed that distinctive form of genius, blent of meekness and severity, which goes to make the great churchman. And this carried him through to final triumph, and enabled him, despite the persistent hatred of which he was the object, to become one of the most respected men in Cambridge. He was ready, when the occasion required, to endure the worst insults. But he could also crush his opponents with a look,[3] invoke the aid of the police, and punish those who insulted him with public humiliations, even with imprisonment. Under his orders was ranged a little army of 120 enthusiasts, organized on the Wesleyan model in groups of twenty, who met regularly for meditation in common, public confession, and the management of a charitable fund. In the neighbourhood, he had his " circuit " of parishes which he visited periodically. At Cambridge, Simeon recruited a body of young Evangelical clergy, whom he scattered later throughout the kingdom to leaven insensibly Anglican preaching with the spirit of the new pietism.[4]

The Cambridge group were supported by another group at Clapham near London. This was a group of laymen who linked the Evangelical clergy with the world of politics and business to which they themselves belonged. Its members were men of wealth, who provided funds for the construction of chapels, and the purchase of advowsons.[5] In this way they enabled the clergymen trained by Simeon to employ freely under their patronage the new methods of evangelization, secure from episcopal interference. Their leader was Wilberforce, distinguished as a parliamentarian, famous as a philanthropist.

[1] Carus, *Life of Simeon*, p. 373, Simeon to the Rev. Thomas Thomason, August 16, 1813.
[2] See the description of his style of living in Arthur Young's *Autobiography*, p. 399.
[3] " Two young men . . . came into my church in a most disorderly way ; and as usual I fixed my eye upon them with sternness, indicative of my displeasure. One of them was abashed ; but the other, *the only one that ever was daring enough to withstand my eye* . . . " (Carus, *Life of Simeon*, p. 92). [4] Carus, *Life of Simeon*, chap. vii. pp. 137 sqq.
[5] For the rumours current about this see *Zeal without Innovation*, pp. 149-50.

From 1795 to 1808 he lived at Clapham, on Battersea Rise. His neighbours were the Thorntons, bankers and philanthropists ; Zachary Macaulay, the editor of the *Christian Observer* ; Lord Teignmouth, formerly Governor-General of India ; James Stephen, the lawyer. This group of pietists had chosen as their parish clergyman John Venn, son of the celebrated Henry Venn. To their receptions at Clapham there gathered a motley throng of Anglican clergymen, Nonconformist ministers, gentlemen of means, lawyers, business men, and representatives of all the oppressed races on earth—Spaniards and Portuguese from Europe and America, Negroes, Hindus. It required all Wilberforce's tact and affability to secure harmony even for a single evening among guests so ill-assorted as these.

The Clapham group, it was called the Clapham sect, consisted chiefly of Members of Parliament. There they were joined by other members ; country gentlemen such as Sir Richard Hill had been formerly, and Thomas Babington was at present, Nonconformists of the mercantile class like Thomas Thompson, the Methodist banker of Hull, William Smith and Joseph Butterworth. Together they formed a little party of their own filled with self-importance, " the party of the Saints," to use the mocking epithet of their opponents. Though William Smith belonged to the Opposition, the Saints were generally speaking Conservatives, and voted for Pitt and his successors. But they stood for independence and morality. In 1795 Wilberforce had braved Pitt's anger and jeopardized his own popularity by speaking in favour of peace. In 1805 he had voted for the trial of Lord Melville, and in 1809 for an inquiry into the Duke of York scandal. In a political crisis the independence of Wilberforce and his friends might threaten the existence of the Cabinet. From the depths of Gloucestershire the famous Hannah More, novelist, theologian, reformer of morals, evangelist of the poor, founder of schools, and a woman who treated on an equal footing with bishops, collaborated with the Saints by her writings and philanthropic activities. No picture of the evangelical group would be complete which left unmentioned so notable a celebrity. Equally with Wilberforce and Simeon, she was one of the " great men " of the party.

A religious party must possess a common belief. The Evangelicals plainly belonged to the Calvinist tradition. But their Calvinism was of a very mild variety. When at the close of the 18th century an exceedingly long and exceedingly violent theological controversy had arisen between the Arminians of the school of Wesley and the Calvinists who followed Whitefield,[1] the " Saints " had carefully avoided taking part in it. If they did not accept Wesley's Arminianism it was because they rejected certain of his private opinions, the doctrine of instantaneous

[1] Hunt, *Religious Thought*, vol. iii. pp. 297 sqq ; Overton, *Evangelical Movement*, pp. 120 sqq.

conversion, that God in an instant by a sudden miracle transfers sinners to a state of grace, and the doctrine of perfection, that a sinner once saved can never relapse. But on the other hand, they were repelled by the extravagance of orthodox Calvinism. They rejected the paradox, too subtle and too immoral for their liking, that all works are essentially worthless. "How I hate," wrote Hannah More in 1802, "the little narrowing names of Arminian and Calvinist. . . . *Bible* Christianity is what I love ; that does not insist on opinions indifferent in themselves."[1] "I began," wrote Isaac Milner, "to study the controversy when a very strong Arminian. *Very close thought shook my Arminianism.* . . . But I think I have learned where to stop. Calvin is much too systematical for me."[2] "Though a moderate Calvinist myself, I think," wrote Simeon, "the great mass of Calvinists are wrong." [3] Wilberforce could even write in 1822 that every year he became "more impressed with the unscriptural character of the Calvinistic system." [4] Nothing places in a clearer light the decay of the old dogmatic Calvinism than the aversion to it displayed towards the close of the 18th century by the leaders of the last great Protestant revival, by the Arminian Wesley and by the moderate Calvinists of the Evangelical party. The Evangelicals accepted as a general principle the dogma of justification by faith, but they declined to speculate on the niceties of the doctrine. They were not theologians but men of emotion and action. Their Calvinism, if we are entitled to use the term to describe their position, was a sentimental and a practical Calvinism—one might almost say, an undoctrinal Calvinism.

This feature of Evangelicalism made it easy for its adherents to work with Protestants of every denomination. For while the Evangelicals maintained the theological principle which was the common foundation of all the doctrinal systems of Protestantism, they systematically refused to interest themselves in the theological differences which held Protestants apart. And their philanthropic activity constituted a bond with the Nonconformists, their fellow philanthropists. Here also was common ground on which they continually met. "These city people are better than at our end of the town," [5] wrote Wilberforce at the outset of his career as a religious reformer after dining with some of his new friends. Sprung himself from the gentry, he found himself introduced into the world of commerce. There he met indeed a majority of Anglicans but Dissenters also, and he did not fail to appreciate the earnestness and zeal of the latter.

Some of these were Methodists, but their number was few ; for

---

[1] W. Roberts, *Memoirs of the Life and Correspondence of Mrs. Hannah More*, vol. iii. p. 196 (extract from her diary, July 8, 1802).

[2] Mary Milner, *Life of Isaac Milner*, p. 660.

[3] Carus *Life of Simeon*, p. 418, Simeon to the Rev. W. Carus Wilson, October 11, 1815.

[4] *Life of Wilberforce*, vol. v. p. 162.

[5] April 1790 (*Life*, vol. i. p. 265).

Methodism, a new sect, drew its adherents chiefly from the lower and lower middle classes. Others were members of a sect of which no mention has hitherto been made, so eccentric is its character, and so difficult is it to classify or describe, the " Friends " or " Quakers." The sect was revolutionary in its obstinate refusal to take oaths in the courts, to pay tithes, and to perform military service, but of all revolutionary groups it was the most peaceable. For Quakers condemned rebellion equally with war and for the same reason, and offered the Government only a passive resistance. They deliberately rejected all forms of worship, or courtesy. But this contempt for forms had itself degenerated into a rigid formalism. Public opinion, if it laughed at the comic aspects of Quakerism, respected the solemn silence of their meetings, which contrasted strikingly with the noisy and emotional services of the new sects, their honesty, their spirit of order and economy, their unwearied and enlightened charity. Wilberforce's friends worked side by side with rich Quakers, and respected business men of the three old denominations—Independents, Baptists, and Presbyterians. Among the latter, however, were Socinians and Rationalists. But even with these the Evangelicals were willing to enter into friendly relations. They were indeed on good terms with avowed Liberals, attached to no denomination, and with Free Thinkers who made no secret of their hostility to religion. It was enough, if their friends were animated by a sincere and practical zeal for the reformation of abuses, and the crusade against ignorance and vice. By a strange paradox men who were Protestant to the backbone, zealots for the dogma of justification by faith, were so devoted to philanthropy that on the common ground of good works they were reconciled with the most lukewarm Christians, even with declared enemies of Christianity.

But as the Evangelicals thus entered into frequent relations with heretics of every kind they condemned themselves to increasing isolation and suspicion within the Anglican communion. The existence of numerous and powerful Protestant sects has always been a source of weakness to the party within the Church of England which emphasizes most strongly her Protestant character. With few exceptions the Episcopal Bench adopted an attitude of frank hostility. Bishop Porteus of London, indeed, inclined to Evangelical views. But he had died in 1810, and in 1811 his successor had issued a charge fulminating in the most violent language against traitors more dangerous to the Church than avowed Nonconformists.[1] Bishop Yorke, of Ely, had protected Simeon against the local persecution to which he had been exposed. But he died in 1811 and his successor, Dampier, employed every means in his power to annoy Simeon and check his irregular propaganda.[2]

[1] See a criticism of the charge illustrated by quotations in the *British Review*, 1811 (vol. i. pp. 418 sqq.).
[2] Carus, *Life of Simeon*, pp. 234, 276, 326 sqq.

Who were the Bishops on whom the Evangelicals could now count for protection ? Shute Barrington of Durham and Henry Bathurst of Norwich. These prelates, however, tolerated the Evangelicals rather from a broad-minded and liberal temper than from any sympathy with their views. And there was also Bishop Burgess of St. David's, who was active in the moral reform of his clergy, an ardent supporter of the propaganda for the abolition of slavery, and a friend of Hannah More. In 1815 they won an important victory. Dr. Ryder, the brother of an influential minister, was appointed to the see of Gloucester. "This is a wonderful event," exclaimed Simeon. "He is truly, and in every respect, a man of God. . . . He preached for me at Trinity, not two years ago, and I for him at Lutterworth, not half a year ago. Does it not appear that God is with us of a truth ?" [1] But Simeon's very delight proves that the gain of a seat on the Episcopal Bench was a rare, almost a miraculous, success for the Evangelicals.

The party was a minority not only of the Episcopate but of the Church as a whole. It consoled itself for this by regarding itself as the salt of the Church. What was the number of true Christians ? Simeon was asked the question by the agriculturist Arthur Young, himself a convinced pietist.[2] The Quaker Fry estimated their numbers at 3,000,000 ; but Simeon considered his estimate too optimistic. At Cambridge he knew only 110 "vital Christians," that is only 1 per cent. of the inhabitants. The Evangelicals managed to persuade first themselves, then by degrees the general public, that they were the only true Christians. Did Coleridge repudiate his youthful pantheism and return to orthodox Christianity ? At once the rumour spread that he had turned Methodist.[3] Did Lord Eldon allow himself to write a long private letter filled with pious reflections ? He judged it prudent to explain to his correspondent at the close that his piety must not be taken as proof that he had joined the Saints.[4] Never in the history of Anglicanism had any party exercised so profound an influence. Never had any party been in such a false position.

The Reform of Ecclesiastical Abuses.

Did the abuses which disgraced the Establishment cry for reformation ? The Saints were ready to undertake the task. To adopt the

[1] Carus, *Life of Simeon*, p. 406, Simeon to the Rev. T. Thomason, May 19, 1815. Cf. *ibid.*, p. 372.

[2] Arthur Young, *Autobiography*, p. 398.

[3] *Journal of Lady Holland*, vol. ii. p. 238 (1808) : " His nature is radically bad, he hates and envies all that are good and celebrated, and to gratify that spleen he has given into Methodism. . . ."

[4] Twiss, *Life of Lord Eldon*, vol. ii. p. 64, April 7, 1808 : " Though I write in this style and have been very unwell and still am not as I should be, and however grave you may think me, don't think me a ' saint ' ; I mean a ' modern saint.' The more I see of that character, the less I like it."

language of one of their pamphleteers,[1] they sought to expel from the parsonage Parson Dolittle and Parson Merryman and to replace them by Parson Lovegood.[1] They desired numerous churches, resident parsons, well-paid curates. Already in 1783 Wilberforce expressed his belief that his friendship with Pitt had placed him in a position to effect much in the way of reform. Reforming statutes he thought would be his for the asking, even the appointment of a bishop chosen by himself.[2] But we have already remarked the poor success of his efforts to secure bishoprics. And his attempts at legislation were thwarted by Episcopal opposition. He failed to carry a Bill to facilitate the construction of churches by private persons through granting the advowsons to those who had borne the expense of their erection.[3] The Bishops were far too ill-disposed towards these proprietary chapels which escaped their control, were strongholds of the semi-heretical Evangelicals, and were even on occasion shared with Nonconformists.[4] Wilberforce and his friends were more successful in their attempts to deal with the non-residence of vicars and the pauperism of curates, but only after long struggles marked by countless vicissitudes. Their history is not without interest, for it casts a brilliant light on the attitude and power of each of the rival parties then contesting the government of the Anglican Church.

In 1796 Parliament passed an Act enabling bishops to raise the stipends of the curates in their diocese to £75 instead of the previous maximum of £50.[5] The cost of living had risen and curates had an equal right to consideration with other minor officials. Their stipend was deducted from the stipend of their vicars, who were thus submitted to an indirect and inadequate penalty for non-residence. Wilberforce desired a more radical measure, but had failed to secure a hearing.[6] And, moreover, we must take into consideration the character of the Act as a whole. Bishops were given power to fix the stipends of curates at their uncontrolled discretion, and power also, for any cause they deemed good and reasonable, to revoke curates' licenses summarily and without process of law. The curates' sole appeal was to the Archbishop, who was to decide by a summary procedure. Thus the object of the Act was apparently to strengthen the position of the Episcopate. It offered greater satisfaction to the High Church than to the Low Church party.

Five years passed by. The vicars' non-residence began to be

---

[1] *Village Dialogues between Farmer Littleworth and Thomas Newman, Rev. Messrs. Lovegood, Dolittle, and Others*, by Rowland Hill, 2nd ed., 1801.

[2] *Life of Wilberforce*, vol. ii. p. 200.

[3] *Ibid.*, vol. ii. p. 362, Wilberforce to William Hey, September 9, 1800.

[4] Danteny's *Guide to the Church*, quoted by Overton, *English Church in the 19th Century*, p. 148.

[5] 36 Geo. III, cap. 83.

[6] *Life of Wilberforce*, vol. ii. pp. 146–7. The debates have left no record in the *Parliamentary History*. H. of C., May 5, 1796 (*Parliamentary Register*, vol. xliv. pp. 598–9).

felt as a scandal. There existed an Act of Henry VIII never since repealed,[1] prohibiting, under severe penalties pluralism, non-residence and clerical trading or farming. Moreover, this old Act gave private persons the right to prosecute for its infringement and even promised them a reward, if successful in proving their charge. Two or three lawyers realized that there was money to be made out of the Act and began the prosecution on a large scale of churchmen who had violated its provisions. The High Church took alarm. They procured first the passage of a Bill suspending for a year all prosecutions for breaches of Henry's Act.[2] Then Sir William Scott, brother of the Lord Chancellor and an orthodox High Churchman, carried a Bill which mitigated very considerably legislation so galling to the clergy.[3]

Henceforward, it was legal for a clergyman to manage a farm, if he had obtained his bishop's consent. The right of non-residence, that is, of absence for a period exceeding three months, was granted *ipso facto* to clergymen who held certain specified diocesan offices, and bishops were given the power to grant permission for non-residence in a number of cases, which the Act enumerated in detail and which included the simultaneous possession of several benefices, and they were even permitted to go further and grant this licence outside the cases specified by the Act. On this occasion the Evangelicals were apparently divided. Grant spoke in favour of the Act. Simeon's brother criticized it in a speech approved by Wilberforce. He denounced " a new order of ecclesiastical law " which " went to place an unconstitutional power in the hands of the bishops."[4]

On the whole the Act of 1803 plainly constituted a victory for the High Church. Sir William Scott completed the Act of 1803 by two further Bills. The object of one of these was to indemnify curates who might find themselves suddenly deprived of their curacies because the bishop had enforced residence on their vicars.[5] It was passed this same year.[6] The object of the other was to complete the Act of 1796 and to encourage the residence of curates by improving their financial position. But the Bill, though introduced four times in succession in both Houses,[7] was finally rejected. The Bill provided that when the annual value of a benefice exceeded £400 the bishop

---

[1] 21 Henry VIII, cap. 13.

[2] H. of C., June 9, 19, 1801 (*Parliamentary History*, vol. xxxv. pp. 1549 sqq.).

[3] 43 Geo. III, cap. 84. H. of C., April 7, May 21, 1802 ; April 6, May 26, June 10, 1803. H. of L., June 10, 1803 (*Parliamentary History*, vol. xxxvi. pp. 463, 882, 1514, 1579).

[4] H. of C., May 31, 1802. Cf. *Life of Wilberforce*, vol. iii. p. 49.

[5] H. of L., December 12, 1803 (*Parl. Deb.*, vol. i. p. 1760).

[6] 44 Geo. III, cap. 4.

[7] First by Sir William Smith, then by Perceval, then by Porteous. H. of C., December 1 and 2, 1803 ; H. of L., December 12, 1803 ; H. of C., April 30, May 6, 21, 30, July 4, 1805 ; H. of C., April 14, 25, 1806 ; H. of C., February 9, 10, April 12, 13, May 10, June 8, 14, 1808 ; H. of L., June 21, 22, 27, 28, 1808 (*Parl. Deb.*, vol. i. pp. 1577, 1578, 1760 ; vol. iv. pp. 510, 611 ; vol. v. pp. 41, 152, 737 ; vol. vi. pp. 741, 922 ; vol. x. pp. 407, 413 ; vol. xi. pp. 54, 61, 141, 833, 876, 958, 975, 1086, 1893). Cf. Hodgson, *Life of Porteous*, p. 243.

could assign a fifth part of the income to the curate, if that fifth did not exceed £200 or £250 a year. The opponents of the Bill stigmatized it as an equalitarian and Jacobin measure. Every rector and vicar, they maintained, had a right to the full income of his benefice, and the State could not transfer a portion of that income to a curate without violating the property of the lay patron and the incumbent. One is accustomed to arguments of this sort from the opponents of reform; but in this instance they were used by Whig speakers.[1]

Behind the Bill they scented the activity of the Evangelicals, and this prejudiced them against it from the outset. For they had no affection for the Low Church party since it had become imbued with this new spirit, a spirit as unlike the spirit of the old Low Church party, which had been consistently Latitudinarian and devoted to the Whigs, as the new Dissent, permeated by Methodism, was unlike the old Rationalist Nonconformity.[2] Nor had they failed to remark the alliance between the Evangelicals and the High Church party to carry the Bill. The "Saints" had desired stricter legislation which would have imposed on vicars an unconditional obligation to set aside a fixed portion of their stipend for their curates. Since that was beyond their reach,[3] they acquiesced in a Bill which abandoned the curate to the discretion of his diocesan. By this concession they purchased the support of the High Church party and the bishops. The Archbishop of Canterbury expressed his satisfaction that the new Bill restored to the bishops a power they had exercised in the primitive Church and had only lost after the Reformation.[4] It is not, therefore, surprising that the Whigs should oppose legislation which revived the traditions of Catholicism, restricted lay patronage in the interest of the hierarchy, struck a blow at Erastianism, and strengthened clericalism in the Church of England. The Bill was rejected. And even the Act of 1803, inadequate and conservative as it was, was never applied. Vicars neglected to obtain from their diocesan a renewal of their license for non-residence. The bishops neglected to draw up, as the Act prescribed, an annual list of non-resident clergy. The abuse of non-residence prevailed even more widely than before.

But the influence of the Evangelicals was on the increase. Perceval, who became Prime Minister in 1809, favoured them. Lord Harrowby, a Cabinet Minister, was himself an Evangelical. He it was who in

[1] Beside the debates in the House, the articles in the *Edinburgh Review* afford samples of the criticisms directed by the Opposition against the new ecclesiastical legislation (see *Edinburgh Review*, April 1803, No. 22, *Sturges on the Residence of the Clergy* (vol. ii. pp. 202 sqq.); January 1805, No. 10, *Observations on Dr. Sturges' Pamphlet respecting the Non-residence of the Clergy* (vol. v. pp. 301 sqq.).

[2] See especially the speeches of Creevy and Windham, H. of C., June 8, 1808 (*Parl. Deb.*, vol. xi. pp. 833–4, 839). Cf. *Life of Wilberforce*, vol. iii. pp. 364 sqq.

[3] See the reservations made by William Smith and Wilberforce in their speeches on behalf of the Bill (H. of C., June 8, 1808). *Ibid.*, pp. 835–6, 837–8.

[4] H. of L., June 27, 1808 (*Parl. Deb.*, vol. xi. p. 1091).

1815 secured the nomination of his brother, Dr. Ryder, to the see of Gloucester. In 1810 Perceval obtained from Parliament a grant of £100,000 to improve the condition of the poorer clergy. Lord Harrowby supported the grant in the House of Lords, but dwelt on its inadequacy.[1] Legislation, he urged, of a more comprehensive character was necessary to cure the evils under which the Church suffered and to enable her to check the continuous progress of Nonconformity. The clergy must be compelled to keep their parsonages in repair. In too many parishes they were either non-existent or uninhabitable ; which provided the clergy with a welcome excuse for non-residence. The law should define the maximum distance between the livings which might be held by one incumbent. And in every instance the bishop should assign the curate a fixed stipend, which in poor livings might absorb the total value of the benefice. And a Government subsidy should secure a minimum stipend, graduated in accordance with the size of the parish, to all clergymen without exception. The Bill introduced by Lord Harrowby in 1812, and through his efforts passed into law the following year, gave a partial effect to these extensive proposals.[2]

Henceforward, in parishes where the population did not exceed 300, a curate possessed the right to a minimum stipend of £80, or to a stipend equal to the value of the living if its annual value did not exceed £80. This minimum stipend was increased, when the population of the parish exceeded 300, and again when it exceeded 500. If the annual value of a benefice exceeded £400, the bishop was given power to assign £100 to the curate, and to make him a further allocation proportionate to the size of the parish. The Saints gave their unreserved support to Lord Harrowby's Bill.[3] But this time the High Church party were hostile.[4] In the House of Lords the bishops were loud in their protests against a Bill which, they declared, destroyed the Anglican hierarchy, arrayed curates against their vicars, and imposed rigid rules on the heads of the Church instead of leaving

[1] H. of L., June 1810 (*Parl. Deb.*, vol. xvii. pp. 752 sqq.).

[2] 53 Geo. III, cap. 149. H. of L., June 18, 26, 1812 ; H. of L., March 11, 23, May 17, 21, 1813 ; H. of C., July 5, 8, 13, 1813 (*Parl. Deb.*, vol, xxiii. pp. 592, 771 ; vol. xxv. pp. 2, 256 ; vol. xxvi. pp. 210, 295, 1115, 1171, 1197).

[3] See especially the speeches of Wilberforce, Thomas Thompson, H. Thornton, H. of C., July 8, 1813 (*Parl. Deb.*, vol. xxvi. p. 1171). Cf. *Parl. Deb.*, vol. xxvi. p. 299 : " The Earl of Radnor said, that one object of the Bill had been stated to be the discouragement of sectaries. He did not think it had that tendency ; and it would be found, on the division, that the friends of sectaries would vote for it."

[4] For the High Church opposition see a letter from Copleston to his father, January 29, 1814 (*Memoir of Copleston*, p. 47) : " The leading partisans who assume that title (of High Churchmen) appear to me only occupied with the thought of converting the property of the Church to their private advantage, leaving the duties to be performed how they can." Copleston contributed to the *Quarterly Review* for October 1813 an article in support of the new Act (Art. 3, *The Earl of Harrowby's Speech on the Curacy Bill*, vol. x. pp. 49 sqq.). Cf. *Letters of the Earl of Dudley to the Bishop of Llandaff*, p. 6, letter written January 28, 1814.

them, like the earlier Acts, the unfettered exercise of their discretion. On this occasion, there is no doubt, the advantage rested with the Evangelicals.

Then the High Church party took the offensive. The Act of 1803 had not been regularly applied, and it contained clauses maintaining the old right of private prosecution. The clergy, once more exposed to the unwelcome attentions of the informer, were loud in their demands for relief. Parliament acted, as it had acted thirteen years earlier. To put a stop to the prosecution of vicars [1] the operation of the Act of 1803 was suspended for a year, and the suspension annually renewed till 1817, when the Archbishop of Canterbury introduced and carried an Act of general scope consolidating previous measures, a miniature code of canon law.[2] The Acts of 1803 and 1813 were refurbished and combined in one Act. Curates were given the right of farming even without the bishop's consent, provided the farm did not exceed eighty acres. Otherwise episcopal authority was strengthened. Private persons lost the right of prosecution. On the whole the Act of 1817 was a High Church victory. But its complicated provisions bore the marks of the long conflict between the rival parties, their diverse demands, their respective defeats.

Foreign Missions and Bible Societies.

When from the reform of the internal organization of the Church, we turn to the encouragement of her foreign missions, we find the Evangelicals faced by the same prejudices. In 1776 they had founded the Society for Missions in Africa and the East. Simeon advised the foundation, John Venn, the parson of Clapham, took the chair at the first meetings, Henry Thornton was the first treasurer. The society was strictly Anglican, and to make its Anglicanism plain the founders in 1812 changed its name to the Church Missionary Society. But from what quarter was its inspiration derived? Plainly from Methodism and the new Dissent. When the 18th century opened and for many years to come there was not a single Protestant missionary in the entire world with the exception of the small German group of the Moravian Brethren. Under the direct influence of the Moravians Wesley had revived the missionary spirit among the Protestants of England. The Methodists were the first to organize, in 1787, a regular system of foreign missions. Wilberforce and Henry Thornton were among the subscribers. In 1792 the Baptists followed

[1] H. of C., November 17, 20, 24, 1813; March 24, 28, 30, 31, April 4, 26, 1814 (*Parl. Deb.*, vol. xxvii. pp. 128, 168, 193, 355, 371, 385, 395, 409, 551).
[2] 57 Geo. III, cap. 99. It was again Sir William Scott, who had taken the initiative three years earlier (H. of C., May 9, 1814, *Parl. Deb.*, vol. xxvii. p. 741). See H. of L., June 12, 1816; H. of C., May 16, 1817 (*Parl. Deb.*, vol. xxxiv. p. 1084, vol. xxxvi. p. 683).

their example. In 1795 the Evangelicals founded, before their Anglican society, a London Missionary Society, based on the principle of united action by all denominations of orthodox Christians. Since Nonconformist missionaries were now scattered throughout the British colonies, wherever there were aborigines or slaves to be converted, in Nova Scotia, Jamaica, Trinidad, on the West Coast of Africa, among the Hottentots, in the East Indies, it was natural that the High Church party should regard with suspicion the Evangelical Society for Missions. Could such a society be trusted to combat heartily the Nonconformist missionaries ? On the contrary, was not the Society openly encouraging these missionaries, even making them frequent grants and seeking only to supplement their work by action on similar lines ? Two incidents, still recent in 1815, had revealed the depth of the gulf which on these matters divided the Evangelicals from the Anglican hierarchy.

The first of these incidents had arisen from the action of the Bible Society,[1] another missionary society founded by the Evangelicals in 1804. There was already in existence a society dating from the close of the 17th century, the Society for Promoting Christian Knowledge, composed exclusively of Anglicans, of which the archbishops and bishops were ex-officio members, and whose object was the free distribution of Bibles and Books of Common Prayer. But this old society, confident in its official status, had gone to sleep. When during the last decade of the 18th century the Welsh Methodists had appealed to it for the Bibles they needed, it had been unable to satisfy the request. Then the Methodists and their fellow Nonconformists took action, and with the assistance of the Anglican Evangelicals formed a large society for the printing and free circulation of Bibles. In a short time the society had become very wealthy. The founders had reckoned on an annual income of £10,000, in 1812 it exceeded £50,000.[2] From 1809 they built up their organization on a prearranged plan and aimed at the foundation of a branch in every county. But when in 1811 they contemplated the foundation of branches at Oxford and Cambridge the High Church Anglicans took alarm. They had no wish to see a breach made in the fortresses of the Establishment through which Methodism might find an entrance.

When, under Simeon's influence, 200 undergraduates undertook to found the branch at Cambridge, Marsh, a professor who since 1805 had waged a theological war against the Evangelicals, publicly denounced the scheme. To ask Anglicans, he said, to join a society

[1] Its original title was " A Society for Promoting a more Extensive Circulation of the Scriptures at Home and Abroad." For this title, at the suggestion of Hughes, was substituted The British and Foreign Bible Society (Owen's *History of the British and Foreign Bible Society*, vol. i. p. 32).

[2] Canton, *History of the British and Foreign Bible Society*, vol. i. pp. 50–1. Owen, *History of the British and Foreign Bible Society*, vol. ii. p. 348, gives a different and a higher figure for the year 1813 (£76,455 1s.). The number of Bibles distributed was 202,580.

whose object was the distribution of Bibles and nothing except Bibles, was to confuse the Anglican Church with the sects ; for the doctrinal basis of the Church was not the Bible only, but the Bible with the official commentary contained in the Book of Common Prayer. Isaac Milner, who occupied a position of authority, being the master of a college and a dignitary of the Church, had no wish to appear the leader of an undergraduate revolt even in the cause of religion.[1]   But Wilberforce agitated in London.   And as a result of his activities, a member of the royal family, and chancellor of the University, the Duke of Gloucester accepted the presidency of the Cambridge branch.   The branch was founded, and Milner, now sure of his ground, addressed the inaugural meeting.   Another branch was founded at Oxford.[2] By 1814 there was not a county that did not possess its branch of the Bible Society.   The High Church attack had failed.   But the mutual antagonism persisted, and the old Society for Promoting Christian Knowledge continued to compete with the Bible Society.

The other incident belongs to 1813.   Parliament was discussing the renewal of the East India Company's charter.   It was a principle with the Company to respect the native religions.   Not only did it abstain from missionary activity of any kind, it discouraged private missionary enterprise by every means in its power.   Long had the Saints been scandalized by this policy of religious indifference.   Twenty years earlier, at the previous renewal of the Charter, they had secured the adoption by the Commons of a series of resolutions affirming the obligation of Parliament to work for the religious welfare of the British possessions in India.[3] Since the resolutions had remained a dead letter, no Act being passed to carry them into execution, the Evangelicals proceeded to attempt the conquest of India by more direct methods.   With Lord Teignmouth, Charles Grant and Robert Thornton, Evangelicalism penetrated to the heart of the East India Company.   The Company thus inspired by a new spirit regarded the Christian missions in a more favourable light.   These missions were the Danish Mission, established for a century past at Trinquebar, the Baptist Mission in Bengal, the Evangelical Mission on the Coromandel coast.   The Company consulted Simeon in the appointment of their official chaplains, and appointed Henry Martyn, Buchanan and Thomason.[4]   But in 1806 the influence thus directly exercised by the Evangelicals over the Company received a setback.   A serious mutiny of the native sepoys occurred at Vellore. It was attributed by the Indian Government to the belief of the natives

[1] Mary Milner, *Life of Isaac Milner*, pp. 463 sqq.   Cf. Gunning, *Reminiscences of Cambridge*, vol. ii. pp. 278 sqq.

[2] *Life of Wilberforce*, vol. iii. pp. 559–60.

[3] *Ibid.*, vol. ii. pp. 24, 25, 27.   See on pages 392–3 the text of the articles Wilberforce desired to introduce into the Charter.

[4] For the Evangelical chaplains see *Life of Mrs. Sherwood*, pp. 353 sqq.

that the English were intending their forcible conversion to Christianity. The Saints, no longer in favour with the Company, realized the necessity of invoking further parliamentary assistance.[1] It is easy to anticipate the difficulties which confronted them in this course.

If they merely proposed to organize in India one or two dioceses, served by a regular hierarchy of priests, the High Church clergy would have no quarrel with their plans.[2] But in that case the Evangelicals would incur the suspicion of the Methodist and other Nonconformist missionaries, enthusiasts for the conversion of India, but by no means disposed to see Indian Christianity identified with episcopacy and submitted to the control of the Church of England. If, on the other hand, it were proposed to grant an absolute liberty of missionary propaganda in India and to open that vast territory to the missionaries' uncontrolled activities, the High Church party would be in arms against the proposal. The only missionaries then in India were either Baptists or Evangelicals, whom public opinion confused with the Nonconformists under the common designation of Methodist. And the bishops were little disposed to see the respectability of English religion compromised in Asia by the invasion of a host of unwashed enthusiasts. Moreover, although the influence of Perceval and Lord Harrowby had disposed the Government favourably to the Evangelicals, the temper of the majority in the House was uncertain. The Evangelicals were in an awkward predicament. Agitation outside the House was difficult. If a campaign of petitions were organized, the Dissenters would sign *en masse*. But for that very reason Anglicans would refuse to sign and the total impression produced on Parliament would be unfavourable. Notwithstanding these difficulties Wilberforce and his friends contrived to win a partial success.

They began by obtaining from the Cabinet and the Legislature the appointment of a bishop for India and three archdeacons.[3] There remained the more delicate problem of the missions. They secured the insertion into the Charter of a clause investing the Board of Control in London with authority to overrule decisions of the Company refusing a license to a missionary.[4] Though this fell far short of unfettered

---

[1] For the Protestant missions to India and the Vellore disturbances see *Edinburgh Review*, April 1808, Art. 4, *Indian Missions* (vol. xii. pp. 151 sqq.). The article is hostile to the Evangelicals.

[2] See Pellew, *Life of Lord Sidmouth*, vol. iii. p. 103, Bishop Huntingdon's letter to Lord Sidmouth, April 17, 1813 : " America had never been lost if an Episcopal Church had long ago been established there ; and I am persuaded now, the strongest means through which you can secure any degree of real attachment to this country will be through the Episcopalians. . . . In my discourse before the ' Society for the Propagation of the Gospel in Foreign Parts,' I made allusion to the policy of securing the affections of the rising generations in New South Wales by establishing an Episcopal Church, before separatists had prejudiced their minds against our constitution, civil and religious. On the same grounds of policy an Episcopal Church establishment seems essential in India."

[3] 53 Geo. III, cap. 155, sec. 49.

[4] 53 Geo. III, cap. 155, sec. 43. For the circumstances under which the articles of the

religious freedom, it was more than the Evangelicals had dared to hope. The first bishop sent to India, Middleton, was, as we should expect, a High Churchman. But he had the wisdom to adopt a conciliatory attitude towards the Evangelical missionaries and chaplains and administered his diocese to their entire satisfaction.

Moral Reforms.

Thus even in the interior reform of the Anglican Church the Evangelicals in spite of the opposition of the vast majority of the clergy always took the offensive and won many victories. And they were even more successful when they undertook the reform not of the Church but of the national morality. It is even arguable that in many ways the dubious position occupied by the Evangelicals on the border line between the Church and Nonconformity enlarged their sphere of action. Outside the Establishment they came to the assistance of the Methodists and other Nonconformist pietists, and protected them against the contempt and hostility of the clergy. And meanwhile, they exercised on the upper classes a direct influence akin to that exercised by the Methodists on the masses. In the 18th century the English aristocracy, gentry, and upper middle class had been Free Thinkers and loose livers, cynics, critics of established institutions and received ideas, republicans. As late as 1794 Isaac Milner, writing to a correspondent, expressed the disgust he felt for their conduct. " Now in general," he wrote, " the lower orders only regard such things " (the Gospel), " and the great and the high have, all over Europe, forgotten that they have souls."[1] But the French Revolution had opened the eyes of the gentry and the wealthy traders to the risks to which their light attitude towards religion was exposing that social order of which they were the principal beneficiaries. And the Evangelicals appealed successfully to this new attitude to support their propaganda.

Even if a gentleman were personally devoid of justifying faith he respected its presence in his neighbours and encouraged it among the poor as the surest guarantee of law and order, if not of salvation. The names of Voltaire and Rousseau had become objects of universal execration. At the second entry of the Allies into Paris a leading article in *The Times* expressed its desire for the demolition of Voltaire's statue. " We would grind to powder the statue of the vain, obscene, heartless, atheistical Voltaire."[2] And a few years earlier during a period of public panic when the entire nation was in dread of a French invasion, Lord Exeter at his Stamford seat had made a public bonfire of the

---

new Charter dealing with religion were passed, see especially the *Life of Wilberforce*, vol. iv. pp. 9 sqq., 100 sqq. The report of the sittings in the *Parliamentary Debates* is obviously careless and incomplete.

[1] Mary Milner, *Life of Isaac Milner*, p. 100. [2] *The Times*, July 10, 1815.

works of Voltaire, Rousseau, and other apostates from Christianity.[1] A few of the old Whigs were left to lament this change of public opinion. "The natural tendency of the excesses of the French Revolution," wrote Thomas Moore, "was to produce in the higher classes of England an increased reserve of manner, and, of course, a proportionate restraint on all within their circle, which have been fatal to conviviality and humour, and not very propitious to wit, subduing both manners and conversation to a sort of polished level, to rise above which is often thought almost as vulgar as to sink below it."[2] The aristocracy abandoned its former friendship with men of letters. Sport, politics, the preservation of social order, and morality, now constituted the only fashionable topics.

Formerly, in the days of William of Orange and Louis XIV, of Lord Chatham and Louis XV, the English regarded their country as the citadel of freedom at war with a "Turkish" despotism. No doubt during the first fifteen years of the 19th century they still cherished the same belief; but the word "liberty" no longer bore for them the sense it had borne for their fathers. They now understood by liberty restraint self-imposed and freely accepted as opposed to restraint forcibly imposed by the Government. England was contrasted with Napoleonic France, as being at once the home of liberty and of virtue. Probably the vast majority of Englishmen, despite so much bitter strife of ideas and interests, would have agreed in this belief. "It is to the cultivation of the moral qualities," wrote the *Morning Chronicle*, the leading organ of the Liberal Opposition, "that England is indebted for her power and influence, from the want of them France may be mischievous but she never will be great."[3] And this change in the opinion entertained of themselves by the English was undoubtedly the result of the Methodist propaganda continued by the Evangelicals.

The nineteenth-century Englishman was distinguished from the continental European, and it was a distinction of which he was proud, by a feature which, if superficial, was none the less characteristic, his strict observance of the Biblical Sabbath. And this Sabbath observance was unquestionably a direct result of the Methodist and Evangelical revival. The Saints had indeed never succeeded in obtaining from Parliament the legal prohibition of every kind of work and amusement for one entire day every week, nor even an Act prohibiting the publication of Sunday newspapers.[4] But they did not abandon the attempt. To obtain their end they had recourse to other means.

In 1787 the King had issued, at their instance, a proclamation condemning Sabbath-breaking, blasphemy, drunkenness, obscene literature, immoral amusements. They had proceeded to found for

[1] *Journal of Lady Holland*, vol. ii. p. 250.   [2] Moore, *Life of Sheridan*, p. 217.
[3] *Morning Chronicle*, February 2, 1815.
[4] *Life of Wilberforce*, vol. ii. pp. 338, 424.

the enforcement of the proclamation a large and important society,[1] which included in its membership the entire bench of bishops, members of both Houses, and wealthy merchants. " In our free state," wrote Wilberforce, " it is peculiarly needful to obtain these ends by the agency of some voluntary association ; for thus only can those moral principles be guarded which of old were under the immediate protection of the Government. It" (the association) "is to us, like the ancient censorship, the guardian of the religion and morals of the people."[2] The Society, reorganized fifteen years later under the name of the Society for the Suppression of Vice, carried on a vigorous warfare against blasphemous or obscene publications, brothels, and fortune tellers. But its principal object was the observance of the Sunday rest.[3] It kept its eye on the days chosen for markets, on the days when the aristocracy took its pleasures, on the days when the militia manœuvred. When employers were inclined to oppose a movement which deprived them of labour one day every week the Evangelicals pointed out that it was to their advantage to command a religious and obedient proletariat.[4] Why had France, even the France of the counter-revolution, failed to learn the lesson ? When Louis XVIII left England to return to his kingdom, he chose a Sunday to begin his journey. " What ingratitude," exclaimed Wilberforce, "and without temptation. What folly ! Is this the Roman Catholic religion ? Is it philosophical enlargement of mind ? . . . How sad that none should have the courage to tell them. O shame, shame. Forgive, O Lord, and punish not our land for this ingratitude and cowardice."[5]

The activity of the Saints was displayed in other and less questionable forms. Although within the last twenty years duels between men in high position continued to engage the attention of the British public, among them a duel between the Premier and the Leader of the Opposition, and a duel between two members of the same Cabinet, the custom was obviously on the decline. In the Army and Navy duelling had been rigidly suppressed.[6] This was a result of Evangelical propaganda.[7] And to the

---

[1] Its full title was " The Society for Enforcing the King's Proclamation against Immorality and Profaneness." [2] *Life of Wilberforce*, vol. i. pp. 131–2.

[3] *Society for the Suppression of Vice*, 1825, pp. 7 sqq.

[4] Arthur Young, *Lincolnshire*, 1799, p. 438 : " I know nothing better calculated to fill a country with barbarians ready for any mischief, than extensive commons and Divine Service only once a month. . . . To the scandal of the kingdom, of the legislature, of the executive, of the laws, therefore to the scandal of the magistracy, we see carriers' wagons and stage coaches crowding the roads on Sunday ; add to this the fields full of workmen and where soon would divine worship be found ? Do French principles make so slow a progress, that you should lend them such helping hands ? "

[5] *Life*, vol. iv. p. 180 ; *Journal*, April 24, 1814.

[6] See in Brenton, *Life of Lord St. Vincent*, vol. i. pp. 409 sqq., the Admiralty prohibition of a duel to which Sir John Orde had challenged Lord St. Vincent. In 1812 a court martial cashiered a lieutenant " for scandalous and infamous behaviour " because he had tried to compel officers to settle their quarrels by a duel (*Examiner*, November 1, 1812).

[7] After Pitt's duel with Tierney, Wilberforce entertained the idea of procuring from Parliament a resolution of censure (*Life*, vol. ii. pp. 281–2).

same propaganda must be ascribed the protests raised every day more loudly against the brutal amusements not only of the lower classes, but of the aristocracy itself. Such were the fights between professional boxers to which the population of the large towns eagerly gathered. And there were cock-fights, bear-baiting and bull-baiting. A bear or a bull was tied to a post and worried by a pack of dogs, and the fight, cleverly interrupted at the right moment, could be continued over several days before the bear or bull was killed.[1] The Saints made repeated attempts to obtain from Parliament an Act protecting animals from human cruelty, and in the Upper House they had the warm support of Lord Erskine.[2] There were lengthy debates on the question in which the best speakers in Parliament took part. Windham was a zealous advocate of these cruel sports. He denounced the Methodist-Jacobin conspiracy to make the lower classes serious, gloomy, critical and discontented. He won the day. The Act demanded by the Evangelicals was not passed and bull-baitings were still carried on amid shouts of Windham and Liberty.[3] But was there any need for new legislation? In 1811 the Attorney-General was consulted and declared that in his opinion since bull-baiting took place on the King's highway and thus impeded traffic and rendered it dangerous, it constituted what English law terms a nuisance and was therefore an offence.[4] And was it even necessary to invoke the help of the Courts? The number of bull-baitings and bear-baitings was decreasing every year.[5] The Evangelical propaganda had rendered legal prohibition superfluous.

The Evangelicals were also engaged in an attempt to protect the children of the working class against the oppression of employers. We have already seen the part they took in the legislation regulating the conditions under which pauper children worked in the factories.[6]

---

[1] At a fight in Lancashire the right to strangle one's opponent was recognized, also to beat him to death with iron-rimmed clogs (Baines, *Lancashire*, vol. iii. pp. 75–6). The *Examiner* for February 19, 1815, contains an account of a sport similar to bull-baiting practised at Penzance. "On Saturday week, near Penzance, some men and boys, accompanied by *two young women*, amused themselves with *tail-piping* a dog, which they had procured for that purpose. Having fastened a bullock's horn to its tail, they turned the affrighted animal loose and followed it with brutal exultation. . . . The practice of tail-piping or, as it is there called *pralling* dogs, we believe, ranks as an amusement next to bull-baiting in the estimation of the lower orders in the neighbourhood of Penzance."

[2] Campbell, *Lives of the Lord Chancellors*, vol. vi. pp. 607 sqq. See *Parl. Deb.*, H. of C., April 18, 1800; June 12, 13, 15, 1809. H. of L., May 15, June 2, 1809; April 17, May 8, 14, 1810. (*Parl. Hist.*, vol. xxxv. pp. 202 sqq. *Parl. Deb.*, vol. xiv. pp. 989, 1029, 1071; pp. 553, 830; vol. xvi. pp. 630, 846, 880.)

[3] *Life of Wilberforce*, vol. ii. pp. 365–6. Cf. Howitt, *Rural Life of England*, 1840, p. 522.

[4] Langford, *Century of Birmingham Life*, vol. ii. p. 270.

[5] This was the chief argument employed by the opponents of legal prohibition. See in the *Anti-Jacobin Review*, vol. vi. (1800), p. 218, an article on *A Letter to the Right Hon. William Windham on his late Opposition to the Bill to prevent Bull-baiting*, by an old M.P. (Sir Richard Hill). According to Sir William Pulteney (H. of C., April 18, 1800), bull-baiting, common in Staffordshire and Rutland, was unknown in Yorkshire and Northumberland.

[6] See above Book II, chap. ii. pp. 269 sqq.

MORAL REFORMS

They were equally concerned in an effort to improve b̲
ment the condition of the children employed as chim̲
London.[1]   The reform of the prison system and the pena̲
indeed directly due to the Evangelicals.   Bentham was̲
Voltaire and Helvetius, Romilly a disciple of Bentham.̲
Howard, the first prison reformer, had been a Dissenter, an̲
Fry and William Allen, who devoted their lives to improving̲
ment of criminals, were Quakers.   Their philanthropic activity had
not been uninfluenced by the Evangelical revival.   And Wilberforce
was in full sympathy with all these reformers.   Every time Romilly
brought forward in the Commons the abolition of the death penalty
for an offence, Wilberforce intervened in the debate to support Romilly's
proposal with his influence.[2]   When in 1812 the revolutionary democrat,
Sir Francis Burdett, demanded the abolition of flogging in the Army,
Romilly rose in support of his motion, while making reservations as to
several opinions voiced by Sir Francis in his speech, and Wilberforce
in his turn expressed his assent with further reservations to the views
of Romilly.[3]   How came the Evangelicals to temper their austere
code with so much mercy ?   Had they been influenced unconsciously
by humanitarian Liberalism ?   Possibly, but the Evangelicals could
defend themselves from the charge of inconsistency.   " The barbarous
custom of hanging," Wilberforce had written as early as 1787, " has
been tried too long, and with the success which might have been expected
from it.   The most effectual way to prevent greater crimes is by
punishing the smaller, and by endeavouring to repress that general
spirit of licentiousness, which is the parent of every species of vice."[4]
It was by a severe public morality that the Evangelicals hoped to render
the criminal code unnecessary.

The Abolition of the Slave Trade.

Among all the reforms of which the Evangelical party were justly
proud, the most glorious was the abolition of the slave trade.   The
agitation dated from the period between the American War of Independence and the French Revolution.   About 1788 the abolitionists
expected a speedy victory from the skilful organization of their

[1] An Act had already been passed in 1788 (28 Geo. III, cap. 48).   From *The Philanthropist*
we learn of four societies founded respectively in 1773, 1780, 1788 and 1799 to protect these
chimney sweeps (vol. v. pp. 341–2), and of another founded in 1803, of which the Bishop of
Durham was president (vol. vii. pp. 27 sqq.).   A Bill which passed the Commons in 1814 was
thrown out by the Lords.   See also H. of C., June 5, 25, 1817 (*Parl. Deb.*, vol. xxxvi. pp. 889–90,
1155–7).
[2] H. of C., May 1, 1810 (*Parl. Deb.*, vol. xvi. pp. 773–4) ;   *Life of Wilberforce*, vol. iii.
pp. 440, 444, 504.
[3] H. of C., March 13, 1812 (*Parl. Deb.*, vol. xxi. p. 1287).   " Most vilely used in the
newspapers," Wilberforce remarks in his *Journal*, March 23 (*Life*, vol. iv. p. 18).
[4] *Diary*, June 12, 1787 (*Life*, vol. i. p. 131).

mmittees of propaganda, the wide circulation of their pamphlets, their public meetings, their petitions. But the French Revolution postponed their triumph. The abolition of the slave trade was identified with total emancipation, and that in turn with Jacobinism. And the Convention seriously compromised the friends of the negroes with the British public, when it conferred French citizenship on Wilberforce in recognition of his campaign against the slave trade. Year after year from 1789 to 1800, Wilberforce and his friends made vain efforts to obtain even a gradual or a partial abolition. From 1800 to 1804 they kept silence, judging it the most prudent course to abstain from any further proposals. Later when the anti-Jacobin scare had become weaker their propaganda regained ground in Government circles. In 1805, a few months before his death, Pitt forbade by an Order in Council the importation of slaves into the colonies recently conquered. In 1806 the Fox-Grenville Ministry introduced a series of measures which led up to the passage in the following year of an Act of Total Abolition.[1]

The legislation thus obtained must not be allowed to remain a dead letter. To secure the execution of the Act Wilberforce and his allies founded the African Institution.[2] They obtained from the Government the establishment of a strict watch on the African coast to prevent an illegal traffic in slaves by British subjects. They obtained Government support for the colony they had established at Sierra Leone to present the world with an example of a European colony among a negro population which was not based on slavery.[3] They obtained further official action to prevent the illegal introduction of new slaves into the British West Indies, and the passage in 1811 of an Act of Parliament punishing traffic in slaves with fourteen years' deportation.[4] The naval victories of Great Britain rendered their task easier. Every time a French colony was occupied by the English, so much more ground was lost to the slave trade. And since the Governments of Spain and Portugal had become dependent on Great Britain, it might be hoped that Britain would force them to abolish the slave trade in their colonies. On the eve of peace the House of Commons by a unanimous vote enjoined the Cabinet to solicit from all the sovereigns of Europe the immediate and universal abolition of the slave trade.[5]

For the moment the resolution was fruitless. Lord Castlereagh, who had been one of the few obstinate opponents of abolition in the

---

[1] 46 Geo. III, cap. 52 ; 46 Geo. III, cap. 119 ; 47 Geo. III, sess. 1, cap. 36.

[2] *Life of Wilberforce*, vol. iii. p. 360 ; *Life of William Allen*, vol. i. pp. 85, 86, 91, 112, 138 sqq., 184 sqq., 223 sqq., 258.

[3] In 1791. *Life of Wilberforce*, vol. i. pp. 305, 307, 323. Its success was not great. See complaints in the Commons, April 8, 1811 (*Parl. Deb.*, vol. xix. pp. 731 sqq.).

[4] 51 Geo. III, cap. 23. Bill introduced by Brougham (H. of C., March 5, 1811, *Parl. Deb.*, vol. xix. pp. 233 sqq.).

[5] H. of C., May 2, 1814 (*Parl. Deb.*, vol. xxvii. p. 641).

Commons, was satisfied to obtain in the first Treaty of Paris the promise of Louis XVIII that he would take the necessary steps to effect abolition at the end of five years. Thus the slave trade was readmitted for a period of five years into all the colonies now restored to France from which it had been banished, as men had believed, for ever.[1] It was impossible to refuse recognition to a treaty definitely concluded and duly signed : but how then could Spain and Portugal be refused the five years' postponement granted to France ? All that Lord Liverpool and Lord Castlereagh could do to satisfy public opinion was to obtain at Vienna a prohibition of the slave trade along the entire west coast of Africa from Cape Formosa. But Napoleon on his return from Elba delivered the abolitionists from the impasse. To conciliate Liberal opinion he decreed the abolition of the slave trade. This made it easy, when the second Treaty of Paris was concluded with Louis XVIII, to avoid the mistake made in 1814 and to obtain immediate abolition.[2]

The abolition of the slave trade was now complete. We have called it the work of the Evangelicals. The statement, however, requires qualification. The Evangelicals had possessed allies whose power was far, very far, from negligible. That the Methodists, like Wesley himself, had always been convinced abolitionists scarcely detracts from the importance of the part played by the Evangelicals, for between the Evangelicals and the Methodists the relationship was extremely close. Evangelicalism was, after all, but a variety of Methodism. But side by side with the Methodists and the Evangelicals, the Dissenters of the old school had fought from the beginning for the abolition of the slave trade. The Baptists as a body had supported the movement.[3] So also had the Quakers. In 1787 two-thirds of the Abolitionist Committee were Quakers.[4] Now, among these Dissenters were many Socinians, many Rationalists, some who were practically Deists. In the United States the abolitionist movement was born of an alliance between the Quakers and the adherents of natural religion, Franklin, Tom Paine and their disciples. And since the opinion of the majority in the British Parliament from 1788, an opinion more or less openly expressed, was in favour of abolition, why was it that the arrival in office of Fox, an anti-clerical Whig, effected a settlement of the question within a

---

[1] See the important debates in the Commons on June 6, 1814 (*Parl. Deb.*, vol. xxvii. p. 1083). See also H. of L., June 27th ; H. of C., June 27th ; H. of L., June 28, 29, 30, July 11, 14, 1814 (*Parl. Deb.*, vol. xxviii. pp. 268, 299, 362, 417, 466, 655, 699).

[2] We realize the importance which the question possessed for the British Government when we see Lord Liverpool on July 7, 1815, little over a fortnight after Waterloo. urge Lord Castlereagh to insist on this point in his negotiations with King Louis (Yonge, *Life of Lord Liverpool*, vol. ii. p. 189.)

[3] Clarkson, *History of the Abolition*, vol. i. pp. 443, 568-9.

[4] Clarkson, *ibid.*, vol. i. pp. 110 sqq., 442, 444-5. For the part played by the Quakers, cf. *Life of William Allen, passim*.

few months ?[1] If Fox had not then become Premier, but the Tory party had held office continuously from 1784 to 1815, can we feel any confidence that one or other among Pitt's mediocre successors, the Duke of Portland, Perceval, or Lord Liverpool, would have taken the initiative and abolished the slave trade ? Would not Rose and Lord Castlereagh have opposed the reform ? And in view of the manner in which parliamentary institutions functioned in England at the beginning of the 19th century can we conceive a parliamentary majority capable of imposing so radical a measure on an apathetic or hostile administration ?

Obviously the Evangelical party cannot claim the sole glory of this decisive blow to slavery. Neither Thomas Clarkson nor Granville Sharpe belonged to the party, and their part in the abolitionist campaign was as considerable as that of Wilberforce himself. In fact Evangelicalism played here a rôle similar to that which it has played in all the humanitarian movements of modern England. It constituted a link, effected a transition between Anglicanism and Dissent, between the governing classes and the general public, as represented by the great middle class. It prevented the formation of a reactionary group and won the support of the gentry and nobility, sometimes even of a member of the Royal Family, for a movement initiated by shopkeepers and preachers. And the action of the party was decisive in securing from Parliament the legislation which embodied the dictates of the national conscience.

Till 1806 it had acted under great difficulties. There were so many prejudices to be overcome, so many interests were compromised. But from the passage of the decisive Act of 1806 the anti-slavery campaign enjoyed a free course. Henceforward the entire British Empire had an interest in the universal abolition of the slave trade. Failing this England would find that, carried away by an outburst of humanitarian zeal, she had acted against her commercial interest and had ruined her colonies for the profit of their rivals. Hence the universal outburst of public opinion in 1814 whose violence was so disconcerting to the lukewarmness of ministers and diplomatists. " I was not aware," wrote Wellington, whom long absence abroad had made a stranger in his native land " (till I had been some time here) of the degree of frenzy existing here about the slave trade."[2] " The nation," wrote Lord Castlereagh on the eve of signing the Treaty of Paris, " is bent upon this object. I believe there is hardly a village that has

---

[1] Cf. the speech of G. Philips, H. of C., June 27, 1814 (*Parl. Deb.*, vol. xxvii. p. 289), and Wilberforce, *Journal*, June 29, 1806 : " Oh that I might be the instrument of bringing him to the knowledge of Christ ! I have entertained now and then a hope of it. . . . I quite love Fox for his generous and warm fidelity to the Slave Trade cause " (*Life*, vol. iii. p. 268).

[2] Wellington to Sir Henry Wellesley, London, July 29, 1814 (*Suppl. Disp.*, vol. ix. p. 165). Cf. three letters from Wellington to Wilberforce, December 1814 (*Papers of Wilberforce*, pp. 144 sqq.).

not met and petitioned upon it : both Houses of Parliament are pledged to press it : and the ministers must make it the basis of their policy."[1]

THE JEWS, THE SCOTTISH PRESBYTERIANS, THE CATHOLICS, THE QUESTION OF CATHOLIC EMANCIPATION.

Other Religious Bodies. The Jews.

We have described the influence exercised by the Methodist revival on the religious life of the nation. We have witnessed the Dissenting sects awaking from their lethargy and increasing enormously the numbers of their adherents, and in the Establishment we have seen the Low Church party operative as an energetic minority. We have described the wider influence exercised by the Evangelical revival through the mediation of the churches upon the morality of the entire nation, the growth of a spirit at once philanthropic and conservative, a spirit of social reform and individual piety. But there existed in the United Kingdom religious bodies upon whom this Evangelical movement had exercised no influence whatsoever. What then had been their influence on the national intelligence and morality ?

Let us turn first to the Jews. There were scarcely more than 20,000 Jews in the country, domiciled in London and the large provincial towns.[2] But their numbers were being daily increased by the immigration of Jews from Portugal or Germany. Their wealth was constantly increasing and was no longer concealed. In every town where there was a Jewish colony, sumptuous edifices were replacing the old synagogues formerly hidden away in the slums.[3] They had long been exposed to the persecution which was their universal lot, and had not yet obtained the right of naturalization on the same terms as Christians. But their unpopularity was on the decline. In 1810 Cobbett, an anti-Semite, expressed his indignation that in modern dramas the part of moralist and virtuous sage was often given to a Jew.[4] The system of national loans had constantly compelled Chancellors of

[1] *Correspondence of Lord Castlereagh*, vol. x. p. 73, Lord Castlereagh to Sir Henry Wellesley, August 1, 1814.

[2] F. H. Goldsmid, *Remarks on the Civil Disabilities of British Jews*, 1830, pp. 69 sqq., and J. E. Blunt, *Jews in England*, 1830, p. 75, give the following statistics : In London, 18,000 ; in the rest of England, 9,000. Total 27,000. These figures, which are extremely arbitrary, were based on (1) The number of Jewish burials in London, (2) The supposition that the number of Jews in the provinces must be at least equal to half the number of the London Jews.

[3] For instance, the Steel Street synagogue was erected at Liverpool in 1808 (Baines, *Lancashire*, vol. iv. p. 107) ; the Severn Street synagogue at Birmingham in 1809 (Langford, *Century of Birmingham Life*, vol. ii. p. 237) ; and at Manchester a synagogue was built in Halliwell Street (Margoliouth, *The Jews in England*, vol. iii. p. 124).

[4] *Political Register*, October 8, 1818 (vol. xviii. p. 522). See especially Cumberland's Comedy, *The Jew*.

the Exchequer to have recourse to their assistance. Scions of the Whig aristocracy, plunged in debt, had opened to the Jews the door of good society in return for pecuniary advances. And, after all, anti-Semitic prejudice cannot be so strong in a community of traders and bankers, as in a nation whose organization is military, must be weaker in a country where a crowd of sects live peaceably side by side than in a country where the national religion is imposed on every citizen.

A series of famous names illustrates the importance of the English Jews in the life of their adopted country. To the business world belonged Gideon Sampson, the celebrated banker of the period of the Seven Years' War, whose son became an Irish peer, the two brothers Goldsmid, ruined in 1810, and Nathan Meyer Rothschild. Employed to arrange all financial transactions between Great Britain and the continental Governments, Rothschild in 1815 was king of the Stock Exchange. But it was not only in finance that Jews won distinction. Gomperz was a first-rate mathematician ; Isaac Disraeli, father of the future statesman, a distinguished man of letters ; Ricardo founded a new school of economics. But none of these men, whether financiers or thinkers, engaged in any distinctively Jewish propaganda, religious or political, peaceful or revolutionary. Often they even abandoned their religion. Gideon Sampson's family became Christian, Isaac Disraeli allowed his children to be baptized, Ricardo was himself a convert to Christianity.[1] In short, the Jews as a body appear to have exercised no collective influence on the religious life of Britain. And in this they were distinguished from two other religious societies, both of whom exerted a profound influence on the national character and which therefore we must consider at greater length. They were the Scottish Presbyterians and the Catholics of Great Britain and Ireland.

The Scottish Presbyterians.

North of the Tweed the Methodist propaganda exercised practically no effect. Wesley often visited Scotland. But his account in the *Journal* of these northern tours leaves us with the impression that he was in a foreign land whose manners and needs he had the greatest difficulty to understand.[2] Whitefield had preached in Scotland with more success. Aided by a number of Presbyterian ministers he had conducted several revivals on a large scale.[3] Nevertheless, Methodism

---

[1] According to Margoliouth (*The Jews in England*, vol. iii. p. 125), these conversions were numerous. In Manchester many Jews attended Socinian chapels instead of the synagogue, and even orthodox Christian churches.

[2] See especially *Journal*, June 2, 22, 23, 1766 (*Works*, vol. iii. pp. 239, 242).

[3] Tyerman, *Life of Whitefield*, vol. i. pp. 497 sqq. and *passim*.

took no root in Scotland. In 1815 there were at most 9,000 Scottish Methodists as against 200,000 in England.[1] In Scotland the sermons of Wesley and Whitefield did not, as in England, minister to the needs of the moment. Scotland had different religious traditions, other desires.

The history of Scottish Presbyterianism throughout the entire 18th century is the history of a stubborn contest between two powerful parties in the Church, the Popular party and the Liberal party. The Popular party was the orthodox party. It maintained the obligation for all members of the Church of Scotland to accept in its integrity the dogmatic system of Calvinism. But it was termed popular, because it also defended against the attacks of the opposite party the right of the faithful to elect their pastors. For Calvinism is pre-eminently democratic Christianity. What could the Methodist preachers from England do to assist the Popular party in the Presbyterian Church? They were either Wesleyans or disciples of Whitefield. In the former case they were Arminians, and on that ground alone tainted in the eyes of the Scottish pietists with heresy, if not with infidelity. In the latter case their orthodoxy indeed was beyond question. But they brought with them no new truth and could only offer to a national party, whose organization was already powerful, the unwelcome aid of the foreigner. And whether followers of Wesley or of Whitefield, they were either in favour of episcopacy or indifferent to forms of Church government. Hence their message, confined to the sphere of personal religion, was out of harmony with the republican zeal of the orthodox Presbyterians. And the abuses against which they waged war in England were on the whole absent in Scotland. There a clergy, provided with adequate stipends, performed its duties conscientiously.[2] Pluralism, non-residence, miserably paid curacies were unknown. Would the Methodists conduct Sabbatarian propaganda in Edinburgh or Glasgow? On this point Scotland set the example to England. The scrupulous observance in Scotland of the law of Sunday rest was proverbial.

Meanwhile, in the Presbyterian Church of Scotland the Popular party steadily lost ground to their Liberal opponents. An unending and embittered strife was engaged between the two parties in those half-clerical, half-lay assemblies by which the Church was governed. The 900 Scottish parishes were divided into districts, each with its lay president, its elder. And each parish was governed by a council of elders under the presidency, the " moderation " it was termed, of the minister of the parish. Several parishes were united in a presbytery,

---

[1] 6,000 members, 9,000 including children; 11 circuits, 18 preachers (Sinclair, *Scotland*, vol. iv. p. 9).

[2] An Act of 1810 (50 Geo. III, cap. 84) raised the minimum stipend of a Scottish minister to £150. The Treasury defrayed the necessary cost (Grub, *Ecclesiastical History of Scotland*, vol. iv. p. 156).

to which each parish sent a minister and an elder. The presbytery, acting as an ecclesiastical court of second instance, decided on appeal cases judged previously by the parochial councils. But its specific function was the approbation of candidates for ordination, the delivery of licenses to preach. Several presbyteries were grouped to form a provincial synod. At the head of the entire system was the General Assembly, which consisted of representatives of all the Presbyteries together with representatives of the royal boroughs and the universities.

The Assembly met once a year in Edinburgh. A Royal Commissioner, the head of a noble family, presided and opened the discussions by an " address from the throne." A debate on the address followed. The Assembly then proceeded to the transaction of business, either in committee or in full session, and it was decided whether a particular question of detail or principle, of organization or doctrine, should be submitted to the examination of the presbyteries. Since the Act of Union in 1707 had deprived Edinburgh of her Parliament, religious disputes had kept alive in Scotland party spirit and political passions. The meeting of the General Assembly played the same rôle in the social life of Edinburgh, as the meeting of Parliament in the social life of London.[1] Through the channel of the Synods and Presbyteries these disputes engaged the attention of the entire country and penetrated to the most remote districts. Thus religion joined hands with law to develop in Scotland a logical and juristic temper. Unlike English Evangelicalism, the Christianity of the Scottish Presbyterian was intellectual and argumentative. And his observation of the Scotch might well confirm Wesley in his dislike of theological disputes. Reasoning leads to rationalism and unbelief.

As was pointed out above, the dispute between the two parties in the Church of Scotland presented two aspects. One of these was the dogmatic. From the beginning of the 18th century the orthodox Calvinists suffered a series of defeats. The majority in the Assembly refused to condemn books delated by the orthodox party as Arian or Socinian, or even condemned books whose extreme Calvinism had been denounced by the Liberals. A few orthodox ministers seceded in their indignation from the national Church in 1733 and founded a sect which was soon itself split into hostile sects.[2] But their exodus only strengthened the position of the Liberal party within the Church. In the universities, the seminaries of the Scottish clergy, the triumph of the Liberals was even easier. Their predominance dates from 1737

[1] Cockburn, Life of Jeffrey, pp. 179 sqq.
[2] The Burghers and Antiburghers in 1746 (Grub, Ecclesiastical History of Scotland, vol. iv. p. 75). The Antiburghers were themselves split in 1804 by the formation of the Constitutional Associate Presbytery (id. ibid., pp. 150 sqq.) ; the Burghers, in 1799, by the formation of the Associate Presbytery (id. ibid., pp. 164–5).

when, in the University of Glasgow, Hutcheson began to teach natural religion and the ethics of the greatest happiness of the greatest number.[1] After this came the period of Adam Smith and Reid at Glasgow, of Robertson and Ferguson at Edinburgh. And though Reid refuted Hume he did not excommunicate him. He was, on the contrary, Hume's personal friend. " If you," he wrote to Hume, " write no more on morals, politics and metaphysics, I am afraid we shall be in want of subjects."[2] And Reid was a member of the party which protected Hume against the persecution of the bigots and prevented his citation before the bar of the Assembly, as the orthodox desired, to hear the solemn condemnation of his teaching.

Beside dogma, the dispute turned on ecclesiastical organization. Both parties accused each other of destroying the balance of the Presbyterian system. The Liberals charged the orthodox with attempting to transform a Presbyterian into a Congregational Church, by making each parish an autonomous religious unit with free choice of its pastor and uncontrolled by any superior authority. The Church of Scotland, they urged, was not an anarchic Church which fulfilled the ideal of the English Independents, but a democratic Church whose pastors and faithful were implicitly pledged to submit to the majority decisions of the hierarchy of Assemblies by which the Church was governed. The Popular party replied by declaring that they would willingly have obeyed the decisions of the Synods and the General Assembly, had not the original constitution of the Church been gravely tampered with in other respects. An Act of 1711 [3] passed in London had established in Scotland the system of lay patronage and given the Crown or the great landowners the right to appoint the parochial ministers. Therefore they were justified in their revolt against the decisions of a majority of pastors who had not been regularly elected by the people according to the original system. Here also in the 18th century the Liberal party triumphed. It was in vain that the Popular party secured certain modifications of the Act of 1711, and a resolution of the Assembly in 1736, that in the choice of ministers account should be taken of the wishes of the congregation.[4] The Liberals ignored the resolution of 1736, applied the Act of 1711 to the letter, forcibly imposed on unwilling parishes ministers chosen by lay patrons, and finally compelled a number of Popular ministers to secede and found a new separatist Church.

Such was the trend of events throughout the 18th century. The Liberals successfully maintained their position against the orthodox, and supported an aristocratic system of Church government because it protected them against the fanatical Calvinism of the lower classes.

---

[1] Rae, *Life of Adam Smith*, pp. 12–13 ; W. R. Scott, *Francis Hutcheson*, pp. 57 sqq.
[2] Hunt, *Religious Thought*, vol. iii. p. 324.   [3] 10 Anne, cap. 12.
[4] MacKerrow, *History of the Secession Church*, 1841, p. 97.

But at the close of the century the situation entirely changed. After the French Revolution opposition between the cause of the people and the cause of intellectual freedom was no longer possible. The Popular party insensibly tended to become the champion of the rights of the individual reason, and under the leadership of Sir Harry Moncrieff began to regain the ascendancy in the Church. In 1805 it was proposed to annul the nomination to the chair of mathematics at Edinburgh University of John Leslie, a doctor, who was accused of having adopted in his scientific treatises the philosophy of Hume. The affair made a powerful stir in Edinburgh society. And it was the Popular party who, in alliance with Dugald Stewart and the intelligentsia, won the victory for Leslie.[1] Does this mean that the Popular party in becoming Liberal repudiated its ancient Calvinist tradition? Far from it. In 1811 Thomas MacCrie published a *Life of John Knox*. The appearance of the book marked an epoch in the history of Scottish thought. Hitherto it had been the fashion in Liberal circles to depreciate the memory of the man who introduced Calvinistic puritanism into Scotland. Mr Crie's book was a defence of Knox by an enlightened democrat. It had scarcely appeared before the leading Liberal organ, the *Edinburgh Review*, took the book under its patronage.[2]

In this way came into being in the Scotland of the early 19th century a Rationalist Protestantism or Intellectual Calvinism, a faithful expression of the paradox inherent in the national mentality. For that mentality betrays a curiously double character. On the one hand Scotland is the home of philosophic idealism, of intuitionist metaphysics. But it is equally a country scrupulously observant of the religious traditions of the past, a country where every Sunday the current of social life ceases to flow, every street is empty, every church filled to overflowing. And yet in spite of these contrasts the national character is eminently homogeneous. All Scotsmen, whatever their religious persuasion, are Scottish and proud to be Scottish. They are all filled with admiration for their fellow countrymen as a body and with contempt for the English. Men whose attitude towards Christian dogma is of the freest feel an affection for religious customs which are as much

[1] For the affair of Leslie see a minutely detailed account in the *Edinburgh Review* for October 1805, No. 13, *Professor Stewart's Statement of Facts* (vol. vii. pp. 113 sqq.). The article is by Horner ; also Grub, *Ecclesiastical History of Scotland* (vol. iv. pp. 153–5). For the aversion with which the spirit which prevailed in the Scottish universities inspired the English Evangelicals, see *Life of Wilberforce* (vol. ii. p. 142). " Against Dundas I recommend and will cultivate in myself a propensity to direct hostilities. Reared as he has been in the small metaphysics of Scotland, and cramped by his country's imitative adoption of French philosophy, I can only see in the influence of such a man the approaches of French morals, French politics, French atheism " (*ibid.*, vol. iii. p. 229). " His connexion with Dundas was Pitt's great misfortune. Dundas was a loose man, and had been rather a disciple of the Edinburgh school in his youth."

[2] *Edinburgh Review*, July 1812, No. 39, Art. 1, *MacCrie's Life of John Knox* (vol. xx. pp. 1 sqq.). Remark, however, the qualifications of MacCrie's thesis made four years later by the same review, September 1816, No. 53, Art. 8, *Toleration of the Reformers* (vol. xxvii. pp. 163 sqq.).

national as religious. And those even who have rejected these practices are still attached more or less consciously, more or less avowedly to moral traditions inherited from the religion of their fathers. Instances are not far to seek. Thomas Erskine, the friend of Maurice and the Duchesse de Broglie, was a Free Thinker professing strange religious views peculiar to himself and taking no part in the worship of any religious body. But all his life long he would speak with emotion of the " Calvinian atmosphere " in which he had been brought up and of a religion " which makes God all and the thought of Him all in all, and makes the creature almost as nothing before Him."[1] Thomas Carlyle refused to enter the ministry. He no longer believed in Christianity. But he remained a mystic and was fully aware that he owed his mysticism to the education of his home, to the separatist sect, of which his parents were members, to the preachers of that sect—" men so like evangelists in modern vesture . . . I have nowhere met with among Protestant or Papal clergy in any country in the world," and to the humble village chapel, " rude, rustic, bare," . . . " but more sacred to me than the biggest cathedral."[2] And he will consecrate his entire life as a writer to the celebration of Puritan heroism. But the case of James Mill is perhaps the most typical. Mill was an avowed Free Thinker, an opponent of the Christian creed, especially in its Calvinist form. But read his son's picture of his father : " He had scarcely any belief in pleasure. . . . He deemed very few ' pleasures ' worth the price which, at least in the present state of society, must be paid for them. . . . He thought human life a poor thing at best, after the freshness of youth and of unsatisfied curiosity had gone by. . . . For passionate emotions of all sorts, and for everything which has been said or written in exaltation of them, he professed the greatest contempt. He regarded them as a form of madness."[3] This utilitarian is a Stoic, even an ascetic, and we cannot fail to recognize in his instinctive asceticism the stamp of his early education.

The life led by Thomas Carlyle and James Mill during their child-hood and youth was the life of every poor Scotsman who desired to win through to success. Parents, schoolmaster and minister determine that he shall enter the ministry. They teach him reading, writing, arithmetic, and elementary Latin. He is then sent to the University to prepare for Ordination. But as he follows the lectures of Dugald Stewart, Thomas Brown, Playfair and Leslie, the student feels his orthodoxy undermined, abandons all thought of the ministry, and in search of an arena more worthy of his ambition goes up to London, where he will become a political pamphleteer or journalist, a Government official, a statesman. He reaches the capital assured of his intellectual

[1] *Letters of Thomas Erskine*, ed. Hanna, 1877, vol. ii. pp. 321, 369.
[2] J. A. Froude, *Thomas Carlyle, A History of the First Forty Years of his Life*, vol. i. pp. 11-12.
[3] John Stuart Mill, *Autobiography*, pp. 48, 49.

and moral superiority to the English around him.   He does not distinguish between these two diverse species of excellence, and is apt therefore to believe that, if he appears better endowed intellectually than others, it is simply that his industry has enabled him to extract more profit from intellectual endowments common to all men alike. And this determination, as he is well aware, is the gift of his Calvinist education.   In this way the Scottish Presbyterians, hard on others, hard on themselves, unwearied thinkers, contributed to nineteenth-century England an element of intellectual virility which would have been wanting had the country been entirely abandoned to the emotionalism of the Wesleys and the Wilberforces.

The Catholics of Ireland and Great Britain.

Equally with the Scottish Presbyterians, though for different, indeed opposite reasons, Catholics turned a deaf ear to the Methodist preacher. Seventeen times Wesley crossed St. George's Channel and traversed on horseback the whole of Ireland.   The conversion of Catholic Ireland was his avowed ambition.   But whatever proselytes were made in Ireland by the Wesleyan, and still more by the Calvinistic Methodists, all belonged to the colonists of English or Scottish origin, were Protestants, Dissenters, Presbyterians, Quakers.[1]   Wesley himself admitted that out of every hundred Catholics ninety-nine remained faithful to the religion of their fathers.   In 1814 Wakefield declared that he did not know a single instance in which a Catholic had been converted.[2]

When the itinerant preachers of Methodism, nicknamed the Swaddlers or Cavalry Preachers, traversed the villages in pairs, preaching the one in English, the other in Gaelic, the Catholic priests forbade their flocks to attend their sermons.   If on occasion the prohibition were not obeyed, the priests took a whip and dispersed the audience.[3]   In 1816, in County Kerry, a woman named Catherine Healy called herself "the Holy Woman" and claimed to be the recipient of new revelations of a doctrinal character.   But the Bishop of Limerick condemned her in a pastoral letter read from the pulpit, and Catherine Healy found no disciples.[4]   What, indeed, was the need to which the Methodist evangel could appeal ?   The common people of Ireland, unlike the English poor, possessed a poor, resident and conscientious clergy, and a cult saturated with the miraculous, and speaking daily to the imagination.[5] Catholic devotion was impervious to Protestant piety.

---

[1] Letter to Blackwell, Dublin, August 13, 1747 (*Works*, vol. xii. p. 157).

[2] Wesley, *Journal*, August 15, 1747 (*Works*, vol. ii. p. 67) ; Wakefield, *Ireland*, vol. ii. p. 67.   The extreme paucity of sincere conversions among the common people does not contradict what has been said already of conversions for interested and political motives frequent in the 18th century among the wealthy.

[3] Wakefield, *Ireland*, vol. ii. p. 555.   [4] *Annual Register*, 1816, Chron., p. 26.

[5] See the interesting reflexions suggested by John Jebb to Southey when the latter was preparing his Life of Wesley (Forster, *Life of Jebb*, p. 134).

In the United Kingdom as a whole the Catholics were a minority, though a powerful minority, in Ireland a majority. What, then, was the proportion of Catholics to the entire population of Ireland ? It is difficult to answer with any approach to accuracy. According to Newenham they constituted four-fifths of the population; six-sevenths, or even more than that, according to Wakefield. Their numbers exceeded four, possibly five, millions.[1] Only in the north-east, in the district around Belfast, did the number of Protestants equal the number of Catholics. In the centre, the west, and the south the Protestants were a mere handful. This Catholic population consisted of an aristocracy, ancient and poverty-stricken, for it had been stripped of its possessions by the English invaders—an aristocracy ill-educated indeed, but men of honour and universally respected—a middle class comprising numerous wealthy members, the graziers, or middlemen of whom we have already spoken, a class which the poor hated and everyone despised, and finally a vast proletariat ignorant, miserably poor, superstitious and disorderly. The organization of the Church had preserved the form it had possessed when the Catholic Church was the official Church of the country.[2] There were twenty-six dioceses, governed by four archbishops and twenty-two bishops. The dioceses were regularly divided into parishes, which were served by 1,000 parish priests assisted by over 800 curates or coadjutors. The obedience displayed by the common people of Ireland towards their priests was regarded as the extreme of servility, and Protestant landlords often made use of the priest to maintain order. If a theft had been committed they applied to the priest to discover the thief. If a popular rising threatened, they would consult with the priest on the best means of preventing it. Nevertheless, the priests were well aware that the docility of their flocks was not unlimited.

If the Irish loved their clergy, it was not only because they were good Catholics ; it was also, and this perhaps was the predominant motive, because they saw in their priests the defenders of their nationality. To be sure the Catholic Church in Ireland did not possess the venerable privileges enjoyed by her Gallican sister. While Charles Edward, the Jacobite Pretender, lived, episcopal nominations were in his hands. And after his death the Irish officers, in the pay of the great continental Governments, had provided through the embassies many candidates with an effective recommendation. But about 1785 propaganda had decided that henceforward no account should be taken of recommendations by the laity. When a see fell vacant it was the custom to hold a

---

[1] For the number of Irish Catholics see Wakefield, *Ireland*, vol. ii. pp. 585 sqq., 591 sqq., 630–1. Cf. *Edinburgh Review*, July 1806 (vol. viii. p. 317) ; October 1807 (vol. xi. p. 122).

[2] For the organization of the Catholic Church in Ireland, see Wakefield, *Ireland*, vol. ii. pp. 548 sqq. ; also *Memoirs and Correspondence of Viscount Castlereagh*, vol. iv. pp. 97 sqq., *Abstract of the Returns of the several Roman Catholic Bishops of Ireland relative to the State of their Church*, 1801.

meeting of the clergy of the diocese which postulated the appointment of one of their number to replace the late prelate. The bishops of the province also met and submitted to the Pope a list of two or three names; and, practically speaking, the Pope always gave effect to these local recommendations.

Stripped of all their former possessions the Irish Catholic clergy depended exclusively for their support on the voluntary offerings of the faithful. Wakefield calculated that the Irish people, besides paying tithe to the Established Church, gave £500,000 to the Catholic Church.[1] The bishops received from the lower clergy what was termed the cathedraticum, procuration or proxy. Parish priests regularly contributed two guineas, curates a guinea. They increased their income by reserving to themselves *in commendam* the titles of one or two parishes, and by selling marriage licenses. From all these sources united the best-paid bishop in Ireland received an income of £550. The average episcopal income did not exceed £300.[2] The parish priests, who themselves kept curates at a fixed stipend, received the offerings of their parishioners at Christmas and Easter. These offerings, payable in money or in kind, and whose amount varied according to the means of each family, ran from a shilling to a guinea. At a marriage they received an additional offering. Half the year they dined with their parishioners. Their average income, which varied enormously in different localities, may be estimated at £65.[3] Obviously no legislation guaranteed to the Irish priest the enjoyment of this income. He was therefore financially dependent upon his flock.

At times this dependence was felt as a heavy burden. "The priest," in the words of a contemporary witness, "must follow the impulse of the popular wave, or be left behind on the beach to perish. . . . ' Live with me and live as I do ; oppress me not with superior learning or refinement, take thankfully what I choose to give you, and earn it by compliance with my political creed or conduct.' Such, when justly translated, is the language of the Irish cottager to his priest."[4] However diverse their respective constitutions, the Catholic Church in Ireland and the Presbyterian Church of Scotland possessed one feature in common. Both were national Churches. Lacking a Parliament to voice his desires the Irish like the Scottish peasant found in his Church the only society which opposed an impassable barrier to the encroachments of the central government. For the Irishman obedience to his priests was a means, and the only means at his disposal, of asserting

---

[1] *Ireland*, vol. ii. pp. 562–4.

[2] *Memoirs and Correspondence of Lord Castlereagh*, vol. iv. pp. 97–8.

[3] After the expenses of the curate have been deducted, who, in addition to his board and lodging, received a horse and £10 pocket money (*Memoirs and Correspondence of Lord Castlereagh*, vol. iv. p. 99 ; cf. pp. 130–1).

[4] Dr. Stock, Protestant Bishop of Waterford, quoted by Wakefield, *Ireland*, vol. ii. p. 557.

his independence against the Parliament at Westminster and the English Crown.

There was a constant stream of immigrants from Ireland to Scotland and England. Thus Irish Catholicism overflowed into Great Britain. There were several thousand Catholics in London and Liverpool. This was due to the large Irish immigration into these towns. But Great Britain possessed also its native Catholics, themselves divisible into two sections. One section consisted of the remnants of the pre-Reformation Catholic population in the Highlands of Scotland, in Lancashire and Staffordshire, which had remained faithful to the old religion through two centuries of persecution. The other section was composed of old families among the nobility and gentry scattered throughout all the counties of England. Each of these families, with its Catholic servants and tenants and the chaplain who formed part of the family, consituted a little island of Catholicity amid the ocean of Protestantism. The total number of Catholics, according to calculations whose accuracy is merely approximate, was about 60,000 for England, 30,000 for Scotland.[1]

To be sure a tiny minority. Nevertheless, the Catholics of Great Britain, whose leaders were the heads of noble families of the highest rank and most ancient lineage, regarded themselves and were regarded by others as occupying a position far superior to the Irish proletariat, as the flower of Catholicism in the United Kingdom.[2] Since the relaxation of the penal laws many English Catholics no longer made it a point of honour to be loyal to the faith of their fathers. Among these was the Duke of Norfolk, the friend of Fox and one of the Whig leaders. But even the large majority, who regarded conversion to Protestantism as dishonourable, were, when all is said, country gentlemen, closely akin in ideas and manners to their Protestant neighbours.[3] They were equally attached to the Throne, since there was no longer a Catholic claimant, equally attached also to the English traditions of

[1] These figures are mere guesswork; they are based on the calculations made by the Rev. Joseph Berington in his work *The State and Behaviour of English Catholics from the Revolution to the Year 1780*, 1780, p. 111. But even for 1780 the correctness of Berington's figures is doubtful. See the contradictory figures supplied in 1773 and in 1786 by the Vicars Apostolic ot London (Ward, *Dawn of the Catholic Revival*, p. 30). Between 1780 and 1818 the Irish immigration may have increased the number of Catholics in England. Later between 1830 and 1840 Manning and Gladstone estimated the number of Catholics in England and Wales as over 200,000, as possibly even 300,000 (Shane Leslie, *Henry Edward Manning, His Life and Labours*, 1921, pp. 35, 63). For the year 1840 they obtained the figure of 223,987 by multiplying by 137·5 the number of Catholic marriages. For Scotland the total of 30,000 is given by Amherst (*History of Catholic Emancipation*, vol. i. p. 279). Sinclair (*Scotland*, vol. iv. p. 9) puts the figures at 27,000, and in the very same work, vol. i. p. 21, at 50,000, possibly a printer's error for 30,000.

[2] Berington, *State and Behaviour* . . . 1780, p. 120 : 8 Peers, 19 Baronets, and about 150 gentlemen of landed property.

[3] Cobbett, *Rural Rides*, October 30, 1821. "To be sure the Roman Catholic religion may, in England, be considered as a *gentleman's religion*, it being the most *ancient* in the country."

self-government, equally opposed to every kind of bureaucracy whether in Church or State. What had been the organization of the Catholic Church in England under the penal laws, how was it still organized in 1815 ? There were no provinces or regular dioceses. Four Vicars Apostolic, appointed by Rome, administered without the normal forms of government the four districts into which England was divided. There was no parochial organization within the district, and the Vicar Apostolic had but a vague idea of the number of priests under his authority. The priests were chaplains attached to the nobility and gentry. They had been chosen by the wealthy laymen, who provided their board and lodging, not by the bishops. It was therefore but natural that these laymen came to regard themselves as the protectors of their Church, authorized by the very fashion in which English Catholicism was organized to control ecclesiastical affairs.

When at the close of the 18th century they formed a committee to obtain the abolition of the penal laws, they were with difficulty persuaded to admit a clerical minority to their deliberations. They declared themselves prepared to take an oath, formulated by themselves, which refused the Pope all temporal jurisdiction, definitely restricted his spiritual authority, and expressly condemned his claim to infallibility. They drew up an entire scheme for the reform of the ecclesiastical organization, and demanded that the Vicars Apostolic, too directly subject to the *curia* be replaced by regular bishops, whose canonical status would render their authority beyond dispute. These bishops were to be appointed by the inferior clergy, and even by the laity. Certain members of the committee laid their plans before the Duke of Norfolk. He gave them a sympathetic hearing, but added his ironical congratulations : " I applaud you for this ; it is just what I ought to wish. You are following my example. You will soon become good Protestants ; *I have been only thirty-five years beforehand with you.*"[1] These Cisalpine Catholics, as they termed themselves in distinction from the Ultramontanes, were the more impatient for entire emancipation in proportion to their sense of kinship in thought and feeling with their Protestant compatriots.

In fact Catholic Emancipation had already made very considerable progress. The application of the severe penal laws, which from the beginning of the 18th century had weighed heavily on the Catholics of the three kingdoms, was already lenient in the early years of the

---

[1] *Life and Speeches of Daniel O'Connell*, vol. i. p. 372. James Barry's *Letter to the . . . Society for the Encouragement of Arts* (1793) is a typical expression of English Cisalpinism. Barry attacks the great rulers who founded English Protestantism, Henry VIII and Elizabeth (pp. 16–17), shows how disastrous to the Papacy itself had been the claim to political power (pp. 24–5), quotes a number of Catholic authorities in favour of the principle of popular sovereignty (pp. 57–8), points out the existence of a democratic Catholicism before the Reformation, and its survival in the Swiss cantons, and expresses his hope of the establishment in France of a Gallican and democratic Catholicism (pp. 67 sqq.).

reign of George III. Informations were not lodged against those who had infringed the provisions of the penal code, and when on occasion informers forced a prosecution, the judges taxed their ingenuity to mitigate the law by decisions as favourable as possible to Catholics. From 1771 a series of Relief Acts had been passed to modify the penal laws. In Ireland an Act of 1771 permitted Catholics for the first time, on conditions defined by the Act, to hold land on a long lease. An Act of 1774 provided for Catholics a special form of the oath of allegiance. An Act of 1778 placed Catholics on an equality with Protestants as regards the ownership and leasehold of land. Two Acts of 1782 granted Catholics freedom of worship and education, and an Act of 1793 admitted them to the franchise and to commissions in the Army below the rank of colonel. In England an Act of 1778 [1] provided for Catholics an oath modelled on the Irish formula of 1774, and repealed several provisions of the penal laws. Henceforward a Catholic could acquire land, by inheritance or purchase, and could open a school without incurring the penalty of imprisonment for life. No longer would the priest, the bishop, the Jesuit be at the mercy of the informer. An Act of 1791 [2] completed the Act of 1778, and on the fulfilment of certain legal formalities granted Catholics, clerical and lay, freedom of worship. In 1793 [3] the concessions secured by the English Catholics were extended to the Catholics of Scotland.

Was this complete civil emancipation? No. In Scotland Catholics still lacked the right to open schools. Neither in England nor in Scotland had they the right to celebrate in public their marriages and funerals. The Catholic service was performed at the house. In church, or at the grave, a clergyman conducted the service. Was it complete political emancipation? Far from it. A Catholic could be a barrister but he could not be judge of a High Court. In Great Britain he neither possessed the franchise nor could he hold even a subordinate rank in the Army or the Navy. Nowhere in the United Kingdom had he the right to command a regiment or a vessel of the line, to occupy a post in the administration, to be elected to the Commons, to take his seat in the Lords. But after such rapid progress within the space of twenty years was not the work of emancipation on the verge of completion? Since the opening of the 19th century the question had been agitated, and had absorbed a large part of the attention of statesmen. The influence of the Catholics of the United Kingdom on the intellectual

---

[1] 18 Geo. III, cap. 60.   [2] 31 Geo. III, cap. 32.

[3] 33 Geo. III, cap. 44. The oath exacted from Catholics is identical in the Irish Act of 1774, the English Acts of 1778 and 1791, and the Scottish Act of 1793. But a formula by which Catholics dissociated themselves from the cause of the Jacobite pretenders disappeared after 1791. On the other hand the formulæ in which Catholics repudiated certain doctrines of intolerance towards heretics and infidels, " commonly attributed to the Church of Rome," were modified in the Scottish oath of 1793, which mentioned heretics only, not infidels. Two later Acts of 1803 (43 Geo. III, cap. 30) and 1813 (53 Geo. III, cap. 128) were concerned only with matters of detail. Their object was to harmonize conflicting provisions of the older Acts.

life of the nation was slight,[1] on the economic even slighter.[2] But indirectly they affected profoundly the fate of England. For the question of Catholic emancipation paralysed, and, as long as it remained unsolved, would continue to paralyse the efforts of reformers.

The Problem of Emancipation, its various Aspects.

When in the year 1800 Pitt carried through the Union of Great Britain and Ireland he hoped to make the Union popular with the Irish Catholics by granting to them and to their English and Scottish co-religionists complete political emancipation, including the right to sit in Parliament. But he was thwarted by the obstinate refusal of King George, and resigned office. In 1807 the ministry of All the Talents made another but a less radical attempt to give relief to Catholics by opening to them all ranks in the Army and Navy. But not only did George III refuse his consent to the introduction of the Bill, he even demanded from the Cabinet a promise never to bring it forward again, and the ministry resigned. Year after year a Catholic petition was presented to Parliament asking for emancipation. In 1812 a majority of 129 in the Commons voted that the petition be taken into consideration, and in the Lords a motion in favour of the Catholics was only lost by one vote. At this moment there was a split in the Tory Party, and the Opposition seemed on the eve of taking office. It was the universal belief that as 1806 had witnessed the abolition of the slave trade, 1812 would be the year of Catholic emancipation, and the favourable motion in the Commons would be speedily followed by an Act to give it effect. But a Bill brought forward in the Commons in 1813 failed to pass the House. Continental victories had secured the position of the Cabinet, and once more Catholic emancipation was postponed. Would the postponement be a lengthy one? And what were the obstacles opposed by public opinion to a reform whose ultimate adoption seemed inevitable?

Were these obstacles of a religious character? Obviously Catholicism and Protestantism represent opposite and mutually exclusive views of Church government and Christian dogma, indeed of religion and life as a whole. And the very period when Parliament initiated a policy of tolerance for Catholics witnessed an outbreak of Protestant feeling in England. Two years after the Relief Act of 1778 the Gordon Riots broke out against Catholics, and for several days filled

---

[1] The historian Lingard, the novelist Mrs. Inchbald, the painters Barry and Mulready, the historian Charles Butler, the theologian and archæologist Joseph Milner, are the most eminent Catholic names during this period. But the two celebrated actors, Kemble and his sister Mrs. Siddons, no doubt did more to make their Church popular than all these intellectuals together.

[2] Berington, *State and Behaviour* . . . 1780, p. 121. " At this hour there are not more than two Catholics of any note who are even engaged in mercantile business."

the streets of London with bloodshed and incendiarism.   Many people accused the Methodists of having fomented the riot.   Had not Wesley uttered a public protest against any amelioration of the penal laws ? [1] When the Relief Act of 1791 was under discussion, the abolitionist leader, Granville Sharpe, founded a Protestant Union to oppose the Bill.[2]   But we must not forget that since these events twenty-five, and thirty-five years respectively, had passed by and several causes had conspired to render English Protestants more tolerant towards their Catholic fellow countrymen.

In the first place, the apologists of Protestantism presented their religion as essentially individualist in character, and delighted to identify, if only in word, the cause of Protestantism with the cause of freedom of conscience.   To justify the persecution of Catholics they were obliged to employ very subtle arguments.   And secondly, the most purely Protestant among the Protestants were the Dissenters who, like the Catholics, though not to the same extent, had been victims of Anglican intolerance.   In 1807 the Tories had run an election on the " No-Popery " cry, and had worked hard to detach the Dissenters from the Whigs by appealing to their anti-Catholic prejudices.   But the Dissenters had been rewarded for their Tory vote, by a Tory attempt to carry an Act restricting their freedom of organization. And there was yet a third factor at work, perhaps the most influential of the three.   The anti-religious philosophy of the 18th century, and the French Revolution which embodied that philosophy in action, had imparted a new aspect to the problem of toleration.   The modern Babylon was no longer Rome but Paris, Anti-Christ no longer the Pope but Voltaire.   Thus the antipathy felt by the English Protestant for absolute and open infidelity led him to regard with more indulgence all forms of religion and especially Catholicism.   " True enough," wrote Hannah More in one of her anti-Jacobin tracts, " the French had but a poor sort of religion, but bad is better than none." [3]   Among the " Saints," Henry Thornton from 1805 was a convinced advocate of emancipation, and Wilberforce, who had always been disposed to extend the fullest toleration to Catholics,[4] in 1812 and in 1813 supported their admission to Parliament.[5]   In circles widely remote from these there was a movement of reaction against the eighteenth-century ideal, classical, profane, and pagan.   And the reaction favoured Catholicism.   In the Christian and Catholic Middle Ages men of

---

[1] See the account given by Amherst, *History of Catholic Emancipation*, vol. i. pp. 145 sqq. ; also Wesley, *Works*, vol. x. pp. 153 sqq.

[2] Charles Butler, *Historical Memoirs*, vol. iv. p. 411.

[3] Hannah More, *Village Politics*.

[4] See his attempt in 1797 to open the militia to Catholics (*Life*, vol. ii. pp. 222–3). " My own final judgment," he wrote in 1808 in his *Journal*, " is not made up on the Catholic question.   I strongly incline to their coming into Parliament, though not to their seeing with other men's (priests') eyes " (*Life*, vol. iii. p. 362).

[5] See his letter to William Hey, February 22, 1813 (*Life*, vol. iv. pp. 95 sqq.).

letters discovered new sources of inspiration. Wordsworth in the *Excursion* contrasts with the hell of the modern factory the peace of the ancient cathedral,[1] admires and describes Gothic ruins,[2] and is indignant at the thought of the disorders which accompanied the Reformation, of the altars destroyed, the religious scattered. In Scott's *Waverley* all the Calvinists are ridiculous or odious ; Charles Edward, the Catholic Pretender, is on the contrary idealized, and the heroic Flora MacIvor, also a Catholic, concludes the novel with her entrance into a Benedictine convent.[3]

Wordsworth and Scott were notwithstanding Tories, and the Tories opposed Catholic emancipation. In ecclesiastical affairs their legislation was guided by the opinions of the High Church party. Why, then, did the High Church party adopt this attitude of determined hostility to Catholicism ? Of the two parties which contested the government of the Church of England was it not the High Church which tended to counteract the Protestantism of the Establishment, and which insisted on precisely those aspects of the Anglican ideal which approximated to the Catholic ? But if in 1815 one or two theologians,[4] Alexander Knox [2] or Daubeny, had reached this philosophic presentation of Anglicanism, they were a mere handful.[5] Three-quarters of a century after the Low Church revival the High Church was still asleep. And it would not awake from its slumber till the realization of Catholic emancipation had suddenly altered the respective strength of the two political parties, and that in turn had caused a profound revolution in the national life. Meanwhile the High Church was a party without an ideal. And a party of men in office. For the Anglican bishops a rival hierarchy of Catholic prelates was a disagreeable prospect. Essentially also a Government party. The arguments with which the High Church opposed Catholic emancipation were not theological but political.

The Catholic Church, urged the opponents of emancipation, was not a Christian sect like the others and must therefore be submitted to a special control. In virtue of a constitution at once autocratic and bureaucratic, its entire structure rested on a foundation of passive obedience to an absolute ruler, who was at the same time a foreign

---

[1] Book VIII.   [2] Book VIII.

[3] The *Quarterly Review*, January 1814 (vol. x. pp. 404–5) remarks that " a . . . reasonable apprehension is that to which many Protestants are not insensible, that the cause of Popery will be eventually a gainer, from the play which its system gives to religious feeling," but appears in this to be thinking chiefly of Germany. " One of the remarkable effects of mysticism has been that some of its principal supporters in the North of Germany have gone over to the Roman Catholic opinions."

[4] Typical expressions of their standpoint will be found in *Thirty Years' Correspondence between Knox and Jebb*; letters from Knox to Jebb, June 13, 1811 ; January 5, March 8, September 13, 1813 ; and from Jebb to Knox, March 7, 1813.

[5] See for this group the copious details, too copious one is inclined to think in view of its practical insignificance, in Overton, *English Church in the 19th Century*, pp. 25 sqq.

monarch. The Catholic Church was and desired to be a State within the State. It was all very well for Catholics to declare that their obedience was due to the Pope only in spiritual matters. Between spiritual and temporal the line was difficult to draw, and Catholics left the Pope to draw it. Was it not an article of the Catholic faith that no one was bound to keep faith with heretics ? That the Pope could dispense Catholics in advance from the obligation of their oaths, and absolve them for the guilt of their violation ? Of what use was it to extract from Catholics the express repudiation of these tenets, when their affirmations, even when sanctioned by oath, must always be suspect ? Was it prudent to abandon the penal laws which had freed England for a century from the troubles occasioned in so many Continental nations by the struggle between the Clergy and the Government ? But in the course of the last fifty years these arguments had obviously lost much of their old plausibility. The memories of the *Armada*, blest by the Pope, and of the two last Stuarts, Catholics and traitors to the nation, had begun to fade into the distance. It was in vain that a sour fanatic like Dr. Duigenan, or a pedant like Sir John Cox Hippisley, insisted on the danger to national unity to be feared from the political interference of the Holy See. The House of Commons heard their harangues with a growing impatience, and they caused even more amusement than irritation. For the European situation had entirely changed.

Between 1792 and 1795 England had witnessed the arrival on her shores of the entire body of the French clergy proscribed by the Jacobins, and had taken pride in extending to them a lavish hospitality. Scarcely fifteen years after the Gordon Riots a public subscription for the exiled priests brought in £33,775. The Government, with the approval of Parliament and of public opinion, granted them a regular monthly allowance—£10 to bishops, £1 15s. to ordinary priests. The religious houses founded on the Continent in penal times, at Paris, Douai, St. Omer, and Liège for the education of Catholic children, or as seminaries for the English Catholic clergy, were transported to England with the connivance of the Government, and this monastic revival aroused only a few feeble protests in the Commons.[1]

In Scotland, the Government appointed a Catholic chaplain to a regiment of Catholic Highlanders, and even made grants to the Catholic clergy and their two seminaries. In Ireland, Parliament voted an annual grant of £8,000 to the new seminary at Maynooth for the training of the Irish priesthood.[2] When, in 1800, the Cardinal of York, the last representative of the Stuarts, was compelled to leave Rome by the French occupation, and lost his ecclesiastical revenues, the King,

[1] Ward, *Dawn of the Catholic Revival*, vol. ii. pp. 1 sqq., 69 sqq., 163 sqq. ; H. of C., May 22, 1800 (*Parl. Hist.*, vol. xxxv. pp. 340 sqq.).

[2] Wakefield, *Ireland*, vol. ii. pp. 446 sqq.

on Pitt's recommendation, granted him a pension of £4,000.[1] How could one speak seriously of a Catholic peril when the Catholic Church, spoiled and oppressed, was a pensioner on the charity of Protestant England ? Surely such a Church deserved pity rather than hatred.

There followed in France the autocracy of Napoleon. After an attempt by the Concordat and the organic articles to subordinate the French clergy to the civil Government, Napoleon finally carried the Pope into France, with the intention of making him the instrument of his designs. Napoleon's policy supplied the English anti-Catholics with new arguments. Suppose, they urged, Pius VII died in his prison, and Napoleon secured the election to the Papacy of his uncle, Cardinal Fesch, would not this involve the total subjection of the Holy See to the Empire, and consequently open to French influence an entrance into the Kingdom through the Irish and English Catholics ? To this the advocates of emancipation replied that if the Papacy submitted to such bondage the Catholic world would withdraw its obedience from a Government thus degraded, that a slavery so complete was hardly conceivable, and that even Cardinal Fesch, once Pope, would be in a position to defy the Emperor.[2]

Then came the overthrow of the French Empire, and at once all these fears became groundless. Pius VII returned to his capital under the protection of the British Army. His Secretary of State, Cardinal Consalvi, had long been the friend of English statesmen.[3] It was to the influence of Lord Castlereagh that he owed his seat at the Congress of Vienna beside the Allied sovereigns and their representatives. To secure the integrity of its territory against the ambitions of Austria the Holy See counted on the support of the British Cabinet.[4] The Pope had become the client of England.

Should we conclude from these facts that the political objections to emancipation were entirely chimerical ? This would be the case were our statement complete. But one objection has been left unexamined. The vast majority of Catholics in the United Kingdom were Irish. Therefore whenever the question of Catholic emancipation was raised it involved the Irish question, and for British statesmen Ireland was the subject of legitimate anxiety.

The Emancipation Question and the Irish Question.

In Ireland Pitt had sought the simultaneous settlement of the political and of the religious problem. If he deprived Ireland of her

[1] Lord Stanhope, *Life of Pitt*, vol. ii. p. 182.
[2] *Life and Speeches of Daniel O'Connell*, vol. ii. p. 234.
[3] *Memoirs and Correspondence of Lord Castlereagh*, vol. iv. p. 224, letter from the Rev. P. Macpherson to Sir J. C. Hippisley, Rome, July 18, 1800.
[4] *Edinburgh Review*, December 1816, No. 54, Art. 2, *Catholic Question*, vol. xxvii. p. 321.

Parliament, he intended in return to grant Irish Catholics the right to sit in both Houses of the United Parliament. And he wished at the same time to establish both Irish Catholicism and Irish Presbyterianism, which was very powerful in the north-east of Ireland. The State would pay the Catholic priests and the Presbyterian ministers, and would obtain in return a control over the choice of both. In this way the priests and ministers, instead of fomenting rebellion as they had done during the previous decade, would become Government officials with an interest in the maintenance of order.

The English Government expected the Presbyterians to raise difficulties. Jealously republican, accustomed to regard their Church as a strictly independent community, they were little likely to accept Government control. With the Catholics Pitt hoped for an easier success,[1] for the laity were not accustomed to control the choice of their clergy, and the clergy accepted Pitt's scheme. Ten bishops, and among them two archbishops who had met by accident at Dublin in 1799, had drawn up, signed and transmitted to Lord Castlereagh a formal declaration to that effect.[2] The name of every nominee to a bishopric was to be submitted for the approval of the British Government before it was sent up to Rome. Every appointment of a parish priest was to be notified by the bishop with an attestation that he had taken the oath of allegiance. But when Pitt's Government failed to open to Irish Catholics the Westminster Parliament the prelates changed their attitude. They dared not brave Irish public opinion by accepting the revenues held out to them at the very moment when the hopes of their lay co-religionists had been disappointed.[3] Nevertheless in spite of repeated failures the British Government continued to expect good results from the Union. It must, they thought, accustom Irish and English Catholics to common action in defence of their common interests. " It may," wrote Sir Arthur Wellesley in 1807 to Lord Hawkesbury, " have the effect of moderating their party violence ; at all events it will give us an additional channel for knowing their secrets."[4] Events very quickly gave these hopes the lie.

In 1808 the secret, hitherto successfully guarded, of the negotiations between Lord Castlereagh and the ten bishops on the eve of the Union leaked out. John Milner, Vicar Apostolic of the Midland District and the London agent of the Irish bishops, admitted that the report was well founded, and that in 1799 ten Irish prelates had in fact accepted a Government veto on episcopal appointments. The supporters of Catholic emancipation, Henry Grattan and Lord Ponsonby, made

[1] *Memoirs and Correspondence of Lord Castlereagh*, vol. iv. pp. 223 sqq., Lord Castlereagh's letter to Addington, July 21, 1802.
[2] The text will be found in Wakefield, *Ireland*, vol. ii. pp. 514–15.
[3] H. of C., May 13, 1813, Lord Castlereagh's speech (*Parl. Deb.*, vol. xxvi. p. 155).
[4] Yonge, *Life of Lord Liverpool*, vol. i. p. 263.

haste to argue that the fears expressed by its opponents were without foundation, and that complete equality of legal rights could be granted to Catholics without imperilling national unity. But a division was immediately revealed among the Catholics of the United Kingdom.

The more wealthy Catholics, noblemen, gentlemen, and members of the middle class, landowners, barristers and merchants, were eagerly waiting for the passage of the Act which would enable them to take an active share in the political life of the nation. They had not the least objection to grant the Government in return a veto on episcopal nominations. There was nothing in such a veto that conflicted with Catholic discipline. In Canada the British Government, as the successor of France since the Seven Years' War, actually appointed the Catholic bishops.

Poor Catholics, on the other hand, had no direct interest in such legislation. They could never become officers in high command, judges or members of Parliament. And in Ireland these poor Catholics were opposed to the veto for a very good reason, not religious, but political. The veto would give the Government in London a control over the choice of the Irish clergy, and this would complete the Act of Union by a further assault upon their national freedom.

A party was formed in Ireland whose programme was opposition to the veto. Its leader, an orator whose eloquence never flagged, was the young barrister, Daniel O'Connell. O'Connell refused to divorce the cause of Catholic emancipation from the cause of Irish emancipation. If one must be sacrificed to the other, it should be the former, not the latter cause.[1] He proved himself so skilful an agitator that he intimidated the Irish hierarchy. Less than four months after the debate in Parliament, during which the secret of their concessions had been made public, the Irish bishops, gathered in a meeting convened for the purpose, declared unanimously that it was inexpedient to make any change in the canonical form hitherto followed in the appointment of Catholic bishops.[2] The Popular party, led by O'Connell, with its programme of unyielding resistance, made continual progress at the expense of the aristocratic and moderate party, led by Lord Fingall. When in June 1812 the Opposition secured the passage by the Commons of a motion in favour of Catholic emancipation, which was carried by a considerable majority, it revealed a glaring divergence between the Catholics and their supporters in Parliament. The latter had obtained

[1] *Life and Speeches of O'Connell*, vol. i, p. 86, speech delivered on December 29, 1810 : " We would fain excite a national and Irish party capable of annihilating any foreign oppressor whatsoever " ; also pp. 54–5, speech on September 18, 1810 : " Nay, were Mr. Perceval to-morrow to offer me the Repeal of the Union upon the terms of re-enacting the entire penal code, I declare from my heart and in the presence of my God that I would most cheerfully embrace his offer."

[2] *Edinburgh Review*, November 1810, No. 33, Art. 1, *Catholic Question* (vol. xvii. pp. 1 sqq., especially 26 sqq.).

their majority by accepting conditional emancipation—emancipation accompanied by a system of securities. The overwhelming majority of Irish Catholics—that is to say, the overwhelming majority of the Catholics of the United Kingdom—desired and were actually demanding at a series of extremely violent meetings the total and *unconditional* repeal of the penal laws.[1]

During the spring of 1813 a Catholic Emancipation Bill was introduced in the Commons. The original draft was the work of Grattan, but Canning added a number of articles embodying the desired securities, and Grattan accepted these articles in the belief that it was impossible to pass the Bill on any other terms.[2] What, then, were these securities? First, an oath very long and detailed and directly inspired by " Cisalpinism " ; secondly, the establishment of a Board of Commissioners, to be chosen by the Crown from the leading representatives of British Catholicism, the Peers and great landlords. When Rome proposed a successor to a vacant bishopric the Board should possess the right to examine his credentials, and after such examination accord or refuse the candidate the testimonial of loyalty and peaceable behaviour, without which he could not be appointed ; and all bulls and other Papal documents must be submitted to the examination of the Board, which would refuse to permit their circulation, if in the opinion of the Board they were opposed to the law of the land. Probably this scheme also was of Cisalpine inspiration. The Catholic gentry would have been delighted to introduce into the administration of the Church the principle of aristocratic self-government after the approved British pattern. Generally speaking, all, or almost all, the English Catholics accepted Canning's plan, and among them three of the four Vicars Apostolic. But Catholic Ireland was in arms. O'Connell expelled the " vetoists " from the Catholic Board, a committee that had been formed in Ireland for Catholic defence.[3] The bishops denounced the scheme as schismatic.[4] It was impossible, urged the anti-vetoists, to regulate the relations between Church and State without an agreement with the Pope, and the Pope, then the prisoner of Napoleon, was inaccessible.

But even in the Pope's absence Rome possessed an ecclesiastical authority for the transaction of current business. In February 1814 the English statesmen and the Catholic moderates obtained from Mgr. Quarantotti, the head of propaganda, an unreserved approbation

---

[1] Meeting of June 18, 1812 (*Life and Speeches of O'Connell*, vol. i, pp. 168 sqq.).

[2] For the text of Grattan's Bill, see H. of C., April 30, 1813 (*Parl. Deb.*, vol. xxv. pp. 1108 sqq.) ; and for Canning's additional articles, H. of C., May 11, 1813 (*Parl. Deb.*, vol. xxvi. pp. 88 sqq.). For the final text of the Bill after its amendment in committee, see H. of C., May 20, 1813 (*Parl. Deb.*, vol. xxvi, pp. 270 sqq.).

[3] Catholic Meeting at Cork, August 30th (*Life and Speeches of O'Connell*, vol. ii. pp. 7 sqq.).

[4] General Meeting of the Roman Catholic Prelates of Ireland, May 27, 1813 (*Life and Speeches of O'Connell*, vol. i. p. 320).

of the Bill of 1813. This, however, altered nothing. The Irish intransigents refused to admit his competence, and appealed to the Sovereign Pontiff in person.[1]   Indeed, they went even further, and declared that if the Pope were to ratify Quarantotti's decree they would not yield. " I am sincerely a Catholic," declared O'Connell, " but I am not a *Papist*. . . . In spiritual matters, too, the authority of the Pope is limited. . . . Let our determination never to assent reach Rome."[2]

Meanwhile Pius VII returned to Rome. Anti-vetoists and vetoists dispatched rival deputations to lay their case before him. The anti-vetoists were represented by Murray, coadjutor of the Archbishop of Dublin, and by John Milner ; the vetoists by Poynter, Vicar Apostolic of the London district. Pius VII found himself in a difficult position. For all their unguarded language, the Irish Catholics were defending the right of the Catholic Church to unrestricted freedom. On the other hand, the Pope had no desire to quarrel with the British Government, nor, indeed, could he afford a breach. In April 1815 a letter from Cardinal Litta, the prefect of propaganda, attempted to hold a balance between the two parties. The oath was rejected and with it the Board of Commissioners. But a modified form of veto was suggested. From the list of candidates proposed for every vacant bishopric the Crown should have the right to demand the elimination of a certain number of names, but must always leave enough names for the Holy See to make a choice. But even this was too great a concession for Irish intransigence. O'Connell accused Milner of betraying the cause of those whom he represented in Rome ;[3] and the Irish bishops, while protesting their veneration for the Sovereign Pontiff, unanimously expressed their persistent anxiety at " a determination of His Holiness adopted, not only without our concurrence, but in direct opposition to our repeated resolutions." [4]

" The English do not dislike us as Catholics ; they simply hate us as Irish." In speaking thus [5] O'Connell no doubt described correctly the true character of English hostility to Catholicism. The speaker himself by his agitation did much to strengthen the anti-Irish prejudice, and his semi-religious, semi-political agitation aggravated the agrarian disorders already described. The mass of the proletariate, indeed, still lacked sufficient class-consciousness to enter into the agitation, but its inertia was daily decreasing. The Catholic Board, twice dissolved, was re-constituted in 1815 as the Catholic Association, and it was O'Connell's avowed intention to make every parish priest the

---

[1] Resolutions passed by the Bishops, May 27, 1814 (*Life and Speeches of O'Connell*, vol. ii. p. 149).

[2] January 24, 1815 (*Life and Speeches*, vol. ii. p. 178).

[3] Ward, *Eve of Catholic Emancipation*, vol. ii. p. 147.

[4] August 23, 24, 1815 (*Life and Speeches of O'Connell*, vol. ii. p. 206).

[5] May 29, 1813 (*ibid.*, vol. i. p. 344).

official agent of the revolutionary societies which he had organized.[1] Is it surprising that in London there was a reaction of opinion unfavourable to Catholicism ?

A majority of the Commons, and possibly even of the Lords, would have admitted to Parliament a Lord Petre, an Earl of Shrewsbury, a Sir John Throckmorton and a Charles Butler ; but no one cared to face the prospect of a party of demagogues—intransigent, rebellious and separatist—sitting in Westminster as representatives of the Irish counties. Those who had hesitated were strengthened in their doubts. Such was Wilberforce, whose state of mind is a faithful reflexion of the changes of public opinion. In a speech, delivered in 1814, he asks in accents of irritation whether the Irish must not be regarded as among the races unworthy of freedom.[2] The most convinced supporters of emancipation could not forgive O'Connell and his followers for having so brutally dismissed Grattan, after long years of unwearied labour on behalf of Irish independence and Catholic emancipation, merely because Grattan had not indeed proposed, but had judged it prudent to accept, the system of securities devised by Canning. " I mean," Grattan declared, " to support the Catholic question with a *desperate* fidelity." [3] It was the courage of despair. During the century now opening the Irish question was destined alternately to accelerate and to retard the movement of reform. In 1815 it retarded reform. For the moment, by universal consent, the cause of Catholic emancipation was at a low ebb ; and this was the result of Irish violence.

[1] H. of C., May 17, 1814 ; speech of Sir John Cox Hippisley (*Parl. Deb.*, vol. xxvii. p. 931).
[2] H. of C., July 20, 1814 (*Parl. Deb.*, vol. xxvii. p. 808).
[3] H. of C., May 30, 1815 (*Parl. Deb.*, vol. xxxi. pp. 522–3).

CHAPTER II

FINE ARTS, LITERATURE, SCIENCE

THE FINE ARTS.

Patronage of Artists.

DURING the opening years of the 19th century Methodism and Evangelicalism had imbued English society with their *ethos*. And it was precisely in the middle class, whose social importance was increasing with the progress of the industrial revolution, that this Protestant revival first took root. The middle class, therefore, was not only deprived by their eagerness to accumulate wealth of the leisure necessary for the appreciation of the Fine Arts, it was imbued with a spirit of positive antipathy towards the artistic. The Protestant pietist was an iconoclast who rejected as sheer paganism every attempt to idealize natural form. The conscience of the individual believer was a sanctuary where God was present to his worship. But no symbol could represent His Presence, however imperfectly, to the imagination. If a Puritan merchant deigned to accord any attention to the Fine Arts, he was actuated not by any æsthetic ideals, but by the hope that the improvement of artistic technique might indirectly improve the processes of industry. Since 1754 there had existed in London a " Society for the Encouragement of Arts," and the society was flourishing. The first exhibition of paintings had been held on its premises, and it offered annual prizes for drawing. But its full title was "Society for the Encouragement of Arts, *Manufactures and Commerce* in Great Britain," and the title reveals its founders' real object.[1] Two or three hundred youths studied

---

[1] Taylor, *Fine Arts in England*, vol. ii. p. 169. " They entered into subscriptions, and offered rewards for the discovery of native cobalt, and the smalt, zaffer, etc., prepared for it, and for the cultivation of madder and other substances used in the process of dyeing and in the manufacture of cottons." Cf. the inaugural address delivered by the painter West in 1792, on his election to the Presidency of the Royal Academy : " Here ingenious youth are instructed in the Art of design ; and the instruction acquired in this place has spread itself through the various manufactures of this country, to which it has given a taste that is able to convert the most common and simple materials into rare and valuable articles of commerce. These articles the British merchant sends forth into all the quarters of the world, where they stand preeminent over the productions of other nations (Galt, *Life of West*, vol. ii. p. 747). Cf. the programme

the Fine Arts in London. How many of these would become in the strict sense of the term painters or sculptors? Five or six was the estimate of the *Edinburgh Review*. "The rest," continued the *Review*, "spread themselves through our various manufactures, of porcelain, pottery, foundery, cotton-printing, etc., and give them that elegance of design and beauty of finish, which, added to our superiority in capital and machinery, secures to them the command of the markets throughout the world."[1] Thus did the manufacturer make the artist his tool. Apart from this service to himself he disdained the artist's life as useless, idle and sensual. The entire energy of the English capitalist was directed to the improvement of the tools and methods of manufacture and to the better organization of industry, and apart from these ends of immediate utility, to purposes more general indeed, but still utilitarian, philanthropy and political reform. If he rested every seventh day it was to pray, not to enjoy life.

If these were the new interests of the middle class, interests inimical to artistic culture, were any counteracting influences at work in England? The Court perhaps? When George III ascended the throne he was the first of his dynasty to manifest a desire to give the monarchy its legitimate place among the national institutions. And the revival of monarchy had reacted on the Fine Arts. British artists were divided into rival coteries. The King decided to take one of these groups under his protection and to establish it as the "Royal Academy of Arts in London, for the purpose of cultivating and improving the Arts of Painting, Sculpture and Architecture."[2] The Royal Academy consisted of forty members, a proof of the royal purpose to imitate the French monarch and the French Académie des Beaux Arts. Its membership was recruited by cooptation. Its government was a president assisted by a council of eight. The members elected a secretary and an archivist. The King nominated a treasurer. Nine "visitors," historical painters, eminent sculptors or other qualified artists, arranged classes of drawing from models, four professors taught anatomy, architecture, painting and perspective, and these nine visitors and four professors were elected by the Academy and removable by the King. Reynolds had been the first president. Indeed, the accession of George III marks the transition from the period of Hogarth to the period of Reynolds.

Hogarth had been a popular artist, hostile to the aristocracy. He had preferred to depend for his livelihood on the sale of his engravings than to enter the clientele of a nobleman. The foe of corporations, he

---

of the British Institution (see below p. 493): "To improve and extend our manufactures by that degree of taste and elegance of design which are to be exclusively derived from the cultivation of the Fine Arts and thereby to increase the general prosperity and resources of the empire."

[1] *Edinburgh Review*, September 1814, No. 46, Art. 1; Northcote's *Life of Reynolds* (vol. xxiii. p. 269).

[2] See Sandby, *History of the Royal Academy*, vol. i. pp. 45 sqq.

had prevented the British painters founding an Academy during his lifetime. Reynolds, on the contrary, was a man of the world and a born Academician. He was the first artist to receive a title since the accession of the House of Hanover. He was a fashionable portrait painter, also a painter of large mythological and historical groups ; he decorated churches and palaces. His inaugural speech at the Academy is an excellent statement of his aims. After paying his homage to the " influence of Majesty," against which the Whigs were opening their campaign, he preached to the students " an implicit obedience to the *rules of art*, as established on the practice of the great masters . . . perfect and infallible guides," and expressed the hope that the new institution " may answer the expectation of its Royal Founder, . . . that the present age may vie in arts with that of Leo X and that the dignity of dying art . . . may be revived under the reign of George III." Reynolds died in 1792.[1] West and Lawrence divided the succession. West became President of the Royal Academy, Lawrence the Court painter. Never before had British art enjoyed a period of equal brilliance, and the Academy could claim the credit without fear of contradiction. The King subjected the Academy to a rigorous control, and in 1806 for political reasons he refused to appoint Smirke archivist.[2] The social position of an artist was immediately raised by the fact of his inclusion in the official hierarchy. The Academy gave an annual dinner to which 140 guests were invited, at which all the distinguished members of Government circles were entertained on a footing of equality by painters, sculptors and architects who possessed the diploma. The artist, therefore, was now treated as a gentleman, not as formerly, as an artisan. On ceremonial occasions the Academician took precedence of a " master of arts." Himself and his eldest son had a right to the title of esquire.[3] Though since Reynolds no artist had received a baronetcy, two architects, Chambers and Soane, the engraver Strange, and the painter Lawrence had been knighted. When the President of the Academy, West, refused a knighthood, he justified his refusal by his religious scruples as a Quaker ; but popular report found the true reason in a pride which disdained a distinction not hereditary.[4] The painter Opie who died in 1808 was buried, like Reynolds, in Westminster Abbey.

A social barrier had fallen. Artists had been admitted to the ruling class, and apparently by the action of the monarch. We must not, however, overlook the limitations which confined royal influence in this direction. King George attempted conscientiously to play

1 Quoted by Sandby, *History of the Royal Academy*, vol. i. pp. 45 sqq.
2 *Life of Haydon*, vol. i. pp. 24–5.
3 *Minutes of Evidence before Select Committee on Arts and Principles of Design*, 1836, pp. 794 sqq.
4 Sandby, *History of the Royal Academy*, vol. i. p. 296.

the part of patron of the arts. Unhappily, he lacked the vocation. He was a countryman, devoted to farming and hunting, and his interests were bounded by the domestic circle. Artists had more to hope from his son the Prince of Wales, who spent lavishly and loved luxury and pleasure. But since his advent to power as Regent all his actions were subject to the jealous scrutiny of Parliament. His private means were not inexhaustible and he was not free to regulate his own expenditure. The entire weight of commerce and industry in the House of Commons opposed the addition of useless expenses to the crushing burden of the war debt. To the great Whig families the Regent was the object of implacable hatred, a liar and a traitor. And the gentry viewed with suspicion everything that might increase unduly the prestige of the Crown.

The true rulers of the country were the nobility and gentry. And it was they who, by commissioning portraits at high prices, gave art its direction. If the Royal Academy had succeeded, the measure of its success had been determined by the extent of their patronage. And in fact the novel institution had been the object of lively opposition and had not been suffered to enjoy an uncontested supremacy. It was accused of servility to the Government. Barry and Haydon conducted campaigns whose echoes spread far and wide against a body they judged inimical to the unfettered development of genius. Though the hostile groups which had preceded the foundation of the Royal Academy, the "Society of Artists," and "the free Society of Artists" were extinct by the end of the 18th century, other groups had been formed independent of the Academy, though not directly competing with it.[1] Until 1798 the choice of an artist to design a public monument had been left to the official society. But the favouritism displayed by the Academicians, their tendency to manipulate unfairly open competitions, and to monopolize commissions, provoked lively complaint. In 1798 the House of Commons appointed a "Committee of Taste" composed of amateurs, taken in part from the Members of Parliament, to which these nominations were henceforth transferred.[2] And when about the beginning of the new century public opinion was convinced that the Government did not yet afford sufficient encouragement to art, no appeal was addressed to the Royal Academy, no new official society was demanded. A number of noblemen with the assistance of a few wealthy bankers founded by subscription a free society. The "British Institution for the development of the Fine

---

[1] *Society of Painters in Water Colours*, 1805; *The Associated Artists in Water Colours Society of Engravers, under the Patronage of H.R.H. the Prince of Wales*, 1803.
[2] Prince Hoare, *Epochs of the Arts*, 1813, pp. 229–33. The commission was universally known as the "Committee of Taste"; but its official title was "Commission for the Erection of Public Monuments." An additional committee was subsequently appointed to choose the site of monuments in cathedrals. On this committee six members of the Royal Academy were added to the members of the Committee of Taste (*ibid.*, pp. 258–9). Cf. Barry, *A Letter to the Dilettanti Society*, 1797.

Arts" founded in 1805 awarded prizes, possessed a permanent picture gallery and opposed to the Academy exhibition its annual or rather its half-yearly exhibitions.[1] To be sure the Institution disclaimed any systematic opposition to the spirit of the official society. Nevertheless, the circumstances of its foundation and the success it achieved are symptomatic of the national temper. In England the power of the monarch was swamped by the influence of the aristocracy.

Music, Architecture, Sculpture, Painting.

Royal patronage, noble patronage : these were the influences which in England supplied the lack of patronage by a middle class too hard worked and too puritanic to encourage art, and which stimulated artistic progress. But we must not be too dogmatic in our statements. It is not easy to establish between the Fine Arts and other social phenomena relations sufficiently simple for the convenience of the historian. Natural endowment is a necessary, if not a sufficient condition of artistic achievement, and the causes of its existence or non-existence lie outside the sphere of history. How, for example, can we explain by the influence of pietism the worthlessness of British music ? No doubt the English eighteenth-century Puritan proscribed every branch of art, even music, and refused to admit hymns into his worship. Nevertheless, of all the arts music must have suffered the least from this proscription. What, then, was the reason that in spite of the Puritans eighteenth-century England possessed dramatists and painters but lacked musicians ? Moreover, in this respect, as in so many others, the new puritanism, the puritanism of Wesley, marked a transition. Far from excluding hymnody the Methodists made hymn-singing a distinctive feature of Evangelical worship. Both Charles Wesley and John Wesley himself were the authors of hymns which became classics, and they stimulated an entire literary movement which would culminate in 1833 in the publication of Edward Bickersteth's *Christian Psalmody* whose circulation reached 150,000 copies.[2] And if the Church of England at first discouraged hymn-singing as tainted by its Methodist associations she encouraged instrumental music as a reaction against hymnody and as a counter attraction. Towards the close of the 18th century Burney introduced professional singers into Anglican churches.[3] A few years later Sydney Smith remarks the growing employment of music to attract congrega-

---

[1] Taylor, *Fine Arts in England*, pp. 214 sqq ; Galt, *Life of West*, vol. ii. pp. 179 sqq. The first exhibition of the *British Institution* was identical in character with the exhibition of the Royal Academy. The second was of a more special character and henceforward the plan of the exhibition differed from year to year. In 1813 there was an exhibition of Reynolds ; in 1814 of Hogarth, Wilson, Gainsborough, and Zaffany ; in 1815 of the Flemish and Dutch masters ; in 1816 of the Italian and Spanish.

[2] Overton, *Evangelical Movement*, pp. 124 sqq. ; *English Church*, pp. 132 sqq.

[3] Overton, *English Church*, pp. 133-4.

tions, and notices the erection of a large number of organs in churches throughout the provinces.[1] This rivalry should have effected a revival of sacred music. That this was not the case was surely no fault of the prevailing pietism. Must we not rather conclude a racial incapacity ?

To turn from music to architecture. Here the operation of the environment is easier to discern. The enormous towns now springing up on all sides were of a uniform ugliness, an ugliness which occasioned no discomfort to the capitalists who built them. Four brick walls pierced by windows, soon black with grime, served according to the arrangement of the interior as house, factory or church. These buildings which boasted no style of architecture whatsoever were dumped down at haphazard. Thus as street was added to street villages grew into towns, towns into cities. No Government department intervened in the process, national, provincial, or municipal. There was no general plan, no expression of the will of the community. " In future times," wrote Lady Holland in 1800, " when this little island shall have fallen into its natural insignificancy, by being no longer possessed of a fictitious power founded upon commerce, distant colonies, and other artificial sources of wealth, how puzzled will the curious antiquary be when seeking amidst the ruins of London vestiges of its past grandeur." She explains the meanness of everything throughout England " by the spirit of 'independence' and 'selfishness'" engendered by a commercial civilization. "Hence there is no ambition, no desire of perpetuating by great works fame to posterity."[2] The brothers Adam, who were architects, remarked how the " bigoted zeal " and the "superstitious pomp " of Roman Catholicism had favoured the artistic achievement of Italy. " Neither," they continued, " has the form of our Government nor the decent simplicity of our religion, ever demanded any such exertion ; nor is it probable that they ever will while we continue a free and flourishing people."[3] The Tory spirit, once more awake in England since the accession of George III, reacted against this extreme of religious and commercial individualism ; but the results of this reaction were disappointing. We have seen how ineffective, on the whole, the Tory revival had proved. Take ecclesiastical architecture. The Tories erected no churches. They abandoned the field to the Nonconformists, who multiplied their hideous meeting-houses. Take civil architecture. The Government was thwarted by the jealousy and parsimony of the Commons. When Carlton House was connected with the northern suburbs by the opening of Regent Street, an imposing thoroughfare elaborately designed, protests were raised which had not yet ceased.[4] Moreover, this Georgian architecture bore the stamp of its origin. It was academic and artificial.

[1] Lady Holland, *Memoir of the Rev. S. Smith*, 1855, vol. i. p. 49.
[2] *Journal*, vol. ii. p. 54.
[3] *The Works in Architecture of Robert and James Adam*, vol. i., 1778, Preface to Part IV.
[4] H. of C., February 15, 1816 (*Parl. Deb.*, vol. xxxii. pp. 576–7).

"The buildings of the Ancients," wrote Robert Adam, "are in Architecture what the works of Nature are with respect to the other Arts; they serve as models which we should imitate, and as standards by which we ought to judge."[1] The principle here enunciated moulded ever more tyrannically the taste of British architects. Sir William Chambers' Somerset House, built at the end of the 18th century, was no doubt a work of the classic style in which free invention was combined with imitation. But as time passed the Græco-Roman models were copied with an ever-increasing servility. For a century past the "Dilettanti Society"[2] had dispatched missions to Italy, Greece and Asia Minor. Dawkins and Wood published their *Baalbek*, Adam his *Spalatro*, Stuart his *Athens*. All these archæological treatises served as guides to the English architects. The middle class in the industrial centres followed suit. Whenever they required a town hall, an exchange, a bank, they planted haphazard amid the chaos of narrow streets a sham temple turned out to order by an Academician. At the Bank of England business men passed beneath the Arch of Constantine to receive their money in the Roman temple of the Sun and Moon.

It is more surprising that British architects were unable to create an original style of domestic architecture adapted to the requirements of the fine, spacious and free existence spent on their country seats by the nobility and gentry. Over two hundred mansions had been built in the course of the 18th century. In 1815 the movement had not slackened. But the artistic worth of all these country houses, the seats of the aristocracy, was very slight. Can it be that the eighteenth-century Englishman, aristocrat and bourgeois alike, was an individualist who disdained to display his wealth to the curiosity of the passer-by, and reserved for the interior of his home ingenious arrangement and luxurious furniture? Was not the most distinctive feature of English domestic architecture precisely the central hall, invisible from without, an adaptation of the Mediterranean Patio to a cold and rainy climate.[3] The suggestion would be plausible had the exterior of the mansion been unpretentious. Unfortunately, the owners followed the advice of the professional architect whose ideal was the vast size and classical style of Latin antiquity. But since the remains of ancient architecture were the ruins of public buildings architects set themselves the problem of building houses which should be as habitable as possible while resembling not the private houses of the ancients, for which evidence was wanting,[4] but Roman or Greek temples.

[1] R. Adam, *Ruins of the Palace . . . at Spalatro*, Pretace.

[2] For the circumstances of its foundation, its aristocratic composition, and its activities, see Taylor, *Fine Arts in England*, vol. ii. pp. 158 sqq.

[3] Fergusson, *History of the Modern Styles of Architecture*, 3 Ed., vol. ii. p. 91.

[4] It was precisely to fill this lacuna that R. Adam had undertaken his study of Diocletian's Dalmatian Palace, *Ruins of the Palace at Spalatro*, Introduction, p. 3. John Hall, *Origin . . . of Gothic Architecture*, pp. 135 sqq., remarks with justice that the classical style is inapplicable even to a Christian church without alterations which change its character completely.

A few owners rebelled and demanded a style more national, less artificial. But exchanging one form of archæology for another they sought their models in the mediæval architecture of England.1 Fifty years earlier Horace Walpole had initiated the Gothic revival by building a sham abbey at Strawberry Hill. In 1815 Beckford was engaged upon his sham abbey at Fonthill, a ridiculous piece of scene painting hastily put together which had already fallen once and was destined to a second fall.2 An entire school of antiquarians furnished architects with the necessary models. John Britton published in 1807 the first volume of his *Architectural Antiquities of Great Britain*; Sir James Hall in 1813 his *Essay on the Origin, History and Principles of Gothic Architecture*. And Catholics began to exploit, for apologetic purposes, the nascent enthusiasm for the art of the Middle Ages. John Milner, Vicar Apostolic of the Midland District, urged the fundamental Catholicism of the Gothic style in a work which attracted considerable attention.3 But in reality the Gothic fashion was as insincere as the neo-classical. There were not even two rival schools inspired by opposite convictions. The selfsame architects, clever men of business, men like Wilkins and Nash, worked in either style indifferently, and produced to suit the whim of their client, a Doric portico, or a decorated façade, at need even a Chinese pagoda.

In sculpture and painting the efforts of the Royal Academy to create a grand style achieved a measure of success. Thomas Banks had founded for the first time in English history a national school of sculpture. Flaxman who enjoyed a European reputation, Chantrey, Westmacott, Wyatt, were artists of considerable merit. In Benjamin West England possessed a successful historical painter. Fifty years before our date West had effected an artistic revolution by depicting the men and women who figured in his pictures in the exact costume of their period and profession. Though now seventy years of age he continued to produce, and the subjects which he undertook were increasingly ambitious.4 It was said that between 1769 and 1801 he had received £34,787 for pictures commissioned by the King. In 1811 the British Institution bought for 3,000 guineas his picture of "Christ Healing the Sick" and gave it to the nation.5 But

1 Eastlake, *History of the Gothic Revival*, pp. 57–8, remarks that restorations in the original style of country houses and castles had never ceased entirely.

2 Fergusson, *History of the Modern Styles of Architecture*, vol. ii. pp. 96 sqq.

3 Is this the reason that Eastlake in his *History of the Gothic Revival* makes no mention of Milner ? See his protest (p. 59) against " the vulgar superstition which then and long afterwards identified the Pointed Arch with the tenets of Rome." For Milner's work, see *Quarterly Review*, October 1811, Art. 111, *Milner's Ecclesiastical Architecture* (vol. vi. pp. 62 sqq.).

4 See Prince Hoare's appreciation of West in 1813, *Epochs of Art*, p. 221 : "Above the sportive, desultory trains of Venetian grouping, he ranks with the more chaste composers of the Florentine and Lombard schools ; and surpassing many, is excelled by few."

5 Taylor, *Fine Arts in England*, p. 224 ; Carey, *Observations . . . on . . . Decline of . . . Historical Painting*, p. 64. According to Carey's estimate, subscriptions, the sale of an engraving of the picture, and the receipts of the exhibition brought the British Institution about £13,000.

the current code of morality restricted the patronage of King and Government. Artists were faced by the prudery of the Court. We are told that King George refused to sit to Gainsborough to mark his disapproval of the artist's personal immorality, and that the latter was therefore compelled to study the monarch unobserved and paint him from memory.[1] They were faced by Puritan bigotry. When in 1773 the painters of the Academy offered to decorate the interior of St. Paul's at their own expense the Archbishop of Canterbury and the Bishop of London refused the offer as calculated to arouse the cry of Popery.[2] And they were faced by the parsimony of the Exchequer. It was in vain that the Royal Academy made repeated attempts to obtain a grant of £5,000 to open a Gallery of Honour which should contain a permanent exhibition of the best examples of contemporary painting.[3] Parliament voted the erection of two monuments to celebrate the victories of Trafalgar and Waterloo.[4] But the Waterloo memorial was never carried out. Such was the strength in the Commons of the spirit of opposition, so pettifogging was the meanness of the middle class, so intense the indifference of the gentry to the embellishment of the capital. The aristocracy, whose patronage exercised a decisive influence on the development of the fine arts, demanded portraiture. Economic reasons, therefore, explain the uninterrupted victory of the portrait painters in the struggle which they had waged for the past fifty years with the historical painters.[5] It was by his portraits that Reynolds had accumulated a fortune of £100,000.[6] A portrait by Lawrence cost in 1815 300 guineas and would shortly cost 700.[7] It was in vain that the Royal Academy had been founded for the purpose of enabling a British artist to paint, without starvation, subjects other than portraits; in vain that the British Institution excluded portraits from its annual exhibition. Despite every effort to the contrary the English school remained a school of portraiture. Gainsborough had died in 1788, Reynolds in 1792, Romney in 1802, Hoppner, the favourite painter of the Prince of Wales, in 1810, and the Scottish artist Raeburn had but a few more years

1 Memoirs and Correspondence of Viscount Combermere, vol. i. p. 333.

2 Sandby, History of the Royal Academy, vol. i. pp. 145–8; Pye, Patronage of British Art, pp. 217–18. Pye, however, remarks that the prejudice had already grown weaker, as was shown by the decoration of churches at Rochester, Winchester, and Salisbury, also of St. Stephen's, Walbrook and St. Margaret's, Westminster. Prince Hoare, Epochs of the Arts, p. 259, adds the chapel of the Foundling Hospital. See the protests of contemporary painters against this Puritanism, also Barry, Inquiry, chap. v. (Works, vol. ii. p. 210); Carey, Observations . . . on . . . Decline of . . . Historical Painting, p. 13. Cf. Literary Works of Sir Joshua Reynolds, vol. ii. p. 338.

3 Minutes of Evidence for Select Committee on Arts and Principles of Design, 1836, p. 1106.

4 H. of C., February 5, 1816 (Parl. Deb, vol. xxxii. pp. 311 sqq.).

5 For this bitter contest see Barry, Inquiry, chap. x. (Works, vol. ii. pp. 246 sqq.); Life of Haydon, vol. i. passim.

6 Biographie Universelle, art. Reynolds.

7 Journal of a Tour . . . by a French Traveller, 1815, vol. i. p. 39.

to live. But Lawrence was in full possession of his faultless technique. The Regent had entrusted to Lawrence the decoration of a State apartment at Windsor Castle to commemorate the victories of 1814 and 1815. Not, however, with battle scenes. In obedience to public taste and the force of circumstances the Regent commissioned a gallery of portraits. So Lawrence renewed the days of Rubens and Van Dyck, and went abroad to execute the royal command by obtaining sittings from all the sovereigns of Europe. It was the supreme moment of English portraiture.

Webster tells us how he abandoned architecture in 1803 because he had not found in that profession the pecuniary advantages he had at first expected. He therefore determined to become a landscape painter, since landscape painting was at that time a highly " lucrative profession."[1] At the beginning of the century the landscape painters constituted with the portrait painters the glory of English art. They had slowly emancipated themselves from the foreign influences under which they had grown up. Dutch influence is evident in Gainsborough, and in Crome, the founder of the Norwich school ; French and classical influence can be seen in Wilson and is obvious in the pictures of Turner's first manner. Nevertheless, these masters possess an original quality common to them all. Before Turner's art had reached its perfection, or Constable had made his reputation, they constituted already a school in the strictest sense of the term.[2] They created a new tradition the offspring of a land of mist and cloudy skies. For they discovered the beauty of an atmosphere which possessed a life of its own and in which every object was bathed. This type of art of a supreme chastity and permeated by a vague mysticism awoke less than any other the hostility of the Evangelicals. And an aristocracy of country dwellers appreciated this effort to maintain the love of nature, more vigorous and unimpaired than in any other country in Europe, at a time when in England beyond any other European country industrialism and its urban type of civilization were making such gigantic strides. And it is, no doubt, to the same influence that we should ascribe the vogue enjoyed by the genre painting, a little picture depicting a scene of everyday life, especially of country life. Morland was

[1] Bence Jones, *History of the Royal Institution*, p. 194.
[2] In 1815 Turner exhibited a classical painting, " Dido building Carthage." See the eulogy in the *Examiner*, May 28, 1815 : " Gaspar and Nicholas Poussin may have painted nobler grown trees, and have been more careful in detail and finishing ; Rubens may have had even a bolder flush of colour, and Claude more refinement ; but combining all Mr. Turner's other capabilities with that best of all qualities, a creative imagination, not one of the great Masters was more significant and inspiring than the Professor of Perspective to the Academy." In all Turner exhibited eight pictures, which included besides the Dido " The Eruption of the Souffrier Mountains " and " Crossing the Brook." The *Examiner* contained the following criticism of Constable's exhibition : " It is a pity that Mr. Constable's pencil is still so coarsely sketchy. There is much sparkling insight and a general character of truth in 268, ' Village in Suffolk,' and in 245, ' Boat Building.' "

dead, but Wilkie was the fashion and Mulready was winning his first successes. In the Academy exhibition of 1815 they were represented by two of their most celebrated pictures, Wilkie's " Distraining for Rent," Mulready's " Idle Boys."

Possibly the development in England of landscape painting, genre painting, and above all of portraiture had disappointed the hopes of those who had founded the Royal Academy to encourage the grand style in art, and historical painting in particular. For even in the Academy the historical painters were outnumbered by the portrait painters, landscape painters and genre painters. Engravers on the other hand were excluded. By the constitution of the Academy they were allowed six seats among the associates, who lacked the vote and were even excluded from the library. Landseer wasted his energy in fruitless efforts to obtain better treatment for himself and his fellows. He demanded the election of four engravers and the addition to the annual exhibition of a room of engravings. His attempts failed, and the indignant engravers refused their candidature for the six seats among the associates which had been alloted to them.[1] Academicians persisted in their contempt for engraving, as an art altogether subordinate, a mere technical process, serviceable for the dissemination of works of art, in fact, a craft not a fine art. Such obstinacy is amazing, and all the more amazing, when we consider that for the past thirty years England had produced the best engravers in Europe.

The entire English school of engraving owed its existence to Alderman Boydell, a good artist and a sucessful man of business. He had commissioned from the best painters a series of pictures whose subjects were taken from the plays of Shakespeare. The pictures were to serve as models to Woollett, Earlom and Sharpe, and to form a permanent exhibition of modern painting, the celebrated *Shakespeare Gallery* in Pall Mall.[2] And the growth in England of the trade in engravings had profoundly affected the economic situation of the English artist. Henceforth he depended not as formerly on royal or noble patronage but on the anonymous patronage of the public who purchased on a large scale the engravings of his work.[3] The engraving could either be sold singly or incorporated in a book. It might be the portrait of a celebrity, or the illustration of a novel or book of travels.[4] In any case painter and engraver became producers whose productions were retailed by the publisher. Thus engraving considered as a trade occupies a position intermediate between painting and literary production.

[1] Sandby, *History of the Royal Academy*, vol. i. pp. 134–6, 273–4; *Minutes of Evidence before Select Committee on Arts and Principles of Design*, 1836, pp. 1308, 1226–1328.

[2] Sandby, *History of the Royal Academy*, vol. i. p. 165.

[3] Pye, *Patronage of British Art*, p. 141.

[4] For the early days of book illustration in England see Pye, *Patronage of British Art* pp. 246–7.

DRAMA AND LITERATURE.

Patronage of men of letters.

The Government extended its patronage not to artists alone, but also to men of letters. England possessed her poet laureate, who for a salary of £100 per annum held himself in readiness to celebrate in verse victories by land or sea, and the birth, marriage or death of members of the Royal Family. The State also awarded pensions, offices and sinecures to men of letters. Southey, poet laureate since 1813, received beside his official emoluments a pension of £145. At the age of twenty-seven the poet Campbell was granted a pension of £200. The influence of Lord Moira secured for Thomas Moore the post of Registrar of the Bermudas. He resided in England while a substitute performed his official duties in Bermuda. In 1820 the Regent will appoint the dramatist George Colman, lieutenant of the Yeomen of the Guard, and remit the purchase money. Authors often owed Government favours to noble influence. But the heads of noble families, landed gentlemen, bankers, even manufacturers, were sometimes their immediate patrons. Coleridge was on the verge of entering the Unitarian ministry to obtain a livelihood when the Wedgwoods came to his assistance ; and they paid later the entire expense of his tour in Germany. Wordsworth, Southey and Thomas Moore all accepted the assistance of a wealthy patron. Even the new philanthropic movement applied its energy in this direction. A group of important landowners and merchants formed in 1790 an association, known as the Literary Fund, to assist indigent authors. The fund gave an annual dinner at which the members exchanged compliments and the authors thanked their benefactors in verse.[1] " Poetry, as *the wise* know," wrote one of his correspondents in 1808 to Constable, the publisher, " requires judgment, genius and *patronage*."[2]

But at the very time when this letter was written the patronage of literature whether official or private was passing out of fashion.

Noble patronage was condemned by public opinion with an ever-increasing severity. In a novel, whose object was to attack patronage of every description, Miss Edgeworth introduces the drawing-room bard, the tame author, and portrays him as a miserable creature, a figure of fun.[3] Writers who consented to accept the patronage of the Literary Fund were the object of universal derision.[4] The laureateship had

[1] For the Society for the Establishment of a Literary Fund, the circumstances of its foundation, its composition, statutes and resources, see Lettsome, *Hints Designed to Promote Beneficence, Temperance, and Medical Science*, vol. ii. pp. 237 sqq.

[2] A. Murray to A. Constable, April 6, 1808 (*Archibald Constable*, vol. i. p. 263).

[3] *Patronage*, chap. xxii.

[4] Byron, *English Bards and Scotch Reviewers*, vol. i.–ii. with the note ; *Quarterly Review*, September 1812, Art. 6, *D'Israeli's Calamities of Authors* (vol. viii. pp. 122–3 ; the article is Southey's).

long since lost its ancient prestige, and was finally discredited when in 1790 Pitt gave it to an unknown poetaster named Pye as payment for political services. At Pye's death in 1813 the Regent offered the laureateship to Scott. But he refused and secured Southey's appointment in his place. It was not only that Southey was the older man and extremely poor. Scott shrank from the ridicule which attached to the title. " I should be mortified," wrote the Duke of Buccleugh, " to see you hold a situation which by the general concurrence of the world is stamped ridiculous."[1] There were those who desired the State to do for writers what it had done for painters, sculptors and architects and found an institution similar to the French Academy.[2] But the scheme proved abortive. And though 1823 would witness the foundation of a Royal Society of Literature, it degenerated into a mere " Académie des Inscriptions." When Canning was asked to patronize the scheme, he refused. " I am really of opinion," he replied, " with Dr. Johnson that the multifarious personage called The Public is, after all, the best patron of literature and learned men."[3] No longer was the Court or even the nobility arbiter of the world of letters. The managers of theatres and the publishers, middlemen between the author and his public, had succeeded to their position as rulers of the literary world.

Drama.

English drama made neither reputations nor fortunes. Since Otway tragedy was dead. Home's *Douglas*, already half a century old, and far more recently Joanna Baillie's tragedies of character, were artificial and unsuccessful attempts. Gloomy and mediæval dramas were, indeed, manufactured by the score, and Maturin's *Bertram* had scored in 1815 a striking success. But nobody regarded these new productions, even if successful, as destined to become classics. During the early years of George III, in the days of Sheridan and Goldsmith, comedy had shone with the parting brilliance of sunset. But Sheridan was no more, and years before his death the politician had killed the dramatist. Though Charles Dibdin, George Colman junior, and Prince Hoare were still writing light comedy, which was facile and amusing, the decadence was none the less rapid and incontestable. Theatre managers had supplied the deficiencies of the national drama by adaptations of French pieces, ancient or modern. Remarking the unpopularity of French literature since 1792 they turned to Germany for a new source of dramatic supply, and for the past twenty years the

---

[1] Lockhart, *Memoirs of the Life of Sir Walter Scott*, vol. iii. p. 79.
[2] See *Quarterly Review*, September 1812, Southey's article above-mentioned.
[3] Smiles, *Murray*, vol. i. p. 237.

Londoner had wept over the tragedies of Kotzebue.[1]   English drama
was on the brink of the grave.

By a remarkable paradox England, destitute of great dramatists,
was rich in great actors.   In default of modern drama they drew Shakespeare from oblivion, and thereby won their own laurels.   Garrick had
initiated the revival.   But Garrick presented a Shakespeare adapted to
eighteenth-century taste.   When in 1783 Kemble made his first appearance at Drury Lane as Hamlet, he announced his intention to play the
tragedy as originally written by Shakespeare.[2]   And he wore the costume
of the period in which the action was imagined to take place.   Assisted
by the painter, William Capon, and influenced by the Gothic revival
Kemble effected a revolution in stagecraft.[3]   And so thorough was
the conversion of the public that the reform which he had initiated was
soon felt to be inadequate.   In spite of his promises he still presented
an adapted Shakespeare, and Leigh Hunt, after witnessing what he
termed a " farcical representation " of the *Tempest*, swore that never
again would he watch Shakespeare acted.[4]   Even Kemble's acting
seemed cold and mannered[5] since, in the January of 1814, Kean had
revealed his powers in the part of Shylock and a few months later as
Richard III.   Kean's acting was violent, exaggerated and brutal,
and he pushed realism to affectation.   " Our styles of acting," Kemble
told a friend " are so totally different, that you must not expect me to
like that of Mr. Kean ; but one thing I must say in his favour—he
is at all times terribly in *earnest*."[6]   But the Shakespearian revival
ushered no revival of British drama.   As Shakespeare was more
frequently acted and better interpreted, the exhaustion of dramatic
genius in England was more painfully evident.

To what cause must the decay of the drama be attributed ?   Many
observers ascribed it to the legal regulations which controlled the stage
in England.   A statute of 1737 had not only subjected all plays to the
preliminary censorship of the Lord Chamberlain, but had imposed
severe restrictions on the number of theatres.[7]   Henceforward neither
the Crown by letters patent nor the Lord Chamberlain by licence
could authorize dramatic representations outside the City of Westminster
and places of royal residence.   The erection of a theatre in any English
town would require a special Act of Parliament.   Certainly a larger

[1] Boaden, *Life of Mrs. Jordan*, vol. ii. pp. 34, 43–5.

[2] Boaden, *Memoirs of . . . Kemble*, vol. i. p. 88.

[3] *Ibid.*, vol. ii. pp. 160–1.

[4] *Examiner*, July 23, 1815 : " Even those daubs of pictures, formerly exhibited under the
title of the Shakespeare Gallery, had a less evident tendency to disturb and distort all the previous
notions we had imbibed in reading Shakespeare. . . . And be it observed further, that these
same anomalous, unmeaning, vulgar and ridiculous additions, are all that *take* in the present
farcical representations of the *Tempest*."

[5] *Examiner*, February 5, 1815.

[6] Boaden, *Memoirs of . . . Kemble*, vol. ii. p. 555.

[7] 10 Geo. II, cap. 28.   See also 25 Geo. II, cap. 36.

measure of freedom had been bestowed by a statute of 1788 which invested the magistrates at Quarter Sessions with authority to grant licenses.[1] But even this measure of liberty was seriously restricted. The magistrates were empowered to authorize theatrical representations " for a limited time," they could not license " a constant and regular " theatre. Nor had they power to grant licenses within a radius of twenty miles of Westminster, London and Edinburgh, fourteen miles of Oxford and Cambridge, ten miles of a royal residence, eight miles of a theatre already licensed by letters patent. And if the provincial theatre secured new facilities by the legislation of 1788, the system of monopoly obtaining in London was unaffected by the Act. Whereas under Elizabeth London with a population of 230,000 possessed seventeen theatres, and Paris in 1815 with a population of 548,000 possessed twenty-three, contemporary London with its population of a million possessed no more than a dozen. Of these twelve theatres only two, in virtue of letters patent granted by Charles II, enjoyed an unrestricted liberty. One of these was Covent Garden, burnt in 1809 and re-erected on a magnificent scale by Robert Smirke with a façade in the classical style copied from the Parthenon. The other was Drury Lane, burnt a few months after the destruction of Covent Garden, and rebuilt in the same style by Benjamin Wyatt. The little theatre at the Haymarket and the Lyceum were only licensed for the summer months and their repertoire was restricted to light comedy. And these four were the only theatres in the strict sense of the term to be found in London.

Thirty years previously Palmer had attempted to open a new theatre in the East End in the neighbourhood of the Tower. But the management of Covent Garden and Drury Lane protested, and Palmer's Royal Theatre was condemned to be one of the second-rate theatres, theatres such as the Amphitheatre at Westminster Bridge, the Circus at St. George's Fields, Sadler's Wells at Islington,[2] where pantomimes and farces were acted and circus performances given. The managers of the large theatres were clever politicians who utilized aristocratic patronage and interested influential Members of Parliament in their undertakings. Whitbread, the leader of the Popular party in the Commons, had become towards the close of his life a member of the managing committee of Drury Lane. In this way, whenever the authorization of a new theatre was brought before Parliament, the monopoly secured zealous advocates, even among the most active members of the Liberal Opposition.[3] We might be tempted to ascribe the paralysis of drama to these legal restrictions.

[1] 28 Geo. III, cap. 30. See the preamble : " Whereas it may be expedient to permit and suffer, in towns of considerable resort, theatrical representations for a limited time and under regulations ; in which, nevertheless, it would be highly impolitick, inexpedient and unreasonable to permit the establishment of a constant and regular theatre."

[2] Charles Dibdin, *History and Illustrations of the London Theatres*, p. 87.

[3] James Lawrence, *Dramatic Emancipation*, 1813, in the *Pamphleteer*, vol. ii. pp. 385-6.

The day, however, would come when the Act of 1788 would be repealed and the theatre released from its bondage ; and the decadence of British drama would not be arrested. We are therefore compelled to seek its cause elsewhere, possibly in the growth of Puritanism. Eighteenth-century actors had remarked that a provincial audience was more strait-laced than a London audience, and that many pieces could be staged in London whose production would be impossible elsewhere. By degrees the severity of the provinces spread to the capital. A middle-class audience drawn from the social *milieu* most profoundly affected by Evangelical beliefs would no longer tolerate the witticisms at the expense of Methodists and Quakers which were the traditional eighteenth-century method of extracting a laugh from the theatregoer. If Leigh Hunt in his articles of dramatic criticism was never weary of praising the *Beggar's Opera*, his motive was the desire to check the growing unpopularity of Gay's masterpiece. Modern cant found this rogues' comedy vulgar and demanded cuts.[1] " We are drilled, " he complained, " into a sort of stupid decorum, and forced to wear the same dull uniform of outward appearance."[2] The nobility and gentry of the provinces had little opportunity to patronize the drama, and the private theatricals which were the fashion during the closing years of the 18th century could not supply the want of theatres. And in the large towns the Puritan bourgeoisie neither went to the theatre themselves nor desired the local authorities to patronize the stage. They were too busy, too serious ; and they did not approve of pleasure.

The stage about 1815 occupied a very curious position. The growth of Puritanism had not resulted in the degradation of the comedian to the legal status of " vagabond " out of which the 18th century had raised him.[3] Garrick and Kemble were prominent members of the middle class, who moved in good society, and were universally respected.[4] In London comedians dined with the Regent at Carlton House.[5] On tour they received invitations from the gentry.[6] Nor was social

---

H. of C., April 28, 1813, Whitbread's speech ; H. of L., June 27, 1814, Lord Holland's speech (*Parl. Deb.*, vol. xxv. pp. 1096 sqq. ; vol. xxviii. pp. 418–19).

[1] *Examiner*, June 18, 1815, November 5, 1815. Miss Laetitia Hawkins, *Anecdotes*, vol. i. 1822, pp. 99–100, judges the piece exactly as Leigh Hunt accused the public of judging it. " That vulgar caricature," she calls it. The *Eclectic Review*, an Evangelical organ, denounced in January 1807 the grossness of Shakespeare (Doran, *English Stage*, vol. iii. p. 331). Wilberforce was invited by his friends in 1811 to consider the advisability of founding a moral theatre : " Sir Thomas Bernard's plan of an Alfred Theatre by private subscription—no promiscuous admission—select plays and actors—all *pour la morale*." Wilberforce, however, expressed distrust of the proposal, which was not sufficiently strict for his approval (*Life*, vol. iii. p. 497).

[2] *Examiner*, August 20, 1815.

[3] 10 Geo. II, cap. 28, had repealed, so far as comedians were concerned, 12 Anne, st. 2, cap. 23.

[4] Laetitia Hawkins, *Anecdotes*, vol. i., 1822, pp. 21 sqq. For Mrs. Siddons, see Madame D'Arblay, *Diary and Letters*, ed. 1854, vol. ii. pp. 164–5.

[5] Doran, *English Stage*, vol. iii. p. 346.

[6] Dibdin, *Reminiscences*, vol. i. pp. 174–5, 205, 206–7 ; vol. ii. pp. 278–9.

propriety outraged when an actress made a brilliant match. The rigid code of the middle class would never be able to gain a complete triumph over the habits acquired by the upper classes during the previous century. Nevertheless the theatre was being increasingly abandoned to the common people.

In 1815 a traveller remarks that it was not the fashion in London to spend the evening at the theatre.[1] Except for a row of boxes, the very arrangement of the theatre sacrificed the comfort of the wealthy play-goer, whether fashionable or bourgeois. He was squeezed on the narrow benches of the pit, for the French orchestra stall was still unknown. Above the boxes the gallery occupied a very important position. There, facing the stage, sat *the Gods,* otherwise the populace, and interrupted the representation with its jokes, applauding, booing, throwing orange-peel. To the right and left were free entrances for the light women of the neighbourhood ; for the management had devised this method of attracting the men.[2] Nowhere in Europe were the theatres more rowdy. When in 1809 the management of Covent Garden had attempted to raise the price of seats, the O.P. (Old Prices) demon-strations[3] had stopped all performances for two months. There had been a riot at the Opera in 1813,[4] riots at Drury Lane and Covent Garden in 1815.[5] A popular audience demands a popular performance. Therefore while the polite and polished drama, the comedy of manners and the comedy of character, were declining and on the verge of ex-. tinction, the harlequinade flourished. Kemble and Kean were content to " revive " Shakespeare, but Grimaldi created an original type, the English clown. Nevertheless a middle class, careful for the respectability of the nation, supervised the amusements of the populace. If the English clown was brutal, he was not obscene.

Publishers and Authors.

If the theatre was at a standstill, the publishing trade was making enormous strides. The development dated from the 18th century. The first important publishing houses in England had been founded by Jacob Tonson and Bernard Lintot shortly after the Revolution of 1688. The London firm of Longmans dates from 1724. During the early years of George III's reign, Elliot of Edinburgh earned the

---

[1] *Journal of a Tour* . . . *by a French Traveller,* 1815, vol. i. pp. 89 sqq. Cf. Leigh Hunt, *Autobiography,* p. 134.

[2] James Lawrence, *Dramatic Emancipation* in *Pamphleteer,* vol. ii. pp. 384–5. *Report of Select Committee on Dramatic Literature,* 1832, p. 27 : " I think it is a most decided objection to any man carrying his wife or sister to the theatre, when he is compelled to take them through a crowd of women of notoriously bad character."

[3] Dibdin, *History of the London Theatre,* pp. 19 sqq. According to Boaden the riot was not without a political aspect (*Memoirs of Kemble,* vol. ii. p. 500 sqq.). Cf. Boaden, *Memoirs of Mrs. Siddons,* vol. ii. p. 369–70.

[4] *Examiner,* May 16, 1813.   [5] *Ibid.,* July 23, 1815.

jealousy of the entire trade by his daring ventures and by the high prices he paid to authors. The standing of Miller of Albemarle Street won him the soubriquet of "Lord Albemarle." Joseph Johnson, the publisher of Liberal Nonconformity, gave dinners attended by Price, Priestley, Fuseli the painter, Gilbert Wakefield, and Mary Wollstonecraft. But it was only within the last twenty years that the touch of the industrial revolution had transformed the venerable guild of publishers, the Stationers' Company.[1]

Formerly competition between publishers was practically non-existent. Books were often published cooperatively by several members of the company or by the company as a whole.[2] Moreover, every publisher was at the same time a retail bookseller, and business between publishers was a process of barter, each publisher exchanging a portion of his own stock for a corresponding quantity of books published by the other houses. But the publisher was now a publisher first and foremost, his retail trade an unimportant extra, his concession to the established tradition, though also continued because his shop served as a *salon* where authors, critics and men of literary taste could meet, discover the public demand and acquire a personal influence over the world of letters.[3] He now refused country orders, and purchase had replaced barter in business relations between publishers. Once a year he held a *Trade Sale*. All the booksellers, both those of Paternoster Row and the Edinburgh booksellers, were invited to a dinner at a hotel. After dinner the stock of which the publisher wished to dispose was sold by auction. This arrangement enabled a publisher to sell his stocks quickly, and at the same time the custom of trade dinners was introduced into the book trade.

On the eve of the trade sale publishing houses had no ready money. Their effects had accumulated in the publisher's safe, and their commitments were on so large a scale that the debts of a single firm might exceed £40,000.[4] A financial crisis selected the solid firms by extinguishing the imprudent. The new system of industry and commerce was marked by the supremacy of a few energetic leaders compelled at every instant to employ all their resourcefulness in the defence of their sovereignty. The book trade, equally with the iron or the cotton trade, possessed its "kings" in 1815. Constable reigned in Edinburgh, Murray in London. Constable exploited Sir Walter Scott, Murray Byron. Constable shared with Jeffrey the editorship of the *Edinburgh Review*,

[1] For the changes effected, see Smiles, *Murray*, vol. ii. p. 508.

[2] F. Espinasse, *Histories of Publishing Houses* (*Critic*, April 7, 1860, new series, vol. xx. p. 435).

[3] David Constable to his Father, November 2, 1813 : " It invites literary men to come about you, which I think one of the greatest pleasures of the bookselling profession, and appears to me to make the distinction between the person who is merely a *wholesale dealer*, and him who makes it his profession as well for the advancement of learning as for his emolument " (*Archibald Constable*, vol. ii. p. 114).

[4] Rob. Cathcart to A. Constable, May 2, 1812 (*Archibald Constable*).

the famous critical review whose foundation marked an era in the history of English literature and which was the organ of advanced Liberalism. Murray was editor of the *Quarterly Review*, founded to oppose the *Edinburgh*. Its director was Gifford, its inspiration Canning. Murray, heir to a firm already solidly established, and better educated than his rival, professed all the tenets—ethical, religious and political— of the respectable Conservative. Unlike Murray, Constable, a man of the people, displayed the manners of a parvenu. Overweening, despotic and daring, he pursued his road to bankruptcy. Constable was the " Napoleon " of publishing,[1] Murray " the Prince " of booksellers.[2]

It is astonishing at first sight to remark no apparent decrease in the price of books. New books were very expensive, more expensive indeed than at the commencement of the reign.[3] A short poem by Byron, for instance the *Bride of Abydos* or the *Corsair*, was priced at 6s. 6d., a new novel in two or three octavo volumes between 12s. and 18s. But these figures do not represent the true cost of books. Hookham and Lane had already founded large circulating libraries, in which a single copy served the needs of a great number of readers.[4] And since the publishers were no longer interested in the retail trade and sold their stocks below the published price, booksellers were free to sell below the nominal price. James Lackington had inaugurated the system in 1790,[5] and his example had been followed throughout the entire trade. Again, if first editions were expensive, reprints of popular works were soon issued at a lower figure. A publisher named Harrison had begun in 1779 the system of publication by instalments, in weekly parts of two octavo columns, and priced at 6d.[6] His *Novelists' Magazine* had been followed by the *New Novelists' Magazine*, by the *British Classics* and the *Sacred Classics*. When Hume's *History of England* went out of copyright, two popular editions in parts were published by rival houses, and both were successful. In 1815 the leading publishers were still opposed to this method. Publication in parts, the " number trade " seemed to them unworthy of their reputation ; and they were afraid that a cheap reprint of a successful work would reduce their unsold copies to waste paper or check the circulation of the

---

[1] " The grand Napoleon of the realms of print " (Lockhart, *Life of Sir Walter Scott*, vol. vii. p. 351).

[2] Washington Irving, *Sketch Book*, Preface.

[3] Knight, *Shadows of the Old Booksellers*, Appendix, pp. 263 sqq. The *Market of Literature* records during the first forty years of the reign an increase of price ranging between 50 per cent. and 100 per cent. : " The 2s. 6d. duodecimo had become 4s., the 6s. octavo 10s. 6d., and the 12s. quarto £1 1s." ; and during the following period (1800–27) a further increase in price : " The 4s. duodecimo of the former period became 6s., or was converted into a small octavo at 10s. 6d. ; the 10s. 6d. octavo became 12s. or 14s., and the guinea quarto very commonly £2 2s."

[4] *Ibid.*, pp. 25–6.

[5] *Ibid.*, p. 254. Hitherto booksellers had destroyed a portion of the stock purchased by auction at the Trade Sale and had sold the remainder at the published price.

[6] Rees and Britton, *Reminiscences of Literary London*, pp. 21 sqq.

first edition. But they would be obliged to adopt the new methods at no distant date. Within a few years Constable, and Murray in imitation of Constable, would be selling quite recent novels in a single 6s. volume and would thus multiply tenfold the number of readers.[1]

How large was the public reached by the publishers of London and Edinburgh ? It is difficult to arrive at an exact estimate. The combined circulation of the *Edinburgh* and the *Quarterly* extended to 20,000 copies.[2] These 20,000 purchasers, who represented perhaps 100,000 readers, constituted the élite of the British public. It was calculated that Longman spent £300,000 on the publication of *Chambers's Cyclopædia*, revised by Rees. And the enterprise was a success. This implies an enormous number of purchasers.[3] The increase in the number of publications affords another measure of the increase in the number of readers. 327 was the average yearly output during the last decade of the 18th century, 588 during the first twenty-five years of the 19th century.[4] But the most reliable proof of the prosperity of the book trade is afforded by the large profits which authors were beginning to make. The merchants and manufacturers of the new school were essentially optimists who speculated on an unlimited extension of their markets. The book trade was no exception. Constable, Murray and their fellows displayed their optimism by their liberal treatment of authors. It was the etiquette with publishers not to keep too exact an account, to pay more than the stipulated sum, if the success of a work had exceeded the publisher's expectations,[5] to make up totals to a round sum, and occasionally to pay guineas where the agreement was for pounds.[6] Constable made presents to Scott, and furnished Abbotsford.[7] " In your connections with literary men," wrote the publisher Blackwood to Murray, " you have the happiness of making it " (the publishing trade) " a liberal profession, and not a mere business of the pence." [8] Publishers, now the real patrons of English literature, made the fortunes of authors.

---

[1] *Archibald Constable*, vol. iii. p. 359.

[2] *Memoirs, Journal and Correspondence of Thomas Moore*, vol. ii. p. 40, Jeffrey to Thomas Moore, September 14, 1814 : " It is something to think that at least 50,000 people will read what you write in less than a month. We print now nearly 13,000 copies." Smiles, *Murray*, vol. i. p. 366, John Murray to Lord Byron, September 12, 1816 : " My *Review* is improving in sale beyond my most sanguine expectations. I now sell nearly 9,000. Even Perry says the *Edinburgh Review* is going to the devil." *Ibid.*, p. 372, to the same, January 22, 1817 : " I now this time print 10,000 of my *Review*." *Ibid.*, vol. i. p. 204, Southey to Bedford (1817) : " . . . Murray . . . prints 10,000 and fifty times ten thousand read its contents, in the East and in the West." *Ibid.*, vol. ii. p. 4, John Murray to James Hogg, January 24, 1818 : " . . . the *Quarterly Review*, of which, by the way, the number printed is now equal to that of the *Edinburgh Review*, 12,000, and which I expect to make 14,000 after two numbers."

[3] Rees and Britton, *Reminiscences of Literary London*, p. 53.

[4] Knight, *Shadows of the Old Booksellers*, p. 275. New publications between 1800–27, 19,860 ; if we deduct a fifth for reprints we obtain a yearly average of 588. New publications 1792–1802, 4,096 ; deducting a fifth as before, a yearly average of 327.

[5] Smiles, *Murray*, vol. ii. pp. 129–30.   [6] *Archibald Constable*, vol. iii. p. 165.

[7] *Ibid.*, vol. iii. p. 228.   [8] Smiles, *Murray*, vol. i. p. 456.

For serious works dealing with religion, philosophy, science and travel an author might receive up to £1,000, even £1,500. In 1812 Constable paid Dugald Stewart £1,000 for a preface on *The Progress of Philosophy* to introduce the *Supplement of the Encyclopædia Britannica*, and an equal sum to Playfair for a sketch of *The Progress of Mathematics and Physics*.[1] Fashionable novelists received for a novel £1,500, £2,000, even £3,000.[2] Poets fared as well as novelists and their emoluments increased every year. In 1805 Scott received from Longmans £500 for the copyright of the *Lay of the Last Minstrel*[3] and in 1807 for *Marmion* 1,000 guineas payable in advance. " It was a price," he said later with a laugh, " that made men's hair stand on end."[4] In 1814 he received 1,500 guineas for half the copyright of *Lord of the Isles*, the other half remaining his property.[5] Byron in 1812 received £600 for the first two cantos of *Childe Harold*, 1,000 guineas in 1813 for the *Giaour* and *Bride of Abydos*, £2,000 in 1816 for the third canto of *Childe Harold*.[6] In 1814 Thomas Moore was looking for a publisher to buy a poem. Longmans agreed to pay 3,000 guineas, but asked to see the poem. Murray agreed to dispense with the inspection of the verses, but offered only £2,000. Moore finally agreed with Longmans to take £3,000 for a poem still unwritten, the poem to be at least equal in length to Scott's *Rokeby*.[7] And the second-rate poets benefited by the rise in prices. When Crabbe in 1818 offered Murray his *Tales from the Hall*, Murray offered to purchase the copyright of his entire works for £3,000. Authors had now become so exacting that Crabbe at first refused and sought, in vain, better terms from another publisher.[8]

The authors, thus released from penury and Bohemia, adapted themselves in different ways to the novel conditions. When Crabbe received his £3,000 he was as delighted as a happy child, and hurried off with his banknotes to Trowbridge to show them to his son.[9] Byron remembered that he was a Lord, affected to despise payment, refused to negotiate directly with his publisher and abandoned the money he

---

[1] *Archibald Constable*, vol. ii. pp. 318, 322.   [2] *Ibid.*, vol. ii. p. 70.

[3] Lockhart, *Life of Sir Walter Scott*, vol. ii. p. 196.

[4] *Ibid.*, vol. iii. p. 4 ; Smiles, *Murray*, vol. i. p. 76.

[5] Lockhart, *Life of Sir Walter Scott*, vol. iv. p. 345.

[6] Smiles, *Murray*, vol. i. pp. 211, 221, 367.

[7] *Memoirs, Journal and Correspondence of Thomas Moore*, vol. ii. pp. 57, 58.

[8] Smiles, *Murray*, vol. ii. p. 72 ; *Memoirs, Journal and Correspondence of Thomas Moore*, vol. ii. pp. 235–8. The great reviews were still important sources of income to authors. When Constable founded the *Edinburgh*, he made the experiment of paying his contributors highly, at the rate of ten guineas a page, three times the rate paid by the older reviews, and fifty guineas a number to the editor. The rate per page rose later to twenty guineas. (Cockburn, *Life of Jeffrey*, vol. i. p. 134 ; vol. ii. p. 74.) The *Quarterly* paid the same rates. See Southey's letter to Coleridge : " The most profitable line of composition is reviewing. . . . I have not yet received so much for the *History of the Brazils* " (in three volumes) " as for a single article in the *Quarterly* " (Smiles, *Murray*, vol. ii. p. 39).

[9] *Memoirs, Journal and Correspondence of Thomas Moore*, vol. ii. p. 259.

had earned to poor friends.[1] The aged Southey, whose character was methodical and industrious, turned out epics and reviews with the diligence and regularity of a conscientious workman.[2] Scott was a daring speculator, who got on all the better with Constable because he regarded authorship as Constable regarded publishing.

Scott wrote to get rich, to purchase an estate, to become a great landlord. He began by putting his money into a printing and publishing business in order to receive from his works a double profit, the publisher's as well as the author's. The business was doing badly when Constable bought it. Henceforward the great publisher and the great author worked in partnership. Constable paid Scott fixed sums in promissory notes in return for an undertaking to deliver a poem or a novel by a fixed date. If the undertaking was not fulfilled, and the novel was not delivered by the promised date, Scott redeemed his promise by undertaking to deliver an additional novel by a later date. " They talk," he wrote, " of a farmer making two blades of grass grow where one grew before, but you, my good friend, have made a dozen volumes, where probably but one would have existed."[3] There remained the possibility of Scott's death in the interval. Constable had taken the precaution of insuring Scott's life. But perhaps Scott might have outwritten his welcome. Constable experienced occasional qualms on that score. A fellow publisher warned him that " Bank of England notes fall in value by an over-issue."[4] When this happened, instead of the publisher jogging the author, the author pushed the publisher forward : " I am wholly against any *hiatus* in these works, " Scott told his friend Mr. Cadell. " I have five or six subjects in my head. . . . Some other person may enter into the arena, and give me a heavy oar to work to make up to him again. . . . I am now young and healthy and strong ; some two or three years hence it is hard to say how I may be."[5] Thus in turn did these two men of business spur each other along the road to ruin.

The Novel.

Writers had become well-to-do members of the middle class. No longer were they retainers of king or noble. Their sole patrons now were their readers, for whose consumption they produced in concert with the publisher such literary wares as they deemed most saleable. But the public demanded novels. Author and publisher fed the demand

[1] *Works of Lord Byron : Letters and Journals*, ed. Prothero, vol. iii. pp. 41 sqq. Smiles, *Murray*, vol. i. pp. 354–6.

[2] " Literature is now Southey's trade ; he is a manufacturer, and his study is his workshop." H. C. Robinson, quoted by Smiles (*Murray*, vol. ii. pp. 39–40).

[3] March 23, 1823, *Archibald Constable*, vol. iii. p. 207.

[4] June 12, 1823, *Ibid.*, vol. iii. p. 267 n.

[5] Cadell to Constable, February 5, 1823 (*Ibid.*, vol. iii. pp. 238–9).

with a supply almost excessive. More novels appeared during the opening years of the 19th century than in the period of Fielding and Richardson, of Smollett and Sterne. But the type of novel now in demand was no longer the type popular in the 18th century. Therefore a different type of novel was now written.

Horace Walpole had inaugurated a literary revolution by the publication of his *Castle of Otranto* in 1764. It was a stupid novel, whose literary merit did not surpass the architectural worth of its author's Gothic pile at Strawberry Hill. Nevertheless, its success calls for explanation. Walpole, a sceptic and a *dilettante*, had a sense for the demand of the moment. He perceived that the time was ripe for a double reaction, against the realism of the English novel, and against the classical manner of the French. By this first attempt he fixed the romantic scenery of the imaginative novel, the mediæval castle with a ruined wing untenanted or abandoned to the family ghost. He distributed the casts—the ill-used wife, the cruel husband, his immured victim, the boastful and cowardly retainer. He had thus drawn up the recipe whose application would for a good half-century enable novelists of the " school of terror " to frighten readers out of their wits with no chance of failure and with the expenditure of a minimum of energy. Miss Clara Reeve was the first to follow in Walpole's traces with her *Old English Baron*, " a Gothic history." Further causes supervened to assist the progress of the new school. The French Revolution placed an abyss between the literature of England and France. Meanwhile German literature was coming to birth, a literature of sentiment, romance and unbridled fancy. To put the imagination to school in Germany and to compose Gothic romances was to collaborate with the anti-Gallican and anti-Jacobin movement. Mrs. Radcliffe published her celebrated novels, the masterpieces of the school, her *Sicilian Romance*, *Forest Romance*, *Mysteries of Udolpho* and *Italian*. In his *Monk*, Lewis combined terror with impropriety. Mrs. Roche's *Children of the Abbey* enjoyed a success almost equal to the success of the *Mysteries of Udolpho*. " During my confinement," wrote Lady Holland in 1800, " I have been reading (among other things) multitudes of novels, most of them sad trash, abounding with the general taste for spectres, hobgoblins, castles, etc."[1]

Nevertheless the modern rationalism set limits to this renaissance of fancy. In the manifesto with which he prefaced the *Castle of Otranto* Horace Walpole did not pose as the uncompromising foe of realism. He claims for his novel a position intermediate between the novel of the old style, where " all was imagination or improbability," and the modern novel, " where nature is always intended to be copied . . . and the resources of fancy have been dammed up by a strict adherence to common life." While he would leave his imagination free " to

<hr/>

[1] *Journal of Lady Holland*, January 12, 1800 (vol. ii. p. 41).

expatiate through the boundless realms of invention," he would make his characters act according to the rules of probability, "as it might be supposed mere men and women would do in extraordinary positions."[1] And it was also due to his realism, his desire to keep close to nature, that he attempted to combine in his novel comedy and tragedy, "clowning and sublimity"; in this the disciple of a greater model than Voltaire, Shakespeare himself. And Mrs. Radcliffe never really quits the sphere of real life. For she is careful to reassure the reader at the end of the story, not only by an exact adjustment of fortune to merit, but by a natural explanation of all the happenings which in the course of the tale had appeared preternatural.

The last representative of the school of terror was the Irish writer Maturin. But in the preface to his *Pour et Contre*, which appeared in 1818, Maturin admits the very indifferent success of his earlier novels, *The Wild Irish Boy*, *Montorio* and *The Milesian Chief*, and ascribes it to their lack of "reality and of probability," because the characters, situations and language had been drawn solely from his imagination.[2] The new novel he now offered to the public was devoid of striking incidents and was a copy of everyday life. Even during the last years of the 18th century, when the school of terror was at the summit of its popularity, the style had been an artificial product. In 1815 it was on the decline. Indeed, the British public had never been condemned to an exclusive diet of Gothic romance. The realist novel[3] had survived Fielding and Smollett. But its character had been modified. It had lost its old brutality, its crude masculinity. Indeed, it could scarcely have been otherwise. For the novel was now the monopoly of women. Robert Bage, whose political novels had been popular towards the end of the last century, had just died. Henry Mackenzie, the author of the *Man of Feeling*, and William Godwin, the author of *Caleb Williams*, were ghosts of their former selves. The sole exception, Maturin, does not invalidate the general rule. In the opening years of the century library shelves were laden with the works of women. The fact measures the emancipation of the Englishwoman. But it was an emancipation whose character is difficult to define.

Legislation shows scarcely a trace of it. The political emancipation of woman was obviously non-existent and remote from actualities.

---

[1] Preface to the 2nd edition. Cf. Preface to the 1st edition, pp. 7–8 : "If this *air of the miraculous* is excused, the reader will find nothing else unworthy of his perusal. Allow the possibility of the facts, and all the actors comport themselves as persons would do in their situation. There is no bombast, no similes, flowers, digressions or unnecessary descriptions. . . . The characters are well drawn, and still better maintained." And Miss Clara Reeve in the *Old English Baron* confines within even narrower limits that element of the marvellous, whose recipe she had learnt from Walpole (W. Scott, *Lives of the Novelists*, vol. ii. p. 174).

[2] Quoted in the *Edinburgh Review*, June 1818, No. 59, Art. 9, *Women, or Pour et Contre* (vol. xxx. p. 235).

[3] English writers termed a story of the imaginative type a romance, a story of the realist type a novel. See the definitions in Clara Reeve, *Progress of Romance*, pp. 6, 7, 111.

Mary Wollstonecraft's *Defence of the Rights of Woman* had awoken a very feeble response from public opinion. Even her personal emancipation was merely beginning. Though by a clever use of trustees wealthy women had secured " in equity " the protection of their marriage portion against the exploitation of their husbands, " according to the common law " the wife had no right to her personal fortune.[1] She had not even the refuge of divorce, a privilege reserved to the very rich ; for every divorce required a special Act of Parliament. It was not to law but to custom that the Englishwoman owed a degree of personal freedom unknown apparently in any Continental country. For example, in England the love match was the rule, and normally at least, a girl was allowed the choice of her husband. It was otherwise in France and Germany. Nevertheless, the Englishwoman did not take advantage of her greater degree of personal liberty to claim the right to think, live or write as her male contemporaries thought, lived and wrote. On the contrary, in the pride of her stricter morality, she sought to impose on the male sex that modesty of conduct and language which the world exacted from a respectable woman, or a girl who had been well brought up. This was undoubtedly a result of the Evangelical propaganda. Feminine virtue was portrayed in its most aggressive form in the novels of Christian propaganda written by Hannah More and Mrs. Sherwood. Elsewhere the same influence was at work, though in a more indirect and attenuated form. Passing over the names of Mrs. Inchbald, Mrs. Opie, Miss Owenson and Miss Mary Brunton, we come to the greatest women novelists of the period—Miss Burney, Miss Edgeworth and Miss Austen. While Mrs. Radcliffe doted, these three women maintained the realist tradition. But all three were ignorant of the brutal and unclean aspects of life, and confined themselves to a minutely detailed study of the world open to the observation of a girl of good education and quick understanding.

The subject of Miss Burney's novels is always the same. A young girl, in consequence of unforeseen misfortunes, finds herself plunged suddenly into the difficulties of life, and the novel is the account of her difficulties. Tragedy is by no means wanting ; but the interest of Miss Burney's work lies in her accurate description of the thousand and one incidents of everyday life—her picture of a ball, of an evening at Vauxhall, of a middle-class London family living beyond their means, of a noble family bullied by a pompous and stupid father. Miss Burney's novels are akin to the genre painting and the caricature. And her tone was scrupulously moral. Miss Burney deserved her position as lady-in-waiting at the rigid and prudish Court of Windsor. " She has as much virtue of mind," said her father's old friend Samuel Johnson, when as an enthusiastic admirer of the young novelist he introduced

---

[1] For the jurisprudence on these points, see Professor A. V. Dicey's interesting remarks, *Law and Opinion in England*, pp. 369–73.

her to his friends, " as knowledge of the world," and " with all her skill in human nature," is at the same time "as pure a little creature." [1]

With Miss Edgeworth the novelist was a schoolmistress. Her avowed purpose was to illustrate for the imagination the moral precepts taught in the educational works of herself and her father. Her *Moral Tales* and her *Popular Tales* displayed in action the *Practical Education*, her *Tales of Fashionable Life* the *Essays on Professional Education*.[2] Miss Edgeworth's morality had nothing of the supernatural. Whether preaching or story-telling, her feet were firmly planted on the earth. Occasionally she was content to tell a story for its own sake. The sole object of her Irish stories is to describe for the English reader the picturesque disorder and innate generosity characteristic of her countrymen. The remarks of the critics enable us to understand the qualities which the public appreciated in works which passed for masterpieces. "The quintessence of common sense," declared the *Edinburgh Review*.[3] " Miss Edgeworth," observed the *Quarterly*, " is, if we may be allowed to coin a word, an anti-sentimental novelist."[4]

With Miss Austen this feminine realism attains its perfection. While the 18th century lasted she sought a publisher in vain. The 19th century brought her a publisher and an audience. *Sense and Sensibility* appeared in 1811, *Pride and Prejudice* in 1813, *Mansfield Park* in 1814, *Emma* in 1815. The petty jealousies and hatreds, the littleness and the meanness which characterized social relations in the country and the provincial town, were portrayed by Jane Austen with a merciless, if unembittered pencil. " Have for the first time," wrote Gifford to Murray, " looked into *Pride and Prejudice*, and it is really a very pretty thing. No dark passages ; no secret chambers ; no wind-howlings in long galleries ; no drops of blood upon a rusty dagger— things that should now be left to ladies' maids and sentimental washer-women."[5] And in a review he welcomes the appearance " within the last fifteen or twenty years " of a type of novel which, " instead of the splendid scenes of an imaginary world," is " a correct and striking representation of that which is daily taking place."[6]

The novel of Fielding and Smollett was the novel of the old Whig England—insubordinate, riotous, licentious. The novel of Mrs. Radcliffe was the novel of Tory England—counter-revolutionary, Francophobe, chivalrous, romantic. The novel of Miss Burney, Miss Edgeworth and Miss Austen was the novel of the new Eng-

[1] Madame D'Arblay, *Diary and Letters*, vol. ii. p. 4.
[2] See R. L. Edgeworth's preface to the *Tales of Fashionable Life*, 1809, p. 4.
[3] *Edinburgh Review*, February 1815, No. 48, Art. 3, *Standard Novels and Romances* (vol. xxiv. p. 334).
[4] *Quarterly Review*, January 1814, Art. 1, *Miss Edgeworth's Patronage* (vol. x. p. 305).
[5] Gifford to Murray, 1815 (Smiles, *Murray*, vol. i. p. 282).
[6] *Quarterly Review*, October 1815, Art. 9, *Emma* (vol. xiv. pp. 192–3).

land, the England of middle-class respectability and virtuous common sense, the child of Evangelicalism and industrialism.

Suddenly in 1814 the world of letters was startled by a new novel. Nothing presaged its appearance, and for years to come its author would be anonymous. It related the adventures of a young man named *Waverley*, a colourless and indecisive figure who during the last Jacobite rising in the middle of the 18th century was tossed to and fro between the Whigs and Tories, carried in succession from England to Scotland, from the Lowlands to the Highlands. The public were entertained by its descriptions of a barbarous and heroic society, its episodes of love and war. The author persevered, and *Waverley* opened the long series of " historical novels " by Walter Scott.

Were the Waverley novels the resurrection under a new form of the romance discredited by the extravagancies of Mrs. Radcliffe and her followers ? Undoubtedly the psychological appeal was the same. But Scott revived the romance by making the romance realistic. He himself informs us that his object in *Waverley* was to do for Scotland what Miss Edgeworth had done for Ireland,[1] to utilize the romance to describe the manners of a past state of society, and relate as truthfully as possible the history of a period and country.[2] It is usual to contrast the novel of Scott with the novel of Balzac. But in reality the contrast has been exaggerated. Not only is there plenty of romanticism in Balzac ; there is also plenty of realism in Scott. In many respects Balzac is essentially Scott's successor and disciple, who merely transposes Scott's procedure by applying to contemporary society the methods of the historical novel which Scott had applied to the past. Scott indeed lacks Balzac's depth and genius. The psychology of his heroes is adapted exactly to the intelligence of the schoolroom, and it was, in fact, among children of fifteen that the novels found faithful readers for an entire century. These boys and girls were delighted with the idea of learning history while reading novels. Scott addressed an audience eager at once for extraordinary adventures and the acquisition of knowledge.

Poetry.

The literary revolution which had given birth to the school of terror, to the romance, exercised on English poetry an influence of the same order, but more decisive and more profound. The imagination of

---

[1] General Preface to the *Waverley Novels*, 1829.

[2] *Waverley*, chap. i., Introductory, *sub finem :* " It is from the great book of Nature . . . that I have adventurously essayed to read a chapter to the public " ; also chap. v., *sub finem :* " I beg pardon, once and for all, of those readers who take up a novel merely for amusement. . . . My plan required that I should explain the motives on which its action proceeded. . . . I do not invite my fair readers . . . into a flying chariot drawn by hippogriffs, or moved by enchantment. Mine is a humble English post-chaise, drawn upon four wheels, and keeping His Majesty's highway."

the poets broke the bonds imposed by French classicism, invented freer rhythms and sought new themes in the Christian chivalry of the Middle Ages. The German origin of the Romantic movement is indubitable. Scott began his poetical career by translating German ballads. Then Coleridge, by the publication of *Christabel*, proved that English as well as German poets could draw on the sources of national legend. Then Scott set himself to edit the old Scottish ballads, and finally composed original poetry in the irregular metre which Coleridge had employed in *Christabel*, and published in rapid succession the *Lay of the Last Minstrel*, the *Lady of the Lake*, and *Marmion*. These were short romances filled with adventure and picturesque scenery. And there were occasional touches of the preternatural. The author was not a great poet. He himself disclaims that ambition.[1] But his verse is living and dramatic. It obtained a success beyond all expectation ; and it provoked a host of imitators, who soon wearied the public. Then a new style of ornament suddenly replaced in English poetry the mediæval bric-à-brac introduced by Scott.

The English had begun to realize that the war had not excluded them from the entire Continent of Europe. British troops had never quitted Sicily, and the British possessed another foothold in Portugal. From garrison to garrison the traveller could reach Greece, and beyond Greece Constantinople, the Bosphorus, and Asia. In 1809 the young Lord Byron, disgusted by the reception of his first volume of poems, hurled an insolent defiance at his critics and set out to discover the East. English men of letters had already sought inspiration in that quarter. Beckford's *Vathek* was preeminently a gorgeous picture of the East, not a didactic novel in the Voltairian style. And Southey was at work on *Kehama*. But Byron was the first to reveal to the British public the Mediterranean world as a magnificent reality of which every man, if he would, might be spectator, and where, given sufficient bravery, he might play an active part. The two first cantos of *Childe Harold* are the account of Byron's voyage. The *Giaour* appeared in May 1813, the *Bride of Abydos* before the end of the year, the *Corsair* at the beginning of 1814, and in the same year *Lara*. The public became familiar with a new type of scenery and a new jargon, with Ramadan and Baïram, Maugrebins and Mamelukes, Caïques and Tophaïks, Yatagans and Jerreeds. And from the notes they learned that an emir is distinguished by his green robe,[2] and that when a Turk lost his

---

[1] *Rokeby*, preface : " I shall not, I believe, be accused of ever having attempted to usurp a superiority over many men of genius, my contemporaries ; but, in point of popularity, not of actual talent, the caprice of the public had certainly given me such a temporary superiority over men, of whom, in regard to poetical fancy and feeling, I scarcely thought myself worthy to loose the shoe-latch. On the other hand, it would be absurd affectation in me to deny that I conceived myself to understand more perfectly than many of my contemporaries the manner most likely to interest the great mass of mankind."

[2] *The Giaour*, 357.

temper "his beard curled." "I don't care," [1] Byron wrote to his publisher, "one lump of sugar for my *poetry*, but for my *costume* and my *correctness*; on those points I will combat lustily." [2] Six months had revolutionized the fashion in poetry. Scott replied to *Childe Harold* by *Rokeby*. Then the tide submerged him, and he abandoned poetry for prose. Byron had dethroned him and wore his crown. "Sir Walter reigned before me."

Whatever Byron might say, the change from Scott's romanticism to his own was no mere change of scenery. Byron's poetry was before all things personal, and the philosophy he versified was the antithesis of Sir Walter's moral idealism. Childe Harold was Byron himself, Conrad the Corsair his oriental incarnation. The Corsair became Lara. But what was Lara's country or epoch? Byron had renounced his oriental scene-painting—indeed, local colour of any kind. *Lara* is the direct precursor of *Manfred* and *Cain*, poems of philosophic rebellion, the apotheosis of a Satanic individualism.

The Byronic hero bids defiance to authority in every shape, to monarch, noble, and plutocrat. He rouses to revolt the pauper at home, the Greek in the Levant. And the leader of the rebels hates the very authority he wields. The taciturn despot Conrad disappears one night and abandons to its fate the horde of bandits which he rules. What is command, asks Manfred, but another slavery? From top to bottom society is nothing but a fabric of conventions, illusions and lies. Byron would shatter the idols. Patriotism, glory, honour, he denies them all. He rejects the entire system of hopes and fears on which human morality has been founded. He denies Providence and immortality. And if, after all, God did exist, and the soul were immortal, it would still be a duty to defy God. He is, to be sure, omnipotent. But what reason other than His omnipotent will can He produce in justification of the monstrous commands He lays upon us, the miserable destiny to which He condemns us? Since we are rational beings, we have the power to judge the tyrant who destroys us. For all eternity, damned without hope, but for ever free, we can defy the authority of God. "How?" Lucifer inquires of Cain.

> . . . By being
> Yourself in your resistance. Nothing can
> Quench the mind, if the mind will be itself
> And centre of surrounding things—'tis made
> To sway.[3]

In common with the whole of Europe, British society had been stirred its depths. The war had been followed by riots. But the rebellious

---

[1] *The Giaour*, 593.

[2] Byron to John Murray, November 14, 1813 (*Works, Letters and Journal*, ed. Prothero, vol. ii. p. 283).

[3] *Cain*, Act I, Scene 1.

proletariat of the provinces had neither read Byron nor heard his name. And the educated middle class, who constituted the backbone of the Liberal Opposition, did not know what to make of this strange ally from the ranks of the nobility. Byron's true affinity was with the old Whig aristocracy, rebellious on principle, rather than with the new Opposition, hardworking men of business, whose objection to the aristocracy in power was precisely their dissolute morals and disorderly finance, and who loved everything that Byron hated—order, peace, civilization and comfort. Byron compelled admiration by the ascendancy of personal genius and by the very amazement he created. But in the country of his birth he was an anomaly. Since he met with nothing but mortification from his fellow-countrymen, he twice abandoned England for the Continent. The youthful Shelley, still unknown and, like Byron, a rebel against the beliefs and laws of his country, shared his voluntary exile. But was it, after all, voluntary? If both poets went to live in Italy, it was because British society had refused them a place. "The man who is exiled by a faction," wrote Byron, "has the consolation of thinking that he is a martyr; he is upheld by hope and the dignity of his cause, real or imaginary; he who withdraws from the pressure of debt may indulge in the thought that time and prudence will retrieve his circumstances; he who is condemned by the law has a term to his banishment, or a dream of its abbreviation, or, it may be, the knowledge or the belief of some injustice of the law, or of its administration in his own particular; but he who is outlawed by general opinion, without the intervention of hostile politics, illegal judgment or embarrassed circumstances, whether he be innocent or guilty, must undergo all the bitterness of exile, without hope, without pride, without alleviation. This case was mine."[1]

Let another ten years pass. Byron is dead. The poet Thomas Moore and his publisher Murray are his literary executors. In their possession are the poet's memoirs. Murray reads the manuscript, judges it scandalous and libellous. He summons his intimate friends and in their presence consigns the manuscript to the flames. No one can now read a work, which was perhaps a masterpiece. Murray has sacrificed a fortune, but he has saved British respectability.[2]

The success of Byron's poems would be inexplicable, if they had expressed no sentiments save hatred and scorn for everything which the English regarded with affection or reverence. Byron loved nature and the English loved nature with him. And he loved the sea whose praise is sung in every canto of *Childe Harold*, is indeed a *motif* never left long unheard from the moment of the hero's farewell to his native land to the majestic Invocation to the Ocean which concludes the poem.

---

[1] *Some Observations upon an Article in Blackwood's Magazine*, No. 39, August 1815. (*Works of Byron, Letters and Journals*, ed. Prothero, vol. iv. p. 478.)

[2] Smiles, *Murray*, vol. i. pp. 442–3.

And his fellow countrymen born in an island and accustomed to regard the sea as their bulwark and their empire loved it with him. But his passion for nature insensibly acquired a character more tender and more religious. When about 1816 he came under the poetic and philosophic influence of Shelley it became coloured with a vague pantheism. To be absorbed in nature is to be united with the universal being.

> I live not in myself but I become
> Portion of that around me, and to me
> High mountains are a feeling.[1]

And it is a reconciliation in the bosom of deified nature with humanity itself.

> To fly from, need not be to hate mankind ;
> All are not fit with them to stir and toil,
> Nor is it discontent to keep the mind
> Deep in its foundation.[2]

It is to return to the source of life, to discover the secret of immortality.

> And when at length the mind shall be all free
> From what it hates in this degraded form,
> When elements to elements conform
> And dust is as it should be, shall I not
> Feel all I see, less dazzling but more warm ?
> The bodiless thought ? The spirit of each spot ?
> Of which, even now, I share at times the immortal lot.[3]

When Byron ceases to talk the language of devils and damned souls, and worships nature, his inspiration is akin to Wordsworth's own, and Wordsworth was, or was on the verge of becoming, England's national poet.[4]

It was in 1798 that Wordsworth and Coleridge had jointly published the *Lyrical Ballads*. Then Coleridge forsook poetry for metaphysics. The popular favourites were Scott and Byron, Mrs. Radcliffe and Kotzebue. " The invaluable works of our older writers," wrote Wordsworth sadly, " I had almost said the works of Shakespeare and Milton are driven into neglect by frantic novels, sickly and stupid German tragedies, and deluges of idle and extravagant stories in verse."[5] He

---

[1] *Childe Harold*, Canto 3, st. 72.   [2] *Ibid.*, Canto 3, st. 69.
[3] *Ibid.*, Canto 3, st. 74.
[4] For the Wordsworthian quality in Byron, see *Memoirs, Journal and Correspondence of Thomas Moore*, vol. iii. p. 161 ; G. Brandes, *Hauptströmungen*, . . . vol. iv., *Der Naturalismus in England*, p. 47.
[5] *Poems . . . including Lyrical Ballads and the Miscellaneous Pieces of the Author, with additional Poems, a new Preface and a Supplementary Essay in two Volumes*, London 1815. Wordsworth, however, had miscalculated ; his hour had not yet come. See *Edinburgh Review*, November 1814, No. 47, Art. 1, Wordsworth's *Excursion* (vol. xxiv. pp. 1 sqq.) ; also *Quarterly Review*, October 1815, Art. 10, Wordsworth's *White Doe* (vol. xiv. pp. 201 sqq.).

ascribed this morbid fashion to the craving for violent sensations natural to a period of profound disturbance. But he continued to write without regard to the favour of the public. The *Prelude*, the most penetrating of his philosophic poems, was written in 1805. When peace was restored he hoped that his time had perhaps arrived. Not only did he publish in 1814 his *Excursion*, a curious poem at once theological and bucolic, half didactic and half descriptive ; in 1815 he offered the public a second edition of his early poems and prefaced it by a literary manifesto, a declaration of principles.[1]

His poetical system was concerned with form and matter alike. For the form of poetry, Wordsworth denied the existence of a " poetic diction." A poet should be able to evoke the most poignant and the most profound emotions with the words and phrases of everyday life. For the matter, he denied the existence of a specific class of subjects which alone were capable of poetical treatment. The true poet has no need of extraordinary adventures, preternatural happenings or of the mysterious atmosphere in which events are clothed by distance in time or space. The joys and sorrows of daily life, the peaceful landscapes of the English country-side possess sufficient beauty. To render that beauty the poet need only describe them with a scrupulous veracity of detail. Does this mean that Wordsworth's theory of poetry reduces itself to the defence of prosaic realism ? that his object is to justify little descriptive sketches after the manner of Crabbe, the poetical counterpart of the genre paintings of Wilkie and Mulready ? There is much more than this in Wordsworth. He is not satisfied with correcting the literary taste of his readers. He has a further aim in view : " to reform and purify " their " moral sentiments." His often prosaic realism cloaks an ethical, indeed a religious purpose.

Everything in nature merits the observation and description of its humblest details because everything is the creation of a Will infinitely good. Wordsworth's poetry is based on a fundamental optimism, on the conviction of an essential harmony between nature and man. But unhappily, as man develops the consciousness of his existence as an independent individual, capable of 'thinking his own thoughts, and acting in accordance with his own will or caprice, he destroys this harmonious correspondence with the environment in which the Creator has ordained his birth. Civilization, the artificial life of the city, have blinded him to the true relationship between natural objects and himself. It is therefore the task of the philosopher by his appeal to reason, and of the poet by his more direct appeal to the feelings, to reconcile man with nature and with God. How should the poet, thus invested by Wordsworth with the mantle of the theologian, fulfil his august function ? By making every poem a continuous symbol, expressive of the intimate bond between the human soul and the universe.

[1] Preface, 1815.

> To every natural form, rock, fruits or flower,
> Even the loose stones that cover the highway,
> I gave a moral life : I saw them feel,
> Or linked them to some feeling.[1]

Thus is man reunited with his native environment and his passions are disciplined. The very fact of employing verse as his medium furnishes the poet's narrative or description with a measure which restrains the movements of emotion. Man is restored by art to that natural serenity which is his *summum bonum*.

> From nature doth emotion come, and moods
> Of calmness equally are nature's gift :
> This is her glory : these two attributes
> Are sister horns that contribute her strength.
> Hence genius born to thrive by interchange
> Of place and excitation, finds in her
> His best and purest friend ; from her receives
> That energy, by which he seeks the truth,
> *From her that happy stillness of the mind*
> *Which fits him to receive it when unsought.*[2]

Too often Wordsworth's poetry is as commonplace as prose, as dull as a sermon. But if we resign ourselves to the soft and equable current of these innumerable lines of blank verse, we cannot fail to experience the serene and pure loveliness of the emotions which he is analysing, and of the landscapes which he describes. And we shall understand the quality of his appeal to the English mind. To be sure Wordsworth does not, like the popular preacher, urge the fear of hell or man's need of a supernatural redemption. Sin and damnation play little part in his creed of optimism. He is the son not of Wesley but of Rousseau. But however little Methodists and Evangelicals might relish Rousseau's natural religion, his philosophy was the first emotional and Christian reaction against the critical rationalism of the 18th century. And in spite of themselves the Evangelicals felt his influence.

Bowles, Wordsworth's precursor, was an Anglican parson, and it was his conversion to Christianity which made Cowper the poet of nature before Bowles. Gisborne, the author of *Walks in the Forest*, was also an Evangelical ; and a most sincere love of nature is displayed throughout the *Journal* of Wilberforce.[3] We may repeat about the

---

[1] *Prelude*, Book III.　　　　　　[2] *Ibid.*, Book XIII, opening.

[3] See especially his letter to Miss Wilberforce (Stock), April 16, 1786 : " I was out before six, and made the fields my oratory, the sun shining as bright, and as warm as at Midsummer. I think my own devotions become more fervent when offered in this way amidst the general chorus, with which all nature seems on such a morning to be swelling the song of praise and thanksgiving, and except the time that has been spent at church and at dinner (and neither in the sanctuary nor at the table, I trust, had I a heart unwarmed with gratitude to the Giver of all good things) I have been all day basking in the sun " (*Life*, pp. 110–11). Or again in 1812 : " Yesterday, I was fully occupied until the evening, when it would have been almost sacrilege and ingratitude not to walk for half an hour at least enjoying one of the finest sun-settings and

nature poets our earlier remarks about the landscape painters. British life possessed a twofold aspect. It was half urban, half rural. As the industrial revolution progressively concentrated labour in the towns, the country districts, deserted by the artisan and the labourer, were becoming enormous parks, solitudes abandoned to the contemplation of the artist. In the country he found rest, lived at peace with his Creator and almost fancied himself in Eden.

THE CULTIVATION OF THE NATURAL SCIENCES EDUCATIONAL INSTITUTIONS.

Protestantism and Science.

A superstitious literalism in the interpretation of the Bible discourages the exact observation of natural fact. And religious emotion may easily produce a distrust of natural science, with its claims to infallibility and universal validity. In England, however, the period which witnessed the Methodist propaganda and the revival of orthodox Protestantism witnessed also a series of important scientific discoveries which followed one another in rapid succession. One of two things, therefore, is certain ; either we have exaggerated the part played by the Methodist revival in the formation of the national character, or this revival was after all less unfavourable to the scientific spirit, than would appear at first sight. In the first place, Protestantism is a book religion, a thoughtful and serious religion. From every Christian, worthy of the name, it demands a knowledge of the Bible, and thus encourages its adherents to learn reading and to that degree at least favours, if not the higher studies, at least elementary education. And secondly it was among the middle class, the mercantile and industrial class, that the new propaganda obtained the largest number of converts. But the manufactures which were now coming into existence and spreading so rapidly needed engineers and scientific experts. Moreover, the very sight of machinery inclines the mind to seek a mechanical explanation of all natural phenomena, and among them of human society. We must examine the entire system of education in Great Britain from the elementary schools to the Universities ; and we must endeavour to determine the action on British education of these two forces, the Protestant revival and the industrial revolution. Wherever neither of these two forces was operative, we shall discover complete stagnation ; where, on the contrary, either or both had made itself felt, vitality and progress.

moon-risings which my eyes ever beheld " (*ibid.*, vol. iv. p. 71). Cowper's poetry aided him to understand and love the beauties of nature (*ibid.*, vol. iii. pp. 417, 419, 420). Similar impressions are recorded by other Evangelicals, for instance by John Newton (Colquhoun, *Wilberforce and his Friends*, vol. i. p. 101), Lord Muncaster (*id. ibid.*, p. 138), and Porteus (R. Hodgson, *Life of Porteus*, pp. 29, 98).

Elementary Education.

As the rapid diffusion of scientific knowledge is only rendered possible by a well-organized system of education, so in turn the possibility of such a system depends on an extensive and systematic provision for elementary education. Calvinistic Scotland held up its system of elementary schools as a model to the entire United Kingdom. A statute of 1696, modified in 1803, provided for the lodging and salary in every parish of a schoolmaster to be appointed by the local landowners and the minister.[1] The Scottish system was not strictly speaking a system of free education ; but pauper children were educated at the expense of the parish, and the others paid only a trifling fee for their schooling. They paid 1s. 6d. a quarter for instruction in reading, 2s. or 2s. 6d. for reading and arithmetic together, and as much for Latin ; for Latin was taught in the elementary schools of Scotland.[2] Nor was it a system of compulsory education ; but it was in fact universal. When a peasant was too poor to pay the master for the whole year, he made his children work on the land during the summer and sent them to school during the winter. When the area of a parish extended over many square miles, and it was, therefore, impossible for the children to attend school daily, the schoolmaster became an itinerant teacher and was lodged in turn by the inhabitants of the parish.

But we must not seek a relation of cause and effect between this development of primary education and the progress of industry. On the contrary, the growth of manufactures was accompanied by the decline of popular education.[3] The parishes were swamped in a chaos of houses and factories, and like the church, the school ceased to be a centre of social life. The children, conscripts of the factory, no longer possessed the time for education. All, or almost all, could still read ; but the number of those who could not write was on the increase. Individual philanthropists were forced to supply as best they could the deficiencies of the official system by opening free schools in the poor quarters, or, like Dale and Owen, by attempting to educate the children in the factories where they worked. It was not in the manufacturing districts of the Clyde ; it was in the country, and even in the Highlands, that travellers remarked the surprising contrast between the lack of material comforts, a squalor almost " Irish," and the universal zeal for education, the schools crammed with pupils, the reading-room and

---

[1] 45 Geo. III, cap. 54. Till 1803 the master's salary ranged between a minimum of 200 Scottish marks (about £11 2s.), and a maximum of 300 marks (about £16 13s.). The Act of 1803 raised the minimum figure to 300 marks (about £16 13s.), the maximum to 400 marks (about £22 4s.).

[2] Adolphus, *British Empire*, vol. iv. p. 249. Cf. Froude, *Thomas Carlyle : a History of the First Forty Years of his Life*, vol. i. pp. 5–6 ; Bain, *James Mill*, pp. 6–7.

[3] Chalmers, *System of Parochial Schools*, pp. 15, 16.

library in every village.[1] Intellectual Scotland was the old Scotland, rural and Calvinistic. And its capital was Edinburgh—the city not of the manufacturer and the merchant, but of the theologian, the lawyer and the University professor.

England possessed nothing similar. The endowed schools were private religious foundations, where poor children received free education ; sometimes also, free lodging, board and clothing. The oldest of these dated from the Middle Ages. The majority were about a century old. These were the charity schools founded by the Society for Promoting Christian Knowledge.[2] But many of these had deteriorated. The nominal schoolmaster had made his post a sinecure, pocketed the bulk of the salary and delegated the work to a substitute miserably paid.[3] Nor was their number sufficient to supply the needs of a large nation. Only 150,000 children attended these schools.[4] The dames' schools were institutions of a humbler type. Old women eked out a livelihood by taking charge of little children and giving them lessons in reading for about 3d. a week. When in 1819 the attempt was made for the first time to draw up educational statistics the number of children attending the dame schools would be estimated at about 53,000.[5]

There remains a third type of school ; the schools of industry, opened in certain districts to provide pauper children with the rudiments of education, and to teach them a trade. But we must not forget how scanty was the ground covered by the schools of industry. Out of the 194,914 Poor Law children between the ages of five and fourteen only 21,600 enjoyed the benefit even of the extremely elementary education imparted in these schools.[6] And we have now described the entire provision for primary education made by eighteenth-century England. To be sure, many reformers during the last fifty years had been scandalized by the educational condition of the country. Adam Smith,[7] himself a Professor of Glasgow University, and later Malthus,[8] had help up Scotland as a model for English imitation. And circumstances

---

[1] R. Ayton, *Voyage round Great Britain*, vol. ii. p. 117 ; vol. iii. (continuation by W. Daniell), p. 17 ; vol. iv. p. 78–9.

[2] Lecky, *History of England in the 18th Century*, vol. iii. p. 32.

[3] H. of C., June 20, 1816, Brougham's speech (*Parl. Deb.*, vol. xxxiv. p. 1233) ; July 7, 1817, Brougham's speech (*Parl. Deb.*, vol. xxxvi. pp. 1303–4).

[4] *A Digest of Parochial Returns : Education of the Poor*, vol. iii. p. 224. Statistics for 1819, 165,433, of whom 125,843 attended schools termed " ordinary," 39,590 schools termed " new."

[5] The exact figure was 53,624 (*A Digest*, . . . vol. iii. p. 224). By " Dames' Schools " are meant, in the words of the introduction, " not only those kept by females, but also preparatory schools for very young children generally."

[6] Colquhoun, *Treatise on Indigence*, 1806, p. 142.

[7] *Wealth of Nations*, Book V, chap. i., Part 3, Art. 2 (Thorold Rogers' ed, vol. ii. p. 369.)

[8] *Principle of Population*, Book IV, chap. ix.

had apparently conspired to present the British legislature with an opportunity to introduce a system of elementary education more liberal even than the Scottish. When Sir Robert Peel and Robert Owen were utilizing the provisions of the old Poor Law to introduce the first legal interference with child labour, it would surely have been possible to make further use of the Poor Law, and organize a system of popular education. Why could not elementary education have been treated as a form of poor relief and free schools provided from the poor rate ? But it was in vain that Pitt in 1796, as part of his extensive scheme of Poor Law reform, proposed the universal provision of schools of industry.[1] It was in vain that Whitbread ten years later reopened the question and demanded in every parish a school, where children between seven and fourteen should have the right to free education for two years.[2] Pitt's Bill was not even put to the vote. Whitbread's Bill, passed as a matter of form by the Commons, was thrown out by the Lords. Only one instance can be found of State action and that of a most indirect nature. In 1812, on the motion of Wilberforce, an Act was passed by which the endowed schools were placed under the control of the Court of Chancery, to ensure the observance of the founder's wishes.[3] And the Act was a dead letter ; had indeed, in the course of interminable debates, undergone several amendments which had weakened it considerably. If in the course of the past half-century popular education had made undeniable progress no credit was due to the State. It was the free initiative of private individuals, which had compensated in some measure for the inertia of the public authorities.

In 1780 at Gloucester a local journalist named Robert Raikes had founded with the help of an Anglican clergyman the first Sunday school. Every Sunday the children were taken twice to church, were taught the catechism and received elementary instruction from a teacher, who was either paid or gave his services as a charity. Raikes found imitators. In large towns such as Leeds and Birmingham a methodical system was adopted. The town was divided into districts and in each district two Sunday schools were opened—one for boys, the other for girls. In 1785 a *London Society for the establishment of Sunday Schools*

---

[1] Eden, *State of the Poor*, vol. iii. p. 308, Appendix No. 11, *Mr. Pitt's Speech and Heads of his Bill for the Relief of the Poor*. See also Bentham's criticisms of Pitt's Bill, *Observations on the Poor Bill*, etc. (*Works*, ed. Bowring, vol. viii. pp. 369–439).

[2] See the debates, H. of C., February 19, April 24, July 13, August 4, 1807 ; H. of L., August 11, 1807 (*Parl. Deb.*, vol. viii. p. 865 ; vol. ix. pp. 423, 798, 1049*, 1174). The scheme was revived by Robert Owen in 1813. See *Diary of Lord Colchester*, April 30, May 4, 1813 (vol. ii. pp. 444–5).

[3] 52 Geo. III, cap. 101. An Act to provide a summary remedy in cases of abuses of trusts created for charitable purposes. Cf. *Observations on the Amended Bill now Depending in the House of Commons " for the Registering and Securing of Charitable Donations for the Benefit of Poor Persons in England*," by A. Higham, January 1810. See also H. of C., January 9, 1812 (*Parl. Deb.*, vol. xxi. p. 108), April 29, 1812 (*Parl. Deb.*, vol. xxii. p. 1119). For the agitation which culminated in the passage of the Act, see T. Bernard, *Of the Education of the Poor*, pp. 43, 45, 306 sqq.

was founded, and in 1803 a *Sunday School Union*, whose activity embraced the whole of England. In 1820 it was calculated that 477,225 children in England and Wales attended the Sunday schools.[1] What were the influences to which the movement owed its success? The sentimental humanitarianism whose foremost representative was Jean Jacques Rousseau had awakened the public conscience to a keener sense of duty to children. This occasioned a revival of interest in the theory of education and the publication of the first children's books written expressly for their amusement and instruction. It is probable that however little they might desire or even be conscious of it, writers so rigidly orthodox as Mrs. Trimmer and Mrs. Sherwood were under the influence of Rousseau, when they created in England a literature for children. Nevertheless, the inspiration of the Sunday school movement was obviously religious and Evangelical. Its object was the sanctification of the Lord's Day and the salvation of souls.

John Wesley encouraged the movement. Henry Thornton was a member of the managing committee of the London Society from its foundation in 1785. Hannah More, at the suggestion of Wilberforce,[2] devoted ten years of her life to the foundation of Sunday schools in Gloucestershire. During these years she was the object of violent attacks from the local gentry and farmers, and from the Tory Press. Her schools, declared her opponents, were a danger to public order, the lower classes would learn in these schools to think for themselves, they were hotbeds of sedition political and religious, of Methodism, of Jacobinism. The charge of Jacobinism was an absurdity, the charge of Methodism was not so absurd. Hannah More's schoolmasters did occasionally set up as preachers, and transform her school into a Nonconformist *meeting-house*.[3]

Joseph Lancaster, a Quaker, opened in 1798 a small school in London in which he claimed to apply new educational principles. He reformed discipline through appealing to the motive of respect for the opinion of our fellows, by means of a rational method of honours and humiliations. He introduced original methods of learning to write and calculate with a slate and pencil; and he also borrowed from an Anglican clergyman named Dr. Bell the system of teaching by monitors. The master was assisted by a number of subordinate teachers taken from the pupils themselves, each of whom took charge under the master's super-

---

[1] *A Digest*, vol. iii. pp. 1171, 1275. The figure for England was 452,817, for Wales 24,408. Brougham (June 28, 1820, *Parl. Deb.*, new series, vol. ii. p. 62) gives a different and a considerably lower figure, only 100,000.

[2] *Life of Wilberforce*, vol. i. pp. 246–7, letter to Hannah More, October 1789.

[3] For all this see Roberts, *Memoirs . . . of Mrs. Hannah More*, vol. ii. pp. 178, 215 sqq.; vol. iii. pp. 101 sqq., 115 sqq., and 254. See, for the schools founded by Mrs. Hannah More, T. Bernard, *Education of the Poor*, pp. 112 sqq. For the Nonconformist Sunday schools and the attempts made by the Anglican clergy to obtain their condemnation, as an infringement of the Conventicle Act, see the *Times*, August 7, 1811.

vision of a little band of ten children. Thanks to this economical system " one master could teach a thousand ; or even a greater number of children, not only as well, but a great deal better, than they can possibly be taught by the old methods, and at an expense of less than five shillings a year for each." [1] Lancaster interested in his school his co-religionists, who were wealthy and always ready to spend money on philanthropy ; and he secured the patronage of Lord Somerville, the Duke of Bedford, and two princes. In 1805 his school, now a free school, contained provision for 1,000 pupils. It served also as his training college. His monitors were apprentices of the scholastic profession, trained to undertake the management of other schools founded in the provinces on the same pattern.[2] But Lancaster was a bad administrator, and squandered his funds. In 1807 he found himself faced with a deficit of £3,000. His friends came to his assistance and founded the *Royal Lancastrian Institution*, which became in 1814, when further extravagancies had led to the final ejection of Lancaster, under the title of the *British and Foreign School Society*, a powerful agency for the promotion of popular education.

What elements composed this group of educators ? When Wilberforce was pressed to accept the position of vice-president on the committee of the Lancastrian Institution he refused. He had no liking for a method of education which rested entirely on emulation and vanity. But he took a fortnight to consider his decision.[3] And the active members of the Institution were precisely those philanthropic Nonconformists, Quakers or members of the three primitive denominations who enjoyed so high a degree of his regard and sympathy, with whom he had so often worked.[4] Side by side with them were to be found Bentham and his friends, men of no religion, steeped in the ideas of eighteenth-century France. They were attracted by the experimental and mechanical character of Lancaster's educational methods. It was at the Lancastrian Institution that James Mill was initiated into the propaganda of the reformers ; and it was there that Brougham made the acquaintance of Mill, and through Mill of Bentham.[5] They founded a branch of the Society at Westminster. Bentham offered his house for use as a school, and composed, as a programme of studies, his *Chresto-mathia*, a treatise on Utilitarian Education.[6] Between believers and

[1] *Edinburgh Review*, November 1810, Art. 3, *Education of the Poor* (vol. xvii. p. 67).
[2] For the growth of the system in England, see *The Philanthropist*, vol. i. pp. 118 sqq. (1811).
[3] *Life of Wilberforce*, vol. iii. p. 478.
[4] For the part played by Quakers in the Lancastrian Institution, see *Life of William Allen*, vol. i. pp. 93 sqq., 109 sqq., 112, 113, 114, 132, 151 sqq., 166.
[5] For the Benthamite element see Graham Wallace, *Life of Francis Place*, pp. 93 sqq. ; also my own *Formation du Radicalisme Philosophique*, vol. ii. pp. 247 sqq.
[6] *Chrestomathia : being a Collection of Papers, explanatory of the Design of an Institution proposed to be set on foot under the name of the Chrestomathic Day School, for the use of the Middling and Higher Ranks in Life (Works*, ed. Bowring, vol. viii. pp. 1 sqq.).

rationalists collisions were inevitable. But the alliance subsisted. The Benthamites were the theorists of the industrial revolution, the mouthpiece of the class in which on the other hand the Evangelical propaganda had made the most marked progress. The School Society, therefore, was a perfect expression of the mentality of the young middle class—half Protestant, half industrial, passionately philanthropic.

Religiously the Lancastrian schools were neutral schools or, to speak more accurately, were neutral as between the different Christian sects. The reading of the Bible was obligatory, but it was unaccompanied by commentary or catechism. To use the formula of James Mill, whose private convictions favoured a more radical type of neutrality, they were schools for all, not for Churchmen only. Hence the hostility of the High Church party.

Mrs. Trimmer denounced a method of education which destroyed first the fear of man, then the fear of God, and stigmatized Lancaster's schools as training schools for the army of the approaching revolution.[1] For Daubeny Lancaster was a deist, a new Julian the Apostate, an emissary of Satan.[2] In a public lecture Coleridge, who had now become the philosopher of the High Church party, read a passage from the book in which Lancaster explains his method, denounced his schools, which he compared to prisons or convict stations, and flung the book to the ground with a theatrical gesture of disgust.[3] Something must be done to counteract the mischief. Anglicans remembered that the system of teaching by monitors was after all the invention of an Anglican. They set up Bell against Lancaster. The Archbishop of Canterbury entrusted Bell with the management of a charity school, the Bishop of Durham gave him a rich living. In 1811 there was formed under the patronage of the entire Episcopate a rival society to the Lancastrian Association, the "National Society for the Education of the Poor in accordance with the Principles of the Established Church."

The directors of the National Society were animated by a spirit narrowly clerical and Tory.[4] In 1812, at the very moment when the New Toleration Act was being passed, the Bishops attempted to confine admission to the Society's schools to children who attended the Anglican church on Sunday. The result of such a decision would have been to force into the Lancastrian schools the masses who floated between the Church and Methodism, were willing that their children should be

[1] *Edinburgh Review*, October 1806, No. 17, Art. 12, *Mrs. Trimmer on Lancaster's Plan of Education* (vol. ix. pp. 177 sqq.).

[2] *Edinburgh Review*, November 1810, No. 33, Art. 3, *Education of the Poor* (vol. i. pp. 69, 83).

[3] *Quarterly Review*, October 1811, Art. 15, *Bell and Lancaster's System of Education* (vol. vi. p. 285).

[4] The spirit which inspired the founders of the society is evident from the fact that the term "national" was only adopted under protest. Since the word was derived from French, it was suspect of Jacobinism (Overton, *English Church*, p. 239).

taught the Anglican Catechism, but who often preferred to hear in the Wesleyan chapel a more homely and more fervent preacher than the clergyman of the Establishment. After six months' resistance the Episcopate yielded.[1] Here also the Evangelicals had exercised a moderating influence. Nevertheless, the new society was a creation of the High Church, in which the Evangelicals played a very subordinate part. Certainly they were not hostile nor even indifferent to the education of the lower classes. Wilberforce and his friends had been the first to plan, between 1802 and 1804, an Anglican scheme of primary education.[2] But owing to the force of circumstances they had been squeezed out between the Dissenters and Rationalists of the *British and Foreign Society* on the one hand, and the High Churchmen of the *National Society* on the other.

Pessimists still complained and declared the results of these educational efforts extremely unsatisfactory. In 1806 Colquhoun estimated at 2,000,000 the number of children in England and Wales who received no education whatever.[3] The philologist Alexander Murray maintained in 1810 that three-quarters of the agricultural labourers were unable to read.[4] When the first official statistics were compiled in 1819 the number of children attending school in England and Wales amounted to a fifteenth of the entire population; in Scotland, where a knowledge of reading was believed to be universal, to a tenth.[5] But these figures require interpretation.

In the first place this proportion is an average. In certain western [6] and midland [7] counties and in the four northern counties [8] the proportion approached, equalled or even exceeded the Scottish figure. In England as in Scotland, although to a lesser degree, a popular Protestantism deeply rooted in the national character favoured the education

---

[1] For the question, see *Diary of Lord Colchester*, January 1812 *passim*, and then May 4th and June 18th, 24th, 27th (vol. ii. pp. 352 sqq.).

[2] *Life of Wilberforce*, vol. iii. p. 72; T. Bernard, *Education of the Poor*, pp. 240 sqq.

[3] Colquhoun, *Treatise on Indigence*, p. 143.

[4] *Archibald Constable*, vol. i. p. 295, A. Murray to A. Constable, December 29, 1810.

[5] *Digest of Parochial Returns*, 1819, vol. iii. pp. 1171*, 1275* : (1) *England and Wales.—* Total population, 10,155,328; number attending school, 674,883 children. (2) *Scotland.—* Total population, 1,885,688; number attending school, 176,525 children.

[6] H. of C., April 24, 1807, Mr. Davies Giddy's speech : " That in a part of England that he lived in (in Cornwall) education was pretty generally diffused, at least so much of it, that almost every person there had learned reading, writing and something of arithmetic (*Parl. Deb.*, vol. ix. p. 543). Nevertheless, the statistics of 1819 do not show that in Cornwall the proportion of children attending school exceeded the average for the entire country. On the other hand, they show for the adjoining county of Devonshire out of a population of 383,308 a school attendance of 30,633. The proportion is a twelfth.

[7] Derbyshire one-twelfth, Lincolnshire one-eleventh, Nottingham one-eleventh, Rutland one-ninth.

[8] Northumberland one-tenth, Durham one-eleventh, Cumberland one-ninth, Westmorland one-ninth. H. of C., April 24, 1807, Whitbread's speech : " Westmorland, the best educated county in England " (*Parl. Deb.*, vol. ix. p. 550). See also, for the schools in the northern counties, Tuke, *North Riding*, 1800, pp. 317-18.

of the people. This was the reason that the agricultural counties which had been hardly touched by the new industrial civilization, counties such as Devónshire, Lincolnshire and Westmorland, contained so very few illiterates ; that during the 18th century so many celebrated men, engineers like Scott and Telford, political writers like Gifford and Cobbett, scientists and scholars like Dalton and Porson had risen from the ranks of the people ; that the development of manufacturers could draw from the country the necessary staff of engineers and foremen. Again the immediate effect of the industrial revolution, since it involved child labour, had been to lower the standard of popular education. The number of illiterates was nowhere greater than in Middlesex and Lancashire,[1] precisely the two industrial centres of the nation. But these conditions aroused the zeal of the philanthropists. Evangelicals and Nonconformists began a campaign against this glaring abuse by the foundation of new educational institutions. Such was the success of their propaganda among the governing classes that in 1815 no Member of Parliament would have dared to maintain, as had been maintained during the anti-Jacobin scare, that the promotion of popular education was the work of an anarchist and a revolutionary. The two great parties now vied with each other in the attempt to capture the popular mind by the foundation of the larger number of schools. Undoubtedly the statistics of 1819 do not enable us to gauge accurately the effects of their rivalry. They merely inform us of the number of children attending school in England at that date ; they do not inform us whether their numbers were on the increase, were stationary or on the decline. But we may, however, call attention to the fact that of the 650,000 English children attending school, close on 150,000 attended schools founded since 1803 where the methods of Bell and Lancaster were applied. We can only conclude that, if the number of illiterates was still enormous, it was rapidly decreasing.[2]

Secondary Education. The Public Schools.

If the English were disposed to admit the superiority of the Scottish system of primary education they were by no means prepared to extend

---

[1] Proportion of school attendance in Middlesex one-twenty-fourth, in Lancashire one-twenty-first.

[2] *Digest of Parochial Returns*, 1819, vol. iii. pp. 1171*. Children in endowed schools, 165,433 ; in unendowed schools, 478,849. Total 644,282. In new endowed schools, 39,590 ; in new unendowed day schools, 105,582. Total 145,172. And these statistics take no account of the Sunday schools. If the Sunday schools were taken into account the proportion of school attendance to the total population would practically equal the proportion in Scotland. Scotland, 1,805,688 : school attendance inclusive of Sunday schools, 229,974 (proportion almost equals one-eighth). England, 9,543,610 : school attendance inclusive of Sunday schools, 1,115,099 (proportion equals one-eighth). Wales, 611,718 : school attendance inclusive of Sunday schools, 55,009 (proportion equals one-fourteenth). Obviously the education given in the Sunday schools was elementary in the extreme. Nevertheless, those who had attended a Sunday school cannot be regarded as absolutely illiterate.

that admission to what we now term secondary education. In Scotland secondary education among the upper classes was domestic, education by a private tutor, a poor devil wretchedly paid, known as the dominie. For children of the middle classes, as for the hard-working children of the proletariat, it was an education in the day schools which existed in every town large or small throughout the Kingdom. Of these the most celebrated was the High School of Edinburgh.[1]

The English, on the other hand, had adopted the boarding-school system. But the English boarding school bore no resemblance whatever to the boarding school, as organized on the Continent by the Jesuits and later by the Napoleonic university. The English boarding school was unique, unlike any other educational establishment in the world ; and the English were intensely proud of it and saw in it one of the sources of their national greatness. "The Battle of Waterloo," said Wellington, "was won on the playing fields of Eton."[2] All the English boarding schools were originally religious foundations—royal foundations like Eton and Westminster, or the foundations of wealthy benefactors, like Charterhouse and Merchant Taylors' School ; and they had been founded for the free education of a fixed number of poor children. From the beginning paying pupils had been admitted in addition to the scholars. When the number of these paying pupils did not exceed the number of scholars, the school, attended by a small number of children, had remained the primitive grammar school, a charitable institution with very little prestige. In other schools, on the contrary, the paying pupils had become the majority.[3] In this way arose the great public schools of modern England—Eton, Winchester, Westminster, Charterhouse, Rugby, and Harrow—to which the nobility and gentry were practically obliged to send their children.[4]

The teaching given in these schools was, in conformity with the traditional spirit of the grammar school from which they were descended, exclusively literary and classical. The boys composed Latin "declamations" and Latin and Greek verse. Arithmetic, algebra, geometry, and geography were taught only as extra subjects, and in a very elementary form, during the few hours of study on holidays and half-holidays.[5] It was in vain that the middle-class opposition, the group of Benthamites, were already protesting against an education devoid of every "utilitarian" feature and ill-adapted to the needs of a practical

---

[1] Cockburn, *Memorials*, pp. 3 sqq., 249 ; Adolphus, *British Empire*, vol. iv. pp. 260–1.

[2] Even if the saying is apochryphal (Percy M. Thornton, *Harrow School and Surroundings*, p. 352), the legend is typical.

[3] At Harrow in 1816 out of 295 boys there were only three scholars. In 1818 and 1819 the number of scholars, in spite of all the efforts made to increase it, did not exceed ten (Percy M. Thornton, *Harrow School and Surroundings*, p. 230).

[4] Adolphus, *British Empire*, vol. iii. pp. 73 sqq. See, for a criticism of the system, *Edinburgh Review*, August 1818, No. 32, Art. 3, *Public Schools of England* (vol. xvi. pp. 326 sqq.).

[5] Sir C. H. Maxwell Lyte, *Eton College*, pp. 321 sqq.

age. The parents whose sons went to a public school were deaf to these complaints. They were not educating their sons for commerce; they were indifferent to science. What they valued in the great public schools of the country was their aristocratic and manly system of education, if indeed we can speak of a system, where there reigned a sovereign contempt for system of any kind.

The masters taught their classes, and in cases of serious insubordination they interfered and flogged the offenders. Otherwise they left the boys to themselves. There were no masters, like the French *maîtres d'études*, whose province was the continual maintenance of discipline. Discipline was left in the hands of the older boys, the members of the sixth form, which constituted the senate, the ruling aristocracy of the public school. Servants were few or none. The boys, therefore, must provide their own service. The younger boys, the members of the lower forms, were the fags of the older boys, waxed their shoes, boiled the water for their tea, carried their cricket balls and bats. An enormous society of boys between the ages of eight and eighteen governed by an unwritten code of its own making, an almost free republic of 100, 200 or 500 members, a club where even before adolescence a boy was imbued with the spirit of an aristocratic nation : such was the English public school.

The British aristocracy was not a closed caste. The public schools were not open only to the sons of gentlemen and closed to commoners. A great manufacturer, a wealthy banker, had only to renounce commerce for his son and send him to a public school and the University : henceforward his son belonged to the ruling class and lived on a footing of equality with the sons of noblemen and gentlemen who had been his school-fellows. Moreover, the British aristocracy was an aristocracy of equals, not nicely graded like the German aristocracy. And this lesson also was learned at the public school. The son of the noblest and wealthiest parents began as a fag, the humblest ended as a member of the Sixth. Common membership of the same school, a source of pride to all the boys alike, levelled every distinction of wealth or rank.[1] When a little English boy of eight left his home to enter a public school his family felt that he was really going out into the world.[2] No longer will his father kiss him on the cheek ; he will treat him henceforward as one gentleman treats another. When ten years later the same boy, now a young man, exchanges Eton or Winchester for Oxford or Cambridge he will nurse the conviction, exaggerated sometimes to the pitch of absurdity, that experience has nothing further to teach him.

---

[1] Bulwer, *England and the English*, p. 159. "Boys at a public school are on an equality" (p. 160). "At no place are the demarcations of birth and fortune so faintly traced as at a school."
[2] *Journal of Lady Holland*, vol. ii. p. 236 : "On Monday, the 17th (January 1808), we took Charles to Eton. He is now launched into the sea of human affairs ; the *world* of a public school he will find very different from the world seen from under the paternal roof."

Bring him face to face with a young man of the same age, who, for special reasons, has received a private education at home : how striking is the contrast between the confidence and conceit of the former, the timidity and awkwardness of the latter. They had not undergone the same initiation ; they did not belong to the same world.[1]

On the whole the public school belonged to the old England of the 18th century. The new moral forces, whose influence was, as we have seen, so powerful among the middle class, had not yet penetrated these citadels of aristocracy. Just as the public-school education was neither scientific nor commercial, but exclusively classical, so among masters and boys alike Evangelicalism was unknown. The masters were Anglican clergymen of the old type and the religion of a public school, if we can call it religion, was crude in the extreme. The prevailing morality was the morality of the tribe, tyrannical, often barbarous. The bullying was severe and the fags were often tortured by their fag-masters. As among the Spartan youth, certain forms of theft were accounted permissible, even honourable, and landlord and farmer in the neighbourhood of a public school must be prepared for constant raids. Rebellions against masters were frequent. Byron began his career as a rebel in the great Harrow mutiny which broke out in 1808 against an unpopular headmaster.[2] Games were played with a savagery which knew no rules. They had not yet been submitted to the scientific, almost pedantic regulation which they would receive a few years later. The first cricket match between Harrow and Eton was played in 1796, without the knowledge of the respective authorities, and all the boys who took part in it were flogged.[3] It was not until 1822 that the first official match would be played between the two schools and that Eton would engage professional instructors for cricket.[4] Nevertheless, we should beware of exaggerating, as many English writers are inclined to exaggerate, the importance of the reforms effected in the discipline of the public schools during the first half of the 19th century. When in 1827 Thomas Arnold will begin his reform he will make no revolutionary changes ; he will proceed along the lines already laid down. He will need only to make use of the group morality already existing in a barbarous form ; to appeal to the corporate pride of the boys, especially of the senior boys ; to subject the customs of the school to the control, sometimes visible, more often invisible, of the masters ; and he will

---

[1] Miss Austen, *Sense and Sensibility*, chap. xxxvi : "... talking of his brother, and lamenting the extreme *gaucherie* which he really believed kept him from mixing in proper society, he candidly and generously attributed it much less to any natural deficiency, than to the misfortune of a private education, while he himself, though probably without any particular, any material superiority by nature, merely from the advantage of a public school was as well fitted to mix in the world as any other man."

[2] Percy M. Thornton, *Harrow School and Surroundings*, p. 219.

[3] Sir C. H. Maxwell Lyte, *Eton College*, p. 369.

[4] C. Wordsworth. *Annals of my Early Life*, pp. 9 sqq.

transform Rugby, to employ his own expression, into a nursery of "Christian gentlemen."

When a boy left school he proceeded to the University. He became a *student* at one of the four Scottish universities, Edinburgh, Glasgow, St. Andrews, Aberdeen, or an *undergraduate* of Oxford or Cambridge. To these two terms corresponded two distinct types of university.

The Scottish Universities.

The Scottish universities can hardly be regarded as institutions of higher education.[1] The student entered at about the age of fourteen—sometimes even younger ; some students were barely ten on leaving either a grammar school, or in the majority of cases one of those parochial schools in which, as we know, Latin was taught. A four-year course was the rule, or in technical terminology a course of four consecutive sessions. The first of these sessions was spent in completing the very elementary knowledge of Latin which the Scottish boy brought with him to the university, and in beginning the study of Greek. With the second session the studies, though still elementary—the students were only fifteen or sixteen—changed their character. Logic was compulsory. Cockburn has told us what a revelation the first lectures of Finlayson were to himself and his fellow students. " Until we heard him, few of us knew that we had minds : and still fewer were aware that our intellectual operations had been analysed, and formed the subject of a science."[2] The course of logic was followed in the third year by moral philosophy, which comprised a smattering of metaphysics, moral philosophy in the strict sense, the philosophy of history, and political economy. At Edinburgh, Glasgow and St. Andrews there was a special course of political economy. After the course of moral philosophy came the course of natural philosophy, in other words of physics and chemistry. When to these courses we add the special course of mathematics, which in the second and third years served as a preparation for the course of natural philosophy, and remember that in the three universities of Edinburgh, Glasgow and St. Andrews, and the two colleges of Aberdeen, neither the subjects taught nor the order in which they were taught were identical, we obtain an idea, which, if lacking in detail, is quite sufficient for our purpose, of the curriculum of the four universities. It is the curriculum, comprehensive without being overburdened, of a superior type of secondary education. England did not possess its equivalent.

When this four-year course had been completed, it was followed

[1] For the system of studies in the Scottish universities see an excellent article, written from the English standpoint—fifteen years later, indeed, than our period, but of which we can, nevertheless, make use with the necessary reservations (*Quarterly Journal of Education*, vol. iv. pp. 21 sqq., 234 sqq.).

[2] *Memorials*, p. 21.

by years of specialized and professional study. Suppose the student now eighteen years old intended to enter the ministry : he could either live in the country, acting possibly as a schoolmaster, and content himself with an annual visit to the university to attest his presence by reading a sermon ; or he could remain at the university and follow a four-year course of theology. If he wished to become a barrister or a doctor, he was provided at Edinburgh and Glasgow and, up to a certain point, at the Marischal College in Aberdeen, with excellent schools of law and medicine which enjoyed a world-wide reputation.

The English readily found fault with the system of education followed in the Scottish universities. They pointed to the inadequate teaching of the humanities, of Latin and Greek. The classical course at a Scottish university was identical with the curriculum of an English public school ; nor was it obligatory for students of medicine. Was Presbyterian Scotland so averse to the classics because it cherished Puritan prejudices against pagan antiquity ? They criticized the shortness of the sessions, barely twenty-two weeks in all—from November till Easter. They criticized even the method of teaching. The students were non-collegiate, living in lodgings in the town and only attending the university for lectures. The lectures were public and had degenerated into elaborate displays held before audiences of a hundred or more students. There was no intimacy between professors and students. And they denounced the absence of a qualifying entrance examination, of a serious final examination. Every student who had followed the courses for four years left the university with the degree of M.A. But national jealousy counted for much in these English criticisms, which invited counter criticism.

The quality of the audience to which the Scottish professors lectured was itself a compensation for the alleged deficiencies of the curriculum. A system of scholarships regularly organized opened the universities to the poorest Scotsman, if he were a genuine student. In virtue of a resolution passed by the General Assembly in 1645 every presbytery which comprised at least twelve parishes must provide an annual scholarship of a value not less than £5 12s., and this scholarship was payable for four consecutive years.[1] In this way the replenishment of the Presbyterian ministry was permanently secured. It is true that the scholarship was apparently insufficient to defray the entire cost of life at the university—the fees payable to the professors, which varied with the course and university between ten shillings and three guineas, and the cost of board and lodging. But the poor student knew how to

---

[1] Adolphus, *British Empire*, vol. iv. p. 249. The earliest statistics which deal with the matter, compiled in 1825, give a total of 72 scholars at St. Andrews, 79 at Glasgow, 80 at Edinburgh, and for the two Aberdeen colleges, 134 at King's College (out of a total number of 235 students) and 106 at Marischal College (*Quarterly Journal of Education*, 1832, vol. iv. p. 36).

eke out his resources. His wants were few. Every week a messenger came in from the country, brought him oatmeal, potatoes, salt butter and eggs, and took back linen to wash and clothes to be mended.[1] Between the lectures he repeated them for the benefit of some wealthy student. And during the six months' vacation, indeed the shortness of the session was in part designed to make university life possible for him, he either gained a livelihood as tutor in a noble family or returned to the spade or the plough on his father's farm. For the Scottish student brought with him to the university that enthusiasm for learning which had already during his childhood enabled him to make such an excellent use of the parish school.

And the Scottish professor, though faced with so vast an audience, had devised the means, whatever his critics might allege, of establishing contact with his pupils. The custom which Jardine had introduced at Edinburgh of devoting either a portion of every lecture or an entire lecture once a week to the correction of exercises and oral questions, was becoming more common every year.[2] And if the entrance examination was unknown at Glasgow, Aberdeen and St. Andrews, there was a formal public examination at the beginning or end of every session, calculated to stimulate the ambition of the students. The same object was served by the prizes which had been founded for the students who composed the best essays. Sometimes these prizes were awarded by the vote of the students. And if the Scottish professor was less occupied by teaching than the professors of other universities, the students benefited by the provision of distinguished teachers to whom the six months' vacation gave sufficient leisure to compose the works which rendered them famous. The neglect of the classics is undeniable. But it was precisely because the classics did not occupy a predominant position in the curriculum that the education given at the Scottish universities possessed that philosophic and scientific character which was its distinctive feature. Even the course of rhetoric was marked by a scientific and abstract quality. We should, indeed, describe it as a course of æsthetics, in which, in the language of an official report, it was the aim of the professor " to invest criticism with the character of a science by relating the productions of genius to the operations of our physical and mental nature."

Alone in the United Kingdom the Scottish universities possessed an original school of philosophy. The tradition had been continued for three-quarters of a century—at Glasgow by Hutcheson, Adam Smith and Reid, at Aberdeen by Beattie, at Edinburgh by Dugald Stewart and Thomas Brown. For the historian of philosophy the Scottish philosophers are preeminently critics of the systems of Berkeley, Hume

[1] J. A. Froude, *Thomas Carlyle*, vol. i. pp. 20 sqq.
[2] *Appendix to General Report of Commissioners on the Universities and Colleges of Scotland,* 1831, p. 246.

and Hartley. But we must be sure that we understand the nature of their criticism. In Berkeley they criticized his idealism, in Hume his scepticism. That is to say they rejected the metaphysical conclusions which these philosophers believed themselves to have reached by the application of their method. But they did not reject the method itself. They criticized also the psychologists of Hartley's school, who explained our entire mental life by a mechanical association of ideas, without however drawing an idealist or sceptical conclusion. But their criticism was motived by a distrust of Hartley's generalizations as unwarrantably rash, and by the suspicion that his system was too simple to explain the complex phenomena of psychology. Thomas Brown, who had occupied Dugald Stewart's chair since 1810, followed so closely the French ideologists of the school of Condillac that he was even charged with plagiarism.[1] And his famous analysis of the origin of the idea of space is in perfect conformity with the principles of the Hartleians. In short, the entire question debated between Berkeley, Hume and the followers of Hartley on the one hand, and the Scottish philosophers of " common sense " on the other, is confined to the application of a method, admitted as their common starting-point by all the disputants alike, the method initiated by Locke. For all alike philosophy is reducible ultimately to psychology, and is essentially experimental and positive. In his important *Dissertation on the Progress of Philosophy*, published in 1815, Dugald Stewart, the most illustrious member of the Scottish school, maintained that by metaphysics we must understand " not Ontology or Pneumatology, but the Inductive Philosophy of the Human Mind."[2]

The teaching of science was as well organized in the Scottish university as the teaching of philosophy. All the great British physicians of the 18th century, with the exception of the brothers Hunter, had been Scottish professors. Black, the eighteenth-century physicist who was the immediate precursor of modern chemistry and anticipated most closely the modern theory of heat, lectured at Glasgow, and it was in his laboratory that Watt began his researches. And Watt, alone of the great English inventors, worked from the standpoint of theoretical, not merely of applied, science. Black's work on latent heat had been continued by his pupil Irvine, a professor at the same university, and later by Crawford, whose first experiments were made at Glasgow. Leslie, who published in 1804 a classic " on the nature and propagation of heat," lectured at Edinburgh University. Robison and Playfair were professors of repute. To all these savants the universities made very considerable grants of money for the purchase of the necessary apparatus. In 1831 the Professor of Physics at Edinburgh, even when

---

[1] Sir William Hamilton, *Discussions on Philosophy and Literature*, etc., 3rd ed., 1866, p. 44.

[2] *Preface to the First Dissertation, Supplement to Encyclopædia Britannica*, vol. i. p. 17.

lamenting the inadequate equipment of his laboratory, will be obliged to admit that no institution in Britain possessed as good a laboratory.[1]

The Scottish universities were centres of an intense intellectual activity. The closing years of the 18th century and the opening years of the 19th marked the zenith of their greatness. Not only the students, but the entire intelligentsia of Edinburgh, were to be seen taking notes at Dugald Stewart's lectures.[2] Around the universities debating societies flourished, at which, in virtue of a tradition almost unquestioned, the students possessed entire liberty to raise any question they pleased, theoretical or practical.[3] A society of this kind was the Academical Society at Edinburgh, founded in 1796 and now on the decline. Another was the Speculative Society, which dated from 1764 and was enjoying undiminished prosperity. It was at the Speculative Society that about the year 1800 the youthful adherents of the two political parties had engaged stirring contests. Lord Henry Petty, sent by his father, Lord Lansdowne, to make a course of studies at Edinburgh, took part in these debates, and there made the acquaintance of the men who were later, as orators or publicists, to constitute the principal support of the Liberal Opposition—Brougham, Horner and Jeffrey. For if the English decried the system which obtained at the Scottish universities, their actions gave their criticism the lie. It had formerly been the fashion among the nobility to complete the education of a young nobleman by a "grand tour" on the Continent in the company of a tutor. Twenty-five years of Continental war had rendered the tour impossible, and it was now to Edinburgh University that noblemen often sent their sons on leaving the public school to complete their education before going up to Oxford or Cambridge. We have already had occasion to depict the spirit of Scotland, at once liberal and austere. To a laxer England Scottish Calvinism was a teacher of serious morality and serious thought.

Oxford and Cambridge.

Very different was the system followed at Oxford and Cambridge.[4] For over a century the nominal professors had lacked an audience. Both universities had alike degenerated into agglomerations of independent "colleges." The college was a species of lay monastery where celibate fellows resided with their pupils. There was no division of

[1] *Appendix to General Report*, 1831, p. 134.
[2] Cockburn, *Life of Jeffrey*, pp. 119; *Memorials*, pp. 174–5.
[3] Cockburn, *Life of Jeffrey*, vol. i. pp. 51 sqq.; *Memorials*, pp. 27 sqq., 73–4; *Memoirs . . . of Francis Horner*, vol. i. p. 56.
[4] To be complete mention must be made of Dublin University. It consisted merely of a single college, where the tutorships had become sinecures, since the students were no longer in residence and put in an appearance at Trinity College, only to receive their degrees. The entire importance of Trinity College lay in the fact that it was a stronghold of English Protestantism in Ireland.

labour between the colleges. Every college claimed to teach every subject the student needed to learn. There was little or no division of labour between the tutors of the same college. Every tutor had the charge of a certain number of pupils, whose entire course he directed by lectures delivered to a class, or by individual tuition. Not apparently a system favourable to education. But the defenders of the English university maintained that the system possessed great moral advantages, that it brought teacher and pupil into close personal contact. They also called attention to the fact that the English universities were attended by students of riper years than the students of a Scottish university. The young Englishman was eighteen, not fourteen, years old when he arrived at the university. One thing at any rate is certain—the important part played by the two Universities in the intellectual and moral life of the nation. Was this position justified ? If so, what was its justification ?[1]

Oxford was preeminently the Tory university. Every new intellectual movement was an object of suspicion or abhorrence whether it were Methodism, which, though born like so many religious movements at Oxford, had not prospered at its birthplace, or the Jacobinism of the French revolutionaries and of those Englishmen whose sympathies lay to a certain extent with them. A number of students suspected of Wesleyan leanings had been sent down. No town in England had subscribed more liberally to the fund on behalf of the *emigré* priests. It is true that in 1809 Lord Grenville, the Leader of the Opposition, author of the Act which abolished slavery and a supporter of Catholic emancipation, had been elected chancellor of the university in opposition to Lord Eldon, the intimate friend and political adviser of King George. But such manifestations of independence were few. The High Church reigned at Oxford. It was not the spiritual and other-worldly High Church that would be born in fifteen years' time, but the High Church of the 18th century, with its stolid conservatism and imperturbable apathy. The descriptions of Gibbon,[2] Bentham,[3] and Jeffrey[4] have rendered the intellectual torpor of Oxford a byword. There was a complete absence of rivalry between colleges or individuals. Men did not become undergraduates or fellows by passing an examination or even by election. The great public schools enjoyed a monopoly of scholarships and fellowships alike and distributed them at their unfettered discretion. Wealthy students kept hounds, passed entire nights over the bottle, gambled for high stakes. Nor did the University impose

---

[1] See, for an excellent description of the teaching given at the Universities, its deficiencies, the progress actually accomplished, and a comparison with the Scottish universities, the *Quarterly Review*, June 1827, Art. 8, *State of the Universities* (vol. xxxvi. pp. 216 sqq.). The article was the work of Charles Lyell. (Smiles, *Murray*, vol. ii. p. 267).

[2] *Autobiography*, chap. iii. ed. 1897, pp. 66–7.

[3] *Works*, ed. Bowring, vol. x. pp. 36 sqq.

[4] Cockburn, *Life of Jeffrey*, vol. i. pp. 35 sqq.

on candidates for the degree of "Bachelor of Arts" any examination worthy of the name. Three questions made public in advance in theology, logic and grammar, the answers to which existed in a stereotyped form and passed from candidate to candidate, followed by a dinner with the Regent Master who had questioned the candidate, constituted the entire examination.[1] "Except praying and drinking, I see nothing else that it is possible to acquire in this place," wrote Jeffrey to a friend in Scotland.[2] Such Oxford remained until the end of the 18th century. Since that time several reforms had been effected. The repute enjoyed by the Scottish universities, the even greater repute of the German universities, and the fall of the old Sorbonne made the continuance of this torpor impossible. In 1800 a system of genuine examinations was organized.[3] After two years at the University the undergraduate who wished to be promoted to the rank of *Sophista generalis* must construe to the satisfaction of a board of examiners whose impartiality was beyond question a passage, no longer made public in advance, from a Greek and a Latin author. And there was a further optional examination in Aldrich's *Manual of Logic* and in Euclid's *Elements*. For the B.A. degree there was an examination at the end of three years in religion, in logic, on Aristotle's *Rhetoric* and *Ethics*, in mathematics. This examination proving too difficult to attract more than four or five candidates a year, new regulations were introduced in 1807,[4] which transformed a qualifying into a classifying examination. Thus established on a definite basis the reform, if we may trust contemporary witness, awoke at Oxford an intellectual ambition hitherto unknown.

To obtain better tutors the colleges were beginning to abolish the public-school monopoly and to open their fellowships to all comers. And to raise the quality of their students they were instituting entrance examinations, and terminal examinations upon the term's work. When Ward visited Oxford he noticed the improved tone of the University. There was less ragging and less drunkenness. He describes the examination, at which he was himself present, of a brilliant scholar, who answered questions for five consecutive hours before a crowded hall. "I regard," he writes, "the institution of these examinations as

---

[1] Cox, *Recollections of Oxford*, pp. 35–6.

[2] Cockburn, *Life of Jeffrey*, vol. i. pp. 39–40.

[3] *Statutes*, vol. ii. pp. 29 sqq. See for a summary of the reforms, *A Reply to the Calumnies of the Edinburgh Review*, 1810, by E. Copleston, pp. 138 sqq. ; Cox, *Recollections of Oxford*, pp. 45–6. Cf. Charles Lyell, *Travels in North America*, 1845, vol. i. pp. 270 sqq.

[4] *Statutes*, vol. ii. pp. 64–5. Candidates were divided into three classes. The first was the class of "honours" men, the second also bestowed the right to be enrolled on the register of the University, and by an additional statute passed in 1809 (*Statutes*, vol. ii. p. 401), the third class was thrown open to all who chose to present themselves, except those, to use the words of a defender of the system, "who displayed an extreme incapacity or an extraordinary lack of scholastic education or had been flagrantly idle during their life at the University."

one of the most important national improvements that has taken place in my time."[1] But before we decide whether this enthusiasm was justified, we must investigate more closely the degree, and above all the real character, of the progress accomplished.

It was not in the very least an improvement in the teaching of science. No doubt mathematics entered into the scheme of the new examinations. But they counted for practically nothing. Pure mathematics alone were concerned and the standard was elementary. In 1815 the thought had occurred to no one of setting up a special board of examiners in mathematics.[2] For the natural sciences there had existed at Oxford since the 18th century public lectures in " experimental philosophy," astronomy, mineralogy and botany, and in 1803 a Chair of Chemistry had been established. But these courses were optional and no examination was attached. Hearers were few or none. Even the Chairs of Medicine had become sinecures. The examinations in this faculty were a pure formality. The same indifference was shown towards the attempts that were made to impart a scientific character to the study of humanity, social or individual. The Faculty of Law might have been utilized for this purpose. But at Oxford the Faculty of Law was no less a sham than the Faculty of Medicine. There was no Chair of Political Economy : the occupant of the recently established Chair of Modern History was expected to throw out passing allusions to the new economic theories. " The best works in political economy," wrote Copleston, the Provost of Oriel, " as well as in the elements of law and politics, are in the hands of many students with the full approbation of those who regulate their studies ; although it is never forgotten that to lay a foundation of liberal literature, ancient and modern, before any particular pursuit absorbs the mind is our main business."[3]

The English were a nation of manufacturers and merchants governed by an aristocracy who made it a point of honour to appear ignorant, indeed to be ignorant of the economic foundation on which rested both the national greatness and their own. And it was at Oxford that this aristocracy finished its education. It would have none of a scientific education which it scorned as plebeian and materialist. It demanded

[1] Letters to Ivy, December 27, 1812 (p. 182). Cf. Coleridge, Biographia Literaria, 1817, chap. iii. pp. 67–8 : " To those who remember the public schools and universities some twenty years past, it will appear no ordinary praise in any man to have passed from innocence to virtue, not only free from all vicious habit, but unstained by one act of intemperance or degradations akin to intemperance."

[2] Quarterly Review, article quoted above (vol. xxxvi. pp. 257–8).

[3] A Reply to the Calumnies, . . . p. 154. Cf. the opinions on political economy expressed on p. 172 : " However important and even necessary it may be, it is a subordinate and not the predominant concern in public affairs—not less than the management and improvement of an estate in private life is an inferior duty to the education of children, the maintenance of character and the guiding of a house. . . . Its great leading principles, however, are soon acquired ; the ordinary reading of the day supplies them."

an education exclusively classical. And Oxford knew nothing of
the methods by which German scholars were transforming the study
of the classical texts : the *Edinburgh Review* criticized severely the
costly editions issued by the Oxford University Press which were over a
century behind the productions of the German school.[1]

Cambridge differed from Oxford. There the college fellowships
had never been monopolized by the public schools, and the masters
had therefore more liberty to appoint competent tutors. Relations
between tutors and pupils were more friendly than at Oxford.[2] Just
as the Oxford tradition was Tory, the Cambridge tradition was Whig.
The obligation of subscription to the thirty-nine articles had been
abolished altogether in 1775 for the undergraduates, and for Bachelors of
Arts a formula had been drawn up in language deliberately ambiguous.[3]
In 1793 the Jacobinism of the fellows and undergraduates of St. John's
College and Trinity College had alarmed the authorities.[4] If Oxford
was the stronghold of the High Church, Cambridge, where Milner
and Simeon taught and preached, was, as we have seen, a centre of
Evangelical activity. This occasioned an inevitable *rapprochement*
with Dissent. The Baptist preacher Robert Hall attracted to his
chapel not only the normal meeting-house congregation—shopkeepers,
farmers and artisans—but a large number of members of the University,
both tutors and undergraduates.[5] In 1809 the Duke of Grafton,
Chancellor Elect of the University, openly attended in London the
Unitarian chapel in Essex Street.[6] For the past thirty years Cambridge
had been distinguished by its zeal for the abolition of the slave trade.[7]
Nothing of the kind would have been possible at Oxford.

And we must remark another important difference. At the end
of the 17th century, when Newton was making the discoveries to which
he owes his renown, Cambridge had established the examination known
as the mathematical tripos. Cambridge therefore had possessed for
over a century a system of genuine examinations, and a system whose
character was distinctively scientific and modern.

The lectures in physics, chemistry and anatomy were better attended
than at Oxford.[8] Clarke, who had occupied since 1803 the new

[1] *Edinburgh Review*, July 1809, No. 28, Art. 10, *The Oxford Edition of Strabo* (vol. xiv. pp. 429 sqq.).

[2] Peacock, *Life of Young*, p. 120 ; C. Wordsworth, *Annals of my Early Life*, pp. 35 sqq.

[3] C. H. Cooper, *Annals of Cambridge*, vol. iv. pp. 336, 390.

[4] For the episode of Frend's expulsion see Gunning, *Reminiscences of Cambridge*, vol. i. pp. 280 sqq.

[5] O. Gregory, *A Brief Memoir of the Life of Robert Hall*, pp. 111-12.

[6] Campbell, *Lives of the Chancellors*, vol. vii. p. 234. "The King said . . . 'it would be hard if Cambridge had a Unitarian Chancellor and Oxford a Popish one.'"

[7] Clarkson, *Abolition of the Slave Trade*, vol. i. pp. 203 sqq., 456-7. In 1818 a Dissenter was on the point of occupying a Chair at Cambridge. *Quarterly Review*, July 1818, Art. 10; *Cambridge Botanical Professorship* (vol. xix. pp. 434 sqq.).

[8] *Quarterly Review*, article quoted above (vol. xxxvi. p. 263).

Professorship of Mineralogy, was a scientist of distinction.[1] For the past twenty years Farish had been lecturing on chemistry and applied mechanics to audiences which approached a hundred. For his practical work and his demonstrations he had at his disposal a fine laboratory equipped with a steam engine.[2] While Oxford, faithful to the scholastic tradition, was teaching Aristotle's *Logic* and *Ethics*, Aristotle was unknown at Cambridge. Newton's *Principia*, and in philosophy Locke's *Essay* and the works of Paley, were the foundation of the Cambridge course. And candidates were examined not only on Locke and Paley, but on Hume, Butler, Clarke, and Hartley.[3] No systematic courses were yet given in political economy ; but the deficiency had for many years been keenly felt by many tutors. Paley had introduced lectures on political economy into his course of moral philosophy. In 1799 Ingram had demanded the institution of a Professorship in Economics,[4] and his desire was to be fulfilled in 1816. And the scientific character of the education given at Cambridge was apparent even in classics and theology. Porson, who had died in 1809, had been one of the greatest Hellenists in Europe. Marsh, the foe of the Bible Societies, was the only member of the Church of England who attempted to apply to the Bible the methods of German criticism. If further evidence be desired of the spirit of scientific rationalism which prevailed at Cambridge, here is a conclusive, if external, proof. The critics of the *Edinburgh Review*, whose attacks upon the University of Oxford were so unsparing, treated the sister University with indulgence or passed it over in silence ; and silence is a species of indulgence. But when all has been said, we must admit that the methods employed at Cambridge in teaching natural science were in many respects open to complaint, and invited criticisms of a similar nature to the criticisms that were urged against the methods of contemporary Oxford. As at Oxford, the courses in science were optional. A series of unassuming lectures delivered to an audience whose attendance was not compulsory, they were elementary in the extreme. Newton's chair was occupied by a theologian, Milner, and Gunning in his witty and entertaining *Reminiscences of Cambridge* describes his lectures in optics as mere " exhibitions of the magic lanthorn."[5] Moreover, the teaching of mathematics was submitted to a traditional routine. A Newtonian scholasticism reigned at Cambridge as the Aristotelian scholasticism at Oxford.[6] All

1 G. Dyer, *History of the University of Cambridge*, 1814, vol. . p. 216.

2 *Life of William Allen*, vol. i. p. 77. See the interesting conspectus of his course published by Farish under the title *A Plan of a Course of Lectures on Arts and Manufactures, more particularly such as relate to Chemistry*, 1st ed., 1796.

3 *Cambridge University Calendar* for the year 1814, p. 259.

4 G. Dyer, *History of the University of Cambridge*, 1814, vol. i. p. 220.

5 Gunning, *Reminiscences of Cambridge*, vol. i. p. 259.

6 For this Newtonian idolatry and its effects, see *Edinburgh Review*, January 1808, p. 22 n., Art. 1, La Place, *Traité de Mécanique céleste* (vol. xi. pp. 249 sqq.) ; also Peacock, *Life of Young*, p. 186.

the progress effected since Newton in the study of the differential and integral calculus was deliberately ignored, and the antiquated method of fluxions obstinately maintained. Few Englishmen, therefore, were capable even of understanding the great works of the contemporary French mathematicians. Astronomical mechanics and mathematical physics were alike unknown at Cambridge. And the ignorance of Cambridge hindered the development of these branches of science throughout the whole of England.

To sum up, the University of Oxford, although important reforms had been made in the methods of study, was exclusively literary and classical and despised or ignored the sciences. The University of Cambridge, where the intellectual interest had always been more serious, had indeed been affected by the modern developments in natural science, but could not be considered in any degree the home of active scientific research. Both Universities were suffering from a radical evil common to both alike, and due to the composition of their student body. No doubt at Cambridge, and even at Oxford, there had been for many years past an élite who worked hard, who even at times overworked themselves to prepare for an examination.[1] But the great mass of undergraduates were deliberately idle.

Neither University educated doctors ; and barristers learnt their profession in London. If future doctors and barristers spent a short period at Oxford or Cambridge, it was either under the compulsion of the rules of their profession or because it was the correct thing to do from the social standpoint, and the body of which they hoped to be members was aristocratic. All candidates for Ordination passed through the University. But as we have seen, the national Church in England made no claim to be intellectual. The vast majority of undergraduates were drawn from the nobility and gentry.[2] The ambition of the ablest was to play a part in the political and parliamentary life of the country. These men asked from their teachers a sufficient stock of philosophic and historical commonplaces, a few tricks of oratory, and some reminiscences of the classics. And they wanted nothing further. For the rest the University was entirely and exclusively a club of young men who had come up on leaving their public school to learn the art of spending money. During the seven months of term the wealthiest could spend several thousands. It was difficult to live

[1] See the favourable account of Cambridge which, in 1811, John Campbell, the future Lord Campbell, wrote to his father (*Life of John, Lord Campbell*, vol. i. p. 265). The testimony of a Scotsman is above suspicion. Cf. Lyell, *Travels in North America*, 1845, vol. i. pp. 286-7.

[2] This accounts for their small number, 3,000 between Oxford and Cambridge in 1827, according to Lyell's estimate (*Quarterly Review*, vol. xxxvi. p. 240), as against 4,000 at the Scottish Universities. But Lyell adds that the number of students at the two English Universities " has greatly increased of late." Ward (*Letters to Ivy*, December 27, 1812, p. 183) reckons for Oxford " 700 to 800 young people . . . including the representatives of at least half the great families in the Kingdom."

in a town where these rich spendthrifts set the fashion, under £100 to £150 a year.[1] The poor student was condemned to a precarious and humiliating existence in an environment necessarily unfavourable to serious study. We can now appreciate the reason of the immense social importance of Oxford and Cambridge, the reason also why their social importance was so disproportionate to their scientific. Were there perhaps outside the Universities other institutions that could be relied upon to further the progress of science ?

Other Scientific Bodies.

The Royal College of Physicians of London, a sixteenth-century foundation, possessed both the authority and the duty to organize and control in London the teaching of medicine, and in this way to further the progress of the biological sciences. It had been founded by Henry VIII at the advice of his court physician, Linacre, to protect the public from quacks by the establishment of what we may term a supreme council of the profession. Eight *electi* chosen by cooptation and themselves appointing an annual president had been charged with the supervision of the London doctors who constituted the associates, the *socii*. With the process of time the constitution of the college became increasingly elaborate and hierarchic. It now consisted of a treasurer, a keeper of the archives, a librarian, and a bedel, not to mention the four censors elected annually. As a weapon against the increasing competition of Scottish doctors, it had been decided that no one should be admitted as an associate who had not taken a degree at Oxford or Cambridge. For the others, whose professional merit could not be ignored, a subordinate rank had been created in the hierarchy of the profession, the rank of *permissi* or licentiates. And occasional attempts were made to compel candidates for the rank of licentiate to spend two months at Oxford or Cambridge. The total number of members amounted to fifty associates and fifty licentiates.

Undeniably this policy of exclusion raised the standing of the profession. London doctors could accumulate enormous fortunes. We hear of a doctor about 1815 who made over £20,000 a year.[2] The standing of the medical profession was perhaps slightly inferior to the standing of the two other liberal professions.[3] Members of noble

[1] Our figure is a mean between the figure given by Huber for the 18th century (*The English Universities*, vol. ii. pp. 329 sqq.) and the figure given by his translator, Fr. Newman, for 1843 (*ibid.*, p. 230 n.).

[2] According to Laetitia Hawkins (*Anecdotes*, vol. i., 1822, p. 249), £8,000 a year was regarded as a very large income for a doctor at the close of the 18th century. When she wrote it was said that one doctor in London was making £22,000.

[3] Beddoes, *A Letter to Sir Joseph Banks on the . . . Discontents . . . in Medicine*, 1808, summarized by Stock, *Memoir of . . . Beddoes*, p. 375 : " Hence . . . has arisen the marked distinction between the three liberal professions . . . that while honours and distinctions await eminence or influence in the other two, the votary of medicine is considered as, of necessity, excluded from every public honour." The distinction was apparently still more marked in

families did not enter it, nor could any doctor obtain a peerage. On the other hand, no Dissenter could become an associate, since only members of the Church of England could take a degree at Oxford or Cambridge. During his years at the University an associate had mixed with the future dignitaries of Church and State, the members of the ruling class. Once established in London he belonged to their world. He might aspire to a knighthood, even to a baronetcy. Of all the countries of Europe England at the opening of the 19th century was the country where the prestige of the medical profession stood highest.

The Royal College of Physicians with its hundred members was obviously incapable of providing all the necessary doctors even for London, not to speak of the provinces. The deficiency of official "physicians" was supplied by the surgeons, members of a subordinate corporation. They possessed their Royal College [1] established in 1800, which was governed by a Court of Assistants, a council of twenty-three inclusive of the Master and two Governors. No one could be admitted to the Royal College of Physicians of London and retain his membership of the Royal College of Surgeons of England. This regulation delineated the respective status of the two bodies. And the surgeons in turn excluded from their Court of Assistants any surgeon who in addition to the exercise of his profession was an *accoucheur* or a chemist. Nevertheless, the chemists, or apothecaries, as they were termed, though they were relegated thus to the lowest degree in the medical hierarchy, and although no professional qualification was required for the practise of their trade, played a very important part in English life. For the provision of surgeons was as inadequate as the provision of physicians. In country districts the treatment of the sick was abandoned almost entirely to the chemist.[2] In the towns and even in London the period was not yet distant when doctors never saw the majority of their patients, and were satisfied with a consultation with the apothecary who sought his advice for serious cases. And the apothecary was still the ordinary medical adviser of the family ; it was only when the illness had become dangerous that the doctor was summoned on the advice of the druggist.[3] In the medical profession

Ireland. Wakefield, *Ireland*, vol. ii. p. 785 : " It is extraordinary that medical men in Ireland are not held in the same estimation as gentlemen of the other liberal professions."

[1] Simon, *English Sanitary Institutions*, p. 69.

[2] *General Report of Commissioners on the Universities and Colleges of Scotland*, 1831, p. 66 : ". . . under this denomination are included nine-tenths of the country practitioners in England. It is only in large towns, and probably rarely even in them, that the different departments of the Physician, Surgeon and Apothecary are kept separate."

[3] And the doctor's function was still almost exclusively diagnosis. Smiles, *Murray*, vol. i. pp. 53–4, I. D'Israeli to John Murray, May 31, 1806 : " Most warmly I must impress on your mind the necessity of taking the advice of a physician. . . . I should imagine that one or two visits will be sufficient to receive some definite notion of your complaint. . . . The expense of a physician is moderate, if the patient is shrewd and sensible. Five or ten pounds this way would be a good deal."

the apothecary bore the same relation to the doctor as, in the law, the attorney bore to the barrister. And just as many famous barristers had received their legal education in the office of an attorney, so many celebrated doctors had begun their médical career in a chemist's shop.

Thus the first effect of organizing the medical profession as a close corporation was to place the vast majority of patients at the mercy of ignorant practitioners. Nor did the system compensate for this unfortunate result by raising the standard of medical knowledge among the members of the Royal College. If among the doctors of Europe the English were the most respected, they were far from being the most learned.

The Scottish universities, and Edinburgh in particular, possessed a medical faculty which enjoyed a high reputation. But the Royal College of London made entrance into the profession difficult alike for the Scotsmen who had studied in these universities and for any Englishman who might desire to do so. At Oxford and Cambridge, at which a long period of attendance was made compulsory by the rules of the Royal College,[1] a medical faculty was for all practical purposes non-existent, the lectures mere displays of oratory, the examinations a farce. And the Royal College of Physicians did nothing, or almost nothing, to supply this lack of medical teaching at the two Universities. At intervals of about twenty years it published a *Pharmacopœia*. In its *Medical Transactions* it printed communications from members. A museum, the Harveian, and a fairly extensive library were attached to the College. And a certain number of lectures which bore the names of their founders—the " Lumleian Lecture," the " Gulstonian Lecture," the " Croonian Lecture," the " Harveian Oration "—were given at regular intervals. The Royal College of Surgeons also possessed its museum, equipped by John Hunter at his private expense, published communications dealing with anatomy and surgery, and gave an annual course of twenty-four lectures. But all these lectures were mere academic displays, of an oratorical rather than a scientific nature. This was the case even when the rules of the foundation prescribed that the lecture should be accompanied by a dissection. When all is said, it is evident that the two colleges were exclusive and reactionary corporations in close alliance with Oxford and Cambridge, not for the encouragement but, on the contrary, for the obstruction of scientific progress.

Was nothing, then, done in London to improve medical training ? We have not yet examined the management of the hospitals ; and it is precisely this examination which will bring home the difficulty of determining for a particular point of time the condition of a social institution in a state of continual change. In the early years of the 19th

[1] For these rules, see Peacock, *Life of Young*, p. 120 sqq.

century the professional tradition in England still declared it beneath the dignity of a doctor of any position to be seen at a hospital. The staff attached to the hospital visited the wards barely once a week. The daily medical work was done by apothecaries. Very few medical students received their training in the hospitals. The right to attend the doctor as a physician's pupil cost about sixteen guineas a term.[1] Salaried posts were obtained by favour or purchase.[2] The rough and ready fashion in which operations were performed, and the almost total absence of accurate observations and records, were a source of frequent complaint. These abuses were of long standing. Nevertheless, they were universally condemned and reform had begun. But the reform was the work of forces entirely foreign to the College of Physicians and the College of Surgeons.

Modern humanitarianism was multiplying the London hospitals. Sir Thomas Bernard, a friend of Wilberforce and a man of vast wealth, spent his energy and devotion in the reform of the great orphanage in the north of London, the Foundlings' Hospital. By the opening year of the new century the necessity of special hospitals for infectious diseases had been realized ; and the example given by their foundation in London had been followed immediately by Manchester and Liverpool. The Society for the Improvement of the Condition of the Poor, the joint foundation of Sir Thomas Bernard, Wilberforce and the Bishop of Durham, was struggling to make the system universal. Between 1800 and 1815 London witnessed the foundation of a Cancer Hospital, two ophthalmic clinics, two societies for the free treatment of hernia, a large number of dispensaries. The propaganda in favour of vaccination dated from 1799. In 1806 for the first time a week passed without a single death in London from smallpox. And obviously the philanthropists who founded hospitals would see that their condition left nothing to be desired, that the administration was conscientious and scientific.

During the closing years of the 18th century two celebrated doctors, Heberden and Abernethy, inaugurated a system of practical training for medical and surgical students in the operating theatres of the hospitals.[3] Nor was this all. In the neighbourhood of the hospitals which were institutions for free treatment, governed by trustees and managed by committees of noblemen, gentlemen and wealthy members of the middle class, there sprung up a considerable number of private medical schools which proved very successful. In these medical students were taught for a fee the knowledge of their profession. The

---

[1] *Life of Sir Robert Christison*, vol. i. pp. 189 sqq., 190–1, 193, 194. Cf. *Journal of a Tour . . . by a French Traveller*, 1815, vol. i. pp. 76–7.

[2] Clarke, *Autobiographical Recollections*, p. 314.

[3] George Macilwain, *Memoirs of Abernethy*, pp. 39–40 ; Perceval, *Medical Ethics*, pp. 204–5, letter from W. Heberden to Dr. Perceval, October 15, 1794.

most celebrated of these schools was the school in Great Windmill Street, off Piccadilly.[1] Thus did unofficial England, the initiative of the individual or, more strictly speaking, of the private and voluntary association, supply the deficiencies of the official corporations, and compel those ancient bodies to adapt themselves to modern conditions. In 1815 after a struggle continued for three years, the apothecaries obtained the legal regulation of their trade and the institution of qualifying examinations.[2] England now possessed a guarantee that in the near future the practice of medicine would no longer be divided between an oligarchy too exclusive and too confident of its privileges to be industrious, and a proletariate of practitioners who offered their patients no proof of the necessary scientific equipment.

Of all the sciences we can discover one, and one alone, towards which the British Government appeared to admit a duty of official patronage. A venerable tradition, dating, perhaps, from the period of judicial astrology, placed astronomy under royal protection. Moreover, the needs of navigation, more urgent in England than in any other country, necessitated the careful observation of the planets and stars, of the tides, of the variation of the compass. The 18th century had produced a host of inventors who successively improved the instruments for their observation and measurement. The labours of George Graham, John Bird, Edward Troughton, and the long line of Dollonds had facilitated astronomical research, and had bestowed on British astronomy its distinctive character as a science of observation rather than a branch of mathematics. William Herschel was, after all, only the greatest of these instrument makers. It was by constructing without assistance or pecuniary resources telescopes sufficiently powerful to discover a new planet, that he attracted the attention of King George and earned his pension from the Government. Private observatories were numerous in England. Observatories were attached to the Universities of Oxford, Cambridge and Dublin. The East India Company had constructed them at Madras, Bombay and St. Helena. Thus had been created a favourable environment for astronomical research. The Royal Observatory founded in 1675, eight years after the Paris Observatory, and distinguished successively by the presence of Halley, Bradley and Maskelyne, benefited by the interest in astronomy. When in 1811 Pond had succeeded Maskelyne as Astronomer Royal, the salary attached to the position had been raised to £600. He renewed the equipment of the observatory and increased the number of his assistants. Greenwich Observatory was a model Government 'laboratory,' whose superiority was recognized throughout Europe.

[1] Clarke, *Autobiographical Recollections*, pp. 8, 9.

[2] 55 Geo. III, cap. 195. For the Apothecaries' Act, its results and the circumstances which led to its passage, see Clarke, *Autobiographical Recollections*, pp. 5 sqq. ; *Life of William Allen*, vol. i. p. 163 ; H. of C., March 26, 1813, November 19, 1813 ; H. of L., July 10, 1815 (*Parl. Deb.*, vol. xxv. pp. 349 sqq. ; vol. xxvii. pp. 164–5 ; vol. xxxi. p. 1143).

Arago would visit Greenwich to study Pond's methods. But what the British Government did for astronomy, it did not do for physics, chemistry or any other branch of natural science.

Nevertheless, England possessed a scientific academy of world-wide repute. The Royal Society of London for Improving Natural Knowledge, a corporation equipped with special privileges and already more than a century old, would appear to have increased its prestige in the scientific world since the accession to the presidency of Sir Joseph Banks, the explorer and botanist, a scientist of distinction, and even more distinguished as a patron of science, a man of good birth, a great landowner, with a wide acquaintance among the aristocracy. To the general satisfaction he made use of the despotic power which he asserted over the officers of the society to maintain a prudent numerical balance between the members who were actually men of science and the aristocrats and bankers who threatened to swamp the society. Through the society his influence made itself felt upon other scientific institutions. He controlled Greenwich Observatory, was consulted as a matter of course about the appointment of the Astronomer Royal, and was a trustee of the British Museum, an enormous storehouse where since 1753 rare books and antiquities of every description had accumulated in disorder. In 1818 he would secure for the Royal Society three permanent seats on the newly constituted Office of Longitudes, and it would be understood that their choice was in his hands. And he wore his presidency in princely fashion, entertained lavishly, even magnificently, at his mansion in Soho Square, kept open house once a week. But whatever the social standing of the society under the presidency of Banks, however useful its functions, it had not been founded for research or education. It was neither a laboratory nor a school. The *Transactions* and the great annual lectures, the *Croonian Lecture* and the *Bakerian Lecture*, provided scientists whose position was recognized an opportunity to publish their latest discoveries. The Royal Society was an admirable instrument for the registration of the progress already accomplished. It could make no direct contribution to its accomplishment.

And the progress made was in fact so rapid that the Royal Society was no longer adequate even to its registration. A host of new societies sprang up around it. We are not speaking of the Royal Society of Edinburgh or of the Royal Irish Academy, both already thirty years old. These two foundations were merely a proof that Scotland and Ireland made it a point of national honour to possess their own scientific academies. We refer to the societies which were being founded in London itself to satisfy the needs of the specialist and assist detailed observations on a large scale. The Linnæan Society, founded in 1788, had received its charter of incorporation in 1802. The Royal Society, its founders explained, by the very fact that its scope embraced every branch of science, could not cope with the minutiæ of Natural History. An institution such as they were founding was indispensable, if the world was to reap the fruits of the toil and expenditure of collectors, the experience of cultivators, the notes of observers.[1] The Geological Society dated from 1807. At that period the public were disgusted by the disputes between the followers of Werner and the followers of Hutton, battles in the clouds remote from solid facts. And William Smith, without guidance or assistance, was accumulating a wealth of discoveries about the geological formations of Britain. The founders of the Geological Society, obeying the motive which inspired the work of Smith, renounced provisionally geological theory and adopted as their exclusive object the collection and publication of the greatest possible number of observations. The Zoological Society, the Horticultural Society, the Medico-Surgical Society, the Society for Animal Chemistry, the Astronomical Society sprang up in rapid succession during these years. Occasionally these new foundations enjoyed the entire approbation of the Royal Society.[2] But more often Sir Joseph Banks took alarm. " I see plainly," he told a friend, " that all these new-fangled associations will finally dismantle the Royal Society and not leave the old lady a rag to cover her."[3] And the Royal Society was in fact swamped by the vast activities which were being carried on around her. How is this outburst of activity to be explained ? What was its origin and its cause ? In Scotland, whether we consider the system of primary education or the universities, the action of a Government inspired by the Protestantism of the national Church is evident. But it was not only in Scotland, it was in England also, that for the past fifty years discovery had followed upon discovery. And with rare exceptions the English Government adopted towards Science an attitude of absolute and impenetrable apathy. It is in Nonconformist England, the England excluded from the national universities, in industrial England with its new centres of population and civilization, that we must seek the institutions which gave birth to the utilitarian and scientific culture of the new era. That culture spread and made its way into the old England of the aristocracy, and even into the Universities. But its birth was elsewhere. The thesis of historical materialism, dubious in its universal application, is to this extent true

---

[1] Weld, *History of Royal Society*, vol. ii. p. 198.

[2] Bence Jones, *The Royal Institution*, p. 261, Sir Joseph Banks' letter to Rumford, April 1804.

[3] Barrow, *Sketches of the Royal Society*, p. 10. Sometimes he made terms with the enemy. In 1809 he obtained the affiliation to the Royal Society of the Society for Animal Chemistry as an assistant society. In recompense for the renunciation of her absolute monarchy over the scientific world the Royal Society would exercise in this way a species of suzerainty over the other Societies. But the plan did not secure general adoption. The Geological Society refused to follow the example of the Society for Animal Chemistry and preserved entire autonomy (Weld, *History of Royal Society*, vol. ii. pp. 237 sqq., 243 ; Woodward, *History of Geological Society*, pp. 25 sqq.). According to F. Galton (*Biometrika*, October 1901, vol. i. p. 9), the Geological Society owed its foundation to a deliberate revolt against the autocracy of Sir Joseph Banks.

of England at the opening of the 19th century. Scientific theory was the offspring of industrial practice. The emotional piety of Evangelical religion and the hunger for experimental knowledge developed at the same time, with the same intensity, and in the same social *milieu*.

VOLUNTARY ORGANIZATION OF SCIENTIFIC ACTIVITY. NATURAL SCIENCE. POLITICAL ECONOMY. THE UTILITARIAN PHILOSOPHY.

The Popular " Library " and " University."

Books were the medium in which the education of the middle class was generated, in a sense, spontaneously. For half a century past the literature of science had been daily enriched by new publications —some more technical, others more popular—adapted thus to the needs of different classes of readers.

The *Encyclopædia Britannica,* planned on the model of the *Encyclopédie* of Diderot and D'Alembert, had passed through five editions since 1771. The first had been in three volumes—the fifth, a quite recent publication, consisted of twenty. And the publisher, Constable, was arranging for an enormous supplement to be written by the most eminent authorities of the day—a collection of scholarly articles designed to present a complete picture of the state of human knowledge about the year 1815. The venerable *Cyclopædia* of Chambers, which had once served as the model of the French *Encyclopédie,* had also passed through several editions. Abraham Rees, after revising it for the first time in 1778, had just undertaken at Longmans' invitation a new edition, which would begin to appear in 1819 and would comprise thirty-nine volumes.

In addition to these works of general information numerous periodicals issued yearly and even monthly kept the public in touch with the progress of science. Nicholson's *Journal* had begun to appear in 1797,[1] Thomson the chemist had just founded the *Annals of Philosophy.*[2] The *Repertory of Arts, Manufactures and Agriculture,* the *Retrospect of Philosophical, Mechanical, Chemical, and Agricultural Discoveries* were two publications of an inferior type, confined to a list of the latest patents, and excerpts from English or French scientific publications. Tilloch's *Philosophical Magazine* aimed at combining amusement with instruction, a combination effected far more completely by the *Repository of Arts, Literature, Manufactures, Fashion and Politics.* Science for the people was an established type of literature.

---

[1] Full title, *A Journal of Natural Philosophy, Chemistry and other Arts.*

[2] *Annals of Philosophy ; or Magazine of Chemistry, Mineralogy, Mechanics, Natural History, Agriculture, and the Arts,* vol. i. January to June, 1813.

We could not, however, explain fully the success achieved by these publications, if we failed to take into consideration the innumerable institutions founded to assist their circulation. The establishment of lending libraries had enabled their subscribers to read a large number of books which they could not have purchased privately. And if the circulating libraries were shops managed by shopkeepers which supplied trashy fiction, the book clubs on the contrary were organized by bodies of disinterested people, whose aim was the acquisition of good books and useful knowledge.[1] Few towns large or small were without a book club. In important centres, such as Liverpool, the organization of the lending libraries was almost perfect. The Athenæum with its 8,000 volumes had been founded by a subscription, which brought in on one day £4,000. Five hundred "proprietors" paid a yearly subscription of two and a half guineas for the use of the library. The Lyceum in the same city, with its 11,000 volumes, had cost the original subscribers £11,000 : its books could be borrowed for an annual subscription of half a guinea.[2] Since the book trade had made such enormous strides, why should not libraries finally take the place which Universities had taken at a period when books were few and speech was the normal method by which men exchanged thoughts ? But libraries suffer from one radical defect. They cannot be centres of original research, laboratories. And in spite of the multiplication of printed matter man feels an irrepressible impulse to communicate his thoughts by word of mouth. To satisfy needs which libraries are incapable of satisfying institutions of a novel type sprang up in the provinces.

At Manchester first, the centre of the cotton industry, a species of local academy, a literary and scientific club, was founded. The foundation was due to the Liberal Dissenters, the members of the Warrington Academy, which had just been transferred to Manchester. Among their number was the doctor and philanthropist Perceval. The Literary and Philosophical Society assumed its permanent shape in 1781, and founded at the same time the College of Arts and Sciences. In the College lectures were given on "applied mechanics, and the principal branches of physics," on " chemistry considered in its relation to arts and manufactures," on " the origin, history and progress of the arts and manufactures and of commerce, on commercial law and the regulation of trade in different countries, commutative justice, and other branches of commercial morality." The object of the Institution was the education of young men between their departure from school and their entrance into business. Every lecturer was paid by his class. After two winter sessions the College failed. But the Society survived and began in 1785 the publication of its *Memorials*. It

[1] See for the organization of the book clubs, *The Critic*, April 7, 1860, p. 435.
[2] R. Ayton, *Voyage round Great Britain* (1815), p. 85.

rose to fame when Dalton began to communicate to it the results of his experiments.

The son of a Westmorland peasant, Dalton had been in succession monitor in an elementary school, schoolmaster and professor of mathematics in the College of Arts and Sciences. Since the College had been closed his sole source of livelihood had been the private tuition he gave in Manchester, and the lectures he delivered in the neighbourhood. The Literary and Philosophical Society furnished him with a laboratory. The instruments at his disposal were of a poor quality and he was an impatient and careless experimenter. But the combination of inadequate apparatus and merely approximate results enabled him in many cases to blame his instrument for the discrepancy between the results actually reached and the demands of the hypotheses which he was seeking to verify. For his genius lay in the formulation of brilliant hypotheses. He was born, to employ the language of his biographer, to be " the lawgiver of chemistry " ; and the boldness of his hypotheses was rewarded by their success.

The investigation of certain meteorological problems led Dalton to the study of vapours, his study of vapours to the study of gases. Alone or in collaboration with Dr. Henry, a Manchester physician, and a translator of Lavoisier, who had introduced into Lancashire new chemical processes for bleaching cloth, he determined the fundamental laws which govern the liquefaction of gases and their mutual combinations. Faithful to the Newtonian tradition, he regarded gases as composed of particles, molecules or atoms. Would not this hypothesis which explained the combination of gases explain also their chemical composition ? In 1802 Dalton discovered that marsh gas and olefiant oil contain for the same quantity of hydrogen, quantities of carbon, one of which is an exact multiple of the other. This would be explained quite simply, if the carbon and the hydrogen were composed of atoms which could unite in the proportion of one to one, one to two, one to three, etc., but could not unite in any intermediate ratio, since the atom is indivisible. Thus were introduced simultaneously into chemistry the law of combination in multiple proportions and the atomic theory, and with these the possibility of prediction. Given knowledge of the relative weight of " the ultimate particles " or "atoms" which composed the structure of a particular body, it would be possible to predict, if not the properties, at least the constitution of an entire series of compounds of which the same simple substances were constituent elements.[1]

In 1804 Dalton explained his system in London. His success was slight. But that same year he was visited at Manchester by the chemist Thomas Thomson, professor at Edinburgh University.

[1] See the account of Dalton's theories by himself, *A New System of Chemical Philosophy*, Part 1, chap. iii., *On Chemical Synthesis*, p. 211.

Thomson had made no original discoveries, and was not therefore prejudiced against Dalton's hypotheses by any preconceived theories. He was a professor who had just published a bulky textbook of chemistry in four volumes, whose avowed aim was to make a stand against the exaggerated deference paid to the French school of chemistry and to rehabilitate the reputation of English chemistry.[1] Thomson was, therefore, disposed to give a sympathetic hearing to the novel theories of his compatriot. Critics charged Thomson with an excessive fondness for speculations on the constitution of matter.[2] This common trait was a further bond between himself and Dalton. The atomic theory won his immediate and enthusiastic adhesion.

It was no doubt at Thomson's invitation that Dalton in 1807 propounded his theory in public lectures at Edinburgh and Glasgow. And in the third edition of his *System of Chemistry*, which appeared the same year, Thomson explained Dalton's theory, though it was as yet unpublished.[3] The same year, at a dinner of the Royal Society Club, Thomson attempted to make the scientists of London understand its importance. He succeeded in convincing Wollaston, a chemist as careful in his experiments as Dalton was bold in the framing of hypotheses. Wollaston, by his proof that the law of multiple proportions was applicable to salts as well as to acids and alkalis, brought a valuable piece of evidence to confirm the Daltonian hypothesis.[4] In France Gay-Lussac accepted Dalton's law and completed it by his law of volumes. Berzelius devised a system of abbreviated notation to express the multiple proportions. As Lavoisier had built a theoretical system out of Priestley's experiments, so Dalton in turn gave a more rigorously scientific form to the theories of Lavoisier and his followers. Priestley was a Unitarian, Dalton a Quaker. Both belonged to the provinces, and moreover to the manufacturing districts in the Centre and North of England. These facts show the importance of the part played in the formation of modern chemistry by the union between the Protestant tradition and the new industry.

Other provincial towns followed the example of Manchester. Birmingham possessed a Philosophical Society, founded in 1800 and occupying freehold premises since 1813.[5] It existed for the study of " natural

[1] *A System of Chemistry*, 1st ed., 1802, vol. i. pp. 8 sqq.

[2] *Edinburgh Review*, April 1804, No. 7, Art. 9, *Dr. Thomson's System of Chemistry* (vol. iv. p. 142).

[3] Vol. iii. p. 424 : " Though the author has not yet thought fit to publish his hypothesis, yet, as the notions of which it consists are original and extremely interesting, and as they are intimately connected with some of the most intricate parts of the doctrine of affinity, I have ventured, with Mr. Dalton's permission, to enrich this work with a short sketch of it."

[4] See Thomas Thomson's communication of January 14, 1808, on Oxalic Acid, and W. H. Wollaston's of January 28, 1808, on Super-Acid and Sub-Acid salts form a connected whole, and their common object is the confirmation of the Daltonian theory (*Phil. Trans.*, 1808, pp. 63, 96). For a complete history of the progress of the atomic theory, see Thomas Thomson, *History of Chemistry*, vol. ii. pp. 285 sqq.

[5] Langford, *A Century of Birmingham Life*, vol. ii. p. 369.

philosophy, moral philosophy, political economy and æsthetics." Lectures were delivered on mechanics, chemistry, mineralogy, and metallurgy.   At Newcastle there was a Literary and Philosophical Society [1] to which George Stephenson sent his son Robert to receive a scientific education, by watching the experiments and hearing the discussions, at a cost of three guineas per annum.[2]   At Bristol Dr. Beddoes, expelled from Oxford in 1792 for " Jacobinism," founded his " Pneumatic Institute " to cure disease by the inhalation of gas. He would have liked to complete it by a large educational establishment ; but lack of funds compelled him to be satisfied with arranging courses of lectures at the Institute itself.   The middle class public flocked to the lectures.   Of these courses some were popular presentations of scientific results ; but others presented a more ambitious character. There were anatomical lectures by the local surgeons, and lectures on chemistry by Dr. Beddoes himself.[3]   A publication entitled " Contributions to Physical and Medical Knowledge, principally from the West of England," was a periodical register of the experiments. Beddoes' assistant in the management of the Institute was a young Cornish Methodist of humble origin named Humphry Davy.   Under Beddoes, Davy completed his scientific training and he published his earliest work in the *Contributions*.

From the University standpoint London was merely a large provincial town.   Scientific education could be organized in London only by the methods employed at Birmingham or Manchester.   Bentham and his friends thought of making use of the Lancastrian association to establish an institute for secondary education, at which mathematics, modern languages, politics and ethics would be taught, and the children of middle-class parents provided with the scientific education at present out of their reach.[4]   The project failed, and many years were to elapse before the Benthamites would succeed in providing the Metropolis with a genuine university.   Meanwhile what provision was made for a Londoner of the middle class who wished to educate himself ?

Subscription lectures were multiplied.   Not only were courses of medicine and anatomy given in the operating theatres of hospitals, but even courses of physics and chemistry.[5]   In 1802 William Allen had lectured on chemistry to audiences of 120.[6]   And more systematic organizations were formed whose exclusive object was the provision of popular lectures on science.   In January 1815 the

[1] Holmes, *Coal Mines of Durham and Northumberland*, 1816, p. 184.

[2] Smiles, *Life of Stephenson*, 5th ed., 1858, pp. 56, 57.

[3] Stock, *Memoir of Beddoes*, pp. 136, 144-5.

[4] See my *Formation du Radicalisme Philosophique*, vol. ii. p. 256.

[5] *Life of Sir Astley Cooper*, vol. i. p. 236.

[6] *Life of William Allen*, vol. i. p. 61. Cf. pp. 2, 62, 73 ; and on the same page (73) we read : " About this period (1804) W. Allen attended a series of conversaziones at Dr. Babington's, where Count Bournon gave instruction in mineralogy, particularly crystallography."

Surrey Institute announced the opening of a course by Mr. John Mason Good " on the passions and affections of the mind, their con- nexion with the organization of the body and their influence on savage and civilized life."[1] At the Russell Institution in Russell Square Mr. Singer delivered a course of lectures on electricity and electro- chemistry at a charge of £1 11s. 6d. to those who were not members of the Institution, of £1 4s. to annual subscribers.[2] Mr. Walker delivered at the Paul's Head, Cateaton Street, his Annual City Course of Philosophy at a charge of a guinea for a course of twelve lectures, or 2s. 6d. a lecture.[3] In 1816 Michael Faraday, a Nonconformist with mystical tendencies, gave six lectures at the City Philosophical Society on " the attraction of cohesion, on radiant matter, on diverse simple bodies." It was at this very Society, which had been founded in 1808 for their mutual education by forty young men of modest origin, that Faraday had begun his scientific studies only three years earlier when a humble apprentice to a bookseller.[4] The Askesian Society had been founded in 1796 by a band of young men who wished to work in cooperation. The Society met at Plough Court, the home of the Quaker philanthropist William Allen, who placed the apparatus of his chemical factory at the disposal of the members for use in their experimental work ; [5] for with the owner's consent any factory could be made in a day into an excellent laboratory. The London Insti- tution, founded in 1805 by voluntary subscription, possessed a very extensive library, a lecture hall and a reading-room.[6] And finally, there was the Royal Institution, with its luxuriously furnished premises in Albemarle Street, in the centre of fashionable London. Among the scientific foundations of London the Institution occupies a place apart ; for here, we have left behind us the type of institution with which we have been lately engaged and are in the neighbourhood of the Royal Society. Insensibly we exchange the company of the middle-class worker for the society of noblemen.

The Royal Institution. Sir Humphry Davy.

The Royal Institution owed its foundation to an adventurer of genius, Count Rumford. He was an American who had provided himself at the Bavarian Court with a German title before he came to

---

[1] *Morning Chronicle*, January 2, 1815. For the Surrey Institution, see Stock, *Memoir of Beddoes*, p. 335.

[2] *Morning Chronicle*, January 6, 1815. [3] *Ibid.*, January 2, 1815.

[4] Bence Jones, *Life and Letters of Faraday*, pp. 52, 57–8.

[5] *Life of William Allen*, vol. i. pp. 26–7, 57, 58, 83. It was the Askesian Society which, at the suggestion of Dr. Babington, who was anxious to further the mineralogical research of the Comte de Bournon, founded first the *Mineralogical Society* (1799–1806), later the *Geological Society* (Woodward, *Geological Society*, pp. 7 sqq.).

[6] Adolphus, *British Empire*, vol. iii. p. 124.

England in 1796. He was associated with Shute Barrington, Wilberforce and Sir Thomas Bernard in the foundation of the Society for Bettering the Condition of the Poor. To further the Society's programme he set himself to study methods of cheap feeding and heating. At once philanthropist and scientist, he invented economical stoves and transformed the theory of heat by important experiments. And he had the further support of Wilberforce and Sir Thomas Bernard in an undertaking which, if not in the strict sense philanthropic, was at least avowedly practical—the foundation of the Royal Institution " for diffusing the knowledge and facilitating the general and speedy introduction of new and useful mechanical inventions and improvements " and " for teaching by regular courses of philosophical lectures and experiments the application of the new discoveries in science to the improvement of arts and manufactures and in facilitating the means of procuring the comforts and conveniences of life." In other words, Rumford wished to found in England an institution similar to the " Conservatoire des Arts et Métiers " in Paris.[1]

Nevertheless, when Rumford in 1800 issued his appeal to the public, it was not received favourably by the manufacturers. Possibly their natural selfishness and distrust took alarm at his request for a supply of models for exhibition. Would not such an exhibition betray their secrets to competitors ? The members of the aristocracy, on the other hand, subscribed liberally. Less secretive than the manufacturers, they were no less in need of machinery for the exploitation of their estates. At the request of the Board of Agriculture Davy gave a course of lectures at the Royal Institution on the chemistry of plants ; and William Allen was charged with the investigation of problems of road transport and the construction of agricultural machinery.[2] Moreover, scientific curiosity, a curiosity which if disinterested was extremely superficial, was spreading among the leisured classes. They had discovered that science was amusing and that a clever lecturer could hold the attention of an ignorant audience by experiments in magnetism and chemistry. The Institution became a fashionable lecture hall, where the lectures were not confined to science. Sydney Smith moralized ; Landseer, Campbell and Coleridge lectured on art and literature. The Royal Institution became the fashion ;[3] but the nature of its success was not so satisfactory. The large audiences were too fashionable. When Dalton gave a course of lectures he spoke above the heads of his audience.[4] Thomas Young proved even more incomprehensible when he explained his revolutionary hypotheses

---

[1] For Rumford's biography and the history of the Royal Institution, see Bence Jones, *The Royal Institution, its Founder and its First Professors*, 1871, especially p. 116.

[2] *Life of William Allen*, vol. i. pp. 111, 122, 132.

[3] Bence Jones, *The Royal Institution*, p. 70.

[4] The official magazine of the Institution did not even publish the text of the lectures See John Dalton, *A New System of Chemical Philosophy*, Part. 1, 1808, Preface. p. 5.

on the nature of light, and dared to question the Newtonian dogma.[1]
The Institution did not want for candid critics.[2] The writers of
the *Edinburgh Review* condemned it as a useless toy, until a series of
sensational discoveries made by Davy with the powerful electric battery
of the Institution bestowed upon it the consecration of success. In
June 1800 Sir Joseph Banks read, as a lecture before the Royal Society,
a communication by Volta on the electricity generated by the mere
contact of conductors of various composition.[3] In his paper Volta
described as a scientific curiosity, and without claiming to draw any sort
of theoretical conclusion from his discovery, the construction of the
pile which has henceforth borne his name. Sir Joseph Banks' lecture
and the subsequent publication of Volta's communication made the
discovery of the Italian electrician known throughout England, and
many men of science constructed Voltaic piles with the object of testing
their power.[4] Nicholson, the editor of the *Journal*, and a surgeon
named Carlisle discovered " by chance " that the Voltaic pile decomposed
water, the hydrogen being attracted to the negative pole, the oxygen
to the positive. Cruikshank proved that the Voltaic pile decomposed
several salts, by an attraction of the alkalis to the positive pole.
Wollaston attempted to show that when chemical changes were produced
in the pile, the chemical not the electrical phenomena were fundamental
and explained the latter.[5] Davy, whom Rumford had brought from
Bristol and who was the most brilliant scientific lecturer at the Royal
Institution, showed that in the decomposition of water by the pile, the
oxygen was attracted to one pole, the hydrogen to the other, whatever
substances animal or vegetable were placed in the intervening space.
To be sure, there was much uncertainty as to the results of these first
experiments. Cruikshank tried in vain to decompose certain salts.
Davy and several other experimenters, English and French, showed
that when water was brought into contact with the pile, a muriatic
or nitro-muriatic acid was produced at the positive pole, and alkaline
fixation at the negative. Did the pile then possess the power to produce
alkalis and acids, and when its contact with salt gave rise to an acid
and an alkali was their production due to the decomposition of the salt
or rather, as appeared to be the case, when the pile acted upon water,
was the sole cause the activity of the pile ?

[1] Even the *Edinburgh Review* was unable to follow him. See *Edinburgh Review*, January
1803, No. 2, Art. 16, *Bakerian Lecture on Light and Colour* (vol. i. pp. 450 sqq.) ; October
1804, No. 9, Art. 7, *Dr. Young's Bakerian Lecture* (vol. v. p. 97).

[2] *Journal of Lady Holland*, March 1, 1800 (vol. ii. p. 52) : " Canning came. . . . He
was witty upon the new Institution, which is a very bad imitation of the *Institut* at Paris ;
hitherto there is only one Professor, who is a Jack-of-all-Trades, as he lectures alike upon
chemistry and shipbuilding." Cf. *ibid.*, pp. 60–1.

[3] *Phil. Trans.*, 1800, Part 2, pp. 403 sqq.

[4] For these experiments and generally for the history of Davy's electro-chemical discovery,
see his *Bakerian Lecture on the Relations of Electrical and Chemical Changes*, June 8, 1826 (*Phil.
Trans.*, 1826, Part 3, pp. 383 sqq.).

[5] *Phil. Trans.*, 1801, Part 2, p. 427.

In 1806 Davy solved the problem. By means of a series of experiments, similar in character to the experiments of Lavoisier, he proved that, whenever the immersion in water of the two poles of the pile was followed by the production of an alkali and an acid, the water was not perfectly pure. The alkali and the acid were products of the decomposition of a salt.[1] In consequence of this discovery Davy continued his experiments from the standpoint reached already by Nicholson, Carlisle and Cruikshank. He proceeded further in the same direction and formulated a law of universal application, " that hydrogen, the alkaline substances, the metals and certain metallic oxides are attracted by negatively electrified metallic surfaces and repelled by positively electrified metallic surfaces, and contrariwise that oxygen and acid substances are attracted by positively electrified metallic surfaces and repelled by negatively electrified metallic surfaces."[2] This rendered possible, if not the identification of chemical with electrical affinity, at least the view that both phenomena were effects of a common cause, and that their intensities were proportional, the degree of the affinity being measured by the difference of the electrical condition.

Electro-chemistry had been born ; and Davy's *Bakerian Lecture*, delivered in the November of 1806 to publish his results to the world, produced a profound impression. The *Edinburgh Review* expressed its surprise that Davy's genius had " escaped unimpaired from the enervating influence of the Royal Institution . . . and had indeed grown prodigiously in that thick medium of fashionable philosophy."[3] But the *Review* was obliged to admit,[4] as Davy himself declared,[5] that the discoveries would have been impossible without the apparatus which the Royal Institution placed at his disposal. And the Institution benefited immediately by Davy's work. A subscription in which all its aristocratic patrons took part brought in £2,000, and the sum was devoted to the construction of a gigantic pile containing 2,000 constituents.[6] With this apparatus Davy continued his researches, and established henceforward as the permanent Bakerian Lecturer, he

[1] *Bakerian Lecture for* 1806, *on some Chemical Agencies of Electricity* (*Works*, vol. v. pp. 4 sqq.).
[2] *Bakerian Lecture for* 1806 (*Works*, vol. v. pp. 28–9).
[3] *Edinburgh Review*, January 1808, No. 22, Art. 8, Davy's *Bakerian Lecture* (vol. xi. p. 390).
[4] *Edinburgh Review*, July 1808, No. 24, Art. 7, Davy's *Bakerian Lecture* (vol. xii. p. 394) :
" Mr. Davy owes much to his indefatigable industry and his knowledge of the subject ; but he owes a great deal more to the powerful instrument which former discoveries put into his hands. Any man possessed of his habits of labour and the excellent apparatus of the Royal Institution could have almost ensured himself a plentiful harvest of discovery."
[5] *Elements of Chemical Philosophy*, Introduction (*Works*, vol. iv. pp. 37–8) : " Nothing tends so much to the advancement of knowledge as the application of a new instrument. The native intellectual powers in different times are not so much the causes of the different success of their labours as the peculiar nature of the means and artificial resources in their possession. . . . Without the Voltaic apparatus there was no possibility of examining the relations of electrical polarities to chemical."
[6] Davy, *Elements of Chemical Philosophy* (*Works*, vol. iv. p. 110), also *Bakerian Lecture for* 1809, *sub finem* (*Works*, vol. v. pp. 282–3).

communicated his results annually to the Royal Society of which the Institution in Albemarle Street had become an annexe. Renouncing hypothesis, for which he professed a distaste,[1] Davy proclaimed his intention to confine himself to the quest of facts. He was the first to decompose the fixed alkalis, and to isolate two new elements, sodium and potassium.[2] For many years the constitution of muriatic and of oxymuriatic acid had eluded the researches of chemists. And the Lancashire manufacturers had a special interest in the inquiry, since Berthollet had taught them the use of oxymuriatic acid to bleach cotton.[3] Davy utilized the great pile of the Royal Institution to prove that so-called oxymuriatic acid was in reality a simple substance, namely chlorine, and that muriatic acid was not oxymuriatic acid minus a portion of its oxygen, but a compound of chlorine and hydrogen.[4] Similarly fluoric acid was a compound of fluorine and hydrogen.[5] These discoveries of substances hitherto unknown were calculated to strike the popular imagination. And if they lacked the importance of the great electro-chemical discovery, they were not without a general bearing. They demolished certain fundamental principles of the Lavoisier school : no longer could oxygen be regarded as the universal generator of acids.[6] Following one after another, and announced in public every year amid the imposing surroundings of a scientific gathering, they carried Davy's fame to its height.

He was acclaimed, not without exaggeration, as a new Lavoisier, a second Newton. While the war was still raging he received a prize from the " Institut " at Paris, and a safe conduct enabling him to travel freely in France. He made a wealthy match, and had received a knighthood. He would soon be a baronet, and on the death of Sir Joseph Banks would succeed him as president of the Royal Society.

[1] *Bakerian Lecture for* 1826 (*Phil. Trans.*, 1826, Part 3, p. 390) : " Believing that our philosophical systems are exceedingly imperfect, I never attached much importance to this hypothesis. . . . I have never criticised or examined the manner in which different authors have adopted or explained it—contented, if in the hands of others it assisted the arrangements of chemistry or mineralogy, or became an instrument of discovery." In the lecture of 1806 Davy was careful to warn his hearers that in the present state of the inquiry, a great extension of this hypothetical part of the subject would be premature (*Works*, vol. v. p. 41).

[2] *Bakerian Lecture for* 1807 (*Works*, vol. v. pp. 57 sqq.).

[3] It was at Manchester that Dr. Henry had discovered, without, however, understanding the cause, that under the action of electricity muriatic acid released hydrogen. His discovery preceded the invention of the pile (*Phil. Trans.*, 1800, pp. 188 sqq.). See also Chevenix's anticipations in this sphere, *Observations and Experiments upon Oxygenized and Hyperoxygenized Muriatic Acid, and upon some Combinations of the Muriatic Acid in its three States*, January 28, 1802 (*Phil. Trans.*, 1802, pp. 165–6).

[4] *Bakerian Lecture for* 1810 (*Works*, vol. v. pp. 284 sqq.).

[5] *Bakerian Lecture for* 1813 (*Works*, vol. v. pp. 408 sqq.).

[6] For a moment Davy was induced to hazard hypotheses about the chemical action of hydrogen as " the principle of inflammability." But he checked himself at once, almost apologized. " Hypotheses," he wrote, " can scarcely be considered as of any value except as leading to new experiments, and the objects in the novel field of electro-chemical research have not been sufficiently examined . . . to enable me . . . to form any general theory concerning them which is likely to be permanent " (*Bakerian Lecture for* 1809 ; *Works*, vol. v. p. 282).

But as his fame increased, his industry decreased. Researches into the constitution of iodine, and the invention of the safety lamp which bears his name, were little to occupy the twenty years of life which followed his work on chlorine and fluorine. The Royal Institution and the Royal Society were aristocratic clubs as well as scientific bodies. And Davy would ruin his health in the endeavour to combine the life of a man of the world with the work of a scientist. But the decline of his inventive power would not injure the progress in England of the science he had founded. And Davy himself detected the man who would be his successor in the field of electro-chemistry. In 1812 he took as assistant in his laboratory a young man named Michael Faraday, whose humble origin and initial struggles we have already mentioned. Thus the line of great physicists which has adorned modern England began with Beddoes, the eccentric chemist of the Pneumatic Association, and passed from Beddoes through Davy to Faraday.

In the preceding pages our object has been not so much to describe the progress of scientific theory as the social organization of scientific research in Britain at the opening of the 19th century. And we have seen that, with the exception of the Scottish universities, the sciences were cultivated by men who belonged to no definite school, who did not conduct their researches on lines previously laid down by a superior authority, who were in the strict sense of the term self-taught. Such were Herschel, Dalton and Davy. Such was Thomas Young, a London doctor, who varied the routine of his profession by the transformation of optics and the translation of Egyptian hieroglyphs. Such also was Sir David Brewster, who had just published his work on the polarization of light and who had never taught except as private tutor in the family of a Scottish nobleman. There existed no scientific body, with its professional code of conduct, prescribing to every worker his proper task, to be accomplished without heed of results, results foreseen for him by others, to be reaped by others after his death. Spontaneously, therefore of necessity imperfectly, the study of natural phenomena took shape in the provinces first, later in London. Hence the peculiar character of British science. Detailed researches, monographs, classifications there are few or none. On the other hand, there are a small number of important discoveries which bestow a new direction on the study of detail. The British scientist, like the British manufacturer, is the lucky inventor, the revolutionary.

This is true of the physicists and chemists whose work we have just described. It is even more true of those whose study was humanity. By these we do not mean the historians. Whatever the value of their work, it is impossible to regard the erudite investigations of Sharon Turner and Lingard, the dogmatic explanations of James Mill or the sweeping generalizations of Hallam, as marking an epoch in the history of human knowledge. We refer to those daring thinkers, taught only by their own reflection, Malthus, Ricardo and Bentham. Their powerful genius transformed the sociological sciences.

The Economists. Malthus and Ricardo.

Malthus' famous work, the *Essay on the Principle of Population*, had appeared in 1798. The father of Thomas Malthus was a Jacobin, an executor of Rousseau's will, and a disciple of the leveller and anarchist William Godwin. But the son did not share his father's humanitarian optimism, and refused to subscribe the creed of Priestley, Condorcet and Godwin, the belief in unlimited progress. He held that humanity had developed in a hostile environment, and was doomed to a never-ending warfare against it—that a life of plenty was not for man. For population tended to increase more rapidly than the means of subsistence. When he came to put in writing his objections to his father's faith, Malthus believed he could enforce his theory by giving it a mathematical form. " Population has," he maintained, " a constant tendency to increase beyond the means of subsistence. . . . Population, when unchecked, increases in a geometrical ratio. . . . The means of subsistence could not possibly be made to increase faster than in an arithmetical ratio." And " the necessary effects of these two different rates of increase, when brought together, will be very striking."

It was a gloomy book. Its conclusions were purely negative. But it appeared during the height of the anti-Jacobin reaction, and the moment was propitious for a refutation of the French Utopias. This amply accounts for the immediate success of the first edition—a small book hastily put together, a mere pamphlet of the moment. But is it a sufficient explanation of the permanent success of the book, of the astounding popularity of the Malthusian doctrine ?

To account for this permanent popularity we must first of all remember that the economists of the British school differed from the physiocrats by regarding labour, not the bounty of nature, as the sole source of wealth, from the Continental economists by finding the standard of value in labour, not in utility. But to maintain that labour is the sole source of wealth and the sole standard of value is to maintain that every pleasure is purchased at the cost of an equivalent or almost equivalent pain, that man is not born to plenty, that a parsimonious nature doles out to him in scanty measure the means of subsistence, and that population exercises on its resources an unremitting pressure. Malthus' doctrine was contained implicitly in the doctrine of all the preceding British economists. It can even be found explicitly, if incidentally, enunciated by Hume, Adam Smith and Stewart. Malthusianism, therefore, confirmed prejudices already dominant in economic science, fitted into the established tradition. This explains a permanent success which survived the accidental popularity enjoyed by the first edition of the *Essay*.

And we must also bear in mind that at the close of the 18th century the Poor Law was a source of perpetual anxiety to the English legislator. His aim was to obtain from the paupers relieved by the public a due return of labour. But during a period of grave distress he felt himself obliged to practise grave relaxations of principle. A host of pamphlets were published, whose authors, in conformity with the principles of Adam Smith and his followers, maintained that the system of poor relief, as it was administered in Great Britain, was opposed to the laws of nature, put a premium on idleness and incompetence, and encouraged the population to outgrow the means of subsistence. Among these pamphlets was Malthus' work.[1] In 1798, at a moment when the guardians were distributing relief with a reckless extravagance, Malthus endowed the economists with arguments of a novel and striking character to denounce the waste and to pass a wholesale condemnation upon the system of Poor Relief.

It would, therefore, be a grave error to treat Malthus, as the student might be led to treat him by a consideration of the circumstances which conditioned the first appearance of his work, as a mere pamphleteer of the counter-revolution. No doubt the harsh attitude which it implied towards the proletariate recommended Malthusianism to the mentality of the middle class. But the English middle class, though it remained sternly opposed to revolution and sentimentality, was increasingly open to the ideas of the Liberal reformers, as the anti-Jacobin panic faded from the public memory. The Tory organ, the *Quarterly Review*, was anti-Malthusian ; the *Edinburgh Review*, the organ of the Radical Opposition, erected Malthusianism into a dogma.

No doubt in its author's pseudo-mathematical statement the Malthusian thesis is not easy to maintain ; it would be difficult even to give it an intelligible meaning. Nevertheless, Malthus' combination of extreme simplicity and apparent scientific accuracy may well have recommended his book to a middle-class public which, though without any very solid education, prided itself on its scientific temper. It was hard to resist the suggestion made, and to refuse to credit the reality of a law stated with such assurance, defined so precisely. In the matter of scientific truth the self-taught man is easily satisfied. Nor is his

---

[1] To realize how closely the work of Malthus is attached to this entire class of literature, see especially the little treatise of John Townshend, *A Dissertation on the Poor Laws by a Well-wisher to Mankind*, 1786. Townshend is a forerunner of Malthus and even, through Malthus, of Darwin himself. We may also consider the following significant passage (*First Report of the Philanthropic Society*, 1789, p. 15) : " So deeply perverted is the whole system of parish government, so defective in execution, as well as wrong in principle, that it falsifies the most substantial maxim in police, that population is the strength and riches of a State. By the creed of an overseer, the number of births is the standard of a nation's decay, and the command to increase and multiply was given as a scourge to mankind."

public more exacting. The historian Hallam would even declare the mathematical formulation of Malthus' principle of population to be as indubitable as the multiplication table.[1] And the day was at hand when Ricardo, more Malthusian than Malthus himself, was going to base on that principle the entire theory of the distribution of wealth, indeed well-nigh the whole of political economy.

The son of a Jewish stockbroker, Ricardo had never received a classical education. In fact his education had scarcely exceeded the standard of what we should now term primary education. Hardly fourteen years of age, he had entered business. In his scanty hours of leisure, and without a teacher, he completed his education as best he could. He studied chemistry and mineralogy, installed a laboratory in his home, was one of the first members of the Geological Society. But his favourite study was political economy. For it was related to the matters which were the subject of his professional work. We have already noticed his share in the controversy occasioned by the depreciation of the banknote, when a series of newspaper articles had revealed his capacity as a thinker. He was already a celebrity, if not yet the head of a school. That position would only be his when another economic question had attracted public attention, and Malthus had distinguished himself by a further discovery.

Since 1805 Malthus had been teaching history and political economy in the college established by the East India Company for the education of its servants. Little by little he had reached an original theory of rent which he regarded as the direct consequence of the *Principle* which he had formulated in 1798.[2] Since population tends to increase more rapidly than the means of subsistence, man is continually obliged to bring under cultivation soils of an inferior quality. Hence of necessity a constant increase in the cost of foodstuffs, which would increase also the reward of labour and of capital employed upon the lands first cultivated, did not both wages and profits tend to the normal level in the manner explained by Adam Smith. Hence, from the more fertile areas arises a surplus which is the income of the landlord— his rent. Thus the increase, nay the very existence of rent, is an effect, not a cause, of the increase in the cost of living. In England economic conditions favoured the acceptance of this theory. On the one hand, the census returns showed a rapid increase of population, and the soil of the United Kingdom was no longer sufficient to feed its inhabitants. On the other hand, rents were continuously rising. Plainly the two phenomena must be related as cause and effect. When the restoration of peace was followed by an agricultural crisis, a Parliamentary Commission was appointed to investigate its causes. A large proportion of

[1] Quoted by Miss Harriet Martineau, *Autobiography*, 1877 ed., vol. i. p. 210.
[2] For the modifications introduced into the passages which deal with rent in the successive editions of the *Principle of Population*, see Bonar, *Malthus and his Works*, p. 222.

the witnesses before this Commission maintained, almost unconsciously, the theory of Malthus.[1] Buchanan, in his edition of the *Wealth of Nations* published in 1814,[2] and the economist West in an essay published in 1815,[3] maintained theories closely akin to the theory of Malthus. Malthus decided that, if he were not to lose his property in the theory, he must no longer delay its publication. He therefore published his essay on " the Nature and Progress of Rent."[4]

This was the signal for Ricardo to intervene. In a short essay " on the Influence of a low Price of Corn on the Profits of Stock,"[5] he accepted the two laws which Malthus had formulated and of which the latter depended upon the former, his law of population, and his law of rent. But he rejected the protectionist consequences which Malthus deduced from his laws in his essay of 1815. And to prove his own doctrine of Free Trade he built upon both an original system of laws regulating the distribution of wealth.

The law of wages is the first consequence of the law of population. According to this law, the amount of wages received by the labourer, the natural price of his labour, is the amount necessary to enable him to subsist and to perpetuate his species " without increase or diminution." For wages cannot decrease without the starvation of the labourer, nor increase without an increase of the population which will reestablish the equilibrium with the means of subsistence.

The law of profits followed. If the amount of wages, as calculated in terms of foodstuffs, remains fixed, that amount, as calculated in terms of money, must constantly increase, since the cost of extracting from the soil an equal amount of nourishment increases constantly, as the increase of population compels the cultivation of inferior soil. But this alteration of wages cannot affect rent which is a fixed quantity. It must therefore affect profits. Thus does the law of differential rent and, by implication, the principle of population explain a phenomenon universally verifiable—the progressive decrease of profits. With the natural progress of society the labourer remains at an equal level of bare subsistence, and the capitalist receives a constantly decreasing income. The landowner alone grows continually more wealthy, and this increase of wealth represents neither labour nor risk. Such was the outline of the system which Ricardo now set himself to develop in all its details and applications. Not till 1817 would he publish, as the fruit

[1] Cannan, *A History of the Theories of Production and Distribution in English Political Economy from 1776 to 1848*, pp. 147 sqq.

[2] *Observations on the Subjects treated of in Dr. Smith's Inquiry into the Nature and Causes of the Wealth of Nations*, vol. iv. pp. 33 sqq.

[3] *An Essay on the Application of Capital to Land . . . by a Fellow of University College*, Oxford, 1815.

[4] *An Inquiry into the Nature and Progress of Rent and the Principles by which it is regulated*, 1815.

[5] *An Essay on the Influence of a low Price of Corn on the Profits of Stock, showing the Inexpediency of Restrictions on Importation*, 1815.

of two years' labour, his classic, the celebrated *Principles of Political Economy and Taxation*.

The character of this famous work is abstract, its style arid. But because Ricardo is a difficult author to read, it does not follow that his work is academic, out of touch with practical life. What indeed was the origin of the principle of population on which the entire edifice is constructed? A pamphlet inspired by the circumstances of the moment, the whim of a publicist, indignant at the maladministration of the Poor Law. What, again, were the books with which in 1809 and in 1815 Ricardo had paved the way for his Political Economy? The reflections of a business man upon a controversy which was occupying Parliament and the Press. The simple notions from which Ricardo sets out in his attempt to construct an entire system of economics, were taken practically unaltered from the phenomena of contemporary life. His new theory of the distribution of wealth was an abstract defence of the passions which were exciting the London mob to riot, and were effecting a coalition of Labour and Capital against the landlord. This explains its immediate adoption as their political creed by an entire party, and the ease and rapidity with which it was popularized. In her *Conversations on Political Economy* which appeared in 1816, and whose aim, as the sub-title informs us, was " to explain in familiar language the elements of that science," Mrs. Marcet explained successfully the entire doctrine of Ricardo without misrepresenting a single point of importance.[1] " I know not why," said the hero of a Bulwer Lytton novel, published a few years later, " this study" (Political Economy) " has been termed uninteresting. No sooner had I entered upon its consideration, than I could scarcely tear myself from it." [2]

The Utilitarians. Bentham and his Disciples.

Thus by 1815 the theories of Malthus had been embodied by Ricardo in the classical tradition of political economy. But contemporaneously Ricardo's teaching was itself incorporated into an entire system of philosophy whose action upon British public opinion would be profound and lasting, the philosophy of Bentham and his school.

Unlike Malthus and Ricardo, Bentham did not achieve an immediate success. His *Introduction to the Principles of Morals and Legislation* had been written about 1775, contemporaneously with the publication of Adam Smith's *Wealth of Nations*, and had been published in 1788 without attracting any attention. The countless manuscripts in which he expounded the plan of an entire system of jurisprudence,

---

[1] *Conversations on Political Economy, in which the Elements of that Science are familiarly explained*, 1816.

[2] Bulwer Lytton, *Pelham*, Book I, chap. xxxvi. 1st ed., 1828, vol. i. p. 336.

wholly different from the established system, emancipated from the domination of metaphysical fictions and founded on the rational and lucid principle of "general utility" or "the greatest happiness of the greatest number," had been composed before the *Introduction* was published. But it was not until 1802 that Dumont published in France the *Traités de Legislation Civile et Penale*. And even after their publication England continued to ignore Bentham, or, if he was known at all, it was not as a writer but as a philanthropist and, moreover, as an unsuccessful philanthropist. Bentham had invented a novel type of prison, a circular prison equipped with a system of central supervision, the Panopticon or house where everything is visible. He had sought to procure its adoption by the British Government, had offered to undertake the financial responsibility and administer himself the institution he proposed. He had even purchased out of his private resources a site for the future prison. But the passage through Parliament of an Act in favour of the scheme had borne no fruit. Neither Pitt nor his successors had given Bentham the support which he had been promised. Already sixty years of age, unknown as a philosopher, impotent as a philanthropist, his fortune devoured by the Panopticon scheme, he believed his career at an end, and his life a failure, when in 1808 he made the acquaintance of James Mill, who had just come up to London from Edinburgh University, and was laboriously earning a livelihood by hard work with his pen. Bentham converted Mill to his philosophy. Mill in return restored Bentham's self-confidence, propagated his ideas, and gathered around him a school of disciples In the history of social science in Britain during the early 19th century the formation of this Benthamite school was an event of the first importance. The Benthamites were in the strictest sense of the term a sect and their influence is comparable in its extent to the influence of the Clapham sect. Possessed by an equal enthusiasm, their inspiration was widely different. Their thoroughgoing rationalism was in striking contrast with the emotionalism of the Evangelicals.

Only seven years had passed since the junction between Bentham and James Mill, only five since Mill had taken a house at Westminster, next door to Bentham's, and already the influence of Benthamism was spreading in every direction. James Mill was expounding its creed in the *Edinburgh Review* and in the *Philanthropist*, the magazine of the Quaker William Allen. In the House of Commons Bentham's lifelong friend, the barrister Romilly, was urging year by year in conformity with his friend's principles a mitigation of the penal code, a reduction in the number of "capital felonies." James Mill introduced Bentham to Robert Owen and Lancaster, indeed, to all who were seeking the reform of society in a system of popular education : we have already seen the share taken by Bentham and his friends in the Lancastrian movement. James Mill became the friend of Ricardo and introduced him to his master : without Mill the *Principles of Political Economy and Taxation* would perhaps never have been written. And finally, it was through Mill that Bentham made the acquaintance of Francis Place, the famous electoral agent of the Westminster constituency. We have remarked the formation at Westminster about the person of Bentham of the youthful party of " Radicals." Fame had come to Bentham and with fame wealth. In 1813 Parliament had voted him a vast indemnity as compensation for the losses incurred in his Panopticon propaganda. A kindly and eccentric old man, owner of a house in town and a country seat, Bentham commanded an army of disciples. The philosophic and social ideas of the 18th century had awoken from a slumber of twenty-five years. What was the common philosophic principle on which the Utilitarians built their jurisprudence, their political economy and their politics ? Man seeks pleasure and avoids pain. This, according to Bentham and his disciples, is the fundamental law of human action. The *summum bonum* is pleasure—not indeed the passing pleasure of the individual, which would render impossible a scientific treatment either of happiness or morality—but " general utility," " the greatest happiness of the greatest number." Hence a rational art of conduct presupposes the knowledge of the conditions which produce pleasure and pain—that the former may be sought, the latter avoided. And this knowledge is in turn only to be obtained by the construction of a psychology modelled on the natural sciences already in existence. But these fall into two classes, the sciences which collect facts, and the sciences which explain and construct a system of laws. It was after the pattern of the latter class, the sciences whose objects are elementary and simple phenomena, that the Utilitarians conceived their new science of human nature.

Such was the spirit of their age and country. It is a current belief that the English are cautious observers, with a keen eye for detail, careful to respect the complexity of nature, as opposed to the French, who delight in intellectual constructions and in generalization. This belief, however, is far from the truth. In reality simplification has been the distinctive character of British thought during the 19th century. British men of science, for the reasons we have already determined— reasons of a strictly historical character—united the inexperience and the boldness, a boldness often successful, of the self-taught man. They were reasoners who sought and discovered simple laws, men of intuition, who claimed to perceive beneath the manifold of natural phenomena, the outlines of a machine, whose parts are few and whose motions are all sensible.[1] It was because it was at once the simplest hypothesis,

---

[1] This explains the small progress made by English scientists of this epoch in higher mathematics. The algorithm of algebra repelled them. They had no liking for this blindfold search of truth. Thomas Young, who cared the most for pure mathematics, avoided symbolic forms of proof, and used as far as possible the language of everyday life, thus making his works

and the most easily visualized that Dalton adopted the atomic theory : it rendered the fundamental composition of bodies visible. And the method of Bentham and his school was Dalton's method applied to the moral sciences. In both departments there was the same simplification, the same "atomism."

The human soul is a compound of elementary feelings, psychical atoms, agreeable feelings and disagreeable feelings, which differ in intensity, duration, number and the manner of their mutual combination.[1] And the laws which govern their association are few and simple, the law of association by likeness, and the law of association by contiguity. Perhaps even these two laws could be reduced to one, the law of association by likeness being a special case of the law of association by contiguity.[2] Bentham had translated a work of the Swedish chemist Bergmann. James Mill was the intimate friend of Thomas Thomson, a defender of the Daltonian atomism. Both were conscious imitators of the methods of the new chemistry. Their ideal moralist, educator and legislator must practise a mental chemistry and must learn from the chemist the art of constructing complex psychoses by the combination of simple elements.

The art of education would thus consist in effecting in the minds of children such an association of ideas that the child could no longer separate his personal happiness from the happiness of his fellows. The art of legislation would consist in producing a similar result in the mind of the adult. By associating the idea of certain actions with the idea of certain penalties the legislator would intimidate the potential criminal and prevent crime. The scientific analysis both of the crime and its penalty into their constituent elements, their atoms, and the establishment of an accurate proportion between both sets of factors, constituted, for the Utilitarian, the entire science of penology. Evidently a science of calculation and reasoning and nothing beyond. The Utilitarians neglected as useless learned research, knowledge of the historical growth of law. Their method was, as they fully realized, in radical opposition to the historical method which the professors of Germany were bringing into fashion. "One might," wrote Bentham in scorn, "open an historical school *à la mode d'Allemagne.* Der Herr Savigny in Germany could furnish admirable masters. . . . To the army and the navy of a country substitute, for example, a history of the wars waged by that

---

more difficult of understanding, by his very attempt to render them more popular (Peacock, *Life of Thomas Young*, pp. 116–17, 183). Similarly, when Berzelius, having accepted the atomic theory, attempted to describe the composition of bodies by formulæ in which the atoms were represented by letters to which were appended coefficients showing the number of atoms in a particular combination, Dalton denounced this new algebra, and described Berzelius' symbols as "horrible." The student of chemistry, he maintained, could as easily learn Hebrew (W. C. Henry, *Memoirs of . . . John Dalton*, p. 124).

[1] Bentham, *Principles of Morals and Legislation*, chap. iv. (*Works*, vol. i. pp. 15 sqq.).
[2] James Mill, *Analysis of the Human Mind*, chap. xi. (ed. 1878, vol. i. pp. 376–7).

same country. . . . to an order on a cook for. dinner substitute a fair copy of the housekeeper's book as kept during the appropriate series of years."[1] These words express the hatred of the reformer for the traditionalist, of the self-educated man for the university scholar.

We may now adopt a slightly different point of view and consider not, as hitherto, the mutual combinations of simple psychoses in the individual consciousness, but the association of individuals to form a society.   Bentham and his followers saw in society only an agglomeration of individuals, by nature existing in mutual isolation, and united solely by deliberate volitions.   A certain proportion of individuals were happy, a certain proportion unhappy.   Which side of the account showed a surplus ?   This was the balance which you must strike whenever you would appreciate a law or a custom.   Such simple operations of addition and subtraction composed the entire intellectual task of the Utilitarian reformer.   And this individualism may be regarded as a kind of sociological "atomism."   It explains the line of reasoning which led the Utilitarians to political radicalism.   And it was the foundation-stone of the entire edifice of the new political economy.

Suppose all the individuals, the atoms, out of which the social body is composed, perfectly selfish, inaccessible to any motive except a self-regarding prudence.   Suppose them also perfectly rational, free from any liability to be blinded by passion.   And finally, suppose them perfectly free, admitting no external constraint in the pursuit of their economic end.   We thus construct a society as unlike any actual human society, as the simplified world of the sciences is unlike the world of sensible experience, but capable of rendering equal service in the explanation of phenomena.   In fact, the hypothesis, precisely because of its simplicity, rendered possible an almost mathematically exact description of several economic phenomena such as the circulation of currency, exchange and banking.   It even provided a sufficiently accurate account of the exchange of manufactured goods.   And Ricardo believed that, when taken in conjunction with the Malthusian law of population, it enabled an equally accurate explanation to be given of the distribution of the profits of labour between the landlord, the capitalist and the labourer.   No attempt was made to discover empirical laws by observation.   Nor was economic theory controlled by statistics.   Political economy, as understood by Ricardo and James Mill, was built up by the series of hypothetical constructions whose character we have explained above.   And this individualist theory was applied by individualist practice.   The Utilitarians regarded the State as in principle incapable of controlling economics.   It must stand

---

[1] Bentham, to his fellow Citizens of France, on Houses of Peers and Senates, 1830 (Works, ed. Bowring, vol iv. p. 425).

aside and leave individuals free to regulate their economic interests, whether as between class and class, or nation and nation.

Thus was erected the finished edifice of Utilitarianism. It was frankly irreligious. Neither as the explanation of history, nor as the foundation of ethics or law did it invoke the supernatural, or any principle transcending sensible experience. Nor is it sufficient to call Utilitarianism irreligious. It was aggressively anti-religious, and regarded religion as a whole and Christianity in particular as the bane of civilization. For religion was of its very nature a form of asceticism, a perversion of feeling which made men desire pain and shun pleasure. And asceticism had produced a taste for slavery of every description, political, legal and economic. Above all, asceticism was responsible for the notion of punishment as an " expiation," which had induced men to regard the infliction of punishment as a good thing in itself, and had thus led to that useless severity of the criminal code against which from the commencement of his literary activity Bentham had never ceased to protest. It would be impossible, without unduly anticipating the future, to relate the campaign of anti-Christian propaganda—no longer deist as in the days of Tom Paine, but frankly atheist—to which the Utilitarians would lend their aid. It dates from the years which followed the conclusion of peace. But even before 1815 the body of doctrines which composed philosophic radicalism exercised in every direction a subversive influence. Thus with Bentham and his friends we are at the opposite pole alike to the Toryism of the Government, and to Evangelical pietism. How then are we to explain the success of the Utilitarian propaganda in face of the hostility of Government, and the influence, felt universally, of the Protestant revival ?

Influence of Benthamism. Utilitarianism and Pietism.

When the Tories wished to discredit Utilitarianism, they denounced it as an unpatriotic philosophy, inspired by foreign ideas, and especially by French ideas. Were not the political principles of the Benthamites the democratic principles of the Jacobins ? Did they not derive their ethics and their jurisprudence from Helvetius and Beccaria, their psychology from Condillac, their philosophy of history and their political economy from Condorcet and Jean-Baptiste Say ? Were they not irreligious Voltairians ? Had not Bentham composed in French and published at Paris his *Traités de Legislation* ?[1] But the Utilitarians could reply with truth that all these so-called French ideas, of whose importation they were accused, were in reality English ideas which had found a temporary home abroad.

Before its appearance in France democracy had been the political

[1] For these French influences, see my *Formation du Radicalisme Philosophique*, vol. i. pp. 23 sqq. ; vol. ii. pp. 219 sqq., 232 sqq. ; vol. iii. pp. 231 sqq. and *passim*.

theory of the Anglo-Saxon rebels in America, and the Americans had themselves taken the principles which inspired their rebellion from Locke and the English republicans of the 17th century. Condillac's psychology had been the psychology of Hartley and Hume before Condillac ever set pen to paper. It was in England that Voltaire had learned to be a Free Thinker. Throughout the anti-Jacobin reaction there had been thinkers—Erasmus Darwin, Thomas Day, Edgeworth, the political agitator Horne Tooke, Unitarians of the school of Priestley —who defended what they believed to be the national tradition against the innovations of the Tories. Among the ideas which composed the Utilitarian system, their economic theories tended more and more to take the first place. And, however great the influence of the French physiocratic school, Hume and Adam Smith were undoubtedly the founders of the new political economy, and the action of this political economy extended far beyond the sphere open to the complete Utilitarian system. The English are a nation of traders and can be governed only by men who possess the commercial mentality. Pitt, the leader of the anti-Jacobins, was a disciple of Adam Smith. Burke, at once the orator and the philosopher of the counter-revolution, was as zealous in the defence of economic individualism, as in the denunciation of political. When the Tories became a party of landlords and country squires, they signed their own death warrant. In this way their economic principles obtained for Utilitarianism an entrance into the governing classes.

Twenty-five years of Tory reaction, a reaction, when all is said, only skin deep, had proved insufficient to destroy intellectual traditions so deeply rooted. And moreover, what official body was in existence on which the party in office could rely to combat the ideas of the Benthamites? The Scottish universities? We have seen the empirical spirit which inspired the philosophers of the Scottish school. If they shrank from the conclusions of Hartley and his followers, their hesitation was due only to the extreme simplicity of the Hartleian generalizations. For they were men of university training, not self-educated men. But at bottom they differed from the radical empiricists only by their greater caution. Was Cambridge less exposed to the infection of Utilitarianism? We have seen that Cambridge had always professed Whig ideas in political philosophy and in philosophy generally. Locke, Paley and Hartley were the philosophers studied at Cambridge. A few years hence Benthamism will be the fashion among the Cambridge undergraduates.[1] There remained the impregnable citadel of Oxford. But Oxford was asleep and no one could possibly regard the remnants of Aristotelian scholasticism taught in her schools as a living intellectual tradition.

To be sure, for the past twenty years there had existed on the

[1] John Stuart Mill, *Autobiography*, pp. 76–7.

Continent a new system of philosophy professed by men of genius, capable of attracting the rising generation and counteracting Utilitarianism. But it was not English. And how many Englishmen were able to read Kant, Fichte and Schelling in the original ? The Scottish professors attempted to make the acquaintance of the new systems through the channel of French interpreters, Madame de Staël and De Gerando : [1] and what they understood, they disliked. Alone in England the poet Coleridge had been deeply influenced by German thought. He had abandoned verse for prose, and exchanged the naturalistic pantheism of his youth for a transcendental theology inspired by Schelling. But Coleridge, far more than Bentham, was an eccentric and lonely thinker. He belonged to no teaching body, to no national tradition. In 1815 his influence still counted for nothing.

England is a free country in which Government pressure plays no part in the formation of public opinion. It is not therefore surprising that the Utilitarian propaganda overcame the opposition of official Conservatism. It is more difficult to understand the influence exercised by Utilitarianism in an environment so impregnated with Evangelical religion as was the England of the early 19th century. Was the action of the two forces successive ? And was Utilitarianism in 1815 a growing force, Evangelicalism on the verge of decline ? Such an explanation would do violence to the complexity of the situation. The fundamental paradox of English society, which it is necessary to explain before we conclude this volume, is precisely the partial junction and combination of these two forces theoretically so hostile.

We have already spoken of the philanthropic activity common to both parties. Utilitarianism was a philosophy wholly practical. Bentham and his friends were ardent advocates of the Panopticon model prison, whose very idea had been conceived by their leader, of Lancaster's model school, and Robert Owen's model factory. They regarded these institutions as " moral " inventions, akin to the important technical inventions which were transforming industry, as " moral " machines ingeniously constructed for the automatic production of virtue and happiness. The Christian philanthropists, whatever their repugnance to such a mechanical conception of psychology and ethics, could not be deaf to the appeal of inventions so beneficent as these. Between the Utilitarians and the " old Dissenters " there existed little short of a permanent alliance. And even the Methodists and Evangelicals sympathized with the Utilitarian philanthropy. As their contribution to the common task the Christians brought their zeal, their missionary spirit, their love for a self-imposed discipline. Nor did the Utilitarians fail to appreciate these qualities. " Townshend," wrote Bentham, " was once what I had liked to have been, a

---

[1] Dugald Stewart, *Dissertations* . . . (*Works*, 2nd ed., 1877, vol. i. pp. 394, 413, 416).

Methodist, and what I should have been, had I not been what I am."[1]
And the Utilitarians contributed their practical sense, their conviction
of the possibility of a social technique, an art of employing the right
means to obtain the desired end. Many Christian philanthropists,
educated in the school of industrialism, shared their convictions on
this point. But we may go further and discover closer affinities
between Benthamite Utilitarianism and Protestant Pietism.

It would be a mistake to establish an irreconcilable opposition between
the Utilitarian ethic and the Christian on the ground that the former
is founded on pleasure, the latter on sacrifice. For Utilitarian morality
cannot be described without qualification as a system of hedonism.
It was based simultaneously on two principles. One of these was no
doubt the identification of the ethical good with pleasure; but the other,
of equal importance with the former, was the duty incumbent upon man,
in virtue of the natural conditions to which his life is subject, to sacrifice
present pleasure to the hope of future pleasure, and to purchase happiness at the cost of labour and suffering. This law of work, implicit in
Bentham's moral arithmetic, was the principle explicitly proclaimed by
the entire system of the classical political economy, and introduced into
Utilitarianism an undeniable element of asceticism.[2] How can we
explain the popularity of the Malthusian thesis at the very period when
public opinion was apparently attached more closely than ever to the
Christian tradition? Undoubtedly it contradicted one of the fundamental doctrines of the Bible. But it also refuted the atheistic humanitarianism of the 18th century, and taught that man is destined by his
very nature to an unending struggle for existence, to a perpetual condition
of hardship. And this appealed to the ascetic and Christian pre-
conceptions of the public. It was in vain that the Benthamites attempted
to reconcile the principle of population with the creed of unlimited
progress, the pessimism of Malthus with the optimism of Condorcet.
Their efforts could not abolish the distinction between the standpoint
of the French Utilitarians and the standpoint of their English teachers.
Benthamism, as its principles were popularized about 1815 by James
Mill the Scotsman, was the French philosophy of the 18th century
adapted to the needs of a nation moulded by a dogmatic and austere
religion.

And moreover, the Utilitarians were individualists. The object
of their entire ethical teaching was to bring home to the individual
that society existed only through him and for his sake, and that it is his
personal duty to maintain his rights and pursue his interest. To be

[1] *Works*, ed. Bowring, vol. x. p. 92. Cf. *ibid.*, p. 508 : "If to be an anti-slavist is to be
a saint, saintship for me. I am a saint!"

[2] For the kinship between economic asceticism and Protestant asceticism, see the subtle,
often indeed the excessively subtle, observations of Max Weber, *Die Protestantische Ethik
und der Geist des Kapitalismus* (*Archiv für Sozial Wissenschaft und Sozial Politik*), 1905, vol. xx.
pp. 1 sqq. ; vol. xxi. pp. 1 sqq.

sure, this individualism was not that theological individualism of the Protestant, whose character has been described above. And moreover, the new type of Protestantism, which sprang from Wesley's preaching in the previous century, was in this respect an enfeebled type. The organization of the Methodist sects was more hierarchic than the organization of the old seventeenth-century sects; and the Evangelicals were Methodists who had refused to break with the Anglican Church. But no Protestant revival could fail to be, in some measure at least, a revival of religious individualism. Between the secular individualism of Bentham and the authoritarian Christianity of the High Churchman, the liberal Protestantism of the Unitarians, Scottish Calvinism, the Methodist sects, the Evangelicalism of the Low Church party, constituted a series of imperceptible transitions. Nor was the individualism of the Utilitarianism radically anti-social. It did not exclude in principle all State intervention. For the Utilitarians looked to the legislature to establish a harmony of interests in the community by imposing obligations sanctioned by penalties. And even where they rejected Government interference, the Benthamites encouraged the formation of voluntary associations whose members would pursue a common end by the free surrender of a portion of their independence. Secular philanthropy and Protestant Dissent stood in equal need of such associations. They were thus among the typical expressions of private initiative in nineteenth-century England. British individualism is a moderate individualism, a mixture whose constituents are often mingled beyond the possibility of analysis, a compound of Evangelicalism and Utilitarianism.

CONCLUSION

FROM whatever point of view we study the institutions of Britain we are brought back to the same formula. England is a free country. But language is not a perfectly accurate instrument, and the same word can bear many meanings. What then are we to understand by British freedom?

After thirty years of Tory reaction, England was a free country. Such was the conclusion of our study of her political institutions. And we meant by this that England was a country in which the executive was systematically weakened in every direction. It would not even be true to say that government was based on the division of powers and that in this division the province of the executive was narrowly limited. On the contrary, the several branches of administration were confused in such a way that all the others encroached on the executive, and that the powers of its nominal head were reduced to a minimum. The actual executive consisted of the group of persons which composed the Cabinet, all members of the Legislature, and responsible to the Legislature. The Justices of the Peace, men of good family, scattered up and down the entire country, united judicial functions with administrative duties of the first importance. A free Press and the right of rebellion, ultimate guarantees of popular liberty against the encroachments of any department of Government, were a very real part of the British Constitution. And the jury system in turn guaranteed the liberty of the Press. The weakness of the Army, a weakness which survived even the large increase of numbers necessitated by a long war, made rebellion a serious possibility. Montesquieu was not wrong in describing the British Constitution as a mixed Constitution equally composed of monarchy, aristocracy and democracy. But it would perhaps be more accurate to term it a confusion of oligarchy and anarchy.

We also pointed out that the economic system of England was a free system, and by that we meant that England was the country in which capitalism had developed more rapidly than in any other country in Europe, and therefore the country in which the system of free contract had superseded most completely the system of custom, corporate trading and State regulation. Mechanical inventions had multiplied until men had come to regard a continual transformation of technical methods as the normal condition of industry. The guilds had disappeared, or had become mere social groups wholly devoid of compulsory powers. The State indeed still protected the manufactures and the agriculture of the nation against foreign competition. But as far as the former were concerned this protection had been rendered unnecessary by the enormous technical superiority of English methods of manufacture over the methods in use abroad. And agrarian protection had become inefficacious and unpopular : for it raised the cost of subsistence above the "natural" level. Therefore the principle of Free Trade was continually gaining ground. Moreover, the progress of Capitalism involved the accumulation of vast wealth in the hands of a few, and this in turn stripped increasing numbers of their property and reduced them to the condition of wage-earners. No legislation regulated the relations between the employer and his hands. The old statutes bore no application to the novel conditions of manufacture. And it was no easy task to build up the new system of laws demanded by the complexity of economic life. Alike in country and town the proletariate formed a disorganized and turbulent mass. The old political Whiggery of the noble families was gradually replaced or overlaid by the economic individualism of the commanders of industry. The political riot which from 1688 to the French Revolution had been the traditional expression of popular feeling in Great Britain gave way to the strike, the riot of the workers, the revolt of the hungry. England was the country of economic freedom, of unbridled competition, of class war.

And finally, if we consider the religious, the ethical and the intellectual conditions in England, we must still term England a free country. For England was a country in which the Established Church, whatever privileges it might enjoy, left the sects outside her borders entire liberty of organization, full power to form a host of little States within the State. Atheism and deism alone were excluded from this toleration, as anti-social systems. But certain sects, whose doctrine was practically indistinguishable from deism, had obtained a legal status and had just been secured by Act of Parliament from the bare possibility of persecution. Of official protection of art, literature or science there was little or none. Although the Tory monarch, George III, had shown signs of a desire to put an end to the traditional inaction of the Crown in this sphere, had founded the Royal Academy, and had encouraged the reorganization and rejuvenation of the Royal Society, all that was best in the intellectual life of Britain developed apart from royal interference. The absence or insufficiency of royal patronage was supplied by the patronage of the aristocracy. And the patronage of the new industrial class counted for even more. Throughout this youthful British society, free from all Court ties, free even from any connexion with the governing aristocracy, independent thinkers were at work, who carried on their experiments and made their discoveries unguided and uncontrolled. Did this lack of organization in the religious and in the scientific world produce the same anarchy which we have remarked in the political and in the economic sphere ? Certainly not, and for the following reason.

The religious bodies whose freedom was respected by the State were societies which, because they lacked the power of legal coercion, were obliged to direct their efforts to the establishment of a powerful moral authority alike over their own members and over society as a whole. And their efforts were successful. They exercised the influence they sought. Not only did they encourage the growth in every sphere of a spirit of free association, and occasion directly or indirectly the mass of voluntary institutions both philanthropic and scientific so characteristic of modern England. They disturbed the torpor of the Government and even of the Established Church. They occupied themselves with the regulation of public morality, compelled the application of existing laws, revived laws which had fallen into abeyance, demanded new legislation. Uniting their influence with the influence of industrialism, they fashioned the character of the English middle class, dogmatic in morals, proud of its practical outlook, and sufficiently powerful to obtain respect for its views from the proletariate on the one hand, from the aristocracy on the other. The ruling classes watched the growth of this new power, whose nature they could not comprehend. They knew that the British Constitution did not give them sufficient strength to repress a general rebellion. And they perceived that the development of industrialism was rendering the social order more unstable and multiplying industrial and political crises. So they called to mind the French Revolution and the American War of Independence and feared " Methodism " almost equally with Jacobinism. Had they understood the situation better, they would have realized that Methodism was the antidote to Jacobinism, and that the free organization of the sects was the foundation of social order in England. " England is a free country " : this means at bottom that England is a country of voluntary obedience, of an organization freely initiated and freely accepted.

BIBLIOGRAPHY

WORKS OF GENERAL REFERENCE[1]

For the period *immediately* preceding 1815 there exists no English history which can claim to be a scientific treatment of the subject.

Lecky (W. E. H.). A History of England in the Eighteenth Century, 1st ed., 8 vols., 1878–90 ; new ed., 7 vols., 1892.

> Concludes with the year 1792.

Massey (W.). A History of England during the Reign of George the Third, 4 vols., 1st ed., 1855–63 ; 2nd ed., 1865.

> Contains interesting details of social life. Nothing after 1802.

Alison (Archibald). History of Europe from the Commencement of the French Revolution in 1789 to the Restoration of the Bourbons in 1815, 1st ed., 10 vols., 1833–42. We have used the 7th ed., 20 vols., 1848.

> An abundantly detailed account of diplomatic, military and economic history ; written from the Tory standpoint.

Jesse (J. Heneage). Memoirs of the Life and Reign of King George the Third, 3 vols., 1867.

> Deals exclusively with political history (Cabinet crises, etc.), superficial.

There have appeared recently a number of textbooks whose value is unequal. All are very elementary.

MacCarthy (Justin). A History of the Four Georges, 4 vols., 1884–1901.

Dorman (M. R. P.). A History of the British Empire in the Nineteenth Century, 2 vols., 1902–4.

> Unfinished ; leaves off at 1815 ; very superficial ; deals exclusively, or almost exclusively, with foreign politics.

Brodrick (the Hon. George C.). The History of England, from Addington's Administration to the close of William IV's Reign (1801–37) . . . completed and revised by J. K. Fotheringham, 1 vol., 1906.

Mathieson (William Law). England in Transition (1789–1832). A Study of Movements, 1920.

Maxwell (Sir Herbert Eustace). A Century of Empire, 1801–1901, 3 vols. ; vol. i (1801–32), 1909.

---

[1] A small number of titles of books, which have appeared since this work was first written in 1913, have been added in order to bring the Bibliography up to date. But the author wishes it to be clearly understood that this translation, though containing a fairly large number of corrections, is not what he would like to call in the full sense of the word a revised edition. All books here mentioned, and which have been published in 1913 and later, should therefore not be taken as having been sources to the present History ; they are merely mentioned because they may convey useful information to our readers.

Good sketches of the general condition of Britain will be found at the beginning of :

Walpole (Spencer). A History of England from the Conclusion of the Great War in 1815, 1st ed., 5 vols., 1878–86 ; new ed. revised., 6 vols., 1890.

Martineau (Miss Harriet). The History of England during the Thirty Years' Peace, 1816–46, 2 vols., 1849–50.

Cory (William). A Guide to Modern English History, 2 vols., 1880–2.
> Valued by English students of history.

In :

The Cambridge Modern History, vol. viii., The French Revolution, 1904, vol. ix, Napoleon, 1906, vol x, The Restoration, 1907,
> The joint work of a number of professors. There are very few chapters on the internal history of England during our period.

For the study of British Diplomacy :

The Cambridge History of Foreign Policy, 1783–1919, edited by Sir A. W. Ward and G. P. Gooch, vol. i (1783–1815), 1922.

Webster (C. K.). British Diplomacy, 1813–15. Select Documents, ed. by ——, 1921.
> A collection of documents, partly new, always well chosen.

For an accurate but dry account of the political institutions of England in 1815, see :

Adolphus (John). The Political State of the British Empire, 4 vols., 1818.

Also for further detail :

Montveran (M. de). Histoire critique et raisonnée de la Situation de l'Angleterre, au 1er Janvier, 1816, sous les rapports de ses finances, de son agriculture, de ses manufactures, de son commerce et sa navigation, de sa constitution et ses lois et de sa politique extérieure, 8 vols., 1819.

But especially

Traill (H. D.) and Mann (J. S.). Social England, a record of the progress of the people in religion, laws, learning and arts, industry, commerce, science, literature and manners, from the earliest times to the present time, by various writers, edited by ——, 6 vols., 1st ed. 1893 ; 2nd ed. 1898. Vol. v (1714–1815), vol. vi (1815–85).
> A storehouse of interesting information concerning the social history of England. Every chapter is the work of a specialist.

Original Sources.

The principal sources are :

> (a) The Collections of Debates.

The Parliamentary Register, or History of the Proceedings and Debates of both Houses . . . 4 series, 1774–1813.

Cobbett's Parliamentary History of England, 1806–28, vols. i–xii 1066–1713, vols. xiii–xxxvi 1743–1803.
> These two collections will often be found to supplement each other most usefully.

introductory to the Study of the Law of the Con-
third edition the work bears the title : Introduction
of the Constitution. 7th ed., 1908.

The Law and Custom of the Constitution : Part I,
Crown, 1st ed., 1886.

sches Staatsrecht, mit Berücksichtigung der für Schott-
Sonderheiten. I. vol. Die Verfassung, 1905; II. vol.
volumes of the Handbuch des Oeffentlichen Rechts
quardsen, von Seydel, G. Jellinek and Piloty).

:

ement de la Constitution et de la Société Politique en

res on the Relation between Law and Public Opinion
Nineteenth Century, 1905,

more philosophical.

YSTEM OF ADMINISTRATION.

HE CENTRAL GOVERNMENT.

BUSES : OFFICIAL DOCUMENTS.

missioners appointed to examine, take and state the Public
ngdom, presented to His Majesty and to both Houses of
he appendices complete, 1783, 1785, 1787.

; and Proceedings thereupon, 1798–1803, with a general
(36 reports).

s of Commissioners, 1802–6 (14 reports).

ng and revising the Civil Affairs of the Navy, 1805. Reports
rs, 1806–9 (13 reports).

ports of Commissioners of Inquiry, 1806–12 (19 reports).
e collection, 1816).

t Committee appointed to draw up Articles of Impeachment
ord Viscount Melville, 1805–6 (3 reports).

taken before the Committee of the Whole House, appointed
Conduct of His Royal Highness the Duke of York, the Com-
with regard to Promotions, Exchanges and Appointments to
he Army and Staff of the Army, and in raising Levies for the

mmittee appointed to examine and consider what regulations
been established in order to control the several Branches of the
ure in Great Britain and Ireland, and how far the same have
nd what further measures can be adopted for reducing any part
nditure, or diminishing the amount of Salaries and Emoluments,
nt to the Public Service, 1807–12 (13 reports).

Cobbett's and (after vol. xxiii.) Hansard's Parliamentary Debates, from 1803, 1st
series, 41 vols., 1803–20.
Index 1834, for the years 1803–30.

(b) Collections of Statutes, especially :

Pickering (D.). The Statutes at large from Magna Charta to 1806, 46 vols., 1672–
1807.
(General indices after vols. xxiv and xxxviii.)

—— The Statutes of the United Kingdom . . . vol. xlvii et sqq.

Chitty (Joseph). A Collection of Statutes of Practical Utility, with notes thereon :
intended as a Circuit and Court Companion, 2 vols., 1829.

(c) Contemporary Magazines, such as :

The Annual Register ; or, a view of History, Politics and Literature.
An annual from 1758.

The Gentleman's Magazine and Historical Chronicle.
A monthly from 1731.
Two indices, 1789 for the years 1731–86, 1821 for 1787–1818.

(d) The great contemporary Reviews :

The Edinburgh Review.
From 1802.
Index to the first 20 vols., 1813 ; to vols. xxi–l, 1832. A Liberal organ.

The Quarterly Review.
From 1809.
Index to first 20 vols. after vol. 20, 1820 ; to vols. xxi–xxxix after vol. xl,
1831. Conservative ; the organ of Canning's group.

(e) Dailies or papers appearing at very frequent intervals :

See above, Book I, chap. ii for a list of the principal newspapers.
We have made frequent use of them.

Cobbett's Annual Register (from 1802) and Political Register (from 1804, the continuation of the former).
A most valuable collection full of documents of every description, also articles
of political criticism or satire.

(f) Biographies, Memoirs, Correspondence :

Their number is very large and taken as a whole are a source of valuable information
to the historian. But as a rule they have been commissioned by the family of their
subject and hence are full of deliberate omissions ; and their compilation has been
too often entrusted to incompetent journalists, who fail to make full use of their
documents. No detailed bibliography can be given here (see the special headings
below), but mention must be made of the excellent

Dictionary of National Biography, edited by Leslie Stephen and afterwards by Sydney
Lee, 1st ed. 1885–1900.

(g) Travels :

These contain much valuable information. This is true of the accounts by
English travellers of journeys in their own country, and even more true of the relations
of foreign travellers. See especially :

Pictet (M. A.). Voyage de trois mois en Angleterre, en Écosse, et en Irlande pendant l'été de l'an ix An xi (1802).

Barber (J. T.). A Tour throughout South Wales and Monmouthshire, 1803.

Warner (Rev. Richard). A Walk through Wales, 1799.

—— A Walk through some of the Western Counties of England, 1800.

—— A Tour through the Northern Counties of England, and the Borders of Scotland, 1802.

—— A Tour through Cornwall in the autumn of 1808, 1809.

Nemnich (P. A.). Neuste Reise durch England, 1807.

Svedenstjerna (Th.). Resa igenom en Del of England, 1804 (German translation from the Swedish, 1807).

Ayton (R.). Voyage round Great Britain, . . . undertaken in the summer of the year 1813, 8 vols., 1814-25. (Continued from vol. iii by W. Daniell.)

Journal of a Tour and Residence in Great Britain during the years 1810 and 1811, by a French traveller [Louis Simond], 1815.

M—— (A. J. B. Defauconpret). Quinze jours à Londres à la fin de 1815, 1816
—— Six mois à Londres en 1816. 1817.

Irving (Washington). The Sketch-book of Geoffrey Crayon, 1st ed., 1820.

Etc., etc.

Dicey (Albert Venn). Lectur
stitution, 1885. From th
to the Study of the Law

Anson (Sir William Reynell).
Parliament ; Part II, T

Hatschek (Dr. Julius). Engl
land und Irland geltende
Die Verwaltung, 1906
der Gegenwart, by Ma

The following work

Boutmy (E.). Le Dévelopl
Angleterre, 1887.

Dicey (Albert Venn). Lect
in England during th

are more general and n

II. THE S

A. T

1. THE REFORM OF A

The Reports of the Com
Accounts of the Ki
Parliament ; with t

Finance Reports, 1797–
index to the whole

Naval Inquiry. Repor

Commission for regulati
of the Commission

Military Inquiry. Re
Index to the entir

Reports from the Sele
against Henry, L

Minutes of Evidence
to investigate the
mander-in-Chief,
Commissions in
Army, 1809.

Reports from the C
and checks have
Public Expendi
been effectual, a
of the said Expe
without detrim

Montesquieu, L

Blackstone (Sir
1765-9.
Its Cons
an actual

De Lolme. Cons
enlarged, unde
English Gover
Government, a

Burke (Edmund).
the 2nd ed. in 1

The Black Book ; or
Violent but
abuses then

Russell (Lord John).
Constitution, from
(greatly enlarged),

Creasy (Edward Shephe
1853. 17th ed. rev
An elementary

Gneist (Rudolph). Das
2 vols., 1857.

Franqueville (Charles de).
de l'Angleterre, 1st ed

Todd (Alpheus). On Parl
New edition abridg

Hearn (William Edward).
ment, 1867 ; 2nd ed.,

May (Sir Thomas Erskine,
England since the accessi
with an additional chapt

Glasson (E. D.). Histoire du
aires de l'Angleterre, comp
leur origine jusqu'à nos jou

Reports from the Select Committee appointed to consider what Offices in the United Kingdom and in the Foreign Dominions of His Majesty come within the purview of the second, third and fourth Resolutions of the House, on the Third Report from the Committee on Public Expenditure of the United Kingdom, 1810–12 (3 reports).

Reports from Select Committee on Sinecure Offices, 1810–12 (3 reports).

Reports from the Select Committee appointed to inquire into and state the Income and Expenditure of the United Kingdom for the year ended the 5th January, 1817, and also to consider and state the probable Income and Expenditure (so far as the same can be estimated) for the years ending the 5th of January 1818, and the 5th of January 1819 respectively ; and also to consider what further measures may be adopted for the Relief of the Country from any part of the said Expenditure, without detriment to the Public Interest (Sinecure Offices), 1819.

A Return of the Number of Persons employed, and Pay, and Salaries granted to such Persons, in all Public Offices or Departments, in the year 1797 ; and in the years 1805, 1810, 1815 and 1819 ; showing the increase in each of these years, as compared with 1797. Also, a Return for 1827, showing the Reduction that has been made since 1819. 1828.

2. Beside the works which give a general account of British political institutions (see especially Gneist) there exists no book dealing with the administrative system except the little work, a mere outline, by

Eaton (Dorman Bridgman). Civil Service in Great Britain ; a history of abuses and reforms and their bearing upon American politics, 1880.

See also Herbert Joyce's monograph :

Joyce (Herbert). The History of the Post Office from its Establishment down to 1836. 1893.

3. THE JUDICATURE, THE BAR, THE ADMINISTRATION OF THE LAW.

(i) *General.*

Cottu (Charles). De l'Administration de la Justice Criminelle en Angleterre et de l'esprit du Gouvernement Anglais 1820, 2nd ed., 1822. (English translation, 1822.)

Pearce (R. R.). A History of the Inns of Court and Chancery ; with Notices of their Ancient Discipline, Rule, Orders, etc., 1848.

(ii) *Biographies.*

Campbell (John, Lord). The Lives of the Lord Chancellors and Keepers of the Great Seal of England, from the earliest times to the reign of King George IV, 1st ed., 8 vols., 1845–8 ; 4th ed., 10 vols., 1856–7.

—— The Lives of the Chief Justices of England, from the Norman Conquest till the death of Lord Tenterden, 3 vols., 1849–57 ; 3rd ed., 4 vols., 1874.

—— Life of John, Lord Campbell, Lord High Chancellor of Great Britain ; consisting of a selection from his autobiography, diary and letters, edited by his daughter, 1881.

Townshend (William Charles). The Lives of twelve eminent Judges of the last and the present century, 2 vols., 1846.

Eldon (Lord Chancellor ——). The public and private Life of ——, with selections from his correspondence by Horace Twiss, 3 vols., 1844.

Kenyon (Lloyd, first Lord ——). The Life of ——, by G. T. Kenyon, 1873.

(iii) *The Reform of Abuses.*

Stephen (Sir James Fitzjames). A History of the Criminal Law of England, 3 vols., 1883.

Bentham (Jeremy). Works, ed. Bowring, 11 vols., 1838–43.

Romilly (Sir Samuel). Memoirs of his Life, written by himself; with a selection from his Correspondence, ed. by his sons, 3 vols., 1840.

B. LOCAL GOVERNMENT.

1. OFFICIAL DOCUMENTS.

Report from the Select Committee appointed to inquire into the state of the Municipal Corporations in England and Wales and Ireland, . . . 1833.

First and Second Reports of the Commissioners appointed to inquire into the Municipal Corporations in England and Wales, 1835, 1837 (Analytical Index, 1839).

First Report of the Commissioners appointed to inquire into the Municipal Corporations in Ireland, 1835.

General Report of the Commissioners appointed to inquire into the state of Municipal Corporations in Scotland, 1835.

2. GENERAL.

Burn (Richard). The Justice of the Peace and Parish Officer, upon a plan entirely new, and comprehending all the Law to the present time, 2 vols., 1755; 29th ed., 5 vols., 1845.

Merewether (H. A.). A Sketch of the History of Boroughs and the Corporate Right of Election, 1822.

—— and Stephens (A. J.). The History of the Boroughs and Municipal Corporations of the United Kingdom from the earliest to the present time, with an examination of records, charters and other documents, illustrative of their constitution and powers, 3 vols., 1835.

Cockburn (A. E.). The Corporations of England and Wales; containing a succinct account of the constitution, privileges, powers, revenues, and expenditure of each corporation; together with details showing the practical working of the Corporate System in each borough or city, and any defects or abuses which have been found to exist. The whole collected and abridged from the reports of the Commissioners for inquiring into Municipal Corporations, 2 vols., 1835.

Smith (J. Toulmin). The Parish: its Obligations and Powers, its Officers and Duties; with illustrations of the practical working of their institution in all secular affairs, 1854.

—— Local Self-Government and Centralization; the characteristics of each, and its practical tendencies as affecting social, moral, and political welfare and progress, including comprehensive outlines of the English Constitution, 1851.

> A protest against the tendency of modern legislation to centralize the administration. It insists on the democratic nature of the old parochial self-government.

Gneist (Rudolf). Geschichte und heutige Gestalt der englischen Communalverfassung oder des Self-government, 2nd ed., 2 vols., 1863,

(Also the work already mentioned of this eminent authority on constitutional law and the system of administration).

Should be supplemented by the first-rate work of :

Redlich (Josef). Englische Lokalverwaltung. Darstellung der inneren Verwaltung Englands in ihrer geschichtlichen Entwicklung und in ihrer gegenwartigen Gestalt, 1901. (English translation with additional matter by F. W. Hirst, 1903.)

And especially by the standard work now in course of publication (6 vols. have appeared, 1924).

Webb (Sidney and Beatrice). English Local Government from the Revolution to the Municipal Corporations Act, 1906.

III. ARMY AND NAVY.

A. GENERAL.

Army Appointments. Report from the Select Committee appointed to inquire into the Establishment of the Garrisons, of Pay and Emolument of General and Staff Officers, and into the Emoluments of Naval Officers holding the Appointments of Vice- and Rear-Admirals of the United Kingdom, or of Generals and Colonels of Marines, and whether any and what Reduction or Alteration can be made in them without detriment to the Public Service, 1833.

Report of Commissioners . . . into Naval and Military Promotion and Retirement, 1840.

B. THE NAVY.

1. OFFICIAL DOCUMENTS.

Navy. Accounts and Papers. Strength of the Navy : Men, Boys, Wages, etc. Account of the Men serving and Sums voted, from 1783 to 1793, 1819.

2. GENERAL HISTORIES.

James (William). The naval history of Great Britain from the declaration of war by France in 1793, to the accession of George IV, 1st ed., in 5 vols., 1822. New ed. with additional matter and notes, . . . by Captain Chamier, in 6 vols., 1837.
Extremely technical. Deals exclusively with the ships and other material equipment of the Navy, and does not treat of the crews. Should be supplemented by the standard work of

Clowes (William Laird). The Royal Navy. A history from the earliest times to the present, 7 vols., 1897–1903. Vol. iv (1775–1802). Vol. v (1803–15).

Also the almost contemporary work by :

Brenton (Captain Edward Pelham). The Naval History of Great Britain from the Year 1783 to 1822, 5 vols., 1825–8.
Contains very intelligent criticism.

See also the excellent picture given by

Dupin (Baron Charles). Voyages dans la Grande-Bretagne, entrepris relativement aux services publics de la Guerre, de la Marine, et des Ponts et Chaussées, de 1816 à 1821. Deuxième Partie Force Navale, 1821.

And the textbook by :

Hannay (David). A short History of the Royal Navy, 1217–1815 ; vol. ii (1689–1815), 1909.

The publications of the Navy Record Society should also be consulted, especially the two volumes edited by M. Julian Corbett, and entitled :

Fighting Instructions (1530–1816). Signals and Instructions (1776–1794).

Chevalier (Edouard). Histoire de la Marine Française sous la première Republique 1886, sous le Consulat et l'Empire, 1806.

For the theory of naval warfare see :

Mahan (Captain A. T.). The Influence of Sea-power upon the French Revolution and Empire, 1793–1812, 2 vols. 1892.

—— Sea-power in its Relations to the War of 1812, 2 vols., 1905.

3. CONTEMPORARY PAMPHLETS DEALING WITH PARTICULAR QUESTIONS.

Butler (Charles). On the Legality of Impressing Seamen, 1778. (See Pamphleteer, No. XXIII, 1824.)

Patten (Philip). The Natural Defence of an Insular Empire, earnestly recommended, with a sketch of a plan to attach real seamen to the service of their country, 1810.

A Letter to the Right Honourable Lord Melville on the present condition of officers in the Royal Navy, by a Post Captain, 1811.

An Inquiry into the present state of the British Navy, together with reflections on the late war with America, and its probable consequences, by an Englishman, 1815.

Napier (Sir Charles). The Navy : its past and present State. In a series of letters, 1851.
    Written between 1816 and 1850.

Cochrane (Thomas, Earl of Dundonald). Observations on Naval Affairs, and on some collateral subjects ; including instances of injustice experienced by the author, 1847.

4. BIOGRAPHIES.

Marshall (Lieut. John). Royal Naval Biography. . . . 12 vols., 1823–35.
    A mere list of the superior officers with short biographical notices.

Mahan (Captain A. T.). Types of Naval Officers drawn from the History of the British Navy, with some account of the conditions of naval warfare at the beginning of the eighteenth century, and of its subsequent development during the said period, 1902.

Collingwood (Lord). A Selection from the Public and Private Correspondence of Vice-Admiral ——, by G. L. Newnham Collingwood, 4th ed., 1829.

Exmouth (Admiral, Viscount). The Life of ——, by E. Osler, 1835.

Jervis (John, Earl of Saint-Vincent). Life and Correspondence of ——, by P. E. Brenton, 2 vols., 1838.

—— Memoirs of ——, by J. S. Tucker, 2 vols., 1844.

Nelson (Admiral Lord). The Life of ———, from his manuscripts, by J. S. Clarke and J. MacArthur, 2 vols., 1809 ; new ed., 1840.

——— Memoirs of the Life of ———, by Thomas Joseph Pettigrew, 2 vols., 1849.

——— Letters and Dispatches of ———, selected and arranged by John Knox, 1886.

Saumarez (Admiral Lord de). Memoirs and Correspondence of ———, by Sir John Ross, 2 vols., 1838.

C. THE ARMY.

1. OFFICIAL DOCUMENTS.

In addition to the documents mentioned under the previous heading, see :

Report of Commissioners for inquiring into the System of Military Punishments in the Army, 1836.

2. GENERAL.

Dupin (Baron Charles). Voyages dans la Grande-Bretagne, entrepris relativement aux services publics de la Guerre, de la Marine et des Ponts et Chaussées, de 1816 à 1821. Première Partie. Force Militaire, 1820.

Clode (C. M.). The Military Forces of the Crown : their Administration and Government, 2 vols., 1869.
　　This remains the standard authority on the subject.

Fortescue (the Hon. J. W.). A History of the British Army.
　　Eleven vols. have already appeared (1923), ending with 1838. Contains many documents hitherto unpublished. It is a pity, from our point of view, that the work should too often degenerate into a history of campaigns. The ground here neglected is however fortunately covered by the same author's smaller work :

——— The County Lieutenancies and the Army, 1803–14, 1 vol., 1909.
　　It deals with the methods of recruiting at this period.

3. HISTORIES OF THE PENINSULA WAR.

Foy (General). Histoire de la Guerre de la Péninsule sous Napoléon, . . . published by la Comtesse Foy, 4 vols., 1827. (English translation, 1827.)
　　The first volume consists of an excellent " Political and Military Description of the contending Powers."

Napier (Major-General W. F. P.). History of the War in the Peninsula and in the South of France, from 1807 to 1814, 6 vols., 1828–40.
　　Concerned almost exclusively with tactics and strategy.

Oman (Sir C. William Chadwick). A History of the Peninsular War.
　　In course of publication, 6 vols. have appeared 1902–22, which bring the history to August 1813. Of very considerable merit as a scientific treatment of its subject.

——— Wellington's Army 1800–1814.

4. BIOGRAPHIES, MEMOIRS, CORRESPONDENCE.

Wellington (Arthur Wellesley, Duke of). The Dispatches . . . from 1799 to 1818, compiled . . . by Lieut.-Colonel Gurwood, 1st ed., 13 vols., 1834–9, with additions,

8 vols., 1844 ; we have used the edition in 12 vols. (1799–1815), 1837–8. Also : Supplementary Dispatches and Memoranda, edited by his son, the Duke of Wellington, 12 vols., 1858–65 ; new series, 3 vols., 1867–8.

Wellington (Arthur Wellesley, Duke of). The Life of ——: the Restoration of the Martial Power of Great Britain, by Sir Herbert Maxwell, 2 vols., 1st ed., 1899 ; 6th ed., 1907.

Combermere (Field-Marshal Viscount). Memoirs and Correspondence of ——, by Mary, Viscountess Combermere and Captain W. W. Knollys, 2 vols., 1866.

IV. THE COLONIES.

1. An interesting General Account.

Egerton (H. E.). A Short History of British Colonial Policy, 1897 (bibliography).

2. Monographs.

Mill (James). The History of British India, 1st ed., 3 vols., 1817 ; 4th ed., with notes and appendix by H. H. Wilson, 9 vols., 1840–8.

Edwards (Bryan). History of the British Colonies in the West Indies, 4th ed., 3 vols., 1807.

Southey (T.). Chronological History of the West Indies, 3 vols., 1827.

Bridges (G.). The Annals of Jamaica, 2 vols., 1827.

Lefroy (Sir J. H.). Memorials of Bermudas, 2 vols., 1877.

Marion (Phillips). A Colonial Autocracy. New South Wales under Governor Macquarie, 1810–21. 1909.

V. PEERAGE.

Debrett (John). The Peerage of Great Britain and Ireland, 14th ed., 2 vols., 1816.

G. E. C. Complete Peerage of England, Scotland, Ireland, Great Britain and the United Kingdom, extant, extinct, or dormant ; alphabetically arranged and edited by ——, 8 vols., 1887–98 ; new ed., V. Gibbs, revised and enlarged, vol. i., 1910 (in course of publication).
    A first-rate genealogical authority.

Lawrence (Sir James). Of the Nobility of the English Gentry, 1825.

John Hampden, Junior. The Aristocracy of England; a history for the people, 1846.

For the orders of Knighthood, see

Nicolas (Sir N. H.). History of the Orders of Knighthood of the British Empire, 4 vols., 1841–2.

VI. THE HOUSE OF COMMONS.

1. Official Documents.

  (i) *Composition of the Commons.*

Return. Members of Parliament. Part II, Parliaments of Great Britain, 1705–96 ; Parliaments of the United Kingdom, 1801–74 ; Parliaments and Conventions of the Estates of Scotland, 1357–1707 ; Parliaments of Ireland, 1559–1800. 1878.

To be supplemented by the following non-official works :

Smith (H. S.). The Parliaments of England, from George I to the present time, 3 vols., 1841.

—— The Register of Parliamentary Contested Elections, 1841.

(ii) *Special Reports and Returns.*

Weymouth and Melcombe Regis Election. Report on Election Petition, with special report on violation of the Treating Act and Abuses in splitting Freeholds, 1812–13.

Returns of Freeholders, registered in Ireland, 1802–3.

Accounts relating to 40s., £20 and £50 freeholders and rent-chargers registered ; inhabitant householders registered ; freemen admitted and sworn ; and number of persons who polled at the last general election, in Ireland, 1824.

Returns of the number entitled to vote at county elections in Ireland, 1825.

Persons registered as freeholders, and admitted as freemen, within the last eight years, in Ireland, 1829.

2. GENERAL WORKS.

The State of the Representation of England and Wales. Delivered to the Society, the Friends of the People, associated for the purpose of obtaining a Parliamentary Reform, on Saturday, February 9, 1793.

A Sketch of the various Proposals for a Constitutional Reform in the Representation of the People, introduced into the Parliament of Great Britain, from 1770 to 1812, by George Wilson Meadley . . . and Algernon Sydney, 1813. (See Pamphleteer, vol. ii. pp. 299 sqq.).

For complete lists see :

Oldfield (T. H. B.). The Representative History of Great Britain and Ireland : being a History of the House of Commons and of the Counties, Cities and Boroughs of the United Kingdom, from the earliest period, 6 vols., 1816.
    The standard authority.

Porritt (E.). The Unreformed House of Commons : Parliamentary Representation before 1832 (vol. i England, vol. ii Scotland and Ireland), 1903.
    A good compilation with a bibliography.

See also

Redlich (Josef). Recht und Technik des englischen Parlamentarismus. Die Geschäftsordnung des House of Commons in ihrer geschichtlichen Entwicklung und gegenwärtigen Gestalt, 1905. (English translation with an additional chapter by Sir Courtenay Ilbert, 3 vols., 1908.)

3. WORKS DEALING WITH LOCAL REPRESENTATION.

Wywill (Rev. Christopher). Political Papers, chiefly respecting the Attempt of the County of York, and other considerable districts, commenced in 1779, and continued during several subsequent years, to effect a Reformation of the Parliament of Great Britain, 4 vols. (no date) ; continued to 1811 in 2 vols. under the title: Political Papers comprising the Correspondence of several distinguished Persons in the years 1792–3.

Ferguson (R. S.) Cumberland and Westmorland M.P.'s from the Restoration to the Reform Bill of 1867 (1660–1867), 1871.

Williams (W. R.). The Parliamentary History of the Principality of Wales, from the earliest times to the present day (1541–1895), comprising lists of the representatives, chronologically arranged under counties, with biographical and genealogical notices of the members, together with particulars of the various contested elections, double returns and petitions, 1895.

—— The Parliamentary History of the County of Hereford, . . . from the earliest times to the present day (1213–1896), with biographical and genealogical notices of the members, 1896.

—— The Parliamentary History of the County of Worcester, . . . 1897

—— The Parliamentary History of the County of Gloucester, . . . 1898.

—— Parliamentary History of the County of Oxford, . . . 1899.

VII. POLITICS OUTSIDE PARLIAMENT.

1. ELECTIONEERING.

Jephson (Henry). The Platform : its Rise and Progress, 2 vols., 1892.

Ostrogorski (A.). La Democratie et l'Organisation des Partis Politiques, 1st vol. (The 2nd deals with the United States of America.)

2. JOURNALISM.

(i) *Official Documents.*

Stamps issued for Newspapers, with the amount of Duties charged thereon, 1814–15. 1822. The same from 1814 to 1824.

Weekly Newspapers published on Saturdays and Sundays, 1821.

Aggregate Number of Stamps issued for Newspapers in Great Britain, 1801 to 1826 ; also in Ireland, 1817 to 1826. 1826–7.

Return of the Ex-Officio Informations filed for Political Libel and Seditious Conduct in the Court of King's Bench in England since 1807, distinguishing those which have been followed up by Prosecution, and those which have not. 1821.

Prosecutions for Libel, Blasphemy and Sedition, 1813–22. 1823.

Prosecutions for Libel, etc. ; a Return of all Prosecutions during the reigns of their late Majesties George III and George IV, either by Ex-Officio Information or Indictment, conducted in the Department of the Solicitor for the Affairs of His Majesty's Treasury. 1830.

(ii) *General.*

Hunt (F. K.). The Fourth Estate ; contributions towards a history of newspapers and of the liberty of the Press, 2 vols., 1850.

Grant (James). The Newspaper Press : its Origin, Progress and present Position, 3 vols., 1871.

VIII. BIOGRAPHIES OF STATESMEN.

1. GEORGE III AND HIS COURT.

George the Third. The Correspondence of King —— with Lord North from 1768 to 1783, ed. W. B. Donne, 2 vols., 1867.

Burney (Frances ——, Madame d'Arblay). Diary and Letters of ——, ed. by her niece (Charlotte Barrett), 1st ed., 7 vols., 1842–6. We have used 2nd ed., 7 vols. 1854.

2. HISTORIES OF A MORE OR LESS BIOGRAPHICAL CHARACTER.

Lewis (Sir George Cornewall). Essays on the Administrations of Great Britain from 1783 to 1830, contributed to the Edinburgh Review, ed. Sir Edmund Head, 1864.

Brougham (Henry, Lord). Historical Sketches of Statesmen in the time of George III, 3 vols., 1839–43.

Fortescue (J. W.). British Statesmen of the Great War, 1793–1814. 1911.

3. BIOGRAPHIES, MEMOIRS, CORRESPONDENCE.

(i) *The Party in Office.*

(*a*) General.

Kebbel (T. E.). History of Toryism, 1789–1881. 1886.
Extremely superficial.

(*b*) Pitt.

Tomline (George). Memoirs of the Life of the Right Honourable William Pitt, 2 vols., 1821.

Stanhope (Earl). Life of the Right Honourable William Pitt, with extracts from his manuscript papers, 4 vols., 1861–2.

Rose (J. Holland). William Pitt and National Revival. 1911.

—— William Pitt and the Great War. 1911.

(*c*) Other Statesmen.

Abbott (Charles, first Lord Colchester). His Diary and Correspondence, ed. by his son Charles, Lord Colchester, 3 vols., 1861.

Addington (Henry ——, Viscount Sidmouth). The Life and Correspondence of ——, by George Pellew, 3 vols., 1847

Canning, Life of ——, by H. M. V. Temperley, 1905.
Stapleton's work (The Political Life of Canning, etc., 1831) deals only with the last period of Canning's political life, 1822–7.

Croker. The —— Papers ; The Correspondence and Diaries of . . . John Wilson Croker, . . . ed. by Louis J. Jennings, 3 vols., 1884.

Jenkinson (Robert Banks, second Earl of Liverpool). The Life and Administration of ——, by Charles Duke Yonge, 3 vols., 1868

Peel (Sir Robert) —— from his private papers, . . . by Charles Stuart Parker, 3 vols., 1899.

Perceval (Right Hon. Spencer). The Life of the ——, by his grandson, Spencer Walpole, 1874.

Rose (Right Hon. George). Diaries and Correspondence, containing original letters of the most distinguished statesmen of his day, ed. by Leveson Vernon Harcourt, 2 vols., 1860.

Stewart (Robert, Lord Castlereagh). Memoirs and Correspondence, ed. by his brother Charles Vane, Marquess of Londonderry, 12 vols., 1848–53.

Temple (Henry John, Viscount Palmerston). The Life of ——, with selections from his Diaries and Correspondence, by the Right Hon. Sir Henry Lytton Bulwer, 3 vols., 1870–4.

Wellesley. Memoirs and Correspondence of the Most Noble Richard, Marquess ——, published by Robert Rouière Pearce, 3 vols., 1846.

The —— Papers. By the Editor of the Wyndham Papers, 2 vols., 1914.

Wilberforce (William). The Life of ——, by his sons, 5 vols., 1st ed., 1838.

—— Private Papers of ——, collected and edited, with a Preface, by A. M. Wilberforce, 1897.

Windham. The —— Papers, with an Introduction by the Earl of Rosebery, 2 vols., 1913.

(ii) *The Opposition.*

(*a*) Fox.

Russell (Lord John). Memorials and Correspondence of Charles James Fox, 4 vols., 1853–7.

—— The Life and Times of Charles James Fox, 3 vols., 1859–66.

(*b*) The Opposition as a Whole.

Fox (Henry Richard, third Baron Holland). Memoirs of the Whig Party during my Time, ed. by his son, Henry Edward, Lord Holland, 2 vols., 1852–4.

—— Further Memoirs of the Whig Party (1807–21), with some miscellaneous reminiscences, . . . ed. by Lord Stavordale, 1905.

Grenville (R. P., Duke of Buckingham). Memoirs of the Court and Cabinets of George the Third, from original family documents, 4 vols., 1853–5.

—— Memoirs of the Court of England during the Regency, 1811–20, from the original family documents, 2 vols., 1856.

Grey. Lord —— of the Reform Bill, by G. M. Trevelyan, 1920.

Holland (Elizabeth, Lady). The Journal of —— (1791–1811), ed. by the Earl of Ilchester, 2 vols., 1908.

Moore (Thomas). Memoirs, Journal and Correspondence of ——, ed. by . . . Lord John Russell, 8 vols., 1853–6.

Shelburne (William, Earl of ——, afterwards first Marquess of Lansdowne). Life of ——, with extracts from his papers and correspondence, 3 vols., 1875–6.

Sheridan (Richard Brinsley). Memoirs of the Life of the Right Hon. ——, by Thomas Moore, 2 vols., 1825.

—— from new and original material, including a manuscript diary of Georgiana, Duchess of Devonshire, by Walter Sichel, 2 vols., 1909.

Sydney Smith. A Memoir of the Rev. ——, by Lady S. Holland, with a selection from his letters, ed. by Miss Austin, 2 vols., 1st ed., 1855.

—— A Sketch of the Life and Times of the Rev. ——, . . . based on family documents and the recollections of personal friends, by Stuart J. Reid, 1884.

Also :

—— La renaissance des idées liberales en Angleterre, par André Chevrillon, 1894.

Ward (John William, first Earl of Dudley). Letters of the Earl of Dudley to the Bishop of Llandaff, 1840.

—— Letters to Ivy (Helen d'Arcy Stewart), from the first Earl of Dudley, ed. by S. H. Romilly, 1905.

(iii) *The Radicals.*

(*a*) General.

Harris (William). The History of the Radical Party in Parliament. 1885.
Extremely superficial.

Kent (C. R.). The English Radicals, 1899.

(*b*) Biographies, Memoirs.

Cartwright (Major John). His Life and Correspondence, ed. by his niece, F. D.
Cartwright, 2 vols., 1826.

Cobbett (William). A Study of His Life as shown in his Writings, by E. J. Carlyle.
1904.

—— The Life and Letters of William ——, in England and America ; based upon
hitherto unpublished family papers, by Lewis Melville, 2 vols., 1913.

Horne Tooke. Memoirs of John ——, interspersed with original documents, by
Alexander Stephens, 2 vols., 1813.

Hunt (Henry). Memoirs, written by himself in His Majesty's Jail at Ilchester, 1820.
Of very slight value.

BOOK II

THE ECONOMIC LIFE OF GREAT BRITAIN

I. GENERAL ACCOUNTS OF ECONOMIC CONDITION IN GREAT BRITAIN.

Macpherson (David). Annals of Commerce, Manufactures, Fisheries and Navigation, with brief notices of the arts and sciences connected with them, containing the commercial transactions of the British Empire and other countries, from the earliest accounts to the meeting of the Union Parliament in January 1801, . . . 4 vols., 1805.

Colquhoun (P.). A Treatise on the Wealth, Power and Resources of the British Empire, etc., 1814.

Chalmers (G.). The State of the United Kingdom at the Peace of Paris, November 20, 1815 ; respecting the people, their domestic energies, their agriculture, their trade, their shipping, and their finances, 1816.

—— Comparative Views of the State of Great Britain and Ireland ; as it was before the war, as it is since the peace, 1817.

Marshall (J.). Digest of all the accounts relating to the population, production, revenues, financial operations, manufactures, shipping, colonies, commerce, etc., of the United Kingdom of Great Britain and Ireland, diffused through more than 600 volumes of journals, reports and papers presented to Parliament during the last thirty-five years, arranged by ——, 1834.

Moreau de Jonnès (A.). Statistique de la Grande-Bretagne et de l'Irlande, 1837–8.

Porter (G. R.). The Progress of the Nation in its various Social and Economic Relations from the Beginning of the Nineteenth Century, 1836–8 ; other eds., 1843, 1847, 1851.

Marx (Karl). Das Kapital, Kritik der Politischen Oekonomie, Buch I, 1st ed., 1867.
> An account, richly furnished with illustrative material, of the great industrial revolution, in which England is taken as the typical example of the great industrial state of modern times.

Held (A.). Zwei Bücher zur socialen Geschichte Englands. 1881.

Toynbee (Arnold). Lectures on the Industrial Revolution in England, with a Memoir by B. Jowett, 1884 ; new ed. with a Reminiscence by Lord Milner, 1908.

Mantoux (Paul). La Révolution Industrielle au XVIIIe siècle, Essai sur les Commencements de la Grande Industrie Moderne en Angleterre, 1906.
> A first-rate account of the entire industrial revolution, with bibliography.

Cunningham (W.). The Growth of English Industry and Commerce in Modern Times. Vol. iii. Modern Times. Laissez-faire, 1907.

Smart (Professor William). Economic Annals of the 19th Century, 1801–20. 1910.
A useful collection of material bearing on econom cs, gathered from the Parliamentary Debates and the Annual Register.

II. AGRICULTURE.

A. ENGLAND.

1. OFFICIAL DOCUMENTS.

(i) *Parliamentary Reports.*

Report from the Select Committee, appointed to inquire into the Corn Trade of the United Kingdom, 1812–13.

Report from the Select Committee to whom the several Petitions . . . upon the subject of the Corn Laws were referred, . . . 1813–14.

First and Second Reports from the Lords' Committee appointed to inquire into the State of the Growth, Commerce and Consumption of Grain and all Laws relating thereto, 1814–15.

Report on the Nature and Effect of the Game Laws, 1816.

(ii) *Publications by the Board of Agriculture.*

General Report on Enclosures, drawn up by order of the Board of Agriculture, 1808.

Agricultural State of the Kingdom, in February, March and April 1816, being the substance of the replies to a circular letter sent by the Board of Agriculture to every part of the Kingdom, 1816.

Marshall (W.). Review and Complete Abstract of the Reports of the Board of Agriculture, 1808–17.

2. PERIODICAL PUBLICATIONS.

Annals of Agriculture, and other useful Arts, collected and published by Arthur Young, 46 vols., 1784–1815.

The Farmer's Magazine, a periodical work exclusively devoted to agricultural and rural affairs, 26 vols., 1800–25 (index).

3. WORKS DEALING WITH THE CONDITION OF ENGLISH AGRICULTURE, THE LAW OF LANDED PROPERTY, TECHNICAL IMPROVEMENTS, ENCLOSURES, THE AGRICULTURAL LABOURER.

(i) *Contemporary Works.*

Howlett (John). An Inquiry into the Influence which Enclosures have had upon the Population of England. 1786.

—— Thoughts on Inclosure, by a Country Farmer. 1786.

Davies (David, of Barkham). Case of Labourers in Husbandry Stated and Considered, . . . 1795.

Young (Arthur). An Inquiry into the Propriety of Applying Wastes to the better Maintenance and Support of the Poor. 1801.

To which may be added :

Young (Arthur). An Inquiry into the Rise of Prices in Europe during the last Twenty-five Years, compared with that which has taken place in England ; with observations on the effects of high and low prices. 1815.

Humphrey (James). Observations on the Actual State of the English Laws of Real Property, with the outlines of a code, 1st ed. 1827.

Also two works which, though dealing with a period slightly later that our own, afford a picturesque description of the English country-side.

Cobbett (William). Rural Rides, . . . 1st ed., 1830 ; 2nd ed., enlarged, 1853.

Howitt (William). The Rural Life of England, 1st ed., 1837 ; 2nd ed., 1840.

(ii) *The history of English agriculture at the end of the* 18*th century has recently been made the subject of a series of monographs, all of which repay study.*

Scrutton (Thomas Edward). Commons and Common Fields ; or, the History and Policy of the Laws relating to Commons and Enclosures in England, 1887.

Prothero (Rowland E.). The Pioneers and Progress of English Farming, 1888.

Hasbach (Professor Wilhelm). Die englischen Landarbeiter in den letzten hundert Jahren und die Einhegungen, 1894. (English translation by Ruth Kenyon, 1908, with an excellent bibliography).

Curtler (W. H. R.). A Short History of English Agriculture, 1909.

Johnson (A. H.). The Disappearance of the Small Landowner, 1909.

Davies (M. F.). Life in an English Village ; an economic and historical survey of the parish of Corsley in Wiltshire, 1909.

Hammond (John Laurence Le Breton and Barbara). The Village Labourer, 1760–1832 ; a study in the government of England before the Reform Bill. 1911.

Gonner (E. C. K.). Common Land and Enclosure, 1912.

4. BIOGRAPHIES, MEMOIRS.

Sinclair (Sir John, Bart.). Memoirs of the Life and Works of the late Right Hon. ——, by the Rev. John Sinclair, 1837.

Young (Arthur). The Autobiography of ——, with selections from his correspondence, ed. Betham-Edwards, 1898.

Grey (John ——, of Dilston). Memoir of ——, by his daughter, Josephine E. Butler : revised ed., 1874.

Coke (Thomas William, of Holkham, first Earl of Leicester). Coke of Norfolk and his Friends, the Life of ——, by A. M. W. Stirling, 1908.

B. SCOTLAND.

See especially :

Sinclair (Sir John). General Report of the Agricultural State and Political Circumstances of Scotland, drawn up for the consideration of the Board of Agriculture and Internal Improvement, under the directions of the Right Hon. ——, 5 vols., 1814.

Also,

Selkirk (Earl of). Observations on the Present State of the Highlands of Scotland, with a view of the Causes and probable Consequences of Emigration, 1805.

The following works, though of inferior merit, are worth consulting :

Stoddart (John). Remarks on the Local Scenery and Manners in Scotland during the Years 1799 and 1800. 1801.

Irvine (Alexander). An Inquiry into the Causes and Effects of Emigration from the Highlands and Western Islands of Scotland, . . . 1802.

Brown (Robert). Strictures and Remarks on the Earl of Selkirk's Observations, . . . 1806.

C. IRELAND.

1. OFFICIAL DOCUMENTS.

Statement of the Nature and Extent of the Disturbances which have recently prevailed in Ireland, and Measures adopted in consequence thereof. 1816.

Minutes of Evidence, taken before the Select Committee in the last Session of Parliament, on the Disturbances in Ireland. 1825.

Minutes of Evidence, taken before the Select Committee appointed to examine into the Nature and Extent of the Disturbances which have prevailed in those Districts of Ireland which are now subject to the provisions of the Insurrection Act. 1825.

2. GENERAL.

The standard work is :

Wakefield (Edward). An Account of Ireland, Statistical and Political, 1812 (based on observations made in 1808–9).

But the student should also read :

Young (Arthur). A Tour in Ireland ; with general observations on the present state of that kingdom, made in the years 1776–8, and brought down to the end of 1779. 1780–4.

Cooper (George). Letters on the Irish Nation ; written during a visit to that Kingdom in the autumn of the year 1799. 1800.

Newenham (Thomas). A Statistical and Historical Inquiry into the Progress and Magnitude of the Population of Ireland, 1805 ; and : A View of the Natural, Political and Commercial Circumstances of Ireland. 1809.

Curwen (J. C.). Observations on the State of Ireland, Principally directed to its Agriculture and Rural Population, . . . 1818. (A collection of letters giving an account of a journey made in 1813.)

The Dublin Society, following the example set by the English Board of Agriculture, published seventeen reports on the economic conditions in the Irish counties ; see especially :

Townshend (Rev. Horatio). Statistical Survey of the County of Cork, . . . 1810 ; 2nd ed., 1815.

Tighe (William). Statistical Observations Relative to the County of Kilkenny, . . . 1802.

Sigerson (George). History of the Land Tenures and Land Classes of Ireland, with an account of the various secret agrarian confederacies. 1871.

     Elementary : but absolutely reliable.

Bonn (Dr. Moritz Julius). Die englische Kolonisation in Irland, 1896.

     Valuable both for its solid foundation of material, and the original interpretation of the facts collected.

III. INDUSTRY.

A. MINES.

1. COAL.

     (i) *Official Documents.*

Report on the State of the Coal Trade, 1800.

     (ii) *Monographs.*

Gisborne (Rev. Thomas). A General View of the Situation of the Mining Poor, compared with that of some other Classes of the Poor, 1798. (Reports of the Society for Bettering the Condition of the Poor, vol. i, pp. 368 sqq.)

Dixon (Joshua). The Literary Life of William Brownrigg, 1801.

Holmes (J. H. H.). A Treatise on the Coal Mines of Durham and Northumberland, . . . 1816.

Nelson Boyd (R.). Coal Pits and Pitmen ; a short history of the coal trade and the legislation affecting it, 1872.

Fynes (Richard). The Miners of Northumberland and Durham, a History of their Social and Political Struggles, . . . 1873.

Galloway (Robert L.). Annals of Coal Mining and the Coal Trade, the Invention of the Steam Engine and the Origin of the Railway, 1898.

—— Papers relating to the History of the Coal Trade and the Invention of the Steam Engine, . . . 1906.

Jevons (H. Stanley). The British Coal Trade, 1915.

2. COPPER, TIN, LEAD.

     (i) *Official Documents.*

Report on the State of the Copper Mines and Copper Trade, 1799.

     (ii) *General Works.*

Hunt (Robert). British Mining ; a treatise on the history, discovery, practical development and future prospects of metalliferous mines in the United Kingdom, 1884 ; 2nd ed. revised, 1887.

     (iii.) *Monographs.*

        (*a*) Copper and Tin.

An Address to the Gentlemen of the County of Cornwall on the Present State of Mining in that County, . . . 1772.

Myce (W.). Mineralogia Cornubiensis ; a treatise on minerals, mines and mining, . . . 1778.

     Contains a detailed account of the organization of labour in the mines.

A Brief Address on Mining in Cornwall, demonstrating some of the advantages resulting to commerce, and the profit to capitalists, by investment in those national undertakings ; by the Secretary to the Kellewerris and West Tresavean Mining Companies. 1835.

(b) Lead.

Hardy (William). The Miner's Guide ; or, Compleat Miner, containing I . . . II, The Customs, Laws, and Articles of the High and Low Peak, . . . 1748.

Hall (Frederick). An Appeal to the Poor Miner and to every Nobleman, Gentleman and Tradesman in the Kingdom, who feels interested in a Miner's Fate, 1818.

B. METAL WORKING.

Gibbons (William). A reply to Sir Lucius O'Brien, Baronet ; in which that part of his letter to the author which most particularly respects the present state of the Iron Trade between England and Ireland is considered. 1785.

[Needham (M.)]. Library of Useful Knowledge. Manufacture of Iron. 1831.

Scrivenor (H.). A Comprehensive History of the Iron Trade throughout the World, from the earliest records to the present period, . . . 1841.

Hall (John). The Iron Trade, with remarks, pointing out the true cause and cure for its existing state of depression. 1843.

Wilkie (George). The Manufacture of Iron in Great Britain ; with remarks on the employment of capital in ironworks and collieries. 1857.

Jeans (J. S.). Steel : its History, Manufacture, Properties and Uses. 1880.

Fell (Alfred). The Early Iron Industry of Furness and District ; an historical and descriptive account from the earliest times to the end of the 18th century, with an account of Furness ironmasters in Scotland (1726–1800). 1908.

C. MANUFACTURE OF MACHINERY AND TOOLS, THE TOY TRADE, HARDWARE, CUTLERY.

We can utilize :

1. A NUMBER OF LOCAL HISTORIES.

Pye (Charles). A Description of Modern Birmingham ; whereunto are annexed observations made during an excursion round the town in the summer of 1818, including Warwick and Leamington [1820.]

Hutton (William). The History of Birmingham ; continued to the present time by Catherine Hutton, 4th ed. 1819.

Langford (John Alfred). A Century of Birmingham Life ; or, a chronicle of local events, from 1741 to 1841, compiled and ed. by ——. 1868.

Hunter (Joseph). Hallamshire, the History and Topography of the Parish of Sheffield in the County of York ; with historical and descriptive notices of the parishes of Ecclesfield, Hansworth, Treeton and Whiston, and of the Chapelry of Brad-field, 1819 ; new ed., enlarged, by A. Gatty, 1869.

2. A FEW BIOGRAPHIES.

Smiles (Samuel). Industrial Biography : Ironworkers and Toolmakers, new ed., 1879 ;

And several other biographies by the same author, which will be given below under " Transport."

D. TEXTILE MANUFACTURES.

1. COTTON, SILK AND WOOL.

Taylor (W. Cooke). Handbook of Silk, Cotton and Woollen Manufactures, 1843.

2. COTTON.

(i) *Official Documents.*

Minutes of Evidence taken before the Select Committee, to whom the Petitions presented to the House in this Session relating to Act 39 and 40 Geo. III, " for settling disputes between Masters and Workmen engaged in the Cotton Manufacture, were referred," 1802–3.

Report from the Select Committee appointed to consider of the most speedy and effectual mode of adjusting such differences as may arise between Masters and Workmen engaged in the Cotton Manfacture, . . . 1803–4.

Minutes of Evidence taken before the Select Committee to whom the Petition of Journeymen Calico Printers in the counties of Leicester, Derby, Chester and Stafford, in England, and in the counties of Lanark, Renfrew, Dumbarton, Stirling and Perth, in Scotland, was referred, 1803–4.

Report from the Select Committee to whom it was referred to examine into the matter of the Minutes of Evidence taken before the foregoing Committee, 1806.

Report from the Committee on Petitions of several Cotton Manufacturers and Journeymen Cotton Weavers, together with the Minutes of Evidence, . . . 1808.

Report on the Cotton Weavers' Petition, 1809.

Report from the Committee on Dr. Cartwright's Petition respecting his Weaving Machine, together with the Minutes of Evidence, . . . 1808.

Report from the Select Committee to whom the Petition of Richard Ainsworth, of Bolton (Lancaster), Cotton Manufacturer, and that of Journeymen Cotton Weavers resident in England, were severally referred. 1808.

Report from the Select Committee to whom the Petition of several Journeymen Cotton Weavers resident in England, that of the Cotton Manufacturers and Operative Weavers in Scotland, and the foregoing Report were severally referred. 1809.

Report from the Select Committee to whom the Petition of Manufacturers and Artisans in Manchester, that of Weavers and Spinners of Cotton, Handicraft, Artists and Labourers, resident in Bolton (Lancaster) ; those of persons residing in Paisley, and of Heritors, Manufacturers, Merchants, Mechanics and Labourers resident in Lancaster, Ayr and Renfrewshire were referred. 1810–11.

The following works on factory legislation are confined, so far as our period is concerned, to the cotton industry :

Report of the Minutes of Evidence taken before the Select Committee on the State of the Children employed in the Manufactories of the United Kingdom. 1816.

Report from the Select Committee to whom the Bill to regulate the Labour of Children in Mills and Factories of the United Kingdom was referred. 1831–2.

First Report of the Central Board of His Majesty's Commissioners, appointed to collect information in the manufacturing districts, relative to the Employment of Children in Factories and as to the propriety and means of curtailing the hours of their labour, with Minutes of Evidence and Reports of District Commissioners. 1833.

(ii) *Monographs.*

Kennedy (John). Observations on the Rise and Progress of the Cotton Trade in Great Britain . . . (in Memoirs of the Literary and Philosophical Society of Manchester, 2nd series, vol. iii. 1819).

Guest (Richard). A Compendious History of the Cotton Manufacture ; with a disproval of the claim of Sir Richard Arkwright to the invention of its ingenious machinery. 1823.

Radcliffe (William). Origin of the new System of Manufacture, commonly called " Power Loom Weaving," and the Purposes for which this System was Invented and brought into Use ; fully explained in a narrative, containing William Radcliffe's struggle through life to remove the cause which has brought this country to its present crisis, written by himself. 1828.

Gaskell (P.). The Manufacturing Population of England, . . . 1833.

—— Artisans and Machinery ; the moral and physical condition of the manufacturing population considered, with reference to mechanical substitutes for human labour. 1836.

> A second and enlarged edition of the preceding. It deals exclusively with the cotton industry.

Baines (Edward). History of the Cotton Manufacture in Great Britain . . . (1835)

—— History of the County Palatine and Duchy of Lancaster, 4 vols., 1836.

Ure (A.). The Cotton Manufacture of Great Britain, systematically investigated, 1836.

Schulze-Gaevernitz (G. von). Der Grossbetrieb, ein wissenschaftlicher und socialer Fortschritt, 1892.

> This work deals only with the cotton industry.

Daniels (George A.). The Early English Cotton Industry, with some unpublished letters of Samuel Crompton ; Introductory chapter by George Unwin, 1920.

Also the two following works on the history of factory legislation :

Plener (Ernest Edler von). Die englische Fabrikgesetzgebung. (English translation, 1873.)

Hutchins (B. L.) and Harrisson (A.). A History of Factory Legislation, with a Preface by Sidney Webb. 1903.

For the condition of labour see the important statistical work of :

Wood (G. W.). History of Wages in the Cotton Trade during the past Hundred Years. 1910.

> This work forms part of a larger work on the fluctuation of wages in British industry during the 19th century, which has been published in the Journal of the Royal Statistical Society.

See, finally, for a complete and vivid picture of the Lancashire cotton industry, its employers and factory hands, and of the factory legislation, the excellent work of :

Owen (Robert). The Life of ——, written by himself, with selections from his writings and correspondence, vol. i. (the only volume ever published). 1857.

3. WOOL.

(i) *Official Documents.*

Report from the Select Committee on the Petition of persons concerned in the Woollen Trade and Manufactures in the counties of Somerset, Wilts and Gloucester, 1802–3.

Report from the Select Committee on the Petitions of Merchants and Manufacturers concerned in the Woollen Manufacture in the county of York and town of Halifax (York), 1802–3.

Report of the Select Committee on the Petition of the Manufacturers of Woollen Cloth in the county of York, 1803–4.

Minutes of Evidence taken before the Committee, to whom the Bill, respecting the Laws relating to the Woollen Trade, is committed, 1803.

Report and Minutes of Evidence, on the State of the Woollen Manufacture in England, and the Use of Machinery, 1806.

A document of the first importance.

(ii) *General.*

Hirst (W.). History of the Woollen Trade during the last Sixty Years. 1844.

James (J.). History of the Worsted Manufacture in England from the Earliest Times. 1857.

Dechesne (L.). L'Evolution Economique et Sociale de l'Industrie de la Laine en Angleterre. 1900.

Lipson (E.). English Woollen and Worsted Industries. 1920.

4. SILK.

For this manufacture, which was in a state of decline, no general work exists, but a few official documents are at the student's disposal :

Report from Committee on Silk Ribbon Weavers' Petitions, 1818.

First and Second Reports of Minutes of Evidence taken before the Committee appointed to consider of the several Petitions relating to Ribbon Weavers, 1818.

5. LINEN.

Warden (A. J.). The Linen Trade, Ancient and Modern, 1st ed., 1864 ; 2nd ed., 1867.

E. HOSIERY.

1. OFFICIAL DOCUMENTS.

Report on Framework Knitters' Petitions, complaining of the deceitful manufacture of goods. 1812.

Second Report on the same subject, and describing the different modes of making stockings. 1812.

Report and Minutes of Evidence of Framework Knitters, on their Petition, respecting the mode of manufacturing stockings. 1819.

2. GENERAL.

Felkin (W.). History of the Machine-wrought Hosiery and Lace Manufactures. 1869.

> A work of considerable interest ; the author was a manufacturer who had taken a personal share in the suppression of labour riots.

See also :

Blackner (John). The History of Nottingham, embracing its antiquities, trade and manufactures, from the earliest authentic records to the present time. 1815.

F. TRANSPORT ; MEANS OF COMMUNICATION.

1. OFFICIAL DOCUMENTS.

(i) *Roads.*

Reports on the state of the Highways, 1808–21 (7 reports).

(ii) *Navigation.*

British and Foreign Vessels and Tonnage, and number of men and boys employed in navigating the same in the several ports of Great Britain, 1810–12.

British and Foreign Tonnage, and number of foreign seamen and vessels entered inwards and cleared outwards at the ports of the United Kingdom, 1812.

Vessels entered and cleared in Great Britain, 1812.

British and Foreign Vessels and Tonnage, and number of men and boys, . . . 1817.

British and Foreign Vessels, with their Tonnage, and number of men and boys employed in navigating the same, entered inwards and cleared outwards at the several ports of Great Britain, from or to all parts of the world, 1817.

2. GENERAL.

Dupin (Baron Charles). Voyages dans la Grande-Bretagne, 2nd ed., Part III. Force Commerciale. Section des Travaux Publics et d'Association. Voies publiques, Places, Rues, Routes, Canaux, Ponts et Chaussées, 2 vols. 1826.

Phillips (J.). A General History of Inland Navigation, Foreign and Domestic ; containing a complete account of the canals already executed in England, with considerations on those projected, . . . 1792.

Lindsay (W. S.). History of Merchant Shipping and Ancient Commerce, 4 vols. 1874–6.

> (Vol. ii extremely superficial.)

3. BIOGRAPHIES.

Smiles (Samuel). Lives of the Engineers, new and revised ed. ; vol. i, Harbours, Lighthouses, Bridges ; . . . vol. ii, History of Roads ; . . . vol. iii, The Steam Engine ; . . . vol. iv, The Locomotive, 1874.

—— The Life of George Stephenson, Railway Engineer, 5th ed., 1858.

G. THE EMPLOYERS.

1. THE ORGANIZATION OF BRITISH INDUSTRY.

Observations on Public Institutions, Monopolies, Joint-Stock Companies, and Deeds of Trust ; showing the advantages the public derive from Competition in Trade, . . . 1807.

Joint-Stock Companies with Transferable Shares : Report of the Arguments, upon the application to the Court of King's Bench, for leave to file an Information against Mr. Ralph Dodd, upon the Statute of 6 Geo. I, cap. 18.   1808.

Levy (Hermann).   Monopole, Kartelle und Trusts in ihren Beziehungen zur Organisation der Kapitalistischer Industrie ; Dargestellt an der Entwicklung in Grossbritannien, 1909.

2. COMMERCE AND COMMERCIAL POLICY : ORDERS IN COUNCIL : BLOCKADE OF THE CONTINENT.

(i) *Official Documents*.

(a) Tariffs.

Mascall (E. J.).   A Practical Book of Customs, with Excise, upon all Foreign Articles Imported.   1801.

—— A Digest of the Duties of Customs and Excise, etc. ; the whole brought up to July 5, 1809.   1809.

(b) Imports and Exports : Statistics.

An Account of the real value of Exports from Great Britain in the years, 1805, 1806, 1807, 1808, 1809, 1810, 1811 respectively, distinguishing generally the countries to which the goods were exported, 1812.

An Account of the real value of exports from Great Britain to all parts of the world, in the years 1805, 1806, 1807, 1808, 1809, 1810 and 1811 respectively, distinguishing British Produce and Manufactures from Foreign and Colonial Merchandise ; distinguishing the Amount to the North of Europe, to Spain, to Portugal, to other Parts of Europe, to Asia, to Africa, to the United States of America, and to all other parts of America, 1812.

An Account of the Imports and Exports of all Merchandise of Great Britain, to and from Foreign Countries ; in the years ending January 5, 1792, 1804 and 1814 ; distinguishing the Official from the Real Value, 1814.

An Account of the Official Value of the Exports from Great Britain, in each year from 1792 to 1816, both inclusive ; distinguishing the value of British Produce and Manufactures, from that of Foreign and Colonial Merchandise, 1817.

(c) Orders in Council.

Minutes of Evidence taken at the Bar of the House upon taking into consideration the Petition of several Merchants in Liverpool, and also the Petition of several Merchants and Manufacturers of Manchester who are extensively concerned in the trade to the United States of North America, respecting the Orders in Council, 1808 ; reprinted 1812.

Minutes of Evidence, taken before the Committee of the whole House, to whom it was referred to consider of the several Petitions which have been presented to the House in this Session of Parliament relating to Orders in Council.   1812.

(ii.) *Contemporary Works ; the Controversy occasioned by the Orders in Council*.

Stephen (John).   War in Disguise, or the Frauds of Neutral Flags.   1805.

Spence (William).   Britain Independent of Commerce.   1807.

Mill (James).   Commerce Defended, . . . 1807 ; 2nd ed., 1808.

Bosanquet (Charles).   Thoughts on the Value, to Great Britain, of Commerce in General, and on the Value and Importance of the Colonial Trade in Particular. 1808.

Chalmers (Thomas). An Inquiry into the Extent and Stability of National Resources. 1808.

Phillimore (J.). Reflections on the Nature and Extent of the Licence Trade. 1811.

West (Sir Edward). Letter on the Licence Trade. 1812.

3. THE EAST INDIA COMPANY.

 (i) *Official Documents.*

Minutes of Evidence respecting the Renewal of the Company's Charter, 1812–13.

4. PROTECTION OF AGRICULTURE ; THE CORN LAWS.

 (i) *Official Documents.*

The reports enumerated above, under " Agriculture."

 (ii) *Contemporary Works.*

Malthus (T. R.). Observations on the Effects of the Corn Laws, and of a Rise or Fall in the Price of Corn on the Agriculture and General Wealth of the Country, 1814.

[West (Sir Edward)]. Essay on the Application of Capital to Land ; with observations showing the impolicy of any great restriction on the importation of corn, . . . by a Fellow of University College, Oxford. 1815.

Malthus (T. R.). An Inquiry into the Nature and Progress of Rent, and the Principles by which it is Regulated. 1815.

—— The Grounds of an Opinion on the Policy of Restricting the Importation of Foreign Corn. . . . 1815.

Ricardo (D.). An Essay on the Influence of a Low Price of Corn on the Profits of Stock ; showing the inexpediency of restrictions on importations, . . . with remarks on Mr. Malthus' two last publications. . . . 1815.

5. GENERAL.

Levi (Leone). The History of British Commerce and of the Economic Progress of the British Nation, 1763–1878. 1880.

Rose (John Holland). England's Commercial Struggle with Napoleon. . . . 1902.

Cunningham (Aubrey). British Credit in the last Napoleonic War. . . . 1910.

H. THE PROLETARIATE.

1. ORGANIZATION : STANDARD WORKS.

Brentano (Lujo). On the History and Development of Gilds, and the Origin of Trade Unions. 1870.

Webb (Sidney and Beatrice). The History of Trade Unionism. 1896.

Howell (George). Labour Legislation, Labour Movements and Labour Leaders. 1902.

2. POVERTY.

Eden (Sir F. M.). The State of the Poor, or a history of the labouring classes in England, from the Conquest to the present period, 3 vols., 1797.

Colquhoun (P.). A Treatise on Indigence ; exhibiting a general view of the national resources for productive labour. . . . 1806.

And the two more recent volumes, at once scholarly and impassioned :

Hammond (J. L. and Barbara). The Town Labourer (1760–1832). The New Civilisation, 1917.

—— The Skilled Labourer (1760–1832), 1919.

3. LABOUR TROUBLES, THE LUDDITES ; A FEW OFFICIAL DOCUMENTS.

Report of the Committee of Secrecy on Papers relating to certain violent Proceedings in several Counties of England. 1812.

Proceedings at York Special Commission (January 2–12, 1813). 1813.

The Trials of all the Prisoners at the Special Assizes for the County of Lancaster, commencing May 23, 1812.

Charlotte Brontë's novel, Shirley. 1849.
    An historical source for the riots in Yorkshire.

IV. CREDIT.

1. THE BANKING SYSTEM.

   (i) *Official Documents.*

An Account of the Number of Country Banks in England and Wales for which Licences to issue Promissory Notes have been taken out in each Year, from 1808 to 1818. . . . 1819.

   (ii) *General.*

Macleod (H. D.). The Theory and Practice of Banking, 2 vols., 1st ed., 1855–6 ; 5th ed., 1892–3.

Bagehot (W.). Lombard Street ; a description of the Money Market. 1873.

Rae (George). The Country Banker : his Clients, Cares and Work, from an experience of forty years. 1885.

Lawson (W. J.). The History of Banking ; with a comprehensive account of the origin, rise and progress of the banks of England, Ireland and Scotland, 1st ed., 1852 ; 2nd ed., enlarged, 1855.

Kerr (A. W.). History of Banking in Scotland, 1884.

Two works by

Francis (John). History of the Bank of England, its Times and Traditions. 1847.

—— Chronicles and Characters of the Stock Exchange. 1849.
    Primarily collections of anecdotes.

   (iii) *Monographs, Biographies.*

Forbes (Sir William). Memoirs of a Banking House. 1860.

Hughes (L.). Liverpool Banks and Bankers, 1760–1837. 1905.

2. SUSPENSION OF CASH PAYMENTS, FINANCIAL CRISES, THEIR EXPLANATION.

   (i) *Official Documents.*

Report, together with Minutes of Evidence and Accounts, from the Select Committee appointed to inquire into the cause of the High Price of Gold Bullion, . . . 1810.

First and Second Reports from the Committee of Secrecy appointed to consider of the State of the Bank of England, with reference to the expediency of the Resumption of Cash Payments at the period fixed by law. 1819.

First and Second Reports by the Lords' Secret Committee, appointed to inquire into the same subject. 1819.

(ii) *Contemporary Controversy.*

The Iniquity of Banking ; or banknotes proved to be an injury to the public, and the real cause of the present exorbitant price of provisions, 2nd ed., 1797.

The Utility of Country Banks considered. 1802.

Thornton (Henry). An Inquiry into the Nature and Effects of the Paper Credit of Great Britain. 1802.

Guineas an Unnecessary and Expensive Incumbrance on Commerce ; or, the impolicy of repealing the Bank Restriction Bill considered. 2nd ed., with an Appendix, 1803.

King (Peter, seventh Lord King). Thoughts on the Effects of the Bank Restrictions, 1st ed., 1803 ; 2nd ed., enlarged, 1804.

Bosanquet (Charles). Practical Observations on the Report of the Bullion Committee. 1st ed., 1810 ; 2nd ed., enlarged, 1810.

Ricardo (David). High Price of Bullion a Proof of the Depreciation of Bank Notes. 1811.

—— Reply to Mr. Bosanquet's Practical Observations on the Report of the Bullion Committee. 1811.

A pamphlet which appeared in 1811, entitled :

Resolutions proposed to the House of Commons on the Report of the Committee appointed to inquire into the High Price of Bullion, by Francis Horner and the Right Hon. N. Vansittart, also the several divisions which took place in consequence of the same ——, to which is added, a list of publications occasioned by the Report of the Committee. 1811.

Contains a list of 60 works, which appeared between 1802 and 1811.

Cobbett (William). Paper against Gold ; containing the History and Mystery of the Bank of England, the funds, the debt, the sinking fund, the bank stoppage, the lowering and the raising of the value of paper-money ; and showing that taxation, pauperism, poverty, misery and crimes have all increased, and ever must increase, with a funding system. 1817.

A collection of articles from the Political Register, 1810–11.

(iii) *General Works, worthy of mention, are :*

Tooke (Thomas). A History of Prices and of the State of the Circulation from 1793 to 1837. 1838.

Juglar (Clément). Des Crises Commerciales et de leur retour periodique en France, en Angleterre et aux États-Unis, 1st ed., 1862 ; 2nd ed., 1889.

V. NATIONAL FINANCE.

A. GENERAL.

Pebrer (Pablo). Taxation, Revenue, Expenditure, Power, Statistics and Debt of the whole British Empire ; their origin, progress and present state, with an estimate of the capital and resources of the Empire and a practical plan for applying them to the liquidation of the National Debt ; the whole founded on, and illustrated by, official tables, and authentic documents. 1833.

Doubleday (Thomas). A Financial, Monetary and Statistical History of England, from the Revolution of 1688 to the present time ; derived principally from official documents. In seventeen letters addressed to the young men of Great Britain, 1847.

    Extremely superficial.

B. THE NATIONAL DEBT.

1. OFFICIAL DOCUMENTS.

Total amount of money raised in each year from 1790 to 1815 ; sums issued on account of the interest of the National Debt, the reduction of the National Debt, or of general expenditure ; capital of funded and unfunded debt. 1814–15.

2. CONTEMPORARY CONTROVERSY.

Paine (Thomas). The Decline and Fall of the English System of Finance. 1796.

Morgan (William). Facts Addressed to the Serious Attention of the People of Great Britain respecting the Expense of the War, and the State of the National Debt. 1796.

—— Additional Facts Addressed, etc. 1796.

—— An Appeal to the People of Great Britain on the Alarming State of the Public Finances and of Public Credit. 1797.

—— A Comparative View of the Public Finances from the Beginning to the Close of the Late Administration. 1801.

Gentz (Frédéric). Essai sur l'état actuel de l'Administration des Finances et de la Richesse Nationale de la Grande-Bretagne. 1800.

Grellier (J. J.). The Terms of all the Loans which have been raised for the Public Service during the last Fifty Years ; with an introductory account of the principal loans prior to that period. 1799.

—— The History of the National Debt, from 1688 to the Beginning of 1800 ; with a preliminary account of the debts contracted previous to the era. 1810.

Hamilton (Robert). An Inquiry Concerning the Rise and Progress, the Redemption and Present State, and the Management, of the National Debt of Great Britain, 1st ed., 1813 ; 2nd ed., enlarged, 1814 ; 3rd ed., further enlarged, 1818.
    The standard authority on the subject.

Ricardo (David). Essay on the Funding System, 1820 (published in the supplement to the 6th ed. of the Encyclopædia Britannica . . . Works, ed. MacCulloch, pp. 513 sqq.).

C. TAXATION.

1. OFFICIAL DOCUMENTS.

In addition to the large collection of annual budgets we may mention the following Parliamentary papers :

Gross and net produce of revenue collected in England and Scotland during fourteen years, ending 1815 ; also, gross and net produce of war taxes during the like period, 1814–15.

An account or estimate of the gross and net assessments of the Property Tax for five years, ending April 5, 1814, distinguishing the several classes : annual value of lands, tenements and hereditaments ; and duty arising from profits of professions, trades and offices, 1814–15.

2. GENERAL.

Sinclair (Sir John). The History of the Public Revenue of the British Empire, 1785 ; Part II, 1789 ; Part III, 1790 ; 3rd ed., 3 vols., 1803–4.

Dowell (Stephen). A History of Taxation in England from the Earliest Times to the Present Day. 1st ed., 1884 ; 2nd ed., 1888.

—— A History and Explanation of the Stamp Duties ; containing remarks on the origin of stamp duties, a history of the duties in this country from their commencement to the present time. . . . 1873.

D. RATES : THE POOR LAW.

1. OFFICIAL DOCUMENTS.

Local Taxation, Poor Rates, County Rates, Highway Rates, Church Rates, . . . 1839.

Report from the Committee on Poor Houses and Poor Rates, 1813.

Report from the Select Committee on the Poor Laws, with the Minutes of Evidence, . . . 1817.

2. CONTEMPORARY CONTROVERSY ON THE ADMINISTRATION OF THE POOR LAW.

In addition to the works, already mentioned, of Sir F. M. Eden and Colquhoun (p. 545), see

Malthus (T. R.). An Essay on the Principle of Population, . . . 1st ed., 1798 ; 2nd ed., enlarged, 1803 ; 3rd ed., 2 vols., 1807 ; 5th ed., 1817 ; 6th ed., 1826.

Rose (Right Hon. George). Observations on the Poor Laws and on the Management of the Poor in Great Britain. . . . 1805.

—— Observations on Banks for Savings. 1816.

Weyland (John). Observations on Mr. Whitbread's Poor Bill, and on the Population of England ; intended as a supplement to a short inquiry into the policy, humanity and past effects of the Poor Laws, 1807.

—— The Principle of the English Poor Laws, illustrated from the evidence given by Scottish Proprietors (before the Corn Committee), on the connection observed in Scotland between the price of grain and the wages of labour. 1815.

Clark (William). Thoughts on the Management and Relief of the Poor ; on the causes of their increase, and on the measures that may be best calculated to amend the former, and check the latter. 1815.

3. GENERAL.

Nicholls (Sir George). A History of the English Poor Law, in connection with the legislation and other circumstances affecting the condition of the people. 1854.

—— A History of the Scotch Poor Law, in connection with the condition of the people, 1856.

—— A History of the Irish Poor Law, in connection, . . . 1856.

BOOK III

RELIGION AND CULTURE

I. RELIGION.

A. GENERAL.

Hunt (John). Religious Thought in England, from the Reformation to the End of the Last Century, . . . 3 vols., 1870–3.
> A summary of the religious doctrines taught during this period ; vol. iii deals with the 18th century.

Haweis (Rev. T.). An Impartial and Succinct History of the Rise, Declension, and Revival of the Church of Christ ; from the birth of our Saviour to the present time, with faithful characters of the principal personages. 1800.
> Vol. iii. Evangelical.

Timpson (Rev. T.). British Ecclesiastical History ; including the religion of the Druids, the introduction of Christianity into Britain, and the rise, progress and present state of every denomination of Christians in the British Empire. 1838.
> Nothing more than a textbook. But the portion of the work which deals with the 18th and 19th centuries is founded on a rich collection of material.

Stoughton (John). Religion in England from 1800 to 1850 ; a history, with a postscript on subsequent events, 2 vols., 1884.

B. THE CHURCH OF ENGLAND.

1. ECCLESIASTICAL LAW.

Burn (Richard). Ecclesiastical Law, 1st ed., 1763 ; 7th ed., in 4 vols., 1809.

2. OFFICIAL DOCUMENTS.

Abstracts, presented to the House of Commons, of Returns relative to the Clergy ; also further Papers respecting Non-Residence. 1808.

Abstracts, presented to the House of Commons, of Returns made to the Privy Council of Great Britain by the several Archbishops and Bishops, relative to the Residence of the Clergy in their respective Dioceses, in the years 1804, 1805, 1806, 1807 and 1808. 1809.

An Abstract of Returns respecting Non-Residence for the year ending March 25, 1808, including only Livings under the value of £150 per annum. 1810.

An Abstract of Returns respecting Non-Residence for the year ending March 25, 1809. 1812.

Abstract of the Number and Classes of Non-Resident Incumbents, and of the Number of Resident Incumbents, according to the Diocesan Returns for the year 1810. 1812.

Abstract of the Number of Resident and Licensed Curates, with the amount of the Salaries of Curacies, according to the Diocesan Returns for the year 1810. 1812.

Abstract of the Number of Resident and Licensed Curates, with the amount of the Salaries of Curacies, according to the Diocesan Returns for the year 1811. 1812–13.

Abstract of the total Number of Parishes in each Diocese in England and Wales, containing a Population of 1,000 Persons and upwards ; the number of Churches and Chapels therein ; the number of persons they will contain ; and the number of Dissenting Places of Worship therein. 1812.

Report of the Commissioners, appointed by His Majesty to inquire into the Ecclesiastical Revenues of England and Wales. 1835.

3. CONTEMPORARY PUBLICATIONS.

A Report from the Clergy of a District in the Diocese of Lincoln, convened for the purpose of considering the state of religion in the several Parishes of the said District. 1800.

Cove (Rev. Morgan). An Essay on the Revenues of the Church of England ; with an inquiry into the necessity, justice and policy of an abolition or commutation of tithes, 1st and 2nd ed., 1797 ; 3rd ed., 1816.

Cockburn (Rev. W.). Strictures on Clerical Education in the University of Cambridge, 1809.

The State of the Established Church ; in a series of letters to the Right Hon. Spencer Perceval, Chancellor of the Exchequer, 2nd ed., 1810.

4. GENERAL.

Abbey (Charles J.) and Overton (John H.). The English Church in the Eighteenth Century, 2 vols., 1878.

Overton (John H.). The English Church in the Nineteenth Century (1800–33). 1894.

> Works full of information and usually safe guides, though the authors, two High Churchmen, are not absolutely impartial.

Cornish (F. Warre). History of the English Church in the Nineteenth Century. 2 vols., 1910.

Mathieson (William Law). English Church Reform (1815–40). 1924.

5. BIOGRAPHIES, MEMOIRS, CORRESPONDENCE.

Jebb (John) and Knox (Alexander). Thirty Years' Correspondence Between ——, ed. Forster, 2 vols., 1834.

Jebb (John). Life of ——, Bishop of Limerick, by Charles Forster. 1851.

> But practically all the outstanding figures of Anglicanism in the opening years of the 19th century were Evangelicals. For their biographies see the following section.

BIBLIOGRAPHY

C. THE EVANGELICAL PARTY.

1. CONTEMPORARY LITERATURE.

Gisborne (Thomas). An Inquiry into the Duties of Men in the Higher Rank and Middle Classes of Society in Great Britain, 1st ed., 1797; 2nd ed., 2 vols., 1795.

> Contains very little theology; a useful book for the study of social life.

Wilberforce (William). A Practical View of the Prevailing Religious System of Professed Christians in the Higher and Middle Classes in this Country, contrasted with Real Christianity, 1797, 15th ed., 1824.

> May be regarded as the party manifesto. It provoked a war among the theologians. *See especially :*

Daubeny (Charles). A Guide to the Church; in several discourses, to which are added two postscripts : the first to those members of the Church who occasionally frequent other places of public worship, the second to the clergy, Addressed to William Wilberforce, Esq., M.P., 1798.

> High Church.

Hill (Sir Richard). An Apology for Brotherly Love and for the Doctrines of the Church of England, in a series of letters to the Rev. Charles Daubeny. 1798.

> Evangelical.

Overton (John). The True Churchman Ascertained; or an apology for those of the Regular Clergy of the Establishment who are sometimes called Evangelical Ministers, . . . 1801.

> Evangelical.

Daubeny (Rev. Charles). Vindiciæ Ecclesiæ Anglicanæ; in which some of the false reasonings, incorrect statements, and palpable misrepresentations in a publication entitled The True Churchman Ascertained, by John Overton, A.B., are pointed out. 1803.

> High Church.

[Bean (Rev. James)]. Zeal without Innovation; or, the Present State of Religion and Morals Considered. 1808.

> A moderate criticism of the Evangelicals.

———

Marsh (Herbert). An Inquiry into the Consequences of Neglecting to Give the Prayer Book with the Bible, interspersed with remarks on some late speeches at Cambridge and other important matter relative to the British and Foreign Bible Society. 1812.

Otter (Rev. William). A Vindication of Churchmen who become Members of the British and Foreign Bible Society, in a letter to a friend at Cambridge; being an answer to Dr. Marsh's pamphlet upon that subject. 1812.

Milner (Rev. I). Strictures on some of the Publications of the Rev. Herbert Marsh, D.D., intended as a reply to his objections against the British and Foreign Bible Society. 1813.

2. GENERAL.

Overton (John Henry). The Evangelical Revival in the Eighteenth Century, 1886; new ed., 1900.

Stock (Eugene). The History of the Church Missionary Society : its environment, its men and its work. For the period before 1848, see vol. i. 1899.

Owen (Rev. John). The History of the Origin and First Ten Years of the British and Foreign Bible Society. 2 vols., 1816.

Canton (William). A History of the British and Foreign Bible Society. For the period before 1834, see vol. i. 1904.

3. BIOGRAPHIES.

Stephen (Right Hon. Sir James). Essays in Ecclesiastical Biography and other Subjects. 1st ed., 1849.

Colquhoun (J. C.). William Wilberforce : his friends and his times, 1866.

These two biographies taken together present a picture of the Evangelical party as a body. The former is authoritative.

Milner (Isaac). The Life of ——, ... by Mary Milner, 1842.

More (Mrs. Hannah). Memoirs of the Life and Correspondence of ——, by William Roberts, 4 vols., 1834.

Porteus (Right Reverend Beilby ——, Bishop of London). The Life of the ——, by the Rev. Robert Hodgson. 1811.

Sherwood (Mrs.). The Life of ——, edited and abridged by Isabella Gilchrist. 1917.

—— The Life and Times of —— (1775–1851), from the Diaries of Captain and Mrs. Sherwood, ed. F. J. Harvey Darton. 1910.

Shore (John, Lord Teignmouth). Memoirs of the Life and Correspondence of ——, by his son. 2 vols., 1843.

Simeon (Rev. Charles). Memoirs of the Life of the ——, with a selection from his writings and correspondence, by the Rev. William Carus. 1847.

Wilberforce (William). The Life of ——, by his sons, R. I. and S. Wilberforce, 5 vols., 1st ed. 1838.

D. NONCONFORMITY.

1. THE OLD DENOMINATIONS (PRESBYTERIANS, INDEPENDENTS, BAPTISTS).

(i) *General.*

Bogue (David) and Bennett (James). History of Dissenters, from the Revolution in 1688 to the year 1808, 4 vols., 1808–12, with

Bennett (James). The History of Dissenters (from 1808–38), 1839,

Remains the standard authority.

Skeats (H. S.). A History of the Free Churches of England, from A.D. 1688 to A.D. 1851, 1868 ; new ed., revised and continued to 1891, by C. S. Miall, 1891.

Adds hardly anything to Bogue and Bennett. *See also :*

Evans (John). A Sketch of the Denominations into which the Christian World is Divided ; accompanied with a persuasive to religious moderation, 1st ed., 1795 ; 9th ed., 1807.

(ii) *Works relating*

(*a*) To a particular sect.

Waddington (John). Congregational History.

An enormous compilation ; the entire work extends from 1200–1880. See the following vols. :

Waddington (John). Congregational History, 1700–1800 ; in relation to contemporaneous events, education, the eclipse of faith, revivals and Christian missions. 1876.

—— Congregational History, continuation to 1850 ; with special reference to the rise, growth and influence of institutions, representative men, and the inner life of the Churches. 1878.

Ivimey (Joseph). A History of the English Baptists, vol. iii ; comprising the principal events of the history of Protestant Dissenters, from the Revolution in 1688 till 1760, and of the London Baptist churches during that period, 1824. Vol. iv, comprising the principal events of the history of the Protestant Dissenters during the reign of George III, and of the Baptist churches in London, with notices of many of the principal churches in the country during the same period. 1830.

Lindsey (Rev. Theophilus). Memoirs of the Late ——, M.A. ; including a brief analysis of his works, together with anecdotes and letters of eminent persons, his friends and correspondents. Also, a General View of the Progress of the Unitarian Doctrine in England and America, by Thomas Belsham. 1812.

(b) To a particular sect, or to all the Dissenting bodies, in a particular locality. See especially :

Coleman (Thomas). Memorials of the Independent Churches in Northamptonshire. 1853.

Sibree (John) and Caston (M.). Independency in Warwickshire, . . . 1855.

Miall (James G.). Congregationalism in Yorkshire, . . . 1868.

Halley (Rev. Robert). Lancashire : its Puritanism and Nonconformity, 2 vols., 1869.

Urwick (William). Historical Sketches of Nonconformity in the County Palatine of Chester, . . . 1864.

—— Nonconformity in Hertfordshire, . . . 1884.

—— Nonconformity in Worcester, . . . 1897.

Densham (W.) and Ogle (J.). The Story of the Congregational Churches of Dorset, . . . 1899.

Congregational Historical Society Transactions, from 1904.

(iii) Works which we have found useful in our study of the older sects.

(a) Biographies.

Hall (Robert). A Brief Memoir of the Life of ——, by Olinthus Gregory, 1833.

Hinton (Rev. James). A Biographical Portraiture of the Late ——, Pastor of a Congregational Church in Oxford, by his son, J. Howard Hinton. . . . 1824.

(b) Works of controversy.

Pierce (James). The Western Inquisition ; or, a relation of the controversy which has been lately among Dissenters in the West of England. 1720.

An Inquiry into the Causes of the Decay of the Dissenting Interest ; in a letter to a Dissenting minister. 2nd ed., 1730.

Doddridge (Philip). Free Thoughts on the most Probable Means of Reviving the Dissenting Interest, occasioned by the late inquiry into the cause of its decay ; addressed to the author of that inquiry (Works, 1802, vol. iv. pp. 199 sqq.).

Plain Reasons : I, For Dissenting from the Communion of the Church of England ; II, Why Dissenters are not, nor can be guilty of schism, in peaceably separating from the places of public worship in the Church of England ; and III, Several common objections brought by Churchmen against Dissenters, Answered by a true Protestant, 23rd ed., to which is added, a Letter to a Divine in Germany, giving a brief but true account of the Protestant Dissenters in England. By the late Rev. Edmund Calamy, . . . 1736.

The Causes and Reasons of the Present Declension among the Congregational Churches, in London and the Country, in a letter addressed to the pastors, deacons and members of those Churches, by one of that denomination, interspersed with reflections on Methodism and Sandemanianism, 1766.

Brine (John). A Refutation of Arminian Principles ; delivered in a pamphlet, entitled The Modern Question, concerning repentance and faith, examined with candour, . . . in a letter to a friend, 1743.

Fuller (Andrew). The Gospel Worthy of all Acceptation ; or, the duty of sinners to believe in Jesus Christ, 1785, 2nd ed., with corrections and additions, to which is added an appendix, on the question whether the existence of any holy disposition of heart be necessary in order to believe in Christ, 1801.

Robinson (R.). A Plan of Lectures on the Principles of Nonconformity, for the Instruction of Catechumens, 1778 ; 6th ed., 1797.

Kingsbury (William). An Apology for Village Preachers ; or, an account of the proceedings and motives of Protestant Dissenters, and serious Christians of other denominations, in their attempts to suppress infidelity and vice, and to spread vital religion in country places—especially where the means of pious instruction among the poor are rare ; with some animadversions on an " Anonymous Appeal to the People," and replies to objections, 1798.

Hall (Robert). Modern Infidelity Considered with Respect to its Influence on Society, . . . 1800.

Bright (J. S.). Apostolical Independency ; exemplified in the history, doctrines, discipline, and ordinances of the Congregational Churches, commonly called Independent. 1842.

Porter (S. T.). Lectures on the Ecclesiastical System of the Independents, 1856.

Hinton (John Howard). A Review of the Congregational System, in connection with a department of its local history, being the first circular letter of the Berks and West London Association [1826 ?].

(iv) *Nonconformist Periodicals.*

The Protestant Dissenter's Magazine, 6 vols., 1794–9.
> Organ of the older Nonconformity.

The Evangelical Magazine, from 1793.
> Organ of the new Evangelical Nonconformity.

Less exclusively theological :

The Eclectic Review, from 1805.

The British Review and London Critical Journal, from 1811.

2. METHODISM.

(i) *General.*

Stevens (Abel). History of the Religious Movement of the Eighteenth Century called Methodism ; considered in its different denominational forms and in its general relation to Protestantism, revised and corrected by Rev. William Willey, 3 vols., 1863–5.

(ii *Wesleyan Methodism.*

Wesley (John). Works, 4th ed., 14 vols., 1840-2.

Southey (Robert) The Life of Wesley, and the Rise and Progress of Methodism, 2 vols., 1st ed., 1820.

     A popular work, but of high quality and still very well worth reading.

Tyerman (Rev. L.). The Life and Times of the Rev. John Wesley, 3 vols., 1870-1.

Léger (Augustin). L'Angleterre Religieuse et les Origines du Méthodisme au XVIIIᵉ Siècle. La Jeunesse de Wesley. 1910.

Lelièvre (Mathieu). John Wesley, Sa Vie et son Œuvre, 3rd ed., 1891.

Smith (George). History of Wesleyan Methodism, 2nd ed., corrected, vol. i, Wesley and his Times, 1859 ; vol. ii, The Middle Age (to 1805), 1862 ; vol. iii, Modern Methodism, 1862.

Crowther (Jonathan). A Portraiture of Methodism ; or, the history of the Wesleyan Methodists, showing their rise, progress and present state, . . . 1815.

Jackson (Thomas). The Centenary of Wesleyan Methodism ; a brief sketch of the rise, progress and present state of the Wesleyan Methodist Societies throughout the World. 1839.

Turner (George). The Constitution and Discipline of Wesleyan Methodism, in which various misrepresentations of its leading principles are exposed, and its present form is vindicated. 1850.

Minutes of the Methodist Conferences, from the first held in London by the late Rev. John Wesley, M.A., in the year 1744, vol. i., 1812.

Arminian Magazine ; consisting of extracts and original translations on Universal Redemption, 20 vols., 1778-97. Continued under the title : The Methodist Magazine.

Wesley Historical Society, proceedings and publications, from 1896-7.

Osborn (G.). Outlines of Wesleyan Bibliography ; or, a record of Methodist literature from the beginning, 1869.

(iii) *Other Methodist bodies.*

Tyerman (Rev. L.). The Life of the Rev. George Whitefield, . . . 1876-7.

General Rules of the Government of the New Connexion of Methodists, 1803.

[Blackwell (John)]. Life of the Rev. Alexander Kilham, formerly a preacher under the Rev. J. Wesley and one of the founders of the Methodist New Connexion in the year 1797, including a full account of the disputes which occasioned the separation. 1838.

Ryder (Rev. Thomas). The Spiritual Life and Aims of the Methodist New Connexion, 1897.

Crothers (Rev. T. D.), T. Rider, W. Longbottom, W. J. Townshend, G. Packer. The Centenary of the Methodist New Connexion, 1897.

Petty (John). The History of the Primitive Methodist Connexion, from its origin to the Conference of 1860, . . . new ed., 1864.

(iv) *Anti-Methodist Literature.*

Strictures on Methodism, by a careful observer.

Ingram (R. A., B.D.). The causes of the increase of Methodism and Dissension, and of the popularity of what is called Evangelical Preaching, and the means of obviating them, considered in a sermon, . . . 1807.

[Leigh Hunt]. An Attempt to show the Folly and Danger of Methodism, by the editor of the Examiner, 1809.

Methodism Displayed and Christianism Detected ; intended as an antidote against, and a preservative from, the delusive principles and unscriptural doctrines of a modern set of seducing preachers, and as a defence of the Regular and Orthodox Clergy from their unjust reflections. By a member of the Church of England, 1813.

Ward (Valentine). Free and Candid Strictures on Methodism, and especially its finances, . . . 1818.

E. PHILANTHROPY: THE REFORM OF PUBLIC MORALITY.

The Reports of the Society for Bettering the Condition and Increasing the Comforts of the Poor, 5 vols. (1798–1808).

A fine record of philanthropic achievement. From this compilation Holy-oake (G. J.) drew the material for his popular work—

Self-Help a Hundred Years Ago, 1888.

Dobbs (A. E.). Education and Social Movements (1700–1850), 1919.

The Philanthropist, or repository for hints and suggestions calculated to promote the comfort and happiness of man [ed. by W. Allen], 7 vols., 1811–19 ; also Allen's Biography :

Allen (William). Life of ——, with selections from his correspondence, 3 vols., 1846–7.

Highmore (A.). Pietas Londiniensis ; the history, design and present state of the various public charities in and near London. 1810.

—— Philanthropia Metropolitana : a view of the charitable institutions established in and near London, chiefly during the last twelve years. 1822.

Lettsom (John Coakley). Hints Designed to Promote Beneficence, Temperance and Medical Science, 3 vols , 1st ed., 1801 ; new and enlarged ed., 1816.

On the abolition of the slave trade :

Clarkson (Thomas). A History of the Abolition of the Slave Trade, 2 vols., 1839.

——A Biographical Sketch of ——, with occasional brief strictures on the misrepresentations of him contained in the Life of William Wilberforce, . . . by Thomas Taylor, 1839.

A curious picture of the manners of the period, the brutal sports, the gaming-houses and races will be found in the works of Pierce Egan, and especially in :

Pierce Egan. Life in London ; or, the day and night scenes of Jeremy Hawthorn, Esq., and his elegant friend Corinthian Tom, accompanied by Bob Logic, the Oxonian, in their rambles and sprees through the Metropolis, 1st ed., 1821.

F. SCOTTISH PRESBYTERIANISM.

Sack (D. Karl Heinrich). Die Kirche von Schottland, Beiträge zu deren Geschichte und Beschreibung, 2 vols., 1844–5.

Grub (George). An Ecclesiastical History of Scotland, from the introduction of Christianity to the present time. See for the period 1721–1857, vol. iv, 1861.

MacKerrow (Rev. John). History of the Secession Church, revised and enlarged, 1841.

Struthers (Gavin). The History of the Rise, Progress and Principles of the Relief Church, embracing notices of the other religious denominations in Scotland, 1843.

BIBLIOGRAPHY

G. THE CATHOLICS.

1. CONTEMPORARY LITERATURE.

[Berington (Rev. Jos.)]. The State and Behaviour of English Catholics, from the Reformation to the Year 1780, with a view to their present number, wealth, character, etc. In two parts, 1780.

—— The History of the Decline and Fall of the Roman Catholic Religion in England, during a period of two hundred and forty years, from the reign of Elizabeth to the present time, including the Memoirs of Gregorio Panzani, . . . 1813.

Butler (Charles). Historical Memoirs of the English, Irish and Scotch Catholics, from the Reformation to the present time. 2 vols., 1819.

    Berington and Butler were Cisalpines.

Milner (John). Supplementary Memoirs of English Catholics, addressed to Charles Butler, Esq., 1820.

    Ultramontane.

2. GENERAL WORKS.

Flanagan (Canon). History of the Church in England, from the earliest period to the establishment of the Hierarchy in 1850. 2 vols., 1857.

Amherst (W. J.). The History of Catholic Emancipation and the Progress of the Catholic Church in the British Isles (chiefly in England), from 1771 to 1820. 2 vols., 1886.

    Ultramontane. Without value for the historian.

Ward (Bernard). The Dawn of the Catholic Revival in England, 1781–1803. 2 vols., 1909.

—— The Eve of Catholic Emancipation ; being the history of the English Catholics during the first thirty years of the 19th century. Vols. i and ii, 1912.

    Excellent works, based on the records.

3. BIOGRAPHY.

Husenbeth (F. C.). The Life of the Right Rev. John Milner, 1862.

See also, as concerned with the question of Catholic emancipation in Ireland,

O'Connell (Daniel). The Life and Speeches of ——, ed. by his son, John O'Connell. 2 vols., 1846.

Grattan (Henry). Memoirs of the Life and Times of the Right Hon. ——, by his son, Henry Grattan, 5 vols., 1839–46.

H. THE JEWS.

Goldsmid (F. H). Remarks on the Civil Disabilities of British Jews. 1830.

Blunt (J. E.). A History of the Establishment and Residence of the Jews in England, with an inquiry into their civil disabilities. 1830.

Margoliouth (Rev. Moses). The History of the Jews in Great Britain. 3 vols., 1851.

Picciotto (James). Sketches of Anglo-Jewish History. 1875.

Schaible (K. H.). Die Juden in England vom achten Jahrhundert bis zum Gegenwart. Ein kulturgeschichtliches Bild. 1890.

II. FINE ARTS, LITERATURE, SCIENCE.

A. FINE ARTS.

1. GENERAL.

Strange (Sir Robert). An Inquiry into the Rise and Establishment of the Royal Academy. 1775.

Barry (James). An Inquiry into the Real and Imaginary Obstructions to the Acquisition of the Arts in England. 1775.

—— A Letter to the Right Honourable the President, Vice-Presidents, and the rest of the Noblemen and Gentlemen of the Society for the Encouragement of Arts, Manufactures and Commerce, . . . 1793.

—— A Letter to the Dilettanti Society, respecting the obtention of certain matters essentially necessary for the improvement of public taste, and for accomplishing the original views of the Royal Academy of Great Britain, 1798.

—— The Works of ——, 2 vols., 1809.

Dallaway (Rev. James). Anecdotes of the Arts in England ; or, comparative observations on architecture, sculpture and painting, . . . 1880.

Hoare (Prince). Epochs of the Arts, 1813.

Taylor (N. S.). The Origin, Progress and Present Condition of the Fine Arts in Great Britain and Ireland, 2 vols. (the 2nd vol.), 1841.

Pye (John). Patronage of British Art ; an historical sketch, comprising an account of the rise and progress of art and artists in London, from the beginning of the reign of George II, 1845.

Sandby (William). The History of the Royal Academy of Arts, from its Foundation in 1768 to the Present Time, with biographical notices of all its members, 2 vols., 1862.

2. PAINTING.

[Carey (William)]. The National Obstacle to the National Public Style Considered ; observations on the probable decline or extinction of British historical painting, from the effects of Church exclusion of paintings, 1825.

Barry, Opie and Fuseli. Lectures on Painting, by the Royal Academicians ——, ed. . . . by Ralph N. Wornum, 1848.

Wornum (Ralph Nicholson). The Epochs of Painting ; a biographical and critical essay on painting and painters of all times and many places, 1864.

> Chapter xxxii is a collection of biographical notices of all the English painters since the Renaissance.

West (Benjamin). The Life and Studies of ——, President of the Royal Academy of London, . . . compiled from materials furnished from himself, by John Galt, 2 vols., 1816, 1820.

Haydon (Robert). Life of ——, Historical Painter, from his autobiography and journals. Ed. and compiled by Tom Taylor, 3 vols., 1853.

3. ARCHITECTURE.

(i) *General.*

Fergusson (James). History of the Modern Styles of Architecture, 3rd ed., revised ; 2nd impression by Robert Kerr, 2 vols., 1902.

(ii) *The Classical Style.*

Stuart (James) and Revett (Nicholas). The Antiquities of Athens Measured and Delineated, vol. i, 1762 ; other volumes by different hands, 1787, 1794, 1816.

[Wood (R.) and Dawkin]. Les Ruines de Palmyre, autrement dite Tedmor, au Désert. A Londres chez A Millar dans le Strand, 1753.

R. Adam. Ruins of the Palace of the Emperor Diocletian at Spalatro in Dalmatia, 1763.

[Robert and James Adam]. The Works in Architecture of ——, vol. i containing the five following numbers, viz. : 1. the Seat of the Duke of Northumberland, at Sion ; 2. the Villa of the Earl of Mansfield, at Kenwood ; 3. the Seat of the Earl of Bute, at Luton Park ; 4. the Public Buildings ; 5. the Designs for the King and Queen, and the Princess Dowager of Wales, 1778.

(iii) *The Gothic Revival.*

Milner (Rev. John). The History, Civil and Ecclesiastical, and Survey of the Antiquities of Winchester, 2 vols. [1798].

—— A Dissertation on the Modern Style of altering Ancient Cathedrals, as exemplified in the Cathedral of Salisbury, 1798.

Warton (Rev. T.). Rev. J. Bentham, Captain Grose and the Rev. J. Milner, . . . Essays on Gothic Architecture, . . . 1800.

Milner (Rev. John). A Treatise on the Ecclesiastical Architecture of England during the Middle Ages, 1811.

Britton (John). The Architectural Antiquities of Great Britain ; represented and illustrated in a series of views, elevations, plans, sections, and details, of various ancient English edifices, with historical and descriptive accounts of each, 5 vols., 1807-27.

Hall (Sir James). Essay on the Origin, History and Principles of Gothic Architecture, 1813.

Eastlake (Charles L.). A History of the Gothic Revival ; an attempt to show how the taste for mediæval architecture which lingered in England during the last two centuries has since been encouraged and developed, 1872.

4. MUSIC.

Burney (Charles). A General History of Music, from the earliest ages to the present period, 4 vols., 1776–89 (see the concluding chapter).

Forsyth (Cecil). Music and Nationalism ; a study of English opera, 1912.

B. LITERATURE.

1. GENERAL WORKS.

The Cambridge History of Modern Literature, ed. by A. W. Ward and A. R. Waller. 14 vols., 1907–16.
> Vol. xi, The Period of the French Revolution. Vol. xii, The Nineteenth Century.

Taine. Histoire de la Littérature Anglaise, 4 vols., 1st ed., 1863-4. English translation, 1st ed., 1871.

Oliphant (Mrs.). The Literary History of England in the end of the Eighteenth and beginning of the Nineteenth Century, 3 vols., 1882.

Goss· (Edmund). A Short History of Modern English Literature, 1898.

Also the two following works :

Craik (George L.). A Compendious History of English Literature and of the English Language, from the Norman Conquest, with numerous specimens, 2 vols., 1864 (the second volume).

Chambers's Cyclopædia of English Literature, new ed. by David Patrick ; a history, critical and biographical, of authors in the English tongue from the earliest times till the present day, with specimens of their writings, 3 vols., 1901 (vols. ii and iii).

> The series is rather an anthology of specimen passages than a literary history.

2. NOVELISTS AND POETS.

(i) *General Works.*

C. R. [Clara Reeve]. The Progress of Romance, through times, countries and manners, . . . 1785.

Scott (Sir Walter). Lives of the Novelists, 1825.

Dunlop (John Colin). History of Prose Fiction, 1st ed., 1814 ; new ed., revised with notes.

> A concise textbook of the history of the novel from its beginnings. Chapter xiv (p. 46) traces the history of the English novel.

Brandes (George). Die Literatur des neunzehnten Jahrhunderts in ihren Hauptströmungen dargestellt, iv. vol. Der Naturalismus in England, 1900.

Courthope (W. J.). A History of English Poetry ; vol. vi. the Romantic Movement in English Poetry. Effects of the French Revolution, 1910.

(ii) *Biographies, Memoirs, Correspondence.*

Burns (Robert). ——, by Auguste Angellier, 2 vols., 1893.

Byron (Lord). Letters and Journals . . . ed. by R. E. Prothero, 6 vols., 1898–1900.

—— Correspondence. Ed. John Murray. 2 vols., 1922.

Coleridge. La Vie d'un Poète, by Joseph Aynard, 1907.

Crabbe. Un Poète Réaliste Anglais, 1754–1832, by René Huchon, 1906. (English translation, 1907.)

Hunt (Leigh). The Autobiography of —— ; a new ed., revised by the author, with further revision and an introduction by his eldest son, 1860.

Jeffrey (Lord). Life of ——, with a selection from his correspondence, by Lord Cockburn, 2 vols., 1852.

Lamb (Charles). The Complete Correspondence and Works of ——, with an essay on his life and genius by Thomas Purnell, aided by the recollections of the author's adopted daughter, 4 vols., 1870.

—— The Life of ——, by E. V. Lucas. 2 vols. 1st ed. 1905 ; 2nd ed. revised 1907.

Rogers (Samuel). —— and his Circle, by R. Ellis Roberts.

Scott (Sir Walter, Bart.). Memoirs of the Life of ——, by John Gibson Lockhart. 1st ed., 7 vols., 1837–8. We have used the latest ed., in 10 vols., 1902–3.

Seward (Anna). Biography entitled : A Swan and her Friends, by E. V. Lucas.

Southey (Robert). The Life and Correspondence of ——, edited by his son, C. C. Southey, 6 vols., 1849–50.

Wordsworth. La Jeunesse de ——, by Emile Legouis, 1896. (English translation, 1897.)

(iii) *Publishers and Booksellers.*

Constable (Archibald). —— and his Literary Correspondents ; a memorial by his son, Thomas Constable, 3 vols., 1873.

Murray (John). A Publisher and his Friends ; memoir and correspondence of the late ——, with an account of the origin and progress of the house, 1768–1843. 1891.

Rees (Thomas). Reminiscences of Literary London, from 1779 to 1853, . . . with extensive additions by John Britton ; edited by a book-lover, 1896 (1st ed. printed for private circulation, 1853).

Knight (Charles). Shadows of the Old Booksellers, 1865 ; new ed. [1908].

3. DRAMA.

(i) *Official Documents.*

Report from the Select Committee on Dramatic Literature, with the Minutes of Evidence, 1832.

> Many years later than our period. Nevertheless, it contains useful material.

(ii) *General.*

Lawrence (James). Dramatic Emancipation, or, strictures on the state of the theatres, and the consequent degeneration of the drama ; on the partiality and injustice of the London managers ; on many theatrical regulations ; and on the regulations on the Continent for the security of literary and dramatic property, particularly deserving the attention of the subscribers for a third theatre, 1813.

> Reprinted in the Pamphleteer, vol. ii. pp. 369 sqq.

Dibdin (Charles, Jr.). History and Illustrations of the London Theatres ; comprising an account of the origin and progress of the drama in England, with historical and descriptive accounts of the Theatre Royal, Covent Garden, Drury Lane, Haymarket, English Opera House, and Royal Amphitheatre, 1826.

[Genest]. Some Account of the English Stage, from the Restoration in 1660 to 1830, 10 vols., 1832.

> Vols. vii. (1790–1805) and viii. (1805–19).

Doran (Dr.). " Their Majesties' Servants." Annals of the English Stage from Thomas Betterton to Edmund Kean (published and corrected by Rob. W. Law), 3 vols., 1888.

> Vol. iii extends from the death of Foote to the death of Kean.

Nicholson (Watson). The Struggle for a Free Stage in London, 1906.
> Contains a bibliography.

(iii) *Collections of Plays.*

Inchbald (Mrs.). The British Theatre ; or, a collection of plays . . . acted at the Theatres Royal, . . . 25 vols., 1808.

—— A Collection of Farces and other After Pieces, . . . 7 vols., 1815.

Dibdin (T. S.). The London Theatre ; a collection of the most celebrated dramatic pieces, . . . 26 vols., 1815–18.

(iv) *Biographies.*

Colman. Memoirs of the —— Family, . . . 2 vols., 1841.

Dibdin (Thomas). The Reminiscences of ——, 2 vols., 1827.

Inchbald (Mrs.). Memoirs of ——, . . . by James Boaden, 2 vols., 1833.

Jordan (Mrs.). The Life of ——, . . . by James Boaden, 2 vols., 1831.

Reynolds (Frederick). The Life and Times of ——, written by himself, 2 vols., 1827.

Kemble (John Philip). Memoirs of ——, . . . by James Boaden.

Siddons (Mrs.). Memoirs of ——, . . . by James Boaden, 2 vols., 1827.

C. SCIENCE, EDUCATION.

1. EDUCATIONAL INSTITUTIONS.

(i) *Elementary Education.*

A Digest of Parochial Returns made to the Select Committee appointed to inquire into the Education of the Poor ; Session 1818, 3 vols., 1819.

Of the Education of the Poor ; being the first part of a Digest of the Reports of the Society for Bettering the Condition of the Poor, and containing a selection of those articles which have a reference to education, 1809.

Chalmers (Thomas). Considerations on the System of Parochial Schools in Scotland, and on the advantage of establishing them in large towns, 1819.

(ii) *Secondary Education.*

Ackermann (Rudolph). The History of the Colleges of Winchester, Eton and Westminster, with the Charterhouse, the Schools of St. Paul's, Merchant Taylors', Harrow and Rugby, and the free school of Christ's Hospital, 1816.

Rugby. Recollections of ——, by an old Rugbeian, 1848.

Eton. A History of —— College, by H. C. Maxwell Lyte, 1st ed., 1875 ; 4th ed., 1911.

Harrow. —— School and its Surroundings, by Percy M. Thornton, 1885.

Arnold (Thomas). The Life and Correspondence of ——, by Arthur Penrhyn Stanley, 1st ed., 2 vols., 1844.

(iii) *The Universities.*

(*a*) The English Universities.

Huber (V. A.). The English Universities, . . . translated from the German and abridged by Francis W. Newman, 2 vols., 1843.
  The text is accompanied by critical notes, often of importance.

Mansbridge (Albert). The Older Universities of England : Oxford and Cambridge, 1923.

Oxford University Statutes, translated by G. R. M. Ward, vol. ii containing the University Statutes from 1767 to 1850. 1851.

Oxford University Calendar, from 1810.

[Copleston (Edward)]. A Reply to the Calumnies of the Edinburgh Review against Oxford, containing an account of studies pursued in that University, 2nd ed. 1810.

—— Memoir of ——, with selections from his diary and correspondence, by William James Copleston, 1851.

Cox (G. V.). Recollections of ——, 1868.

Statuta Universitatis Cantabrigiensis, 1785.

Statutes of the University of Cambridge, with some Acts of Parliament relating to the University. 1882.

Cambridge University Calendar, from 1796.

Jebb (Rev. John). Remarks upon the Present Mode of Education in the University of Cambridge ; to which is added a proposal for its improvement. 1773.

Dyer (G.). History of the University and Colleges of Cambridge ; including notices of the founders and eminent men, 2 vols., 1814.

Cooper (C. H.). Annals of Cambridge, 4 vols., 1852 (vol. iv., 1688–1849).

Gunning (Henry). Reminiscences of the University, Town and County of Cambridge, 2 vols., 1854.

Winstanley (D. A.). The University of Cambridge in the Eighteenth Century. 1923.

    (*b*) The Scottish Universities.

Report made to His Majesty by a Royal Commission into the State of the Universities of Scotland, 1831.

For the study of the Scottish intelligentsia in the 18th and 19th centuries, the following biographies are of value :

Hutcheson (Francis). His Life, Teaching and Position in the History of Philosophy, by W. R. Scott. 1900.

Smith (Adam). Life of ——, by John Rae. 1895.

Mill (James). A Biography, by A. Bain 1882.

Carlyle (Thomas). A History of the First Forty Years of his Life, by A. Froude, 2 vols., 1882.

And especially the two works by

Cockburn (A.) Memorials of his Time, 1856.

—— Life of Lord Jeffrey, with a selection from his correspondence, 2 vols., 1852.

    (iv) *Medicine*.

Statuta Collegii sive Communitatis Medicorum Londiniensis, 1745.

Bye-Laws, Ordinances, Rules and Constitutions, Made and Ordained by the Master, Governors and Court of Assistants, of the Royal College of Surgeons in London, 1802. 1806.

A Letter from a Physician in Town to his Friend in the Country, concerning the disputes at present subsisting between the Fellows and Licentiates of the College of Physicians in London, 1753.

Gregory (John). Lectures on the Duties and Qualifications of a Physician, 1770 ; other eds., 1772, 1805.

Percival (Thomas). Medical Ethics ; or, a code of institutes and precepts, adapted to the professional conduct of physicians and surgeons : 1. In hospital practice ; 2. In private, or general practice ; 3. In relation to apothecaries ; 4. In cases which may require a knowledge of law ; to which is added an appendix, containing a discourse on hospital duties, also notes and illustrations, 1803.

—— The Works, Literary, Moral and Medical of ——, . . . to which are prefixed memoirs of his life and writings, and a selection from his literary correspondence ; new ed., 4 vols., 1807.

Simon (Sir John). English Sanitary Institutions, reviewed in their course of development, and in some of their political and social relations, 1890.

    Chapter v is a compendium of the history of the medical corporations.

Munk (William). The Roll of the Royal College of Physicians of London; comprising biographical sketches of all the eminent physicians, from 1518 to 1828, 2nd ed., revised and enlarged, 3 vols., 1828.

Abernethy (John). Memoirs of ——, by George MacIlwain, 3rd ed., 1856.

Christison (Sir Robert). The Life of ——, edited by his sons; vol. i. Autobiography, 1885.

Clarke (J. F.). Autobiographical Recollections of the Medical Profession, 1874.

Cooper (Sir Astley). The Life of ——, Bart., by B. B. Cooper, 2 vols., 1843.

Knighton (Sir William). Memoirs of ——, Bart., by Lady Knighton, 1838.

(v) *Learned Societies.*

(a) The Royal Society.

The standard authority is :

Weld (C. R.). A History of the Royal Society, with Memoirs of the Presidents, . . . 2 vols., 1849.

See further :

Kippis (Andrew). Observations on the Late Contests in the Royal Society, 1784.

Barrow (Sir John). Sketches of the Royal Society, and Royal Society Club, 1849.

Huggins (Sir William). The Royal Society, or Science in the State and in the Schools, . . . 1906.
    Merely a collection of academic orations.

Maiden (J. H.). Sir Joseph Banks, the " Father of Australia," 1909.

(b) Other Societies.

Jones (Dr. Bence). The Royal Institution : its Founder and its First Professors, . . . 1871.

Woodward (H. B.). The History of the Geological Society of London. 1907.

2. THE PROGRESS OF SCIENCE.

(i) *The Natural Sciences.*

(a) General.

Thomson (Thomas). History of the Royal Society from its Institution to the end of the Eighteenth Century, 1812.
    This is not so much a history of the Royal Society, as a sketch of scientific progress, based on a methodical use of the Philosophical Transactions.

—— The History of Chemistry, 2 vols., 1830–1.
    An excellent history of the Atomic Theory.

Whewell (William). History of the Inductive Sciences, from the earliest to the present time, 1st ed., 1837 ; 3rd ed., enlarged, 1857.

Leslie (Sir John). Dissertation exhibiting a general view of the progress of Mathematical and Physical Science (Encyclopædia Britannica, vol. i, 1842).

Ostwald (W.). L'Evolution d'une Science, la Chimie, translated from the German by Marcel Dufour, Paris, 6th ed., 1910.

(b) Biographies.

Beddoes (Thomas). Memoirs of the Life of ——, by John Edmonds Stock, 1811.

Dalton (John). Memoirs of the Life and Scientific Researches of ——, by W. C. Henry, 1854.

—— Religio Chemici, Essays, by George Wilson, 1862.
> Contains an essay on Dalton and an essay on Wollaston.

Davy (Sir Humphry). Life of ——, Bart., by J. A. Paris, 2 vols., 1831.

—— Memoirs of ——, Bart., by John Davy, 2 vols., 1836.

—— Fragmentary Remains, Literary and Scientific, of ——, with a sketch of his life and selections from his correspondence, edited by his brother John Davy, 1858.

—— Grosse Männer, by W. Ostwald, 2nd ed., 1910.
> Contains a chapter on Davy.

Faraday. The Life and Letters of ——, by H. Bence Jones, 2 vols., 1870.

Herschell (Sir William). Analyse Historique et Critique de la Vie et des Travaux de ——, by D. F. J. Arago, 1843.

——. His Life and Works, by Edward S. Holden, 1881.

Rumford (Baron). See the work of Bence Jones mentioned above, History of the Royal Institution, etc.

Young (Thomas). Life of ——, by George Peacock, 1855.

(ii) *The Moral Sciences.*

(a) General.

Stephen (Leslie). The English Utilitarians, 3 vols., 1900, vol. i. Jeremy Bentham ; vol. ii. James Mill.

Halévy (Elie). La Formation du Radicalisme Philosophique, 3 vols., 1901-4.

Cannan (Edwin). A History of the Theories of Production and Distribution in English Political Economy, from 1776 to 1848. 1893.

(b) Biographies.

Malthus. —— and His Work, by James Bonar, 1885.

Mill (James). ——, a Biography, by Alexander Bain, 1822.

Mill (John Stuart). Autobiography, 1873.

Ricardo (David). ——, a Centenary Estimate, by J. H. Hollander, 1910.

From this bibliography we have omitted the original scientific works which appeared during our period. We have omitted also contemporary novels and poems. It may be added that all the important works on economics which appeared during our period will be found under the appropriate headings in the bibliography of Book II (Economic Life).

INDEX

Cobbett's and (after vol. xxiii.) Hansard's Parliamentary Debates, from 1803, 1st series, 41 vols., 1803–20.
>   Index 1834, for the years 1803–30.

(b) Collections of Statutes, especially :

Pickering (D.). The Statutes at large from Magna Charta to 1806, 46 vols., 1672–1807.
>   (General indices after vols. xxiv and xxxviii.)

—— The Statutes of the United Kingdom . . . vol. xlvii et sqq.

Chitty (Joseph). A Collection of Statutes of Practical Utility, with notes thereon : intended as a Circuit and Court Companion, 2 vols., 1829.

(c) Contemporary Magazines, such as :

The Annual Register ; or, a view of History, Politics and Literature.
>   An annual from 1758.

The Gentleman's Magazine and Historical Chronicle.
>   A monthly from 1731.
>   Two indices, 1789 for the years 1731–86, 1821 for 1787–1818.

(d) The great contemporary Reviews :

The Edinburgh Review.
>   From 1802.
>   Index to the first 20 vols., 1813 ; to vols. xxi–l, 1832. A Liberal organ.

The Quarterly Review.
>   From 1809.
>   Index to first 20 vols. after vol. 20, 1820 ; to vols. xxi–xxxix after vol. xl, 1831. Conservative ; the organ of Canning's group.

(e) Dailies or papers appearing at very frequent intervals :

See above, Book I, chap. ii for a list of the principal newspapers.
>   We have made frequent use of them.

Cobbett's Annual Register (from 1802) and Political Register (from 1804, the continuation of the former).
>   A most valuable collection full of documents of every description, also articles of political criticism or satire.

(f) Biographies, Memoirs, Correspondence :

Their number is very large and taken as a whole are a source of valuable information to the historian. But as a rule they have been commissioned by the family of their subject and hence are full of deliberate omissions ; and their compilation has been too often entrusted to incompetent journalists, who fail to make full use of their documents. No detailed bibliography can be given here (see the special headings below), but mention must be made of the excellent

Dictionary of National Biography, edited by Leslie Stephen and afterwards by Sydney Lee, 1st ed. 1885–1900.

(g) Travels :

These contain much valuable information. This is true of the accounts by English travellers of journeys in their own country, and even more true of the relations of foreign travellers. *See especially :*

Pictet (M. A.). Voyage de trois mois en Angleterre, en Écosse, et en Irlande pendant l'été de l'an ix An xi (1802).

Barber (J. T.). A Tour throughout South Wales and Monmouthshire, 1803.

Warner (Rev. Richard). A Walk through Wales, 1799.

—— A Walk through some of the Western Counties of England, 1800.

—— A Tour through the Northern Counties of England, and the Borders of Scotland, 1802.

—— A Tour through Cornwall in the autumn of 1808, 1809.

Nemnich (P. A.). Neuste Reise durch England, 1807.

Svedenstjerna (Th.). Resa igenom en Del of England, 1804 (German translation from the Swedish, 1807).

Ayton (R.). Voyage round Great Britain, . . . undertaken in the summer of the year 1813, 8 vols., 1814–25. (Continued from vol. iii by W. Daniell.)

Journal of a Tour and Residence in Great Britain during the years 1810 and 1811, by a French traveller [Louis Simond], 1815.

M—— (A. J. B. Defauconpret). Quinze jours à Londres à la fin de 1815, 1816
—— Six mois à Londres en 1816. 1817.

Irving (Washington). The Sketch-book of Geoffrey Crayon, 1st ed., 1820.

Etc., etc.

BOOK I

POLITICAL INSTITUTIONS

I. GENERAL.

Montesquieu, L'Esprit des Lois, 1748.

Blackstone (Sir William). Commentaries on the Laws of England, 4 vols., 1st ed., 1765-9.

> Its Constitutional theory follows Montesquieu closely—some passages are an actual translation of Montesquieu.

De Lolme. Constitution de l'Angleterre, 1st ed., 1771. (First English edition, enlarged, under the title : The Constitution of England, or an Account of the English Government ; in which it is compared with the Republican form of Government, and occasionally with the other monarchies in Europe, 1775.)

Burke (Edmund). The Works of the Right Honourable ——. We have used the 2nd ed. in 16 vols., 1803-27.

The Black Book ; or Corruption Unmasked, . . . 1820.

> Violent but extremely well informed. It enumerates all the politica abuses then prevalent.

Russell (Lord John). An Essay on the History of the English Government and Constitution, from the reign of Henry VII to the present time, 1821 ; 2nd ed. (greatly enlarged), 1823 ; new ed., 1865.

Creasy (Edward Shepherd). The Rise and Progress of the English Constitution, 1853. 17th ed. revised ; 1907.

> An elementary textbook.

Gneist (Rudolph). Das heutige Englische Verfassungs-und Verwaltungsrecht, 2 vols., 1857.

Franqueville (Charles de). Les Institutions Politiques, Judiciaires, et Administratives de l'Angleterre, 1st ed., 1863 ; new ed., in 3 vols., 1887.

Todd (Alpheus). On Parliamentary Government in England, 2 vols., 1867-9.
New edition abridged and revised by S. Walpole, 2 vols., 1892.

Hearn (William Edward). The Government of England : its Structure and Development, 1867 ; 2nd ed., 1887.

May (Sir Thomas Erskine, Baron Farnborough). The Constitutional History of England since the accession of George III, 1760-1860, 2 vols., 1861-2 ; new ed. with an additional chapter, 1879.

Glasson (E. D.). Histoire du Droit et des Institutions Politiques, Civiles et Judiciaires de l'Angleterre, comparés au Droit et aux Institutions de la France depuis leur origine jusqu'à nos jours, 2 vols., 1882.

Dicey (Albert Venn). Lectures introductory to the Study of the Law of the Con-
    stitution, 1885. From the third edition the work bears the title : Introduction
    to the Study of the Law of the Constitution. 7th ed., 1908.

Anson (Sir William Reynell). The Law and Custom of the Constitution : Part I,
    Parliament ; Part II, The Crown, 1st ed., 1886.

Hatschek (Dr. Julius). Englisches Staatsrecht, mit Berücksichtigung der für Schott-
    land und Irland geltenden Sonderheiten. I. vol. Die Verfassung, 1905 ; II. vol.
    Die Verwaltung, 1906 (2 volumes of the Handbuch des Oeffentlichen Rechts
    der Gegenwart, by Marquardsen, von Seydel, G. Jellinek and Piloty).

The following works :

Boutmy (E.). Le Développement de la Constitution et de la Société Politique en
    Angleterre, 1887.

Dicey (Albert Venn). Lectures on the Relation between Law and Public Opinion
    in England during the Nineteenth Century, 1905,

are more general and more philosophical.

II. THE SYSTEM OF ADMINISTRATION.

A. THE CENTRAL GOVERNMENT.

1. THE REFORM OF ABUSES : OFFICIAL DOCUMENTS.

The Reports of the Commissioners appointed to examine, take and state the Public
    Accounts of the Kingdom, presented to His Majesty and to both Houses of
    Parliament ; with the appendices complete, 1783, 1785, 1787.

Finance Reports, 1797-8 ; and Proceedings thereupon, 1798-1803, with a general
    index to the whole (36 reports).

Naval Inquiry. Reports of Commissioners, 1802-6 (14 reports).

Commission for regulating and revising the Civil Affairs of the Navy, 1805. Reports
    of the Commissioners, 1806-9 (13 reports).

Military Inquiry. Reports of Commissioners of Inquiry, 1806-12 (19 reports).
    Index to the entire collection, 1816).

Reports from the Select Committee appointed to draw up Articles of Impeachment
    against Henry, Lord Viscount Melville, 1805-6 (3 reports).

Minutes of Evidence taken before the Committee of the Whole House, appointed
    to investigate the Conduct of His Royal Highness the Duke of York, the Com-
    mander-in-Chief, with regard to Promotions, Exchanges and Appointments to
    Commissions in the Army and Staff of the Army, and in raising Levies for the
    Army, 1809.

Reports from the Committee appointed to examine and consider what regulations
    and checks have been established in order to control the several Branches of the
    Public Expenditure in Great Britain and Ireland, and how far the same have
    been effectual, and what further measures can be adopted for reducing any part
    of the said Expenditure, or diminishing the amount of Salaries and Emoluments,
    without detriment to the Public Service, 1807-12 (13 reports).

Good sketches of the general condition of Britain will be found at the beginning of :

Walpole (Spencer). A History of England from the Conclusion of the Great War in 1815, 1st ed., 5 vols., 1878–86 ; new ed. revised., 6 vols., 1890.

Martineau (Miss Harriet). The History of England during the Thirty Years' Peace, 1816–46, 2 vols., 1849–50.

Cory (William). A Guide to Modern English History, 2 vols., 1880–2.
    Valued by English students of history.

In :

The Cambridge Modern History, vol. viii., The French Revolution, 1904, vol. ix, Napoleon, 1906, vol x, The Restoration, 1907,
    The joint work of a number of professors. There are very few chapters on the internal history of England during our period.

For the study of British Diplomacy :

The Cambridge History of Foreign Policy, 1783–1919, edited by Sir A. W. Ward and G. P. Gooch, vol. i (1783–1815), 1922.

Webster (C. K.). British Diplomacy, 1813–15. Select Documents, ed. by ——, 1921.
    A collection of documents, partly new, always well chosen.

For an accurate but dry account of the political institutions of England in 1815, see :

Adolphus (John). The Political State of the British Empire, 4 vols., 1818.

Also for further detail :

Montveran (M. de). Histoire critique et raisonnée de la Situation de l'Angleterre, au 1er Janvier, 1816, sous les rapports de ses finances, de son agriculture, de ses manufactures, de son commerce et sa navigation, de sa constitution et ses lois et de sa politique extérieure, 8 vols., 1819.

But especially

Traill (H. D.) and Mann (J. S.). Social England, a record of the progress of the people in religion, laws, learning and arts, industry, commerce, science, literature and manners, from the earliest times to the present time, by various writers, edited by ——, 6 vols., 1st ed. 1893 ; 2nd ed. 1898. Vol. v (1714–1815), vol. vi (1815–85).
    A storehouse of interesting information concerning the social history of England. Every chapter is the work of a specialist.

Original Sources.

The principal sources are :
    (a) The Collections of Debates.

The Parliamentary Register, or History of the Proceedings and Debates of both Houses . . . 4 series, 1774–1813.

Cobbett's Parliamentary History of England, 1806–28, vols. i–xii 1066–1713, vols. xiii–xxxvi 1743–1803.
    These two collections will often be found to supplement each other most usefully.

WORKS OF GENERAL REFERENCE[1]

For the period *immediately* preceding 1815 there exists no English history which can claim to be a scientific treatment of the subject.

Lecky (W. E. H.). A History of England in the Eighteenth Century, 1st ed., 8 vols., 1878–90 ; new ed., 7 vols., 1892.
> Concludes with the year 1792.

Massey (W.). A History of England during the Reign of George the Third, 4 vols., 1st ed., 1855–63 ; 2nd ed., 1865.
> Contains interesting details of social life. Nothing after 1802.

Alison (Archibald). History of Europe from the Commencement of the French Revolution in 1789 to the Restoration of the Bourbons in 1815, 1st ed., 10 vols., 1833–42. We have used the 7th ed., 20 vols., 1848.
> An abundantly detailed account of diplomatic, military and economic history ; written from the Tory standpoint.

Jesse (J. Heneage). Memoirs of the Life and Reign of King George the Third, 3 vols., 1867.
> Deals exclusively with political history (Cabinet crises, etc.), superficial.

There have appeared recently a number of textbooks whose value is unequal. All are very elementary.

MacCarthy (Justin). A History of the Four Georges, 4 vols., 1884–1901.

Dorman (M. R. P.). A History of the British Empire in the Nineteenth Century, 2 vols., 1902–4.
> Unfinished ; leaves off at 1815 ; very superficial ; deals exclusively, or almost exclusively, with foreign politics.

Brodrick (the Hon. George C.). The History of England, from Addington's Administration to the close of William IV's Reign (1801–37) . . . completed and revised by J. K. Fotheringham, 1 vol., 1906.

Mathieson (William Law). England in Transition (1789–1832). A Study of Movements, 1920.

Maxwell (Sir Herbert Eustace). A Century of Empire, 1801–1901, 3 vols. ; vol. i (1801–32), 1909.

---

[1] A small number of titles of books, which have appeared since this work was first written in 1913, have been added in order to bring the Bibliography up to date. But the author wishes it to be clearly understood that this translation, though containing a fairly large number of corrections, is not what he would like to call in the full sense of the word a revised edition. All books here mentioned, and which have been published in 1913 and later, should therefore not be taken as having been sources to the present History ; they are merely mentioned because they may convey useful information to our readers.

BIBLIOGRAPHY